Stanley Gibbons

# Great Britain

Specialised Stamp Catalogue
Volume 4

D1066882

*Photo:* National Postal Museum

**The Machin Head**

Stanley Gibbons

# Great Britain

## Specialised Stamp Catalogue

Volume 4
Queen Elizabeth II
Decimal Definitive Issues

Sixth Edition

Stanley Gibbons Publications Ltd
London and Ringwood

**By Appointment to
Her Majesty the Queen
Stanley Gibbons Ltd, London
Philatelists**

Published by **Stanley Gibbons Publications Ltd.**
Editorial, Sales Offices and Distribution Centre:
5 Parkside, Christchurch Road, Ringwood,
Hants BH24 3SH.

© **Stanley Gibbons Publications Ltd 1991**

**ISBN 0–85259–294–9**

1st edition—October 1976
　Reprinted—November 1977, July 1978
2nd edition—April 1979
3rd edition—November 1981
4th edition—May 1985
5th edition—March 1988
6th edition—July 1991

Item No. 2820 (91)

**Typeset by Black Bear Press Limited, Cambridge
Printed in Great Britain by Butler & Tanner Ltd., Frome,
Somerset**

# Contents

# Stanley Gibbons Addresses

HEAD OFFICE, 399 STRAND, LONDON WC2R 0LX

**Auction Room and Specialist Stamp Departments.** Open Monday–Friday, 9.30 a.m. to 5 p.m.

**Shop.** Open Monday 9.30 a.m. to 5.30 p.m., Tuesday–Friday 8.30 a.m. to 5.30 p.m. and Saturday 10.00 a.m. to 4.00 p.m.
**Telephone 071-836 8444 and Telex 28883 for all departments.**

RINGWOOD OFFICE

**Stanley Gibbons Publications and Promotions,** 5, Parkside, Christchurch Road, Ringwood, Hants BH24 3SH. Telephone 0425 472363.

· OVERSEAS BRANCHES

**Stanley Gibbons (Australia) Pty. Ltd.,** P.O. Box 863J, Melbourne 3001, Australia. Telephone (01 0613) 670 3332 and Telex AA 37223.

**Stanley Gibbons (Singapore) Pte. Ltd.,** Raffles City, P.O. Box 1689, Singapore 9117, Republic of Singapore. Telephone (010 65) 336 1998.

Stanley Gibbons Publications Ltd. has overseas agents and distributors for Australia, Austria, Belgium, Canada, Denmark, France, Germany, Hong Kong, Israel, Japan, Luxembourg, Netherlands, New Zealand, Scandinavia, South Africa, Switzerland, United States and West Indies. Please contact the Ringwood address for details.

---

**Great Britain Philatelic Societies**

**The Great Britain Philatelic Society.** Hon. Membership Secretary: A. J. Walker, 42 Jesmond Road, Newcastle-upon-Tyne NE2 4PQ.

**The British Decimal Stamps Study Circle.** The Secretary: P. Daniels, 70 Moor Park Close, Rainham, Gillingham, Kent ME8 8QT.

**The Great Britain Decimal Stamp Book Study Circle.** Hon. Membership Secretary: A. J. Wilkins, 3 Buttermere Close, Brierley Hill, West Midlands, DY5 3SD.

# Preface

It is twenty years since the first Decimal Machin stamps appeared. The 1p., unchanged in design since 1971, has been in use longer than any other Great Britain low value definitive since the King George V 1d. value introduced in 1912 and current for the following twenty-two years. If the 1p. Machin survives until 1994 it will equal the twenty-three year record held by the 1841 1d. red.

The Machins are not the simplest issue to collect—escalating postage rates and the increasing pace of modern technology have seen to that, but their study is a fascinating one.

This sixth edition of the *Great Britain Specialised Catalogue Volume* 4 covers all Decimal definitives from 1970 until the end of 1990. The Machins are here, from ½p. to £5, with comprehensive details of papers, phosphor, perforation types, booklet panes, errors and varieties with a coverage going far beyond that provided in the standard catalogues. New sections have been added for Machin booklet panes printed in lithography, the NVI (No Value Indicated) provisional issues of 1989 and 1990, the Castle high values based on photographs taken by Prince Andrew, the Greetings stamps (introduced in 1989 to encourage the growth of greetings by post) and the Penny Black Anniversary series of "short-term" definitives issued in 1990 to mark the 150th anniversary of the Penny Black.

In the existing sections the major innovation has been the introduction of the Barcode stamp booklets in 1987 as part of a massive increase in stamp availability from commercial outlets. Some of these booklets contain stamps not available from other sources and there are clear indications that some of these may become key values for the Machin collector.

Prices in this new edition have been carefully revised and there is now a 10p. minimum. Errors and varieties continue in demand and many of the Machin folded booklet panes have required substantial increases. Certain Machin and Regional plate blocks from values produced by lithography are becoming increasingly scarce.

We are grateful to all those collectors and dealers who have helped with the new edition. John Deering, the modern G.B. correspondent of *Gibbons Stamp Monthly*, has provided much assistance and we would also like to thank Alan Bond, Mike Holt and Alan Wilson for details of individual items. Specialist collectors who have provided help include Jim Dutton, B. Snook and Ian de la Rue Browne.

Collectors are reminded that Decimal commemoratives now form the fifth volume in this series. A new edition is expected towards the end of this year.

It is not known when, or indeed if, the Decimal Machins are to be replaced. Whatever is to be their future this series of stamps will provide a rich field of modern philatelic study for many years to come.

D. J. Aggersberg
R. H. Oliver

---

## Specialised Numbers Changed in Section UD

| Old Nos. | New Nos. | Old Nos. | New Nos. | Old Nos. | New Nos. |
|----------|----------|----------|----------|----------|----------|
| U128/30 | U129/31 | U261 | U275 | U272/3 | U298/9 |
| U140 | U139c | U262/3 | U279/80 | U274 | U301 |
| U232/42 | U235/44 | U264 | U283 | U276/8 | U304/6 |
| U243/8 | U245/50 | U265 | U285 | U281/3 | U310/12 |
| U250/4 | U254/8 | U266 | U288 | U290/1 | U321/2 |
| U258/60 | U264/6 | U267/70 | U291/4 | U300/10 | U330/7 |

# Introductory Notes

**Detailed Introductory Notes**

Before using the catalogue it is most important to study the "General Notes" as these detail the technical background of the issues in question. These "General Notes" will be found at the beginning of each section and also indicate some of the areas which are beyond the scope of this work.

**Arrangement of Lists**

The Machin and Regional issues are dealt with value by value. The order of listing is as follows:

- A. Basic listing of single stamps from sheets, booklets and coils according to paper and gum with errors and varieties.
- B. List of cylinder or plate blocks according to paper and gum combinations quoting ink and phosphor cylinder numbers and priced according to perforation types.
- C. Illustrations of the listed cylinder varieties.
- D. Details of constant minor sheet flaws without illustrations and prices but quoting positions on stamps.
- E. Information relating to coils.
- F. Withdrawal dates.

If there is a deliberate change in the number of phosphor bands this is treated as a separate issue which is then listed in the same order shown above.

Booklet Panes are listed separately in Sections UE and UH under the illustrations of complete panes and according to paper and gum, with errors and cylinder varieties and all priced according to perforation types. These are followed by illustrations of cylinder varieties and lists of booklet pane cylinder numbers appear at the end of each group of a particular face value.

**Catalogue Numbering**

Basic catalogue numbers bear the prefix letter which denotes its Section of the catalogue. This is followed by the related number in the 1992 editions of the *Part I (British Commonwealth)* and *G.B. Concise Catalogues.*

Shades, where there is more than one, are denoted by bracketed numbers, *e.g.* (1) Ultramarine, (2) Pale ultramarine for stamp No. U104, the Machin 3p FCP/GA with two phosphor bands.

Varieties have a letter identification, *e.g. a.* Phosphor omitted, *b.* (short description of cylinder variety) and related varieties to item *b*, will be listed as *ba., bb.,* etc.

Booklet panes have numbers prefixed with the letters UB or ULP in combination with other letters signifying the class of booklet.

In Appendix J the booklets have the same numbers and prefix letters as are used in the *G.B. Concise Catalogue.*

**Prices**

Prices quoted in this Catalogue are those which Stanley Gibbons Ltd. estimate will be their selling prices at the time of publication. They are for stamps of fine condition for the particular issue, unless otherwise indicated; those of lesser quality may be offered at lower prices.

In the case of unused stamps, our prices are for stamps unmounted mint. Prices for used stamps refer to postally used copies.

All prices are subject to change without prior notice and Stanley Gibbons Ltd. may from time to time offer stamps below catalogue price in consequence of special purchases or particular promotions. Subscribers to new issues are asked to note that the prices charged for them contain an element for the service rendered and so may exceed the prices shown when the stamps are subsequently catalogued.

No guarantee is given to supply all stamps priced, since it is not possible to keep every catalogued item in stock.

If a variety exists on more than one *shade*, the price quoted is for the commoner shade; it will be worth correspondingly more on a scarcer shade.

Cases can exist where a particular stamp shows more than one of the listed varieties. It might, for example, have a cylinder flaw as well as a broad phosphor band, both of which are listed but priced separately. It is not practical to cover every possible combination but the value of such items may be established by adding the difference between the price of the basic stamp and the dearest variety to the catalogue price of the cheapest variety.

*Cylinder blocks* are priced according to the type of perforator used. This takes account of the state of the perforations on all four sides of the sheet, not just the corner where the cylinder number appears. Note that a full specification of a cylinder block should quote the basic number of the stamp; cylinder number; phosphor cylinder number and displacement if any; with or without dot; perforation type; and type of paper and gum wherever such alternatives exist.

Prices for *cylinder flaws* are for single stamps and extra stamps required to make up positional blocks would be charged as normals. However all cylinder flaws and other varieties listed under *booklet panes* are priced for the complete pane.

Prices for *cylinder blocks containing listed varieties* are indicated by an asterisk and include the cost of the variety.

The prices quoted for *booklet panes* are for panes with good perforations and complete with the binding margin. Prices for complete booklets are for those containing panes with average perforations as it is unusual for all panes in the booklet to show full perforations on the guillotined sides. The same principle applies to folded booklets (see notes under Section UE sub-section B).

## Items Excluded

In dealing with *varieties* and *minor constant flaws* we record only those for which we can vouch, namely items we have seen and verified for ourselves. It should be recognised, however, that some flaws described as constant may be transient: they may develop in size to be sufficiently noticeable to be worth retouching.

To qualify for listing, *imperforate errors* must show no sign of indentation, i.e. blind perforations, on any side of a pair. Such part-perforated varieties can occur in "Jumelle" printings after re-starting the press during a run and are caused by the pins on the perforating drum only gradually coming into contact with the female cylinder so that some rows will show signs of indentation.

*Colour shifts* due to faulty registration range from minor shifts to quite spectacular varieties. As it is very difficult to draw a line between major and minor shifts we have not listed any.

We likewise exclude: doctor blade flaws; paper creases; partially omitted colours; and misplaced perforations.

We do not quote for traffic light blocks, gutter margins or positional blocks showing various sheet markings other than cylinder blocks but when available they will be supplied at appropriate prices.

Finally, we make no mention whatever of unusual items in a form not issued by the Post Office. In recent years many philatelic items have been prepared privately, with or without Post Office authority, some having postal validity. Many are made for laudable purposes, such as for the promotion of philatelic events, exhibitions and society anniversaries, or for charitable causes, but others have been purely commercial productions. They can be such things as legitimate postal issues with overprints in the margins, black prints, specially prepared packs and booklets made up from sheet stock. Their variety seems endless and their status is arguable.

## Correspondence

Letters should be addressed to the Catalogue Editor, Stanley Gibbons Publications Ltd., 5, Parkside, Christchurch Road, Ringwood, Hants BH24 3SH, and return postage is appreciated when a reply is sought. New information and unlisted items for consideration are welcomed.

Please note we do not give opinions as to the genuineness of stamps, nor do we identify stamps or number them by our Catalogue.

### To order from this Catalogue

Always quote the *Specialised Catalogue* number, mentioning *Volume 4, 6th Edition*, and where necessary specify additionally the precise item wanted.

### Guarantee

All stamps supplied by Stanley Gibbons Ltd., are guaranteed originals in the following terms:

If not as described, and returned by the purchaser, we undertake to refund the price paid to us in the original transaction. If any stamp is certified as genuine by the Expert Committee of the Royal Philatelic Society, London, or by B.P.A. Expertising Ltd., the purchaser shall not be entitled to make any claim against us for any error, omission or mistake in such certificate.

Consumers' statutory rights are not affected by the above guarantee.

### Expertisation

We do not give opinions as to the genuineness of stamps. Expert Committees exist for this purpose and enquiry can be made of the Royal Philatelic Society, 41 Devonshire Place, London W1N 1PE or B.P.A. Expertising Ltd., P.O. Box 163, Carshalton Beeches, Surrey SM5 4QR. They do not undertake valuations under any circumstances and fees are payable for their services.

### National Postal Museum Archive Material

During 1984 and 1985 surplus GB material from the National Postal Museum archives was included in three auction sales. The lots offered were mostly imprimaturs, which were handstamped on the reverse to indicate origin, and specimen overprints. All the material offered in these auction sales was issued before decimalization and does not affect the listings in this volume.

### Symbols and Abbreviations

| | |
|---|---|
| † | (in price column) does not exist. |
| — | (in price column) exists, but no market price is known. |
| | (a blank in the used price column conveys the same meaning). |
| * | (against the price of a cylinder block) price includes a listed variety. |
| FCP | Fluorescent coated paper. |
| GA | Gum arabic. |
| mm. | Millimetres. |
| No. | Number. |
| OCP | Original coated paper. |
| Phos. | Phosphor. |
| ptg. | Printing. |
| PVA | Polyvinyl alcohol (gum). |
| PVAD | Polyvinyl alcohol (gum) with dextrin added. |
| R. | Row (thus "R. 6/4" indicates the fourth stamp from the left in the sixth horizontal row from the top of a sheet of stamps). |
| Th. | S.G "Thirkell" Position Finder. The letters and figures which follow (e.g. Th. E5) pinpoint the position of the flaw on the stamp according to the grid engraved on the Finder. |

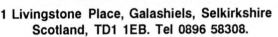

# COMPLETE YOUR SET

No stamp collector likes to have incomplete sets – whether you are talking about Tudor Crowns, St Edward Crowns or the Crown of the SG Catalogue range – the **Great Britain Specialised Catalogue.**

Volume 1 (item 0285) **Queen Victoria**

Volume 2 (item 0286) **King Edward VII to King George VI**

Volume 3 (item 2810) **Queen Elizabeth II pre-decimal issues**

Volume 4 (item 2820) **Queen Elizabeth II decimal definitive issues**

Volume 5 (item 2891) **Queen Elizabeth II decimal special issues**

Volumes 1 & 2 are available either case bound or paperback.

# SECTION UC

# Machin Decimal Issues

## 1970–74. Recess-printed

## General Notes

**INTRODUCTION.** The four "high values" were issued on 17 June 1970 in advance of decimalisation which was introduced on 15 February 1971. These values were brought into use early to accustom the public to the changeover and followed the introduction of the 10p. and 50p. coins. The £1 value differs only slightly from its predecessor and was issued in sheets of 100 instead of 40.

**PRINTERS.** As with the £.s.d. Machin high values the decimal equivalents were recess-printed by Bradbury, Wilkinson & Co. on rotary sheet-fed machines. They were issued in sheets of 100 arranged in ten rows of ten stamps.

**PLATES.** In place of the usual procedure used for the pre-decimal Machin high values by which the die was rocked in by means of a transfer roller to construct each individual plate, for each of the 10p., 20p. and 50p. values and later the redrawn £1, this process was only used to produce a "master" plate of 100 units (10 × 10). From this a matrix was taken and used to make the individual printing plates. It follows, therefore, that any flaws on the "master" plate will be reproduced in all the printing plates derived from it.

For all values at first only plates comprising one pane of 100 units were produced, used two at a time positioned on opposite sides of the printing cylinder, so that one revolution of the press produced two separate sheets of stamps. The plates were usually successively numbered, but not necessarily so.

Later, for all values except the 10p., plates comprising two panes each of 100 units separated by a gutter of one stamp width wide, were made, the plate number of the right-hand pane bearing the suffix letter A. These double-pane plates were produced entire from a second matrix built up from two images of the master plate—thus accounting for the flaws which occur on the original single-pane plates being repeated on each pane of the double-pane plates.

Like the single-pane plates, the double-pane plates were used two at a time so that an examination of the printed, perforated and guillotined sheets would show an alternating repeat sequence of the two plate numbers, either with or without the A, but never mixed. This can be clearly seen in the post office "lifts". Old plates were sometimes re-chromed and used again.

**PAPER.** All paper used was without watermark. At first the printers were supplied by the Post Office with paper which was lightly coated, giving only slight reaction to the silver test for chalky paper. There is hardly any response for the 10p. which had phosphorised paper and the remainder of this paper was used up for the 50p. stamps in 1973 which do show slight reaction. In the text this is all described as "Post Office Paper".

From 1973 Bradbury, Wilkinson began printing on clay-coated paper supplied by them which is whiter and does respond more readily to the silver test. This is described as "Bradbury's Paper".

**GUM.** Only PVA gum was used.

**PERFORATION.** All values are comb perforated 12 with perforation Type K which is described in Appendix I. This perforation Type is the same for sheets printed from both single and double-pane plates.

The sheets from double-pane plates were sometimes cut into single width sheets and perforated with a single comb as used for normal single-pane sheets. Later double comb perforators were used, making this unnecessary. See under "Guide Holes" below.

**WITHDRAWAL.** The 10p., 20p. and 50p. values were gradually replaced by stamps in the small-sized photogravure issue and stocks of the recess-printed stamps remained on sale at the Edinburgh Philatelic Bureau and philatelic counters until exhausted. The £1 value was replaced by the large format photogravure issue of 2 February 1977.

**POST OFFICE TRAINING SCHOOLS.** The 20p. and 50p. values are known overprinted with two thick vertical bars for use at counter training schools. Their issue to the public was unauthorised and we therefore do not list them.

### SHEET MARKINGS

**Perforation Guide Holes.** On 20p. double-pane sheets that have been divided by cutting through the narrow gutter margin and perforated on a single-comb machine, unboxed guide holes are

**1**

found in left and right margins of row 6 in both panes. They are invariably found on Plates 17/A and 18/A, when doubtless no double-comb perforators were available. Thereafter sheets from many 20p. double-pane plates can be found either with or without guide holes, dependent upon whether they were divided before or after perforating.

Plate Number

**Plate Numbers.** In bottom margin below R. 10/9.

**Register Cross.** This has been seen in the right-hand margin opposite row 8 on some single plates of the 10p., 20p. and 50p., caused by bad trimming resulting in an extra-wide margin.

Total Sheet Value

**Total Sheet Values.** The "TOTAL SHEET VALUE" and amount was introduced in the high values for the first time on all values of the decimal issue. They occur four times in the sheet, opposite rows 2/4 and 7/9 reading up at left and down at right.

**U3.** Queen Elizabeth II
(Des. after plaster cast by Arnold Machin)

# 1970–74. Type U3

## 10p. (1970)
### 1970 (17 JUNE).   PHOSPHORISED PAPER
**Post Office Paper**

| | | | |
|---|---|---|---|
| U37 (=S.G.829) | Cerise    .. .. .. .. .. .. .. .. | 1·00 | 75 |
| | *a.* Neck retouch .. .. .. .. .. .. .. .. | 4·00 | |

**Plate Numbers (Blocks of Four)**

| Pl. No. | | | Pl. No. | | | Pl. No. | | |
|---|---|---|---|---|---|---|---|---|
| 3 | .. | .. 15·00 | 7 | .. | .. 15·00 | 11 | .. | .. 15·00 |
| 4 | .. | .. 15·00 | 8 | .. | .. 15·00 | 12 | .. | .. 22·00 |
| 5 | .. | .. 28·00 | 9 | .. | .. 17·00 | 13 | .. | .. 28·00 |
| 6 | .. | .. 15·00 | 10 | .. | .. 15·00 | | | |

**PLATE VARIETIES**
**Listed Plate Flaw**

U37*a*
Retouch in neck under necklace
(R. 7/8)
Although visible on all plates, this is most prominent
on Plates 3 and 4 (illustrated from Pl. 3)

**Minor Constant Flaws**

Pls.   3/4 7/8 Circle of dots in right-hand gutter margin (Th. H10). This is included with variety
U37*a*

Pls.   3/13 7/9 Single dot in left-hand gutter (left of Th. F1) and two dots in upper gutter (above
Th. A1)

Doubtless the dots on R. 7/8 were removed from Plate 5 onwards when attempts were made
to repair the listed retouch.

**WITHDRAWN**   2.75

The 10p. was printed on phosphorised paper to continue the experiment started on the 1s.6d.
Machin to provide information as to the effect of weather conditions upon the phosphor. No
doubt the objective was to see these effects on a recess-printed stamp as the results could be
better evaluated. When the experiment was discontinued the stamp was replaced by the 10p. photogravure on 11 August 1971 but it continued to be available at the Philatelic Bureau and at philatelic
counters until February 1975.

# 20p. (1970–73)

## 1970 (17 JUNE)

### A. Post Office Paper

| | | | |
|---|---|---|---|
| U38 | Olive-green .. .. .. .. .. .. .. .. | 80 | 30 |
| | *a.* Uncoated paper* .. .. .. .. .. | | |

*This is not as apparent as uncoated photogravure issues where there is normally a higher degree of chalk-surfacing. This is known only as a block of four with Plate No. 5.

### Plate Numbers (Blocks of Four)

Post Office Paper

Single Pane Plates

| Pl. No. | | | Pl. No. | | | Pl. No. | | |
|---|---|---|---|---|---|---|---|---|
| 3 | .. .. | 7·50 | 9 | .. .. | 7·50 | 15 | .. .. | 12·00 |
| 4 | .. .. | 7·50 | 10 | .. .. | 15·00 | 16 | .. .. | 12·00 |
| 5 | .. .. | 7·50 | 11 | .. .. | 8·50 | 21 | .. .. | 16·00 |
| 6 | .. .. | 8·50 | 12 | .. .. | 8·00 | 22 | .. .. | 16·00 |
| 7 | .. .. | 8·50 | 13 | .. .. | 8·00 | | | |
| 8 | .. .. | 7·50 | 14 | .. .. | 8·00 | | | |

Double Pane Plates

| | | | | | | | | |
|---|---|---|---|---|---|---|---|---|
| 17 | .. .. | 15·00 | 30 | .. .. | 7·50 | 41 | .. .. | 75·00 |
| 17A | .. .. | 15·00 | 30A | .. .. | 7·50 | 41A | .. .. | 75·00 |
| 18 | .. .. | 7·50 | 31 | .. .. | £450 | 42 | .. .. | 12·00 |
| 18A | .. .. | 7·50 | 31A | .. .. | £550 | 42A | .. .. | 12·00 |
| 19 | .. .. | 7·50 | 33 | .. .. | 9·00 | 43 | .. .. | 12·00 |
| 19A | .. .. | 7·50 | 33A | .. .. | 9·00 | 43A | .. .. | 12·00 |
| 20 | .. .. | 7·50 | 34 | .. .. | 9·00 | 44 | .. .. | 70·00 |
| 20A | .. .. | 7·50 | 34A | .. .. | 9·00 | 44A | .. .. | 65·00 |
| 25 | .. .. | 7·50 | 35 | .. .. | 18·00 | 45 | .. .. | 18·00 |
| 25A | .. .. | 7·50 | 35A | .. .. | 18·00 | 45A | .. .. | 18·00 |
| 26 | .. .. | 7·50 | 37 | .. .. | 18·00 | 46 | .. .. | 12·00 |
| 26A | .. .. | 7·50 | 37A | .. .. | 18·00 | 46A | .. .. | 12·00 |
| 27 | .. .. | 7·50 | 38 | .. .. | 18·00 | 47 | .. .. | 9·00 |
| 27A | .. .. | 7·50 | 38A | .. .. | 18·00 | 47A | .. .. | 9·00 |
| 28 | .. .. | 7·50 | 39 | .. .. | 18·00 | 48 | .. .. | 12·00 |
| 28A | .. .. | 7·50 | 39A | .. .. | 18·00 | 48A | .. .. | 12·00 |
| 29 | .. .. | 7·50 | 40 | .. .. | 12·00 | | | |
| 29A | .. .. | 7·50 | 40A | .. .. | 12·00 | | | |

### B. Bradbury's Paper (30. 11.73†)

| | | | |
|---|---|---|---|
| U39 (=S.G.830) | Olive-green .. .. .. .. .. .. .. .. | 70 | 15 |

†This is the date officially announced but the earliest recorded appearance, in commercial use of this paper was March 1974. This paper supplied by the printers is whiter than that supplied by the Post Office.

**Phosphorised Paper.** It has been confirmed that part of the balance of the phosphorised paper ordered for the 10p. was later used in the ordinary course for the 20p. value, probably in conjunction with Plates 21 and 22. However, unlike the 50p. value, no copies of the 20p. have so far been reported but they could exist.

### Plate Numbers (Blocks of Four)

Bradbury's Paper

Double Pane Plates

| Pl. No. | | | Pl. No. | | | Pl. No. | | |
|---|---|---|---|---|---|---|---|---|
| 49 | .. | 25·00 | 55 | .. .. | 12·00 | 62 | .. .. | 4·00 |
| 49A | .. .. | 15·00 | 55A | .. .. | 12·00 | 62A | .. .. | 4·00 |
| 50 | .. .. | 10·00 | 56 | .. .. | 6·00 | 63 | .. .. | 4·00 |
| 50A | .. .. | 10·00 | 56A | .. .. | 6·00 | 63A | .. .. | 4·00 |
| 51 | .. .. | 6·00 | 57 | .. .. | 8·00 | 64 | .. .. | 4·00 |
| 51A | .. .. | 6·00 | 57A | .. .. | 8·00 | 64A | .. .. | 4·00 |
| 52 | .. .. | 4·00 | 58 | .. .. | 5·00 | 65 | .. .. | 11·00 |
| 52A | .. .. | 4·00 | 58A | .. .. | 5·00 | 65A | .. .. | 11·00 |
| 53 | .. .. | 50·00 | 59 | .. .. | 12·00 | 66 | .. .. | 12·00 |
| 53A | .. .. | 18·00 | 59A | .. .. | 12·00 | 66A | .. .. | 12·00 |
| 54 | .. .. | 6·00 | 61 | .. .. | 4·00 | | | |
| 54A | .. .. | 6·00 | 64A | .. .. | 4·00 | | | |

A feature of the single plate printings of the 20p. value is two dots in the form of a colon placed to the left of the plate number as illustrated above.

**WITHDRAWN** 9.77

## 50p. (1970–74)

### 1970 (17 JUNE)
#### A. Post Office Paper

| | | | |
|---|---|---|---|
| U40 | Deep ultramarine .. .. .. .. .. .. .. 1·60 | 60 |
| | *a.* Thinner uncoated paper* .. .. .. .. .. .. 25·00 | |

*This is not as apparent as uncoated photogravure issues where there is normally a higher degree of chalk-surfacing. These occurred on Plates 8 and 9.

**Plate Numbers (Blocks of Four)**
Single Pane Plates
Post Office Paper

| Pl. No. | | Pl. No. | | Pl. No. | |
|---|---|---|---|---|---|
| 4 | .. .. 12·50 | 8 | .. .. 12·50 | 11 | .. .. 12·50 |
| 5 | .. .. 14·00 | 9 | .. .. 12·50 | 12 | .. .. 65·00 |
| 6 | .. .. 14·00 | 10 | .. .. 12·50 | 13 | .. .. 60·00 |
| 7 | .. .. 12·50 | | | | |

#### B. Post Office Phosphorised Paper (1.2.73)

| | | |
|---|---|---|
| U41 | Deep ultramarine .. .. .. .. .. .. 2·00 | 60 |

This cannot be distinguished without the use of an ultra violet lamp. The sole purpose of this issue was to use up some of the surplus paper of the 10p.

**Plate Numbers (Blocks of Four)**
Post Office Phosphorised Paper

| | | | | | |
|---|---|---|---|---|---|
| 14 | .. .. 18·00 | 17 | .. .. 18·00 | 20 | .. .. 30·00 |
| 15 | .. .. 18·00 | 18 | .. .. 35·00 | 21 | .. .. 30·00 |
| 16 | .. .. 18·00 | 19 | .. .. 55·00 | | |

#### C. Bradbury's Paper (20.2.74†)

| | | |
|---|---|---|
| U42 (=S.G.831) | Deep ultramarine .. .. .. .. .. .. 1·40 | 40 |

†This is the date officially announced but the earliest recorded appearance, in commercial use of this paper was March 1974. This paper supplied by the printers is whiter than that supplied by the Post Office.

**Plate Numbers (Blocks of Four)**
Bradbury's Paper

| | | | | | |
|---|---|---|---|---|---|
| 12 | .. .. 24·00 | 16 | .. .. 15·00 | 20 | .. .. 7·00 |
| 13 | .. .. 24·00 | 17 | .. .. 15·00 | 21 | .. .. 7·00 |
| 14 | .. .. 15·00 | 18 | .. .. 15·00 | | |
| 15 | .. .. 15·00 | 19 | .. .. £100 | | |

The first plates to appear on the Bradbury paper were numbers 20 and 21 in March 1974 after which earlier plates were brought back into use, presumably while the double pane plates were being prepared.

Double Pane Plates on Bradbury's Paper

| | | | | | |
|---|---|---|---|---|---|
| 22 | .. .. 50·00 | 25 | .. .. 7·00 | 28 | .. .. 25·00 |
| 22A | .. .. 50·00 | 25A | .. .. 7·00 | 28A | .. .. 25·00 |
| 23 | .. .. 10·00 | 26 | .. .. 7·00 | | |
| 23A | .. .. 10·00 | 26A | .. .. 7·00 | | |
| 24 | .. .. 7·00 | 27 | .. .. 7·00 | | |
| 24A | .. .. 7·00 | 27A | .. .. 7·00 | | |

**PLATE VARIETIES**

**Minor Constant Flaws**

All plates

7/1     Extension of bottom frame line into right-hand margin
10/2
10/7 } Extension of bottom frame line into left-hand margin
10/8

WITHDRAWN     No. U41, Aug. 1975, but put back on sale at Philatelic Bureau in Jan. 1976 and
again withdrawn June 1976
No. U42, November 1977

U4          Queen Elizabeth II          U5
Value redrawn
(Des. after plaster cast by Arnold Machin)

# £1 Type U4.   (1970)

New plates were made from the same master die as the £1 pre-decimal issue but in single pane settings of 100 (10 × 10) in place of the plates of four panes each of 40 (8 × 5). Plate blocks of four from Plate 3 of the decimal issue can easily be distinguished from Plate 3 blocks of the pre-decimal issue (No. U36 in Vol. 3 of this catalogue), as they show part of the "TOTAL SHEET VALUE" inscription in the margin opposite R. 9/10.

However, specialists may also recognise single copies of the decimal issue by studying the background shading under a strong magnifying glass, particularly in the top left and bottom right corners. The pre-decimal issue has thicker horizontal lines of shading whilst the decimal issue has thicker vertical lines, each caused by the direction in which the transfer roller was rocked, both plates being produced by the conventional process of rocking in impressions from the die.

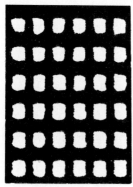
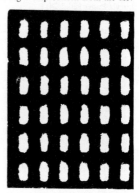

U36                                  U43
Pre-decimal issue                    Decimal issue
Thicker horizontal lines             Thicker vertical lines
(Illustrations taken from top left corner)

## 1970 (17 JUNE)
**Post Office Paper**

U43 (=S.G.790)          Bluish black     .. .. .. .. .. .. .. ..    3·00    1·60

**Plate Numbers (Blocks of Four)**
Single Pane Plates

| | Pl. No. | | | | Pl. No. | | | |
|---|---|---|---|---|---|---|---|---|
| | 2 | .. | .. £6000 | | 3 | .. | .. 22·00 | |

**WITHDRAWN**   Sept. 1974, but put back on sale at Philatelic Bureau in Sept. 1975 and withdrawn again in Mar. 1976.

---

# £1 Type U5.   (1972–73)

Unlike No. U43, the plates were made by the method employed for the 10p., 20p. and 50p. as described in the General Notes.

## 1972 (6 DECEMBER).   REDRAWN VALUE
**A. Post Office Paper**

U44                     Bluish black     .. .. .. .. .. .. .. ..    3·25    1·00

**Plate Numbers (Blocks of Four)**
Post Office Paper. Single Pane Plates

| | Pl. No. | | | | Pl. No. | | | |
|---|---|---|---|---|---|---|---|---|
| | 4 | .. | .. 15·00 | | 7 | .. | .. 15·00 | |

**B. Bradbury's Paper** (27.9.73†)

U45 (=S.G.831*b*)        Bluish black     .. .. .. .. .. .. .. ..    2·75    75

†This is the date officially announced but the earliest recorded appearance, in commercial use of this paper was October 1973.

**Plate Numbers (Blocks of Four)**
Bradbury's Paper
Single Pane Plates

| | | | | | | | | | | | |
|---|---|---|---|---|---|---|---|---|---|---|---|
| 4 | .. | .. 15·00 | 8 | .. | .. 14·00 | 10 | .. | .. 30·00 |
| 7 | .. | .. 15·00 | 9 | .. | .. 14·00 | 11 | .. | .. 30·00 |

Double Plane Plates

| | | | | | | | | | | | |
|---|---|---|---|---|---|---|---|---|---|---|---|
| 12 | .. | .. 14·00 | 14 | .. | .. 13·00 | 15 | .. | .. 13·00 |
| 12A | .. | .. 14·00 | 14A | .. | .. 13·00 | 15A | .. | .. 13·00 |
| 13 | .. | .. 13·00 | | | | | | |
| 13A | .. | .. 13·00 | | | | | | |

## PLATE VARIETIES
**Minor Constant Flaws**
All plates   7/9 Small coloured dot in margin at bottom right corner (Th. K9)
Pls. 12, 13 10/9 and 10/10 Small coloured blemish in margin between the two stamps (Th. A9–10)
Pl. 13      10/9 Extension of right-hand frame line into bottom margin

**WITHDRAWN**   No. U45, 11.78

## Presentation Packs

UPP3 No. 18 (17.6.70) 10p., 20p. and 50p  ..   ..   ..   ..   ..   ..   ..   ..   7·00

A red slip-in wallet bearing the Royal Arms and inscribed "BRITISH POST OFFICE" containing a set of the twelve low values and four high values was on sale at face value at the G.P.O. Stand at the NABA Philatelic Exhibition held at Basle in June 1971. The ten Postage Due stamps were also on sale in a separate wallet. (*Price for the two wallets* £50.)

They were also sold at later foreign exhibitions where the British Post Office had a stand such as Scandinavia, San Francisco, etc., as an introductory offer of the decimal stamps. This did not apply to Regional or Special issues.

UPP4 No. 38 (25.11.71) 20p., 50p. and £1  ..   ..   ..   ..   ..   ..   ..   ..   8·00

This pack originally contained the £1 No. U43 (in cellophane wrapper) but at some later stage the redrawn £1 stamps, Nos. U44/5, were included instead (in polythene wrapper).

**Withdrawn**   No. UPP3, 24.11.71; No. UPP4, 9.76

**Quantity Sold**   No. UPP3, 42,330

## First Day Covers

On official cover prepared and issued by the Post Office and stamps franked with a commemorative postmark.

| | | |
|---|---|---|
| UFD1 (17.6.70) | 10p., 20p. and 50p.  ..   ..   ..   ..   ..   ..   .. | 5·50 |
| | *a.* Plus £1 (U43) ..   ..   ..   ..   ..   ..   .. | 10·00 |
| UFD2 (6.12.72) | £1 (U44)   ..   ..   ..   ..   ..   ..   ..   .. | 7·00 |

# SECTION UD

# Machin Decimal Issues

## 1971–90. Sheet and Coil Stamps in Photogravure

---

## General Notes

**INTRODUCTION.** Decimal currency was introduced in Great Britain on 15 February 1971 and the new stamps were ready for general use on that day. However, a country-wide postal strike had been in operation before 15 February and did not end until 10 March 1971. All but a few Crown post offices were closed but most sub-offices remained open. However, distribution of supplies of the decimal issues had started before the strike and we understand that it was possible to purchase all issues, including booklets and coils, at some places on 15 February. Special arrangements were made to cater for first day covers as explained in the notes at the end of this Section.

**ARRANGEMENT.** Following the precedents laid down in the earlier volumes, this Section takes each value in turn and follows its history through the different papers and gums employed and phosphor band changes.

The general arrangement is to show in Section UD first the basic listing according to papers and gums, followed by errors and varieties. This is followed by illustrations of the listed varieties and a record of minor constant sheet flaws. This is followed by a record of any coils issued. Cylinder blocks are listed with the basic stamps.

In Section UE we list separately the booklet panes and the varieties on them and set out according to perforator types. See the separate General Notes to that section.

Section UF contains the multi-value coil strips in photogravure.

At the end of these notes there is a table of Machin issues printed in photogravure setting out which values occurred in each state and quoting their catalogue numbers for easy reference.

**PRINTERS AND SHEET ARRANGEMENTS.** All the photogravure Machin decimal issues with the exception of No. U162/ were printed by Harrison & Sons. The stamps were printed on continuous reels of paper "on the web" usually in double pane sheets, i.e. 400 stamps consisting of two panes (no dot and dot) each of 200 stamps arranged in twenty rows of ten stamps, the panes being guillotined before issue. Single pane printings, usually no dot, occur and a dagger is used to indicate where the dot cylinder from this printing does not exist. Exceptionally one half of the printing may not be issued as in the case of the 4½p. cylinder 1 dot. Another example of single pane cylinder printing arose due to the diminishing pressure at the sides of cylinders 13 and 14 when only the central part of the cylinder was etched. The old Halley press was used for these printings and the missing phosphor variety on cylinder 14 can be attributed to machine failure. Some 10p. stamps printed on a Chambon press from cylinders 7, 8 and 9 were double pane (no dot), but both panes were identical and were separated by a gutter margin. This was the only occasion that a low value definitive has appeared in this format.

The various arrangements of the sheets printed for making up into booklets are described in the Introduction to the Booklets Appendix and some are illustrated in the Perforators Appendix.

The vertical delivery coil cylinders used on the "Jumelle" press have a circumference of 21 stamps and are divided into rolls numbered 1 to 12. Cylinder R4, used for the first printings of the 1p. EL coils, was a double pane cylinder (no dot and dot), producing 504 stamps at each revolution. All other vertical delivery coil cylinders are single pane producing 252 stamps at a time. The sideways delivery cylinders (including the multi-value coils) have a circumference of 25 stamps and are divided into rolls numbered 1 to 10, producing 250 stamps at each revolution.

Vertical delivery coils have, since 1977, been printed by cylinders which were also employed for single value booklet panes.

**MACHIN PORTRAIT.** As with the £.s.d. low values, the design was from a plaster cast by Arnold Machin. Several plaques were obtained from the plaster mould of the original cast and of these Harrisons used two and made a master negative of each.

**Head B.** This head, always on a solid ground, is from Negative I and has the curved "shadow" below the bust (illustrated in the Introduction to Section XB). It has two curved shadows in the hair and irregularities in the pearls of the necklace. It was used for the 1, 1½, 2, 3p. (both colours), 4p. (three colours), 5½, 6½, 7, 8, 9p. (U171/3), 10p. (U182/3), 11½p., drab (UMFB 23/4) and £1 to £5.

Head B1   Head B2

Head high      Head low
*(Actual size)*

The Type B1 head underwent a modification late in 1976 when a new multipositive was introduced. The first state had a missing screening dot in the bottom left frame about 1 mm. from the left, appearing as a slight nick. This was corrected in what has come to be described as Head B2, with the base nearer to the bottom frame line, as shown in the actual size illustration above.

**9**

Head B

Head C

Two curved shadows in hair
Pearls irregular (one missing)

One curved shadow in hair
Pearls regular

Head D

As Head C but with strengthened outline
at back of hair, collar and front of dress

The following is a list of Head Type B2 stamps and sources which also exist with Head B1. The 11½p. drab was the highest denomination, excluding £1 to £5, to have both Head Types after which Head B2 was used on values with solid ground.

1p.  No. U59 from Panes UMFB1/2
     No. U60 from Panes UMFB3/6 and UMFB19/20
     No. U61 from Panes UMFB7, UMFB12, UMFB31 and UMFB34
     No. U63 from sheets Cylinder 14 and 13p. multi-value coil
     No. U64 from sheets Cylinder 14
     No. U65 from Panes UMFB39/41
     No. U66 from Pane UMFB42
     No. U67 from Pane UWB31

2p. Myrtle-green No. U80 from Panes UWB7/8 and UWB11
No. U81 from Panes UMFB9/10 and UMFB14/17
No. U82 from sheets Cylinder 13
No. U83 from sheets Cylinders 13 and 14

3p. Bright magenta No. U110 from sheets Cylinder 43; Pane UWB16
No. U111 from sheets Cylinder 43
No. U111*a* from 15p. multi-value coil
No. U113 from Pane UWB11

4p. Greenish blue No. U127(2) from 13p. multi-value coil
No. U129 from Pane UMFB34
No. U130 from Pane UWB23
No. U131 from Pane UWB23

6½p. No. U142 from sheets Cylinders 9, 11; Panes UFB1/2 and vertical RL coil
Nos. U144/5 from Panes UMFB3/4

7p. Purple-brown No. U154 from sheets Cylinders 14, 20, 21, 22; Panes UFB5/6, UMFB7/8
and vertical XL coil
Nos. U155/6 from Panes UMFB5/6

8p. No. U162 from sheets Cylinder 10: Panes UFB9/10, UMFB11/13 and vertical AL coil
Nos. U163/4 from Panes UMFB9/10

11½p. Drab No. U201 from sheets Cylinder 1, 3; Panes UFB17/18, UMFB25 and vertical EL coil
Nos. U202/3 from Panes UMFB19/22

**Head C.** This derives from Negative II and gives a three-dimensional effect. It has a single curved shadow in the hair and the pearls of the necklace are complete. It was used for the values with light to dark gradated backgrounds, namely the ½, 2½p. (both colours), 3½p. bronze-green, 5p. (both colours), 6, 7½, 8½, 9p. deep violet, 9½, 12, 13p. olive-grey, 15½, 18p. deep violet, 19½, 25, 28 and 31p.

**Head D.** This is also from Negative II and is basically a Type C head amended by strengthening the outline of the head and particularly around the collar in order to separate the head from the pale background. It was used for the 3½p. purple-brown, 4½, 10p. orange-brown, 10½p, (both colours), 11, 12½, 13p. pale chestnut, 14, 16, 16½, 17p. three colours, 17½, 20, 23 and 50p.

**MULTIPOSITIVES.** A multipositive is a glass photographic plate on which the master negative is projected, using a step and repeat camera. A manual operation initially, this was later automated. For the decimal Machin issues two multipositives are used, one for the head and background and the other for the value. The head multipositive is common to all the values of each head type, but more than one of the second multipositive may be used for any individual value, particularly if issued in different forms (sheet stamps, booklets or coils). The use of a new value multipositive is often indicated by a variation in the shape and thickness of the figures of the letter "p", and the more important of these variations are listed and illustrated as different value types.

A lack of uniformity in the figures and their placing, combined with increases in postal rates (resulting in values such as the 19½p. which overfilled the available space), led the Post Office to commission Jeffery Matthews to redesign the value tablets in 1982. This new generation of sleeker figures, which are to become standard, first appeared on the 20½p. value issued on 30 March 1983. Although described in the Catalogue as additional value types they are not treated as minor varieties and are, accordingly, listed with whole numbers since the restyled value is very different from that it replaced.

Another variation under this heading stems from changes in the relative position of the two multipositives. In the days of the manual step and repeat process this could result in "floating values" where the position of the value tablet in relation to the bust could vary on a single sheet, but because each stamp could be fractionally different from its neighbour they are not listed. However, even after the process was automated, the introduction of a new cylinder could result in a change of the value position or "setting" and this would be indicative of that particular printing as occurred on the 12p. two 8 mm. bands printed on the Jumelle and Chambon presses. For the specialist constant "settings" are often a valuable indicator of printing source, but the variations are too numerous to list here.

Varieties and minor flaws sometimes occur on multipositives and may therefore be found on different cylinders and also in different values. Sometimes they are retouched individually on the cylinders affected and these retouches are likely to vary from one another.

**DIRECTION OF PRINTING.** It is known that some sheet stamps have been printed both upright (from bottom to top) and inverted and others inverted only, but this is outside the scope of this catalogue. However, the direction of the printing is an important factor in plating varieties on booklet panes. The method for distinguishing the direction of the printing is described in Appendix I under the Booklet Perforator Type APPLL.

**PAPER.** Unwatermarked chalk-surfaced paper was used for all values. There have been a few instances where the coating has been omitted. Such varieties do not respond to the chalky test (applying silver to see if it will produce a black line) and may be further distinguished from the normal chalk-surfaced paper by the fibres which clearly show on the surface, resulting in a rougher impression and less definition to the screening dots. Stamps showing signs of poor impression due to insufficient ink (which are known as "dry prints") are sometimes confused with uncoated paper.

**Original Coated Paper (OCP) and Fluorescent Coated Paper (FCP).** OCP is the original coated paper which is off-white. Late in 1971 the printers introduced fluorescent coated paper (FCP) which gives a clearer impression. It is much whiter and reacts clearly under an ultra violet lamp, although it can also be distinguished by the naked eye. It also gives a much stronger chalk reaction. It is fugitive under prolonged exposure to ultra violet light as well as to sunlight. The two papers are distinguished in the lists.

**Phosphorised Paper.** For a description of phosphorised paper see the note after Phosphor Cylinder Numbers.

**Paper Thickness.** Variations in the thickness of paper sometimes occur in the making and are undetected where the finished reel conforms to the prescribed weight. Within the reel there may be sections where the paper is unusually thick or thin; such items are outside the scope of this catalogue. Thinner paper was deliberately introduced for the multi-value coils with PVAD gum to help prevent them from sticking in the machines. We list these as well as the 3p. from an issue of 30p. Booklets containing Pane UB38 FCP/PVA.

**Glossy Paper.** A number of stamps were originally reported on "glazed" paper, due to their glossy or shiny appearance. Some are quite distinct, but the cause was due to the action of the printing cylinder giving a shine to the finished product in a buffing action rather than by any additive. There is bound to be some variation between different printings and so we make no attempt to list them.

**Gum.** Polyvinyl alcohol (PVA) was used for all values of the original decimal issue of February 1971 and it occurred on the fluorescent coated paper as well as the original coated paper. Exceptionally gum arabic was retained for the multi-value coil because this was perforated by the Swedish "lawnmower" rotary perforator, which was unsatisfactory with PVA gum.

PVA is almost invisible except that a small amount of pale yellowish colouring matter was introduced to make it possible to see that the stamps had been gummed. It sometimes has a mottled effect.

Gum Arabic (GA) is the normal shiny gum. When the Swedish perforator was pressed into use to maintain supplies of sheet stamps, gum arabic was introduced for the ½p., 2½p., 3p. (2 bands and centre band), 4p. and 6p. values.

From 1973 dextrin was added to the PVA gum (PVAD). Because this is virtually colourless a bluish green colouring matter was added to distinguish it from the earlier pure PVA. It was introduced for use with the rotary perforator attached to the "Jumelle" press and is now the standard gum used for all sheets, booklet panes and coils.

**PERFORATION.** All stamps in this Section are perforated 15 × 14 as for the £.s.d. issues. The horizontal perforation is very close to the three-quarters mark and so this is sometimes described elsewhere as 14½ × 14.

A number of different perforators were used for both sheets and booklet panes and these are described and illustrated in Appendix I. The cylinder number blocks are listed according to the different perforation types illustrated in Appendix I.

**PHOSPHOR BANDS.** The purpose of these is to activate the Automatic Letter Facing machines and to sort the mail into first and second class. Further technical information is given in the Introduction to Section S in Vol. 3 of this catalogue. See also an article by Aubrey Walker on "Printed Phosphor and Phosphor-coated Stamp Paper" in the April 1977 issue of the *Philatelic Bulletin* published by the Philatelic Bureau. Suffice it to say, however, that so far as this volume is concerned, all the phosphor used was applied by photogravure cylinders and normally reacts with a violet afterglow under ultra violet light.

**New Phosphor Ink.** In July 1986 the 12p. bright emerald with a centre phosphor band was issued as an experiment using a phosphor ink designed to overcome the problem of band discolouration. It had been realised for some time that certain stamp colours were tinting the phosphor as it was applied. The new phosphor ink is based on a change in the solvent employed which makes it impervious to the coloured ink used for the stamps. Further changes to the chemical make-up of the resins used in the ink and the phosphor ensured that the phosphor had improved protection when in contact with moisture so that the important phosphor signal was not reduced. The ink was developed by Harrisons and gradually replaced the original. Detection is possible under ultra violet light as the original appears dark in comparison with the new ink which is very pale. In the lists we make a distinction only when both inks have been employed on the same issue or when an error has been made.

**Phosphor Reacting Green.** Phosphor, which under u.v. light gives a green reaction, was used by mistake for a printing of the 2½p. value in 1972 and listed as No. U87b. This, although mixed with the violet phosphor, was of sufficient strength to cause problems. It is quite easy to identify and reacts to short wave ultra-violet light in the 2000–3000 Ångstrom range.

**Phosphor Contamination.** In 1973 the violet phosphor became contaminated with an inorganic phosphor based on zinc sulphide of a type used by certain overseas postal administrations. This was a weak mixture which had no effect on the normal reaction of the letter facing machinery. Although the reaction is generally greenish, it is quite different from the green phosphor of No. U87b.

Moreover, the light exhibited by zinc sulphide is yellow and this is the colour quoted by a Post Office technical official, so we have adopted this term.

The yellow phosphor reacts after irradiation by longwave ultra violet light at 3650 Ångstroms and is distinct from the violet phosphor which only responds briefly to shortwave UV light. However, it is only seen under certain conditions. In the absence of an ultra violet lamp which is completely enclosed, the examination should take place in darkness after allowing some minutes for the eyes to adjust to the dark. Irradiation should take place with the eyes closed and then opened after the lamp has been switched off when the phosphorescence should be visible for a period of up to 15 seconds. This longwave reaction can be seen using a shortwave lamp if the stamp is covered by a piece of plastic (such as the transparent material from a Hawid strip) to absorb and eliminate the shortwave UV light.

We record the stamps affected in footnotes under the basic stamps in Section UD together with details of the source of the printing. They all relate to a short period around May 1973. Usually only part of the printings was affected.

| Value | Cat. No. | Paper/Gum | Source |
|---|---|---|---|
| ½p. (I) | U48 | FCP/PVA | UB25 (Cyl. B17) |
| ½p. (II) | U48c | FCP/PVA | USB3 |
| 1p. | U57 | FCP/PVA | USB7 |
| 1½p. | U72 | FCP/PVA | USB7 |
| 2p. | U78 | FCP/PVA | USB3 (cyl. B7) |
| 2½p. (I) · | U87 | FCP/PVA | Cyl. 11 (phos. 8) |
| 2½p. (II) | U87f (centre band) | FCP/PVA | UB32 (Cyl. B19) |
| 2½p. (II) | U92 (band left) | FCP/PVA | USB10 |
| 3p. | U103 | FCP/PVA | Cyls. 8 (phos. 7), 10 (phos. 7) |
| 3p. | U103 | FCP/PVA | UB38 (Cyl. B27) |
| 3p. | U103 | FCP/PVA | USB10 (Cyl. B9) |
| 3p. | U103 | FCP/PVA | UB40 (Cyl. B14) |
| 4p. | U123 | FCP/GA | Cyl. 4 (phos. 7) |
| 6p. | U144 | FCP/GA | Cyl. 4 (phos. 7) |

The sources of the booklet panes so far recorded are as follows:—

| Pane Cat. No. | Booklet Value | Booklet Cat. No. | Date |
|---|---|---|---|
| USB3 | 10p. | DN61/2 | Aug. and Oct. 1973 |
| USB7 | 10p. | DN61 | Aug. 1973 |
| UB38 | 30p. | DQ71/2 | June and Aug. 1973 |
| USB10, UB25, 32 and 40 | 50p. | DT12 | Aug. 1973 |

The yellow phosphor mixture has also been found in Regional issues where they are recorded in the General Notes.

This discovery is treated in considerable detail in articles by J. E. Thompson in the December 1978 issues of *The Bookmark* and *Guidec*.

**Phosphor bands printed under the printing ink.** It has been reported that values from certain printings have the phosphor bands below the ink. With the exception of booklet pane No. UB47a which has cream-tinted phosphor, we do not list these stamps as varieties as they are difficult to distinguish. All are on fluorescent coated paper with PVAD gum.

| Cat. No. | Value | Cyl. No. | Phos. Cyl. No. | Perf. Type |
|---|---|---|---|---|
| U133 | 4½p. | 3, 7 | 26 | A |
| U146 | 6p. | 8 | 26 | A |
| U146e | 6p. | 4 | 7 | A |
| U153 | 7p. | 3 | 26 | A |
| U154 | 7p. | 14 | 29 | A |
| U161 | 8p. | 3 | 26 | A |
| U175 | 9p. | 11, 16 | 7 | A |
| U184 | 10p. | 3 | 7 | A |
| U198 | 11p. | 4 | 30 | RE |
| U212 | 12½p. | 2 | 20 | RE |

**Band Widths.** The bands are normally 9½ mm. wide and are placed over the sides of the stamps to give one band on each side. However, 8 mm. bands were used for the 50p. UMFB3/6, 9/10, 14/15, 19/20, 23/4 and 26/7 multi-value booklet panes. Where only one band is required to denote second-class post a narrow 4 mm. band is placed in the centre of the stamp. Where a one-band stamp is *se-tenant* with a two-band one the single band appears at one or other side of the stamp and not in the centre except for the *se-tenant* panes in the Christmas booklets.

From 8 January 1985 a 4.5 mm. centre band was introduced for the first time on 13p. second-class stamps contained in the stitched sponsored booklets. These were later used in machine booklets; the sheets continue to use the standard 4 mm. bands.

On the 5 September 1988 50p. and £1 booklets were issued containing 19p. values with a narrow band of 3.5 mm. These narrow bands in new phosphor ink are difficult to measure but they appear to vary between 3 and 4 mm. particularly on the later 22p. values with imperforate edges.

**Phosphor Bands Omitted.** Phosphor bands are sometimes omitted in error and these are listed. Sometimes "dry prints" of the phosphor occur giving a visible impression of the band (screening) but having no phosphor reaction under the ultra violet lamp. These are not listed. The omission of phosphor on stamps printed on the "Jumelle" press can occur on full sheets as a result of the phosphor ink running out and not being noticed but more often it occurs through stopping and restarting the machine. In this event the omission is much more likely to affect only parts of the sheet or even a part of a stamp. Stamps with partially omitted phosphor are not listed unless this affects the number of bands. The 9½p. with missing band, Nos. U181*b/c* are examples.

**"All-over" Phosphor.** Stamps are frequently reported with "all-over" phosphor but most of these are due to the inefficiency of the phosphor doctor blade, allowing the phosphor ink to creep under and extend over the stamp. The degree of phosphor wash is thus variable. In this catalogue, only the more marked examples are listed and other irregularities of the phosphor doctor blade, such as stamps with "extra bands" may be recorded in a footnote.

We list the 9p. violet from Cylinder 16, the 10½p. yellow and the 50p. with "all-over" phosphor as these all have a *thick* coating of phosphor with which the phosphor doctor blade was unable to cope. On the 6½p. two bands and centre band there was a weak viscosity of the phosphor ink which extended under the doctor blade to give a thin overall coating and these are recorded in footnotes.

**Pre-printed "All-over" Phosphor Paper.** In October 1979 the 1p., 2p. and 10p. orange-brown were issued on "all-over" phosphor paper; the phosphor was printed first by a cylinder (P35 or P37) with 150 screen and the ink was printed over the phosphor coating rather than on the coated paper. The ink cylinder has a 250 screen and the result was a very blurred impression. In order to identify these stamps it is necessary to use a magnifying lens with the printed surface of the stamp at an angle to the light source and not overhead. The phosphor screen shows best on the unprinted area of the stamp.

**Misplaced Phosphor Bands.** Phosphor bands are sometimes found misplaced but they are not listed unless they affect the number of bands, i.e. one broad band instead of two bands. These are very popular with collectors and are described as one broad band left, right or centre but we do not make these distinctions. Nor do we list misplaced centre bands as a general rule as this can be a matter of degree.

**Phosphor Bands Inverted Printing.** Examples are included in the cylinder block listings which show inverted printing of the phosphor cylinder. The first number which appears in between the two panes will be located on dot blocks when the margin is wide. Therefore no dot blocks will show ink cylinder number only and the dot block will show the same plus an inverted phosphor number. We do not give prices for inverted phosphor cylinder numbers located outside the cylinder block format.

**PHOSPHOR SCREENS.** The phosphor bands were applied in photogravure, some of the cylinders having a 150-screen and others a 250-screen. Screens are measured by the number of screening dots in a square inch, so that a 250-screen is much finer than a 150 screen, the dots being closer together. The apparent absence of a screen on parts of a printing is due to the cylinder being clogged.

The phosphor is printed by a cylindrical drum and on some cylinders the "ends" do not join properly, causing a kink in the phosphor band, which may appear as a horizontal line across the band. On some cylinders the ends do not join at all and so a phosphor insert has to be applied to the cylinder. Screen joins can only be found on stamps printed vertically as on stamps printed sideways the phosphor bands run across the cylinder.

Stamps showing phosphor joins are collected by specialists but are outside the scope of this catalogue.

We do not distinguish these screens in the lists where single stamps are concerned, but as the phosphor cylinders used in the decimal issues have distinctive numbers it is possible to relate the phosphor screens to the cylinder numbers as follows:—

**Sheet Stamps**

| 2 Band Cylinders | | Centre Band Cylinders | "All-over" Phosphor Cylinders |
|---|---|---|---|
| 150 Screen | 250 Screen | 150 Screen | 150 Screen |
| 7 | 1 | 1 (Enschedé) | P35 |
| 10* | 2 | 5 | P37 |
| 11* | 4 | 8 | |
| 12* | 22* | P9 | |
| 13 | | 14 | |
| 13A | | 14A | |
| 17 | | 18 | |
| P21 | | P19* | |
| 26 | | 20 | |
| 28† | | 27† | |
| 30 | | 29 | |
| P33 | | 31 | |
| 34 | | P39 | |
| P36 | | 41 | |

*These have only been used for Regional stamps.
†Used only for coils and folded booklets.

## Booklet Panes

All have 150-line screens apart from a small part of the 1p./1½p. horizontally *se-tenant* pane No. USB7 from the 10p. booklets of February and April 1973 which had 250-line screens. These are very scarce.

## Coils

As there is no set pattern about these the screens are indicated in the lists.

**PHOSPHOR CYLINDER NUMBERS.** The phosphor cylinder numbers were introduced as a regular feature in the decimal issues. They can be identified under ultra violet light.

At first they were unsynchronised and so could be found anywhere in the left-hand margin of both panes. Very soon however, they were synchronised in the box to the left of the ink cylinder number. Sometimes they were displaced but also synchronised in the wrong place.

Some phosphor cylinder numbers on sheet stamps are prefixed by the letter "P" and where the letter is normally visible it is shown in the lists. It sometimes happens that part of the cylinder number is guillotined off.

**Phosphor Cylinder Number Displacements.** The phosphor cylinder numbers are listed under the cylinder blocks of six and in conjunction with the ink cylinder numbers. Where they are displaced within a block of 10 stamps (2 × 5) this is indicated by a figure showing the distance in millimetres between the base of the ink cylinder box and the base of the phosphor cylinder number. A plus sign indicates displacement above the box and a minus sign a displacement below it. *Any variations of less than 20 mm. are ignored.* The figure in brackets given after this measurement indicates the row against which the phosphor cylinder number appears.

Blocks of ten are quoted for State 3 of phosphor cylinder 2 and other displacements falling between rows 16 and 17/18 are also quoted in blocks of ten. If more than one displacement exists outside the block of ten the range of displacement is given for the record but cylinder blocks of six will be identical and the prices the same.

We do not usually quote for displaced cylinder numbers on their own. Prices for larger pieces than blocks of ten with ink cylinder numbers are not quoted.

**Cylinder Number Characteristics.** Some cylinder numbers exist in various states or have certain characteristics. All are synchronised except where otherwise mentioned.

Cyl.
1. This is always shown reversed, with the serif on the right. It is printed very wide to the left of the first vertical phosphor band. Consequently on about 95% of the dot panes it is guillotined off and appears in the right-hand margin of the no dot panes.
2. This exists in several states:—

    *State* 1. Small 2 which is 1¼ mm. high on no dot panes and 2 mm. high on dot panes. Unsynchronised. Described as S2.

    *State* 2. An additional large 4 mm. 2 was engraved on the cylinder approximately 41 mm. below the small 2, but still unsynchronised. Described as L2, S2.

    *State* 3. As State 2 but synchronised. Later the large 2 of the dot pane was re-engraved inverted; the large 2 of the no dot pane was strengthened, giving a thicker appearance. Described as L2, S2 Re-engraved.
4. This exists in two states:—

    *State* 1. Small 4 about 2 mm. on both panes. Unsynchronised. Described as S4.

    *State* 2. Large 4 about 4 mm. superimposed over the small 4. Synchronised. Described as L4.
8. This was not engraved on the dot cylinder and dot cylinder blocks show only the inverted "T" of the phosphor box.
17. and 20. On the no dot cylinder blocks only traces of these numbers may be visible and sometimes they are not visible at all. In such instances they may be identified by a study of the phosphor "inserts" in the adjacent phosphor bands.
26. This was not engraved on the dot cylinder and dot cylinder blocks show neither phosphor cylinder number nor phosphor box.
29.
30. } The phosphor numbers are engraved sideways instead of upright.
31.

**Inverted Phosphor Cylinder Numbers.** Occasionally the phosphor cylinder was applied inverted and in such instances the no dot cylinder blocks show no phosphor cylinder number but on the dot pane part of the cylinder number appears inverted on the cylinder block and the whole number occurs inverted in the right-hand margin. If trimmed wide the margin will show the inverted number on the dot pane.

**PHOSPHORISED PAPER.** On 13 November 1974 the 4½p. value, then the first class letter rate stamp was issued on paper with phosphor incorporated in the coating in addition to the usual 2 bands. This was to test the efficacy of paper treated with a phosphor coating. The experiment was repeated with the 8½p. value issued on 24 March 1976 but on this occasion the stamp was printed on phosphorised paper without phosphor bands. From 15 August 1979 phosphorised paper was accepted for use generally, this paper replacing phosphor bands on most values other than those required for the basic second class rate.

The phosphorised paper used for the initial printings of the 11½p., 13p. and 15p. values issued on 15 August 1979 gave a weak after-glow in response to ultra violet light. Later printings were issued which gave a stronger after-glow. The 10p. stamp (U185) which was printed on the Chambon press, was similarly treated with the weak phosphor additive and the stamps were, in consequence issued with 2 phosphor bands in addition. This was done in order that letters, franked with these stamps received first class handling when sorted by the automatic sorting machinery.

The inter-action of chemicals in the drying process produces stamps on phosphorised paper which have either a matt or a glossy surface. The glossy stamps tend to have a photo-negative effect when the printed surface is angled so that light reflects from it. Stamps thus treated are mentioned in a footnote.

**Phosphorised (Advanced Coated) Paper.** In order to resolve the problem of ink absorption in the drying process, the chemists at the printer's laboratories developed a different method of combining phosphor with fluorescence. It became necessary to increase the amount of fluorescent brightener to reduce longwave ultra violet sensitivity. Under ultra violet light the improved fluorescent property in the paper coating gives a stronger result than before and this paper has been employed for most values. Sheet printings of the 15½p. followed by the 1p. and 16p. were the first three values to appear on this Advanced Coated Paper.

**Fluorescent Brightener Omitted.** Occasionally the fluorescent additive in the coating is omitted in error and these stamps give a dull response under ultra-violet light. They are distinguished in the lists as fluorescent brightener omitted. Outside the scope of this catalogue are stamps showing reduced optical brightening or fluorescent additives which exist on some printings. Their existence does not imply the re-introduction of phosphorised (fluorescent coated) paper *after* the use of advanced coated paper.

**UNDERPRINTS.** Symbols, printed in pale blue ink over the gum, denote that the stamp was issued in a booklet sold at a discount rate. The stamps thus marked were identifiable for post office accounting purposes.

**VARIETIES IN SHEETS.** We have only listed cylinder varieties that we have actually seen and know to be constant in the position given. Others have been reported and may be added in future editions as specimens become available for illustration.

The position is indicated by stating the cylinder number, whether no dot or dot pane, followed by the position, giving first the horizontal row and then the position in it. Thus "Cyl. 15 no dot, R. 10/3" means cylinder 15 no dot, the third stamp in the tenth row down. Where the same cylinder is used on a different stamp, e.g. variation in number of bands, paper, gum etc., the varieties on that cylinder will recur, unless corrected by retouching, and they are then listed again. Under the variety illustration we give the catalogue numbers relating to the particular variety. See also note about varieties under "Multipositive" above.

The prices are for single stamps and extra copies needed to make positional blocks will be charged as normals.

**MINOR CONSTANT FLAWS.** These are so numerous that they are merely recorded without illustrations. Their location on the stamp is indicated, where helpful by reference to the S.G. "Thirkell" Position Finder, an essential tool for identifying flaws. The recording of these flaws, often insignificant in themselves, will prove an aid in identifying a particular cylinder and will also serve to show that the flaw has been considered for listing as a variety but rejected as being too minor. Again we have only recorded what we have actually seen but the picture is necessarily incomplete as we have not been able to view full sheets from every cylinder. We do not record minor constant flaws on coils or booklet panes.

**COIL VARIETIES.** These are listed under the sheet stamps and the Roll number is given where it is known. This number is printed on the outer wrapper of the coil and corresponds to the row in the sheet before reeling.

The sheet arrangements of the coils are described under "Printers and Sheet Arrangements" earlier in these notes. Varieties on the 1p. EL coil printed from Cylinder R4 will occur on half the coils bearing the roll numbers as this was a double pane cylinder, but all the others are single pane cylinders.

The 6½, 7, 8, 8½, 9, 10 and 12p. coils were all printed from double pane cylinders on the "Jumelle" press. There were twelve rolls for vertical delivery coils and ten for sideways delivery coils (including multi-value coils) and constant varieties will be repeated on every 21st stamp on vertical delivery rolls and on every 25th stamp on sideways delivery rolls. The Chambon press has been employed to print booklet panes and vertical delivery coils from the same single pane cylinder and constant varieties will be repeated on every 12th stamp.

Horizontal coils printed by single pane cylinders on the Chambon press will show constant varieties repeated on every 16th stamp. This includes the 1p. SC and 12p. SA coils and onwards all prefixed S.

*Prices for coil varieties are for single stamps but they are best collected in the centre of a strip of five.*

**SHADES.** There is quite a range of shades in the low value decimal stamps but we only list a few which are more easily identifiable. A detailed list of shades is not advisable where there are a number of intermediates and one does not know what the future may bring. We shall review the position in later editions.

**DATES OF ISSUE.** So far as possible stamps are listed according to paper and gum in the order in which they appeared. Sometimes a change of paper or gum came out in booklets before sheet issues but we quote the earliest known date. Naturally some issues of booklets contain different mixtures of papers or gums within the same "issue". For instance stocks of booklet sheets left over after making up an order for booklets with a particular dated cover were generally used up together with a new printing for the next dated issue of booklets.

**WITHDRAWAL DATES.** Stamps with inappropriate phosphor bands for contemporary usage were generally withdrawn or stocks allowed to run out at post offices but they continued to remain on sale for some time at the Philatelic Bureau in Edinburgh and other Philatelic Sales Counters. There have been some instances of stamps being brought back on sale at the Bureau after having previously been withdrawn. The withdrawal dates quoted refer only to the Philatelic Bureau and where there have been temporary withdrawals this information is given.

**POST OFFICE PRESENTATION PACKS.** They are listed at the end of the Section.

**FIRST DAY COVERS.** These are listed after the Presentation Packs but we only quote for official covers prepared and issued by the Post Office and cancelled by "FIRST DAY OF ISSUE" circular postmarks.

**"UNPRINTED STAMPS".** Widely trimmed sheet margins sometimes produce the effect of unprinted stamps as illustrated above. The blank paper often has the phosphor bands printed as on the normal stamps. In the Machin, Regional and Postage Due stamps they come from either left- or right-hand margins and they may also occur at the top or bottom of Machin issues printed by the "Jumelle" machine.

**POST OFFICE TRAINING SCHOOLS.** Special labels were printed for staff decimalisation training but ordinary stamps were also overprinted with two thick vertical bars for use at counter training schools. Their issue to the public was unauthorised and we therefore do not list them.

**SHEET MARKINGS.** We give below the various markings found on the sheets of the low value Machin decimal stamps. Those which apply to other issues are shown in the General Notes to the other Sections. They are particularly helpful in establishing the position of varieties where marginal blocks are available and can also help in identifying the type of perforator used or the type of machine employed for printing etc.

Sheet Cylinder Number          Sheet Marginal Arrows

**Cylinder Number.** Sheet cylinder numbers always occur in the left-hand margin opposite Row 18/1. In double pane cylinders the no dot pane is on the left and the dot pane on the right. The left-hand portion of the box is intended for the phosphor cylinder number which usually requires an ultra violet lamp for identification.

In the bicoloured 9p. and 10p. values the portrait and value cylinder number is placed under the frame cylinder just below the box.

**Marginal Arrows.** These occur in the middle rows of the sheet as an aid to Post Office clerks when breaking up sheets and are printed in the colour of the stamp from the same cylinder. They are therefore to be found above and below vertical rows 5/6 and at sides opposite rows 10/11. On the Chambon printed 10p. (cylinders 7, 8 and 9) the arrows at both sides of the sheet are opposite horizontal rows 5/6 and 16/17. They also occur above vertical rows 5/6 pointing down in the top and gutter margins.

**Marginal Rules.** These are the solid bands of colour which appear below the bottom row of the sheet as illustrated above with the bottom marginal arrow. They are invariably co-extensive, that is with breaks between each stamp, and they are now normally of uniform width.

The 8p. from cylinder 1 printed by Enschedé and the 10p. from cylinders 7, 8 and 9 printed on the Chambon press by Harrison do not have marginal rules.

Perforation Guide Hole               Autotron Mark

**Perforation Guide Holes.** These appear as above opposite rows 14/15 at left on no dot panes and in the right-hand margin of dot panes. The guide hole is only applied with Perforation Type A but the engraved box still appears on sheets with Perforation Types R(S), R or RE. However, they do not occur on the sheets printed from cylinders 13 and 14 of the 8p. or cylinders 7, 8 and 9 of the 10p. values.

The letters "S O N" stand for "Selvedge", "Off-side" and "Near-side" and they appear in the reverse order on the other side of the double-pane sheet.

**Autotron Mark.** This occurs in the colour of the stamp in row 8/9 in the left-hand margin of no dot panes printed by the "Jumelle" press (Perforation Type R or RE). Some single colour Halley sheet printings exist with these marks as the cylinders were originally intended for the Jumelle press.

Bicolour printings:

9p. to cyl 4A 4B and 10p. to cyl 5A 4B the autotron marks appear on dot pane below columns 2/3 (light colour) columns 3/4 (dark colour).

9p. and 10p. cyl 8A 6B (Jumelle printings) the autotron marks appear on the no dot pane below columns 7/8 (dark colour) and columns 8/9 (light colour).

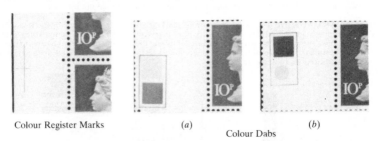

Colour Register Marks            (a)                              (b)

Colour Dabs

**Colour Register Marks.** Bicolour printings:

9p. to cyl 4A 4B and 10p. to cyl 5A 4B the colour register marks appear in the left hand margin on the no dot pane against rows 1/2 and also rows 17/18. Similarly in the right hand margin on the dot pane.

**18**

9p. and 10p. cyl 8A 6B (Jumelle printings) the colour register marks appear in the left hand margin on the no dot pane against rows 1/2 and also rows 19/20. Similarly in the right hand margin on the dot pane.

On the £1.41, £1.50 and £1.60 values the cross in the top margin above vertical row 4 on the no dot pane was changed to a 3 mm diameter circle over the cross.

**Colour Dabs.** These appear in two forms: as (a) on the bicoloured 9p., and 10p. up to cylinders 5A–4B, and as (b) on cylinders 8A–6B. Later printings of the 10p. cylinders 8A–6B showed the orange-brown dab as square but the original round dab was still visible. They occur between the panes opposite row 19 and may appear at right of no dot pane or at left of dot pane according to the width of the selvedge.

**Total Sheet Values.** As an aid to counter clerks in stocktaking and in selling stamps by the sheet, the "TOTAL SHEET VALUE" and amount is printed in the margins, four times in the sheet on each pane opposite rows 5/7 and 15/17 reading up at left and down at right. On the 8p. printed from cylinder 14 the inscriptions are opposite rows 5/6 and 15/16. The inscription in the sheets printed by the Chambon press is in the top and gutter margins above vertical rows 4/7.

**Sheet numbers.** Most sheets are serially numbered in black after printing for checking purposes but the numbers are liable to be placed anywhere in the margins and so are of no use for identifying a position. They are not of much help in establishing whether a sheet occurred early or late in a printing either as a particular printing was not necessarily numbered from 1 and several machines may have been used. However, in the past, Halley press printings show sheet numbers which have irregularly aligned figures. Timson and Thrissell printings show sheet numbers reading downwards instead of upwards.

Jumelle printings are serially numbered with six digits, for example 003166, placed in the vertical margin sideways reading up or down. Usually a number in the left margin indicates no dot; the dot side will have the number in the right margin.

**Checkers' Marks.** These are small encircled numbers applied with a rubber stamp in a variety of colours. They are applied by Post Office checkers when counting the sheets delivered by the printer. As with sheet numbers they are liable to placed anywhere in the sheet margins.

**Varieties in Cylinder Blocks.** Where a cylinder block contains a listed variety the price is adjusted accordingly and bears an asterisk.

**Enschedé Sheet Markings.** Marginal arrows occur above and below vertical rows 5/6 and opposite rows 10/11 at both sides. The sheet value inscriptions are as the "Jumelle" printing except they occur opposite rows 5/6 and 15/16 reading up at left and down at right. The cylinder number is as described for the "Jumelle". The press used was a Palatia machine and there were no other sheet markings.

## Check List of Machin Photogravure Issues

The check list gives the sources of every basic stamp listed, indicating whether it can come from sheets, booklets or coils.

Under "Phosphor bands" 1L = band at left, 1R = band at right, C = centre band and Phos paper = phosphorised paper.

Under "Paper" OCP = original coated paper, FCP = fluorescent coated paper, ACP = advanced coated paper.

Under "Gum" GA = gum arabic, PVA = polyvinyl alcohol, PVAD = polyvinyl alcohol with dextrin.

½p. Turquoise-blue

| Spec. Number | S.G. Standard Number | Phosphor Bands | Paper | Gum | Source |
|---|---|---|---|---|---|
| U46 | — | 2 (9·5 mm.) | OCP | PVA | Sheets, 10 p. m/v coil (UMC6), 10p. Booklets (DN46/50), 25p. Booklets (DH39/43), 50p. Booklets (DT1/3). |
| U47 | — | 2 (9·5 mm.) | OCP | GA | 5p. m/v coil (UMC1). |
| U48 | — | 2 (9·5 mm.) | FCP | PVA | Sheets, 10p. Booklets (DN51/65), 25p. Booklets (DH44/52), 50p. Booklets (DT5/12), £1 Wedgwood Booklet (DX1). |
| U49 | X841Eg | 2 (9·5 mm.) | FCP | GA | Sheets, 5p. m/v coil (UMC 2). |
| U50 | X841 | 2 (9·5 mm.) | FCP | PVAD | Sheets, 5p. m/v coil (UMC 3/4), 10p. m/v coil (UMC5), 10p. Booklets (DN66/75). |
| U51 | X842 | 1L (Narrow) | FCP | PVA | £1 Wedgwood Booklet (DX1). |
| U52 | — | 2 (8 mm.) | FCP | PVAD | 50p. Booklets (FB1, FB14/16, FB19/23). |
| U53 | X843 | 1C (4 mm.) | FCP | PVAD | 10p. m/v coil (UMC1), 10p. Booklets (FA4/8). |
| U54 | X924 | Phos paper | FCP | PVAD | Sheets, 12½p. m/v coil (UMC10). |

1p. Crimson

| Spec. Number | S.G. Standard Number | Phosphor Bands | Paper | Gum | Source |
|---|---|---|---|---|---|
| U55 | — | 2 (9·5 mm.) | OCP | PVA | Sheets, Coils, 10p. m/v coil (UMC6), 10p. Booklets (DN46/50). |
| U56 | — | 2 (9·5 mm.) | OCP | GA | 5p. m/v coil (UMC1). |
| U57 | — | 2 (9·5 mm.) | FCP | PVA | Sheets, 10p. Booklets (DN51/65). |
| U58 | X844Eg | 2 (9·5 mm.) | FCP | GA | Coils, 5p. m/v coil (UMC2) |
| U59 | X844 | 2 (9·5 mm.) | FCP | PVAD | Sheets, 5p. m/v coil (UMC3/4), 10p. m/v coil (UMC5), 10p. Booklets (DN66/75, FA1/3). |
| U60 | — | 2 (8 mm.) | FCP | PVAD | 50p. Booklets (FB1/8, FB14/16). |
| U61 | X845 | 1C (4 mm.) | FCP | PVAD | 10p. m/v coil (UMC7/8), 10p. Booklets (FA4/11), 50p. Booklets (FB24/30, FB45a). |
| U62 | X846 | "All-over" phos | FCP | PVAD | Sheets. |
| U63 | X925 | Phos paper | FCP | PVAD | Sheets, 13 m/v coil (UMC11). |
| U64 | — | Phos paper | ACP | PVAD | Sheets, Coils. |
| U65 | — | 1C (4·5 mm.) | FCP | PVAD | 50p. Booklets (FB34/6, FB43/5). |
| U66 | X847 | 1L (Narrow) | FCP | PVAD | 50p. Booklets (FB37/41). |
| U67 | X847Ea | 1R (Narrow) | FCP | PVAD | £5 P & O Booklet (DX8). |

| Spec. Number | S.G. Standard Number | Phosphor Bands | Paper | Gum | Source |
|---|---|---|---|---|---|

**1½p. Black**

| Spec. Number | S.G. Standard Number | Phosphor Bands | Paper | Gum | Source |
|---|---|---|---|---|---|
| U71 | — | 2 (9·5 mm.) | OCP | PVA | Sheets, 10p. Booklets (DN46/50). |
| U72 | — | 2 (9·5 mm.) | FCP | PVA | Sheets, 10p. Booklets (DN51/65). |
| U73 | X848 | 2 (9·5 mm.) | FCP | PVAD | Sheets, 10p. Booklets (DN67/75). |

**2p. Myrtle-green**

| Spec. Number | S.G. Standard Number | Phosphor Bands | Paper | Gum | Source |
|---|---|---|---|---|---|
| U76 | — | 2 (9·5 mm.) | OCP | PVA | Sheets, 10p. m/v coil (UCM6), 10p. Booklets (DN46/50). |
| U77 | — | 2 (9·5 mm.) | OCP | GA | 5p. m/v coil (UMC1). |
| U78 | — | 2 (9·5 mm.) | FCP | PVA | Sheets, 10p. Booklets (D51/65). |
| U79 | X849Eg | 2 (9·5 mm.) | FCP | GA | 5p. m/v coil (UMC2). |
| U80 | X849 | 2 (9·5 mm.) | FCP | PVAD | Sheets, 5p. m/v coil (UMC3/4), 10p. m/v coil (UMC5), 10p. Booklets (DN66/75), £3 Wedgwood Booklet DX2, £4 S.G. Booklet (DX3). |
| U81 | — | 2 (8 mm.) | FCP | PVAD | 50p. Booklets (FB9/13). |
| U82 | X850 | "All-over" phos | FCP | PVAD | Sheets. |
| U83 | X926 | Phos paper | FCP | PVAD | Sheets. |
| U84 | X928 | Phos paper | ACP | PVAD | 14p. m/v coil (UMC13). |

**2p. Deep green**

| Spec. Number | S.G. Standard Number | Phosphor Bands | Paper | Gum | Source |
|---|---|---|---|---|---|
| U85 | X927 | Phos paper | ACP | PVAD | Sheets. |

**2½p. Magenta**

| Spec. Number | S.G. Standard Number | Phosphor Bands | Paper | Gum | Source |
|---|---|---|---|---|---|
| U86 | — | 1C (4 mm.) | OCP | PVA | Sheets, Coils, 25p. Booklets (DH39/43), 50p. Booklets (DT1/3). |
| U87 | — | 1C (4 mm.) | FCP | PVA | Sheets, 25p. Booklets (DH44/52), 50p. Booklets (DT4/12), £1 Wedgwood Booklet (DX1). |
| U88 | X851Eg | 1C (4 mm.) | FCP | GA | Sheets, Coils. |
| U89 | X851 | 1C (4 mm.) | FCP | PVAD | Sheets. |
| U90 | — | 1L (Narrow) | FCP | PVA | £1 Wedgwood Booklet (DX1). |
| U91 | — | 1L (Narrow) | OCP | PVA | 50p. Booklets (DT1/3). |
| U92 | — | 1L (Narrow) | FCP | PVA | 50p. Booklets (DT4/12). |
| U93 | X852 | 1L (Narrow) | FCP | PVA | £1 Wedgwood Booklet (DX1). (Thin figures). |
| U94 | — | 1R (Narrow) | FCP | PVA | £1 Wedgwood Booklet (DX1). |
| U95 | X852Ea | 1R (Narrow) | FCP | PVA | £1 Wedgwood Booklet (DX1). (Thin figures). |
| U96 | X853 | 2 (9·5 mm.) | FCP | PVAD | Sheets. |

**2½p. Rose-red**

| Spec. Number | S.G. Standard Number | Phosphor Bands | Paper | Gum | Source |
|---|---|---|---|---|---|
| U97 | X929 | Phos paper | FCP | PVAD | Sheets, 11½p. m/v coil (UMC9). |
| U98 | X854 | 2 (8 mm.) | FCP | PVAD | 50p. Booklets (FB17/18). |

| Spec. Number | S.G. Standard Number | Phosphor Bands | Paper | Gum | Source |
|---|---|---|---|---|---|

**3p. Ultramarine**

| | | | | | |
|---|---|---|---|---|---|
| U101 | X855 | 2 (9·5 mm.) | OCP | PVA | Sheets, Coils, 30p. Booklets (DQ56/9), 50p. Booklets (DT1/3). |
| U102 | — | 2 (9·5 mm.) | OCP | GA | Coils. |
| U103 | — | 2 (9·5 mm.) | FCP | PVA | Sheets, 30p. Booklets (DQ60/72), 50p. Booklets (DT4/12), £1 Wedgwood Booklet (DX1). |
| U104 | X855Eg | 2 (9·5 mm.) | FCP | GA | Sheets, Coils. |
| U107 | X856Eg | 1C (4 mm.) | FCP | GA | Sheets. |
| U108 | X856 | 1C (4 mm.) | FCP | PVAD | Sheets, Coils, 30p. Booklet (DQ74), 50p. Booklet (DT14). |
| U109 | — | 1C (4 mm.) | FCP | PVA | Sheets, 30p. Booklet (DQ73), 50p. Booklet (DT13). |

**3p. Bright magenta**

| | | | | | |
|---|---|---|---|---|---|
| U110 | X930 | Phos paper | FCP | PVAD | Sheets, 11½p. m/v coil (UMC9), £4 Royal Mint Booklet (DX4). |
| U111 | — | Phos paper | ACP | PVAD | Sheets. |
| U111b | X930c | Phos paper | ACP | PVAD | 15p. m/v coil (UMC14) (Narrow value). |
| U112 | X857 | 2 (8 mm.) | FCP | PVAD | 50p. Booklets (FB19/23). |
| U113 | — | 2 (9·5 mm.) | FCP | PVAD | £4 S.G. Booklet (DX3). |

**3½p. Bronze-green**

| | | | | | |
|---|---|---|---|---|---|
| U114 | X858 | 2 (9·5 mm.) | OCP | PVA | Sheets. |
| U115 | — | 2 (9·5 mm.) | FCP | PVA | Sheets, 35p. Booklets (DP1/3), 50p. Booklet (DT13). |
| U116 | X858Eb | 2 (9·5 mm.) | FCP | PVAD | Sheets, Coils, 50p. Booklet (DT14). |
| U117 | — | 2 (9·5 mm.) | OCP | PVAD | Sheets. |
| U118 | X859 | 1C (4 mm.) | FCP | PVAD | Sheets, 35p. Booklet (DP4), 85p. Booklet (DW1). |

**3½p. Purple-brown**

| | | | | | |
|---|---|---|---|---|---|
| U119 | X931 | Phos paper | FCP | PVAD | Sheets. |
| U120 | — | Phos paper | ACP | PVAD | £4 Royal Mint Booklet (DX4). |
| U121 | X860 | 1C (4 mm.) | FCP | PVAD | 50p. Booklets (FB24/6). |

**4p. Ochre-brown**

| | | | | | |
|---|---|---|---|---|---|
| U122 | — | 2 (9·5 mm.) | OCP | PVA | Sheets. |
| U123 | X861Eg | 2 (9·5 mm.) | FCP | GA | Sheets. |
| U124 | — | 2 (9·5 mm.) | FCP | PVA | Sheets. |
| U125 | X861 | 2 (9·5 mm.) | FCP | PVAD | Sheets. |

| Spec. Number | S.G. Standard Number | Phosphor Bands | Paper | Gum | Source |
|---|---|---|---|---|---|
| | | **4p. Greenish blue** | | | |
| U126 | X862 | 2 (8 mm.) | FCP | PVAD | 50p. Booklets (FB17/18). |
| U127 | — | Phos paper | FCP | PVAD | 12½p. m/v coil (UMC10), 13p. m/v coil (UMC11). |
| U128 | X932 | Phos paper | ACP | PVAD | 13p. m/v coil (UMC12), 14p. m/v coil (UMC13). |
| U129 | X863 | 1C (4 mm.) | FCP | PVAD | 50p. Booklets (FB27/30). |
| U130 | X864 | 1R (Narrow) | FCP | PVAD | £5 Times Booklet (DX6). |
| U131 | X864Ea | 1L (Narrow) | FCP | PVAD | £5 Times Booklet (DX6). |
| | | **4p. New Blue** | | | |
| U132 | X933 | Phos paper | ACP | PVAD | Sheets, 17p. m/v coil (UMC15). |

| Spec. Number | S.G. Standard Number | Phosphor Bands | Paper | Gum | Source |
|---|---|---|---|---|---|
| | | **4½p. Grey-blue** | | | |
| U133 | X865 | 2 (9·5 mm.) | FCP | PVAD | Sheets, Coils, 45p. Booklets (DS1/2), 85p. Booklet (DW1). |
| U134 | — | 2 (9·5 mm.) + Phos paper | FCP | PVAD | Sheets. |

| Spec. Number | S.G. Standard Number | Phosphor Bands | Paper | Gum | Source |
|---|---|---|---|---|---|
| | | **5p. Pale violet** | | | |
| U135 | — | 2 (9·5 mm.) | OCP | PVA | Sheets. |
| U136 | — | 2 (9·5 mm.) | FCP | PVA | Sheets. |
| U137 | X866 | 2 (9·5 mm.) | FCP | PVAD | Sheets. |
| U138 | X934 | Phos paper | FCP | PVAD | Sheets. |
| | | **5p. Claret** | | | |
| U139 | X867 | 1C (4·5 mm.) | FCP | PVAD | 50p. Booklets (FB35/6, FB43/5). |
| | | **5p. Dull red-brown** | | | |
| U140 | X935 | Phos paper | ACP | PVAD | Sheets. 17p. m/v coil (UMC15). |

| Spec. Number | S.G. Standard Number | Phosphor Bands | Paper | Gum | Source |
|---|---|---|---|---|---|
| | | **5½p. Violet** | | | |
| U141 | X868 | 2 (9·5 mm.) | FCP | PVAD | Sheets. |
| U142 | X869 | 1C (4 mm.) | FCP | PVAD | Sheets. |

| Spec. Number | S.G. Standard Number | Phosphor Bands | Paper | Gum | Source |
|---|---|---|---|---|---|
| | | **6p. Light emerald** | | | |
| U143 | — | 2 (9·5 mm.) | OCP | PVA | Sheets, 10p. m/v coil (UMC6). |
| U144 | X870Eg | 2 (9·5 mm.) | FCP | GA | Sheets. |
| U145 | — | 2 (9·5 mm.) | FCP | PVA | Sheets. |
| U146 | X870 | 2 (9·5 mm.) | FCP | PVAD | Sheets, 10p. m/v coil (UMC5), 10p. Booklets (FA1/3). |

| Spec. Number | S.G. Standard Number | Phosphor Bands | Paper | Gum | Source |
|---|---|---|---|---|---|

### 6½p. Greenish blue

| Spec. Number | S.G. Standard Number | Phosphor Bands | Paper | Gum | Source |
|---|---|---|---|---|---|
| U148 | X871 | 2 (9·5 mm.) | FCP | PVAD | Sheets. |
| U149 | X872 | 1C (4 mm.) | FCP | PVAD | Sheets, Coils, 65p. Booklet (FC1). |
| U150 | — | 1C (4 mm.) | FCP | PVA | Sheets. |
| U151 | X873Ea | 1L (Narrow) | FCP | PVAD | 50p. Booklet (FB1). |
| U152 | X873 | 1R (Narrow) | FCP | PVAD | 50p. Booklet (FB1). |

### 7p. Purple-brown

| Spec. Number | S.G. Standard Number | Phosphor Bands | Paper | Gum | Source |
|---|---|---|---|---|---|
| U153 | X874 | 2 (9·5 mm.) | FCP | PVAD | Sheets. |
| U154 | X875 | 1C (4 mm.) | FCP | PVAD | Sheets, Coils, 10p. m/v coil (UMC1), 10p. Booklets (FA4/8), 70p. Booklets (FD1/7). £1·60 Christmas Booklet (FX1). |
| U155 | X876Ea | 1L (Narrow) | FCP | PVAD | 50p. Booklets (FB2/8). |
| U156 | X876 | 1R (Narrow) | FCP | PVAD | 50p. Booklets (FB2/8). |

### 7p. Brownish red

| Spec. Number | S.G. Standard Number | Phosphor Bands | Paper | Gum | Source |
|---|---|---|---|---|---|
| U157 | X936 | Phos paper | FCP | PVAD | Sheets. |

### 7½p. Pale chestnut

| Spec. Number | S.G. Standard Number | Phosphor Bands | Paper | Gum | Source |
|---|---|---|---|---|---|
| U158 | — | 2 (9·5 mm.) | OCP | PVA | Sheets. |
| U159 | — | 2 (9·5 mm.) | FCP | PVA | Sheets. |
| U160 | X877 | 2 (9·5 mm.) | FCP | PVAD | Sheets. |

### 8p. Rosine

| Spec. Number | S.G. Standard Number | Phosphor Bands | Paper | Gum | Source |
|---|---|---|---|---|---|
| U161 | X878 | 2 (9·5 mm.) | FCP | PVAD | Sheets. |
| U162 | X879 | 1C (4 mm.) | FCP | PVAD | Sheets, Coils, 10p. m/v coil (UMC8), 10p. Booklets (FA10/11) 80p. Booklet (FE1), £1·80 Christmas Booklet (FX2). |
| U163 | X880Ea | 1L (Narrow) | FCP | PVAD | 50p. Booklets (FB9/10). |
| U164 | X880 | 1R (Narrow) | FCP | PVAD | 50p. Booklets (FB9/10). |

| Spec. Number | S.G. Standard Number | Phosphor Bands | Paper | Gum | Source |
|---|---|---|---|---|---|

**8½p. Yellow-green**

| | | | | | |
|---|---|---|---|---|---|
| U166 | X881 | 2 (9·5 mm.) | FCP | PVAD | Sheets, Coils, 85p. Booklet (FF1). |
| U167 | X937 | Phos paper | FCP | PVAD | Sheets. |
| U168 | — | 2 (8 mm.) | FCP | PVAD | 50p. Booklet (FB1). |

**9p. Orange and black**

| | | | | | |
|---|---|---|---|---|---|
| U171 | — | 2 (9·5 mm.) | OCP | PVA | Sheets. |
| U172 | — | 2 (9·5 mm.) | FCP | PVA | Sheets. |
| U173 | X882 | 2 (9·5 mm.) | FCP | PVAD | Sheets. |

**9p. Violet**

| | | | | | |
|---|---|---|---|---|---|
| U174 | — | 2 (9·5 mm.) | FCP | PVAD | Sheets. (With varnish). |
| U175 | X883 | 2 (9·5 mm.) | FCP | PVAD | Sheets, Coils, 90p. Booklets (FG1/8), £1·60 Christmas Booklet (FX1). (Without varnish). |
| U176 | — | 2 (8 mm.) | FCP | PVAD | 50p. Booklets (FB2/8). |

**9½p. Purple**

| | | | | | |
|---|---|---|---|---|---|
| U181 | X884 | 2 (9·5 mm.) | FCP | PVAD | Sheets. |

**10p. Orange-brown and chestnut**

| | | | | | |
|---|---|---|---|---|---|
| U182 | X885 | 2 (9·5 mm.) | FCP | PVA | Sheets. |
| U183 | — | 2 (9·5 mm.) | FCP | PVAD | Sheets. |

**10p. Orange-brown**

| | | | | | |
|---|---|---|---|---|---|
| U184 | X886 | 2 (9·5 mm.) | FCP | PVAD | Sheets, £1·80 Christmas Booklet (FX2). |
| U185 | — | 2 (9·5 mm.) + Phos paper | FCP | PVAD | Sheets. |
| U186 | — | 2 (8 mm.) | FCP | PVAD | 50p. Booklets (FB9/10). |
| U187 | X887 | "All-over" phos | FCP | PVAD | Sheets, Coils, £1 Booklet (FH1). |
| U188 | — | Phos paper | FCP | PVAD | Sheets. |
| U189 | X938 | Phos paper | ACP | PVAD | Sheets. |
| U190 | X888 | 1C (4 mm.) | FCP | PVAD | Sheets, Coils, £1. Booklets (FH2/4), £2·20 Christmas Booklet (FX3), £3 Wedgwood Booklet (DX2). |

| Spec. Number | S.G. Standard Number | Phosphor Bands | Paper | Gum | Source |
|---|---|---|---|---|---|
| U191 | X889Ea | 1L (Narrow) | FCP | PVAD | 50p. Booklets (FB11/13), £3 Wedgwood Booklet (DX2). |
| U192 | X889 | 1R (Narrow) | FCP | PVAD | 50p. Booklets (FB11/13). |
| U193 | X886b | 2 | FCP | PVAD | £4 Christian Heritage Booklet (DX5). (Narrow figures). |

**10p. Dull orange**

| | | | | | |
|---|---|---|---|---|---|
| U194 | X939 | Phos paper | ACP | PVAD | Sheets. |

**10½p. Yellow**

| | | | | | |
|---|---|---|---|---|---|
| U196 | X890 | 2 (9·5 mm.) | FCP | PVAD | Sheets. |

**10½p. Dull blue**

| | | | | | |
|---|---|---|---|---|---|
| U197 | X891 | 2 (9·5 mm.) | FCP | PVAD | Sheets. |

**11p. Brown-red**

| | | | | | |
|---|---|---|---|---|---|
| U198 | X892 | 2 (9·5 mm.) | FCP | PVAD | Sheets. |
| U199 | X940 | Phos paper | FCP | PVAD | Sheets. |

**11½p. Ochre-brown**

| | | | | | |
|---|---|---|---|---|---|
| U200 | X941 | Phos paper | FCP | PVAD | Sheets. |

**11½p. Drab**

| | | | | | |
|---|---|---|---|---|---|
| U201 | X893 | 1C (4 mm.) | FCP | PVAD | Sheets, Coils, £1·15 Booklets (FI1/4), £2·55 Christmas Booklet (FX4). |
| U202 | X894Ea | 1L (Narrow) | FCP | PVAD | 50p. Booklets (FB14/18), £1·30 Booklets (FL1/2). |
| U203 | X894 | 1R (Narrow) | FCP | PVAD | 50p. Booklets (FB14/18), £1·30 Booklets (FL1/2). |

**12p. Yellowish green**

| | | | | | |
|---|---|---|---|---|---|
| U204 | X942 | Phos paper | FCP | PVAD | Sheets, Coils, £1·20 Booklets (FJ1/3). |
| U205 | — | 2 (8 mm.) | FCP | PVAD | 50p. Booklets (FB11/13). |
| U206 | X895 | 2 (9·5 mm.) | FCP | PVAD | £2·20 Christmas Booklet (FX3), £3 Wedgwood Booklet (DX2). |

| Spec. Number | S.G. Standard Number | Phosphor Bands | Paper | Gum | Source |
|---|---|---|---|---|---|
| | | **12p. Bright emerald** | | | |
| U207 | X896 | 1C (4 mm.) | FCP | PVAD | Sheets, Coils, £1·20 Booklets (FJ4/6). |
| U208 | X896Eu | 1C (4 mm.) | FCP | PVAD | Sheets. (Multi-star underprint). |
| U209 | X897Ea | 1L (Narrow) | FCP | PVAD | £1·50 Booklets (FP1/3), £5 British Rail Booklet (DX7). |
| U210 | X897 | 1R (Narrow) | FCP | PVAD | £1·50 Booklets (FP1/3), £5 British Rail Booklet (DX7). |
| U211 | — | 1C (4·5 mm.) | FCP | PVAD | 50p. Booklet (FB34), £5 British Rail Booklet (DX7). |

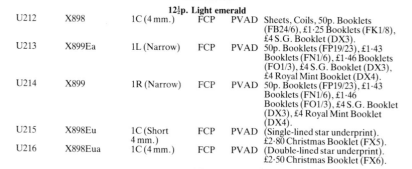

| | | **12½p. Light emerald** | | | |
|---|---|---|---|---|---|
| U212 | X898 | 1C (4 mm.) | FCP | PVAD | Sheets, Coils, 50p. Booklets (FB24/6), £1·25 Booklets (FK1/8), £4 S.G. Booklet (DX3). |
| U213 | X899Ea | 1L (Narrow) | FCP | PVAD | 50p. Booklets (FP19/23), £1·43 Booklets (FN1/6), £1·46 Booklets (FO1/3), £4 S.G. Booklet (DX3), £4 Royal Mint Booklet (DX4). |
| U214 | X899 | 1R (Narrow) | FCP | PVAD | 50p. Booklets (FP19/23), £1·43 Booklets (FN1/6), £1·46 Booklets (FO1/3), £4 S.G. Booklet (DX3), £4 Royal Mint Booklet (DX4). |
| U215 | X898Eu | 1C (Short 4 mm.) | FCP | PVAD | (Single-lined star underprint). £2·80 Christmas Booklet (FX5). |
| U216 | X898Eua | 1C (4 mm.) | FCP | PVAD | (Double-lined star underprint). £2·50 Christmas Booklet (FX6). |

| | | **13p. Olive-grey** | | | |
|---|---|---|---|---|---|
| U217 | X943 | Phos paper | FCP | PVAD | Sheets. |
| | | **13p. Pale chestnut** | | | |
| U218 | X900 | 1C (4 mm.) | FCP | PVAD | Sheets, Coils, 50p. Booklets (FB27/30, FB45a), £1·30 Booklets (FL3/11). |
| U219 | X901Ea | 1L (Narrow) | FCP | PVAD | £1 Booklets (FH6/13), £1·54 Booklets (FQ1/4), £4 Christian Heritage Booklet (DX5), £5 Times Booklet (DX6). |
| U220 | X901 | 1R (Narrow) | FCP | PVAD | £1 Booklets (FH6/10), £1·54 Booklets (FQ1/4), £4 Christian Heritage Booklet (DX5), £5 Times Booklet (DX6), FB39/41. £5 P & O Booklet (DX8). |
| U221 | — | 1C (4·5 mm.) | FCP | PVAD | £5 Times Booklet (DX6), 50p. Booklets (FB35/6, 43/5), 52p. Barcode Booklet (GA1), £1·30 Barcode Booklet (GI1), £5 P & O Booklet (DX8) |
| U222 | X900Eu | 1C (4 mm.) | FCP | PVAD | (Double-lined star underprint). £1·30 Christmas Booklet (FX9). |

| Spec. Number | S.G. Standard Number | Phosphor Bands | Paper | Gum | Source |
|---|---|---|---|---|---|

**13½p. Purple-brown**

| | | | | | |
|---|---|---|---|---|---|
| U224 | X944 | Phos paper | FCP | PVAD | Sheets. |

**14p. Grey-blue**

| | | | | | |
|---|---|---|---|---|---|
| U225 | X945 | Phos paper | FCP | PVAD | Sheets, Coils, £1·40 Booklets (FM1/4). |
| U226 | X902 | 2 (8 mm.) | FCP | PVAD | 50p. Booklets (FB14/16), £1·30 Booklets (FL1/2). |
| U227 | — | 2 (Short 9·5 mm.) | FCP | PVAD | £2·55 Christmas Booklet (FX4). |

**14p. Deep blue**

| | | | | | |
|---|---|---|---|---|---|
| U228 | X903 | 1C (4 mm.) | FCP | PVAD | Sheets, Coils, 56p. Barcode Booklets (GB3/4), £1·40 Barcode Booklets (GJ1, 3). |
| U229 | X904 | 1R (Narrow) | FCP | PVAD | 50p. Booklets (FB51/4), £1 Booklets (FH14/15, 17). |
| U230 | — | 1C (4·5 mm.) | FCP | PVAD | Coil, 56p. Barcode Booklets (GB1/2). |

**15p. Ultramarine**

| | | | | | |
|---|---|---|---|---|---|
| U231 | X946 | Phos paper | FCP | PVAD | Sheets. |

**15p. Bright blue**

| | | | | | |
|---|---|---|---|---|---|
| U232 | X905 | 1C (4 mm.) | FCP | PVAD | Sheets, Coils. |
| U233 | X906 | 1L (Narrow) | FCP | PVAD | 50p. Booklet (FB55). |
| U234 | X906Ea | 1R (Narrow) | FCP | PVAD | £5 London Life Booklet (DX11). |

**15½p. Pale violet**

| | | | | | |
|---|---|---|---|---|---|
| U235 | X947 | Phos paper | FCP | PVAD | Sheets, Coils, £1·55 Booklets (FR1/6). |
| U236 | — | Phos paper | ACP | PVAD | Sheets. |
| U237 | X907 | 2 (8 mm.) | FCP | PVAD | £1·43 Booklets (FN1/6). |
| U238 | — | 2 (9·5 mm.) | FCP | PVAD | £4 S.G. Booklet (DX3). |
| U239 | X907Eu | 2 (Short 9·5 mm.) | FCP | PVAD | (Star underprint). £2·80 Christmas Booklet (FX5). |

| Spec. Number | S.G. Standard Number | Phosphor Bands | Paper | Gum | Source |
|---|---|---|---|---|---|

**16p. Olive-drab**

| Spec. Number | S.G. Standard Number | Phosphor Bands | Paper | Gum | Source |
|---|---|---|---|---|---|
| U240 | X948 | Phos paper | ACP | PVAD | Sheets, Coils. |
| U241 | — | Phos paper | FCP | PVAD | £1·60 Booklets (FS1, 3/4). |
| U242 | X908 | 2 (9·5 mm.) | FCP | PVAD | £1·46 Booklets (FO1/3). |
| U243 | X948Eu | Phos paper | FCP | PVAD | ("D" underprint). £1·60 booklet (FS2). |

**16½p. Pale chestnut**

| U244 | X949 | Phos paper | FCP | PVAD | Sheets. |
|---|---|---|---|---|---|

**17p. Light emerald**

| U245 | X950 | Phos paper | FCP | PVAD | Sheets. |
|---|---|---|---|---|---|

**17p. Grey-blue**

| U246 | — | Phos paper | FCP | PVAD | Sheets, Coils. |
|---|---|---|---|---|---|
| U247 | X951 | Phos paper | ACP | PVAD | Sheets, £1 Booklet (FH5). £1·70 Booklets (FT1/3, 5/7), £4 Christian Heritage Booklet (DX5), £5 Times Booklet (DX6), £5 British Rail Booklet (DX7). |
| U248 | X909 | 2 (9·5 mm.) | FCP | PVAD | 50p. Booklet (FB33), £1·50 Booklets (FB1/3), £1·54 Booklets (FQ1/4), £4 Christian Heritage Booklet (DX5), £5 Times Booklet (DX6), £5 British Rail Booklet (DX7). |
| U249 | X951Eu | Phos paper | FCP | PVAD | ("D" underprint). £1·70 Booklet (FT2). |
| U250 | X909Eu | 2 (9·5 mm.) | FCP | PVAD | (Multi-star underprint). 50p. Booklets (FB31/3). |

**17p. Deep blue**

| U251 | X910 | 1C (4 mm.) | FCP | PVAD | Sheets, Coils. |
|---|---|---|---|---|---|
| U252 | X911Ea | 1L (Narrow) | FCP | PVAD | 50p. Booklet (FB57). |
| U253 | X911 | 1R (Narrow) | FCP | PVAD | 50p. Booklet (FB57), £1 Booklet (FH21). |

**17½p. Pale chestnut**

| U254 | X952 | Phos paper | FCP | PVAD | Sheets. |
|---|---|---|---|---|---|

| Spec. Number | S.G. Standard Number | Phosphor Bands | Paper | Gum | Source |
|---|---|---|---|---|---|

**18p. Deep violet**

| U255 | X953 | Phos paper | FCP | PVAD | Sheets. |
|---|---|---|---|---|---|

**18p. Deep olive-grey**

| U256 | X954 | Phos paper | ACP | PVAD | Sheets, Coils, 72p. Barcode Booklet (GC1), £1·80 Barcode Booklet (GK1), £5 P & O Booklet (DX8). |
|---|---|---|---|---|---|
| U257 | — | Phos paper | FCP | PVAD | Coils, £1·80 Booklets (FU1/5). |
| U258 | X912 | 2 (9·5 mm.) | FCP | PVAD | 50p. Booklets (FB37/41), £1 Booklets (FH6/13), £5 P & O Booklet (DX8). |

**19p Bright orange-red**

| U259 | X955 | Phos paper | ACP | PVAD | Sheets, Coils, 76p. Barcode Booklets (GD1/4), £1·90 Barcode Booklets (GL1, 3). |
|---|---|---|---|---|---|
| U260 | X913 | 2 | FCP | PVAD | 50p. Booklets (FB51/4), Booklets (FH14, 15, 17) |

**19½p. Olive-grey**

| U264 | X956 | Phos paper | FCP | PVAD | Sheets. |
|---|---|---|---|---|---|

**20p. Dull purple**

| U265 | X914 | 2 (9·5 mm.) | FCP | PVAD | Sheets. |
|---|---|---|---|---|---|
| U266 | X957 | Phos paper | FCP | PVAD | Sheets. |

**20p. Turquoise-green**

| U267 | X958 | Phos paper | ACP | PVAD | Sheets. |
|---|---|---|---|---|---|

**20p. Brownish black**

| U268 | X959 | Phos paper | ACP | PVAD | Sheets, Coils. |
|---|---|---|---|---|---|
| U269 | X915 | 2 (9·5 mm.) | FCP | PVAD | 50p. Booklet (FB55), £5 London Booklet (DX11) |

| Spec. Number | S.G. Standard Number | Phosphor Bands | Paper | Gum | Source |
|---|---|---|---|---|---|

**20½p. Ultramarine**

| U275 | X960 | Phos paper | FCP | PVAD | Sheets. |

**22p. Blue**

| U279 | X961 | Phos paper | FCP | PVAD | Sheets. |

**22p. Yellow-green**

| U280 | X962 | Phos paper | ACP | PVAD | Sheets. |

**22p. Bright orange-red**

| U281 | X963 | Phos paper | ACP | PVAD | Sheets, Coils. |
| U282 | X916 | 2 | FCP | PVAD | £1 Booklet (FH21). |

**23p. Brown-red**

| U283 | X964 | Phos paper | FCP | PVAD | Sheets. |

**23p. Bright green**

| U284 | X965 | Phos paper | ACP | PVAD | Sheets. |

**24p. Violet**

| U285 | X966 | Phos paper | ACP | PVAD | Sheets. |

**24p. Indian red**

| U286 | X967 | Phos paper | ACP | PVAD | Sheets. |

**25p. Purple**

| U288 | X968 | Phos paper | FCP | PVAD | Sheets. |

| Spec. Number | S.G. Standard Number | Phosphor Bands | Paper | Gum | Source |
|---|---|---|---|---|---|

**26p. Rosine**

| Spec. Number | S.G. Standard Number | Phosphor Bands | Paper | Gum | Source |
|---|---|---|---|---|---|
| U291 | — | Phos paper | FCP | PVAD | Sheets. |
| U292 | X969 | Phos paper | ACP | PVAD | Sheets. |
| U293 | X917 | 2 | FCP | PVAD | £5 P & O Booklet (DX8). |
| U294 | X969a | Phos paper | ACP | PVAD | (Thin figures). £1·04 Barcode Booklet (GE1). |

**26p. Drab**

| | | | | | |
|---|---|---|---|---|---|
| U295 | X970 | Phos paper | ACP | PVAD | Sheets. |

**27p. Chestnut**

| | | | | | |
|---|---|---|---|---|---|
| U296 | X971 | Phos paper | ACP | PVAD | Sheets, £1·08 Barcode Booklets (GF1/2). |

**27p. Violet**

| | | | | | |
|---|---|---|---|---|---|
| U297 | X972 | Phos paper | ACP | PVAD | Sheets. |

**28p. Deep violet**

| | | | | | |
|---|---|---|---|---|---|
| U298 | — | Phos paper | FCP | PVAD | Sheets. |
| U299 | X973 | Phos paper | ACP | PVAD | Sheets. |

**28p. Ochre**

| | | | | | |
|---|---|---|---|---|---|
| U300 | X974 | Phos paper | ACP | PVAD | Sheets. |

**29p. Ochre-brown**

| | | | | | |
|---|---|---|---|---|---|
| U301 | X975 | Phos paper | FCP | PVAD | Sheets. |

**29p. Deep mauve**

| | | | | | |
|---|---|---|---|---|---|
| U302 | X976 | Phos paper | ACP | PVAD | Sheets. |

**30p. Deep olive-grey**

| | | | | | |
|---|---|---|---|---|---|
| U303 | X977 | Phos paper | ACP | PVAD | Sheets. |

| Spec. Number | S.G. Standard Number | Phosphor Bands | Paper | Gum | Source |
|---|---|---|---|---|---|

**31p. Purple**

| U304 | — | Phos paper | FCP | PVAD | Sheets. |
| U305 | X978 | Phos paper | ACP | PVAD | Sheets. |
| U306 | X918 | 2 (9·5 mm.) | FCP | PVAD | £5 British Rail Booklet (DX7). |

**31p. Ultramarine**

| U307 | X979 | Phos paper | ACP | PVAD | Sheets. |

**32p. Greenish blue**

| U308 | X980 | Phos paper | ACP | PVAD | Sheets. |

**33p. Light emerald**

| ·U309 | X981 | Phos paper | ACP | PVAD | Sheets. |

**34p. Ochre-brown**

| U310 | — | Phos paper | FCP | PVAD | Sheets. |
| U311 | X982 | Phos paper | ACP | PVAD | Sheets. |
| U312 | X919 | 2 (9·5 mm.) | FCP | PVAD | £5 Times Booklet (DX6). |

**34p. Deep bluish grey**

| U313 | X983 | Phos paper | ACP | PVAD | Sheets |

**35p. Sepia**

| U314 | X984 | Phos paper | ACP | PVAD | Sheets. |

**37p. Rosine**

| U316 | X985 | Phos paper | ACP | PVAD | Sheets. |

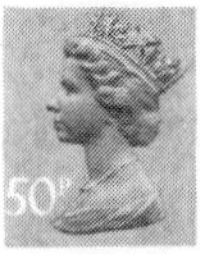

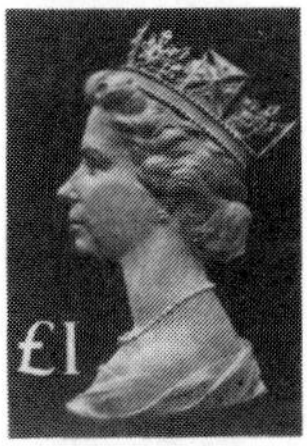

| Spec. Number | S.G. Standard Number | Phosphor Bands | Paper | Gum | Source |
|---|---|---|---|---|---|

**50p. Ochre-brown**

| U321 | X920 | 2 (9·5 mm.) | FCP | PVAD | Sheets. |
| U322 | X986 | — | FCP | PVAD | Sheets. |

**50p. Ochre**

| U323 | X987 | — | FCP | PVAD | Sheets. |
| U324 | X921 | 2 (9·5 mm.) | FCP | PVAD | £5 London Life Booklet (DX11). |

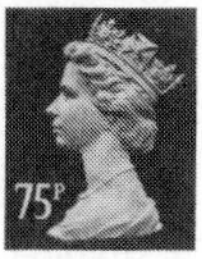

**75p. Grey-black**

| U325 | X988 | — | FCP | PVAD | Sheets. |

**HIGH VALUES**

**£1**

| U330 | 1026 | — | FCP | PVAD | Sheets. |

**1·30**

| U331 | 1026b | — | FCP | PVAD | Sheets. |

**£1·33**

| U332 | 1026c | — | FCP | PVAD | Sheets. |

**£1·41**

| U333 | 1026d | — | FCP | PVAD | Sheets. |

**£1·50**

| U334 | 1026e | — | FCP | PVAD | Sheets. |

**£1·60**

| U335 | 1026f | — | FCP | PVAD | Sheets. |

**£2**

| U336 | 1027 | — | FCP | PVAD | Sheets. |

**£5**

| U337 | 1028 | — | FCP | PVAD | Sheets. |

**U6** Queen Elizabeth II
(Des. after plaster cast by Arnold Machin)

# Type U6
## ½p. Turquoise-blue   (1971–80)

**Two Value Types**

Type I.  Thin value
Type II. Thick value. Occurs in USB2 and UMFB7 booklet panes.

I        II

## 1971 (15 FEBRUARY).   TWO 9·5 mm. PHOSPHOR BANDS. TYPE I

**A. ORIGINAL COATED PAPER. PVA GUM**

| | | | | | | | | |
|---|---|---|---|---|---|---|---|---|
| U46 | Turquoise-blue | .. | .. | ' .. | .. | .. | .. | 10 | 10 |
| | *a*. Phosphor omitted | | .. | .. | ' .. | .. | .. | 10·00 |
| | *b*. One broad band .. | | .. | .. | .. | .. | .. | 30·00 |
| | *c*. Type II (14.7.71).. | | .. | .. | .. | .. | .. | 2·25 | 50 |
| | *ca*. Phosphor omitted | | .. | .. | .. | .. | .. | £140 |
| | *cb*. One broad band .. | | .. | .. | .. | .. | .. | £200 |
| | *d*. Spur on foot of P | | .. | .. | .. | .. | .. | 2·00 |
| | *e*. Deformed base to 2 | | .. | .. | .. | .. | .. | 2·00 |
| | *f*. Dark flaw below collar .. | | .. | .. | .. | .. | 2·25 |
| | *h*. White patch on shoulder | | .. | .. | .. | .. | 2·00 |
| | *i*. Vertical scratch behind head | | .. | .. | .. | .. | 2·00 |
| | *j*. Coloured lines behind shoulder | | .. | .. | .. | 2·00 |
| | *k*. Deformed base to 2 | | .. | .. | .. | .. | .. | 2·00 |
| | *l*. Retouch by dress | | .. | .. | .. | .. | .. | 1·50 |

No. U46 Type I also exists from 10p. G3 multi-value coils issued about March 1977.

**Cylinder Numbers (Blocks of Six unless otherwise stated)**

Perforation Type A

| Cyl. No. | Phos. No. | | | | No dot | Dot | |
|---|---|---|---|---|---|---|---|
| 2 | L2, S2 | .. | .. | .. | 20·00 | 20·00 | Block of ten |
| 2 | L2, S2 | + 20 mm. (18) .. | | .. | 35·00 | 25·00 | |
| 2 | L2, S2 | Re-engraved | .. | .. | 15·00 | 15·00 | Block of ten |
| 2 | L4 | .. | .. | .. | .. | 2·00 | 2·00 | |
| 4* | L4 | .. | .. | .. | .. | 10·00 | 10·00 | |

*Cyl. No. 4 is printed in the left-hand box and the phosphor number occurs in the right-hand box.

**B. ORIGINAL COATED PAPER. GUM ARABIC.** 5p. Multi-value coil only (15.2.71)

| | | | |
|---|---|---|---:|
| U47 | Turquoise-blue | .. .. .. .. .. | 40 |
| | *a.* Phosphor omitted | .. .. .. .. | 50·00 |
| | *b.* One broad band .. | .. .. .. .. | 10·00 |
| | *c.* Missing pearl in necklace | .. .. .. | 2·50 |
| | *d.* Shoulder scratch .. | .. .. .. .. | 2·25 |
| | *i.* Vertical scratch behind head | .. .. .. | 3·00 |

**C. FLUORESCENT COATED PAPER. PVA GUM** (17.9.71)

| | | | |
|---|---|---|---:|
| U48 | Turquoise-blue | .. .. .. .. .. | 60 |
| | *a.* Phosphor omitted | .. .. .. .. | 95·00 |
| | *b.* One broad band .. | .. .. .. .. | £300 |
| | *c.* Type II (6.10.71).. | .. .. .. .. | 1·40 |
| | *ca.* Phosphor omitted | .. .. .. .. | £160 |
| | *cb.* One broad band .. | .. .. .. .. | 30·00 |
| | *d.* Spur on foot of P | .. .. .. .. | 2·25 |
| | *e.* Deformed base to 2 | .. .. .. .. | 2·50 |
| | *f.* Dark flaw below collar .. | .. .. .. | 2·50 |
| | *g.* Phosphor printed on both sides (ex. UWB3).. | .. | £150 |

Examples of No. U48 from booklet pane No. UB25 (Cyl. B17) and of U48*c* from booklet pane No. USB3 exist with contaminated "yellow phosphor". *Price mint* (No. U48) £9 *or* (No. U48*c*) £4·50.

**Cylinder Numbers (Blocks of Six)**

Perforation Type A

| Cyl. No. | Phos. No. | | | | | No dot | Dot |
|---|---|---|---|---|---|---|---|
| 2 | 1 | .. | .. | .. | .. | 5·00 | 12·00 |
| 2 | —* | .. | .. | .. | .. | — | 3·50 |
| 2 | 7 | .. | .. | .. | .. | 3·50 | 3·50 |

*Cyl. 2 without phosphor number on dot pane can be either displaced or guillotined off, identifiable only by the insert.

Phosphor Cylinder Displacement. Phosphor cyl. 1 is known displaced up the margin 417 mm. opposite row 1.

**D. FLUORESCENT COATED PAPER. GUM ARABIC** (22.9.72)

| | | | |
|---|---|---|---:|
| U49 (=S.G.X841Eg) | Turquoise-blue | .. .. .. .. | 10 |
| | *a.* Imperforate (pair) | .. .. .. .. | £900 |
| | *b.* Imperforate top margin.. | .. .. .. | £225 |
| | *d.* Spur on foot of P | .. .. .. .. | 2·00 |
| | *e.* Deformed base to 2 | .. .. .. .. | 2·00 |
| | *f.* Flaw below collar retouched (white) .. | .. .. | 2·00 |

**Cylinder Numbers (Blocks of Six)**

Perforation Type R(S)

| Cyl. No. | Phos. No. | | | | | No. dot | Dot |
|---|---|---|---|---|---|---|---|
| 2 | 7 | .. | .. | .. | .. | 4·50 | 4·50 |

**E. FLUORESCENT COATED PAPER. PVAD GUM** (10.9.73)

| | | | | |
|---|---|---|---:|---:|
| U50 (=S.G.X841) | Turquoise-blue | .. .. .. .. .. | 10 | 10 |
| | *a.* Phosphor omitted | .. .. .. .. | 1·00 | |
| | *ab.* Left-hand band omitted.. | .. .. .. | 60·00 | |
| | *ac.* Right-hand band omitted | .. .. .. | 60·00 | |
| | *b.* One broad band .. | .. .. .. .. | 1·00 | |
| | *c.* Thinner paper (5p. multi-value coil) .. | .. .. | 7·50 | |
| | *d.* Type II (12.11.73) | .. .. .. .. | 75 | 50 |
| | *da.* One broad band .. | .. .. .. .. | 10·00 | |
| | *db.* Phosphor omitted | .. .. .. .. | 50·00 | |
| | *e.* Long diagonal scratch (*Strip of three*).. | .. .. | 4·00 | |
| | *f.* Scratch under chin | .. .. .. .. | 2·00 | |
| | *g.* Dark spot above central cross .. | .. .. | 1·75 | |
| | *h.* White patch on shoulder | .. .. .. | 1·75 | |
| | *i.* Vertical scratch behind head | .. .. .. | 1·90 | |
| | *j.* Coloured lines behind shoulder | .. .. .. | 2·00 | |
| | *k.* Deformed base to 2 | .. .. .. .. | 1·75 | |
| | *l.* Retouch by dress | .. .. .. .. | 2·00 | |
| | *m.* Line of dots on dress | .. .. .. .. | 2·00 | |
| | *n.* With varnish coating (6.77) | .. .. .. | 40 | |

On No. U50*n* the varnish coating completely covers the phosphor bands so that they do not react under ultra-violet light, nor does the fluorescent paper. Cylinder flaws usually found from Cyl. 8 are less prominent due to the varnish coating.

**Cylinder Numbers (Blocks of Six unless otherwise stated)**
Perforation Type R

| Cyl. No. | Phos. No. | | | | | No dot | Dot | |
|---|---|---|---|---|---|---|---|---|
| 7 | 17 | +42 mm. (17) | .. | | .. | 18·00 | 14·00 | Block of ten |
| 7 | 17 | .. | .. | .. | .. | 1·00 | 1·00 | |
| 8 | 17 | .. | .. | .. | .. | 1·00 | 1·00 | |

Perforation Type RE

| 7 | 17 | .. | .. | .. | .. | 1·00** | 1·50 |
|---|---|---|---|---|---|---|---|
| 8 | 17 | .. | .. | .. | .. | 1·00** | 1·50 |
| 8 | 17 | —20 mm. (20) | .. | | .. | 75·00 | 75·00 |
| 8 | 17 | With varnish coating | | .. | | 18·00 | 15·00 |
| 8 | P21 | .. | .. | .. | .. | 1·40 | 1·40 |
| 8 | 30 | .. | .. | .. | .. | 80 | 80 |

**Same prices as perforation type R with single extension holes in left margin.

## 1972 (24 MAY). ONE NARROW PHOSPHOR BAND AT LEFT. TYPE I. FLUORESCENT COATED PAPER. PVA GUM

Wedgwood booklet pane UWB4 only
U51 (=S.G.X842)    Turquoise-blue    ..    ..    ..    ..    ..    .. 65·00  25·00
✐ No. U51 also exists used from uncut sheet stock separated by hand for use on first day covers with Wedgwood postmarks and these always have untrimmed perforations on all four sides of the stamp.
No. U51 in a very pale shade derives from pane UWB4c.

## 1977 (26 JANUARY). TWO 8 mm. PHOSPHOR BANDS. TYPE I. FLUORESCENT COATED PAPER. PVAD GUM

50p. booklet panes UMFB3/4, UMFB19/20 (26.1.81) and UMFB26/27 (1.2.82)
U52    Turquoise-blue    ..    ..    ..    ..    ..    .. 50    50
       *b.* Short phosphor band at bottom left (1.2.82) ..    .. 2·00
       *c.* Short phosphor band at bottom right (1.2.82)    .. 2·00

## 1977 (14 DECEMBER). ONE 4 mm. PHOSPHOR BAND AT CENTRE. TYPE I. FLUORESCENT COATED PAPER. PVAD GUM

10p. multi-value G4 coil only
U53 (=S.G.X843)    Turquoise-blue    ..    ..    ..    ..    .. 30    20
       *b.* Dark spots around eye ..    ..    ..    ..    .. 2·00
       *c.* Red flaw above eye    ..    ..    ..    ..    .. 2·00
       *d.* Spot in band of crown ..    ..    ..    ..    .. 1·50
       *e.* Type II (Pane UMFB7) (8.2.78)    ..    ..    .. 30    20
       *ea.* Phosphor omitted    ..    ..    ..    ..    .. 5·00

## 1980 (10 DECEMBER). PHOSPHORISED (FLUORESCENT COATED) PAPER. TYPE I. PVAD GUM

U54 (=S.G.X924)    Turquoise-blue    ..    ..    ..    ..    .. 10    10
       *a.* Imperforate (pair)    ..    ..    ..    ..    .. £125
       *b.* Long diagonal scratch (*strip of three*) ..    .. 2·00
       *c.* Patch over central cross..    ..    ..    ..    .. 2·50
       *d.* Retouched scratch    ..    ..    ..    ..    .. 5·00
       *e.* Retouch on cheek    ..    ..    ..    ..    .. 3·00
       *f.* Dark spot above central cross ..    ..    ..    .. 2·00
       *g.* Fluorescent brightener omitted    ..    ..    ..

No. U54 is known on phosphorised paper with either a shiny ink surface which gives a photo-negative reflection or a matt surface without the negative effect.
No. U54g derives from the 12½p. multi-value coil, UMC11 and is printed on chalk-surfaced paper but without the fluorescent additive which was probably omitted in error. Perfect unmounted examples are rare and care should be exercised when buying this stamp. Horizontal waxed strips were used to mount the strips on Reader's Digest cards and most examples show gum disturbance and in this condition No. U54g is £90 *each.*

**Cylinder Numbers (Blocks of Six)**
Perforation Type RE

| Cyl. No. | | | | | No Dot | Dot |
|---|---|---|---|---|---|---|
| 7 | .. | .. | .. | .. | 1·00 | 1·00 |
| 8 | .. | .. | .. | .. | 1·00 | 1·00 |

**CYLINDER VARIETIES**
Listed flaws

U46*d*, U48*d*, U49*d*
(Cyl. 2 no dot, R. 2/8)
(Later retouched)

U46*e*, U48*e*, U49*e*
(Cyl. 2 dot, R. 20/9)

U47*c*
2nd ½p. in 5p. multi-value
coil in every fifth
position

U47*d*
(Roll 8)
(2nd ½p. in 5p. multi-value
coil in every 5th position)

U46*f*, U48*f*    U49*f*
Retouched state
(Cyl. 2 dot, R. 2/9)

White patch on shoulder due to missing screening dots
(1st ½p. in 5p. PVAD and 10p. G3 multi-value coils, Roll No. 8
in every 5th position. Also confirmed with additional dark dot
below necklace on 1st ½p. Roll No. 10 in 5p. multi-value coil
PVAD and with dot retouched in 10p. G3 multi-value coils
OCP/PVA and FCP/PVAD)

U46*h*, U50*h*

Vertical scratch originally
on 2nd ½p. of 5p. multi-
value coil OCP/GA in
every 5th position and
then weaker on 5p. PVAD
coil and 10p. G3 PVAD
and OCP/PVA coils

Two blue and one
red short vertical
lines in back-
ground (1st ½p. in
10p. G3 multivalue
coils in every 5th
position)
(Later retouched)

U46/7*i*, U50*i*
(Cyl. R6, Roll 8)

U46*j*, U50*j*

| U46k, U50k | U46l, U50l | U50f |
| (Roll 8) | (Roll 10) | (Cyl. 7 dot, R. 16/9) |
| | | (Later retouched) |

(Both on 1st ½p. of 10p. G3 multi-value coil
in every 5th position)

The deformed 2 shown above may be a multipositive flaw corresponding to the sheet flaw listed as
Nos. U46e, U48e and U49e.

U50g, U54f
(Cyls. 7 and 8 dot, R. 20/6)

U50m
(2nd ½p., Cyl. R6, Roll No. 7
in 5p. multi-value coil in
every 5th position)
(Retouched on 10p. G3 coil)

(U50g was retouched on 2½p. Cyl. 19 and 3½p. Cyls. 9 and 12, all
dot. Occurs on 3½p. Cyl. 11, 6p. Cyl. 8 and 7½p. Cyl. 5, all dot)

U50e, U54b

Long horizontal scratch from necklace of left stamp through right stamp extending to foot of bust on
next stamp (Cyls. 7 and 8 no dot, R. 3/3–3/5). This flaw is faint on No. U54 (Cyl. 7)

♦ Nos. U50e and U50g are multipositive flaws on 2½p. Cyl. 19, also see minor constant flaw list; 3½p.
♦ Cyls. 9, 11 and 12; 5p. and 6p. Cyl. 8 and 7½p. Cyl. 5. Both flaws were retouched on later printings of
♦ some values.

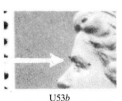

| U53b | U53c | U53d |
| (1st ½p., Cyl. R10, Roll 1) | (2nd ½p., Cyl. R10, Roll 4) | (1st ½p., Cyls. R9 and R10, |
| | (Later retouched) | Roll 6) |

(All from G4 10p. multi-value coil in every 5th position)

No. U53b was repaired on Cyl. R9, appearing as pale spots.
No. U53d is a multipositive flaw which also occurs on the 9p. DS horizontal coil in Roll 5.

U54c
(Second Reader's Digest coil in
every 4th position, Cyl. R11, Roll 6)

U54d
Retouched scratch
(Cyl. 7 no dot, R. 12/2,
late printing only)

U54e
Retouch on cheek
(Cyl. 8 no dot, R. 20/10,
late printing only)

For further flaws on ½p. stamps in booklet panes, see under Nos. UB23, UB25, USB1/4, UWB4, UMFB1/3 and UMFB7.

**Minor Constant Sheet Flaws**

Cyl. 2   5/2 and 6/2 Coloured scratch from bottom of design of 5/2 (Th. E6) to crown of 6/2 (Th. B5)
9/2 and 10/2 Similar scratch from Queen's collar on 9/2 (Th. E6) to crown on 10/2 (Th. B5)
6/7 Diagonal scratch from Queen's ear to neck (Th. D4–F3)
16/1 White specks under Queen's necklace (Th. F4)
16/7 Coloured scratch from Queen's chin to P of value (Th. E2–F2)

Cyl. 2.   7/4 Blue line in margin at bottom left
8/5 Diagonal scratch from Queen's collar to hair (Th. G3–E4)

Cyl. 7   3/6 Dark patch over crown (Th. A4)
6/10 Circle of dots in front of Queen's nose (Th. C1)
11/7 Spot in base of collar (Th. G4)
20/3 Small retouch behind Queen's necklace (Th. E5)

Cyl. 7.   1/2 Two white spots in Queen's hair (Th. C4)
6/7 Diagonal scratch from Queen's ear to neck (Th. D4–F3)*
13/6 Dark patch behind Queen's shoulder (Th. D4–F3)*
15/1 Blue diagonal line in left margin (Th. C)
15/2 Blunted 2 at bottom left
15/8 Retouch in background at top left (Th. A2)
19/6 Dark spot behind crown (Th. C6)
19/7 Hairline scratch behind collar (Th. G5–G6)*
20/7 Inverted U-shaped scratch behind crown (Th. B6)

Cyl. 8   3/6 Dark patch over crown as on Cyl. 7 is retouched (Th. A4)
6/10 As Cyl. 7 but fainter
20/3 As Cyl. 7

Cyl. 8.   2/9 Squiggle in front of Queen's eye (Th. C2)
6/7 As Cyl. 7
10/4 Pale oval right of Queen's neck (Th. E5)
16/7 Blue spot on Queen's forehead (Th. C2–C3)
19/7 As Cyl. 7
20/7 As Cyl. 7
20/10 White spot right of collar (Th. G6)

Some of the flaws on Cyls. 7 and 8 are multipositive flaws which also recur on the 2½p. Cyl. 19 and 3½p. Cyls. 9, 11 and 12.

*The flaws recorded on Cyl. No. 7 are less prominent on the phosphorised paper printing, and those marked with an asterisk are not visible on No. U54.

**WITHDRAWN**   No. U50 30.4.82; No. U54 28.6.85

# 1p. Crimson   (1971–87)

**Two Value Types**

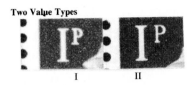

I          II

Type I.    Close value

Type II.   P spaced wider to the right of figure. Pane UMFB12.

## 1971 (15 FEBRUARY).   TWO 9·5 mm. PHOSPHOR BANDS. TYPE I
### A. ORIGINAL COATED PAPER. PVA GUM

| | | | | | | | |
|---|---|---|---|---|---|---|---|
| U55 | Crimson | .. | .. | .. | .. | .. | .. 25  25 |
| | *a.* Imperforate (vert. coil)* | .. | .. | .. | .. | |
| | *b.* Pair, one imperforate 3 sides (vert. coil)* | .. | .. | |
| | *c.* Phosphor omitted | .. | .. | .. | .. | .. 3·50 |
| | *d.* Left-hand band omitted.. | .. | .. | .. | .. £250 |
| | *e.* One broad band .. | .. | .. | .. | .. .. 35·00 |
| | *f.* Screened figure 1 | .. | .. | .. | .. | .. 3·00 |
| | *g.* White spots on neck | .. | .. | .. | .. | .. 2·50 |
| | *h.* Screened loop to P | .. | .. | .. | .. | .. 1·50 |
| | *i.* Semi-circle around front curl | .. | .. | .. | .. 1·50 |
| | *j.* Shoulder scratch .. | .. | .. | .. | .. | .. 2·50 |
| | *k.* Chipped P | .. | .. | .. | .. | .. | .. 2·50 |
| | *l.* Green marks in dress | .. | .. | .. | .. | .. 3·50 |

No. U55 also exists from 10p. G3 multi-value coils issued about March 1977.

*Nos. U55*a*/*b* come from a vertical strip of eight of the vertical coil. It comprises two normals, one imperforate at sides and bottom, one completely imperforate, one imperforate at top, left and bottom and partly perforated at right due to the bottom three stamps being perforated twice. No. U55*b* is also known from another strip having one stamp imperforate at sides and bottom.

**Cylinder Numbers (Blocks of Six unless otherwise stated)**

Perforation Type A

| Cyl. No. | Phos. No. | | | | | No dot | Dot | |
|---|---|---|---|---|---|---|---|---|
| 1 | S2 | .. | .. | .. | .. | 50·00 | 50·00 | |
| 1 | — | .. | .. | .. | .. | 2·50 | 2·50 | |
| 1 | L2, S2 | .. | .. | .. | .. | 2·75 | 2·75 | Block of ten |
| 1 | L4 | .. | .. | .. | .. | 1·50 | 1·50 | |
| 3 | 1 | .. | .. | .. | .. | 2·00 | 5·00 | |
| 3 | — | .. | .. | .. | .. | † | 1·75 | Guillotined off on dot |

### B. ORIGINAL COATED PAPER. GUM ARABIC. 5p. Multi-value coil only (15.2.71)

| | | | | | | | |
|---|---|---|---|---|---|---|---|
| U56 | Crimson | .. | .. | .. | .. | .. | .. 40 |
| | *a.* Phosphor omitted | .. | .. | .. | .. | .. 45·00 |
| | *b.* One broad band .. | .. | .. | .. | .. | .. 5·00 |
| | *c.* Malformed P | .. | .. | .. | .. | .. | .. 2·00 |
| | *d.* Vertical white line between 1 and P | .. | .. | .. 2·00 |
| | *e.* Vertical dark line at upper right | .. | .. | .. 2·00 |

### C. FLUORESCENT COATED PAPER. PVA GUM (6.10.71)

| | | | | | | | |
|---|---|---|---|---|---|---|---|
| U57 | Crimson | .. | .. | .. | .. | .. | .. 1·40 |
| | *a.* Phosphor omitted | .. | .. | .. | .. | .. 25·00 |
| | *b.* One broad band .. | .. | .. | .. | .. | .. £225 |
| | *c.* Screened figure 1 | .. | .. | .. | .. | .. 4·00 |
| | *d.* White spots on neck | .. | .. | .. | .. | .. 3·00 |

Examples of No. U57 from booklet pane No. USB7 exist with contaminated "yellow phosphor". *Price mint £5.*

**Cylinder Numbers (Blocks of Six unless otherwise stated)**

Perforation Type A

| Cyl. No. | Phos. No. | | | | No dot | Dot | |
|---|---|---|---|---|---|---|---|
| 1 | L2, S2 | Re-engraved | .. | .. | 14·00 | 14·00 | Block of ten |
| 3 | 7 | .. | .. | .. | 8·00 | 8·00 | |

**D. FLUORESCENT COATED PAPER. GUM ARABIC** 5p. Multi-value coil and vertical coil (9.72)

| | | | | | | |
|---|---|---|---|---|---|---|
| U58 (=S.G.X844Eg) | Crimson | .. | .. | .. | .. | 10 |
| | *c.* White spots in neck (partly retouched) | | .. | .. | 2·50 |
| | *d.* Screened loop to P | | .. | .. | 2·50 |
| | *e.* Semi-circle around front curl | .. | .. | .. | 2·50 |
| | *f.* Dark spot in hair | .. | .. | .. | .. | 2·00 |
| | *g.* Repair in neck | .. | .. | .. | .. | 2·00 |
| | *h.* Gash in forehead | .. | .. | .. | .. | 2·00 |
| | *i.* Screened base to P | .. | .. | .. | .. | 2·00 |

**E. FLUORESCENT COATED PAPER. PVAD GUM** (10.9.73)

| | | | | | | | |
|---|---|---|---|---|---|---|---|
| U59 (=S.G.X844) | Crimson | .. | .. | .. | .. | 10 | 10 |
| | *a.* Phosphor omitted | .. | .. | .. | .. | 2·00 |
| | *b.* One broad band .. | .. | .. | .. | 1·40 |
| | *c.* Thinner paper (5p. multi-value coil) | .. | .. | 8·00 |
| | *d.* Shoulder scratch .. | .. | .. | .. | 1·00 |
| | *e.* Chipped P | .. | .. | .. | .. | 1·00 |
| | *f.* Imperforate (pair) | .. | .. | .. | .. | |
| | *g.* Circular flaw on jaw | .. | .. | .. | 1·50 |
| | *h.* Green marks in dress | .. | .. | .. | 3·00 |

**Cylinder Numbers (Blocks of Six)**

Perforation Type R

| Cyl. No. | Phos. No. | | | | | No dot | Dot |
|---|---|---|---|---|---|---|---|
| 11 | 17 | .. | .. | .. | .. | 75 | 75 |
| 11 | P21 | .. | .. | .. | .. | 1·75 | 1·60 |

Perforation Type RE

| | | | | | | | |
|---|---|---|---|---|---|---|---|
| 11 | 17 | .. | .. | .. | .. | 75** | 1·25 |
| 11 | P21 | .. | .. | .. | .. | 1·75** | 1·25 |
| 11 | 30 | .. | .. | .. | .. | 1·25 | 1·25 |
| 12 | 17 | .. | .. | .. | .. | 3·50 | 4·00 |
| 12 | P21 | .. | .. | .. | .. | 1·00 | 1·00 |
| 12 | 30 | .. | .. | .. | .. | 24·00 | 32·00 |

**Same prices as perforation type R with single extension holes in left margin.

## 1977 (26 JANUARY).   TWO 8 mm. PHOSPHOR BANDS. TYPE I. FLUORESCENT COATED PAPER. PVAD GUM

50p. booklet panes UMFB3/4 (26.1.77), UMFB5/6 (13.6.77) and UMFB19/20 (26.1.81)

| | | | | | | |
|---|---|---|---|---|---|---|
| U60 | Crimson | .. | .. | .. | .. | 40 | 40 |
| | *a.* Short phosphor band at bottom left (ex. UMFB3, 5) .. | | 40 |
| | *b.* Short phosphor band at bottom right (ex. UMFB4, 6) .. | .. | .. | .. | .. | .. | 30 |

## 1977 (14 DECEMBER).   ONE 4 mm. CENTRE PHOSPHOR BAND. TYPE I. FLUORESCENT COATED PAPER. PVAD GUM

10p. G4 and G5 multi-value coils (14.12.77), (16.1.80) and 10p. booklet panes UMFB7 (8.2.78), UMFB11 (17.10.79), UMFB31 (5.4.83), UMFB34 (3.9.84) and UMFB41*a*

| | | | | | | | |
|---|---|---|---|---|---|---|---|
| U61 (=S.G.X845) | Crimson | .. | .. | .. | .. | 20 | 20 |
| | *a.* Type II (4.8.80) .. | .. | .. | .. | .. | 50 | 50 |
| | *b.* White flaw left of earring | .. | .. | .. | 1·50 |
| | *c.* New phosphor ink (ex. UMFB41*a*, 30.10.87) | .. | 75 |
| | *d.* Short band at top (ex. UMFB7) | .. | .. | 80 |

No. U61*c* exists with straight edge at left.

## 1979 (10 OCTOBER).   "ALL OVER" PHOSPHOR (FLUORESCENT COATED) PAPER. TYPE I. PVAD GUM

| | | | | | | | |
|---|---|---|---|---|---|---|---|
| U62 (=S.G.X846) | Crimson | .. | .. | .. | .. | .. | 20 | 20 |

No. U68 is known postmarked at Trafalgar Square, Branch Office on 9 October.

**Cylinder Numbers (Blocks of Six)**

Perforation Type RE

| Cyl. No. | Phos. No. | | | | No dot | Dot |
|---|---|---|---|---|---|---|
| 12 | —* | .. | .. | .. | 1·75 | 1·75 |

*The phosphor cylinder was No. P37 (inverted and unsynchronised) and it is sometimes found in the right-hand margin of the dot panes. *Block of six, price* £7. Not all sheets show the number due to the greater diameter of the cylinder in relation to the ink cylinder.

## 1979 (12 DECEMBER). PHOSPHORISED PAPER. TYPE I. PVAD GUM

### A. FLUORESCENT COATED PAPER

| U63 (=S.G.X925) | Crimson .. .. .. .. .. .. .. | 10 | 10 |
|---|---|---|---|
| | *a.* Imperforate (pair) (Head type B1) .. .. .. | | |
| | *b.* Large flaw on temple .. .. .. .. .. | 6·50 | |
| | *c.* Spot in 1 .. .. .. .. .. .. .. | 2·00 | |
| | *d.* Circular flaw on jaw .. .. .. .. .. | 1·75 | |
| | *e.* Scratch above dress .. .. .. .. .. | 1·75 | |

No. U63 is known on phosphorised paper with either a shiny ink surface which gives a photo-negative reflection or a matt surface without the negative effect.

**Cylinder Numbers (Blocks of Six)**
Perforation Type RE

| Cyl. No. | | | | | No dot | Dot |
|---|---|---|---|---|---|---|
| 12 | .. | .. | .. | .. | 1·00 | 1·00 |
| 14 | .. | .. | .. | .. | 75 | 75 |

Blocks from cyl. 14 no dot with the glossy photo-negative appearance and perforated by the Kampf machine as opposed to the APS perforator (Appendix I, Type R) are scarce. *Price £225 for cyl. 14 no dot. The dot side was not affected.*

Perforation variety
The 17 pin variety as described in Appendix I. *Price for marginal block of 6 £12, cylinder no. 14 dot, block of 6 £22.*

### B. ADVANCED COATED PAPER (4.83)†

| U64 | Crimson .. .. .. .. .. .. .. | 10 |
|---|---|---|
| | *c.* Scratch above dress .. .. .. .. .. | 2·00 |
| | *d.* Spot in 1 .. .. .. .. .. .. | 2·00 |
| | *e.* Large flaw on temple repaired .. .. .. .. | 4·00 |
| | *f.* Oval retouch behind hair .. .. .. .. | 3·00 |
| | *k.* Retouch below bust .. .. .. .. .. | 2·00 |

†No. U64 was first placed on sale at the Philatelic Bureau on 7 January 1986.

**Cylinder Numbers (Blocks of Six)**
Perforation Type RE

| Cyl. No. | | | | | No dot | Dot |
|---|---|---|---|---|---|---|
| 12 | .. | .. | .. | .. | 1·25 | 1·25 |
| 14 | .. | .. | .. | .. | 85 | 85 |
| 15 | .. | .. | .. | .. | 85 | 85 |
| 17 | .. | .. | .. | .. | 85 | 85 |

Perforation variety
The 17 pin variety as described in Appendix I. *Price for marginal block of 6 £5; cylinder no. 14 dot, block of 6 £9.*

## 1986 (29 JULY). ONE 4·5 mm. CENTRE PHOSPHOR BAND. TYPE I. FLUORESCENT COATED PAPER. PVAD GUM

50p. booklet panes UMFB39/41

| U65 | Crimson .. .. .. .. .. .. | 50 | 50 |
|---|---|---|---|
| | *b.* New phosphor ink (27.1.87) .. .. .. .. | 40 | |

No. U65 exists with straight edge at left and with phosphor omitted as listed under pane No. UMFB41*b.*

## 1986 (20 OCTOBER). ONE NARROW PHOSPHOR BAND AT LEFT. TYPE I. FLUORESCENT COATED PAPER. PVAD GUM

50p. booklet pane UMFB42

| U66 (=S.G.X847) | Crimson .. .. .. .. .. .. .. | 75 | 90 |
|---|---|---|---|
| | *a.* One 9.5 mm broad band .. .. .. .. | £150 | |
| | *b.* New phosphor ink (27.1.87) .. .. .. .. | 60 | |

## 1987 (3 MARCH). ONE NARROW PHOSPHOR BAND AT RIGHT. TYPE I. FLUORESCENT COATED PAPER PVAD GUM

£5 P & O booklet *se-tenant* pane UWB31

| | | | | | |
|---|---|---|---|---|---|
| U67 (=S.G.X847Ea) | Crimson | .. .. .. .. .. .. | 75 | 90 |
| | *a*. Error. Original phosphor ink .. | .. .. .. | 10·00 | |

No. U67*a* derives from the 50p. Roman Britain No. 2, St. Albans booklet with reversed phosphor bands. These were found before the normal U67 with bands printed in the new phosphor ink. The 1p. with right band in original phosphor ink with dull reaction also exists from the P & O *se-tenant* booklet pane UWB31*a* of which only five examples were reported.

**CYLINDER VARIETIES**
**Listed Flaws**

U55f, U57c
Lower part of figure 1 screened
(Cyl. 1 dot, R. 1/1)

U55g, U57d, U58c
White spots on neck

Nos. U55*g*, U57*d* and U58*c* are a multipositive flaw which, in the 1p. value occurs in sheets on Cyl. 3 no dot, R. 9/3 on Nos. U55 and U57 and also in vertical coils on Cyl. R4 no dot, Roll 5 on Nos. U55 and U57; the latter being partly retouched.

The flaw can also be found in sheets on the 1½p., 2p., 3p., 4p. and bicoloured 9p. values. See Nos. U71*e*, U72*c*, U76*c*, U78*c*, U103*h*, U104*c*, U107*e*, U122*b*, U171*c*, U172*d* and U173*g*.

U55h, U58d
Screened loop to P
(Cyl. R4 dot, Roll 3)

U55i, U58e
Semi-circle around front curl
(Cyl. R4 no dot, Roll 10)

Both occur on the vertical EL coil

U55j, U59d
Dark scratch in shoulder
(Roll 1)

U55k, U59e
Chipped P in value
(Roll 10)

U55l, U59h
Green marks in dress
(Later removed)

All occur on the 10p. G3 multi-value coil in every fifth position (Cyl. R27)

No. U59*d* is a multipositive flaw which also occurs on the adjoining 2p. value in the same strip. See Nos. U76*d*, U77*e*, U79*b* and U80*d*. It is also found on Roll 10 on 6½p. VS coils and 7p. CS coils, see Nos. U149*i* and U154*h*.

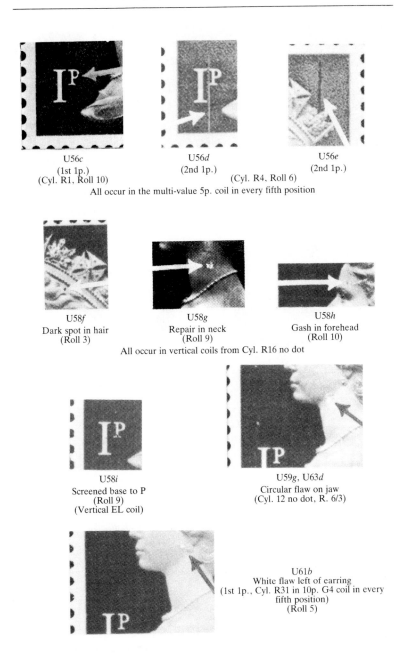

U56c
(1st 1p.)
(Cyl. R1, Roll 10)

U56d
(2nd 1p.)
(Cyl. R4, Roll 6)

U56e
(2nd 1p.)

All occur in the multi-value 5p. coil in every fifth position

U58f
Dark spot in hair
(Roll 3)

U58g
Repair in neck
(Roll 9)

U58h
Gash in forehead
(Roll 10)

All occur in vertical coils from Cyl. R16 no dot

U58i
Screened base to P
(Roll 9)
(Vertical EL coil)

U59g, U63d
Circular flaw on jaw
(Cyl. 12 no dot, R. 6/3)

U61b
White flaw left of earring
(1st 1p., Cyl. R31 in 10p. G4 coil in every
fifth position)
(Roll 5)

No. U61b is a multipositive flaw which also occurs on Cyl. R32 as a small repair and on 7p. CS coil, Roll 6.

U63b
Large flaw on temple
(Cyl. 14 no dot, R. 11/3)

U64e
As No. U63b but flaw
repaired showing solid
eyebrow

U63c, U64d
Spot in 1
(Cyl. 14 dot, R. 6/4)
Later removed but this
first state shows a dotted
line in P. A later second
state shows two breaks
in the loop

U64f
Large oval retouch
(Cyl. 15 dot, R. 3/9)

U64k
Retouch below bust
(Vert. coil QL in
every twelfth position)

For illustration of the multipositive flaw scratch above dress U63e, U64c see 29p. Cyl. 1. This occurs on Cyl. 14 no dot, R. 12/4.

For further flaws on 1p. stamps in booklet panes, see Nos. USB8, UMFB1/3, UMFB5, UMFB7 and UMFB11.

**Minor Constant Sheet Flaws**

| | | |
|---|---|---|
| Cyl. 1 | 2/10 | Horizontal scratch on Queen's shoulder close to collar (Th. F3) |
| | 6/4 | White flaw on Queen's hair (Th. C4) |
| | 8/7 | Retouch on Queen's cheek appearing as "sideburn" (Th. D3) |
| | 18/4 | White dot on Queen's nose (Th. D2) |
| Cyl. 3 | 10/1 | Screening dots in top margin (Th. above A5) (Multipositive flaw) |
| Cyl. 11 | 2/4 | White scratch above front curl of Queen's hair (Th. A2) |
| | 3/4 | Dark spot in Queen's hair (Th. C4) and disturbance at base of collar of dress (Th. G5) |
| | 4/1 | White dots near base of 1 (Th. G1–G2) |
| | 10/2 | Disturbance on Queen's neck (Th. E4) |
| | 17/5 | Small retouch in front of Queen's eye (Th. C2) |
| Cyl. 11. | 6/3 | Dark speck on bust (Th. F3) |
| | 19/7 | White spot touching central cross on crown (Th. A5) |
| | 19/8 | Dark spot in collar (Th. G5) |
| | 20/8 | Horizontal and diagonal scratches on cheekbone (Th. D3) |
| Cyl. 12 | 4/7 | Dark speck on collar of dress (Th. G4) |
| | 7/1 | Two dark specks, one above necklace (Th. E3), other below necklace (Th. F4) |
| | 7/6 | Retouch in hair (Th. B4–C4) |
| | 11/6 | Background retouch in front of Queen's eyebrow (Th. B2) |
| | 15/5 | Dark speck in neck under hair (Th. E4) |

Cyl. 14    5/4 Dark mark on shoulder (Th. F4–G4)
        7/2 White spot on lower band of pearls and hair (Th. C6)
        8/9 Dark mark on dress (Th. G3–G4)
      10/5 White spot below hairline (Th. C3–D3)
      19/5 Dark speck on shoulder (Th. F3)
    19/10 White spot on shoulder (Th. G4)
    20/10 Speck in bottom margin (Th. H5)

Cyl. 14.    2/7 Spot on neck (Th. E4)
        4/9 Spot in top margin (Th. A1 (above))
      5/10 White nick in dress (Th. G4). Later retouched
       7/9 Disturbance on shoulder (Th. F4)
       8/3 Thin white scratch through Queen's face (Th. C3–D3)
       9/9 Two white spots on shoulder (Th. F4) and (Th. G4). Later retouched
     10/3 Speck in 1
     10/7 Pale blemish under 1 (Th. G1)
     13/9 Circular retouch on shoulder (Th. F3)
     14/8 Specks below eye (Th. C2)
     19/7 Scratch across neck (Th. E3–E4)
     20/2 White spot at back of shoulder (Th. F5)
     20/9 Diagonal hairline scratch across shoulder to dress (Th. F5–G4)

Cyl. 15.   14/6 Diagonal hairline across cheek (Th. C3–D3)

**COILS**

Vertical delivery and printed in continuous reels. Cylinder R4 (double pane) was used for PVA and GA and Cylinders R15 and R16 (single pane) for GA only.

Code No.

| Two bands | Issued | Number in roll | Face value | Paper/gum | Screen | Perf. Type |
|---|---|---|---|---|---|---|
| EL | 15.2.71 | 1000 | £10 | OCP/PVA | 250 | Comb |
| EL | 8.73? | 1000 | £10 | FCP/GA | 250 | R(S) |

Phosphorised (advanced coated) paper.

| | | | | | | |
|---|---|---|---|---|---|---|
| QL | 26.7.88 | 1000 | £10 | ACP/PVAD | — | Comb |

Sideways delivery and printed in continuous reels.
Phosphorised (advanced coated) paper.

| | | | | | | |
|---|---|---|---|---|---|---|
| SC | 23.6.87 | 1000 | £10 | ACP/PVAD | — | Comb |

Cylinder Numbers used

| EL | OCP/PVA | R4 |
|---|---|---|
| | FCP/GA | R4, R15, R16 |
| SC | ACP/PVAD | R37 |
| QL | ACP/PVAD | R38 |

**WITHDRAWN** Nos. U55/9, 2.80; No. U62, 3.80; No. U63, 6.1.87

# 1½p. Black   (1971–74)

## 1971 (15 FEBRUARY).   TWO 9·5 mm. PHOSPHOR BANDS

### A. ORIGINAL COATED PAPER. PVA GUM

| U71 | Black .. | | | | | | | 10 | 15 |
|---|---|---|---|---|---|---|---|---|---|
| | *a.* Uncoated paper (1971) .. | | .. | .. | .. | .. | £110 | |
| | *b.* Phosphor omitted | | .. | .. | .. | .. | 10·00 | |
| | *c.* One broad band .. | | .. | .. | .. | .. | 75·00 | |
| | *d.* Malformed 2 | .. | .. | .. | .. | .. | 3·00 | |
| | *e.* Faint spots on neck | | .. | .. | .. | .. | 3·00 | |

**Cylinder Numbers (Blocks of Six unless otherwise stated)**
Perforation Type A

| Cyl. No. | Phos. No. | | | | | No dot | Dot | |
|---|---|---|---|---|---|---|---|---|
| 1 | S2 | .. | .. | .. | .. | 2·00 | 2·00 | |
| 1 | — | .. | .. | .. | .. | 1·75 | 1·75 | |
| 1 | L2, S2 | Re-engraved | .. | | .. | 3·50 | 3·50 | Block of ten |
| 1 | L4 | .. | .. | .. | .. | 2·25 | 2·25 | |

### B. FLUORESCENT COATED PAPER. PVA GUM (6.10.71)

| U72 | Black .. | | | | | | | 1·00 |
|---|---|---|---|---|---|---|---|---|
| | *a.* Phosphor omitted | | .. | .. | .. | .. | 20·00 |
| | *b.* One broad band .. | | .. | .. | .. | .. | £180 |
| | *c.* Faint spots on neck | | .. | .. | .. | .. | 3·75 |

Examples of No. U72 from booklet pane No. USB7 exist with contaminated "yellow phosphor".
*Price mint* £4.50.

**Cylinder Numbers (Blocks of Ten)**
Perforation Type A

| Cyl. No. | Phos. No. | | | | No dot | Dot |
|---|---|---|---|---|---|---|
| 4 | L2, S2 | Re-engraved | .. | .. | 7·50 | 7·50 |

Cylinder blocks of six to show a large phosphor 2 re-engraved £4 *each*.

### C. FLUORESCENT COATED PAPER. PVAD GUM (5.6.74)

| U73 (=S.G.X848) | Black .. | | | | | | | 20 | 15 |
|---|---|---|---|---|---|---|---|---|---|
| | *a.* Phosphor omitted | | .. | .. | .. | .. | £225 | |
| | *b.* Imperforate (pair) | | .. | .. | .. | .. | | |
| | *c.* Imperforate 3 sides (horiz. pair) | | | .. | .. | .. | | |
| | *d.* One broad band .. | | .. | .. | .. | .. | 45·00 | |

**Cylinder Numbers (Blocks of Six unless otherwise stated)**
Perforation Type R

| Cyl. No. | Phos. No. | | | | | No dot | Dot | |
|---|---|---|---|---|---|---|---|---|
| 9 | 17 | .. | .. | .. | .. | 3·50 | 3·50 | |
| 9 | 17 | +35 mm. (17) .. | | .. | | 25·00 | 24·00 | Block of ten |
| 9 | P21 | .. | .. | .. | .. | 2·75 | 2·75 | |

## CYLINDER VARIETIES
**Listed Flaws**

U71*d*
(Cyl. 1 no dot, R. 14/9)

Nos. U71*e* and U72*c* are a multipositive flaw occurring on Cyls. 1 and 4 no dot, R. 9/3, being a fainter state of the 1p. flaw No. U55*g*.
For further flaws on 1½p. stamps in booklet panes, see under Nos. USB7/8.

**Minor Constant Sheet Flaws**
Cyl. 1  10/1  Screening dots in top margin (Th. above A5) (Multipositive flaw as 1p. Cyl. 3)
Cyl. 4  10/1  As Cyl. 1
Cyl. 9  12/2  Small spot on Queen's neck (Th. E3)

**WITHDRAWN**  8.4.78

# 2p. Myrtle-green  (1971–88)

**Three Value Types**

| | |
|---|---|
| I | II | III |

Type I.    Thick value.
Type II.   Thin value. Occurs in UMFB9/10 and UMFB14/15 booklet panes
Type III.  Narrow figures. Occurs on 14p. multi-value coil UMC13 and sheets from cyl. 16 in deep green.

## 1971 (15 FEBRUARY).  TWO 9·5 mm. PHOSPHOR BANDS. TYPE I

**A. ORIGINAL COATED PAPER. PVA GUM**

| | | | | | | | | |
|---|---|---|---|---|---|---|---|---|
| U76 | Myrtle-green.. | .. | .. | .. | .. | .. | 25 | 25 |
| | a. Phosphor omitted | .. | .. | .. | .. | .. 25·00 | |
| | b. One broad band .. | .. | .. | .. | .. | .. 28·00 | |
| | c. Faint spots on neck | .. | .. | .. | .. | .. 1·75 | |
| | d. Shoulder scratch .. | .. | .. | .. | .. | .. 2·00 | |
| | k. White patch. State 1 | .. | .. | .. | .. | .. 2·00 | |

No. U76 also exists from 10p. G3 multi-value coils issued about March 1977.

**Cylinder Numbers (Blocks of Six unless otherwise stated)**
Perforation Type A

| Cyl. No. | Phos. No. | | | | No dot | Dot | |
|---|---|---|---|---|---|---|---|
| 4 | L2, S2 | .. | .. | .. | .. | 3·25 | 3·25 | Block of ten |
| 4 | — | .. | .. | .. | .. | 10·00 | 10·00 | |
| 5 | L2, S2  Re-engraved | .. | .. | 8·50 | 8·50 | Block of ten |

Phosphor Cylinder Displacement. With ink cyl. 4, phos. cyls. L2, S2 are known displaced up the margin 102 mm. opposite row 14.

**B. ORIGINAL COATED PAPER. GUM ARABIC.** 5p. Multi-value coil only (15.2.71)

| | | | | | | |
|---|---|---|---|---|---|---|
| U77 | Myrtle-green.. | .. | .. | .. | .. | .. | 3·00 |
| | a. Phosphor omitted | .. | .. | .. | .. | £175 |
| | b. One broad band .. | .. | .. | .. | .. | 20·00 |
| | c. Pendant variety .. | .. | .. | .. | .. | 5·50 |
| | d. Scratch from top margin through face.. | | .. | .. | 5·50 |
| | e. Shoulder scratch .. | .. | .. | .. | .. | 4·50 |

**C. FLUORESCENT COATED PAPER. PVA GUM** (6.10.71)

| | | | | | | |
|---|---|---|---|---|---|---|
| U78 | Myrtle-green.. | .. | .. | .. | .. | .. | 1·40 |
| | a. Phosphor omitted | .. | .. | .. | .. | £200 |
| | b. One broad band .. | .. | .. | .. | .. | 27·00 |
| | c. Faint spots on neck | .. | .. | .. | .. | 3·25 |

Examples of No. U78 from booklet pane No. USB3 (Cyl. B7) exist with contaminated "yellow phosphor". *Price mint £5.*

**Cylinder Numbers (Blocks of Six)**

Perforation Type A

| Cyl. No. | Phos. No. | | | | No dot | Dot |
|---|---|---|---|---|---|---|
| 4 | 7 | .. | .. | .. | .. | 20·00 | 18·00 |

**D. FLUORESCENT COATED PAPER. GUM ARABIC.** 5p. Multi-value coil only (9.72)

| | | | | | | |
|---|---|---|---|---|---|---|
| U79 (=S.G.X849Eg) | Myrtle-green.. | .. | .. | .. | .. | .. | 2·25 |
| | b. Shoulder scratch.. | .. | .. | .. | .. | 4·00 |

**E. FLUORESCENT COATED PAPER. PVAD GUM.** From sheets, *se-tenant* panes and multi-value coils (10.9.73)

| | | | | | | |
|---|---|---|---|---|---|---|
| U80 (=S.G.X849) | Myrtle-green.. | .. | .. | .. | .. | .. | 20 | 10 |
| | a. Phosphor omitted | .. | .. | .. | .. | 5·00 |
| | b. One 9·5 mm. broad band (Head Type B1, ex. UMC5) | 1·75 |
| | ba. One 6·5 mm. band (ex. UWB8b) | .. | .. | 18·00 |
| | bb. One 9·5 mm. broad band (Head Type B2, booklets) .. | 15·00 |
| | c. Thinner paper (5p. multi-value coil) .. | .. | 24·00 |
| | e. Retouch under chin | .. | .. | .. | .. | 1·60 |
| | f. Retouch left of mouth .. | .. | .. | .. | 1·60 |
| | g. Retouch below chin | .. | .. | .. | .. | 1·60 |
| | h. Rounded bottom left of 2 | .. | .. | .. | 2·00 |
| | i. Retouch over centre of crown .. | .. | .. | 1·50 |
| | j. White spot in fold of dress | .. | .. | .. | 1·75 |
| | k. White patch. State 1 | .. | .. | .. | .. | 3·00 |
| | ka. Green spot. State 2 | .. | .. | .. | .. | 1·75 |
| | l. Shoulder scratch .. | .. | .. | .. | .. | 1·75 |
| | m. Phosphor printed on both sides | .. | .. | £160 |
| | n. Imperforate (horiz. pair) | .. | .. | .. | |

**Cylinder Numbers (Blocks of Six unless otherwise stated)**

Perforation Type R

| Cyl. No. | Phos. No. | | | | | No dot | Dot | |
|---|---|---|---|---|---|---|---|---|
| 11 | 17 | .. | .. | .. | .. | 2·00 | 1·25 | |
| 11 | P21 | .. | .. | .. | .. | 1·50 | 1·25 | |
| 11 | P21 | +27 mm. (17) .. | .. | .. | 60·00 | 60·00 | Block of ten |
| 11 | P21 | +42 mm. (17) .. | .. | .. | 50·00 | 45·00 | Block of ten |

Perforation Type RE

| | | | | | | | |
|---|---|---|---|---|---|---|---|
| 10** | 17 | .. | .. | .. | .. | 1·00 | 1·00 |
| 10 | P21 | .. | .. | .. | .. | 2·75 | 3·00 |
| 10 | 30 | .. | .. | .. | .. | 1·40 | 1·40 |

**The dot was at first omitted on the dot pane of cylinder 10 with phosphor cylinder 17 but the cylinder block can be distinguished from that of the no dot pane by a break in the vertical line of the box. Later the dot was engraved on the cylinder. *Cylinder block of six showing 10 and dot omitted, price £2.*

## 1979 (28 AUGUST).   TWO 8 mm. PHOSPHOR BANDS. TYPE II. FLUORESCENT COATED PAPER. PVAD GUM

50p. booklet panes UMFB9/10 and UMFB14/17 (4.2.80)

| | | | | | | | | | |
|---|---|---|---|---|---|---|---|---|---|
| U81 | Myrtle-green.. | .. | .. | .. | .. | .. | .. | 50 | 40 |
| | *a.* Phosphor omitted | | .. | .. | .. | .. | .. | 5·00 | |
| | *b.* One broad band .. | .. | .. | .. | .. | .. | .. | 5·00 | |

Examples of No. U81 are found with short bands at top or at the bottom on one side. These came from panes UMFB9/10 and 14/17 with phosphor slightly misplaced.

## 1979 (10 OCTOBER).   "ALL OVER" PHOSPHOR (FLUORESCENT COATED) PAPER. TYPE I. PVAD GUM

| | | | | | | | |
|---|---|---|---|---|---|---|---|
| U82 (=S.G.X850) | Myrtle-green.. | .. | .. | .. | .. | .. | 20 | 15 |

**Cylinder Numbers (Blocks of Six)**

Perforation Type RE

| Cyl. No. | Phos. No. | | | | No dot | Dot |
|---|---|---|---|---|---|---|
| 13 | — | .. | .. | .. | 1·75 | 1·75 |
| 13 | P35 | .. | .. | .. | £1500 | † |
| 13 | P37 | .. | .. | .. | £100 | † |

Owing to inverted printing of the phosphor cylinder the phosphor number P37 appeared inverted and unsynchronised in the right-hand margin of the dot panes. *Block of six, price* £10. Later printings had the phosphor cylinder number upright but still unsynchronised so that it appeared in the left-hand margin of the no dot pane. As the diameter of the phosphor cylinders employed in this printing was greater than that of the ink cylinder not all sheets printed show a phosphor number.

## 1979 (12 DECEMBER).   PHOSPHORISED PAPER. PVAD GUM

### A. TYPE I. FLUORESCENT COATED PAPER

| | | | | | | | | |
|---|---|---|---|---|---|---|---|---|
| U83 (=S.G.X926) | Myrtle-green.. | .. | .. | .. | .. | .. | 10 | 10 |
| | *a.* Imperforate (pair) | .. | .. | .. | .. | | | |
| | *b.* Spot in band | .. | .. | .. | .. | .. | 2·00 | |
| | *c.* Scratch above dress | .. | .. | .. | .. | 2·00 | | |

No. U83 is known on phosphorised paper with either a shiny ink surface which gives a photo-negative reflection or a matt surface without the negative effect.

**Cylinder Numbers (Blocks of Six)**

Perforation Type RE

| Cyl. No. | | | | Dot |
|---|---|---|---|---|
| 13 | .. | ... | .. | 1·25 |
| 14 | .. | .. | .. | 1·50 |

### B. TYPE III. ADVANCED COATED PAPER. 14p. Multi-value coil only (5.9.88)

| | | | | | | | |
|---|---|---|---|---|---|---|---|
| U84 (=S.G.X928) | Myrtle-green.. | .. | .. | .. | .. | 20 | 10 |
| | *b.* Damage to background .. | .. | .. | .. | 2·75 | | |

### CYLINDER VARIETIES

**Listed Flaws**

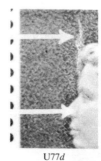

| U77*c* | U77*d* | U80*e* |
|---|---|---|
| Extra earring appearing as pendant | Scratch from top margin extends through face (Cyl. R4, Roll 4) | Retouch under chin (Cyl. 11 dot, R. 2/8) |

(In every fifth position in 5p. multi-value coil)

U80*f*
Retouch by mouth
(Cyl. 10 no dot, R. 11/7)

U80*g*
Retouch below chin
(Cyl. 10 dot, R. 17/3)

U80*h*
Rounded 2
(Cyl. 10 dot, R. 15/4)

U80*i*
Retouch over crown
(Cyl. 10 dot, R. 18/1)

U80*j*
White spot on dress
(10p. G3 multi-value coil in
every fifth position)

U76*k*, U80*k*
State 1. White patch

U80*ka*
State 2. Green spot

No. U76*k* exists on G3 (OCP/PVA printing) and No. U80*k* exists on Roll 10 of G1/2 FCP/PVAD multi-value coils. No. U80*ka* exists on G3 coil. These flaws occur in every fifth position.

Spot in band of crown
(Cyl. 13 no dot, R. 10/1)
(It is faint on 15p. Cyl. 1 no dot)

U83*b*

For illustration of the multipositive flaw U83*c* see 29p. Cyl. 1. This occurs on Cyl. 14 no dot, R. 12/4.

U84*b*
Damage to background
(Fourth Reader's Digest coil
in every 4th position Cyl. R1)

For further flaws on 2p. stamps in booklet panes, see under Nos. USB2/4 and UMFB16/7.

Nos. U76*c*, U78*c* are a multipositive flaw occurring on Cyl. 4 no dot, R. 9/3, being a fainter state of the 1p. variety, No. U55*g*.

The flaw represented by Nos. U76*d*, U77*e*, U79*b* and U80*l* occurs on both the 5p. multi-value coils (on 2p. only) and the 10p. G3 multi-value coils, where it also appears on the adjoining 1p. For details see 1p. flaw No. U59*d*. This shows that the same part of the Head B multipositive was used for several of the 2p. cylinders of the 5p. multi-value coils, as well as for the 2p. and 1p. cylinders of the 10p. G3 multi-value coil.

### Minor Constant Sheet Flaws

Cyl.  4    8/7    Dark spot in band of crown (Th. B4)
Cyl. 10    1/5    Vertical scratch on Queen's neck (Th. E3)
           8/3    White spots on back of collar (Th. G5) and retouch below dress (Th. G4)
           9/7    Small retouch on collar (Th. G3)
          17/5    White patch in right jewel of crown (Th. B5) and small retouch at back of crown
                  (Th. C5–C6)
          18/4    Small retouch under Queen's eye (Th. C3)
          18/6    Dark cut in collar (Th. G3)
Cyl. 10.   2/1    White patch at bottom of hair bun (Th. E5)
           3/5    White spot to right of hair bun (Th. E5)
          13/8    Damage to jaw line (Th. E3)
          15/3    Scratch from Queen's chin to bust (Th. E3–F3)
          16/1    Small white patch at top right corner (Th. A6)
          16/3    White blemish in band of crown (Th. B4)
          17/7    White spot in hair bun (Th. D5)
          18/9    Small retouch behind Queen's neck (Th. E5)
          19/8    Small white spot on Queen's cheek (Th. D3)
          20/2    Circular flaw at bottom left of bust (Th. G2)
Cyl. 11    2/4    Green dots on Queen's neck under necklace (Th. E4)
           7/8    Dark spot in background behind Queen's shoulder (Th. E5)
Cyl. 13    1/7    Small spot below dress (Th. G4)
           1/8    White spot at the back of hair (Th. D5)
           3/2    Small spot below bust (Th. H4)
           4/3    Pale patch at bottom left below 2 (Th. G1)
          10/3    White spot on neck (Th. E3)
          17/6    Three white spots at back of hair (Th. C5)
         17/10    Faint scratch through Queen's hair (Th. G4–G5)
Cyl. 14    7/5    Pale squiggle behind bust (Th. D2)
          11/6    Spot behind nose (Th. D2)
          12/4    Scratch above dress (Th. F5–G3). Multipositive flaw and illustrated under 29p. Cyl. 1
                  no dot.
          17/1    Pale speck in top left corner (Th. A1)
          19/5    Short dark vertical line below front of necklace (Th. F3)
          20/5    Scratch on cheek (Th. D2)
Cyl. 14.   2/7    Spot on neck (Th. E4)
          10/9    Spot in band (Th. B4)
          13/9    Circular retouch on shoulder (Th. F3)
          15/4    Blunt tip to 2
          17/5    White scratch to left of forehead (Th. B2–C2)
          17/6    White speck in top right corner (Th. A6)
          18/6    White speck in front of eye (Th. C2) and speck below chin (Th. E2)
          19/7    Scratch across neck (Th. E3–E4). Multipositive flaw as 22p. blue, Cyl. 4 dot

20/4 Scratch from necklace to base of bust (Th. F4–G4). Multipositive flaw as 3p. magenta, Cyl. 43 no dot

20/9 Diagonal scratch across shoulder (Th. F4–F5). Multipositive flaw as 22p. blue, Cyl. 4 dot

**WITHDRAWN** Nos. U76/80, 5.80; No. U82, 3.80; No. U83, 9.80 but put on sale again at the Philatelic Bureau in May 1981 and withdrawn 9.7.85.

# 2p. Deep Green (1988)

**1988 (26 JULY). COLOUR CHANGED. PHOSPHORISED (ADVANCED COATED) PAPER. TYPE III. PVAD GUM**

| | | | | | | | | |
|---|---|---|---|---|---|---|---|---|
| U85 (=S.G.X927) | Deep green .. | .. | .. | .. | .. | .. | 10 | 10 |
| | *a.* Imperforate (pair) | .. | .. | .. | .. | .. | | |

**Cylinder Numbers (Blocks of Six)**

Perforation Type RE

| Cyl. No. | | | | No dot | Dot |
|---|---|---|---|---|---|
| 16 | .. | .. | .. | 75 | 75 |

**Minor Constant Sheet Flaws**

Cyl. 16    2/2  Pale blemish on jawline (Th. E3)

6/6  Weak diagonal line across shoulder (Th. F3–F5).

10/1  Small retouch in background close to right corner (Th. G6).

Opposite R. 1/15 the O of the "SON" box was not engraved.

Cyl. 16. 13/7  Hairline across shoulder (Th. F4–F8)

The multipositive used for Cyl. 16 was also employed for the 4p., 5p. and 75p., Cyls. 15, 10 and 1.

# 2½p. Magenta   (1971–75)

**Three Value Types**

| I | II | III |

Type I.   Thin value and P (with or without minute scratch in base of small 2)

Type II.   Thicker fraction and P

Type III.   Very thin value and P

The Types were used as follows:—
I.   All sheets except cyl. 19; horiz. and vert. coils; booklet pane UB35 from cyl. B29: Wedgwood 2½p./3p. pane; Wedgwood UWB4c pane from cyl. B22.
II.   Sheets from cyl. 19; booklet panes (except pane UB35 from cyl. B29).
III.   Wedgwood 2½p./½p. panes only from cyls. B20 and B25.

## 1971 (15 FEBRUARY).   ONE 4 mm. CENTRE PHOSPHOR BAND. TYPE I

### A. ORIGINAL COATED PAPER. PVA GUM

| | | | |
|---|---|---:|---:|
| U86 | Magenta .. .. .. .. .. .. .. | 15 | 10 |
| | *a.* Phosphor omitted .. .. .. .. .. | 6·50 | |
| | *b.* Small 2 without serif and scratch through P .. .. | 3·50 | |
| | *c.* Screen damage .. .. .. .. .. | 3·50 | |
| | *d.* Two parallel lines .. .. .. .. | 3·00 | |
| | *e.* Type II (15.2.71). . .. .. .. .. | 1·25 | 60 |
| | *ea.* Phosphor omitted .. .. .. .. | 80·00 | |

**Cylinder Numbers (Blocks of Six)**

Perforation Type A

| Cyl. No. | Phos. No. | .. | .. | .. | .. | No dot | Dot |
|---|---|---|---|---|---|---|---|
| 5 | 5 | .. | .. | .. | .. | 1·25 | 1·25 |
| 5 | — | .. | .. | .. | .. | £100 | £100 |
| 6* | 5 | .. | .. | .. | .. | £500 | £500 |
| 7 | 5 | .. | .. | .. | .. | 1·40 | 1·40 |
| 7 | 5 | +41 mm. (17) | .. | | .. | † | — |
| 8 | 5 | .. | .. | .. | .. | 6·00 | 6·00 |

Phosphor Cylinder Displacement. With ink cyl. 5, phos. cyl. 5 is known displaced up the margin 338 and 400 mm. opposite rows 1 and 2. The 338 mm. displacement is recorded on the dot pane only.
*Collectors are warned that this ink and phosphor combination is common on fluorescent coated paper and the OCP printing should only be purchased with a certificate. Probably no more than five examples survive from the printing prior to the introduction of fluorescent coated paper in Autumn 1971.

### B. FLUORESCENT COATED PAPER. PVA GUM (10.71)

| | | | |
|---|---|---:|---:|
| U87 | Magenta .. .. .. .. .. .. .. | 70 | 15 |
| | *a.* Phosphor omitted .. .. .. .. .. | 9·00 | |
| | *b.* Green phosphor* .. .. .. .. .. | 4·50 | |
| | *c.* Small 2 without serif and scratch through P .. .. | 4·50 | |
| | *d.* White spot in band .. .. .. .. | 3·00 | |
| | *e.* Type II (17.9.71). . .. .. .. .. | 60 | 45 |
| | *ea.* Phosphor omitted (ex. booklets) .. .. .. | 7·00 | |
| | *f.* Long diagonal scratch (Cyl. 19) .. *Strip of three* | 7·00 | |
| | *fa.* Break in necklace (Cyl. 19) .. .. .. .. | 4·00 | |
| | *fb.* Phosphor omitted (ex. sheets, Cyl. 19, deep shade) .. | | |
| | *g.* Type III (24.5.72) .. .. .. .. .. | 2·50 | 2·50 |
| | *ga.* Phosphor omitted .. .. .. .. | £500 | |
| | *h.* Phosphor printed on both sides (ex. UWB3). . .. | £140 | |
| | *i.* Error. Two narrow bands .. .. .. .. | — | |

*Stamps with phosphor reacting green as last used in the Wilding issues come from cylinder 10, phosphor cylinder 8.

Examples of No. U87 from Cyl. 11 (phos. 8) exist with contaminated "yellow phosphor". *Price mint £6.* Also No. U87e from booklet pane No. UB32 (Cyl. B19). *Price mint £12.*

Nos. U87f/fb are all from cylinder 19 Type II in a deeper shade than the printings of 1971.

No. U87i came from pane No. UWB3 where the bands were misplaced. One pane was involved giving 3 examples of U87i.

**Cylinder Numbers (Blocks of Six)**

Perforation Type A

| Cyl. No. | Phos. No. | | | | | No dot | Dot |
|---|---|---|---|---|---|---|---|
| 5 | 5 | .. | .. | .. | .. | 30·00 | 32·00 |
| 6 | 5 | .. | .. | .. | .. | 8·00 | 8·00 |
| 9 | P9 | .. | .. | .. | .. | 5·00 | 5·00 |
| 10 | 8* | .. | .. | .. | .. | 4·00 | 4·00 |
| 10 | — | .. | .. | .. | .. | £110 | £110 |
| 10 | 8* | Green phosphor | | .. | | 95·00 | £130 |
| 10 | P9 | .. | .. | .. | .. | 4·50 | 4·50 |
| 10 | P9 | −38 mm. (20) | .. | | .. | £150 | £150 |
| 11 | 8* | .. | .. | .. | .. | 12·00 | 12·00 |
| 11 | P9 | .. | .. | .. | .. | 3·50 | 3·50 |
| 13 | 14 | .. | .. | .. | .. | 5·00 | 5·00 |
| 13 | — | .. | .. | .. | .. | 28·00 | 25·00 |
| 13 | —† | Box only | | .. | .. | 4·50 | 4·50 |
| 13A | 14 | .. | .. | .. | .. | 4·50 | 4·50 |
| 13A | — | .. | .. | .. | .. | 28·00 | 25·00 |
| 13A | —† | Box only | | .. | .. | † | 4.50 |

*Phosphor cylinder 8 appears on no dot pane but on the dot pane it was not engraved and only the inverted "T" of the box shows.

†Phosphor cylinder 14 was not originally engraved in the phosphor box on cylinders 13 and 13A. On cylinder 13 the inverted "T" of the box shows on no dot and dot but on cylinder 13A this shows in the dot pane only.

Phosphor Cylinder Displacements. With ink cyl. 10, phos. cyl. 8 is known displaced up the margin 95 mm. opposite rows 14/15. With ink cyl. 13 and 13A the phos. cyl. 11 was displaced by 173 mm. opposite row 11.

Perforation Type R

| Cyl. No. | Phos. No. | | | | | No dot | Dot |
|---|---|---|---|---|---|---|---|
| 19 | 18 | .. | .. | .. | .. | 3·50 | 3·50 |
| 19 | 18 | −42 mm. (20) | .. | | .. | 20·00 | 6·00 |

### C. FLUORESCENT COATED PAPER. GUM ARABIC (13.9.72)

| U88 (=S.G.X851Eg) | Magenta | .. | .. | .. | .. | | .. | .. | 15 |
|---|---|---|---|---|---|---|---|---|---|
| | *a.* Imperforate (pair) | | .. | .. | .. | .. | | .. | £225 |
| | *b.* Small 2 without serif and scratch through P | | | .. | | | .. | 3·00 |
| | *c.* White spot in band | | .. | .. | .. | .. | | .. | 2·25 |

**Cylinder Numbers (Blocks of Six)**

Perforation Type R(S)

| Cyl. No. | Phos. No. | | | | | No dot | Dot |
|---|---|---|---|---|---|---|---|
| 9 | 8* | .. | .. | .. | .. | £950 | £950 |
| 9 | P9 | .. | .. | .. | .. | 4·00 | 3·50 |
| 10 | 8* | .. | .. | .. | .. | 3·00 | 3·00 |
| 10 | P9 | .. | .. | .. | .. | 4·50 | 3·75 |
| 11 | 8* | .. | .. | .. | .. | 2·50 | 2·50 |

Perforation Type A

| Cyl. No. | Phos. No. | | | | | No dot | Dot |
|---|---|---|---|---|---|---|---|
| 9 | P9 | .. | .. | .. | .. | 3·50 | 3·50 |
| 11 | P9 | .. | .. | .. | .. | 3·50 | 3·50 |

*Phosphor cylinder 8 appears on no dot pane but on the dot pane it was not engraved and only the inverted "T" of the box shows.

### D. TYPE II. FLUORESCENT COATED PAPER. PVAD GUM. (8.8.73)

| U89 (=S.G.X851) | Magenta | .. | .. | .. | .. | .. | .. | 15 | 10 |
|---|---|---|---|---|---|---|---|---|---|
| | *a.* Long diagonal scratch | | .. | | .. | *Strip of three* | 7·00 | | |
| | *b.* Break in necklace | | .. | .. | .. | .. | .. | 3·50 | |

**Cylinder Numbers (Blocks of Six)**

Perforation Type R

| Cyl. No. | Phos. No. | | | | | No dot | Dot |
|---|---|---|---|---|---|---|---|
| 19 | 18 | .. | .. | .. | .. | 3·00 | 3·00 |

## 1971 (15 FEBRUARY).   ONE NARROW PHOSPHOR BAND AT LEFT
### A. TYPE I. FLUORESCENT COATED PAPER. PVA GUM
Wedgwood Booklet pane UWB4c from cyl. B22 (24.5.72)

U90                  Magenta   ..    ..    ..    ..    ..    ..    ..   26·00

   No. U90 does not have the minute scratch in base of small 2.

### B. TYPE II. ORIGINAL COATED PAPER. PVA GUM. *Se-tenant* 2½p./3p. pane of 6 USB9 (15.2.71)
U91                  Magenta   ..    ..    ..    ..    ..    ..    ..   4·50    4·50

### C. TYPE II. FLUORESCENT COATED PAPER. PVA GUM.
*Se-tenant* 2½p./3p. pane of 6 USB10 (17.9.71)

U92                  Magenta   ..    ..    ..    ..    ..    ..    ..   2·50    2·50

   Examples of No. U92 from booklet pane No. USB10 exist with contaminated "yellow phosphor".
*Price mint* £45.

### D. TYPE III. FLUORESCENT COATED PAPER. PVA GUM.
Wedgwood Booklet Panes UWB3 and UWB4 (24.5.72)

U93 (=S.G.X852)      Magenta   ..    ..    ..    ..    ..    ..    ..   1·75    1·75
                     a. One broad band ..   ..    ..    ..    ..    ..   £325
                     c. Two narrow bands (ex. UWB3d)   ..    ..    ..   £325


## 1972 (24 MAY).   ONE NARROW PHOSPHOR BAND AT RIGHT
## FLUORESCENT COATED PAPER. PVA GUM
### A. TYPE I.* Wedgwood Booklet pane UWB2
U94 (=S.G.X852Ea)    Magenta   ..    ..    ..    ..    ..    ..    ..   1·75    2·25
                     b. Phosphor printed on both sides   ..    ..    ..   £150

   *In this version of Type I there is no minute scratch in the base of the small 2.

### B. TYPE III. Wedgwood Booklet pane UWB3
U95                  Magenta   ..    ..    ..    ..    ..    ..    ..   1·75    2·25


## 1975 (21 MAY).   CHANGE TO TWO 9·5 mm. PHOSPHOR BANDS. TYPE II.
## FLUORESCENT COATED PAPER. PVAD GUM
U96 (=S.G.X853)      Magenta   ..    ..    ..    ..    ..    ..    ..   20    30
                     a. Long diagonal scratch   ..    ..   *Strip of three*   3·50
                     b. Break in necklace   ..    ..    ..    ..    ..   2·50

**Cylinder Numbers (Blocks of Six)**
Perforation Type R

| Cyl. No. | Phos. No. | | | | | No dot | Dot |
|----------|-----------|---|---|---|---|--------|-----|
| 19 | 17 | .. | .. | .. | .. | 2·75 | 2·75 |


**CYLINDER VARIETIES**
**Listed Flaws**

U86b, U87c, U88b
Small 2 without serif and scratch line through P
(No. dot, R. 3/5)

This is a multipositive flaw seen on all sheet cylinders except cyl. 19

U86c
(Vert. coil, Roll No. 11)

U86d
(Horiz. coil, Roll No. 6)

U87d, U88c
(Cyl. 9 no dot, R. 8/9)

U87fa, U89b, U96b
(Cyl. 19 dot, R. 20/10)

Multipositive Flaw

Nos. U87f, U89a and U96a. Cyl. 19 no dot, R. 3/3–3/5 as ½p. No. U50e from cyl. 7 no dot.

For further flaws on 2½p. stamps in booklet panes, see under Nos. UB26/35 and UWB2/3.

**Minor Constant Sheet Flaws**

| Cyl. 6 | 10/5 Coloured dots in base bar of small 2 |
|---|---|
| Cyl. 7 | 6/7 Dark spot in band of crown (Th. B3) |
| Cyl. 9 | 1/2 White speck above crown (Th. A–B5) |
| | 2/9 Cut through top serif of P and severing serif of 2 of fraction |
| | 2/10 Loop of P sliced |
| | 8/2 White speck above crown (Th. A5) |
| | 20/4 Scratch down back of neck (Th. F5) |
| Cyl. 11. | 5/2 Red spot above cross on crown (Th. B5) |
| | 7/1 Diagonal scratch through top of P extending to small 2 |
| | 7/3 Vertical scratch through large 2 |
| Cyl. 19 | 1/3 Retouch under chin (Th. E2) |
| | 3/6 White patch above crown (Th. A4) |
| | 6/10 Circle of dots in front of Queen's nose (Th. C1) |
| | 11/1 Coloured speck in shoulder (Th. F5) |
| | 11/6 White speck under 1 |
| | 12/1 White spot in band of crown |
| | 12/5 White speck in bottom of large 2 |
| | 13/8 Scratch on shoulder (Th. E5) |
| | 20/3 Small retouch behind necklace (Th. E5) |
| Cyl. 19. | 4/6 Retouch behind Queen's hair (Th. D6) |
| | 6/7 Diagonal scratch from Queen's ear to neck (Th. D4–F3) |
| | 15/3 Red specks over Queen's shoulder (Th. F4) |
| | 17/3 Cluster of red specks in front of crown (Th. A3) |
| | 17/5 Two white specks on Queen's cheek bone (Th. C3) |
| | 18/3 Cluster of red spots above crown (Th. A4–A5) |
| | 19/7 Hairline scratch behind collar (Th. G5/6) |
| | 20/6 Retouch above central cross (see ½p. var. U50g) |
| | 20/7 Inverted U-shaped scratch behind crown (Th. B6) |

**COILS**

Centre band. Printed in continuous reels.

| Code No. | Issued | Number in roll | Face value | Paper/gum | Screen | Perf. Type |
|---|---|---|---|---|---|---|
| | | | Vertical delivery | | | |
| CL | 15.2.71 | 1000 | £25·00 | OCP/PVA | 150 | Comb |
| | | | Sideways delivery | | | |
| AS | 15.2.71 | 500 | £12.50 | OCP/PVA | 250 | Comb |
| AS | 8.73? | 500 | £12.50 | FCP/GA | 250 | R(S) |

Cylinder Numbers used

| CL | OCP/PVA R1 | | AS | OCP/PVA R2, R4 |
|---|---|---|---|---|
| | | | | FCP/GA   R4 |

**WITHDRAWN**   Nos. U86/8, 2.78; No. U96, 8.4.78

---

# 2½p. Rose-red   (1981)

## 1981 (14 JANUARY).   COLOUR CHANGED. PHOSPHORISED (FLUORESCENT COATED) PAPER. TYPE II. PVAD GUM

| U97 (=S.G.X929) | Rose-red  .. .. .. .. .. .. .. | 20 | 20 |
|---|---|---|---|
| | a. Eyebrow flaw  .. .. .. .. .. | 2·00 | |
| | b. White flaw in hair  .. .. .. .. | 2·00 | |
| | f. Fluorescent brightener omitted  .. .. .. | 18·00 | |

No. U97 is known on phosphorised paper with either a shiny ink surface which gives a photo-negative reflection or a matt surface without the negative effect.

No. U97f derives from the 11½p. multi-value coil, UMC9 and is printed on chalk-surfaced paper but without the fluorescent additive which was probably omitted in error.

**Cylinder Numbers (Blocks of Six)**

Perforation Type RE

| Cyl. No. | | | | No dot | Dot |
|---|---|---|---|---|---|
| 25 | .. | .. | .. | 1·50 | 1·50 |

## 1981 (26 AUGUST).   TWO 8 mm. PHOSPHOR BANDS. TYPE II. FLUORESCENT COATED PAPER. PVAD GUM

50p. booklet panes UMFB23/24

| U98 (=S.G.X854) | Rose-red  .. .. .. .. .. .. .. | 40 | 40 |
|---|---|---|---|

**CYLINDER VARIETIES**
**Listed Flaws**

U97a

Damage to eyebrow and
small retouch above nose
(First Reader's Digest coil
in every 4th position, Cyl.
R5, Roll 1)

U97b

White flaw in hair
(First Reader's Digest coil
in every 4th position, Cyl.
R5, Roll 10)

For further flaws on 2½p. stamps in booklet panes, see under No. UMFB23.

**Minor Constant Sheet Flaws**

Cyl. 25   6/6   Small white speck in background behind Queen's hair (Th. D6)
           8/10   Horizontal repair from Queen's hair to border (Th. C–D6)
           9/10   Disturbance below small 2
          17/8   White speck on Queen's dress (Th. G4)

Cyl. 25.   5/2   Red spot in large 2 (Th. F1) and another spot below bust (Th. H4)
           8/3   Background blemish to left of chin (Th. E2)
           8/7   Dark speck on lower left of bust (Th. G2)
          8/10   Vertical scratch through Queen's cheek (Th. D3) and blemish between 1 and P
         13/2   Pale blemish on P
         13/3   Spot on edge of dress by Queen's shoulder (Th. G3)

**WITHDRAWN**   26.2.83

# 3p. Ultramarine   (1971–74)

**Two Value Types**

I        II

Type I.   Thin value
Type II.   Bolder value. Occurs only on horizontal and vertical coils

## 1971 (15 FEBRUARY).   TWO 9·5 mm. PHOSPHOR BANDS. TYPE I

**A. ORIGINAL COATED PAPER. PVA GUM**

U101 (= S.G.X855)    Ultramarine ..   ..   ..   ..   ..   ..   ..   20    10
                     *a.* Imperforate coil strip of 5 (Type II) ..   ..   .. £1000
                     *b.* Phosphor omitted   ..   ..   ..   ..   2·00
                     *c.* One broad band ..   ..   ..   ..   ..   £200
                     *d.* Type II (horiz. or vert. coil) (15.2.71)   ..   ..   6·00   3·50

**Cylinder Numbers (Blocks of Six unless otherwise stated)**

Perforation Type A

| Cyl. No. | Phos. No. | | | | | No dot | Dot | |
|---|---|---|---|---|---|---|---|---|
| 2 | L2, S2 | .. | .. | .. | .. | 70·00 | 70·00 | Block of ten |
| 2 | L2, S2 | Re-engraved | .. | .. | .. | 15·00 | 18·00 | Block of ten |
| 2 | L4 | .. | .. | .. | .. | 3·25 | 3·25 | |
| 4 | L2, S2 | Re-engraved | .. | .. | .. | 18·00 | 18·00 | Block of ten |
| 4 | S4 | .. | .. | .. | .. | £150 | £160 | |
| 4 | — | .. | .. | .. | .. | 4·00 | 4·75 | |
| 4 | L4 | .. | .. | .. | .. | 3·00 | 3·00 | |

Ink cyl. No. 4 no dot and dot also exists with phosphor cylinder unnumbered, *price* £50 for block of 40 with complete left-hand selvedge. Cylinder No. 2 no dot has also been reported without a phosphor cylinder number, possibly from an early printing.

**B. TYPE II. ORIGINAL COATED PAPER. GUM ARABIC.** Horizontal coil only (2.73)

U102            Ultramarine ..   ..   ..   ..   ..   ..   .. 50·00

## C. TYPE I. FLUORESCENT COATED PAPER. PVA GUM (17.9.71)

U103

| | | |
|---|---|---|
| (1) Ultramarine .. .. .. .. .. .. | 60 | 40 |
| (2) Pale ultramarine (1972) .. .. .. .. .. | 1·75 | 60 |
| (3) Bluish ultramarine (1973) .. .. .. .. .. | 1·75 | 60 |

    a. Imperforate top margin ..    ..    ..    ..    ..
    b. Phosphor omitted    ..    ..    ..    ..    ..    4·50
    c. One broad band (£1 Wedgwood Booklet)    ..    ..    25·00
    d. Uncoated paper ..    ..    ..    ..    ..    ..    40·00
    e. Thin paper    ..    ..    ..    ..    ..    ..    4·00
    ea. Phosphor omitted    ..    ..    ..    ..    ..    £200
    f. Vertical red line*    ..    ..    ..    ..    ..
    g. Right-hand band omitted (ex. USB10aa)    ..    ..    50·00
    ga. Left-hand band omitted (ex. USB10ab)    ..    ..    50·00
    h. Dark spots on neck    ..    ..    ..    ..    ..    3·50
    i. Vert. scratch and retouch on chin    ..    (vert. pair)    7·00
    j. Solid line through hair ..    ..    ..    ..    ..    5·00
    k. Pale patches by forehead    ..    ..    ..    ..    3·00
    l. Scratch through necklace    ..    ..    ..    ..    3·50
    m. Scar on cheek    ..    ..    ..    ..    ..    3·50

The thin paper comes from part of printings of sheets from cylinders 8 and 21 and from some booklet panes UB38.

Examples of No. U103 from Cyls. 8 (phos. 7), 10 (phos. 7) and booklet pane Nos. UB38 (Cyl. B27), USB10 (Cyl. B9) and UB40 (Cyl. B14) exist with contaminated "yellow phosphor". *Price mint* £2.

*No. U103f is not a cylinder flaw but results from a printing fault. The thin vertical red line ran through vertical row 10 on several sheets from Cyl. 8 no dot, phosphor Cyl. 7, Perf. Type A. It was traced to a faulty transmission roll between units containing ink used for printing the previous stamp, the fault occurring at the beginning of the run of the 3p. stamp.

### Cylinder Numbers (Blocks of Six unless otherwise stated)

Perforation Type A

| Cyl. No. | Phos. No. | | | | No dot | Dot | |
|---|---|---|---|---|---|---|---|
| 2 | L2, S2 | Re-engraved | .. | .. | 20·00 | 24·00 | Block of ten |
| 4 | L2, S2 | Re-engraved | .. | .. | 14·00 | 14·00 | Block of ten |
| 4 | L4 | .. .. | .. | .. | 10·00 | 10·00 | |
| 4 | L4 | +34 mm. (17) | .. | .. | 20·00 | 20·00 | Block of ten |
| 8 | 1 | .. .. | .. | .. | 10·00 | £325 | |
| 8 | — | .. .. | .. | .. | † | 16·00 | Guillotined off on dot |
| 8 | 7 | .. .. | .. | .. | 3·50 | 3·50 | |
| 8 | 7 | +20 mm. (18) | .. | .. | 40·00 | 40·00 | |
| 8 | 7 | +25 mm. (18) | .. | .. | 40·00 | 40·00 | |
| 8 | 7 | −25 mm. (19) | .. | .. | 40·00 | 40·00 | |
| 9 | 1 | .. .. | .. | .. | 3·50 | 32·00 | |
| 9 | — | .. .. | .. | .. | † | 3·50 | Guillotined off on dot |
| 9 | 7 | .. .. | .. | .. | £1800 | £2500 | |
| 10 | 7 | .. .. | .. | .. | 2·00 | 2·00 | |
| 10 | 7 | +20 mm. (18) | .. | .. | 40·00 | 40·00 | Block of ten |
| 10 | 7 | −20 mm. (19) | .. | .. | 35·00 | 35·00 | |
| 10 | 7 | −26 mm. (19) | .. | .. | 35·00 | 35·00 | |
| 12 | 13 | .. .. | .. | .. | 3·25 | 3·25 | |
| 12 | 13 | +20 mm. (18) | .. | .. | 35·00 | 35·00 | Block of ten |
| 12 | 13 | +39 mm. (17-18) | .. | .. | 40·00 | 40·00 | Block of ten |
| 12A | 13 | .. .. | .. | .. | 3·25 | 3·25 | |
| 12A | 13 | +20 mm. (18) | .. | .. | 35·00 | 35·00 | Block of ten |
| 12A | 13 | +39 mm. (17-18) | .. | .. | 40·00 | 40·00 | Block of ten |
| 21 | 17 | .. .. | .. | .. | 2·50 | 2·50 | |
| 21 | — | .. .. | .. | .. | £120 | £140 | |
| 22 | 17 | .. .. | .. | .. | 45·00 | 50·00 | |
| 24 | 1 | .. .. | .. | .. | 10·00 | £120 | |
| 24 | — | .. .. | .. | .. | † | 12·00 | Guillotined off on dot |

Phosphor Cylinder Displacement. With ink cyl. 21, phos. cyl. 17 is known displaced up the margin 87 mm. opposite row 15.

## D. TYPE I. FLUORESCENT COATED PAPER. GUM ARABIC (23.8.72)

| | | | | | | | | | |
|---|---|---|---|---|---|---|---|---|---|
| U104 | (1) | Ultramarine .. | .. | .. | .. | .. | .. | .. | 1·50 |
| (=S.G.X855 Eg) | (2) | Pale ultramarine | .. | .. | .. | .. | .. | .. | 75 |
| | | a. Imperforate (pair) | .. | .. | .. | .. | .. | £225 |
| | | b. Phosphor omitted | .. | .. | .. | .. | .. | 7·00 |
| | | c. Dark spots on neck | .. | .. | .. | .. | .. | 5·00 |
| | | d. Vert scratch and retouch on chin | .. | (*vert. pair*) | 8·00 |
| | | e. Type II (horiz. coil) (2.73) | .. | .. | .. | .. | 25·00 | 7·00 |
| | | f. Scratch through necklace | .. | .. | .. | .. | 4·50 |
| | | g. Scar on cheek | .. | .. | .. | .. | .. | 4·50 |

**Cylinder Numbers (Block of Six unless otherwise stated)**

Perforation Type R(S)

| Cyl. No. | Phos. No. | | | | | No dot | Dot | |
|---|---|---|---|---|---|---|---|---|
| 8 | 1 | .. | .. | .. | .. | 15·00 | £325 | |
| 8 | —* | .. | .. | .. | .. | † | 15·00 | Guillotined off on dot |
| 8 | 7 | .. | .. | .. | .. | 4·50 | 4·50 | |
| 8 | 7 | +25 mm. (17) | .. | .. | £250 | £250 | Block of ten |
| 9 | 7 | .. | .. | .. | .. | 5·50 | 7·00 | |
| 10 | 1 | .. | .. | .. | .. | 10·00 | £100 | |
| 10 | — | .. | .. | .. | .. | † | 10·00 | Guillotined off on dot |
| 10 | 7 | .. | .. | .. | .. | 4·50 | 4·50 | |

*Phosphor cylinder 8 appears on no dot pane but on the dot pane it was not engraved and only the inverted "T" of the box shows.

## 1973 (10 SEPTEMBER).    CHANGE TO ONE 4 mm. CENTRE BAND. TYPE I

### A. FLUORESCENT COATED PAPER. GUM ARABIC

| | | | | | | | | | |
|---|---|---|---|---|---|---|---|---|---|
| U107 | (1) | Ultramarine .. | .. | .. | .. | .. | .. | .. | 30 |
| (=S.G.X856 Eg) | (2) | Bluish ultramarine .. | .. | .. | .. | .. | .. | 1·50 |
| | | a. Imperforate (pair) | .. | .. | .. | .. | .. | £250 |
| | | b. Imperf. between (vert. pair) | .. | .. | .. | .. | £375 |
| | | c. Imperf. horiz. (vert. pair)* | .. | .. | .. | .. | £150 |
| | | d. Phosphor omitted (2) | .. | .. | .. | .. | 75·00 |
| | | e. Faint dots on neck | .. | .. | .. | .. | 4·00 |
| | | f. Screened 3 | .. | .. | .. | .. | .. | 4·00 |
| | | g. White flaw in hair retouched | .. | .. | .. | 3·25 |
| | | h. Pale patches by forehead | .. | .. | .. | .. | 3·00 |
| | | i. White spot above P | .. | .. | .. | .. | 3·00 |

*These come from row 10 of the no dot pane but they are not completely imperforate as there is one hole on each side between the stamps.

**Cylinder Numbers (Blocks of Six)**

Perforation Type A

| Cyl. No. | Phos. No. | | | | | No dot | Dot |
|---|---|---|---|---|---|---|---|
| 8 | 8* | .. | .. | .. | .. | 35·00 | 35·00 |
| 8 | P9 | .. | .. | .. | .. | £140 | 70·00 |
| 31 | 20 | .. | .. | .. | .. | 3·50 | 3·50 |

Perforation Type R(S)

| 8 | 8* | .. | .. | .. | .. | 2·50 | 2·50 |
|---|---|---|---|---|---|---|---|
| 8 | P9 | .. | .. | .. | .. | 42·00 | 28·00 |
| 24 | 8* | .. | .. | .. | .. | 7·00 | 6·50 |

*Phosphor cylinder 8 appears on no dot pane but on the dot pane it was not engraved and only the inverted "T" of the box shows.

### B. FLUORESCENT COATED PAPER. PVAD GUM (10.9.73)

| | | | | | | | | |
|---|---|---|---|---|---|---|---|---|
| U108 (=S.G.X856) | Bluish ultramarine .. | .. | .. | .. | .. | .. | 20 | 25 |
| | a. Phosphor omitted | .. | .. | .. | .. | .. | 14·00 |
| | b. Type II (horiz. or vert. coil) (11.73) | .. | .. | .. | 4·00 | 1·00 |
| | c. White flaw in hair | .. | .. | .. | .. | 10·00 |
| | ca. Ditto, retouched state | .. | .. | .. | .. | 4·00 |
| | d. Indent in right margin | .. | .. | .. | .. | 22·00 |
| | e. Screened 3 | .. | .. | .. | .. | .. | 3·00 |
| | f. Scratch through band to top of stamp.. | .. | 3·00 |
| | g. White spot above P | .. | .. | .. | .. | 3·00 |
| | h. Large spot on temple | .. | .. | .. | .. | 3·00 |
| | i. Retouch above value | .. | .. | .. | .. | 3·75 |

**Cylinder Numbers (Blocks of Six unless otherwise stated)**

Perforation Type A

| Cyl. No. | Phos. No. | | | | | No dot | Dot |
|---|---|---|---|---|---|---|---|
| 31 | 20 | .. | .. | .. | .. | 15·00 | 10.00 |

Perforation Type R

| | | | | | | | | |
|---|---|---|---|---|---|---|---|---|
| 30 | 18 | .. | .. | .. | .. | 2·00 | 2·50 | |
| 30 | 18 | +20 mm. (17–18) | | | .. | 35·00 | 35·00 | Block of ten |
| 30 | 20 | .. | .. | .. | .. | 4·00 | 4·50 | |
| 30 | 20 | −38 mm. (20) | .. | | .. | 50·00 | 50·00 | |
| 30 | 20 | −42 mm. (20) | .. | | .. | 50·00 | 50·00 | |
| 30 | 20 | −46 mm. (20) | .. | | .. | 50·00 | 50·00 | |
| 30 | 20 | +20 mm. (17–18) | | | .. | 35·00 | 35·00 | Block of ten |
| 30 | — | .. | .. | .. | .. | 5·00 | 5·00 | |
| 31 | 18 | .. | .. | .. | .. | 2·25 | 2·25 | |
| 31 | 20 | .. | .. | .. | .. | 2·75 | 2·75 | |
| 38 | 20 | .. | .. | .. | .. | 3·00 | 3·00 | |

Phosphor Cylinder Displacements. With ink cyl. 30, phos. cyl. 20 is known displaced up the margin from 66 to 373 mm. opposite rows 3 to 16. The phosphor band is shifted to the left on displacements of 252, 261 and 265 mm.

### C. FLUORESCENT COATED PAPER. PVA GUM (1.74)

| U109 | | Bluish ultramarine | .. | | .. | .. | .. | .. | 70 |
|---|---|---|---|---|---|---|---|---|---|
| | *b.* | Screened 3 | | .. | .. | .. | .. | .. | 4·00 |
| | *c.* | White flaw in hair retouch | | .. | .. | .. | .. | 5·00 |
| | *d.* | White spot above P | .. | | .. | .. | .. | .. | 3·00 |

**Cylinder Numbers (Block of Six)**

Perforation Type A

| Cyl. No. | Phos. No. | | | | | No dot | Dot |
|---|---|---|---|---|---|---|---|
| 31 | 20 | .. | .. | .. | .. | 6·00 | 7·50 |

**Shades**

There is a wide range of shades in the 3p. value. We have restricted the listing to three shades.

On No. U103 shade (1) occurs on sheets, coils and booklets to early 1972. Shade (2) occurs on cylinder 9 and December 1972 50p. Booklets. Shade (3) occurs on cylinder 24 and August 1973 50p. Booklets.

On No. U104 shade (1) occurs on cylinder 8 (phosphor 1) and shade (2) on cylinders 8 (phosphor 7), 9 and 10.

On No. U107 shade (1) occurs on Cyls. 8 and 31 and shade (2) on Cyl. 24 and part of the Cyl. 8 printing.

### CYLINDER VARIETIES
**Listed Flaws**

| U103*h*, U104*c* | U103*l*, U104*f* | U103*m*, U104*g* |
|---|---|---|
| (Cyl. 8 no dot, R. 9/3) | (Cyl. 9 no dot, R. 2/1) | (Cyl. 9 no dot, R. 6/4) |

Nos. U103*h* and U104*c* are a multipositive flaw being a prominent state of the 1p. flaw, No. U55*g*. On No. U103 it also occurs fainter with phosphor cylinder 7 and is not present with phosphor cylinder 1. It also occurs in a faint state on No. U107, listed as U107*e*.

U103*j*
(Cyl. 12A no dot, R. 7/7)

U103*k*, U107*h*
(Cyl. 24 no dot, R. 6/2)

U103*i*, U104*d*
Vertical scratch from hair to crown on
stamp below, and retouch on chin
(Cyl. 9 dot, R. 17/2 and 18/2)

U108*c*
White flaw in hair

U107*g*, U108*ca*, U109*c*
Retouched state

(Cyl. 31 no dot, R. 1/6)

U108*d*
(Cyl. 31 no dot, R. 2/10)
(Later filled in)
Exists filled in only on
U107 and U109

U107*f*, U108*e*, U109*b*
(Cyls. 30 and 31 no dot,
R. 10/9)

U107*i*, U108*g*, U109*d*
(Cyl. 31 dot, R. 11/1)

| U108f, U110b | U108h | U108i |
|---|---|---|
| (Cyl. 38 no dot, R. 14/4) | (Cyl. 38 dot, R. 1/4) | Retouch above value<br>(Cyl. 31 no dot, R. 5/3) |

For further flaws on 3p. stamps in booklet panes, see under Nos. UB36/42 and USB9/10.

**Minor Constant Sheet Flaws**

| Cyl. 4. | 2/1 | White flaw in crown left of diadem (Th. B4) |
|---|---|---|
| Cyl. 8 | 1/1 | Many small specks in hair (Th. C5–D5) |
| | 7/4 | White blemish in neck (Th. E3) |
| | 10/1 | Screening dots in top margin (Th. above A5) multipositive flaw as 1p. cyl. 3, more prominent on GA) |
| | 10/2 | Small retouch on cheek (Th. C–D3) |
| | 13/4 | Dark speck on cheek (Th. D3) |
| Cyl. 9. | 17/1 | Retouch on cheek (Th. C2–D2) |
| | 17/2 | Retouch on Queen's chin (Th. D–E3) |
| Cyl. 12 | 17/10 | Dark line on Queen's shoulder (Th. F4) |
| Cyl. 24 | 1/2 | Disturbance on collar (Th. G3) |
| Cyl. 31 | 11/5 | White spot on Queen's forehead (Th. B3) |
| | 15/6 | Curved scratch in top right-hand corner (Th. A6) |
| Cyl. 31. | 1/6 | White spots on dress and shoulder (Th. F–G4–5) |
| | 8/6 | White scratch on dress (Th. G4–G5) |
| | 9/7 | White disturbance under necklace (Th. E4–E5) |

**COILS**

Value Type II. Two bands. Printed in continuous reels.

| Code No. | Issued | Number in roll | Face value | Paper/gum | Screen | Perf. Type |
|---|---|---|---|---|---|---|
| | | Vertical delivery | | | | |
| DL | 15.2.71 | 1000 | £30 | OCP/PVA | 250 | Comb |
| | | Sideways delivery | | | | |
| BS | ? | 500 | £15 | OCP/PVA | 150 | Comb |
| BS | 15.2.71 | 500 | £15 | OCP/PVA | 250 | Comb |
| BS | 2.73 | 500 | £15 | OCP/GA | 250 | R(S) |
| BS | 2.73 | 500 | £15 | FCP/GA | 250 | R(S) |

Cylinder Numbers used

| DL | OCP/PVA | R10, R16 (?) | BS | OCP/PVA | R4 (phos. R6) |
|---|---|---|---|---|---|
| | | | | OCP/GA | R4 (phos. R6) |
| | | | | FCP/GA | R4 (phos. R6) |

Value Type II. One centre band. Printed in continuous reels.

| Code No. | Issued | Number in roll | Face Value | Paper/gum | Screen | Perf. Type |
|---|---|---|---|---|---|---|
| | | Vertical delivery | | | | |
| ML | 4.74 | 1000 | £30 | FCP/PVAD | 150 | R(S) |
| | | Sideways delivery | | | | |
| KS | 11.73 | 500 | £15 | FCP/PVAD | 250 | R(S) |

Cylinder Numbers used

| ML | FCP/PVAD | R17 (phos. R9) |
|---|---|---|
| KS | FCP/PVAD | R4 (phos. R5) |

**WITHDRAWN** Nos. U101/4 Feb. 1975 but put on sale again at the Philatelic Bureau in Jan. 1976 and finally withdrawn Feb. 1977
Nos. U107/9, 8.4.78

# 3p. Bright Magenta  (1980–89)

**Two Value Types**

Type I. Wide value. Sheets and booklets
Type II. Narrow value. Multi-value coil, 15p.
No. UMC14

I            II

## 1980 (22 OCTOBER).  COLOUR CHANGED. PHOSPHORISED PAPER. PVAD GUM

**A. TYPE I. FLUORESCENT COATED PAPER**

| | | | |
|---|---|---|---|
| U110 | Bright magenta .. .. .. .. .. .. | 20 | |
| | *a.* Imperforate (horiz. pair) .. .. .. .. | | |
| | *b.* Scratch through band to top of stamp.. .. .. | 2·00 | |
| | *c.* Retouch in hair .. .. .. .. .. | 2·00 | |
| | *d.* Two dots below necklace .. .. .. .. | 1·75 | |
| | *e.* Diagonal scratch.. .. .. .. .. .. | 2·00 | |
| | *f.* Fluorescent brightener omitted .. .. | 2·50 | |
| | *g.* Corner flaw .. .. .. .. .. .. | 1·75 | |

No. U110 is known on phosphorised paper with either a shiny ink surface which gives a photo-negative reflection or a matt surface without the negative effect.

No. U110 is known postmarked at Chelmsford, Essex on 21 October 1980.

No. U110*f* derives from the 11½p. multi-value coil, UMC9 and is printed on chalk-surfaced paper but without the fluorescent additive which was probably omitted in error.

**Cylinder Numbers (Blocks of Six)**

Perforation Type RE

| Cyl. No. | | | | No dot | Dot |
|---|---|---|---|---|---|
| 38 | .. | .. | .. | 2·00 | 2·00 |
| 43* | .. | .. | .. | 1·75 | 1·75 |

*On the dot pane the "3" is close to the perforations and the dot did not appear. The figures are almost 1 mm. inside the box in the no dot but in the dot pane the "3" is level with the tips of the box above and below "3". The dot was later placed after the "3". *Cylinder number* 43 *with dot omitted, price* £2.

Perforation variety

The 17 pin variety as described in Appendix I. *Price for marginal block of* 6 £20; *cylinder no.* 43 *dot, block of* 6 £32.

**B. TYPE I. ADVANCED COATED PAPER** (14.9.83)

| | | | | |
|---|---|---|---|---|
| U111 (=S.G.X930) | Bright magenta .. .. .. .. .. .. | 20 | 20 |
| | *a.* Retouch in hair .. .. .. .. .. .. | 2·00 | |
| | *b.* Type II (ex. UMC14, 10.10.89) .. .. .. | 30 | 25 |

First issued in the Royal Mint booklet, this stamp was later issued in sheet form on 5 May 1987. Stamps from cylinder 43 and 15p. multi-value coil UMC14 have Head B2, whilst those from cylinder 38 have Head B1. Earliest reported date for Head B1 on advanced coated paper was 8 May 1990.

**Cylinder Numbers (Blocks of Six)**

Perforation Type RE

| Cyl. No. | | | | No dot | Dot |
|---|---|---|---|---|---|
| 38 | .. | .. | .. | 1·25 | 1·25 |
| 43 | .. | .. | .. | 1·25 | 1·25 |

*Cylinder number* 43 *with dot omitted, price* £1.75.

## 1982 (1 FEBRUARY).  TWO 8 mm. PHOSPHOR BANDS. FLUORESCENT COATED PAPER. TYPE I. PVAD GUM

50p. booklet panes UMFB26/27

| | | | |
|---|---|---|---|
| U112 (=S.G.857) | Bright magenta .. .. .. .. .. .. | 30 | 25 |
| | *a.* Phosphor omitted (Head type B1) .. .. .. | £750 | |

## 1982 (19 MAY).   TWO 9·5 mm. PHOSPHOR BANDS. FLUORESCENT COATED PAPER. TYPE I. PVAD GUM

"Story of Stanley Gibbons" Booklet *se-tenant* pane UWB11

| U113 | Bright magenta | .. | .. | .. | .. | .. | .. | 1·40 | 1·40 |
|---|---|---|---|---|---|---|---|---|---|
| | *b.* Phosphor omitted (Head type B2) | | .. | .. | .. | 60·00 | | |
| | *c.* One broad band .. | .. | .. | .. | .. | £150 | | |
| | *d.* Phosphor printed on both sides | | | .. | .. | .. | | |

The phosphor band printed at right is short at the top on most examples.

### CYLINDER VARIETIES
### Listed Flaws

For illustration of No. U110*b*, see No. U108*f*

U110*c*
Retouch in hair.
Practically absent on
No. U111*a*
(Cyl. 43 no dot, R. 11/10)

U110*d*
Two dots below necklace
(First Reader's Digest coil
in every 4th position, Cyl. R19, Roll 7)

U110*e*
Diagonal scratch
(First Reader's Digest
coil in every 4th position,
Cyl. R19, Roll 7)

U110*g*
Corner flaw
(First Reader's Digest
coil in every 4th position,
Cyl. R19, Roll 3)

### Minor Constant Sheet Flaws

Cyl. 38   7/9   Red spot on Queen's neck (Th. E4)
10/2   Mark on neck (Th. E4)
Cyl. 38.   4/8   Pale spot above crown (Th. B6)
12/5   Retouch on cheek (Th. D3)
13/8   Mark in top margin (ThA3 (above))
14/10   Dark spot on dress (Th. C3)
18/4   Pale spot on neck (Th. E4)
18/9   Retouch on Queen's cheek (Th. G3)*
19/5   White spot on shoulder (Th. F5)
19/8   Red spot on dress (Th. G5) and pale blemish through top loop of 3*
Cyl. 43   4/5   Retouch in front of neck (Th. F3)
12/4   Scratch above dress (Th. F5–G3)
17/10   Two diagonal scratches across shoulder and dress (Th. G4–G5)
20/4   Scratch from necklace to base of bust (Th. F4–G4)
20/6   Diagonal scratch across shoulder (Th. F3–G4)

R.12/4 is a multipositive flaw appearing more prominently on 29p. Cyl. 1 no dot.

Flaws marked with an asterisk are known on No. U108.

**WITHDRAWN**   No. U110, 4.5.88

# 3½p. Bronze-green   (1971–74)
## 1971 (15 FEBRUARY).   TWO 9·5 mm. PHOSPHOR BANDS
### A. ORIGINAL COATED PAPER. PVA GUM

| | | | | | | | | | |
|---|---|---|---|---|---|---|---|---|---|
| U114 (=S.G.X858) | Pale olive-grey | .. | .. | .. | .. | .. | .. | 30 | 30 |
| | a. Phosphor omitted | | .. | .. | .. | .. | .. | 3·50 | |

**Cylinder Numbers (Blocks of Ten)**

Perforation Type A

| Cyl. No. | Phos. No. | | | | | No dot | Dot |
|---|---|---|---|---|---|---|---|
| 1 | L2, S2 | .. | .. | .. | .. | 7·50 | 7·50 |
| 1 | L2, S2 | Re-engraved | .. | .. | | 7·50 | 7·50 |

Cylinder blocks of six to show a large phosphor 2 only £4.50 *each*.

### B. FLUORESCENT COATED PAPER. PVA GUM (18.7.73)

| | | | | | | | | |
|---|---|---|---|---|---|---|---|---|
| U115 | Bronze-green | .. | .. | | .. | .. | .. | 1·25 |
| | a. Phosphor omitted (ex. pane UB43) | .. | | .. | | | | |
| | b. Long diagonal scratch | | .. | | .. | *Strip of three* | 12·00 | |
| | c. Dark spot above central cross | .. | | .. | .. | .. | 4·50 | |

Five examples of No. U115*a* exist with trimmed perforations from pane No. UB43. Complete panes with missing phosphor are unknown.

**Cylinder Numbers (Blocks of Six)**

Perforation Type A

| Cyl. No. | Phos. No. | | | | | No dot | Dot |
|---|---|---|---|---|---|---|---|
| 9 | 17 | .. | .. | .. | .. | 9·00 | 9·00 |
| 11 | 17 | .. | .. | .. | .. | 18·00 | 20·00 |
| 11 | 17 | +20 mm. (18) | .. | | .. | 20·00 | 22·00 |
| 11 | — | .. | .. | .. | .. | 25·00 | 22·00 |

Perforation Type R

| | | | | | | | |
|---|---|---|---|---|---|---|---|
| 9 | 17 | .. | .. | .. | .. | 10·00 | 10·00 |

Phosphor Cylinder Displacement. With ink cyl. 11, phos. cyl. 17 is known displaced up the margin 100 mm. opposite row 14.

The phosphor cylinder number is very faint or missing on some no dot examples.

### C. FLUORESCENT COATED PAPER. PVAD GUM (22.8.73)

| | | | | | | | | | | |
|---|---|---|---|---|---|---|---|---|---|---|
| U116 | (1) | Bronze-green | .. | .. | .. | .. | .. | .. | 60 | 50 |
| (=S.G.X858Eb) | (2) | Deep olive-brown | .. | .. | .. | .. | .. | .. | £950 | |
| | | a. Imperforate (pair) | .. | .. | .. | .. | .. | .. | £350 | |
| | | b. Phosphor omitted | .. | .. | .. | .. | .. | 8·00 | | |
| | | c. Large retouch under Queen's bust | .. | .. | .. | 5·00 | | | |
| | | d. Thick bottom loop to 3 | .. | .. | .. | .. | .. | 3·50 | | |
| | | e. Damaged top to 3 | .. | .. | .. | .. | .. | 3·50 | | |
| | | f. Nick in bottom loop of 3 | .. | .. | .. | 3·50 | | | |
| | | g. Long diagonal scratch | .. | .. | *Strip of three* | 9·00 | | | |
| | | h. Dark spot above central cross | .. | .. | .. | .. | 3·00 | | |

The deep olive-brown shade is due to faulty mix of the ink and occurred on cylinder 9.

**Cylinder Numbers (Blocks of Six)**

Perforation Type A

| Cyl. No. | Phos. No. | | | | | No dot | Dot |
|---|---|---|---|---|---|---|---|
| 9 | 17 | .. | .. | .. | .. | 7·50 | 6·50 |
| 11 | 17 | .. | .. | .. | .. | 7·00 | 7·00 |

Perforation Type R

| | | | | | | | |
|---|---|---|---|---|---|---|---|
| 9 | 17 | .. | .. | .. | .. | 45·00 | 55·00 |
| 11 | 17 | .. | .. | .. | .. | 4·00 | 4·00 |
| 11 | 17 | +20 mm. (18) | .. | | .. | 22·00 | 22·00 |
| 11 | — | .. | .. | .. | .. | 30·00 | 30·00 |

Phosphor Cylinder Displacement. With ink cyl. 11, phos. cyl. 17 is known displaced up the margin 420 mm. opposite row 1.

**D. ORIGINAL COATED PAPER. PVAD GUM** (January 1974)†

| U117 | Deep olive-green | .. | .. | .. | .. | .. | £125 | 45·00 |
| | *a.* Long diagonal scratch | | .. | .. | *Strip of three* | £450 | |
| | *b.* Dark spot above central cross | .. | | .. | .. | £150 | |

This probably occurred as a result of the use of the wrong paper. The paper is much thicker than the original OCP paper, and the stamp has a highly glossy surface which produces a rich deep olive-green shade, quite distinct fom any of the other printings.

†Exact date of issue not known but one of the earliest reported was 7 January 1974, at Chingford, Essex.

**Cylinder Numbers (Blocks of Six)**

Perforation Type R

| Cyl. No. | Phos. No. | | | | No dot | Dot |
|---|---|---|---|---|---|---|
| 11 | 17 | .. | .. | .. | .. | £1100 | £1700 |

## 1974 (24 JUNE).  CHANGE TO ONE 4 mm. CENTRE BAND. FLUORESCENT COATED PAPER. PVAD GUM

| U118 (=S.G.X859) | Bronze-green | .. | .. | .. | .. | .. | .. | 30 | 15 |
| | *b.* Large retouch under Queen's bust | .. | .. | .. | 4·00 | |
| | *c.* Thick bottom loop to 3 | .. | | .. | .. | .. | 3·25 | |
| | *d.* Damaged top to 3 | .. | .. | .. | .. | .. | 3·25 | |
| | *e.* Nick in bottom loop of 3 | .. | .. | .. | .. | 3·25 | |
| | *f.* Long diagonal scratch | .. | .. | *Strip of three* | 7·00 | |
| | *g.* Dark spot above central cross | .. | .. | .. | .. | 3·00 | |

**Cylinder Numbers (Blocks of Six unless otherwise stated)**

Perforation Type R

| Cyl. No. | Phos. No. | | | | | No dot | Dot | |
|---|---|---|---|---|---|---|---|---|
| 9 | 20 | .. | .. | .. | .. | 22·00 | 20·00 | |
| 11 | 18 | .. | .. | .. | .. | 5·00 | 5·00 | |
| 11 | 18 | +26 mm. (17) | .. | | .. | 25·00 | 25·00 | Block of ten |
| 11 | 18 | +42 mm. (17) | .. | | .. | 60·00 | 60·00 | Block of ten |
| 11 | — | .. | .. | .. | .. | 22·00 | 25·00 | |
| 11 | 20 | .. | .. | .. | .. | 4·50 | 4·50 | |
| 11 | 20 | −20 mm. (19) | .. | | .. | 35·00 | 40·00 | |
| 12 | 18 | .. | .. | .. | .. | 6·00 | 6·00 | |
| 12 | 20 | .. | .. | .. | .. | 8·00 | 7·00 | |

Phosphor Cylinder Displacement. With ink cyl. 11, phos. cyl. 18 is known displaced up the margin 107 and 358 mm. opposite rows 3/4 and 14. The phosphor band is shifted to the left on displacement of 358 mm.

**CYLINDER VARIETIES**
**Listed Flaws**

U116*c*, U118*b*
In addition there is damage on the shoulder
of the Queen's dress
(Cyl. 9 no dot, R. 6/3)
This may also exist on No. U115

| U116*d*, U118*c* | U116*e*, U118*d* | U116*f*, U118*e* |
|---|---|---|
| (Roll No. 5) | (Roll No. 6) | (Roll No. 8) |

(All occur on horizontal coils in every fifth position)

**Multipositive Flaws**
U115*b*, U116*g*, U117*a* and U118*f*. Cyls. 9, 11 and 12 no dot, R. 3/3–3/5 as $\frac{1}{2}$p. No. U50*e*
U115*c*, U116*h*, U117*b* and U118*g*. R. 20/6 as $\frac{1}{2}$p. No. U50*g*. Retouched on cyl. 9 dot, present but later retouched on cyl. 11 dot and present but faint on cyl. 12 dot
   For further flaws on $3\frac{1}{2}$p. stamps in booklet panes, see under Nos. UB43/45.

**Minor Constant Sheet Flaws**

| Cyl. 1 | 19/2 | Retouch on Queen's neck below jawline (Th. at point of intersection of D3–4 and F3–4) |
|---|---|---|
| | 20/2 | Dotted line from back of crown to edge of design (Th. C6) |
| Cyl. 9. | 6/7 | Diagonal scratch from Queen's ear to neck (Th. D4–F3) |
| Cyl. 11. | 6/3 | Dark blemish under Queen's collar (Th. G–H3) |
| | 6/7 | As Cyl. 9. |
| | 15/10 | Diagonal scratch from Queen's eye to top margin (Th. C2–A2) |
| Cyl. 12. | 6/7 | As Cyl. 9. |

**COILS**

Two bands. Printed in continuous reels.

| Code No. | Issued | Number in roll | Face value | Paper/gum | Screen | Perf. Type |
|---|---|---|---|---|---|---|
| | | Vertical delivery | | | | |
| OL | 4·74? | 1000 | £35 | FCP/PVAD | 150 | R(S) |
| | | Sideways delivery | | | | |
| LS | 2·74? | 500 | £17·50 | FCP/PVAD | 250 | R(S) |

Cylinder Numbers used
   OL   FCP/PVAD R4, R5, R8?   LS   FCP/PVAD   R3 (phos. R6)

One centre band. Sideways delivery in continuous reels.

| Code No. | Issued | Number in roll | Face value | Paper/gum | Screen | Perf. Type |
|---|---|---|---|---|---|---|
| PS | 12.74? | 500 | £17·50 | FCP/PVAD | 250 | R(S) |

Cylinder Numbers used
   PS   FCP/PVAD   R3 (phos. R5)

**WITHDRAWN** 9.76

# $3\frac{1}{2}$p. Purple-brown   (1983)

**1983 (30 MARCH).   COLOUR CHANGED. PHOSPHORISED PAPER. PVAD GUM**

**A. FLUORESCENT COATED PAPER**
U119 (=S.G.X931)    Purple-brown    ..    ..    ..    ..    ..    ..    45    30

**Cylinder Numbers (Blocks of Six)**
Perforation Type RE

| Cyl. No. | | | | No dot | Dot |
|---|---|---|---|---|---|
| 17 | .. | .. | .. | 3·00 | 3·00 |

**B. ADVANCED COATED PAPER** Royal Mint *se-tenant* booklet pane UWB15 (14.9.83)
U120          Purple-brown    ..    ..    ..    ..    ..    ..    50    55

**1983 (5 APRIL).   ONE 4 mm. CENTRE PHOSPHOR BAND. FLUORESCENT COATED PAPER. PVAD GUM**

50p. booklet pane UMFB31

| | | | | | | | | | |
|---|---|---|---|---|---|---|---|---|---|
| U121 (=S.G.X860) | Purple-brown | .. | .. | .. | .. | .. | .. | 1·75 | 1.25 |
| | a. Phosphor omitted | .. | .. | .. | .. | .. | 5·50 | |

**WITHDRAWN** No. U119, 28.6.85

# 4p. Ochre–brown   (1971–74)

**1971 (15 FEBRUARY).   TWO 9·5 mm. PHOSPHOR BANDS**
**A. ORIGINAL COATED PAPER. PVA GUM**

| | | | | | | | | |
|---|---|---|---|---|---|---|---|---|
| U122 | Ochre-brown.. | .. | .. | .. | .. | .. | .. | 20 | 20 |
| | a. Phosphor omitted | .. | .. | .. | .. | .. | 30·00 | |
| | b. Faint dots on neck | .. | .. | .. | .. | .. | 3·00 | |
| | c. Left-hand band omitted.. | .. | .. | .. | .. | 35·00 | |
| | d. Right-hand band omitted | .. | .. | .. | .. | 35·00 | |

**Cylinder Numbers (Blocks of Six unless otherwise stated)**

Perforation Type A

| Cyl. No. | Phos. No. | | | | | No dot | Dot | |
|---|---|---|---|---|---|---|---|---|
| 5 | L2, S2 | .. | .. | .. | .. | 7·00 | 6·50 | Block of ten |
| 5 | L2, S2 | −39 mm. (20) | .. | .. | | £800 | † | |
| 5 | — | .. | .. | .. | .. | 28·00 | 50·00 | |
| 5 | L2, S2 | Re-engraved | .. | .. | | 6·00 | 6·00 | Block of ten |
| 5 | L4 | .. | .. | .. | .. | 5·50 | 5·50 | |

Phosphor Cylinder Displacement. Phos. cyls. L2, S2 are known displaced up the margin 216 mm. opposite row 9.

**B. FLUORESCENT COATED PAPER. GUM ARABIC** (31.10.72)*

| | | | | | | | | |
|---|---|---|---|---|---|---|---|---|
| U123 (=S.G.X861Eg) | Ochre-brown.. | .. | .. | .. | .. | .. | .. | 20 |
| | a. Imperforate (pair) | .. | .. | .. | .. | .. | £450 | |

Examples of No. U123 exist with contaminated "yellow phosphor". *Price mint* £16.

**Cylinder Numbers (Blocks of Six)**

Perforation Type R(S)

| Cyl. No. | Phos. No. | | | | | No dot | Dot |
|---|---|---|---|---|---|---|---|
| 4 | 7 | .. | .. | .. | .. | 3·00 | 2·75 |

*Known on cover with unstuck selvedge confirming the gum.

**C. FLUORESCENT COATED PAPER. PVA GUM** (18.7.73)

| | | | | | | | |
|---|---|---|---|---|---|---|---|
| U124 | Ochre-brown.. | .. | .. | .. | .. | .. | 3·50 |

**Cylinder Numbers (Blocks of Six)**

Perforation Type A

| Cyl. No. | Phos. No. | | | | | No dot | Dot | |
|---|---|---|---|---|---|---|---|---|
| 4 | 1 | .. | .. | .. | .. | 22·00 | 30·00 | |
| 4 | — | .. | .. | .. | .. | † | 22·00 | Guillotined off on dot |

**D. FLUORESCENT COATED PAPER. PVAD GUM** (12.11.73)*

| | | | | | | | | |
|---|---|---|---|---|---|---|---|---|
| U125 (=S.G.X861) | Ochre-brown.. | .. | .. | .. | .. | .. | .. | 20 | 20 |
| | b. Top serif in P omitted | .. | .. | .. | .. | .. | 3·00 | |

*Known on cover with unstuck selvedge confirming the gum.

**Cylinder Numbers (Blocks of Six unless otherwise stated)**

Perforation Type R

| Cyl. No. | Phos. No. | | | | | No dot | Dot | |
|---|---|---|---|---|---|---|---|---|
| 12 | 17 | .. | .. | .. | .. | 1·90 | 1·90 | |
| 12 | 17 | +38 mm. (17) | .. | .. | | 4·00 | 4·00 | Block of ten |

**CYLINDER VARIETIES**
**Listed Flaws**

No. U122*b* is a multipositive flaw occurring on Cyl. 5 no dot, R. 9/3, being a fainter state of the 1p. flaw, No. U55*g*.

U125*b*
(Cyl. 12 dot, R. 19/3)

**Minor Constant Sheet Flaws**

| | | |
|---|---|---|
| Cyl. 4 | 1/4 | Loop of P incomplete (Th. F2) |
| Cyl. 4. | 20/9 | Small retouch over necklace (Th. E4) |
| Cyl. 5 | 1/4 | Front loop of P omitted (Th. F2) |
| | 8/7 | Dark spot in band of crown (Th. B4) |
| | 10/1 | Screening dots in top margin (Th. above A5) (Multipositive flaw as 1p. cyl. 3) |
| Cyl. 5. | 3/3 | Dark spots around P of value |
| | 9/3 | Dark spot above Queen's eyebrow (Th. C2) |

These two cylinders are from the same multipositive.

The flaw on Cyl. 5 no dot R. 8/7 is identical to that on the 2p. Cyl. 4 no dot so the same head multipositive was used for these two cylinders and there may be other matched flaws.

| | | |
|---|---|---|
| Cyl. 12. | 1/7 | Small white spot in Queen's hair (Th. C5) |
| | 4/7 | Small pale spots in bust (Th. G4) |
| | 7/1 | Brown spots in horizontal bar of 4 |
| | 10/8 | Small pale spot in bust (Th. G3) |
| | 12/5 | Small pale spot in bust (Th. G3) |
| | 18/4 | White curved scratch to right of top of 4 |

**WITHDRAWN** 6.78

# 4p. Greenish Blue   (1981–85)

**Two Value Types**

I        II

Type I.   Wide value
Type II.  Redrawn value and thinner P

**1981 (26 AUGUST).   COLOUR CHANGED. TWO 8 mm. PHOSPHOR BANDS. TYPE I. FLUORESCENT COATED PAPER. PVAD GUM**

50p. booklet panes UMFB23/24

| | | | |
|---|---|---|---|
| U126 (=S.G.X862) | Greenish blue .. .. .. .. .. | .. 2·00 | 1·75 |
| | *b.* Short phosphor band at bottom left (26.8.81) | .. 3·00 | |
| | *c.* Short phosphor band at bottom right (26.8.81) | .. 3·00 | |

## 1981 (30 DECEMBER).   PHOSPHORISED PAPER. TYPE I. PVAD GUM

**A. FLUORESCENT COATED PAPER.** 12½p. and 13p. Reader's Digest coils

| | | | | | | | | | |
|---|---|---|---|---|---|---|---|---|---|
| U127 | (1) | Greenish blue (coil UMC10) | .. | .. | .. | .. | 25 | 20 |
| (=S.G.X932) | (2) | Pale greenish blue (coil UMC11) .. | .. | .. | .. | 25 | 20 |
| | | *f*. Fluorescent brightener omitted (Shade 1) | .. | .. | | | |

No. U127(1)*f* derives from the 12½p. multi-value coil, UMC10 and is printed on chalk-surfaced paper without the fluorescent additive which was probably omitted in error. The note below ½p. No. U54 describing the strips mounted in special promotion cards also applies here. No. U127(1)*f* with disturbed gum, *price £15 each stamp.*

**B. ADVANCED COATED PAPER.** 13p. and 14p. Reader's Digest coils (3.88)

| | | | | | | | |
|---|---|---|---|---|---|---|---|
| U128 (=S.G.X.932*Ea*) Pale greenish blue .. | .. | .. | .. | .. | .. | 25 | 25 |


## 1984 (3 SEPTEMBER).   ONE 4 mm. CENTRE PHOSPHOR BAND. TYPE II. FLUORESCENT COATED PAPER. PVAD GUM

50p. booklet pane UMFB34

| | | | | | | | | |
|---|---|---|---|---|---|---|---|---|
| U129 (=S.G.X863) | Greenish blue | .. | .. | .. | .. | .. | 75 | 75 |
| | *a*. Phosphor omitted | .. | .. | .. | .. | .. | 85·00 | |


## 1985 (8 JANUARY).   ONE NARROW BAND AT RIGHT. TYPE II. FLUORESCENT COATED PAPER. PVAD GUM

£5 *The Times* booklet *se-tenant* pane No. UWB23

| | | | | | | | | |
|---|---|---|---|---|---|---|---|---|
| U130 (=S.G.X864) | Greenish blue | .. | .. | .. | .. | .. | 1·25 | 1·50 |
| | *a*. Phosphor omitted | .. | .. | .. | .. | £200 | |
| | *b*. Phosphor printed on both sides | .. | .. | .. | £170 | |
| | *c*. One broad band at left .. | .. | .. | .. | £400 | |


## 1985 (8 JANUARY).   ONE NARROW BAND AT LEFT. TYPE II. FLUORESCENT COATED PAPER. PVAD GUM

£5 *The Times* booklet *se-tenant* pane No. UWB23

| | | | | | | | |
|---|---|---|---|---|---|---|---|
| U131 (=S.G.X864*Ea*) Greenish blue | .. | .. | .. | .. | .. | 1·25 | 1·50 |
| | *b*. Phosphor printed on both sides | .. | .. | .. | £170 | |

## 4p. New Blue (1988)

**1988 (26 JULY). COLOUR CHANGED. PHOSPHORISED (ADVANCED COATED) PAPER. PVAD GUM**

U132 (=S.G.X933)    New blue    ..    ..    ..    ..    ..    ..    ..    10    10
                         *b*. Long scratch across head into background    ..    ..    4·00

**Cylinder Numbers (Blocks of Six)**
Perforation Type RE

|  Cyl. No. | | | | No dot | Dot |
| --- | --- | --- | --- | --- | --- |
| 15 | .. | .. | .. | 1·00 | 1·00 |

**CYLINDER VARIETY**
**Listed Flaw**

U132*b*
Long scratch across head into
background
(Sixth Reader's Digest coil in every 4th
position, Cyl. R5, Roll no. not known)

**Minor Constant Sheet Flaws**

Cyl. 15 6/6 Weak diagonal line across shoulder (Th.F3–F5)

Cyl. 15. 13/7 Hairline across shoulder (Th. F4–F8)
    The multipositive used for Cyl. 15 was also employed for the 2p.,5p., and 75p., Cyls.16,10 and 1.

# 4½p. Grey-blue   (1973–74)

## 1973 (24 OCTOBER).   TWO 9·5 mm. PHOSPHOR BANDS. FLUORESCENT COATED PAPER. PVAD GUM

U133 (=S.G.X865)  Grey-blue .. .. .. .. .. .. .. 20   25
      a. Imperforate (pair) .. .. .. .. .. £250
      b. Phosphor omitted .. .. .. .. .. 3·50
      c. One broad band .. .. .. .. .. .. 6·00
      d. Long cylinder scratch across two stamps .. *(Pair)* 12·00
      e. Dark spot on crown .. .. .. .. .. 2·50
      ea. Retouched .. .. .. .. .. .. 2·50
      f. Scratches under bust .. .. .. .. .. 2·50
      g. Gash on cheek .. .. .. .. .. .. 2·50
      h. Gash behind shoulder .. .. .. .. .. 2·50

**Cylinder Numbers (Blocks of Six)**
Perforation Type R

| Cyl. No. | Phos. No. | | | | | No dot | Dot |
|---|---|---|---|---|---|---|---|
| 1 | 17 | .. | .. | .. | .. | † | £950 |
| 3 | 17 | .. | .. | .. | .. | 4·50 | 4·50 |
| 3 | 17 | −33 mm. (20) | .. | | .. | 42·00 | 42·00 |
| 3 | 17 | −26 mm. (19) | .. | | .. | 42·00 | 42·00 |
| 3 | 17 | −22 mm. (19) | .. | | .. | 42·00 | 42·00 |
| 3 | — | .. | .. | .. | .. | 5·00 | 5·00 |
| 7 | 17 | .. | .. | .. | .. | 5·00 | 5·00 |
| 7 | 17 | −31 mm. (20) | .. | | .. | 90·00 | 90·00 |
| 7 | — | .. | .. | .. | .. | 60·00 | 60·00 |

Phosphor Cylinder Displacements. With ink cyl. 3, phos. cyl. 17 is known displaced up the margin from 68 to 431 mm. opposite row 1, 15 and 16. With ink cyl. 7, phos. cyl. 17 is known displaced 102 mm. opposite row 14.

Perforation Type A

| 3 | 26* | .. | .. | .. | .. | 15·00 | † |
|---|---|---|---|---|---|---|---|
| 3 | — | .. | .. | .. | .. | † | 15·00 |
| 7 | 26* | .. | .. | .. | .. | 12·00 | † |
| 7 | — | .. | .. | .. | .. | † | 12·00 |

*The phosphor cylinder number and box were not engraved on the dot pane.

## 1974 (13 NOVEMBER).   TWO 9·5 mm. PHOSPHOR BANDS. PHOSPHORISED (FLUORESCENT COATED) PAPER. PVAD GUM

U134      Grey-blue .. .. .. .. .. .. .. 50   60
      a. Retouched spot on crown .. .. .. .. 3·75

Stamps with two normal phosphor bands were printed on phosphorised paper as an experiment and issued on 13 November 1974. They cannot be distinguished by the naked eye but the entire stamp gives an "after glow" under a short-wave ultra violet light.

**Cylinder Numbers (Blocks of Six)**
Perforation Type R

| Cyl. No. | Phos. No. | | | | | No dot | Dot |
|---|---|---|---|---|---|---|---|
| 7 | 17 | .. | .. | .. | .. | 8·00 | 8·00 |

**CYLINDER VARIETIES**
**Listed Flaws**

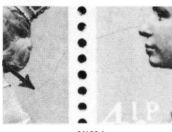

Long cylinder scratch (Cyl. 3 no dot, R. 9/9 and 9/10) (Later retouched)

U133*d*

| U133e | U133ea, U134a |
|---|---|
| Dark spot on tip of crown | Retouched as pale spot |
| (Cyl. 3 no dot. R. 17/10) | (Cyls. 3 and 7 no dot, R. 17/10) |

| U133f | U133g |
|---|---|
| Blue scratches under bust | Gash on cheek |
| and nick in frame | (Cyl. 3 dot, R. 6/9) |
| (Cyl. 3 dot, R. 3/1) | |

U133h.  Gash behind shoulder similar to U133g on adjoining stamp (Later retouched) (Cyl. 3 dot, R. 6/8)

For further flaws on 4½p. stamps in booklet panes, see under No. UB47.

**Minor Constant Sheet Flaws**

Cyl. 3  3/1 Blemish at bottom left of 1 of ½
10/3 Blemish under 4

**COIL**

Sideways delivery and printed on continuous reels.

| Code No. | Issued | Number in roll | Face value | Paper/gum | Screen | Perf. Type |
|---|---|---|---|---|---|---|
| QS | 23.12.74 | 500 | £22·50 | FCP/PVAD | 150 | R |

Cylinder Numbers used:
QS FCP/PVAD R4, R5, R6

**WITHDRAWN**  No. U134, 12.75; No. U133, 9.76

---

# 5p. Pale Violet  (1971–79)

### 1971 (15 FEBRUARY).  TWO 9·5 mm. PHOSPHOR BANDS

**A. ORIGINAL COATED PAPER. PVA GUM**

| U135 | Pale violet | .. | .. | .. | .. | .. | .. | .. | 30 | 30 |
|---|---|---|---|---|---|---|---|---|---|---|
| | a. Phosphor omitted | | .. | .. | .. | .. | .. | £200 | | |

**Cylinder Numbers (Blocks of Six unless otherwise stated)**

Perforation Type A

| Cyl. No. | Phos. No. | | | | | No dot | Dot | |
|---|---|---|---|---|---|---|---|---|
| 2 | L2, S2 | .. | .. | .. | .. | 4·75 | 4·75 | Block of ten |
| 2 | L4 | .. | .. | .. | .. | 2·50 | 2·50 | |

**B. FLUORESCENT COATED PAPER. PVA GUM** (9.71)

| U136 | Pale violet | .. | .. | .. | .. | .. | .. | .. | 2·25 |
|---|---|---|---|---|---|---|---|---|---|
| | a. Phosphor omitted | | .. | .. | .. | .. | .. | £450 | |

As the result of a paper join, a pair of No. U136 exists on uncoated and very substandard paper.

**Cylinder Numbers (Blocks of Six unless otherwise stated)**

Perforation Type A

| Cyl. No. | Phos. No. | | | | No dot | Dot | |
|---|---|---|---|---|---|---|---|
| 2 | L2, S2 | Re-engraved | .. | .. | 32·00 | 32·00 | Block of ten |
| 2 | — | .. | .. | .. | 42·00 | 42·00 | |
| 3 | 7 | .. | .. | .. | 15·00 | 15·00 | |

Phosphor Cylinder Displacement. With ink cyl. 2, phos. cyls. L2, S2 re-engraved are known displaced up the margin 200 mm. opposite row 10.

### C. FLUORESCENT COATED PÁPER. PVAD GUM (5.6.74)

| U137 (=S.G.X866) | Pale violet | .. | .. | .. | .. | .. | .. | .. | 20 | 10 |
|---|---|---|---|---|---|---|---|---|---|---|
| | b. One broad band .. | | .. | .. | .. | .. | .. | 7·00 | |
| | c. With "all over" phosphor | | | .. | .. | .. | £125 | | |
| | d. Long diagonal scratch | | | .. | *Strip of three* | 4·50 | | | |
| | e. Spot on P .. | .. | .. | .. | .. | .. | .. | 1·50 | |

No. U137c is due to a weak mixture of phosphor, with which the doctor blade was unable to cope.

**Cylinder Numbers (Blocks of Six unless otherwise stated)**

Perforation Type R

| Cyl. No. | Phos. No. | | | | No dot | Dot | |
|---|---|---|---|---|---|---|---|
| 8 | 17 | .. | .. | .. | .. | 1·75 | 1·75 | |
| 8 | 17 | +26 mm. (17)* .. | .. | £100 | £100 | Block of ten |
| 8 | 17 | +36 mm. (17)* .. | .. | £100 | £100 | Block of ten |
| 8 | 17 | +40 mm. (17)* .. | .. | £100 | £100 | Block of ten |
| 8 | 17 | +43 mm. (17)* .. | .. | £100 | £100 | Block of ten |
| 8 | 17 | +48 mm. (17)* .. | .. | £100 | £100 | Block of ten |
| 8 | 17 | +64 mm. (16)* .. | .. | £100 | £100 | Block of ten |
| 8 | — | .. | .. | .. | 4·00 | 4·00 | |

*These have one broad band.

Phosphor Cylinder Displacements. Phos. cyl. 17 is known displaced up the margin from 72 to 317 mm. opposite rows 5 to 15. The phosphor band is shfted to give a single broad band on displacements of 72 and 83 mm.

Perforation Type RE

| | | | | | | | |
|---|---|---|---|---|---|---|---|
| 7 | P21 | .. | .. | .. | .. | 1·60 | 1·60 |
| 7 | 30 | .. | .. | .. | .. | 1·60 | 1·60 |
| 8 | 17 | .. | .. | .. | .. | 1·75** | 2·00 |

**Same price as perforation type R with single extension holes in left margin.

On the dot panes of cylinder 8 the dot appears on the left of the cylinder number instead of on the right.

## 1979 (10 OCTOBER). PHOSPHORISED (FLUORESCENT COATED) PAPER. PVAD GUM

| U138 (=S.G.X934) | Pale violet | .. | .. | .. | .. | .. | .. | .. | 30 | 25 |
|---|---|---|---|---|---|---|---|---|---|---|

No. U138 is known on phosphorised paper with either a shiny ink surface which gives a photo-negative reflection or a matt surface without the negative effect.

**Cylinder Numbers (Blocks of Six)**

Perforation Type RE

| Cyl. No. | | | | No dot | Dot |
|---|---|---|---|---|---|
| 7 | .. | .. | .. | 2·00 | 2·00 |

### CYLINDER VARIETIES

**Listed Flaws**

Multipositive Flaw

U137d. Cyl. 8 no dot, R. 3/2–3/5 as ½p. No. U50e, except that it also occurs on R. 3/2 and is very clear on R. 3/5.

U137e

Spot on P
(Cyl. 7 dot, R. 12/2)
(Retouched on No. U138)

**Minor Constant Sheet Flaws**

Cyl. 2    14/5 Diagonal scratch value (Th. G1–F2)

Cyl. 7. 18/10 Dark spot above crown (Th. A3)

Cyl. 8     1/1 Dark spot right of eyebrow (Th. C3)
          4/8 Dark line under necklace (Th. G3)
       10/6 Mark under bust (Th. H3)
       10/7 Dark speck in top of hair in front of crown (Th. B3)
       10/8 Diagonal scratch across cheek (Th. D3–4)
       15/6 Mauve spot on top frame line (Th. A5)
       18/1 White pearl on back of crown (Th. Cg–C6)
       18/6 Dark pearl in bottom of band of crown (Th. B3)

**WITHDRAWN**   Nos. U135/7, 9.80; No. U138, 11.80 but put on sale again at the Philatelic Bureau in May 1981 and withdrawn 26.1.83

## 5p. Claret   (1986–87)

**1986 (20 OCTOBER). COLOUR CHANGED. ONE 4·5 mm. CENTRE PHOSPHOR BAND. FLUORESCENT COATED PAPER. PVAD GUM**

50p. booklet panes UMFB40/1

U139 (=S.G.X867)      Claret ..    ..    ..    ..    ..    ..    1·00   1·00
                     *b*. New phosphor ink (27.1.87)   ..    ..    ..    1·00
                     *c*. One 4 mm. centre band (ex. UMFB41*a*)    ..    1·25
                     *d*. Phosphor omitted    ..    ..    ..    60·00

Booklet pane Nos. UMFB41*a* were issued imperf at left and right with 5p. stamps in positions 3 and 5 with imperf sides at left.

## 5p. Dull Red-brown   (1988)

**1988 (26 JULY). COLOUR CHANGED. PHOSPHORISED (ADVANCED COATED) PAPER. PVAD GUM**

U140 (=S.G.X935)      Dull red-brown    ..    ..    ..    ..    ..    10    10
                     *b*. Circular retouch ..    ..    ..    ..    ..    2·50

**Cylinder Numbers (Blocks of Six)**

Perforation Type RE

| Cyl. No. | No dot | Dot |
|---|---|---|
| 10   ..    ..    ..    .. | 1·00 | 1·00 |

**CYLINDER VARIETY**

**Listed Flaw**

U140*b*
Circular retouch
(Cyl. 10 no dot, R. 4/10)

**Minor Constant Sheet Flaws**

Cyl. 10.   2/2 Pale blemish on jawline (Th. E3)
         3/5 Retouch in background in bottom right corner (Th. G6)
         7/7 Vertical trickle of white specks above forehead (Th. A2–B2)

Cyl. 10. 13/7 Hairline across shoulder (Th. F4–F8)
       19/10 Pale disturbance on folds of dress (Th. G3)

The multipositive used for Cyl. 10 was also employed for the 2p., 4p., and 75p., Cyls. 16, 15 and 1.

# 5½p. Violet    (1973–75)

## 1973 (24 OCTOBER).    TWO 9·5 mm. PHOSPHOR BANDS. FLUORESCENT COATED PAPER. PVAD GUM

| | | | | | | | |
|---|---|---|---|---|---|---|---|
| U141 (=S.G.X868) | Violet.. | .. | .. | .. | .. | .. | .. | 25 | 25 |
| | a. Extra "ear-ring" .. | .. | .. | .. | .. | .. | 1·75 |

**Cylinder Numbers (Blocks of Six)**
Perforation Type R

| Cyl. No. | Phos. No. | | | | | No dot | Dot |
|---|---|---|---|---|---|---|---|
| 2 | 17 | .. | .. | .. | .. | 6·00 | 7·50* |
| 2 | — | .. | .. | .. | .. | 25·00 | 30·00* |

Phosphor Cylinder Displacement. Phos cyl. 17 is known displaced up the margin 219 mm. opposite row 9.

## 1975 (17 MARCH).    CHANGE TO ONE 4 mm. CENTRE BAND. FLUORESCENT COATED PAPER. PVAD GUM

| | | | | | | | |
|---|---|---|---|---|---|---|---|
| U142 (=S.G.X869) | Violet.. | .. | .. | .. | .. | .. | .. | 20 | 20 |
| | a. Uncoated paper .. | .. | .. | .. | .. | .. | £350 |
| | b. Phosphor omitted | .. | .. | .. | .. | .. | 10·00 |
| | c. Extra "ear-ring" .. | .. | .. | .. | .. | .. | 3·00 |
| | d. Cylinder scratch (in horiz block of 20) | | .. | .. | 20·00 |
| | e. Shoulder flaws | .. | .. | .. | .. | .. | 3·00 |

**Cylinder Numbers (Blocks of Six unless otherwise stated)**
Perforation Type R

| Cyl. No. | Phos. No. | | | | | No dot | Dot | |
|---|---|---|---|---|---|---|---|---|
| 2 | 18 | .. | .. | .. | .. | 9·00 | 11·00* | |
| 2 | 20 | .. | .. | .. | .. | 5·00 | 7·00* | |
| 2 | 20 | +37 mm. (17) | .. | .. | 90·00 | £100* | Block of ten |
| 4 | 20 | .. | .. | .. | .. | 4·00 | 4·00 | |
| 4 | 20 | −20 mm. (18) | .. | .. | 70·00 | — | |
| 4 | 20 | −43 mm. (20) | .. | .. | 65·00 | 65·00 | |

Phosphor cylinder number 20 is weak or absent on some no dot examples.
Cyl. 4 dot was originally engraved in reverse and then partially touched out, leaving a faint diagonal stroke from the apex to the right of the extra wide horizontal stroke. In a second state the horizontal stroke is shortened to the usual length.

## CYLINDER VARIETIES
**Listed Flaws**

| U141a, U142c | U142d |
|---|---|
| White spot appearing as extra "ear-ring" (Cyl. 2 dot, R. 19/1) | Long diagonal scratch. Extending across R. 16/1 to16/5 and R. 15/6 to 15/8 as a minor flaw and pronounced on R. 15/9 and 15/10; the latter shown. (Cyl. 2 dot) |

No. U142e (Cyl. No. 4 no dot, R. 20/5) is a multipositive flaw, which occurs in the same position on the no dot panes of the 6½p. Cyl. 4, 7p. Cyls. 3 and 6, also 8p. Cyl. 7. For illustration see under 7p. U153e.

**WITHDRAWN** 23.2.77

# 6p. Light Emerald   (1971–77)

**Three Value Types**

| | | |
|---|---|---|
| I | II | III |

Type I.   Thick value.
          Cyls. 1 and 4
Type II.  Thin value.
          Cyl. 8 and UMFB1/2
          booklet panes
Type III. Very thin value and P.
          10p. G3 multi-value coil

## 1971 (15 FEBRUARY).   TWO 9·5 mm. PHOSPHOR BANDS. TYPE I

### A. ORIGINAL COATED PAPER. PVA GUM

| U143 | Light emerald | .. | .. | .. | .. | .. | .. | 25 | 15 |
|---|---|---|---|---|---|---|---|---|---|
| | a. Uncoated paper .. | .. | .. | .. | .. | .. | 15·00 | |
| | b. Phosphor omitted | .. | .. | .. | .. | .. | 65·00 | |
| | c. Type III (3.77) .. | .. | .. | .. | .. | .. | 2·40 | 1·25 |
| | ca. Flaw over crown .. | .. | .. | .. | .. | .. | 3·50 | |

**Cylinder Numbers (Blocks of Six unless otherwise stated)**

Perforation Type A

| Cyl. No. | Phos. No. | | | | | No dot | Dot | |
|---|---|---|---|---|---|---|---|---|
| 1 | S2 | .. | .. | .. | .. | 7·00 | 7·00 | |
| 1 | — | .. | .. | .. | .. | 2·50 | 2·50 | |
| 1 | L2, S2 | .. | .. | .. | .. | 5·00 | 5·00 | Block of ten |
| 1 | L4 | .. | .. | .. | .. | 3·50 | 3·50 | |

Phosphor Cylinder Displacement. Phos. cyls. L2, S2 are known displaced up the margin 80 mm. opposite row 15.

### B. FLUORESCENT COATED PAPER, GUM ARABIC. (6.6.73)

| U144 (=S.G.X870Eg) | Light emerald | .. | .. | .. | .. | .. | .. | 1·50 |
|---|---|---|---|---|---|---|---|---|
| | b. Incomplete 6 | .. | .. | .. | .. | .. | .. | 3·00 |

No. U144 is only known with contaminated "yellow phosphor".

**Cylinder Numbers (Blocks of Six)**

Perforation Type R(S)

| Cyl. No. | Phos. No. | | | | No dot | Dot |
|---|---|---|---|---|---|---|
| 4 | 7 | .. | .. | .. | 25·00 | 28·00 |

### C. FLUORESCENT COATED PAPER. PVA GUM. (18.7.73)

| U145 | Light emerald | .. | .. | .. | .. | .. | 22·00 |
|---|---|---|---|---|---|---|---|
| | a. Phosphor omitted | .. | .. | .. | .. | £1200 |
| | b. Incomplete 6 | .. | .. | .. | .. | 28·00 |

**Cylinder Numbers (Blocks of Six)**

Perforation Type A

| Cyl. No. | Phos. No. | | | | | No dot | Dot | |
|---|---|---|---|---|---|---|---|---|
| 4 | 1 | .. | .. | .. | .. | £250 | £180 | |
| 4 | — | .. | .. | .. | .. | † | £150 | Guillotined off on dot |

### D. TYPE II. FLUORESCENT COATED PAPER. PVAD GUM (30.10.73)

| U146 (=S.G.X870) | Light emerald | .. | .. | .. | .. | .. | 30 | 15 |
|---|---|---|---|---|---|---|---|---|
| | aa. One broad band .. | .. | .. | .. | .. | 15·00 | |
| | a. Phosphor omitted | .. | .. | .. | .. | £300 | |
| | b. Long diagonal scratch | .. | | *Strip of three* | 7·00 | |
| | c. Dark spot above central cross .. | .. | .. | .. | 2·50 | |
| | d. Type III (3.12.75) | .. | .. | .. | .. | 50 | 50 |
| | da. One broad band .. | .. | .. | .. | .. | 2·00 | |
| | db. Flaw over crown .. | .. | .. | .. | .. | 2·50 | |
| | e. Type I (ex. Cyl. 4) (31.10.77) .. | .. | .. | .. | 30 | 30 |

**Cylinder Numbers (Blocks of Six)**

Perforation Type A

| Cyl. No. | Phos. No. | | | | | No dot | Dot |
|---|---|---|---|---|---|---|---|
| 4 | 7 | .. | .. | .. | .. | 2·00 | 2·00 |
| 8 | 26* | .. | .. | .. | .. | 10·00 | † |
| 8 | — | .. | .. | .. | .. | † | 10·00 |

Perforation Type R

| | | | | | | | |
|---|---|---|---|---|---|---|---|
| 8 | 17 | .. | .. | .. | .. | 1·75 | 1·75 |
| 8 | — | .. | .. | .. | .. | £140 | £150 |
| 8 | P21 | .. | .. | .. | .. | 6·00 | 6·00 |

*The phosphor cylinder number and box were not engraved on the dot cylinder.

On the dot pane of cylinder 8 the dot was first placed in front of the 8 but later this was partly touched out and a prominent dot was inserted after the 8. *Cylinder block showing first state of 8 with dot to left instead of right, price* £10.

Phosphor Cylinder Displacement. Phos. cyl. 17 is known displaced up the margin 425 mm. opposite row 1.

**CYLINDER VARIETIES**

**Listed Flaws**

U143*ca*, U146*db*
From 10p. G3 multi-value
coils in every fifth position
(Roll No. 1)

U144/5*b*
(Cyl. 4 dot, R. 12/4)

**Multipositive Flaws**

U146*b*. Cyl. 8 no dot, R. 3/3–3/5 as ½p. No. U50*e*, but fainter
U146*c*. Cyl. 8 dot, R. 20/6 as ½p. No. U50*g*, but faint

For further flaws on 6p. stamps in booklet panes, see under Nos. UMF1/2.

**Minor Constant Sheet Flaws**

Cyl. 1   20/9 White flaw on bottom jewel at back of crown (Th. C6)
Cyl. 8   10/2 Two white flaws upper left of P and three dark dots to right of it (Th. F2–F3)
Cyl. 8.   6/8 Dark spot in Queen's hair (Th. B3)

**WITHDRAWN**   1.81

# 6½p. Greenish Blue   (1974–77)

## 1974 (4 SEPTEMBER).   TWO 9·5 mm. PHOSPHOR BANDS.
## FLUORESCENT COATED PAPER. PVAD GUM

| | | | | | | | | | |
|---|---|---|---|---|---|---|---|---|---|
| U148 (=S.G.X871) | Greenish blue | .. | .. | .. | .. | .. | .. | 45 | 45 |
| | b. Line in band | .. | .. | .. | .. | .. | .. | 4·00 | |
| | c. Spots in hair | .. | .. | .. | .. | .. | .. | 3·00 | |
| | d. Patch over eye | .. | .. | .. | .. | .. | .. | 2·50 | |
| | e. Dotted line at central cross | .. | .. | .. | .. | .. | 2·25 | |

No. U148 is known with a very wide "phantom" band measuring from 17 mm. to the whole of the stamp, giving it an extra phosphor wash. It was due to a weak mixture of the phosphor ink which leaked under the phosphor doctor blade. This occurred in the first vertical row in a sheet from the no dot cylinder. Examples with, apparently, three phosphor bands are from sheets affected by the malfunction of the doctor blade. *All over phosphor coating from first vertical column, price £150 with left margin.*

### Cylinder Numbers (Blocks of Six)
Perforation Type R

| Cyl. No. | Phos. No. | | | | | No dot | Dot |
|---|---|---|---|---|---|---|---|
| 2 | 17 | .. | .. | .. | .. | 6·50 | 7·50* |

## 1975 (24 SEPTEMBER).   CHANGE TO ONE 4 mm. CENTRE BAND
### A. FLUORESCENT COATED PAPER. PVAD GUM

| | | | | | | | | | |
|---|---|---|---|---|---|---|---|---|---|
| U149 (=S.G.X872) | Greenish blue | .. | .. | .. | .. | .. | .. | 30 | 15 |
| | a. Imperforate (pair) | | .. | .. | .. | .. | .. | £300 | |
| | b. Uncoated paper .. | .. | .. | .. | .. | .. | £160 | |
| | c. Phosphor omitted | .. | .. | .. | .. | .. | 11·00 | |
| | d. Line in band | .. | .. | .. | .. | .. | .. | 6·00 | |
| | e. Spots in hair | .. | .. | .. | .. | .. | .. | 2·25 | |
| | f. Curved line in hair | .. | .. | .. | .. | .. | 2·00 | |
| | g. White patch and retouch in hair | .. | .. | .. | 3·50 | |
| | h. Background retouch and broken cross | .. | .. | 3·50 | |
| | i. Shoulder scratch .. | .. | .. | .. | .. | .. | 1·75 | |
| | j. Dotted line at central cross | .. | .. | .. | .. | 2·50 | |
| | k. Neck flaw .. | .. | .. | .. | .. | .. | 5·00 | |
| | ka. Neck flaw retouched | .. | .. | .. | .. | 4·00 | |
| | l. Curved frame at top right | .. | .. | .. | 3·00 | |
| | m. Dent in top frame | .. | .. | .. | .. | .. | 3·00 | |
| | n. Spot on 6 .. | .. | .. | .. | .. | .. | 2·50 | |
| | o. Shoulder flaws | .. | .. | .. | .. | .. | 2·50 | |

The note under No. U148 also applies to No. U149; the wash occurred in the first vertical row in a sheet from the no dot cylinder. *Price each, £150 mint, with left margin.*

### Cylinder Numbers (Blocks of Six unless otherwise stated)
Perforation Type R

| Cyl. No. | Phos. No. | | | | | No dot | Dot |
|---|---|---|---|---|---|---|---|
| 2 | 20 | .. | .. | .. | .. | 4·00 | 5·50 |
| 4 | 18 | .. | .. | .. | .. | 9·00 | 9·00 |
| 4 | 20 | .. | .. | .. | .. | 1·90 | 1·90 |
| 4 | — | .. | .. | .. | .. | 20·00 | 20·00 |

Phosphor Cylinder Displacement. With ink cyl. 4, phos. cyl. 20 is known displaced up the margin 325 mm. opposite row 5.

Perforation Type RE

| Cyl. No. | Phos. No. | | | | No dot | Dot | |
|---|---|---|---|---|---|---|---|
| 4 | 20 | .. | .. | .. | 1·90** | 1·90 | |
| 4 | 20 | −63 mm. (bot. mar.) | .. | 50·00 | 50·00 | |
| 4 | 20 | −39 mm. (20) | .. | .. | 50·00 | 50·00 | |
| 4 | 20 | −22 mm. (19) | .. | .. | 50·00 | 50·00 | |
| 4 | 20 | +37 mm. (17) | .. | .. | 48·00 | 48·00 | Block of ten |
| 4 | 20 | +45 mm. (17) | .. | .. | 70·00 | 70·00 | Block of ten |
| 4 | 20 | +53 mm. (16) | .. | .. | 70·00 | 70·00 | Block of ten |
| 4 | — | .. | .. | .. | 15·00 | 15·00 | |
| 5 | 20 | .. | .. | .. | 5·50 | 5·50 | |
| 9 | 20 | .. | .. | .. | 1·75 | 1·75 | |
| 9 | 20 | −52 mm. (bot. mar.) | .. | £110 | £110 | |
| 11 | 18 | .. | .. | .. | 5·00 | 5·00 | |

**Same price as perforation type R with extension holes in left margin.

Phosphor Cylinder Displacements. Phos. cyl. 20 is known displaced up the margin from 70 to 373 mm. opposite rows 3 to 15.

**B. FLUORESCENT COATED PAPER. PVA GUM** (12.75)

| U150 | Greenish blue | .. | .. | .. | .. | .. | .. 22·00 |
| | *b.* Curved line in hair | .. | .. | .. | .. | .. 25·00 |

**Cylinder Numbers (Blocks of Six)**
Perforation Type R

| Cyl. No. | Phos. No. | | | | No dot | Dot |
|----------|-----------|---|---|---|--------|-----|
| 4 | 18 | .. | .. | .. | .. £450 | £550 |

## 1977 (26 JANUARY). ONE NARROW PHOSPHOR BAND AT LEFT. FLUORESCENT COATED PAPER. PVAD GUM

50p. booklet pane UMFB4 (6½p. value at right)

| U151 (=S.G.X873Ea) | Greenish blue .. | .. | .. | .. | .. | .. | 60 | 75 |

## 1977 (26 JANUARY). ONE NARROW PHOSPHOR BAND AT RIGHT. FLUORESCENT COATED PAPER. PVAD GUM

50p. booklet pane UMFB3 (6½p. value at left)

| U152 (=S.G.X873) | Greenish blue .. | .. | .. | .. | .. | .. | 60 | 55 |

**CYLINDER VARIETIES**
**Listed Flaws**

| U148*b*, U149*d* | U148*c*, U149*e* | U148*d* |
|---|---|---|
| Heavy coloured line in band of diadem (Cyl. 2 no dot, R. 1/4) | Cluster of coloured spots in hair (Cyl. 2 no dot, R. 12/2) | White patch above eye (Cyl. 2 no dot, R. 13/2) Retouched on No. U149 |

| U148*e*, U149*j* | U149*f*, U150*b* |
|---|---|
| Dotted line at tip of central cross (Cyl. 2 dot, R. 19/2) | Curved line in hair and band (Cyl. 4 no dot, R. 2/4) |

No. U149*i* is a multipositive flaw found on sideways delivery VS coils on roll No. 10. For illustration see No. U59*d* under the 1p. value.

| U149g | U149h | U149k | U149ka |
|---|---|---|---|
| White patch and retouch in hair. Later retouched again with additional dots filling the white area (Cyl. 4 no dot, R. 3/3) | Background retouch and broken cross (Cyl. 4 dot, R. 3/2) | Neck flaw | Retouched (Cyl. 9 no dot, R. 1/10) |

| U149l | U149m | U149n |
|---|---|---|
| Curved frame (Roll No. 5) (Horizontal VS coil) | Dent in top frame (Roll No. 10) | Spot on 6 (Cyl. 11 no dot, R. 12/9) |

For illustration of the multipositive flaw U149o, see U153e under the 7p. value.

For further flaws on 6½p. stamps in booklet panes, see under Nos. UMFB3 and UFB2.

**Minor Constant Sheet Flaws**

Cyl. 2. 2/1 Dark speck on Queen's shoulder (Th. F4)

Cyl. 4 9/1 Retouch to left of Queen's ear (Th. D3)
19/5 Dark dot in band of crown (Th. B4)

Cyl. 4. 2/10 Damaged serif to 2
8/1 Dark speck on Queen's cheek (Th. D3)
13/9 White scratch on Queen's cheek (Th. D3)
20/3 Diagonal scratch through Queen's neck (Th. F3–G4)
20/6 Dark speck on Queen's neck (Th. D–E4)

Cyl. 9 8/1 Diagonal scratch from Queen's nose to necklace (Th. C2–E4)
18/1 to 20/1. Vertical scratch down left margin from Th. D1 on R. 18/1 to Th. C1 on R. 20/1

Cyl. 11 8/1 As Cyl. 9
8/9 Scratch below necklace (Th. F3–F4)
13/5 Small speck in right side of 6

The flaw on Cyls. 9 and 11 no dot, R. 8/1 is a multipositive one which occurs on the 7p. value, Cyl. 14 no dot.

**COILS**

One centre phosphor band. Printed in continuous reels

| Code No. | Issued | Number in roll | Face value | Paper/gum | Screen | Perf. | Type |
|---|---|---|---|---|---|---|---|
| | | Vertical delivery | | | | | |
| RL | 28.1.76 | 500 | £32·50 | FCP/PVAD | 150 | | R |
| | | Sideways delivery | | | | | |
| VS | 13.10.76 | 500 | £32.50 | FCP/PVAD | 150 | | R |

Cylinder Numbers used:

| RL | FCP/PVAD | 7/7. |
|---|---|---|
| VS | FCP/PVAD | R3 (phos. R11) |

Cylinder No. 7 was also used for the 6½p. in booklet panes of ten UFB1/2.

**WITHDRAWN** No. U148, 2.78; No. U149, 9.80

# 7p. Purple-brown   (1975–78)

## 1975 (15 JANUARY).   TWO 9·5 mm. PHOSPHOR BANDS. FLUORESCENT COATED PAPER. PVAD GUM

| | | | | | | | | |
|---|---|---|---|---|---|---|---|---|
| U153 (=S.G.X874) | Purple-brown | .. | .. | .. | .. | .. | .. | 35 | 25 |
| | *a.* Imperforate (pair) | .. | .. | .. | .. | .. | £250 |
| | *b.* Phosphor omitted | .. | .. | .. | .. | .. | 1·25 |
| | *c.* Missing serif to 7.. | .. | .. | .. | .. | .. | 3·50 |
| | *d.* White spot in band | .. | .. | .. | .. | .. | 2·50 |
| | *e.* Shoulder flaws .. | .. | .. | .. | .. | .. | 2·50 |
| | *f.* Scratch down neck | .. | .. | .. | .. | .. | 2·75 |
| | *g.* Neck flaw.. .. | .. | .. | .. | .. | .. | 2·00 |
| | *h.* Retouch on dress | .. | .. | .. | .. | .. | 2·00 |

**Cylinder Numbers (Blocks of Six unless otherwise stated)**

Perforation Type A

| Cyl. No. | Phos. No. | | | | | | No dot | Dot |
|---|---|---|---|---|---|---|---|---|
| 3 | 26* | .. | .. | .. | .. | .. | 10·00 | † |
| 3 | — | .. | .. | .. | .. | .. | † | 10·00 |

Perforation Type R

| | | | | | | | No dot | Dot | |
|---|---|---|---|---|---|---|---|---|---|
| 3 | 17 | .. | .. | .. | .. | .. | 3·25 | 3·25 |
| 3 | P21 | .. | .. | .. | .. | .. | 3·00 | 3·00 |
| 3 | P21 | +23 mm. (17) inverted ptg. | .. | 20·00 | 20·00 | Block of ten |
| 3 | P21 | +48 mm. (16) .. | .. | .. | 35·00 | 35·00 | Block of ten |
| 6 | 17 | .. | .. | .. | .. | .. | 2·75 | 3·00 |
| 6 | P21 | .. | .. | .. | .. | .. | 2·75 | 3·00 |

*The phosphor cylinder number and box were not engraved on the dot cylinder.

## 1977 (13 JUNE).   CHANGE TO ONE 4 mm. CENTRE BAND. FLUORESCENT COATED PAPER. PVAD GUM

| | | | | | | | | |
|---|---|---|---|---|---|---|---|---|
| U154 (=S.G.X875) | Purple-brown | .. | .. | .. | .. | .. | .. | 35 | 20 |
| | *a.* Imperforate (pair) | .. | .. | .. | .. | .. | £100 |
| | *b.* Imperforate top margin.. | .. | .. | .. | .. | £150 |
| | *c.* Missing serif to 7.. .. | .. | .. | .. | .. | 3·00 |
| | *d.* Retouch left of forehead | .. | .. | .. | .. | 1·75 |
| | *e.* Spot in hair .. | .. | .. | .. | .. | .. | 1·25 |
| | *f.* Spot on dress .. | .. | .. | .. | .. | .. | 1·25 |
| | *g.* Faint spots on neck .. | .. | .. | .. | .. | 1·40 |
| | *h.* Dark shoulder scratch .. | .. | .. | .. | .. | 1·40 |
| | *i.* Pale spot below dress .. | .. | .. | .. | .. | 1·25 |
| | *j.* Brown mark on pearls of crown | .. | .. | .. | 1·40 |
| | *k.* Pale patch on neck .. | .. | .. | .. | .. | 1·40 |
| | *l.* Scar on lip .. .. .. | .. | .. | .. | .. | 3·00 |
| | *m.* Short band top and bottom* (15.11.78) | .. | .. | 40 | 40 |
| | *n.* Flaw on front jewel | .. | .. | .. | .. | 1·75 |

*The short phosphor band comes from the £1·60 1978 Christmas Booklet Pane UMFB8. The phosphor covering the printed portion of the design only so as not to overlap on the 9p. stamps. Examples of No. U154 exist with "all over" phosphor coating due to doctor blade malfunction.

**Cylinder Numbers (Blocks of Six unless otherwise stated)**

Perforation Type RE

| Cyl. No. | Phos. No. | | | | | No dot | Dot | |
|---|---|---|---|---|---|---|---|---|
| 8 | 18 | .. | .. | .. | .. | 1·40 | 1·40 |
| 8 | 18 | +23 mm. (18) .. | .. | .. | 18·00 | 18·00 |
| 8 | 18 | +28 mm. (17) .. | .. | .. | 15·00 | 15·00 | Block of ten |
| 8 | 18 | +41 mm. (17) .. | .. | .. | 15·00 | 15·00 | Block of ten |
| 8 | 18 | +47 mm. (16/17) .. | .. | 15·00 | 15·00 | Block of ten |
| 8 | 18 | +48 mm. (16) .. | .. | .. | 15·00 | 15·00 | Block of ten |
| 8 | 18 | +57 mm. (16) .. | .. | .. | 15·00 | 15·00 | Block of ten |
| 8 | 18 | +61 mm. (16) .. | .. | .. | 15·00 | 15·00 | Block of ten |

| Cyl. No. | Phos. No. | | | | | No dot | Dot |
|---|---|---|---|---|---|---|---|
| 8 | 20 | .. | .. | .. | .. | 1·75 | 1·75 |
| 14 | 20 | .. | .. | .. | .. | £100 | 22·00 |
| 14 | 31 | .. | .. | .. | .. | 1·40 | 1·40 |
| 20 | 20 | .. | .. | .. | .. | 1·40 | 1·40 |
| 21 | 20 | .. | .. | .. | .. | 1·40 | 1·40 |
| 21 | 31 | .. | .. | .. | .. | 6·00 | 5·50 |
| 22 | 20 | .. | .. | .. | .. | 2·00 | 2·00 |

Phosphor Cylinder Displacements. With ink cyl. 8, phos. cyl. 18 is known displaced up the margin from 74 to 116 mm. opposite rows 14 and 15.

Perforation Type A

| 14 | 29 | .. | .. | .. | .. | 1·40 | 1·40 |
|---|---|---|---|---|---|---|---|
| 20 | 20 | .. | .. | .. | .. | £1500 | £100 |

## 1977 (13 JUNE).   ONE NARROW BAND AT LEFT. FLUORESCENT COATED PAPER. PVAD GUM

50p. booklet pane UMFB6 (7p. at right)

| U155 (=S.G.X876Ea) | Purple-brown | .. | .. | .. | .. | .. | .. | 60 | 75 |
|---|---|---|---|---|---|---|---|---|---|
| | b. Thin value | .. | .. | .. | .. | .. | .. | 1·25 | |

## 1977 (13 JUNE).   ONE NARROW BAND AT RIGHT. FLUORESCENT COATED PAPER. PVAD GUM

50p. booklet pane UMFB5 (7p. at left)

| U156 (=S.G.X876) | Purple-brown | .. | .. | .. | .. | .. | .. | 60 | 75 |
|---|---|---|---|---|---|---|---|---|---|
| | b. Thin value | .. | .. | .. | .. | .. | .. | 2·25 | |

The thin value varieties occurred in only two positions on the booklet pane cylinder. For illustration see below multi-value panes UMFB5/6.

**CYLINDER VARIETIES**
**Listed flaws**

U153/4c
Missing serif to 7
(Cyls. 3, 6 and 8 dot, R. 5/10)

U153d
White spot in band of diadem
(Cyl. 3 dot, R. 10/10)

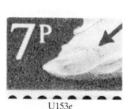

U153e
Flaws on shoulder
(Cyls. 3 and 6 no dot, R. 20/5)

U153f
Straight line from hair to pearls
(Cyl. 6 dot, R. 8/3)

No. U153e is a multipositive flaw which appears on 5½p. Cyl. 4, 6½p. Cyl. 4, 7p. Cyl. 6, 8p. Cyl. 7 all No dot, R. 20/5.

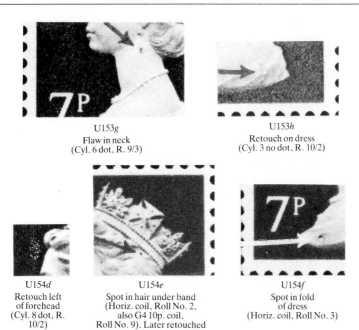

U153*g*
Flaw in neck
(Cyl. 6 dot, R. 9/3)

U153*h*
Retouch on dress
(Cyl. 3 no dot, R. 10/2)

U154*d*
Retouch left
of forehead
(Cyl. 8 dot, R.
10/2)

U154*e*
Spot in hair under band
(Horiz. coil, Roll No. 2,
also G4 10p. coil,
Roll No. 9). Later retouched

U154*f*
Spot in fold
of dress
(Horiz. coil, Roll No. 3)

Faint spots in neck variety No. U154*g* occurs on the horizontal CS coil, Roll No. 10, and is similar to the 1p., No. U55*g*.

Dark shoulder scratch flaw No. U154*h* is a multipositive flaw on the horizontal CS coil. See illustration of No. U59*d* under the 1p. value.

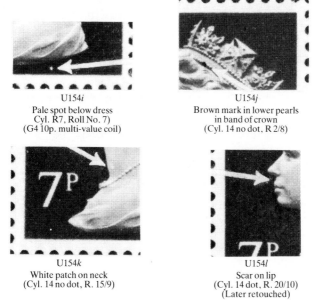

U154*i*
Pale spot below dress
Cyl. R7, Roll No. 7)
(G4 10p. multi-value coil)

U154*j*
Brown mark in lower pearls
in band of crown
(Cyl. 14 no dot, R 2/8)

U154*k*
White patch on neck
(Cyl. 14 no dot, R. 15/9)

U154*l*
Scar on lip
(Cyl. 14 dot, R. 20/10)
(Later retouched)

White flaw on front jewel of crown
(Vert. coil, XL Cyl. 11 no dot)

U154*n*

For further flaws on 7p. stamps in booklet panes, see under Nos. UMFB5/8 and UFB6.

## Minor Constant Sheet Flaws

| | | |
|---|---|---|
| Cyl. 3 | 1/2 | Small retouch on collar of dress (Th. G4) |
| | 7/1 | Small white patch on Queen's jaw (Th. E3) |
| | 8/3 | White scratch across Queen's shoulder (Th. F3–F5) |
| | 9/1 | Retouch on Queen's cheek (Th. D3) |
| | 15/5 | White scratch across Queen's face (Th. D3–D4) |
| Cyl. 3. | 6/6 | Retouch below eye (Th. C–D and 2–3 intersection) |
| | 8/1 | Scratch on cheek (Th. D2–D3) |
| | 9/3 | Dark speck under ear (Th. D4) |
| | 9/9 | Vertical scratch on shoulder (Th. F4–G4) |
| | 19/8 | Diagonal scratch across chin and neck (Th. E3–E4) |
| | 19/10 | White vertical scratch on neck (Th. E4–F4) |
| | 20/1 | White specks in collar (Th. F4–5) |
| | 20/3 | Diagonal scratch across neck and collar (Th. E3–F3) |
| Cyl. 6. | 2/1 | Blemish on lower part of 7 |
| | 16/3 | Mark on Queen's shoulder (Th. E4–F4) |
| Cyl. 8 | 20/5 | Variety U153*e* retouched, but leaving three dots still visible |
| Cyl. 8. | 1/7 | Dark speck on Queen's shoulder (Th. F4) |
| | 2/2 | Two brown spots on Queen's forehead (Th. C3) |
| | 3/7 | Dark speck in Queen's hair (Th. D5) |
| | 4/7 | Slight retouch on Queen's shoulder (Th. F4–F5) |
| | 6/6 | Retouch below Queen's eye (Th. C–D and 2–3 intersection) as on Cyl. 3 dot |
| | 7/7 | Dark speck in Queen's hair (Th. C3) |
| | 9/2 | Brown nick in base of 7 |
| | 9/3 | Dark speck under eye retouched (Th. D2–D3) |
| | 12/3 | Three distinct dots on 7 |
| Cyl. 14 | 8/1 | Diagonal scratch from Queen's nose to necklace (Th. C2–E4)* |
| | 9/6 | Dotted line to right of dress (Th. G6) |
| | 20/7 | Dark dot in band of crown (Th. C5) |

*This is a multipositive flaw which occurs on the 6½p. value, Cyls, 9 and 11 no dot.

## COILS

One centre phosphor band.    Printed in continuous reels

| Code No. | Issued | Number in roll | Face value | Paper/gum | Screen | Perf. Type |
|---|---|---|---|---|---|---|
| | | | Vertical delivery | | | |
| XL | 13.6.77 | 500 | £35 | FCP/PVAD | 150 | R |
| | | | Sideways delivery | | | |
| CS | 16.11.77 | 500 | £35 | FCP/PVAD | 150 | R |

Cylinder Numbers used:

| | | |
|---|---|---|
| XL | FCP/PVAD | 11/11. |
| CS | FCP/PVAD | R2 (phos. R11) |

Cylinder 11 was also used for the 7p. in booklet panes of ten UFB5/6.

**WITHDRAWN**   No. U153, 5.78; No. U154, 12.81

# 7p. Brownish Red   (1985)
## 1985 (29 OCTOBER).   COLOUR CHANGED. PHOSPHORISED (FLUORESCENT COATED) PAPER. PVAD GUM

U157 (=S.G.X936)    Brownish red        ..     ..     ..     ..     ..     ..   2·00   1·50
                    *b*. Dark flaw in dress     ..     ..     ..     ..     ..   3·75

**Cylinder Numbers (Blocks of Six)**

Perforation Type RE

| Cyl. No. | | | | | No dot | Dot |
|---|---|---|---|---|---|---|
| 25 | .. | .. | .. | .. | 12·00 | 12·00 |
| 26 | .. | .. | .. | .. | 12·00 | 12·00 |

**CYLINDER VARIETY**
**Listed Flaw**

U157*b*
Dark flaw on dress
(Cyl. 25 dot, R. 19/7)
Later retouched

# 7½p. Pale Chestnut    (1971–74)

**Two Value Types**

Type I.   Thick value. Cyls. 1 and 3
Type II.  Thinner value. Cyl. 5

I                                    II

## 1971 (15 FEBRUARY).    TWO 9·5 mm. PHOSPHOR BANDS. TYPE I
### A. ORIGINAL COATED PAPER. PVA GUM

| U158 | Pale chestnut.. | .. | .. | .. | .. | .. | .. | 35 | 35 |
|------|----------------|----|----|----|----|----|----|----|----|
|      | *a.* Phosphor omitted | | .. | .. | .. | .. | .. | 15·00 | |

**Cylinder Numbers (Blocks of Six unless otherwise stated)**
Perforation Type A

| Cyl. No. | Phos. No. | | | | | No dot | Dot | |
|------|------|----|----|----|----|--------|------|--------------|
| 1 | S2 | .. | .. | .. | .. | 5·00 | 5·00 | |
| 1 | L2, S2 | .. | .. | .. | .. | 5·50 | 5·50 | Block of ten |
| 1 | — | .. | .. | .. | .. | 3·25 | 3·25 | |
| 1 | L4 | .. | .. | .. | .. | 5·00 | 5·00 | |

Phosphor Cylinder Displacement. Phos. cyls. L2, S2 are known displaced up the margin 70 mm. opposite row 15.

### B. FLUORESCENT COATED PAPER. PVA GUM (Late 1971)

| U159 | Pale chestnut.. | .. | .. | .. | .. | .. | .. | 3·25 | 2·00 |
|------|----------------|----|----|----|----|----|----|------|------|
|      | *a.* Phosphor omitted | | .. | .. | .. | .. | .. | £200 | |
|      | *b.* Sliced loop to P .. | | .. | .. | .. | .. | .. | 7·00 | |

**Cylinder Numbers (Blocks of Six unless otherwise stated)**
Perforation Type A

| Cyl. No. | Phos. No. | | | | | No dot | Dot | |
|------|------|------|----|----|----|--------|------|------------------------|
| 1 | L2, S2 | Re-engraved | .. | .. | 35·00 | 35·00 | Block of ten |
| 3 | 1 | .. | .. | .. | .. | 18·00 | £175 | |
| 3 | — | .. | .. | .. | .. | † | 18·00 | Guillotined off on dot |

### C. TYPE II. FLUORESCENT COATED PAPER. PVAD GUM (1.74)

| U160 (=S.G.X877) | Pale chestnut.. | .. | .. | .. | .. | .. | 30 | 25 |
|------|----------------|----|----|----|----|----|----|----|
| | *a.* Long diagonal scratch  .. | .. | *Strip of three* | 6·00 | | | | |
| | *b.* Dark spot above central cross .. | .. | .. | .. | 2·50 | | | |
| | *c.* Type I (Cyl. 3) (4.74)  .. | .. | .. | .. | 1·75 | | | |
| | *ca.* Sliced loop to P .. | .. | .. | .. | .. | 5·00 | | |
| | *d.* One broad band (Cyl. 3) | .. | .. | .. | £450 | | | |

**Cylinder Numbers (Blocks of Six)**
Perforation Type A

| Cyl. No. | Phos. No. | | | | | No dot | Dot |
|------|------|----|----|----|----|--------|--------|
| 3 | 7 | .. | .. | .. | .. | 20·00 | 20·00 |

Perforation Type R

| 5 | 17 | .. | .. | .. | .. | 1·75 | 1·75 |
|------|------|----|----|----|----|--------|--------|

Perforation Type RE

| 5 | 17 | .. | .. | .. | .. | 1·75** | 1·75 |
|------|------|----|----|----|----|--------|--------|
| 5 | P21 | .. | .. | .. | .. | 3·50 | 4·50 |

** Same price as perforation type R with single extension holes in left margin.

**CYLINDER VARIETIES**
**Listed Flaws**

Sliced loop to P
(Cyl. 3 no dot, R. 9/6)
(See also Pane Nos. UB43/44k)

U159b, U160ca

Multipositive Flaws
U160a.   Cyl. 5 no dot, R. 3/3–3/5 as ½p. No. U50e
U160b.   Cyl. 5 dot, R. 20/6 as ½p. No. U50g

**Minor Constant Sheet Flaws**
Cyl. 1    6/8   White scratch on Queen's forehead (Th. C2)
Cyl. 5.   19/9   White scratch across Queen's shoulder (Th. F5–F6)

**WITHDRAWN**   11.80

# 8p. Rosine   (1973–79)

**1973 (24 OCTOBER).   TWO 9·5 mm. PHOSPHOR BANDS. FLUORESCENT COATED PAPER. PVAD GUM**

U161 (=S.G.X878)    Rosine     ..    ..    ..    ..    ..    ..    25    20
           a. Uncoated paper ..    ..    ..    ..    ..    .. 10·00

**Cylinder Numbers (Blocks of Six)**
Perforation Type A

| Cyl. No. | Phos. No. | | | | No dot | Dot |
|---|---|---|---|---|---|---|
| 3 | 26* | .. | .. | .. | 30·00 | † |
| 3 | — | .. | .. | .. | † | 30·00 |

    *The phosphor cylinder number and box were not engraved on the dot cylinder.
Perforation Type R

| | | | | | | |
|---|---|---|---|---|---|---|
| 3 | 17 | .. | .. | .. | 2·00 | 1·75 |
| 3 | — | .. | .. | .. | 4·00 | 4·75 |
| 3 | P21 | .. | .. | .. | 2·50 | 2·25 |

Perforation Type RE

| | | | | | | |
|---|---|---|---|---|---|---|
| 3 | 30 | .. | .. | .. | 2·00 | 2·00 |

    Phosphor Cylinder Displacement. Phos. cyl. 17 is known displaced up the margin 122 mm. opposite row 13.

**Two Value Types**

U162
HARRISON

U162*l*
ENSCHEDÉ

## 1979 (20 AUGUST).   CHANGE TO ONE 4 mm. CENTRE BAND. FLUORESCENT COATED PAPER. PVAD GUM

| | | | | | | | | |
|---|---|---|---|---|---|---|---|---|
| U162 (=S.G.X879) | Rosine | .. | .. | .. | .. | .. | 25 | 15 |
| | *a.* One short band at top (ex UMFB11) (17.10.79) | | | | .. | 2·75 | |
| | *b.* One short band top and bottom* (14.11.79) .. | | | | | 60 | 60 |
| | *c.* Uncoated paper .. | .. | .. | .. | .. | .. | £550 | |
| | *d.* Imperforate (pair) | .. | .. | .. | .. | .. | £550 | |
| | *e.* Phosphor omitted (Cyl. 14) | .. | .. | .. | .. | £200 | |
| | *f.* Long vertical scratch | .. | .. | .. | (*vert. pair*) | 5·00 | |
| | *g.* Damaged foot to P | .. | .. | .. | .. | .. | 3·00 | |
| | *h.* Spot in hair | .. | .. | .. | .. | .. | 1·50 | |
| | *i.* Spot in band | .. | .. | .. | .. | .. | 2·50 | |
| | *j.* Shoulder flaws | .. | .. | .. | .. | .. | 3·00 | |
| | *l.* Printed by Enschedé** (12.12.79) | .. | .. | .. | 30 | 30 |
| | *la.* Phosphor omitted (Enschedé) .. | .. | .. | .. | £110 | |

*The short phosphor band comes from the £1·80 1979 Christmas Booklet Pane UMFB13. The phosphor covering the printed portion of the design only so as not to overlap on to the 10p. stamps.
**Individual stamps from any position can be distinguished by the slightly forward slope of the P. Laying a rule along the spine of the P so that it projects at top and bottom of the stamp will show, from the left, five perforation holes at the top and slightly over four perforation holes at the bottom of the stamp. This does not apply to Harrison cylinders.

**Cylinder Numbers (Blocks of Six unless otherwise stated)**
HARRISON
Double pane cylinders. Jumelle press
Perforation Type RE

| Cyl. No. | Phos. No. | | | | | No dot | Dot | |
|---|---|---|---|---|---|---|---|---|
| 3 | 20 | .. | .. | .. | .. | 1·75 | 1·75 | |
| 7 | 18 | .. | .. | .. | .. | £140 | £110 | |
| 7 | 20 | .. | .. | .. | .. | 1·75 | 1·75 | |
| 7 | 20 | +24 mm. (17/18) | | .. | .. | 12·00 | 12·00 | Block of ten |
| 7 | 20 | +31 mm. (17) | .. | .. | .. | 12·00 | 12·00 | Block of ten |
| 7 | 20 | +44 mm. (17) | .. | .. | .. | 12·00 | 12·00 | Block of ten |
| 7 | 20 | +50 mm. (16) | .. | .. | .. | 15·00 | 15·00 | Block of ten |
| 7 | 20 | +64 mm. (16) | .. | .. | .. | 15·00 | 15·00 | Block of ten |
| 7 | 20 | (inverted printing) | | .. | .. | 3·50 | 7·00 | |
| 7 | — | .. | .. | .. | .. | 4·50 | 4·50 | |
| 10 | 18 | .. | .. | .. | .. | 1·75 | 1·75 | |
| 10 | 18 | −22 mm. (19) | .. | .. | .. | 2·25 | 2·25 | |

Phosphor Cylinder Displacements. With ink cyl. 7, phos. cyl. 20 is known displaced up the margin from 87 to 131 mm. opposite rows 13 to 15.

Single pane cylinders. Halley press
Perforation Type R (S)

| Cyl. No. | Phos. No. | | | | | No dot |
|---|---|---|---|---|---|---|
| 13 | 39 | .. | .. | .. | .. | 95·00 |
| 14 | 39 | .. | .. | .. | .. | 1·90 |

ENSCHEDE
Perforation Type F (L)*

| 1 | 1 | .. | .. | .. | .. | 2·00 | 2·00 |
|---|---|---|---|---|---|---|---|

The dot was not engraved on the dot pane of the Enschedé printing, however the left-hand cylinder block has the left margin imperforate and the "dot" pane has this margin perforated through.


## 1979 (28 AUGUST). ONE NARROW BAND AT LEFT. FLUORESCENT COATED PAPER. PVAD GUM
50p. booklet pane UMFB10 (8p. at right)
U163 (=S.G.X880Ea)  Rosine    ..    ..    ..    ..    ..    ..    ..    60    60


## 1979 (28 AUGUST). ONE NARROW BAND AT RIGHT. FLUORESCENT COATED PAPER. PVAD GUM
50p. booklet pane UMFB9 (8p. at left)
U164 (=S.G.X880)  Rosine    ..    ..    ..    ..    ..    ..    ..    60    60

**CYLINDER VARIETIES**
Listed Flaws

U162g
Damaged foot to P
(Cyl. 14, R. 15/8)

U162f
Long irregular white scratch
extending from Queen's neck to
stamp below through back of crown
and dress.
(Cyl. 14, R.4/5 and 5/5)

U162i
Spot in band
(Vert. AL coil,
Cyl. 8, Roll 1)

No. U162h is a multipositive flaw occurring on the multi-value 10p. coil G5 in every fifth position, Roll 9 Cyl. R7. See illustration of No. U154e under the 7p. value.

The vertical AL coil and the 80p. booklet panes UFB9/10 were printed from Cylinder 8. Flaw U162i is also listed on this pane.

For illustration of the multipositive flaw U162j, see U153e under the 7p. value.

For further flaws on 8p. stamps in booklet panes, see under Nos. UMFB11 and UMFB13.

**Minor Constant Sheet Flaws**

Cyl.  3  20/5  Small dark flaw on top row of pearls in band of crown (Th. B4)
Cyl. 14  1/3  Mass of white dots on Queen's cheek and hair (Th. C/D 3–4)
        3/3  Pale mark above crown (Th. B6)
        12/2  White dots on Queen's cheek (Th. C/D 3–4)
        15/5  Pale patch on shoulder above dress (Th. F4)
        16/6  Blemish on forehead (Th. C3)

**COIL**

One centre phosphor band. Printed in continuous reels.

| Code No. | Issued | Number in roll | Face value | Paper/gum | Screen | Perf. Type |
|---|---|---|---|---|---|---|
| | | | Vertical Delivery | | | |
| AL | 14.11.79 | 500 | £40 | FCP/PVAD | 150 | R |

Cylinder Number used:

AL  FCP/PVAD  8/8.

Cylinder 8 was also used for the 8p. in booklet panes of ten UFB9/10.

**WITHDRAWN**  No. U161, 11.79; U162 and U162c, 30.4.82

# 8½p. Yellow-green (1975–77)

## 1975 (24 SEPTEMBER). TWO 9·5 mm. PHOSPHOR BANDS. FLUORESCENT COATED PAPER. PVAD GUM

| | | | | | | | | | |
|---|---|---|---|---|---|---|---|---|---|
| U166 | (1) | Light yellowish green (Cyl. 4) | .. | .. | .. | .. | .. | 35 | 20 |
| (=S.G.X881, Eb) | (2) | Yellowish green (Cyl. 6) | .. | .. | .. | .. | .. | 30 | 35 |
| | | a. Imperforate (pair) | .. | .. | .. | .. | .. | £750 | |
| | | b. Phosphor omitted | .. | .. | .. | .. | .. | 1·75 | |
| | | c. Retouch behind head | .. | .. | .. | .. | .. | 2·50 | |
| | | d. Scar on neck | .. | .. | .. | .. | .. | 2·00 | |
| | | e. Damaged loop to 8 | .. | .. | .. | .. | .. | 2·00 | |
| | | f. Line under value.. | .. | .. | .. | .. | .. | 2·00 | |
| | | g. Retouch left of nose | .. | .. | .. | .. | .. | 2·50 | |
| | | h. Cyl. No. in SON box (vertical pair) | .. | .. | .. | .. | 6·00 | |
| | | i. Deformed bottom loop to 8 | .. | .. | .. | .. | 2·00 | |
| | | j. Repaired bottom loop to 8 | .. | .. | .. | .. | 2·00 | |

**Cylinder Numbers (Blocks of Six)**

Perforation Type R

| Cyl. No. | Phos. No. | | | | | No dot | Dot |
|---|---|---|---|---|---|---|---|
| 4 | 17 | .. | .. | .. | .. | 2·50 | 3·00* |
| 4 | P21 | .. | .. | .. | .. | 2·50 | 3·00* |

Perforation Type RE

| | | | | | | | |
|---|---|---|---|---|---|---|---|
| 4 | P21 | .. | .. | .. | .. | 2·50** | 4·00* |
| 4 | P21 | +20 mm. (18) | .. | .. | | 55·00 | |
| 6 | 17 | .. | .. | .. | .. | 5·50 | 5·50 |
| 6 | P21 | .. | .. | .. | .. | 1·75 | 1·75 |
| 6 | P21 | −29 mm. (19/20) | .. | .. | | 10·00 | 10·00 |
| 6 | P21 | −24 mm. (19) | .. | .. | | 10·00 | 10·00 |
| 6 | P21 | −21 mm. (19) | .. | .. | | 10·00 | 10·00 |

** Same price as perforation type R with single extension holes in left margin.

## 1976 (24 MARCH). PHOSPHORISED (FLUORESCENT COATED) PAPER. PVAD GUM

| | | | | | | | | | |
|---|---|---|---|---|---|---|---|---|---|
| U167 (=S.G.X937) | | Yellowish green | .. | .. | .. | .. | .. | 30 | 55 |
| | | e. Damaged loop to 8 | .. | .. | .. | .. | .. | 2·50 | |
| | | f. Line under value.. | .. | .. | .. | .. | .. | 2·50 | |
| | | g. Retouch left of nose | .. | .. | .. | .. | .. | 3·00 | |

This was an experimental issue to test the efficacy of stamps containing a phosphor coating on the paper without the normally overprinted phosphor bands thus distinguishing this experiment from that of the 4½p. which had both (No. U134).

**Cylinder Numbers (Blocks of Six)**

Perforation Type RE

| Cyl. No. | | | | | No dot | Dot |
|---|---|---|---|---|---|---|
| 6 | .. | .. | .. | .. | 4·00 | 4·00 |

## 1977 (26 JANUARY). TWO 8 mm. PHOSPHOR BANDS. FLUORESCENT COATED PAPER. PVAD GUM

50p. booklet panes UMFB3/4

| | | | | | | | | | |
|---|---|---|---|---|---|---|---|---|---|
| U168 | | Yellowish green | .. | .. | .. | .. | .. | 35 | 35 |

**CYLINDER VARIETIES**
Listed Flaws

| U166c | U166d | U166/7e |
|---|---|---|
| Retouch behind head | Scar on neck | Damaged loop to 8 |
| (Cyl. 4 dot, R. 14/8) | (Cyl. 4 dot, R. 18/1) | (Cyl. 6 no dot, R. 2/1) |
| | (Later retouched) | |

No. U166/7e is a multipositive flaw which occurs to a lesser extent on Cyl. 4 but also on the vertical coil, Roll 1 and on booklet pane UFB3, R. 1/1, these being both from Cyl. 3.

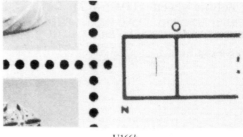

| | |
|---|---|
| U166/7f<br>Line under value<br>(Cyl. 6 dot, R. 3/9)<br>(Later retouched) | U166h<br>Cyl. No. 4 was wrongly engraved in the SON box<br>and partially removed leaving the clear vertical stroke<br>(Cyl. 4 dot, R. 14/10 and 15/10) |

U166/7g
Retouch left of nose
(Cyl. 6 dot, R. 4/1)

U166i
Deformed bottom loop
to 8 (Vert. coil, Cyl. 3 dot,
Roll 1, also sheet Cyl,
6 dot, R. 9/1)

U166j
Repaired bottom
loop to 8
(Horiz. coil, Cyl. R2
dot, Roll 5)

For further flaws on 8½p. stamps in booklet panes, see under Nos. UMFB3/4 and UFB3.

**Minor Constant Sheet Flaws**

Cyl. 4    15/2–14/3   Diagonal scratch from top of crown on 15/2 extending to base of bust on 14/3
          15/5–16/6   Diagonal scratch from back of neck on 15/5 to Queen's hair on 16/6
Cyl. 4.   11/4        Spot in Queen's neck (Th. E3–4)
          14/4        Crescent moon over crown (Th. A4)
          19/2        Screening dots omitted at right edge of design (Th. C6)
Cyl. 6    2/1         Disturbance in front of chin (Th. E2) and small white spot on shoulder (Th. F3–4)
                      (See also Nos. U166/7e)
          5/6         Small retouch at upper right corner (Th. A6)
          5/7         Pale blemish at top right (Th. A6)
          7/1         Dark horizontal scratch from behind crown to frame (Th. C5–6)
          7/2         Scratch on 7/1 extended to Queen's eye (Th. C1–2) and speck at upper right
                      (Th. B6)
          8/3         Large retouched area across back of Queen's shoulder into background (Th.
                      F4–E6)
          10/2        Two specks on dress (Th. G5)
          10/10       Retouch at back of crown (Th. B–C6)
          15/5        Dark horizontal scratch from back of hair (Th. D4–6)
          16/6        Broken diagonal scratch from hair to top left corner (Th. B3–A2)
          18/3        Dark specks in front of Queen's forehead (Th. C2)

**COILS**

Two phosphor bands. Printed in continuous reels

| Code No. | Issued | Number in roll | Face value | paper/gum | Screen | Perf. | Type |
|---|---|---|---|---|---|---|---|
| | | | Vertical delivery | | | | |
| TL | 28.1.76 | 500 | £42.50 | FCP/PVAD | 150 | | R |
| | | | Sideways delivery | | | | |
| WS | 13.10.76 | 500 | £42.50 | FCP/PVAD | 150 | | R |

Cylinder Numbers used:
          TL    FCP/PVAD    3/3.
          WS    FCP/PVAD    R2 (phos. R10)
    Cylinder 3 was also used for booklet panes of ten UFB3/4.

**WITHDRAWN**   No. U166, 10.81; No. U167, 3.78

# 9p. Orange and Black   (1971–74)

## 1971 (15 FEBRUARY).   TWO 9·5 mm. PHOSPHOR BANDS
### A. ORIGINAL COATED PAPER. PVA GUM

| U171 | Yellow-orange and black | .. | .. | .. | .. | .. | 60 | 60 |
|---|---|---|---|---|---|---|---|---|
| | *a.* Phosphor omitted | .. | .. | .. | .. | .. | 65·00 | |
| | *b.* Short tail to 9 | .. | .. | .. | .. | .. | 5·00 | |
| | *c.* Faint spots on neck | .. | .. | .. | .. | .. | 3·00 | |

**Cylinder Numbers (Blocks of Six)**
Perforation Type A

| Cyl. No. | Phos. No. | | | No dot | Dot | |
|---|---|---|---|---|---|---|
| 3A (black)–2B (orange) | 1 | −23 mm. (19) | | † | 10·00 | |
| 3A (black)–2B (orange) | — | .. | .. | 9·00 | 10·00 | Guillotined off on dot |

### B. FLUORESCENT COATED PAPER. PVA GUM (Late 1971)

| U172 | Yellow-orange and black | .. | .. | .. | .. | .. | 2·50 |
|---|---|---|---|---|---|---|---|
| | *a.* Phosphor omitted | .. | .. | .. | .. | .. | 65·00 |
| | *b.* One broad band | .. | .. | .. | .. | .. | 20·00 |
| | *c.* Short tail to 9 | .. | .. | .. | .. | .. | 6·00 |
| | *d.* Faint spots on neck | .. | .. | .. | .. | .. | 3·00 |

**Cylinder Numbers (Blocks of Six)**
Perforation Type A

| Cyl. No. | Phos. No. | | | No dot | Dot | |
|---|---|---|---|---|---|---|
| 3A (black)–3B (orange) | 1 | .. | .. | 16·00 | 35·00 | |
| 3A (black)–3B (orange) | — | .. | .. | 18·00 | 18·00 | |
| 3A (black)–3B (orange) | 1 | +20 mm. (18) | | 22·00 | 42·00 | |
| 4A (black)–4B (orange) | 1 | .. | .. | 22·00 | 50·00 | |
| 4A (black)–4B (orange) | — | .. | .. | † | 22·00 | Guillotined off on dot |

Phosphor Cylinder Displacement. With ink cyl. 3A, 3B, phos. cyl. 1 is known displaced up the margin 107 mm. opposite row 14. No dot blocks of six without a phosphor cylinder number are from the displacement but most dot blocks exist from phos. 1 with the number guillotined off.

### C. FLUORESCENT COATED PAPER. PVAD GUM (22.3.74)*

| U173 | (1) Yellow-orange and black | .. | .. | .. | .. | .. | 1·25 | 60 |
|---|---|---|---|---|---|---|---|---|
| (=S.G.X882) | (2) Pale yellow-orange and black (Cyl. 6B) | .. | .. | .. | .. | 60 | 30 |
| | *a.* Phosphor omitted (2) | .. | .. | .. | .. | .. | 80·00 | |
| | *b.* One broad band (1) | .. | .. | .. | .. | .. | 15·00 | |
| | *c.* One broad band (2) | .. | .. | .. | .. | .. | 3·00 | |
| | *d.* Left-hand band omitted (2) | .. | .. | .. | .. | 38·00 | |
| | *e.* Right-hand band omitted (2) | .. | .. | .. | .. | 38·00 | |
| | *f.* Short tail to 9 (1) | .. | .. | .. | .. | .. | 5·00 | |
| | *g.* Faint spots on neck | .. | .. | .. | .. | .. | 3·00 | |

*Known on cover with unstuck selvedge confirming the gum.

**Cylinder Numbers (Blocks of Six unless otherwise stated)**
Perforation Type A

| Cyl. Nos. | Phos. No. | | | | No dot | Dot | |
|---|---|---|---|---|---|---|---|
| 4A (black)–4B (orange) | 7 | .. | .. | .. | .. | 16·00 | 18·00 | |

Perforation Type R

| | | | | | No dot | Dot | |
|---|---|---|---|---|---|---|---|
| 8A (black)–6B (pale orange) | 17 | (inverted printing) | | .. | 16·00 | 14·00 | |
| 8A (black)–6B (pale orange) | 17 | .. | .. | .. | 6·50 | 6·50 | |
| 8A (black)–6B (pale orange) | 17 | +22 mm. (17) | .. | .. | 65·00 | 65·00 | Block of ten |
| 8A (black)–6B (pale orange) | 17 | +33 mm. (17)* | .. | .. | £160 | £160 | Block of ten |
| 8A (black)–6B (pale orange) | 17 | +39 mm. (17) | .. | .. | 60·00 | 60·00 | Block of ten |
| 8A (black)–6B (pale orange) | — | .. | .. | .. | 50·00 | 50·00 | |

* This occurs on the broad band variety.
Phosphor Cylinder Displacement. Phos. cyl. 17 is known displaced up the margin 122 mm. opposite row 13.

**CYLINDER VARIETIES**
Listed Flaws

Variety        Normal
U171*b*, U172*c*, U173*f*
(Cyls, 3A and 4A, R. 1/10)

Nos. U171*c*, U172*d* and U173*g* are a multipositive flaw occurring on Cyls. 3A and 4A no dot, R. 9/3, being a fainter state of the 1p. flaw, No. U55*g*.

**Minor Constant Sheet Flaws**
Black cyl. 3A no dot in combination with orange cyls. 2B or 3B no dot
   4/8 Vertical scratch down back of crown (Th. B–C5)
   10/1 Screening dots in top margin (Th. above A5) (Multipositive flaw as on 1. cyl. 3)
   11/7 Black dotted line diagonally through P
Black cyl. 3A dot in combination with orange cyls. 2B or 3B dot
   9/1 Blotch on Queen's jawline (Th. D2–3)
   9/2 Rectangular flaw on Queen's jaw (Th. D3)
Black cyl. 4A no dot in combination with orange cyl. 4B no dot
   10/1 Screening dots in top margin (Th. above A5) (Multipositive flaw as on 1p. cyl. 3)

**WITHDRAWN**   3.78

---

# 9p. Violet   (1976–78)

**1976 (25 FEBRUARY).   COLOUR CHANGED. TWO 9·5 mm. PHOSPHOR BANDS. FLUORESCENT COATED PAPER. PVAD GUM**

A. Phosphor Bands over Varnish Coating

U174                Deep violet  ..      ..      ..      ..      ..      ..      ..    60    60

The varnish was applied because the coating and printing were stripping off during the course of production of the initial printing. The effect of the varnish, which cannot easily be detected without the use of a lamp, is to reduce greatly the fluorescent paper reaction under ultraviolet light.

The phosphor bands were applied over the varnish at a separate operation. However No. U174 also exists with the phosphor bands under the varnish. In all probability the bands had been applied in the normal course of printing before the application of the varnish and then some of the varnished sheets failed to receive the phosphor bands on top. It appears that these missing phosphors were detected as the only copies known are singles which were dispensed in the Scottish experimental machine packs. They are extremely difficult to distinguish with certainty so we do not list them. The normal varnished stamps with phosphor bands on top give a very short afterglow under the lamp and those without phosphor on top give almost none.

**Cylinder Numbers (Blocks of Six)**
Perforation Type RE

| Cyl. No. | Phos. No. | | | | | | No dot | Dot |
|---|---|---|---|---|---|---|---|---|
| 12 | 17 | .. | .. | .. | .. | .. | 5·00 | 5·00 |

## B. Without Varnish Coating

| | | | | | | | | | |
|---|---|---|---|---|---|---|---|---|---|
| U175 (=S.G.X883) | Deep violet | .. | .. | .. | .. | .. | .. | 45 | 25 |
| | a. Imperforate (pair) | | .. | .. | .. | .. | .. | £175 | |
| | b. Phosphor omitted | | .. | .. | .. | .. | .. | 1·50 | |
| | c. Right-hand band omitted | | | .. | .. | .. | .. | 18·00 | |
| | ca. Left-hand band omitted | | | .. | .. | .. | .. | 20·00 | |
| | d. Additional phosphor band | | | .. | .. | .. | .. | 20·00 | |
| | e. With "all-over" phosphor | | | .. | .. | .. | .. | 15·00 | |
| | f. Spot in band of crown | | .. | .. | .. | .. | .. | 2·00 | |
| | g. Retouch on collar | | .. | .. | .. | .. | .. | 2·00 | |
| | h. Hole right of collar | | .. | .. | .. | .. | .. | 4·00 | |
| | ha. State 2. Dark patch and white lines | | | .. | .. | .. | .. | 5·00 | |
| | hb. State 3. White patch and white lines | | | .. | .. | .. | .. | 3·50 | |
| | i. Large blemish | | .. | .. | .. | .. | .. | 3·00 | |
| | j. Vertical scratch | .. | .. | .. | .. | (vert. pair) | | 4·00 | |
| | k. Long wavy scratch | | .. | .. | .. | .. | .. | 7·00 | |
| | l. White blob on 9 | .. | .. | .. | .. | .. | .. | 2·00 | |
| | m. Dark scratch on crown | | .. | .. | .. | .. | .. | 2·50 | |
| | n. Short bands at top and bottom (15.11.78)* | | | .. | .. | .. | .. | 45 | 45 |

No. U175c came from a batch of sheets from Cyl. 16 no dot on which the phosphor was omitted except for the first band, covering the left selvedge and the first vertical row of stamps, leaving the right band missing.

No. U175ca came from sheets from Cyl. 27 dot on which the phosphor was omitted from the first vertical row providing further copies of No. U175b and No U175ca from the second vertical row.

The extra phosphor band on No. U175d occurs in various positions between the normal bands and is usually about 7 mm. wide. It came from 90p. booklet panes, usually affecting two of the stamps in the pane, and is due to faulty action of the phosphor doctor blade.

No. U175e comes from sheets which had thick "all-over" phosphor in the first vertical row only. This came from Cylinder 16 no dot and should not be confused with stamps with additional phosphor lines which are quite common and come from Cylinder 12. (*Price* £3.)

*No. U175n (short phosphor bands) comes from the £1·60 1978 Christmas Booklet Pane UMFB8. The phosphor covers the printed portion of the design only so as not to overlap on the 7p. stamps.

**Shades.** There is a wide range of shades in this issue, ranging from violet-blue to blackish violet, but as there are so many intermediate shades it is not practical to list them.

## Cylinder Numbers (Blocks of Six unless otherwise stated)

Perforation Type RE

| Cyl. No. | Phos. No. | | | | | No dot | Dot | |
|---|---|---|---|---|---|---|---|---|
| 11 | P21 | .. | .. | .. | .. | 2·75 | 2·75 | |
| 11 | — | .. | .. | .. | .. | 14·00 | 14·00 | |
| 11 | 30 | .. | .. | .. | .. | £160 | £160 | |
| 11 | 30 | −48 mm. (20) | .. | | .. | £225 | £225 | |
| 12 | 17 | .. | .. | .. | .. | 6·50 | 5·00 | |
| 12 | 17 | −22 mm. (19) | .. | | .. | 50·00 | 75·00 | |
| 12 | 17 | +50 mm. (16) | .. | | .. | 95·00 | £130 | Block of ten |
| 16 | P21 | .. | .. | .. | .. | 2·50 | 2·75 | |
| 16 | P21 | −27 mm. (19/20) | | .. | .. | 5·50 | 5·50 | |
| 16 | 30 | .. | .. | .. | .. | 2·75 | 2·75 | |
| 27 | P21 | .. | .. | .. | .. | 2·75 | 2·75 | |
| 27 | P21 | −27 mm. (19/20) | | .. | .. | 60·00 | 60·00 | |
| 29 | P21 | .. | .. | .. | .. | 16·00 | 16·00 | |
| 29 | 30 | .. | .. | .. | .. | 2·50 | 2·50 | |

Phosphor Cylinder Displacement. With ink cyl. 11, phos. cyl. P21 is known displaced up the margin 190 mm. opposite row 14.

Perforation Type A

| | | | | | | | | |
|---|---|---|---|---|---|---|---|---|
| 11 | 7 | .. | .. | .. | .. | 2·50 | 2·50 | |
| 11 | 7 | −27 mm. (19/20) | | .. | .. | — | £100 | |
| 11 | 7 | −55 mm. (bot. mar.) | | .. | .. | 60·00 | 60·00 | |
| 16 | 7 | .. | .. | .. | .. | 2·50 | 2·75 | |
| 16 | 7 | −52 mm. (20) | .. | | .. | 18·00 | 12·00 | |
| 16 | — | .. | .. | .. | .. | 70·00 | 70·00 | |

Phosphor Cylinder Displacement. With ink cyl. 16, phos. cyl. 7 is known displaced up the margin 72 mm. opposite row 15.

In both panes the figures of Cyl. 11 were engraved with three down strokes and later these were increased to six in combination with Phos. Cyl. P21 and 30.

The dot was not at first engraved on the dot pane of Cyl. 16 with phosphor Cyls. 7 and P21. These can be distinguished from the no dot panes as the ink Cyl. 16 is in the normal size on all printings of the dot pane, whereas the no dot pane has the number hand-engraved in larger figures.

The dot was added on later printings with phosphor Cyl. P21, and with phosphor Cyl. 30 the dot pane always has the dot engraved. The −52 mm. displacement of phosphor Cyl. 7 has only been seen with the dot showing.

The dot pane of Cyl. 27 with phosphor Cyl. P21 also had the dot missing in the first printing but this was very quickly rectified. It can be distinguished from the no dot cylinder block in that the left margin is narrow instead of wide and in the dot pane the 27 is thick instead of being thin and spidery.

### 1977 (13 JUNE).   TWO 8 mm. PHOSPHOR BANDS. FLUORESCENT COATED PAPER. PVAD GUM.

50p. booklet panes UMFB5/6 (13.6.77)

| | | | | | | | | | |
|---|---|---|---|---|---|---|---|---|---|
| U176 | Deep violet | .. | .. | .. | .. | .. | .. | 45 | 45 |

**CYLINDER VARIETIES**
**Listed Flaws**

Multipositive flaw

No. U175f comes from the horizontal DS coil, Roll No. 5. For illustration see No. U53d under the ½p. value.

U175g
Retouch on collar
(Cyl. 16 no dot, R. 15/10)

U175h
Hole right of collar
(Cyl. 16 no dot, R. 19/9)

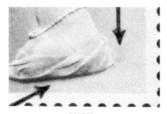

U175ha
Retouched as dark patch
and a series of white
vertical lines below bust

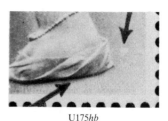

U175hb
Retouched as white patch
and white lines below
bust remain

The original state has been seen with Perf. Type A and the other states with Perf. Type RE.

U175*i*
Large blemish in collar
(Cyl. 27 no dot. R. 2/8)

U175*k*
Long wavy scratch across stamp
Exists from later printing
(Cyl. 27 no dot, R. 19/7)

U175*j*
(Cyl. 27 no dot, R. 15/8 and R. 16/8)

U175*l*
White blob on 9
(Vert. YL coil, Roll 4)

U175*m*
Dark scratch in back of crown
(Vert. YL coil, Roll 6)

Both the vertical YL coils and the 90p. booklet panes were printed from Cylinder 24. Flaws U175*i/j* are also listed on these panes.

For further flaws on 9p. stamps in booklet panes, see under Nos. UFB7/8.

**Minor Constant Sheet Flaws**

Cyl. 11.   3/4 Slight retouch left of dress (Th. G2)
           6/1 Small retouch left of crown (Th. A3)
           7/1 Blemish left of dress (Th. F2–F3)
Cyl. 16   15/8 Small background retouch behind collar (Th. F5)
          20/5 Small white patch under dress at right (Th. G5–G6)
          20/8 Small pale blemish right of 9
Cyl. 16.   3/4 Small retouch below value (Th. G2)
          14/2 Blue dot under necklace (Th. F3)
          15/3 Small retouch in front of dress, right of value (Th. G3)
          20/8 Small retouch under P (Th. F2–G2)
Cyl. 27  20/9 Blemish on tail of 9

**COILS**

Printed in continuous reels

| Code No. | Issued | Number in roll | Face Value | Paper/gum | Screen | Perf. Type |
|---|---|---|---|---|---|---|
| | | Vertical delivery | | | | |
| YL | 13.6.77 | 500 | £45 | FCP/PVAD | 150 | R |
| | | Sideways delivery | | | | |
| DS | 16.11.77 | 500 | £45 | FCP/PVAD | 150 | R |

Cylinder Numbers used:

| YL | FCP/PVAD | 24/24. |
|---|---|---|
| DS | FCP/PVAD | R1 |

Cylinder 24 was also used for the 9p. in booklet panes of ten UFB7/8.

**WITHDRAWN** 12.80

# 9½p. Purple   (1976)

**1976 (25 FEBRUARY).   TWO 9·5 mm. PHOSPHOR BANDS.
FLUORESCENT COATED PAPER. PVAD GUM**

U181 (=S.G.X884)     Purple   ..     ..     ..     ..     ..     ..     ..   45     30
              *a.* Phosphor omitted     ..     ..     ..     ..   .. 15·00
              *b.* Left-hand band omitted..     ..     ..     .. 22·00
              *c.* Right-hand band omitted     ..     ..     .. 20·00
              *d.* White patch in corner   ..     ..     ..     ..   2·50
              *e.* Retouch behind shoulder     ..     ..     ..   2·50

   Minor shades exist, but a few examples were printed in very bright purple due to the use of the wrong ink solvent. Examples should only be purchased with a certificate of genuineness. *Price* £2500 *mint.*
   Nos. U181*b/c* came from sheets on which the phosphor bands were partly omitted due to poor inking.

**Cylinder Numbers (Blocks of Six unless otherwise stated)**
Perforation Type RE

| Cyl. No. | Phos. No. | | | | No dot | Dot | |
|---|---|---|---|---|---|---|---|
| 13 | 17 | .. | .. | .. | 2·75 | 2·75 | |
| 13 | P21 | .. | .. | .. | 5·00 | 4·50 | |
| 13 | P21 | +31 mm. (17) .. | | .. | 80·00 | 80·00 | Block of ten |
| 13 | P21 | +37 mm. (17) .. | | | 80·00 | 80·00 | Block of ten |
| 13 | P21 | +54 mm. (16) .. | | | 80·00 | 80·00 | Block of ten |
| 13 | — | .. | .. | .. | 5·50 | 8·50 | |
| 13 | 30 | .. | .. | .. | 3·00 | 3·00 | |

Phosphor Cylinder Displacement. Phos. cyl. P21 is known displaced up the margin from 68 to 82 mm. opposite row 15.

**CYLINDER VARIETIES**
**Listed Flaws**

U181*d*
White patch in corner
(Cyl. 13 dot, R. 20/4)

U181*e*
Retouch and scratch behind shoulder
(Cyl. 13 dot, R. 11/4)

**Minor Constant Sheet Flaws**
Cyl. 13   15/7 Tail of 9 partly screened
Cyl. 13.   2/8 Retouch in shoulder (Th. F/G–3/4)

**WITHDRAWN**   30.4.82

# 10p. Orange-Brown and Chestnut   (1971–73)

## 1971 (11 AUGUST).   TWO 9·5 mm. PHOSPHOR BANDS
**A. FLUORESCENT COATED PAPER. PVA GUM**

| U182 (=S.G.X885) | Orange-brown and chestnut | .. | .. | .. | .. | 40 | 10 |
|---|---|---|---|---|---|---|---|
| | *a.* Orange-brown omitted .. | .. | .. | .. | .. | £150 | |
| | *b.* Phosphor omitted | .. | .. | .. | .. | 7·50 | |
| | *c.* Imperf. between stamp and top margin | | .. | .. | £450 | | |

**Cylinder Numbers (Blocks of Six)**
Perforation Type A

| Cyl. Nos. | Phos. No. | | | No dot | Dot |
|---|---|---|---|---|---|
| 3A (chestnut)–3B (orange-brown) | 1 | .. | .. | 4·00 | 12·00 |
| 3A (chestnut)–3B (orange-brown) | —* | .. | .. | † | 4·00 |
| 5A (chestnut)–4B (orange-brown) | 1 | .. | .. | 12·00 | £500 |
| 5A (chestnut)–4B (orange-brown) | —* | .. | .. | † | 12·00 |

*Phosphor cylinder 1 was usually guillotined off from the dot selvedge and would appear in the right-hand selvedge of the no dot panes.

**B. FLUORESCENT COATED PAPER. PVAD GUM** (12.11.73)*

U183         Orange-brown and chestnut   ..   ..   ..   ..   70
            *a.* Imperforate (horiz. pair)   ..   ..   ..   ..   £2000
*Known on cover with unstuck selvedge confirming the gum.

**Cylinder Numbers (Blocks of Six)**

Perforation Type A

| Cyl. Nos. | Phos. No. | | | | No dot | Dot |
|---|---|---|---|---|---|---|
| 5A (chestnut)–4B (orange-brown)  1 | | .. | .. | .. | 10·00 | £200 |
| 5A (chestnut)–4B (orange-brown) —* | | .. | .. | .. | † | 10·00 |

Perforation Type R

| | | | | | No dot | Dot |
|---|---|---|---|---|---|---|
| 8A (chestnut)–6B (orange-brown)  17 | −25 mm. (19) | | .. | | 9·00 | 9·00 |
| 8A (chestnut)–6B (orange-brown) P21* | (inverted printing) | | .. | | £175 | £200 |
| 8A (chestnut)–6B (orange-brown) P21 | | .. | .. | | 2·50 | 2·50 |

*Owing to inverted printing of the phosphor cylinder number P21 appears inverted synchronised in the right-hand corner blocks.

**WITHDRAWN**   9.78

# 10p. Orange-brown    (1976–85)

**Two Value Types**

|   |    |
|---|----|
| I | II |

Type I.  Broad O
Type II. Narrow O and thinned at
        top and bottom. £4
        Christian Heritage Booklet

**1976 (25 FEBRUARY).   COLOUR CHANGED. TWO 9·5 mm. PHOSPHOR BANDS. TYPE I. FLUORESCENT COATED PAPER. PVAD GUM**

U184 (=S.G.X886)    Orange-brown   ..   ..   ..   ..   ..   ..   40    20
            *a.* Imperforate (pair)   ..   ..   ..   ..   ..   £250
            *b.* One broad band ..   ..   ..   ..   ..   6·00
            *c.* Phosphor omitted   ..   ..   ..   ..   1·00
            *d.* Short bands at top and bottom (14.11.79)*   ..   ..   50    50
            *e.* Dark shoulder scratch   ..   ..   ..   ..   3·00
        *ea.* Shoulder scratch (retouched state)   ..   ..   3·00
            *f.* Dark mark in hair (Chambon ptg.)   ..   ..   3·00
            *g.* Imperf. between stamp and top margin   ..   ..   £300

*No. U184*d* (short phosphor bands) comes from the £1·80 1979 Christmas Booklet Pane UMFB13. The phosphor covering the printed portion of the design only so as not to overlap on to the 8p. stamp.

**Cylinder Numbers**

Double pane cylinders. Jumelle press.

Perforation Type RE (Block of 6)

| Cyl. No. | Phos. No. | | | | | No dot | Dot |
|---|---|---|---|---|---|---|---|
| 3 | 17 | .. | .. | .. | .. | 3·50 | 3·50 |
| 3 | P21 | .. | .. | .. | .. | 2·10 | 2·10 |
| 3 | 30 | .. | .. | .. | .. | 2·50 | 2·50 |

Perforation Type A (Block of 6)

| | | | | | | | |
|---|---|---|---|---|---|---|---|
| 3 | 7 | .. | .. | .. | .. | 2·75 | 2·75 |

Single pane cylinders. Chambon press (no dot panes only)

| | | | | | | No dot | |
|---|---|---|---|---|---|---|---|
| | | | | | | Block of 6 | Block of 8 |
| 7 | 34 | .. | .. | .. | .. | 4·25 | 18·00 |
| 7 | P36 | .. | .. | .. | .. | 2·10 | 4·00 |
| 9 | 34 | .. | .. | .. | .. | 3·25 | 6·50 |
| 9 | P36 | .. | .. | .. | .. | 2·10 | 3·75 |

**Chambon Printing.** Sheets from cylinders 7 and 9 no dot were each issued in two identical panes separated by a horizontal gutter margin. Therefore cylinder blocks from the upper pane can be found as blocks of 8 including a gutter margin. For note on comb Perf. Type RE see Appendix I.

### 1979 (20 AUGUST). TWO 9·5 mm. PHOSPHOR BANDS. TYPE I. PHOSPHORISED (FLUORESCENT COATED) PAPER. PVAD GUM

| U185 | Orange-brown | .. | .. | .. | .. | .. | .. | 50 | 50 |
|---|---|---|---|---|---|---|---|---|---|
| | b. Dark mark in hair | | .. | .. | .. | .. | .. | 3·00 | |

There is a wide range of shades in this issue, but as there are so many intermediate shades it is not possible to list them.

Copies of No. U185 exist without phosphor bands and are therefore similar to No. U188.

**Cylinder Numbers**

Perforation Type RE (no dot panes only)

| | | | | | | No dot | |
|---|---|---|---|---|---|---|---|
| Cyl. No. | Phos. No. | | | | | Block of 6 | Block of 8 |
| 7 | P33 | .. | .. | .. | .. | 9·00 | 18·00 |
| 7 | P34 | .. | .. | .. | .. | 6·00 | 12·00 |
| 8 | P33 | .. | .. | .. | .. | 15·00 | 30·00 |
| 8 | 34 | .. | .. | .. | .. | 40·00 | 70·00 |
| 8 | P36 | .. | .. | .. | .. | 15·00 | 30·00 |
| 9 | 34 | .. | .. | .. | .. | 6·00 | 14·00 |

**Chambon Printing.** The note describing the sheet format below No. U184 also applies here.

### 1979 (28 AUGUST). TWO 8 mm. PHOSPHOR BANDS. TYPE I. FLUORESCENT COATED PAPER. PVAD GUM

50p. booklet pane UMFB9/10

| U186 | Orange-brown | .. | .. | .. | .. | .. | 45 | 45 |
|---|---|---|---|---|---|---|---|---|

In addition to the narrow bands this issue can be distinguished by the low placing of the value which is level with the Queen's dress.

### 1979 (3 OCTOBER). "ALL OVER" PHOSPHOR (FLUORESCENT COATED) PAPER. TYPE I. PVAD GUM

| U187 (=S.G.X887) | Orange-brown | .. | .. | .. | .. | .. | 30 | 45 |
|---|---|---|---|---|---|---|---|---|
| | b. Shoulder scratch (retouched state) | .. | .. | .. | 2·50 | | | |

**Cylinder Numbers (Blocks of Six)**

Perforation Type RE

| Cyl. No. | Phos. No. | | | | | No dot | Dot |
|---|---|---|---|---|---|---|---|
| 3 | —* | .. | .. | .. | .. | 2·50 | 2·50 |

*The phosphor cylinder employed was P37 and this number is sometimes found in the right-hand margin of the dot panes. The cylinder was inverted and unsynchronised and not all sheets show a phosphor cylinder number owing to the greater diameter on the phosphor cylinder in relation to the ink cylinder. Marginal block of 6 showing P37 inverted *price* £5.

## 1979 (NOVEMBER).    PHOSPHORISED PAPER. TYPE I. PVAD GUM
### A. FLUORESCENT COATED PAPER

| | | | | | | | | |
|---|---|---|---|---|---|---|---|---|
| U188 | Orange-brown | .. | .. | .. | .. | .. | .. | 30 | 30 |
| | b. Dark shoulder scratch | .. | .. | .. | .. | .. | 2·50 | |

For this stamp printed with one centre phosphor band see No. U190b. The Philatelic Bureau gave the date of issue of U188 as 14 December 1983. It is known used on 19 November 1979 from Kingston upon Thames, Surrey.

**Cylinder Numbers (Blocks of Six)**
Perforation Type RE

| Cyl. No | | | | | | No dot | Dot |
|---|---|---|---|---|---|---|---|
| 2 | .. | .. | .. | .. | .. | 2·50 | 2·50 |
| 15 | .. | .. | .. | .. | .. | 2·50 | 2·50 |

### B. ADVANCED COATED PAPER (16.7.85)

| | | | | | | | | |
|---|---|---|---|---|---|---|---|---|
| U189 (=S.G.X938) | Orange-brown | .. | .. | .. | .. | .. | .. | 15 | 20 |

**Cylinder Numbers (Blocks of Six)**
Perforation Type RE

| Cyl. No. | | | | | | No dot | Dot |
|---|---|---|---|---|---|---|---|
| 15 | .. | .. | .. | .. | .. | 2·25 | 2·25 |
| 18 | .. | .. | .. | .. | .. | 2·00 | 2·00 |

## 1980 (4 FEBRUARY).    CHANGE TO ONE 4 mm. CENTRE BAND.
## TYPE I. FLUORESCENT COATED PAPER. PVAD GUM

| | | | | | | | | |
|---|---|---|---|---|---|---|---|---|
| U190 (=S.G.X888) | Orange-brown | .. | .. | .. | .. | .. | 30 | 20 |
| | a. Imperforate (pair) | .. | .. | .. | .. | £225 | |
| | b. Error. Phosphorised paper | .. | .. | .. | 80 | |
| | c. One short band top and bottom (12.11.80)* .. | .. | 40 | 40 |
| | d. Dark shoulder scratch | .. | .. | .. | .. | 2·25 | |
| | e. Retouch in dress .. | .. | .. | .. | 2·00 | |
| | f. Large retouch below chin | .. | .. | .. | 2·50 | |
| | g. Phosphor printed on both sides | .. | .. | 75·00 | |

*No. U190c (short phosphor band) comes from the £2·20 1980 Christmas Booklet Pane UMFB18. The phosphor covers the printed portion of the stamp only so as not to overlap on the 12p. stamps.

**Cylinder Numbers (Blocks of Six unless otherwise stated)**
Perforation Type RE

| Cyl. No. | Phos. No. | | | | | No dot | Dot | |
|---|---|---|---|---|---|---|---|---|
| 2 | 20 | .. | .. | .. | .. | 2·10 | 2·10 | |
| 2 | 20 | −20 mm. (19) .. | .. | 5·50 | 5·50 | |
| 2 | 20 | −30 mm. (20) .. | .. | 5·00 | 5·00 | |
| 2 | 20 | −35 mm. (20) .. | .. | 6·50 | 6·50 | |
| 2 | 20 | Phosphorised paper | .. | 40·00 | 45·00 | |
| 3 | 20 | .. | .. | .. | £190 | £190 | |
| 3 | 20 | +35 mm. (17) .. | .. | £400 | £400 | Block of ten |

## 1980 (4 FEBRUARY).    ONE NARROW BAND AT LEFT. TYPE I.
## FLUORESCENT COATED PAPER. PVAD GUM

50p. booklet panes UMFB15 and 17 (4.2.80) and UWB8 (16.4.80)

| | | | | | | | | |
|---|---|---|---|---|---|---|---|---|
| U191 (=S.G.X889Ea) | Orange-brown | .. | .. | .. | .. | .. | 60 | 60 |
| | b. Phosphor printed on both sides | .. | .. | .. | |
| | c. One 8 mm. broad band .. | .. | .. | .. | 6·00 | |

**1980 (4 FEBRUARY).   ONE NARROW BAND AT RIGHT. TYPE I.
FLUORESCENT COATED PAPER. PVAD GUM**

50p. booklet panes UMFB14 and 16

U192 (=S.G.X889)    Orange-brown    ..    ..    ..    ..    ..    ..    60    60

**1984 (4 SEPTEMBER).   TWO PHOSPHOR BANDS. TYPE II.
FLUORESCENT COATED PAPER. PVAD GUM**

£4 Christian Heritage *se-tenant* booklet pane only

U193 (=S.G.X886b)    Orange-brown    ..    ..    ..    ..    ..    ..    3·00    3·00
                               *b.* Phosphor omitted    ..    ..    ..    ..    ..    £1100

**CYLINDER VARIETIES**
**Listed Flaws**

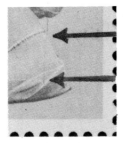

U184*e*, *ea*, U187*b*,
U188*b*, U190*d*
Vertical scratch through shoulder
(Cyls. 2 and 3 dot, R. 20/8)
(The line is faint on Cyl. 2 dot
and was later erased on Cyl. 3 dot,
described as the retouched state)

U183*f*, U185*b*
Dark mark in hair
(Cyl. 9, pane position R. 1/4)
Later retouched on
No. U185

U185*e*
Retouch below fold of dress
(Cyl. 2 no dot, R. 15/2)

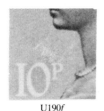

Retouched background
below chin
(Cyl. 2 no dot. R. 17/4)

U190*f*

For **further** flaws on 10p. stamps in booklet panes, see under Nos. UMFB13, UMFB15 and
UFB11/4.

**Minor Constant Sheet Flaws**

Cyl. 2    3/1   Line at bottom right (Th. G6–H6)
            3/3   Retouch in front of Queen's nose (Th. C1–D1)
            4/1   Retouch above 0 of value (Th. E2)
            4/2   Retouch in background at bottom right (Th. G6)
            7/8   Dark spot on shoulder (Th. F4)
            15/3  Sliced top to P
            17/3  Pale spot on neck (Th. E4)

Cyl. 2.    2/6  Vertical hairline in front of Queen's neck (Th. E3–F3)
          12/6  Pale blemish above value (Th. E1)
          18/6  Diagonal line behind Queen's hair (Th. D6)
          18/7  Continuation of the line from 18/6 (Th. C1–B2)
          20/10  Hairline in background to the left of Queen's nose (Th. B2–C1)
  In Cyl. 8 the upper and lower panes are identical and we therefore give the position in the pane.
Cyl. 8    1/5  Pale spot on neck (Th. E4)
          6/2  White spot at lower right in 0 (Th. F2)
          7/5  Dark spot below top margin to left of crown (Th. A3)
          10/2  White speck in hair above necklace (Th. D5)

## COILS

"All Over" phosphor (fluorescent coated) paper. Printed in continuous reels.

| Code No. | Issued | Number in roll | Face Value | Gum | Screen | Perf. Type |
|----------|--------|----------------|------------|-----|--------|------------|
|          |        |                | Vertical delivery | | | |
| BL       | 14.11.79 | 500 | £50 | PVAD | 150 | R |

Cylinder Number used:
  BL "All over" phosphor/PVAD   5/5.
One centre phosphor band. Printed in continuous reels.

| Code No. | Issued | Number in roll | Face Value | Paper/gum | Screen | Perf. Type |
|----------|--------|----------------|------------|-----------|--------|------------|
|          |        |                | Vertical delivery | | | |
| CL       | 11.6.80 | 500 | £50 | FCP/PVAD | 150 | R |

Cylinder Number used:
  CL    FCP/PVA    5/5.
Cylinder No. 5 was also used for the 10p. in UFB11/14.

**WITHDRAWN**    Nos. U184/5, 9.79; No. U187, 9.80; No. U188, 29.2.80 but put on sale again on 14.12.83 at the Philatelic Bureau and withdrawn 31.10.86. It was reissued in May 88 from cyl. no. 18; No. U190, 14.12.84

# 10p. Dull Orange (1990)

## 1990 (4 SEPTEMBER). COLOUR CHANGED. PHOSPHORISED (ADVANCED COATED) PAPER. PVAD GUM

U194 (=S.G.X939)    Dull orange    ..      ..      ..      ..      ..      ..      ..      15      15

**Cylinder Numbers (Blocks of Six)**

Perforation Type RE

| Cyl. No. | | | | | No dot | Dot |
|----------|--|--|--|--|--------|-----|
| 21  ..   | .. | .. | .. | .. | 1·25 | 1·25 |

# 10½p. Yellow    (1976)

## 1976 (25 FEBRUARY).    TWO 9·5 mm. PHOSPHOR BANDS. FLUORESCENT COATED PAPER. PVAD GUM

| | | | | | | | | | |
|---|---|---|---|---|---|---|---|---|---|
| U196 (=S.G.X890) | Yellow | .. | .. | .. | .. | .. | .. | .. | 40 | 30 |
| | a. With "all-over" phosphor | | .. | .. | .. | .. | 7·00 | |

The "all-over" phosphor was applied in error over the normal two phosphor bands.

**Cylinder Numbers (Blocks of Six)**
Perforation Type RE

| Cyl. No. | Phos. No. | | | | | No dot | Dot |
|---|---|---|---|---|---|---|---|
| 1 | 17 | .. | .. | .. | .. | 2·75 | 2·75 |
| 1 | P21 | .. | .. | .. | .. | 3·25 | 3·25 |

**CYLINDER VARIETIES**
**Minor Constant Sheet Flaws**
For list see under 10½p. deep dull blue as the same Cylinder 1 was used.

**WITHDRAWN**    12.78

# 10½p. Deep Dull Blue    (1978)

## 1978 (26 APRIL).    COLOUR CHANGED. TWO 9·5 mm. PHOSPHOR BANDS. FLUORESCENT COATED PAPER. PVAD GUM

| | | | | | | | | |
|---|---|---|---|---|---|---|---|---|
| U197 (=S.G.X891) | Deep dull blue | .. | .. | .. | .. | .. | .. | 60 | 45 |

First day covers posted at Exeter were inadvertently postmarked 25 April.

**Cylinder Numbers (Blocks of Six)**
Perforation Type RE

| Cyl. No. | Phos. No. | | | | | Not dot | Dot |
|---|---|---|---|---|---|---|---|
| 1 | 30 | .. | .. | .. | .. | 3·75 | 3·75 |

**CYLINDER VARIETIES**
**Minor Constant Sheet Flaws**
The flaws are less prominent on the yellow colour No. U196, and those with an asterisk against them are not apparent on that colour.

Cyl. 1
- 1/2 White dot over small 1
- 2/5 Pale blemish above o of value
- 2/7 White spot on Queen's neck (Th. E4)
- 3/8 Hairline from Queen's forehead to left margin (Th. B1–B2)*
- 4/1 Dark dot under Queen's chin (Th. E3)
- 4/8 Retouch under value
- 6/2 White spot in band of crown (Th. B3)
- 8/4 Circle in background in front of Queen's forehead (Th. B1)*
- 10/9 Dark speck behind Queen's hair (Th. D6)*
- 17/7 Curved white scratch in lower right corner (Th. G6–H6)*
- 19/7 Pale blemish in front of Queen's chin (Th. D2)*
- 20/1 White spot on Queen's chin (Th. D2)*

Cyl. 1.
- 1/8 Pale area in top right corner (Th. A6) and scratches on forehead and eye (Th. B–C and 2–3 intersection)
- 3/8 Pale areas and damage to Queen's forehead and hair (Th. B3–C3)
- 10/2 Small nick in bottom frame line (Th. H5)
- 18/2 White speck in band (Th. B4)*
- 18/9 White scratch in Queen's hair (Th. B3–C3) and in band of crown (Th. B4)

**WITHDRAWN**    4.81

**109**

# 11p. Brown-red   (1976–80)

## 1976 (25 FEBRUARY).   TWO 9·5 mm. PHOSPHOR BANDS. FLUORESCENT COATED PAPER. PVAD GUM

| U198 (=S.G.X892) | Brown-red .. | | | | | 60 | 25 |
|---|---|---|---|---|---|---|---|
| | a. Imperforate (pair) | | | | .. £1500 | | |
| | b. Phosphor omitted | | | | .. 2·25 | | |
| | c. Dark scratch at bottom left into margin | | | .. 3·00 | | | |
| | d. Scratch under bust and over crown .. | (vert. pair) | 5·00 | | | | |

**Cylinder Numbers (Blocks of Six)**

Perforation Type RE

| Cyl. No. | Phos. No. | | | | No dot | Dot |
|---|---|---|---|---|---|---|
| 4 | 17 | .. | .. | .. | 3·00 | 3·00 |
| 4 | 30 | .. | .. | .. | 3·50 | 3·50 |
| 4 | 30 | −25 mm. (19) .. | .. | £120 | £120 | |
| 4 | 30 | −31 mm. (20) .. | .. | — | † | |
| 4 | 30 | −57 mm. (bot. mar.) .. | £120 | £120 | | |

## 1980 (27 AUGUST).   PHOSPHORISED (FLUORESCENT COATED) PAPER. PVAD GUM

| U199 (=S.G.X840) | Brown-red .. | | | | | 60 | 75 |
|---|---|---|---|---|---|---|---|
| | a. Scratch under bust and over crown .. | (vert. pair) | 6·00 | | | | |

**Cylinder Numbers (Blocks of Six)**

Perforation Type RE

| Cyl. No. | | | | | No dot | Dot |
|---|---|---|---|---|---|---|
| 4 | .. | .. | .. | .. | 3·75 | 3·75 |

## CYLINDER VARIETIES

**Listed Flaws**

Multipositive Flaw

No. U198c is a multipositive flaw which occurs on the 20p., No. U259e (Cyl. 4 no dot, R. 14/9). No. U259c was retouched on the 11p.

Hairline scratch below bust becoming stronger and extending to cross of crown on stamp below (Cyl. 4 dot, R. 19/9 and 20/9)

U198d, U199a

**Minor Constant Sheet Flaws**

Cyl. 4   6/2  Pale spot in dress (Th. G3)
          6/5  White dot on P (Th. F2)
          9/10 Dark spot under bust (Th. G4)
          10/7 Nick in second 1 (Th. F2)
          18/4 Retouch below chin (Th. E3)

All the above were seen on the phosphorised paper.

**WITHDRAWN**  No. U198, 1.81; No. U199, 2.81

# 11½p. Ochre-brown   (1979)

**1979 (15 AUGUST).   PHOSPHORISED (FLUORESCENT COATED) PAPER. PVAD GUM**

U200 (=S.G.X941)   Ochre-brown.. .. .. .. .. .. ..   50   45

**Cylinder Numbers (Blocks of Six)**
Perforation Type RE

| Cyl. No. | | | | No dot | Dot |
|---|---|---|---|---|---|
| 1 | .. | .. | .. | 3·75 | 3·75 |

# '11½p. Drab   (1981)

**1981 (14 JANUARY).   COLOUR CHANGED. ONE 4 mm. CENTRE PHOSPHOR BAND. FLUORESCENT COATED PAPER. PVAD GUM**

U201 (=S.G.X893)   Drab .. .. .. .. .. .. .. ..   45   30
  *a.* Imperforate (pair) .. .. .. .. ..   £175
  *b.* One short band top and bottom (11.11.81)* .. ..   70   70
  *c.* Phosphor omitted .. .. .. .. ..   5·50

*No. U201*b* (short phosphor band) comes from the £2·55 1981 Christmas Booklet Pane UMFB25. The phosphor covers the printed portion of the stamp only so as not to overlap on to the 14p. stamps.

**Cylinder Numbers (Blocks of Six)**
Perforation Type RE

| Cyl. No. | Phos. No. | | | | No dot | Dot |
|---|---|---|---|---|---|---|
| 1 | 20 | .. | .. | .. | 2·75 | 2·75 |
| 1 | 31 | .. | .. | .. | 10·00 | 10·00 |
| 3 | 31 | .. | .. | .. | 2·75 | 2·75 |
| 3 | — | .. | .. | .. | £110 | £110 |

Phosphor Cylinder Displacement. With ink cyl. 3, phos. cyl. 31 is known displaced sideways and inverted up the margin 100 mm. opposite row 14.

**1981 (26 JANUARY).   ONE NARROW BAND AT LEFT. FLUORESCENT COATED PAPER. PVAD GUM**

50p. booklet panes UMFB20, 24 (11½p. at right) and £1·30 booklet panes UMFB21/22
U202 (S.G.X894Ea)   Drab .. .. .. .. .. .. .. ..   60   60

**1981 (26 JANUARY).   ONE NARROW BAND AT RIGHT. FLUORESCENT COATED PAPER. PVAD GUM**

50p. booklet panes UMFB19, 23 (11½p. at left) and £1·30 booklet panes UMFB21/22
U203 (=S.G.X894)   Drab .. .. .. .. .. .. .. ..   60   60

**CYLINDER VARIETIES**
**Minor Constant Sheet Flaws**

Cyl. 1   7/5 Pale spot on cheek (Th. D3)
Cyl. 3.   4/8 White spot left of central cross on crown (Th. A3)
  9/7 Small spot in band of crown (Th. B4)
  13/9 White blemish below necklace (Th. F3)
  14/8 Diagonal white scratch in background at bottom right (Th. G6)
For further flaws on 11½p. stamps in booklet panes, see under Nos. UMFB19/20 and 22/24.

**COIL**
One centre phosphor band. Printed in continuous reels

| Code No. | Issued | Number in roll | Face value | Paper/gum | Screen | Perf. Type |
|---|---|---|---|---|---|---|
| | | Vertical delivery | | | | |
| EL | 11.3.81 | 500 | £57·50 | FCP/PVAD | 150 | Comb. |

Cylinder number used:
  EL   FCP/PVAD   B5   (B36) phosphor

**WITHDRAWN**  No. U200, 30.4.82; U201, 26.2.83

# 12p. Yellowish Green   (1980)

## 1980 (30 JANUARY).   PHOSPHORISED (FLUORESCENT COATED) PAPER. PVAD GUM

| | | | | | | | | | |
|---|---|---|---|---|---|---|---|---|---|
| U204 | (1) | Yellowish green | .. | .. | .. | .. | .. | 45 | 40 |
| (=S.G.X942) | (2) | Bright green (Cyl. 2) | .. | .. | .. | .. | .. | 1·25 | |
| | | *a.* Background scratches | .. | .. | .. | .. | .. | 3·00 | |
| | | *b.* Long diagonal scratch | .. | .. | .. | .. | .. | 2·50 | |
| | | *c.* Blemish in front of nose | | .. | .. | .. | .. | 2·25 | |

No. U204 (1) is known on phosphorised paper with either a shiny ink surface which gives a photo-negative reflection or a matt surface without the negative effect.

Shade (2) is only found with a shiny ink surface and should not be confused with more minor shades in pale yellowish green.

**Cylinder Numbers (Blocks of Six)**

Perforation Type RE

| Cyl. No. | | | | No dot | Dot |
|---|---|---|---|---|---|
| 2 (Shade.1) | .. | .. | .. | 3·00 | 3·00 |
| 2 (Shade 2) | .. | .. | .. | 18·00 | 18·00 |
| 6 | .. | .. | .. | 4·75 | 4·75 |

Jumelle (U205)        Chambon (U205*a*)

## 1980 (4 FEBRUARY).   TWO 8 mm. PHOSPHOR BANDS. FLUORESCENT COATED PAPER. PVAD GUM

50p. booklet panes UMFB14/17

| | | | | | | | | | |
|---|---|---|---|---|---|---|---|---|---|
| U205 | | Yellowish green | .. | .. | .. | .. | .. | 60 | 60 |
| | *a.* | Chambon printing (25.6.80) | .. | .. | .. | .. | 50 | 50 |
| | *ab.* | Phosphor omitted | .. | .. | .. | .. | 5·00 | |
| | *ac.* | One 8 mm. broad band | .. | | .. | .. | .. | 7·00 | |

No. U205*a* has the value low and to the right close to the Queen's dress from booklet panes No. UMFB16/7. The value placing in Nos. U205*a* and U206 is identical but No. U205*a* can be distinguished by the 8 mm. bands.

## 1980 (16 APRIL).   TWO 9·5 mm. PHOSPHOR BANDS. FLUORESCENT COATED PAPER. PVAD GUM

Wedgwood Booklet panes UWB5 and UWB8

| | | | | | | | |
|---|---|---|---|---|---|---|---|
| U206 (=S.G.X895) | Yellowish green | .. | .. | .. | .. | .. | 45 | 40 |
| | *a.* One 9·5 mm. broad band | .. | .. | .. | .. | 15·00 | |
| | *b.* One 6·5 mm. band | .. | .. | .. | .. | 20·00 | |
| | *c.* Phosphor printed on both sides | .. | .. | .. | 90·00 | |
| | *ca.* Phosphor bands printed on gum only (UWB5*e*) | .. | £100 | |
| | *d.* Short bands top and bottom (12.11.80)* | .. | .. | 50 | 50 |
| | *e.* Short band at left omitted | .. | .. | .. | 55·00 | |
| | *f.* Short band at right omitted | .. | .. | .. | 40·00 | |

*No. U206*d* (short phosphor bands) comes from the £2·20 1980 Christmas Booklet Pane UMFB18. The phosphor covers the printed portion of the stamp only so as not to overlap on to the 10p. stamp.

No. U206 exists with phosphor omitted but as singles would be difficult to distinguish from No. U205*ab* it is only listed when in a complete booklet pane (see Nos. UWB5*a* and UWB8*a*).

**CYLINDER VARIETIES**
**Listed Flaws**

U204*a*
Two diagonal scratches
(Cyl. 2 no dot, R. 19/3)

U204*b*
Long diagonal scratch
(Cyl. 2 dot, R. 14/6)

Blemish in front of Queen's nose
(see also 18p. violet, Cyl. 1, R. 13/2)
(Cyl. 2 and 6, R. 13/2 (later retouched); cyl. 4, Roll 2 in
every 5th position.
Flaw U204*c* is also listed on Panes UWB5 and 8)

U204*c*

For further flaws on 12p. stamps in booklet panes, see under Nos. UMFB15 and UFB15/6.

**Minor Constant Sheet Flaws**

Cyl. 2.   1/7   Diagonal hairline scratch on neck (Th. E3–4)
          5/3   Dot above central cross of crown (Th. B5)
          9/2   Diagonal line below chin (Th. E2–F3)
          11/9  Pale area beneath bust (Th. G4–H5)
          12/6  Diagonal scratch on shoulder (Th. F4–G4)
          13/5  Diagonal scratch behind dress (Th. F6–G6)
          14/10 Blemish at point of Queen's chin (Th. E2)
          18/8  Fine diagonal line from Queen's hair to right margin (Th. D5–6)
          20/9  Blemish above necklace (Th. E4)

**COIL**
Phosphorised (fluorescent coated) paper. Printed in continuous reels

| Code No. | Issued | Number in roll | Face Value | Gum | Perf. Type |
|----------|--------|----------------|------------|-----|------------|
| | | | Vertical delivery | | |
| DL | 11.6.80 | 500 | £60·00 | PVAD | R |

Cylinder Number used:
          DL          Phosphorised (fluorescent coated) paper/PVAD          4/4.

**WITHDRAWN**   No. U204, 9.82

113

## 12p. Bright Emerald   (1985–86)

**1985 (29 OCTOBER).   COLOUR CHANGED. ONE 4 mm. CENTRE PHOSPHOR BAND. FLUORESCENT COATED PAPER. PVAD GUM**

| | | | |
|---|---|---|---|
| U207 (=S.G.X896) | Bright emerald | .. .. .. .. .. 60 | 40 |
| | *b.* Phosphor omitted | .. .. .. .. 8·00 | |
| | *d.* New phosphor ink (7.86) | .. .. .. 60 | |
| | *da.* With "all over" new phosphor ink | .. .. 7·00 | |
| | *e.* White dots variety | .. .. .. .. 3·50 | |
| | *f.* Retouch between value .. | .. .. .. 2·00 | |

The "all-over" phosphor, No. U207*da*, was applied in error and was a very thick coating with which apparently, the phosphor doctor blade was unable to cope.

**Cylinder Numbers (Blocks of Six unless otherwise stated)**
Perforation Type RE

| Cyl. No. | Phos. No. | | No dot | Dot | |
|---|---|---|---|---|---|
| 9 | 18 | .. .. .. | 3·50 | 3·50 | |
| 9 | 18 | +23 mm. (17) .. | 18·00 | 20·00 | Block of ten |
| 9 | 18 | +25 mm. (17) .. | 25·00 | 28·00 | Block of ten |
| 9 | 18 | +50 mm. (16) .. | 30·00 | 30·00 | Block of ten |
| 9 | 20 | .. .. .. | 3·50 | 3·50 | |
| 11 | 18 | .. .. .. | 4·00 | 4·00 | |
| 12 | 18 | .. .. .. | 3·50 | 3·50 | |
| 13 | 18 | .. .. .. | 4·00 | 4·00 | |
| 13 | 18 | (new phos. ink) | 5·00 | 5·00 | |

Perforation variety
The 17 pin variety as described in Appendix I. *Price for marginal block of 6 £7, cylinder no. 12 dot, block of six £12.*

(4)

**1985 (29 OCTOBER).   ONE 4 mm. CENTRE PHOSPHOR BAND. UNDERPRINT TYPE (4) MULTIPLE DOUBLE LINED STAR IN BLUE. FLUORESCENT COATED PAPER. PVAD GUM**

| | | |
|---|---|---|
| U208 (=S.G.X896Eu) | Bright emerald | .. .. .. .. .. .. 60 |
| | *b.* White dots variety | .. .. .. .. 3·50 |
| | *c.* Retouch between value .. | .. .. .. 2·00 |

Underprint **Type (4)** is as shown above but occurs either whole or in part(s) on a single example.

**Cylinder Numbers (Blocks of Six)**
Perforation Type RE

| Cyl. No. | Phos. No. | | No dot | Dot |
|---|---|---|---|---|
| 9 | 18 | .. .. .. .. | 3·75 | 4·00 |
| 9 | 20 | .. .. .. .. | 3·75 | 3·75 |
| 10 | 20 | .. .. .. .. | £400 | — |
| 10 | — | .. .. .. .. | £600 | — |

Phosphor Cylinder Displacement. With ink cyl. 10, phos. cyl. 20 is known displaced up the margin 128 mm. opposite row 13.

**1986 (14 JANUARY).   ONE NARROW BAND AT LEFT. FLUORESCENT COATED PAPER. PVAD GUM**

£1·50 booklet panes UMFB37/38, £5 British Rail booklet pane UWB27

| | | | |
|---|---|---|---|
| U209 (=S.G.X897Ea) | Bright emerald | .. .. .. .. .. 75 | 75 |
| | *b.* One 9·5 mm. broad band | .. .. .. £200 | |

## 1986 (14 JANUARY). ONE NARROW BAND AT RIGHT. FLUORESCENT COATED PAPER. PVAD GUM

£1.50 booklet panes UMFB37/38, £5 British Rail booklet pane UWB27

U210 (=S.G.X897)      Bright emerald      ..      ..      ..      ..      ..      ..      75      75

## 1986 (18 MARCH). ONE 4·5 mm. CENTRE PHOSPHOR BAND. FLUORESCENT COATED PAPER. PVAD GUM

£5 Story of British Rail booklet pane No. UWB26 and 50p booklet pane UMFB39

U211                        Bright emerald      ..      ..      ..      ..      ..      ..      70      70

### CYLINDER VARIETIES
**Listed Flaws**

U207*e*, U208*b*
White dots around Queen's head
(Cyl. 9 no dot, R. 1/2)

U207*f*, U208*c*
Retouch between value
(Cyl. 9 dot, R. 9/10)

**Minor Constant Sheet Flaws**

Cyl.  9    5/4  Retouch below fold of dress (Th. G4)
           19/3  Short line of specks on Queen's neck (Th. E4)
           19/4  Vertical lines on shoulder (Th. F4)
Cyl.  9.   2/2  White mark on face (Th. C3–D3)
           19/1  Pale patch in front of eye (Th. C2)
Cyl. 12    7/3  White patch left of forehead (Th. B2)
           13/1  Two green specks on upper neck (Th. B2)
           14/2  White patch above 1 and similar but smaller mark at top left (Th. E1 and A1)
           20/2  White patch in front of nose (Th. C1)
Cyl. 12.   9/3  Two spots on throat (Th. E4)
           15/1  White patch behind neck (Th. E6)

### COILS

No. U207 one centre phosphor band. Printed in continuous reels

| Code No. | Issued | Number in roll | Face value | Gum | Screen | Perf. Type |
|---|---|---|---|---|---|---|
| | | | Vertical delivery | | | |
| ML | 12.11.85 | 500 | £60 | PVAD | 150 | Comb. |
| | | | Sideways delivery | | | |
| SA | 23.9.86 | 1000 | £120 | PVAD | 150 | Comb. |

Cylinder Numbers used

| ML | FCP/PVAD | B10 | (B62) Phosphor |
|---|---|---|---|
| SA | FCP/PVAD | R1 | (R13) Phosphor |

**WITHDRAWN**   Nos. U207/08, 20.10.87, No. U207*d*, 11.4.89

# 12½p. Light Emerald    (1982–83)

## 1982 (27 JANUARY).   ONE 4 mm. CENTRE PHOSPHOR BAND. FLUORESCENT COATED PAPER. PVAD GUM

| U212 (=S.G.X898) | Light emerald | .. | .. | .. | .. | .. | .. | 45 | 25 |
|---|---|---|---|---|---|---|---|---|---|
| | a. Imperforate (pair) | | .. | .. | .. | .. | .. | £100 | |
| | b. Short band at bottom (19.5.82)* | | | .. | .. | .. | 1·00 | 1·00 |
| | c. Phosphor omitted | .. | .. | .. | .. | .. | 5·50 | |
| | d. Error. Phosphorised paper | .. | .. | .. | .. | 3·00 | |
| | e. Error. Two narrow bands** | .. | .. | .. | .. | 6·00 | |

No. U212 is known postmarked at Cheltenham, Glos. on 1 January 1982 and on later dates, prior to the official date of issue.

No. U212 ocurs with "extra" phosphor bands in addition to the centre band due to faulty action of the doctor blade. Complete "all over" phosphor wash examples are known from Cyl. 11 no dot but as the centre band was still evident we do not list them.

*No. U212b (short phosphor band) comes from £4 "Story of Stanley Gibbons" se-tenant booklet Pane UWB11 (top right stamp) where the phosphor band is short at the bottom so that it did not overlap to the 12½p. below.

**No. U212e came from Cyl. 2 where the normal 4 mm. centre band was printed over the vertical perforations at each side. In theory these bands will be only 2 mm. wide. See also Nos. U213a/b which can be distinguished from No. U212e as the bands on this stamp continue at top and bottom.

### Cylinder Numbers (Blocks of Six unless otherwise stated)
Perforation Type RE

| Cyl. No. | Phos. No. | | | | | No dot | Dot | |
|---|---|---|---|---|---|---|---|---|
| 1 | 20 | .. | .. | .. | .. | 2·75 | 2·75 | |
| 1 | 20 · | +27 mm. (17) | .. | | .. | 7·00 | 7·00 | Block of ten |
| 1 | 31 | .. | .. | .. | .. | 2·75 | 2·75 | |
| 2 | 20 | .. | .. | .. | .. | 2·75 | 2·75 | |
| 2 | —* | .. | .. | .. | .. | 7·00 | 7·00 | |
| 2 | 20 | (inverted printing) | | .. | | 4·50 | 65·00 | |
| 2 | 31 | .. | .. | .. | .. | 3·00 | 3·00 | |
| 2 | 41 | .. | .. | .. | .. | 6·00 | 6·00 | |
| 2 | 41 | Phosphorised paper | | .. | | £500 | £2500 | |
| 10 | 20 | .. | .. | .. | .. | 2·75 | 2·75 | |
| 11 | 18 | .. | .. | .. | .. | 18·00 | 12·00 | |
| 11 | 20 | .. | .. | .. | .. | 2·75 | 2·75 | |
| 11 | 41 | .. | .. | .. | .. | 3·00 | 3·00 | |
| 11 | 41 | +20 mm. (17/18) | | .. | | 10·00 | 10·00 | Block of ten |
| 11 | 41 | +32 mm. (17) | .. | | .. | 10·00 | 10·00 | Block of ten |
| 11 | — | .. | .. | .. | - .. | 3·75 | 3·75 | |

Phosphor Cylinder Displacements. With ink cyl. 11, phos. cyl. 41 is displaced up the margin from 72 to 99 mm. opposite rows 14 and 15.

*The phosphor cylinder 20 appears in the left margin of both panes but as the phosphor was printed before the light emerald no attempt was made to synchronise the printing. Therefore this is a phosphor under ink printing with phosphor cylinder number shift above or below the box.

## 1982 (1 FEBRUARY).   ONE NARROW BAND AT LEFT. FLUORESCENT COATED PAPER. PVAD GUM

50p. booklet panes UMFB27 (12½p. at right), £1·43 booklet panes UMFB28/29, £1·46 booklet panes UMFB32/33 and UWB10/11, 13/14

| U213 (=S.G.X899Ea) | Light emerald | .. | .. | .. | .. | .. | .. | 60 | 60 |
|---|---|---|---|---|---|---|---|---|---|
| | a. Error Two bands (one short at left) | .. | | .. | .. | 18·00 | |
| | b. Error. Two bands (one short at right) | | .. | .. | 18·00 | |
| | c. One 9·5 mm. broad band | .. | | .. | .. | 40·00 | |
| | ca. One broad band (short at top) | .. | | .. | .. | 70·00 | |
| | d. Phosphor printed on both sides | | .. | .. | 60·00 | |
| | e. Left band short at top (19.5.82)* | | .. | .. | 1·10 | |
| | ea. Phosphor printed on both sides | | .. | .. | £160 | |
| | f. One 8 mm. broad band | .. | .. | .. | .. | 25·00 | |

Nos. U213a/b come from panes where the phosphor printing was vertically displaced by one stamp row.

*No. U213e comes from R. 2/3 in the se-tenant pane of the £4 Stanley Gibbons booklet.

## 1982 (1 FEBRUARY). ONE NARROW BAND AT RIGHT. FLUORESCENT COATED PAPER. PVAD GUM

50p. booklet panes UMFB26 (12½p. at left), £1·43 booklet panes UMFB28/29, £1·46 booklet panes UMFB32/33 and UWB10/11, 13/14

| | | | | | | | | | |
|---|---|---|---|---|---|---|---|---|---|
| U214 (=S.G.X899) | Light emerald | .. | .. | .. | .. | .. | .. | .. | 60 | 60 |
| | *a.* Phosphor printed on both sides | | .. | .. | .. | 60·00 |

(1)

## 1982 (10 NOVEMBER). ONE SHORT 4 mm. CENTRE BAND. UNDERPRINT TYPE (1) IN BLUE. FLUORESCENT COATED PAPER. PVAD GUM

1982 Christmas booklet pane UMFB30

| | | | | | | | | |
|---|---|---|---|---|---|---|---|---|
| U215 (=S.G.X898Eu) | Light emerald | .. | .. | .. | .. | .. | .. | 65 |
| | *a.* Phosphor omitted | .. | .. | .. | .. | .. | .. | 45·00 |

The phosphor covers the printed portion of the stamp only so as not to overlap on to the 15½p. stamp.

(2)

## 1983 (9 NOVEMBER). ONE 4 mm. CENTRE BAND. UNDERPRINT TYPE (2) IN BLUE. FLUORESCENT COATED PAPER. PVAD GUM

1983 Christmas booklet pane UFB29

| | | | | | | | |
|---|---|---|---|---|---|---|---|
| U216 (=S.G.X898Eua) | Light emerald | .. | .. | .. | .. | .. | 55 |

Nos. U215/6 were printed with blue star underprint *over* the gum as required by the Post Office for accountancy purposes.

### CYLINDER VARIETIES

**Minor Constant Sheet Flaws**

Cyl. 1   4/10   Horizontal blemish on neck (Th. E3–E4) and spot on Queen's shoulder (Th. F5)
        6/5   Spot below front of bust (Th. H2)
        6/9   Dark spot in Queen's hair (Th. C4)
        9/3   Pale patch at the front of neck (Th. E3)
       11/2   Weak spot below value (Th. G2)
       14/7   Pale spot in background behind dress (Th. G6)
       16/1   Spot on dress (Th. G3) and weak area in loop of large 2
       16/3   Curved scratch through large 2
       16/5   Blemish in background below bust (Th. G4–5 intersection)
       18/1   Spot above crown (Th. A5)
      18/10   Retouch on shoulder above dress (Th. F4)

Cyl. 1.   1/5   White irregular scratch on neck (Th. E4)
        1/9   Diagonal scratch below value (Th. G1)
       2/3   Dark spot above Queen's eyebrow (Th. C3)
       3/2   Pale spot in background at back of crown (Th. B6)
      11/9   Retouches in Queen's hair and background (Th. C4–E5)
      12/1   Small spot in band of crown (Th. B5)
      13/4   Retouch in background above front of necklace (Th. F3)
     15/10   Retouch in background behind crown (Th. D6)
      19/6   Dark spot above crown (Th. B5–6 intersection)
      20/2   White spot between Queen's dress and P (Th. F2)
     20/10   Small spot above crown (Th. A4)

Cyl. 2.    8/5 Blemish below bust (Th. G4)
Cyl. 10    1/8 Diagonal hairline scratch from crown to top right margin (Th. B6)
           1/9 Continuation of scratch on 1/8 at top left corner (Th. A1–A2)
Cyl. 11.   1/5 Pale spot on Queen's cheek (Th. D3)
           1/7 White speck right of Queen's shoulder (Th. G6)
           3/8 Dark speck left of crown (Th. A3)
           4/6 White dot after 2 in ½ (Th. G2)
           8/3 White blob opposite Queen's nose (Th. D1)
           15/7 Weakness to back of crown (Th. C6)
           16/8 Small white dot after P in value

**COIL**

No. U212 one centre phosphor band. Printed in continuous reels

| Code No. | Issued | Number in roll | Face value | Paper/Gum | Screen | Perf. Type |
|---|---|---|---|---|---|---|
| | | Vertical delivery | | | | |
| GL | 1.2.82 | 500 | £62·50 | FCP/PVAD | 150 | Comb. |

Cylinder Number used:

| GL | FCP/PVAD | B1 | | B36 (phosphor) |
|---|---|---|---|---|

**WITHDRAWN**    U212, 28.6.85

# 13p. Olive-grey   (1979)

**1979 (15 AUGUST).   PHOSPHORISED (FLUORESCENT COATED) PAPER. PVAD GUM**

U217 (=S.G.X943)    Olive-grey    ..    ..    ..    ..    ..    ..    ..    60    45

**Cylinder Numbers (Blocks of Six)**

Perforation Type RE

| Cyl. No. | | | | | No dot | Dot |
|---|---|---|---|---|---|---|
| 3 | .. | .. | .. | .. | 3·75 | 3·75 |

On the dot panes the dot appears first followed by "3".

**CYLINDER VARIETIES**

**Minor Constant Sheet Flaws**

Cyl. 3    7/8 Spot on dress (Th. G4)
Cyl. 3.   5/3 Dot above central cross of crown (Th. B5)
          9/9 Weakness in background at lower right (Th. G6)
          17/5 Vertical scratch from serif of 3 (Th. E2–F1)

**WITHDRAWN**    9.82

# 13p. Pale Chestnut   (1984–87)

**1984 (28 AUGUST).   COLOUR CHANGED. ONE 4 mm. CENTRE PHOSPHOR BAND. FLUORESCENT COATED PAPER. PVAD GUM**

| U218 (=S.G.X900) | Pale chestnut.. | .. | .. | .. | .. | .. | 50 | 35 |
|---|---|---|---|---|---|---|---|---|
| | *a*. Imperforate (pair) | .. | .. | .. | .. | .. | £400 | |
| | *b*. Phosphor omitted | .. | .. | .. | .. | .. | 5·50 | |
| | *c*. One broad band .. | .. | .. | .. | .. | .. | 70·00 | |
| | *d*. New phosphor ink (27.1.87) | .. | .. | .. | .. | 50 | |
| | *da*. Imperforate (pair) | .. | .. | .. | .. | £700 | |
| | *f*. Throat and necklace flaw | .. | .. | .. | .. | 3·00 | |

Imperforate edge: No. U218*d* exists with imperforate edge at right from pane UMFB41*a*.

**118**

**Cylinder Numbers (Blocks of Six unless otherwise stated)**

4 mm. Centre Band (No. U218)

Perforation Type RE

| Cyl. No. | Phos. No. | | | | | No dot | Dot | |
|---|---|---|---|---|---|---|---|---|
| 7 | 18 | .. | .. | .. | .. | 3·00 | 3·00 | |
| 7 | 18 | −34 mm. (20) | .. | | .. | 30·00 | 40·00 | |
| 7 | 18 | −42 mm. (20) | .. | | .. | 20·00 | 20·00 | |
| 7 | 18 | −43 mm. (20) | .. | | .. | 20·00 | 30·00 | |
| 7 | 18 | −46 mm. (20) | .. | | .. | 20·00 | 30·00 | |
| 7 | 20 | .. | .. | .. | .. | 15·00 | 15·00 | |
| 14 | 18 | .. | .. | .. | .. | 3·00 | 3·00 | |
| 14 | 18 | −36 mm. (20) | .. | | .. | 20·00 | 20·00 | |
| 14 | 18 | +31 mm. (17) | .. | .. | | — | — | Block of ten |
| 14 | 18 | +48 mm. (16) | .. | .. | | 25·00 | 25·00 | Block of ten |

Perforation variety

The 17 pin variety as described in Appendix I exists on the following:—

| Cyl. No. | Phos. No. | | | | | Dot cyl. block of 6 |
|---|---|---|---|---|---|---|
| 7 | 18 | .. | .. | .. | .. | £400 |
| 7 | 20 | .. | .. | .. | .. | £40 |
| 14 | 18 | .. | .. | .. | .. | £20 |

*Marginal block of 6 without cyl. no. price £12.*

4 mm. Centre Band, New Phosphor Ink (No. U218*d*)

Perforation Type RE

| Cyl. No. | Phos. No. | | | | | No dot | Dot | |
|---|---|---|---|---|---|---|---|---|
| 7 | 18 | .. | .. | .. | .. | £180 | £300 | |
| 14 | 18 | .. | .. | .. | .. | 3·50 | 22·00 | |
| 14 | 41 | .. | .. | .. | .. | 3·00 | 3·00 | |
| 15 | 18 | .. | .. | .. | .. | 3·00 | 3·00 | |
| 15 | 41 | .. | .. | .. | .. | 3·00 | 3·00 | |
| 15 | 41 | +21 mm. (18) | .. | | .. | 7·50 | 7·50 | Block of ten |
| 15 | 41 | +22 mm. (18) | .. | | .. | 7·50 | 7·50 | Block of ten |
| 15 | 41 | +25 mm. (17) | .. | | .. | 7·50 | 7·50 | Block of ten |
| 15 | 41 | +32 mm. (17) | .. | | .. | — | — | Block of ten |
| 15 | 41 | +37 mm. (17) | .. | | .. | 10·00 | 10·00 | Block of ten |
| 15 | 41 | +38 mm. (17) | .. | | .. | — | 10·00 | Block of ten |
| 15 | 41 | +43 mm. (17) | .. | | .. | — | — | Block of ten |
| 15 | 41 | +46 mm. (17) | .. | | .. | — | — | Block of ten |
| 15 | 41 | +47 mm. (16) | .. | | .. | — | 10·00 | Block of ten |
| 15 | 41 | +64 mm. (16) | .. | | .. | — | — | Block of ten |
| 15 | — | .. | .. | .. | .. | 4·50 | 4·50 | |

Phosphor Cylinder Displacements. With ink cyl. 15, phos. cyl. 41 is known displaced up the margin from 68 to 216 mm. opposite rows 10 to 16.

## 1984 (3 SEPTEMBER).   ONE NARROW BAND AT LEFT. FLUORESCENT COATED PAPER. PVAD GUM

£1·54 booklet pane UMFB35/36, £4 Christian Heritage booklet pane UWB18/20 (4.9.84) and £1 booklet panes UMFB43/44

| | | | | | | | | |
|---|---|---|---|---|---|---|---|---|
| U219 (=S.G.X901Ea) | Pale chestnut.. | .. | .. | .. | .. | .. | .. | 60 | 60 |
| | *a.* Error. Two bands (one short at left) | .. | | .. | .. | 5·00 | |
| | *b.* Error. Two bands (one short at right) | | .. | .. | 5·00 | |
| | *c.* Phosphor printed on both sides | .. | .. | .. | 70·00 | |
| | *d.* New phosphor ink (27.1.87) | .. | .. | .. | .. | 80 | |
| | *da.* Error. Two bands (ex. UMFB44) | .. | .. | .. | 10·00 | |

Nos. U219*a/b* come from panes where the phosphor printing was vertically displaced by one stamp row, see UMFB35/6*a.*

Imperforate edge: No. U219*d* exists with imperforate edge at left from pane UMFB44.

No. U219*da* came from £1 Sherlock Holmes booklet No. FH10.

## 1984 (3 SEPTEMBER).   ONE NARROW BAND AT RIGHT. FLUORESCENT COATED PAPER. PVAD GUM

£1·54 booklet pane UMFB35/36, £4 Christian Heritage booklet pane UWB18 and 20 (4.9.84), £5 P & O booklet pane UWB31 and 50p. booklet pane UMFB42

U220 (=S.G.X901)   Pale chestnut. .   ..   ..   ..   ..   ..   60   60
   b. Phosphor printed on both sides   ..   ..   .. 70·00
   d. New phosphor ink (27.1.87)   ..   ..   ..   ..   80

## 1985 (8 JANUARY).   ONE 4·5 mm. CENTRE PHOSPHOR BAND. FLUORESCENT COATED PAPER. PVAD GUM

£5 Story of *The Times* booklet pane UWB22, £5 P & O booklet pane UWB30 and 32, 50p. booklet panes UMFB40/41, 52p. booklet pane UFB47 and £1·30 booklet pane UFB50

U221   Pale chestnut. .   ..   ..   ..   ..   ..   ..   60   60
   b. New phosphor ink (27.1.87)   ..   ..   ..   ..   60

Imperforate edge. No. U221b exists with imperforate edge at right from pane UMFB41.
No. U221 with phosphor omitted is listed under pane No. UMFB41b.

## 1986 (2 DECEMBER).   ONE 4 mm. CENTRE BAND. UNDERPRINT TYPE (2) IN BLUE. FLUORESCENT COATED PAPER. PVAD GUM

1986 Christmas booklet pane UFB32/33

U222 (=S.G.X900Eu)  Pale chestnut. .   ..   ..   ..   ..   ..   ..   55

## CYLINDER VARIETIES

### Listed Flaw

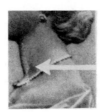

Vertical disturbance
on throat and necklace
(Cyl. 15 dot, R. 15/7)

U218f

### Minor Constant Sheet Flaws

▸ Cyl.   7   1/4  Nick in frame at left (Th. C1)
        7/3  Small weakness in frame at upper right (Th. A6)
        9/4  Disturbance in background opposite Queen's forehead (Th. B1)
        14/1  Retouch above Queen's necklace (Th. E3)
        18/4  Two pale spots in background below chin (Th. E2)
        19/4  Large circular area of weak screening above value
        20/1  White speck above diadem at right (Th. B6)
Cyl.   7.  6/9  White speck on Queen's neck (Th. E3)
        7/1  Disturbance in background opposite Queen's necklace (Th. E6)
        7/8  Nick in frame opposite 1 (Th. F1)
        9/1  White flaw below loop of P
        9/9  Circular pale area in background at left and retouch above dress (Th. B1 and F5)
        10/4  Pale speck below P (Th. G2)
        11/4  Spot touching hair at the front of crown (Th. A3)
        11/7  Pale spot on Queen's cheek (Th. D3)
        15/7  Retouch in front of dress (Th. F2)
        16/10  Retouched pale spot on Queen's shoulder (Th. F4/5)
        17/6  Faint diagonal hairline scratch across bottom right-hand corner (Th. D6–H5)
        19/1  Circular flaw on Queen's shoulder (Th. F3)
        19/9  Repair to bottom left frame below value

Cyl. 14   9/7  Vertical pale smear and retouch by Queen's nose (Th. C1 and D2)
          15/1  Marks in dress (Th. G1–G5)
          16/1  Pale patch in background below top frame (Th. A1–A2)
          19/1  Retouch in wave of hair (Th. B2)
Cyl. 14.  1/2  Pale spot behind Queen's neck (Th. E6)
          1/9  Retouch in background at upper left (Th. A2)
          3/4  White flaw in front of crown (Th. A3)
          4/6  Dark spot to left of 1
          5/6  Stray speck at bottom left corner
          7/7  Background disturbance behind Queen's neck (Th. F5–F6)
          8/2  Dark mark opposite Queen's chin and pale screen above 1
          8/6  Pale spot behind necklace (Th. E5)
          11/9  Pale retouch below jawline (Th. D3–E3)
          13/1  Horizontal dash in margin at top left corner
          14/4  Blemish to right of 1
          16/10  Small break at left frame (Th. E1)
          17/1  Small blemish below Queen's nose (Th. D2). Later retouched but still visible
          19/5  Pale area to left of value (Th. F1–G1)
          19/10  White spot on dress (Th. G3)
          20/1  Pale screening below dress (Th. G4–G5)

**COILS**

One centre phosphor band. Printed in continuous reels

| Code No. | Issued | Number in roll | Face value | Gum | Screen | Perf. Type |
|---|---|---|---|---|---|---|
| | | | Vertical delivery | | | |
| KL | 3.9.84 | 500 | £65 | PVAD | 150 | Comb. |

When the postage rate changed to 13p. the KL roll was reissued on 20 October 1986.

| | | | Sideways delivery | | | |
|---|---|---|---|---|---|---|
| SB | 21.10.86 | 1,000 | £130 | PVAD | 150 | Comb. |

Cylinder Numbers used:

| KL | FCP/PVAD | B7 | (B62) Phosphor |
|---|---|---|---|
| | FCP/PVAD | B12 | (B62) Phosphor |
| SB | FCP/PVAD | R1 | R13 (phosphor) |

**WITHDRAWN**   No. U218, 26.1.88, U218*d*, 4.9.89

# 13½p. Purple-brown   (1980)

**1980 (30 JANUARY).   PHOSPHORISED (FLUORESCENT COATED) PAPER. PVAD GUM**

U224 (=S.G.X944)   Purple-brown   ..   ..   ..   ..   ..   ..   65   60

**Cylinders Numbers (Blocks of Six)**

Perforation Type RE

| Cyl. No. | | | | No dot | Dot |
|---|---|---|---|---|---|
| 1 | .. | .. | .. | 4·25 | 4·25 |

**CYLINDER VARIETIES**

**Minor Constant Sheet Flaws**

Cyl. 1.   1/2  White spot below eye (Th. D2)
          1/3  Blemish on dress (Th. G3)
          19/7  Curved line through neck (Th. E3–E4)
          20/4  Vertical line from necklace to dress (Th. F4–G4)

**WITHDRAWN**   7.82

# 14p. Grey-blue   (1981)

**1981 (14 JANUARY).   PHOSPHORISED (FLUORESCENT COATED) PAPER. PVAD GUM**

| U225 (=S.G.X945) | Grey-blue .. .. .. .. .. .. .. | 50 | 40 |
|---|---|---|---|
| | *a.* Scratch through nose .. .. .. .. .. | 2·75 | |
| | *f.* Fluorescent brightener omitted .. .. .. | 1·50 | |

No. U225 is known on phosphorised paper with either a shiny ink surface which gives a photo-negative reflection or a matt surface without the negative effect.

No. U225*f* came from £1·40 booklet pane UFB20 and is printed on chalk-surfaced paper but without the fluorescent additive, which was probably omitted in error.

**Cylinder Numbers (Blocks of Six)**

Perforation Type RE

| Cyl. No. | | | | | No dot | Dot |
|---|---|---|---|---|---|---|
| 1 | .. | .. | .. | .. | 3·25 | 3·25 |
| 6 | .. | .. | .. | .. | 60·00 | 60·00 |

**1981 (26 JANUARY).   TWO 8 mm. PHOSPHOR BANDS. FLUORESCENT COATED PAPER. PVAD GUM**

50p. booklet panes UMFB19/20 and £1·30 booklet panes UMFB21/22

| U226 (=S.G.X902) | Grey-blue .. .. .. .. .. .. .. | 50 | 45 |
|---|---|---|---|
| | *a.* Short phosphor band at left (6.5.81)*.. .. .. | 50 | 45 |
| | *b.* Short phosphor band at right (6.5.81)* .. .. | 50 | 45 |
| | *ba.* Short right band omitted .. .. .. .. | 40·00 | |
| | *c.* Phosphor omitted .. .. .. .. .. | 28·00 | |

*Nos. U226*a*/*b* (short phosphor bands) come from the £1·30 Panes UMFB21/22. The phosphor band at right or left covers the printed portion of the stamp and side perforations but does not continue at top or bottom. This is to prevent an overlap on to the 11½p. stamp.

No. U226*ba* came from pane UMFB21 on which the phosphor bands were partially omitted.

**1981 (11 NOVEMBER).   TWO SHORT 9·5 mm. PHOSPHOR BANDS. FLUORESCENT COATED PAPER. PVAD GUM**

1981 Christmas booklet pane UMFB25

| U227 | Grey-blue .. .. .. .. .. .. .. | 60 | 60 |
|---|---|---|---|

The phosphor bands do not continue across the top and bottom perforations, but cover the side perforations and printed portion of the stamp only.

**CYLINDER VARIETIES**

**Listed Flaw**

Vertical scratch
through Queen's nose
(Cyl. 1 no dot, R. 8/10)

U225*a*

For further flaws on 14p. stamps in booklet panes, see under Nos. UMFB19, 22 and UFB20.

**Minor Constant Sheet Flaws**

Cyl. 1   1/1  Blemish to right of P (Th. F2)
          3/2  Small retouch in background to left of 1
          8/1  Scratch in background above value (Th. E1–2)
         10/6  White speck on Queen's dress (Th. G4)
         11/1  Small retouch in background behind Queen's hair (Th. D6)
         12/7  Dot on Queen's shoulder (Th. F5)
         16/2  Dot below Queen's eye (Th. C–D2)
         16/5  Pale area below earring (Th. D4)
         20/4  Diagonal scratch behind Queen's dress (Th. F6–G6)

Cyl. 1.  5/3  Vertical scratch from top of stamp to bridge of Queen's nose (Th. A2–C2)
          6/2  Area of dark blue spots behind hair (Th. D, E, F. 6)
        7/10  Horizontal scratch from right margin to Queen's neck (Th. F3–F6)
         9/1  Pale patch over P
        14/6  Pale area in front of forehead (Th. B1–C1)
        14/7  Pale smear by central cross in crown (Th. A5)
        18/3  Fine diagonal line from P to bottom margin
        18/5  Small vertical blemish behind Queen's ear (Th. D4)
        19/6  Circular path beneath chin (Th. E2)

**COIL**

Phosphorised (fluorescent coated) paper. Printed in continuous reels

| Code No. | Issued | Number in roll | Face value | Gum | Perf. Type |
|---|---|---|---|---|---|
| | | | Vertical delivery | | |
| FL | 11.3.81 | 500 | £70 | PVAD | Comb. |

Cylinder Number used:
    FL      Phosphorised (fluorescent coated) paper/PVAD      B3

**WITHDRAWN**  No. U225, 14.1.84

---

# 14p. Deep Blue  (1988)

**1988 (23 AUGUST). COLOUR CHANGED. ONE 4 mm. CENTRE PHOSPHOR BAND. FLUORESCENT COATED PAPER. PVAD GUM**

U228 (=S.G.X903)   Deep blue  ..    ..    ..    ..    ..    ..   45    40
                      *a.* Imperforate (pair)    ..    ..    ..    ..
                      *b.* Phosphor omitted    ..    ..    ..    ..   7·00
                      *c.* Dark spot on hair below crown    ..    ..   3·00

    Examples exist from sheets of cylinder 10 with "all over" phosphor wash on the first three vertical rows due to malfunction of the doctor blade. A 3 mm. band variety came from the first vertical row in the £1.40 Barcode booklets.
    Imperforate edges: No. U228 exists with imperforate edges at right, top, bottom, top and right, bottom and right from panes UFB61, UFB64 and UFB66.
    No. U228*b* came from the 50p. booklet pane UMFB45 and 56p. barcode booklet pane UFB66.

**Cylinder Numbers (Blocks of Six)**

Perforation Type RE

| Cyl. No. | Phos. No. | | | | | No dot | Dot |
|---|---|---|---|---|---|---|---|
| 10 | 41 | .. | .. | .. | .. | 2·75 | 2·75 |
| 11 | 41 | .. | .. | .. | .. | 3·50 | 3·50 |

**1988 (5 SEPTEMBER).  ONE NARROW BAND AT RIGHT. FLUORESCENT COATED PAPER. PVAD GUM**

50p. booklet pane UMFB45 and £1 booklet pane UMFB46

U229 (=S.G.X904)   Deep blue  ..    ..    ..    ..    ..    ..   60    60
    Imperforate edge: No. U229 exists with imperforate edge at left from pane UMFB46. Some examples from this pane show small band at bottom left from the 19p. stamp with left edge imperforate.
    Examples from UMFB45 have a band the height of the stamp or just shorter.

## 1988 (5 SEPTEMBER). ONE 4.5 mm. CENTRE PHOSPHOR BAND. FLUORESCENT COATED PAPER. PVAD GUM

56p. Barcode booklet pane UFB52 and vertical coil
U230                 Deep blue   ..    ..    ..    ..    ..    ..    ..    45    45

**CYLINDER VARIETIES**
**Listed Flaw**

Dark spot below band
of crown (Cyl. 10 no dot,
R. 3/1)

U228c

**Minor Constant Sheet Flaws**

Cyl. 10    4/8   Pale shaded patch on cheek (Th. D3) multipositive flaw (see R. 4/7 on 15p. and 17p.)
           5/7   Smudge on neck (Th. E4)
           6/7   Fine diagonal line across shoulder into dress (Th. F4–G5) multipositive flaw
           6/9   Repair to background at upper right corner (Th. B6)
           19/2  Semi-circular retouch to edge of neck (Th. E3)

The flaw on R. 6/7 is from the multipositive and exists on the same position for the 19p. and 23p. and also on R. 6/6 of the 20p., 28p., 32p. and 35p. issued on 23 August 1988.

**COILS**

One 4 mm. centre band. Printed in continuous reels.

| Code No. | Issued | Number in roll | Face value | Gum | Screen | Perf. Type |
|---|---|---|---|---|---|---|
|  |  |  | Vertical delivery |  |  |  |
| OL | 5.9.88 | 500 | £70 | PVAD | 150 | Comb. |

The OL roll was made available from April 1989 in rolls of 1000 stamps. This was an experimental measure and the code was unchanged.

One 4.5 mm centre phosphor band. Printed in continuous reels.

| | | | Sideways delivery | | | |
|---|---|---|---|---|---|---|
| SD | 5.9.88 | 1000 | £140 | PVAD | 150 | Comb. |

Cylinder Numbers used:
           OL    FCP/PVAD   not know
           SD    FCP/PVAD   R1 (R13) Phosphor

**WITHDRAWN** No. U228, 25.9.90

# 15p. Ultramarine   (1979)

**1979 (15 AUGUST).   PHOSPHORISED (FLUORESCENT COATED) PAPER.
PVAD GUM**

U231 (=S.G.X946)   Ultramarine .. .. .. .. .. .. .. 50   40
                 *a*. Diagonal scratch behind hair .. .. .. .. 2·50
                 *b*. Retouch above crown .. .. .. .. .. 2·50
                 *c*. Scratch above dress .. .. .. .. .. 2·50

No. U231 is known on phosphorised paper with either a shiny ink surface which gives a
photo-negative reflection or a matt surface without the negative effect.

**Cylinder Numbers (Blocks of Six)**
Perforation Type RE

| Cyl. No. | | | | | No dot | Dot |
|---|---|---|---|---|---|---|
| 1 | .. | .. | .. | .. | 3·50 | 3·50 |
| 2 | .. | .. | .. | .. | 3·50 | 3·50 |

**CYLINDER VARIETIES**
**Listed Flaws**

U231*a*
Diagonal scratch behind Queen's hair
(Cyl. 1 dot, R. 20/3)

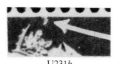

U231*b*
Retouch in background above crown
(Cyl. 1 dot, R. 20/5)

Multipositive Flaw
U231*c*. Cyl. 1 no dot, R. 12/4. See 29p. U301b

**Minor Constant Sheet Flaws**

Cyl. 1   8/1   White scratch in hair to neck (Th. D4–E4)
          10/1   Dark spot in band (Th. B4)
          15/4   Hairline scratch from Queen's chin to P
Cyl. 1.   1/6   Dark mark in background (Th. D6)
         2/10   Faint blemish over Queen's eyebrow (Th. C3)
         3/3   White dot on forehead (Th. B3)
         4/8   Hairline scratch in background extending to bottom margin (Th. A2–H3)
         5/1   Pale area below Queen's dress (Th. G4)
         5/3   Speck on cheek (Th. D3)
         5/8   Continuation of hairline scratch from 4/8 (Th. A3–B3)
        14/6   Two vertical rows of dots on Queen's cheek (Th. C3–D3)
        20/4   Pale vertical line from necklace to shoulder (Th. F4–G4)

**WITHDRAWN** 14.1.84

**Three Value Types**

| | | |
|---|---|---|
| | Type I. | Bold value |
| | Type II. | As Type I, but with thin P. Occurs on 50p. booklet pane UMFB47, horizontal and vertical coils. |
| I      II      III | Type III. | Thin value and P, which is set further to right. London Life *se-tenant* pane UWB33. |

## 15p. Bright Blue (1989)

**1989 (26 SEPTEMBER). COLOUR CHANGED. ONE 4 mm. CENTRE PHOSPHOR BAND. TYPE I. FLUORESCENT COATED PAPER. PVAD GUM**

| | | | | | | | | |
|---|---|---|---|---|---|---|---|---|
| U232 (=S.G.X905) | Bright blue | .. | .. | .. | .. | .. | 25 | 30 |
| | a. Imperforate (pair) .. | .. | .. | .. | .. | £250 | | |
| | b. Phosphor omitted .. | .. | .. | .. | .. | | | |

**Cylinder Numbers (Blocks of Six)**

Perforation Type RE

| Cyl. No. | Phos. No. | | | | No dot | Dot |
|---|---|---|---|---|---|---|
| 3 | 41 | .. | .. | .. | 1·75 | 1·75 |
| 3 | 41 | −22 mm. (19) .. | | .. | 8·00 | 8·00 |
| 3 | — | .. | .. | .. | 15·00 | 15·00 |

Phosphor Cylinder Displacement. Phos. cyl. 41 is known inverted and displaced up the margin 90 mm. opposite row 15.

**1989 (2 OCTOBER). ONE NARROW BAND AT LEFT. FLUORESCENT COATED PAPER. TYPE II. PVAD GUM**

50p. booklet pane UMFB47, horizontal and vertical coils.

| | | | | | | | | |
|---|---|---|---|---|---|---|---|---|
| U233 (=S.G.X906) | Bright blue | .. | .. | .. | .. | .. | 60 | 60 |
| | a. One 3 mm. band at left | .. | .. | .. | .. | 60 | | |

On No. U233a the 3 mm. band is clear of the vertical perforations and should not be confused with the narrow band, No. U233, which covers the perforated edge.

**1990 (20 MARCH). ONE NARROW BAND AT RIGHT. FLUORESCENT COATED PAPER. TYPE III. PVAD GUM**

£5 London Life *se-tenant* booklet pane UWB33

| | | | | | | | | |
|---|---|---|---|---|---|---|---|---|
| U234 (=S.G.X906Ea) | Bright blue | .. | .. | .. | .. | .. | 60 | 60 |

**CYLINDER VARIETIES**

**Minor Constant Sheet Flaws**

Cyl. 3    4/7   Pale shaded patch on cheek (Th. D3) multipositive flaw
            6/6   Fine diagonal line across shoulder into dress (Th. F4–G5) multipositive flaw (see footnote below the flaw list of 14p. deep blue)
          11/5   Pale specks on neck above necklace (Th. E4)
          13/1   Small round omission of colour below necklace (Th. F3)

**COILS**

One 4 mm. centre phosphor band. Printed in continuous reels.

| Code No. | Issued | Number in roll | Face value | Gum | Screen | Perf. Type |
|---|---|---|---|---|---|---|
| | | | Vertical delivery | | | |
| RL | 16.10.89 | 500 | £75 | PVAD | 150 | Comb. |
| | | | Sideways delivery | | | |
| SF | 16.10.89 | 1000 | £150 | PVAD | 150 | Comb. |

RL was later available in rolls containing 1000 stamps. The leader was similar in text, but the number of stamps and face value was changed. It is believed that this larger roll was not available to the public.

Cylinder Numbers used:

| | | | | |
|---|---|---|---|---|
| RL | FCP/PVAD | R2 | (B62) | Phosphor |
| SF | FCP/PVAD | R1 | (B14) | Phosphor |

# 15½p. Pale Violet (1981–82)

**Two Value Types**

Type I.  Pointed tail to 5 and
thin fraction.
Type II.  Blunt tail to 5 and
thicker fraction.

I                        II

## 1981 (14 JANUARY).   PHOSPHORISED PAPER. TYPE I. PVAD GUM
### A. FLUORESCENT COATED PAPER

| | | | | | | | | | |
|---|---|---|---|---|---|---|---|---|---|
| U235 (=S.G.X947) | Pale violet | .. | .. | .. | .. | .. | .. | 50 | 40 |
| | *a.* Imperforate (pair) | .. | .. | .. | .. | £300 | |
| | *b.* Type II (1.2.82) .. | .. | .. | .. | .. | 1·10 | 75 |
| | *ba.* White scratch between 1 and P | .. | .. | 3·00 | |
| | *f.* Fluorescent brightener omitted | .. | .. | 15·00 | |

No. U235 is known on phosphorised paper with either a shiny ink surface which gives a photo-negative reflection or a matt surface without the negative effect.

No. U235*f* was from sheets and is printed on chalk-surfaced paper but without the fluorescent additive which was probably omitted in error.

**Cylinder Numbers (Blocks of Six)**
Perforation Type RE

| Cyl. No. | | | | No dot | Dot |
|---|---|---|---|---|---|
| 3 | .. | .. | .. | .. | 3·50 | 3·50 |

### B. ADVANCED COATED PAPER (9.82)

| | | | | | | | | |
|---|---|---|---|---|---|---|---|---|
| U236 | Pale violet | .. | .. | .. | .. | .. | .. | 2·00 |

**Cylinder Numbers (Blocks of Six)**
Perforation Type RE

| Cyl. No. | | | | No dot | Dot |
|---|---|---|---|---|---|
| 3 | .. | .. | .. | .. | 32·00 | 50·00 |

## 1982 (1 FEBRUARY).   TWO 8 mm. PHOSPHOR BANDS. TYPE II. FLUORESCENT COATED PAPER. PVAD GUM
£1·43 booklet panes UMFB28/29

| | | | | | | | | | |
|---|---|---|---|---|---|---|---|---|---|
| U237 (=S.G.X907) | Pale violet | .. | .. | .. | .. | .. | .. | 45 | 45 |
| | *a.* Short phosphor band at left (1.2.82)* .. | .. | .. | 70 | 70 |
| | *b.* Short phosphor band at right (1.2.82)* | .. | .. | 70 | 70 |
| | *c.* Error. One side band at left | .. | .. | .. | 50·00 | |
| | *d.* Error. One side band at right .. | .. | .. | 50·00 | |

*No. U237*a/b* (short phosphor bands) come from the £1·43 panes UMFB28/29. The phosphor band at right or left covers the printed portion of the stamp and side perforations but does not continue at top or bottom. This is to prevent an overlap on to the 12½p. stamp.

Nos. U237*c/d* came from panes with transposed bands where the phosphor was vertically displaced by one stamp row.

## 1982 (19 MAY).   TWO 9·5 mm. PHOSPHOR BANDS. TYPE I. FLUORESCENT COATED PAPER. PVAD GUM
"Story of Stanley Gibbons" Booklet panes UWB9 and UWB12

| | | | | | | | | | |
|---|---|---|---|---|---|---|---|---|---|
| U238 | Pale violet | .. | .. | .. | .. | .. | .. | 45 | 50 |
| | *a.* Phosphor omitted | .. | .. | .. | .. | 4·00 | |
| | *b.* One 6 mm. band.. | .. | .. | .. | .. | 17·00 | |
| | *c.* One 9·5 mm. broad band | .. | .. | .. | 15·00 | |
| | *d.* Phosphor printed on both sides | .. | .. | £100 | |

Nos. U238*b/c* came from panes where the bands were misplaced to right.

**1982 (10 NOVEMBER).  TWO SHORT 9·5 mm. PHOSPHOR BANDS. TYPE II. UNDERPRINT TYPE (1) IN BLUE. FLUORESCENT COATED PAPER. PVAD GUM**

1982 Christmas booklet pane UMFB30

| | | | | | | | |
|---|---|---|---|---|---|---|---|
| U239 (=S.G.X907Eu) | Pale violet | .. | .. | .. | .. | .. | 85 |
| | *a.* Phosphor omitted | | .. | .. | .. | .. | 75·00 |
| | *b.* Left-hand band omitted.. | | .. | .. | .. | .. | 70·00 |

The note below No. U216 which describes the double-lined star underprint also applies here.

The phosphor bands cover the printed portion of the stamp and the side perforations but do not continue at top or bottom. This is to prevent an overlap on to the 12½p. stamp.

**CYLINDER VARIETIES**

**Listed Flaw**

No. U235*ba* occurs in booklets where it is illustrated as UFB24*a* from cyl. number B7. This cylinder was also employed for the vertical coil HL, Roll No. 10 and the variety occurs in every 12th position.

**Minor Constant Sheet Flaws**

Cyl. 3  1/1  Disturbance in background (Th. H2)
2/5  Dark spot on jawline (Th. D3)
2/7  White patch in band of crown (Th. B3)
6/2  Curved scratch from background to Queen's mouth (Th. C1–D2)
6/3  Curved line above 1 (Th. E2–F2)

Cyl. 3.  1/10  White spot in central cross in crown (Th. B5)
12/6  Retouch below 5 (Th. G2)
13/10  Dark spot in hair (Th. D4)
16/4  Line above crown (Th. A5)
17/3  Pale spot beneath first figure 1 (Th. G1)
17/8  White spot between first 1 and 5 (Th. F1)

**COIL**

Phosphorised (fluorescent coated) paper. Value Type II. Printed in continuous reels

| Code No. | Issued | Number in roll | Face value | Gum | Perf. Type |
|---|---|---|---|---|---|
| | | | Vertical delivery | | |
| HL | 1.2.82 | 500 | £77·50 | PVAD | Comb. |

Cylinder Number used:
| | | |
|---|---|---|
| HL | Phosphorised (fluorescent coated) paper/PVAD | B7 |

**WITHDRAWN**  No. U235, 29.4.84

# 16p. Olive-drab  (1983)

**1983 (30 MARCH).  PHOSPHORISED PAPER. PVAD GUM**

**A. ADVANCED COATED PAPER**

| | | | | | | | | |
|---|---|---|---|---|---|---|---|---|
| U240 (=S.G.X948) | Olive-drab | .. | .. | .. | .. | .. | 60 | 30 |
| | *a.* Imperforate (pair) | .. | .. | .. | .. | £160 | |
| | *b.* Imperforate between stamp and bottom margin | | | .. | 65·00 | |

**Cylinder Numbers (Blocks of Six)**

Perforation Type RE

| Cyl. No. | | | | | No dot | Dot |
|---|---|---|---|---|---|---|
| 2 | .. | .. | .. | .. | 3·75 | 3·75 |
| 3 | .. | .. | .. | .. | 3·75 | 3·75 |
| 4 | .. | .. | .. | .. | 3·75 | 3·75 |

**B. FLUORESCENT COATED PAPER** £1.60 booklet panes UFB25/26 (5.4.83)

| | | | | | | | |
|---|---|---|---|---|---|---|---|
| U241 | Olive-drab | .. | .. | .. | .. | .. | 60 |

Perforation variety

The 17 pin variety as described in Appendix I. *Price for marginal block of 6 £42, cylinder no. 3 dot, block of six* £90.

**1983 (5 APRIL).   TWO 9·5 mm. PHOSPHOR BANDS. FLUORESCENT COATED PAPER. PVAD GUM**

£1·46 booklet panes UMFB32/33

| U242 (=S.G.X908) | Olive-drab | | | | | | | 1·50 | 1·75 |
|---|---|---|---|---|---|---|---|---|---|
| *a.* | Short phosphor band at left (5.4.83)* | | | | | | | 1·50 | 1·75 |
| *b.* | Short phosphor band at right (5.4.83)* | | | | | | | 1·50 | 1·75 |
| *ba.* | Error. Short right band omitted | | | | | | | 50·00 | |
| *c.* | Phosphor omitted | | | | | | | £100 | |
| *d.* | Error. Left-hand band omitted | | | | | | | 50·00 | |

*Nos. U242*a/b* (short phosphor bands) come from the £1·46 panes UMFB32/33. The phosphor band at right or left covers the printed portion of the stamp and side perforations but does not continue at top or bottom. This is to prevent an overlap on to the 12½p. value.

No. U242*ba* came from pane UMFB33 on which the phosphor bands were partially omitted.

**(3)**

**1983 (10 AUGUST).   PHOSPHORISED (FLUORESCENT COATED) PAPER. UNDERPRINT TYPE (3) IN BLUE. PVAD GUM**

£1·60 (sold at £1·45) booklet panes UFB27/8

U243 (=S.G.X948Eu) Olive-drab  ..     ..     ..     ..     ..     ..     ..     75

No. U243 is printed with the underprint *over* the gum as required by the Post Office for accountancy purposes.

**COIL**

Phosphorised (fluorescent coated) paper. Printed in continuous reels

| Code No. | Issued | Number in roll | Face value | Gum | Perf. Type |
|---|---|---|---|---|---|
| | | | Vertical delivery | | |
| JL | 20.4.83 | 500 | £80 | PVAD | Comb. |

Cylinder Number used:

| JL | Phosphorised (fluorescent coated) paper/PVAD | B3 |
|---|---|---|

**WITHDRAWN**   No. U240, 7.2.87

# 16½p. Pale Chestnut   (1982)

**1982 (27 JANUARY).   PHOSPHORISED (FLUORESCENT COATED) PAPER. PVAD GUM**

U244 (=S.G.X949)   Pale chestnut..     ..     ..     ..     ..     ..     ..     85     75

No. U244 is known on phosphorised paper with either a shiny ink surface which gives a photo-negative reflection or a matt surface without the negative effect.

**Cylinder Numbers (Blocks of Six)**

Perforation Type RE

| Cyl. No. | | | | No dot | Dot |
|---|---|---|---|---|---|
| 3 | .. | .. | .. | 5·50 | 5·50 |

**WITHDRAWN**   9.3.85

# 17p. Light Emerald   (1980)

**1980 (30 JANUARY).   PHOSPHORISED (FLUORESCENT COATED) PAPER. PVAD GUM**

| | | | |
|---|---|---|---|
| U245 (=S.G.X950) | Light emerald .. .. .. .. .. .. | 70 | 40 |
| | *a.* Diagonal scratch at lower right and white spot after P | 2·40 | |
| | *f.* Fluorescent brightener omitted .. .. .. | 1·00 | |

No. U245 is known on phosphorised paper with either a shiny ink surface which gives a photo-negative reflection or a matt surface without the negative effect.

No. U245*f* is printed on chalk-surfaced paper but without the fluorescent additive which was probably omitted in error.

**Cylinder Numbers (Blocks of Six)**

Perforation Type RE

| Cyl. No. | | | | | No dot | Dot |
|---|---|---|---|---|---|---|
| 4 | .. | .. | .. | .. | 4·75 | 4·75 |

**CYLINDER VARIETIES**
**Listed Flaw**

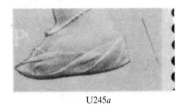

Diagonal scratch at lower right and white spot after P. This exists as a minor flaw on the 14p. Cyl. 1 no dot. (Cyl. 4 no dot, R. 20/4)

U245*a*

**Minor Constant Sheet Flaws**

Cyl. 4.  5/5 Faint vertical white line through face from band of crown to bottom of dress (Th. A3–G3)

7/2 Dark green spot in front of Queen's hair (Th. B2)

9/6 Horizontal line at top left below margin (Th. A2)

10/4 Pale spot opposite Queen's mouth by left margin (Th. D1)

12/9 Curved hairline on shoulder (Th. F5)

14/7 Pale smear from central cross on crown (Th. A5)

15/6 Small white dot behind hair (Th. E5)

18/7 White spot above back of crown (Th. B6)

**WITHDRAWN**   7.82

# 17p. Grey-blue   (1983–86)

**1983 (30 MARCH).   COLOUR CHANGED. PHOSPHORISED PAPER. PVAD GUM**

**A. FLUORESCENT COATED PAPER**

| | | | | | | |
|---|---|---|---|---|---|---|
| U246 | Grey-blue .. .. .. .. .. .. | | | | 60 | |
| | *b.* Vertical scratch .. .. .. .. .. | | | | 3·50 | |
| | *ba.* Vertical scratch retouched .. .. .. | | | | 3·00 | |

For examples of phosphorised paper with two phosphor bands, see below No. U248.

**Cylinder Numbers (Blocks of Six)**

Perforation Type RE

| Cyl. No. | | | | | No dot | Dot |
|---|---|---|---|---|---|---|
| 7 | .. | .. | .. | .. | 4·00 | 4·00 |

**B. ADVANCED COATED PAPER** (19.6.84)

| | | | | | | | |
|---|---|---|---|---|---|---|---|
| U247 (=S.G.X951) | Grey-blue .. .. | .. | .. | .. | .. | 50 | 40 |
| | *a.* Imperforate (pair) .. .. .. .. | | | | £225 | |

130

**Cylinder Numbers (Blocks of Six)**

Perforation Type RE

| Cyl. No. | | | | | No dot | Dot |
|---|---|---|---|---|---|---|
| 7 | .. | .. | .. | .. | 3·25 | 3·25 |
| 10 | .. | .. | .. | .. | 3·25 | 3·25 |
| 11 | .. | .. | .. | .. | 10·00 | 10·00 |
| 13 | .. | .. | .. | .. | 3·25 | 3·25 |
| 15 | .. | .. | .. | .. | 3·25 | 3·25 |

Perforation variety

The 17 pin variety as described in Appendix I. *Price for marginal block of 6* £18, *cylinder no. 10 dot, block of 6* £85; *cylinder no. 13 dot, block of 6* £50.

## 1984 (3 SEPTEMBER).   TWO 9·5 mm. PHOSPHOR BANDS. FLUORESCENT COATED PAPER. PVAD GUM

50p. booklet pane UFB39, £1·50 booklet panes UMFB37/38, £1·54 booklet panes UMFB35/36 and £4 Christian Heritage, £5 *The Times*, £5 British Rail *se-tenant* panes UWB19, UWB23, UWB27

| | | | | | | | |
|---|---|---|---|---|---|---|---|
| U248 (=S.G.X909) | Grey-blue | .. | .. | .. | .. | 75 | 75 |
| | *a.* Short phosphor band at left (3.9.84)* | .. | | .. | .. | 75 | 75 |
| | *b.* Short phosphor band at right (3.9.84)* | | .. | .. | .. | 75 | 75 |
| | *c.* Short phosphor band at bottom right (4.9.84)** | | | .. | 1·00 | |
| | *d.* Short phosphor band at top right (4.9.84)** | | .. | .. | 1·00 | |
| | *e.* Error. One side band at left | .. | .. | .. | 10·00 | |
| | *f.* Error. One side band at right | .. | | .. | .. | 10·00 | |
| | *g.* Two bands short at top (12.8.86) | | .. | .. | 2·00 | |
| | *h.* Error. Phosphorised paper and two bands | .. | | .. | 80·00 | |
| | *ha.* Error. Phosphorised paper and two short bands | | .. | £110 | |
| | *i.* One broad band .. | .. | .. | .. | .. | £250 | |
| | *j.* Phosphor omitted | .. | .. | .. | .. | £125 | |

*Nos. U248*a*/*b* (short phosphor bands) come from the £1·50 and £1·54 panes. The phosphor band at right or left covers the printed portion of the stamp and side perforations but does not continue at top or bottom. This is to prevent an overlap on to the lower denomination.

**Nos. U248*c*/*d* come from the pane UWB19 where the phosphor bands at left are short at top or bottom so that they do not overlap on to the 13p. value printed between Nos. U248*c*/*d*.

Nos. U248*e*/*f* come from £1·54 panes with transposed bands where the phosphor was vertically displaced by one stamp row.

No. U248*g* is from pane position R. 2/1 in 50p. Pictorial Booklet No. FB33*a*, Pond Life Series, No. 2. Nos. U248*h* and *ha* are on phosphorised paper used in error in 50p. Booklet, FB33*a*. The pane is listed under UFB39*a*.

## 1985 (5 MARCH).   PHOSPHORISED (FLUORESCENT COATED) PAPER. UNDERPRINT TYPE (3) IN BLUE. PVAD GUM

£1·70 (sold at £1·55) booklet panes UFB34/35

| | | | | | | | | |
|---|---|---|---|---|---|---|---|---|
| U249 (=S.G.X951Eu) | Grey-blue | .. | .. | .. | .. | .. | .. | 80 |

No. U249 is printed with the underprint *over* the gum as required by the Post Office for accountancy purposes.

## 1985 (4 NOVEMBER).   TWO 9·5 mm. PHOSPHOR BANDS. FLUORESCENT COATED PAPER. UNDERPRINT AS TYPE (4) MULTIPLE DOUBLE LINED STAR IN BLUE. PVAD GUM

50p. booklet pane UFB38

| | | | | | | | |
|---|---|---|---|---|---|---|---|
| U250 (S.G.X909Eu) | Grey-blue | .. | .. | .. | .. | .. | 70 |
| | *a.* Short phosphor bands at top | .. | .. | .. | .. | 1·25 |
| | *b.* Phosphor omitted | .. | .. | .. | .. | 11·00 |
| | *c.* Band at left omitted | .. | .. | .. | .. | 45·00 |
| | *d.* Band at right omitted | .. | .. | .. | .. | 45·00 |

No. U250*a* (short bands at top) came from Pane UFB38. The bands were short so that they did not overlap to the printed label above.

Underprint **Type (4)** is as shown above No. U208 but occurs either whole or in part(s) on a single example.

**CYLINDER VARIETIES**
Listed Flaws

| U246*b* | U246*ba* |
|---|---|
| Vertical scratch | Scratch removed leaving a whitish smear |

(Cyl. 7 dot, R. 18/5)

**Minor Constant Sheet Flaws**

Cyl. 7.  2/10  White patch on P
        3/5  Specks on 7 and P
        4/5  Small specks on 1 and P
        5/6  Several specks on value
        5/7  Specks on 7 and P
      17/4  Small retouch on Queen's jaw (Th. E3)
      17/5  Vertical hairline scratch through dress to frame (Th. F5–H5)
    20/10  Dot below loop P

Cyl. 10   3/4  White flaw in loop of P
        4/9  White speck below earring (Th. D4)
     10/5  Specks on 7 and P
     10/9  As R. 10/5

Cyl. 13   8/9  Small retouch at left (Th. C1)
     11/4  White blemish at right (Th. D6)
    13/10  Speck above crown (Th. A6)

Cyl. 13.  13/5  White spot on fold of dress (Th. G4)
     14/2  Pale spot below frame (Th. A2)
     20/8  Blemish between 1 and 7

**COIL**

Phosphorised (fluorescent coated) paper. Printed in continuous reels

| Code No. | Issued | Number in roll | Face value | Gum | Screen | Perf. Type |
|---|---|---|---|---|---|---|
| | | | Vertical delivery | | | |
| LL | 3.9.84 | 500 | £85 | PVAD | 150 | Comb. |

Cylinder Number used:

| | | |
|---|---|---|
| LL | Phosphorised (fluorescent coated) paper/PVAD | B7 |

**WITHDRAWN** No. U247, 4.86

# 17p. Deep Blue  (1990)

**1990 (4 SEPTEMBER). COLOUR CHANGED. ONE 4 mm. CENTRE PHOSPHOR BAND. FLUORESCENT COATED PAPER. PVAD GUM**

| | | | | | | | | | |
|---|---|---|---|---|---|---|---|---|---|
| U251 (=S.G.X910) | Deep blue | .. | .. | .. | .. | .. | .. | 30 | 30 |
| | *b.* Phosphor omitted | | .. | .. | .. | .. | .. | 6·00 | |

**Cylinder Numbers (Blocks of Six)**
Perforation Type RE

| Cyl. No. | Phos. No. | | | | | No dot | Dot |
|---|---|---|---|---|---|---|---|
| 17 | 41 | .. | .. | .. | .. | 2·10 | 2·10 |

## 1990 (4 SEPTEMBER). ONE NARROW BAND AT LEFT. FLUORESCENT COATED PAPER. PVAD GUM

50p. booklet pane UFB69

| | | | | | | | | No dot | Dot |
|---|---|---|---|---|---|---|---|---|---|
| U252 (=S.G.X911Ea) | Deep blue | .. | .. | .. | .. | .. | .. | 30 | 30 |
| | *a.* One 3 mm. band at left .. | | .. | .. | .. | .. | | 30 | |

On No. U252*a* the 3 mm. band is clear of the vertical perforations so that it differs from the narrow band, No. U253, which covers the perforated edge.

## 1990 (4 SEPTEMBER). ONE NARROW BAND AT RIGHT. FLUORESCENT COATED PAPER. PVAD GUM

50p. booklet pane UFB69 and £1 booklet pane UMFB48

| | | | | | | | | No dot | Dot |
|---|---|---|---|---|---|---|---|---|---|
| U253 (=S.G.X911) | Deep blue | .. | .. | .. | .. | .. | .. | 30 | 30 |

Imperforate edge: No. U253 exists with imperforate edge at left from pane UMFB48.

**CYLINDER VARIETIES**

**Minor Constant Sheet Flaws**

Cyl. 17   4/7   Pale shaded patch on cheek (Th. D3) multipositive flaw (see R. 4/8 on 14p. and R. 4/7 on 15p.)
            5/1   Two pale bands and dots on shoulder (Th. F3–G3)
            5/7   Thin line from hair to dress (Th. E4–G4)
            6/6   Fine diagonal line across shoulder into dress (Th. F4–G5) multi-positive flaw (see 14p. R. 6/7)
          20/2   White flaw at the top of forehead (Th. B3)

**COILS**

One 4 mm. centre phosphor band. Printed in continuous reels.

| Code No. | Issued | Number in roll | Face value | Gum | Screen | Perf. Type |
|---|---|---|---|---|---|---|
| | | Vertical delivery | | | | Chambon |
| UL | 17.9.90 | 500 | £85 | PVAD | 150 | Comb. |
| UL | 17.9.90 | 1000 | £170 | PVAD | 150 | Comb. |

Cylinder Numbers used:
       UL   FCP/PVAD   R2   (B62) Phosphor

# 17½p. Pale Chestnut   (1980)

**1980 (30 JANUARY).   PHOSPHORISED (FLUORESCENT COATED) PAPER. PVAD GUM**

U254 (=S.G.X952)     Pale chestnut. .     . .     . .    . .    . .    . .    . .     80     80
                     *a*. Ear lobe flaw    . .    . .    . .    . .    . .    3·00
                     *b*. Pale spot on cheek    . .    . .    . .    . .    2·75

**Cylinder Numbers (Blocks of Six)**
Perforation Type RE

| Cyl. No. | | | | | No dot | Dot |
|---|---|---|---|---|---|---|
| 1 | . . | . . | . . | . . | 5·00 | 5·00 |

**CYLINDER VARIETIES**
**Listed Flaws**

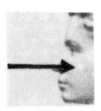

| U254*a* | U254*b* |
|---|---|
| Ear lobe flaw | Pale spot on cheek |
| (Cyl. 1 dot, R. 8/5) | (Cyl. 1 dot, R. 9/1) |

**Minor Constant Sheet Flaws**
Cyl. 1.    1/10 Dark spot between 1 and P of ½p. (Th. F2)
            2/7  Diagonal smear from Queen's hair to right margin (Th. D5–F6)
            6/1  Faint spot above Queen's forehead (Th. A2)
            6/5  Pale mark on cheek (Th. D3)
            7/4  Small nick by neck (Th. E3)
            10/3 White nick in Queen's hair (Th. B3)
            14/5 Small dotted line above Queen's forehead (Th. A3
            14/7 Pale smear from central cross in crown (Th. A5)
            18/10 Two dark patches in front of Queen's mouth (Th. D1–2)
            19/6 Retouch on neck (Th. D4–E4)

**WITHDRAWN**   7.82

# 18p. Deep Violet   (1981)

**1981 (14 JANUARY).   PHOSPHORISED (FLUORESCENT COATED) PAPER. PVAD GUM**

U255 (=S.G.X953)     Deep violet . .     . .     . .     . .     . .     . .     . .     70     75
                     *a*. Retouch behind neck    . .    . .    . .    . .    2·50
                     *b*. Retouch in front of nose    . .    . .    . .    2·75
                     *c*. White scratch across neck    . .    . .    . .    2·75
                     *d*. White scratch behind hair    . .    . .    . .    2·25
                     *e*. Retouched L shaped scratch    . .    . .    . .    3·00

No. U255 is known on phosphorised paper with either a shiny ink surface which gives a photo-negative reflection or a matt surface without the negative effect.

**Cylinder Blocks of Six**
Perforation Type RE

| Cyl. No. | | | | | No dot | Dot |
|---|---|---|---|---|---|---|
| 1 | . . | . . | . . | . . | 4·75 | 4·75 |

**134**

## CYLINDER VARIETIES

### Listed Flaws

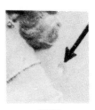

| U255a | U255b | U255c |
|---|---|---|
| Retouch behind neck | Retouch in front of nose | White scratch through |
| (Cyl. 1 no dot, R. 2/10) | (Cyl. 1 no dot, R. 13/2) | neck and background |
| | | (Cyl. 1 no dot, R. 19/9) |

White scratch from Queen's hair
to right hand margin
(Cyl. 1 no dot, R. 19/10)

U255d

Nos, U255b/d are multipositive flaws which also occur to a greater or less extent on 25p. cyl. 2 no dot. A similar flaw to No. U255b exists on the 12p. yellowish green Cyl. 2, R. 13/2.

Multipositive Flaw
   No. U255e from Cyl. 1 dot, R.18/8 is a retouched state of the 25p. flaw from Cyl. 2 dot.

### Minor Constant Sheet Flaws

Cyl. 1
- 1/1 Small retouch below bust (Th. G4)
- 1/8 Diagonal hairline through back of crown (Th. A5–D6)
- 2/9 Diagonal hairline through neck and shoulder (Th. E3–F4) and dark spot above crown (Th. A4)
- 3/6 Small retouch above necklace (Th. E4)
- 4/1 Pale smear in background below bust (Th. H5)
- 4/5 Retouch speck behind band of crown (Th. C5)
- 7/4 Blemish below chin (Th. E2) and dark speck in background above Queen's forehead (Th. B2)
- 8/4 Diagonal line from Queen's nose to the top of 2
- 9/2 Dark spot on hairline above cheek (Th. D3)
- 9/10 Small dark spot in Queen's hair (Th. C4)
- 13/1 Speck behind dress (Th. F6)
- 14/4 Diagonal line through Queen's chin and background (Th. D3–E2)
- 14/9 Short white diagonal line behind Queen's neck (Th. D5–E6)
- 15/2 Small retouch above 8 and P (Th. E2)
- 16/1 Hairline above P and across shoulder (Th. F2–F4)
- 17/8 Vertical line crosses back of crown extending to back of hair (Th. A6–E6)
- 18/10 Diagonal white line across bottom right hand corner (Th. G6)
- 19/3 White scratch above the back of the crown (Th. B6) which continues on 19/4 as a faint line

Cyl. 1.
- 1/5 White spot behind front cross on crown (Th. A3–4) and dark spot on Queen's neck (Th. E3)
- 2/1 Dark vertical scratch above Queen's nose (Th. B2–C2)
- 3/7 Hairline scratch behind Queen's neck (Th. E5–F6)
- 3/9 Pale blemish at left (Th. E1)
- 4/8 Coloured dot on front of neck (Th. E3)
- 6/10 Horizontal blemish behind Queen's hair (Th. D6)
- 7/8 Curved scratch from Queen's neck to margin (Th. G4–H5)

9/6 Diagonal line on Queen's shoulder (Th. F4–G4)
10/6 Two coloured dots right of bust (Th. F6)
12/9 Two dark spots on neck (Th. E4)
15/5 Two white spots in hair (Th. A5–A6)
17/8 Curved scratch on cheek (Th. D3)
18/4 White scratch through base of bust into background at right (Th. E5)
20/2 Two dots above Queen's crown (Th. A5–A6)
Some of these minor flaws are multipositive and exist on 25p. purple.

**WITHDRAWN**  14.1.84

# 18p. Deep Olive-grey  (1984–88)

## 1984 (28 AUGUST). COLOUR CHANGED. PHOSPHORISED PAPER. PVAD GUM

### A. ADVANCED COATED PAPER

U256 (=S.G.X954)  Deep olive-grey  ..  ..  ..  ..  ..  ..  70  60
  *a.* Imperforate (pair)  ..  ..  ..  ..  ..  £160
  *b.* Mark below necklace  ..  ..  ..  ..  ..  3·25

**Cylinder Numbers (Blocks of Six)**
Perforation Type RE

| Cyl. No. | | | | | No dot | Dot |
|---|---|---|---|---|---|---|
| 4 | .. | .. | .. | .. | 4·25 | 4·25 |
| 5 | .. | .. | .. | .. | 4·25 | 4·25 |

Perforation variety
  The 17 pin variety as described in Appendix I. *Price for marginal block of 6 £7, cylinder no. 4 dot, block of 6 £14.*

**B. FLUORESCENT COATED PAPER** £1·80 booklet panes UFB43/44 (20.10.86)
U257  Deep olive-grey  ..  ..  ..  ..  ..  ..  80

**CYLINDER VARIETIES**
**Listed Flaw**

U256*b*
Mark below necklace
(Cyl. 5 no dot, R. 10/8)

**Minor Constant Sheet Flaws**
Cyl. 4.   7/9  Line of specks across Queen's eye, forehead and hair (Th. C2–C5)
      9/3  Dark screening in 1 of value
     13/8  Hairline scratch across shoulder (Th. F4–F5)
     20/10  White spot on shoulder (Th. F4)

**1986 (20 OCTOBER).   TWO 9·5 mm. PHOSPHOR BANDS.
FLUORESCENT COATED PAPER. PVAD GUM**

50p. booklet panes UMFB41/42, £1 booklet panes UMFB43/44 and £5 P & O booklet pane UWB31.

| | | | | | | | | |
|---|---|---|---|---|---|---|---|---|
| U258 (=S.G.X912) | Deep olive-grey | .. | .. | .. | .. | .. | .. | 75 | 75 |
| | a. New phosphor ink (27.1.87) | .. | .. | .. | .. | 75 | |
| | b. Two bands but 3·5 mm. at left.. | .. | .. | .. | 1·00 | |
| | ba. As b but new phosphor ink (27.1.87) .. | .. | .. | 1·00 | |
| | c. Phosphor omitted | .. | .. | .. | .. | 27·00 | |
| | d. One broad band (original phosphor) .. | .. | .. | £150 | |

Slight phosphor misplacement gives stamps showing a short band at top right or a small step at top left. These were from pane No. UMFB42.
Imperforate edges: No. U258a exists with imperforate edge at left or right and No. U258ba at right only from pane UMFB44.

**Coil**

Phosphorised (fluorescent coated) paper. Printed in continuous reels.

| Code No. | Issued | Number in roll | Face value | Gum | Perf. Type |
|---|---|---|---|---|---|
| | | | Vertical delivery | | |
| NL | 20.10.86 | 500 | £90 | PVAD | Comb. |

Cylinder Number used:
NL     Phosphorised (fluorescent coated) paper/PVAD      B2

Phosphorised (advanced coated) paper. Printed in continuous reels.

| | | | Vertical delivery | | |
|---|---|---|---|---|---|
| NL | 3.5.88 | 500 | £90 | PVAD | Comb. |

Cylinder Number used:
NL     Phosphorised (advanced coated) paper/PVAD      B1

**WITHDRAWN**   No. U252, 4.9.89

# 19p. Bright Orange-red   (1988)

**1988 (23 AUGUST). PHOSPHORISED (ADVANCED COATED) PAPER. PVAD GUM**

| | | | | | | | |
|---|---|---|---|---|---|---|---|
| U259 (=S.G.X955) | Bright orange-red | .. | .. | .. | .. | .. | 30 | 35 |
| | a. Imperforate (pair) | .. | .. | .. | .. | £225 | |

Imperforate edges: No. U259 exists with imperforate edges at top or bottom from pane UFB62 and UFB65, and at top, bottom, top and right or bottom and right from UFB67.

**Cylinder Numbers (Blocks of Six)**

Perforation Type RE

| Cyl. No. | | | | | No dot | Dot |
|---|---|---|---|---|---|---|
| 1 | .. | .. | .. | .. | 2·25 | 2·25 |
| 2 | .. | .. | .. | .. | 2·25 | 2·25 |
| 3 | .. | .. | .. | .. | 2·25 | 2·25 |

**1988 (5 SEPTEMBER). TWO PHOSPHOR BANDS (INDIVIDUAL 3 mm. BAND AT RIGHT). FLUORESCENT COATED PAPER. PVAD GUM**

50p. booklet pane UMFB45, £1 booklet pane UMFB46

| | | | | | | | |
|---|---|---|---|---|---|---|---|
| U260 (=S.G.X913) | Bright orange-red | .. | .. | .. | .. | .. | 75 | 75 |
| | b. Two bands (3 mm. at left) | .. | .. | .. | .. | 75 | |
| | c. Two 3 mm. bands | .. | .. | .. | .. | 75 | |
| | d. Phosphor omitted | .. | .. | .. | .. | 2·25 | |

Imperforate edges: No. U260 exists with imperforate edge at right and No. U260b at left from pane No. UMFB46. No. U260c derives from pane No. UMFB45, *se-tenant* with the label.

**137**

**CYLINDER VARIETIES**

**Minor Constant Sheet Flaws**

Cyl. 1  6/7 Fine diagonal line across shoulder into dress (Th. F4–G5) multipositive flaw (see footnote below the flaw list of 14p. deep blue)

**COIL**

Phosphorised (advanced coated) paper. Printed in continuous reels.

| Code No. | Issued | Number in roll | Face value | Gum | Perf. Type |
|----------|--------|----------------|------------|-----|------------|
| | | Vertical delivery | | | |
| PL | 5.9.88 | 500 | £95 | PVAD | Comb. |

This was made available from April 1989 in rolls of 1000 stamps. Prepared as an experiment, the code was unchanged.

Cylinder Number used:
PL        Phosphorised (advanced coated) paper/PVAD   B3

**WITHDRAWN**  No. U255, 25.9.90

# 19½p. Olive-grey (1982)

**1982 (27 JANUARY). PHOSPHORISED (FLUORESCENT COATED) PAPER. PVAD GUM**

U264 (=S.G.X956)   Olive-grey  ..   ..   ..   ..   ..   ..   ..   2·50   1·50

**Cylinder Numbers (Blocks of Six)**

Perforation Type RE

| Cyl. No. | | | | | No dot | Dot |
|---|---|---|---|---|---|---|
| 2 | .. | .. | .. | .. | 16·00 | 16·00 |

**CYLINDER VARIETIES**

**Minor Constant Sheet Flaws**

Cyl. 2  1/3  Two spots in tail of 9
        1/4  Dark spot in front of Queen's nose (Th. D2)
        2/2  Spot on Queen's shoulder (Th. F4)
        2/6  Dark spot close to Queen's neck (Th. E3)
        5/4  Retouch to background below dress (Th. H4)
        9/9  Retouch in hair affecting lower row of pearls in band below central cross of crown (Th. B4–C4)
      20/1  Small retouches in dress (Th. F5 and G4)

**WITHDRAWN**  29.4.84

# 20p. Dull Purple (1976–79)

**1976 (25 FEBRUARY). TWO 9·5 mm. PHOSPHOR BANDS. FLUORESCENT COATED PAPER. PVAD GUM**

U265 (=S.G.X914)   Dull purple ..   ..   ..   ..   ..   ..   ..   75   40
                   *a.* One broad band ..   ..   ..   ..   ..   15·00
                   *b.* Retouch in front of eye ..   ..   ..   ..   2·75
                   *c.* White scar on neck   ..   ..   ..   ..   2·75
                   *d.* Scratch under ear   ..   ..   ..   ..   2·75
                   *e.* Dark scratch at bottom left into margin   ..   ..   2·75

**Cylinder Numbers (Blocks of Six)**

Perforation Type RE

| Cyl. No. | Phos. No. | | | | | No dot | Dot |
|---|---|---|---|---|---|---|---|
| 4 | 17 | .. | .. | .. | .. | 5·00 | 5·00 |
| 4 | P21 | .. | .. | .. | .. | 5·00 | 5·00 |
| 4 | — | .. | .. | .. | .. | £300 | £300 |
| 4 | 30 | .. | .. | .. | .. | 4·75 | 4·75 |

Phosphor Cylinder Displacement. Phos. cyl. P21 is known displaced up the margin 420 mm. opposite row 1.

**1979 (10 OCTOBER). PHOSPHORISED (FLUORESCENT COATED) PAPER. PVAD GUM**

U266 (=S.G.X957)   Dull purple ..   ..   ..   ..   ..   ..   ..   80   20
                   *d.* Scratch under ear   ..   ..   ..   ..   3·00
                   *e.* Dark scratch at bottom left into margin   ..   ..   3·00

No. U266 is known on phosphorised paper with either a shiny ink surface which gives a photo-negative reflection or a matt surface without the negative effect.

**Cylinder Numbers (Blocks of Six)**

Perforation Type RE

| Cyl. No. | | | | | No dot | Dot |
|---|---|---|---|---|---|---|
| 4 | .. | .. | .. | .. | 5·00 | 5·00 |

**139**

**CYLINDER VARIETIES**
**Listed Flaws**

U265*b*
(Cyl. 4 no dot, R. 6/2)

U265*c*
(Cyl. 4 no dot, R. 11/5)
Retouched on No. U266

U265/66*d*
(Cyl. 4 no dot, R. 13/2)

U265/66*e*
(Cyl. 4 no dot, R. 14/9)

Multipositive Flaws
    No. U265*e* occurs on the 11p. value and No. U265*c* was retouched on the 11p.

**Minor Constant Sheet Flaws**
Cyl. 4    20/9  Pale blemishes behind head and neck (Th. D5 and F6)
        20/10 Pale blemish behind bust (Th. G6)

**WITHDRAWN**   No. U265, 12.80; No. U266, 10.81

---

# 20p. Turquoise-green   (1988)
**1988 (23 AUGUST). COLOUR CHANGED. PHOSPHORISED (ADVANCED COATED) PAPER. PVAD GUM**
U267 (=S.G.X958)    Turquoise-green    . .    . .    . .    . .    . .    . .    30    35

**Cylinder Number (Blocks of Six)**
Perforation Type RE

| Cyl. No. | | | | | No dot | Dot |
|---|---|---|---|---|---|---|
| 11    . . | . . | . . | . . | | 2·40 | 2·40 |

**CYLINDER VARIETIES**
**Minor Constant Sheet Flaws**
Cyl. 11    6/6  Fine diagonal line across shoulder into dress (Th. F4–G5) multipositive flaw (see footnote below the flaw list of 14p. deep blue)
Cyl. 11.    3/8  Dark spot on cheek (Th. D3)
        11/8  Solid spot of colour at base of dress (Th. G4)
        13/7  Weak hairline scratch across shoulder (Th. F4–F5) multipositive flaw
        18/10 Small retouch in band of crown below central cross (Th. B4)
        19/7  Dark spot of colour on necklace (Th. F4)

**WITHDRAWN**   28.2.90 but back on sale March 1991

# 20p. Brownish Black   (1989–90)

## 1989 (26 SEPTEMBER). COLOUR CHANGED. PHOSPHORISED (ADVANCED COATED) PAPER. PVAD GUM

U268 (=S.G.X959)   Brownish black   ..   ..   ..   ..   ..   ..   30   30
                    a. Imperforate (pair)   ..   ..   ..   ..   ..

Imperforate edges: No. U268 exists with imperforate edges at left or right from pane UFB68.

### Cylinder Numbers (Blocks of Six)

Perforation Type RE

| Cyl. No. | | | | | No dot | Dot |
|---|---|---|---|---|---|---|
| 12 | .. | .. | .. | .. | 3·00 | 3·00 |

## 1989 (2 OCTOBER). TWO 9.5 mm. PHOSPHOR BANDS. FLUORESCENT COATED PAPER. PVAD GUM

50p. booklet pane UMFB47, £5 London Life se-tenant Pane UWB33.

U269 (=S.G.X915)   Brownish black   ..   ..   ..   ..   ..   ..   30   30
                    b. Phosphor omitted   ..   ..   ..   ..   ..

## CYLINDER VARIETIES

### Minor Constant Sheet Flaws

Cyl. 12   4/7   Retouch to left of ear-ring (Th. D3)
          6/6   Fine diagonal line across shoulder into dress (Th. F4–G5) multipositive flaw (see footnote below flaw list of 14p. deep blue)
          16/5   Straight dark line from Queen's nose to hair (Th. D2—E4)

## COILS

Phosphorised (advanced coated) paper. Printed in continuous reels.

| Code No. | Issued | Number in roll | Face value | Gum | Perf. Type |
|---|---|---|---|---|---|
| | | Vertical delivery | | | |
| TL | 16.10.89 | 500 | £100 | PVAD | Comb. |
| | | Sideways delivery | | | |
| SG | 16.10.89 | 1000 | £200 | PVAD | Comb. |

TL was later available in rolls containing 1000 stamps. The leader was similar in text, but the number of stamps and face value was changed. Prepared as an experiment, it was not available to the public.

Cylinder Numbers used:
          TL   Phosphorised (advanced coated) paper/PVAD   R2
          SG   Phosphorised (advanced coated) paper/PVAD   R3

## 20½p. Ultramarine   (1983)

**1983 (30 MARCH).   PHOSPHORISED (FLUORESCENT COATED) PAPER. PVAD GUM**

U275 (=S.G.X960)    Ultramarine .. .. .. .. .. .. .. 1·10    85
                    *a.* Imperforate (pair)   ..   ..   ..   ..   .. £750
                    *b.* White flaw above large 2   ..   ..   ..   .. 3·00

**Cylinder Numbers (Blocks of Six)**
Perforation Type RE

|         | No dot | Dot  |
|---------|--------|------|
| Cyl. No. |        |      |
| 1  ..   ..   ..   .. | 7·00 | 7·00 |

Perforation variety
   The 17 pin variety as described in Appendix I. *Price for marginal block of* 6 £1000, *cylinder no.* 1 *dot, block of* 6 £1400.

**CYLINDER VARIETIES**
**Listed Flaw**

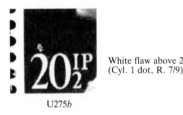

White flaw above 2
(Cyl. 1 dot, R. 7/9)

U275*b*

**Minor Constant Sheet Flaws**
Cyl. 1.    1/1  Small white spot on Queen's cheek (Th. D3)
           3/5  Retouch opposite crown at left side (Th. A2)
           3/6  White patch on Queen's neck (Th. F5)

**WITHDRAWN**   28.6.85

## 22p. Blue   (1980)

**1980 (22 OCTOBER).   PHOSPHORISED (FLUORESCENT COATED) PAPER. PVAD GUM**

U279 (=S.G.X961)    Blue .. .. .. .. .. .. .. 80    45
                    *a.* Imperforate (pair)   ..   ..   ..   ..   .. £150
                    *b.* Thin base to 2   ..   ..   ..   ..   ..   .. 3·00
                    *c.* Foreshortened 2 ..   ..   ..   ..   ..   .. 3·00
                    *d.* Scratch above dress   ..   ..   ..   ..   .. 2·75

   No. U279 is known on phosphorised paper with either a shiny ink surface which gives a photo-negative reflection or a matt surface without the negative effect.
   Covers exist postmarked at Chelmsford on 20 October 1980.
   A printing of this stamp from Cyl. 3 was reported to have an experimental coating but as this did not differ significantly from earlier printings, we do not list it.

**Cylinder Numbers (Blocks of Six)**
Perforation Type RE

|         | No dot | Dot  |
|---------|--------|------|
| Cyl. No. |        |      |
| 3  ..   ..   ..   .. | 4·75 | 4·75 |
| 4  ..   ..   ..   .. | 5·00 | 5·00 |

   Cyl. 4. The dot was omitted but on the no dot pane the figure "4" has a square end at right; on the dot pane it is slanted upwards and the complete right side of the box is weak.

**CYLINDER VARIETIES**
Listed Flaws

|   |   |
|---|---|
| U279*b* | U279*c* |
| Thin base to 2 | Foreshortened 2 |
| (Cyl. 4 no dot, R. 14/1 and 2) | (Cyl. 4 no dot, R. 15/1) |

Similar examples of U279*a* occur in the first row of the no dot and tenth row of the dot pane from Cyl. 3 and in the ninth horizontal row of Cyl. 4, no dot.

Multipositive Flaw
For illustration of No. U279*d*, from Cyl. 4 no dot, R. 12/4, see 29p. Cyl. 1.

**Minor Constant Sheet Flaws**
Cyl. 3.   10/7   Horizontal pale mark below first 2
          10/8   Blemish to top margin from jewels at the top of crown (Th. A4)
         15/10   Diagonal scratch across cheek from Queen's lip to hair (Th. D1–D4)
         20/9   Diagonal hairline flaw across shoulder (Th. F5–G3)
Cyl. 4   11/4   Retouch on shoulder (Th. G2)
         17/3   Spot on first 2
        17/10   Hairline scratch through dress into background at lower left (Th. G4–G5). Multipositive flaw as 29p. Cyl. 1 no dot
Cyl. 4.   19/7   Scratch across neck (Th. E3–E4). Multipositive flaw as 2p. Cyl. 14 dot
         20/9   Diagonal scratch across shoulder (Th. F4–F5). Multipositive flaw as 2p. Cyl. 14 dot

**WITHDRAWN**   29.4.84

# 22p. Yellow-green   (1984)

### 1984 (28 AUGUST).   COLOUR CHANGED. PHOSPHORISED (ADVANCED COATED) PAPER. PVAD GUM

U280 (=S.G.X962)   Yellow-green   .. .. .. .. .. .. 35 45
                   *a*. Imperforate (horiz. pair)   .. .. .. .. £950

**Cylinder Numbers (Blocks of Six)**
Perforation Type RE

| Cyl. No. | | | | No dot | Dot |
|---|---|---|---|---|---|
| 6 | .. | .. | .. | .. 3·00 | 3·00 |
| 10 | .. | .. | .. | .. 2·75 | 2·75 |

Perforation variety
    The 17 pin variety as described in Appendix I. *Price for marginal block of* 6 £30, *cylinder no.* 6 *dot, block of* 6 £50.

**Minor Constant Sheet Flaws**
Cyl. 6   17/8   Spot on shoulder (Th. G4)
Cyl. 6.   4/5   Dark spot between eyebrow and hair (Th. C3)

# 22p. Bright Orange-red   (1990)

**1990   (4   SEPTEMBER).   COLOUR   CHANGED.   PHOSPHORISED (ADVANCED COATED) PAPER. PVAD GUM**

U281 (=S.G.X963)   Bright orange-red  ..     ..     ..     ..     ..     ..     35     35

**Cylinder Numbers (Blocks of Six)**

Perforation Type RE

|  | Cyl. No. | | | | No dot | Dot |
|---|---|---|---|---|---|---|
|  | 10  | .. | .. | .. | .. 2·75 | 2·75 |

**1990   (4   SEPTEMBER).   TWO   PHOSPHOR   BANDS.   FLUORESCENT COATED PAPER. PVAD GUM**

£1 booklet pane UMFB48

U282 (=S.G.X916)   Bright orange-red  ..     ..     ..     ..     ..     ..     35     35
                   *a.* Two 3 mm. bands     ..     ..     ..     ..     ..     35

On No. U282 the left band is across the perforations, but the 3 mm band at right is clear of the vertical edge. No. U282a is the single 22p. value in position R. 2/2 of the pane, below the postcode label.

Imperforate edges: Nos. U282/*a* only exist with imperforate edge at right.

**CYLINDER VARIETIES**

**Minor Constant Sheet Flaws**

Cyl. 10    3/5  Small pale disturbance on shoulder (Th. G4)
           13/8  Scratch above dress (Th. F4–F5) multipositive flaw (see 20p. turquoise-green where
                 it is on R. 13/7)
           20/9  Two dark specks below necklace and one on dress (Th. F3–G3)

**COILS**

Phosphorised (advanced coated) paper. Printed in continuous reels.

| Code No. | Issued | Number in roll | Face value | Gum | Perf. Type |
|---|---|---|---|---|---|
|  |  |  | Vertical delivery | | Chambon |
| WL | 17.9.90 | 500 | £110 | PVAD | Comb. |
| WL | 17.9.90 | 1000 | £220 | PVAD | Comb. |

Cylinder Number used:

WL         Phosphorised (advanced coated) paper/PVAD   R1

# 23p. Brown-red   (1983)

**1983 (30 MARCH). PHOSPHORISED (FLUORESCENT COATED) PAPER. PVAD GUM**

| | | | |
|---|---|---|---|
| U283 (=S.G.X964) | Brown-red .. .. .. .. .. .. .. | 1·40 | 60 |
| | a. Imperforate (horiz. pair) .. .. .. .. | £750 | |
| | b. Retouch on cheek .. .. .. .. .. | 3·50 | |

**Cylinder Numbers (Blocks of Six)**

Perforation Type RE

| Cyl. No. | | | | No dot | Dot |
|---|---|---|---|---|---|
| 1 | .. | .. | .. .. | 8·00 | 8·00 |

Perforation variety
    The 17 pin variety as described in Appendix I is rare on this value.

**CYLINDER VARIETIES**
**Listed Flaw**

U283*b*
Retouch on cheek
(Cyl. 1 dot, R. 2/2)

**Minor Constant Sheet Flaws**

Cyl. 23    2/6  Retouch above crown (Th. A5)
           6/5  Pale spot below necklace (Th. F4)

**WITHDRAWN**   7.9.85

# 23p. Bright Green   (1988)

**1988 (23 AUGUST).  COLOUR CHANGED. PHOSPHORISED (ADVANCED COATED) PAPER. PVAD GUM**

| | | | |
|---|---|---|---|
| U284 (=S.G.X965)   Bright green .. .. .. .. .. .. .. | 35 | 40 |

**Cylinder Numbers (Blocks of Six)**

Perforation Type RE

| Cyl. No. | .. | .. | .. | .. | No dot | Dot |
|---|---|---|---|---|---|---|
| 6 | .. | .. | .. | .. | 2·75 | 2·75 |

**CYLINDER VARIETIES**
**Minor Constant Sheet Flaws**

Cyl. 6    6/7  Fine diagonal line across shoulder into dress (Th. F4–G5) multipositive flaw (see footnote below flaw list of 14p. deep blue)

Cyl. 6.   13/8  Scratch above dress (Th. F4–F5) multipositive flaw (see 20p. turquoise-green where it is on R. 13/7)
          19/7  Weakness in the background at top left (Th. A2)

**WITHDRAWN** 25.9.90

**145**

# 24p. Violet   (1984)
**1984 (28 AUGUST).   PHOSPHORISED (ADVANCED COATED) PAPER. PVAD GUM**

U285 (=S.G.X966)    Violet . .    . .    . .    . .    . .    . .    . .    . .    75    60

**Cylinder Numbers (Blocks of Six)**
Perforation Type RE

| Cyl. No. | | | | | No dot | Dot |
|---|---|---|---|---|---|---|
| 1 | . . | . . | . . | . . | 4·75 | 4·75 |
| 2 | . . | . . | . . | . . | 10·00 | 5·00 |

Perforation variety
   The 17 pin variety as described in Appendix I. *Price for marginal block of* 6 £8, *cylinder no.* 1 *dot, block of* 6 £20.

**WITHDRAWN** 4.9.89

# 24p. Indian Red   (1989)
**1989 (26 SEPTEMBER). COLOUR CHANGED. PHOSPHORISED (ADVANCED COATED) PAPER. PVAD GUM**

U286 (=S.G.X967)    Indian red   . .    . .    . .    . .    . .    . .    . .    40    45
                    *a.* Imperforate (horiz. pair)    . .    . .    . .    . .

**Cylinder Numbers (Blocks of Six)**
Perforation Type RE

| Cyl. No. | | | | | No dot | Dot |
|---|---|---|---|---|---|---|
| 2 | . . | . . | . . | . . | 2·75 | 2·75 |

**CYLINDER VARIETIES**
**Minor Constant Sheet Flaws**
Cyl. 2   1/1 Small speck of colour omitted at back of Queen's neck (Th. F5)
         6/3 Dark spot on hair below band of crown (Th. C5)

# 25p. Purple (1981)

### 1981 (14 JANUARY). PHOSPHORISED (FLUORESCENT COATED) PAPER. PVAD GUM

| U288 (=S.G.X968) | Purple | .. | .. | .. | .. | .. | .. | .. | 90 | 90 |
|---|---|---|---|---|---|---|---|---|---|---|
| | a. Spot on shoulder.. | | .. | .. | .. | .. | .. | 2·75 | |
| | b. Retouch in front of nose | | | .. | .. | .. | .. | 3·25 | |
| | c. White scratch behind hair | | | .. | .. | .. | .. | 3·25 | |
| | d. Dark spot on 2 .. | | .. | .. | .. | .. | .. | 3·25 | |
| | e. L shaped scratch .. | | .. | .. | .. | .. | .. | 3·50 | |
| | f. Semi-circle of dots | | .. | .. | .. | .. | .. | 3·00 | |

No. U288 is known on phosphorised paper with either a shiny ink surface which gives a photo-negative reflection or a matt surface without the negative effect.

**Cylinder Numbers (Blocks of Six)**

Perforation Type RE

| Cyl. No. | | | | | No dot | Dot |
|---|---|---|---|---|---|---|
| 2 | .. | .. | .. | .. | 6·00 | 6·00 |

## CYLINDER VARIETIES

### Listed Flaws

For illustrations of Nos. U288b/c see Nos. U255b and d. These are multipositive flaws which occur on 18p. violet Cyl. 1 no dot, R. 13/2 and R. 19/10.

U288a
Spot on shoulder
(Cyl. 2 no dot, R. 2/7)

U288d
Dark spot on 2
(Cyl. 2 dot, R. 5/7)

U288f
Semi-circle of dots
above pearls
(Cyl. 2 dot, R. 20/6)

Long L shaped scratch
across stamp
(Cyl. 2 dot, R. 18/8)

U288e

**Minor Constant Sheet Flaws**

Cyl. 2   1/1 Small retouch below bust (Th. G4). See also pane No. UFB15
         1/8 Diagonal hairline through back of crown (Th. A5–D6)
         1/10 Dark spot top left (Th. A1)
         2/9 Diagonal hairline through neck and shoulder (Th. E3–F4) and dark spot above crown (Th. A4)
         3/6 Small retouch above necklace (Th. E4)
         4/1 Dark smear in background below bust (Th. G5–H5)
         4/5 Small dot behind band of crown (Th. C5). See also pane No. UFB15
         7/4 Blemish below chin (Th. E2) and dark speck in background above Queen's forehead (Th. B2)
         8/4 Diagonal line from Queen's nose to the top of 2
         9/2 Dark spot on hairline above cheek (Th. D3)
         9/10 Small dark spot in Queen's hair (Th. C4)
         11/7 Dark spot between 2 and 5 (Th. F5)
         11/9 Dark spot above 2 (Th. F1)
         13/1 White speck behind dress (Th. F6)
         14/4 Diagonal line by mouth (Th. D3)
         16/1 Hairline above P and across shoulder (Th. F2–F4)
         19/3 Diagonal hairline above the back of the crown (Th. B6) which continues on 19/4 as a faint line
         19/9 Faint scratch through neck and background (Th. E4–E5)
         20/4 Nick in hair at the back of neck (Th. E5)

Cyl. 2.   1/5 White spot behind front cross on crown (Th. A3–4) and dark spot on Queen's neck (Th. E3)
          2/1 Dark vertical scratch above Queen's nose (Th. B2–C2)
          2/5 White speck in Queen's hair (Th. C2)
          3/3 Damage to base of Queen's bust (Th. G3)
          3/7 Hairline scratch behind Queen's neck (Th. E5–F6)
          3/9 Pale blemish at left (Th. E1)
          4/3 Pale vertical scratch which continues across the corner of 3/3 (Th. A1–H1)
          5/3 Diagonal hairline scratch through value
          6/9 Pale spot behind hair (Th. E5) and diagonal hairline through neck (Th. D3–F5)
          6/10 Horizontal blemish behind Queen's hair (Th. D6)
          7/6 White speck between 2 and 5
          7/8 Curved scratch from Queen's neck to margin (Th. G4–H5)
          9/6 Diagonal line on Queen's shoulder (Th. F4–G4)
          20/2 Two dots above Queen's crown (Th. A5–A6)

Some of the flaws on Cyl. 2 are multipositive flaws which also occur on the 12p. yellowish green, Cyl. 4 booklet pane and 18p. violet Cyl. 1.

**WITHDRAWN**  14.1.84

# 26p. Rosine   (1982–87)

**Two Value Types**

Type I.   Wide figures
Type II.  Narrow figures. £1·04 booklet
pane UFB49

I                II

## 1982 (27 JANUARY).   PHOSPHORISED PAPER. TYPE I. PVAD GUM
### A. FLUORESCENT COATED PAPER
U291              Rosine    ..    ..    ..    ..    ..    ..    ..    90

**Cylinder Numbers (Blocks of Six)**
Perforation Type RE

| Cyl. No. | No dot | Dot |
|---|---|---|
| 2    ..    ..    ..    .. | 5·50 | 5·50 |

Perforation variety
   The 17 pin variety as described in Appendix I. *Price for marginal block of* 6 £75, *cylinder no.* 2 *dot, block of* 6 £170.

### B. ADVANCED COATED PAPER (1984)†
U292 (=S.G.X969)    Rosine    ..    ..    ..    ..    ..    ..    ..    90    30
                    b. Scratch above dress    ..    ..    ..    ..    ..    2·50

**Cylinder Numbers (Blocks of Six)**
Perforation Type RE

| Cyl. No. | No dot | Dot |
|---|---|---|
| 1    ..    ..    ..    .. | 5·50 | 5·50 |
| 2    ..    ..    ..    .. | 5·50 | 5·50 |

   †No. U292 was first placed on sale at the Philatelic Bureau on 24 June 1986 at the same time as the 34p. on advanced coated paper.
Perforation variety
   The 17 pin variety as described in Appendix I. *Price for marginal block of* 6 £800, *cylinder no.* 2 *dot, block of* 6 £1100.

## 1987 (3 MARCH).   TWO PHOSPHOR BANDS. FLUORESCENT COATED PAPER. TYPE I. PVAD GUM
£5 P & O booklet *se-tenant* pane UWB31
U293 (=S.G.X917)    Rosine    ..    ..    ..    ..    ..    ..    ..    5·50    4·50
                    a. Original phosphor ink   ..    ..    ..    ..    ..

   No. U293a came from pane UWB31a with phosphor bands in original phosphor ink which, under ultra violet light, appears dark in comparison with the normal new phosphor ink.

## 1987 (4 AUGUST).   PHOSPHORISED (ADVANCED COATED) PAPER. TYPE II. PVAD GUM
£1·04 booklet pane UFB49
U294 (=S.G.X969a)    Rosine    ..    ..    ..    ..    ..    ..    ..    4·50    3·75

### CYLINDER VARIETIES
Multipositive Flaw
   For illustration of No. U292b, from Cyl. 1 no dot, R. 12/4, see 29p. ochre-brown Cyl. 1

**149**

**Minor Constant Sheet Flaws**

Cyl. 2   16/3  Small white nick in 6 at left
          19/5  Blemish below necklace (Th. F3)

Cyl. 2.   3/7  Right side of 2 damaged
          10/6  Weak loop to 6

**WITHDRAWN**   No. U291, 23.6.87, No. U292, 4.9.89

## 26p. Drab   (1990)

**1990   (4   SEPTEMBER).   COLOUR   CHANGED.   PHOSPHORISED (ADVANCED COATED) PAPER. PVAD GUM**

U295 (=S.G.X970)   Drab ..     ..     ..     ..     ..     ..     ..     ..     40     40

**Cylinder Numbers (Blocks of Six)**

Perforation Type RE

| Cyl. No. | | | | | No dot | Dot |
|---|---|---|---|---|---|---|
| 4 | .. | .. | .. | .. | 3·25 | 3·25 |

**CYLINDER VARIETIES**

**Minor Constant Sheet Flaws**

Cyl. 4.   13/7  Scratch above dress (Th. F4–F5) multipositive flaw (see 20p. turquoise-green)

## 27p. Chestnut   (1988)

**1988 (23 AUGUST).  PHOSPHORISED (ADVANCED COATED) PAPER. PVAD GUM**

U296 (=S.G.X971)   Chestnut     ..     ..     ..     ..     ..     ..     ..     1·00     85

**Cylinder Numbers (Blocks of Six)**

Perforation Type RE

| Cyl. No. | | | | | No dot | Dot |
|---|---|---|---|---|---|---|
| 1 | .. | .. | .. | .. | 6·00 | 6·00 |

**CYLINDER VARIETIES**

**Minor Constant Sheet Flaws**

Cyl. 1    4/1   White specks in front of Queen's nose (Th. C2)
          17/4  Similar flaw to that on R. 4/1 but at top left (Th. B1)
          20/2  Blemish on folds of dress (Th. G3)
          20/10 Pair of dots on shoulder (Th. F4)

Cyl. 1.   5/10  Two dark specks on neck (Th. E3)
          12/9  Wavy line touching the underside of necklace (Th. E4)

**WITHDRAWN**   25.9.90

**150**

# 27p. Violet (1990)

**1990 (4 SEPTEMBER). COLOUR CHANGED. PHOSPHORISED (ADVANCED COATED) PAPER. PVAD GUM**

U297 (=S.G.X972)   Violet.. .. .. .. .. .. .. .. 45   45

**Cylinder Numbers (Blocks of Six)**
Perforation Type RE

| Cyl. No. | | | | No dot | Dot |
|---|---|---|---|---|---|
| 1 | .. | .. | .. | 3·25 | 3·25 |

**CYLINDER VARIETIES**

**Minor Constant Sheet Flaws**
Cyl. 1   20/3  Cluster of specks from a retouch below the front of the necklace (Th. F3)

# 28p. Deep Violet (1983–86)

**1983 (30 MARCH).  PHOSPHORISED PAPER. PVAD GUM**

**A. FLUORESCENT COATED PAPER**

| U298 | Deep violet .. | .. | .. | .. | .. | .. | .. | 75 |
|---|---|---|---|---|---|---|---|---|
| | *a.* Imperforate (pair) | | .. | .. | .. | .. | .. | £975 |
| | *b.* Screen damage .. | | .. | .. | .. | .. | .. | 3·50 |

**Cylinder Numbers (Blocks of Six)**
Perforation Type RE

| Cyl. No. | | | | No dot | Dot |
|---|---|---|---|---|---|
| 1 | .. | .. | .. | 5·00 | 5·00 |

**B. ADVANCED COATED PAPER** (7.10.86)

U299 (=S.G.X973)   Deep violet .. .. .. .. .. .. .. 75   60

**Cylinder Numbers (Blocks of Six)**
Perforation Type RE

| Cyl. No. | | | | No dot | Dot |
|---|---|---|---|---|---|
| 1 | .. | .. | .. | 5·00 | 5·00 |

Perforation variety
 The 17 pin variety as described in Appendix I. *Price for marginal block of* 6 £6, *cylinder no.* 1 *dot, block of* 6 £15.

**CYLINDER VARIETIES**
**Listed Flaw**

U298*b*
Screen damage at top left. There is
a smaller area behind the crown
(Cyl. 1 no dot, R. 6/4)

**Minor Constant Sheet Flaws**

Cyl. 1    5/5  Weakness in background at upper left (Th. A2)
        8/6  Small repair behind dress (Th. F6)
     13/7  Dark blemish below value
     19/2  Curved hairline from right edge and mass of specks below necklace
     20/5  Dark spot behind hair (Th. D6)
Cyl. 1.   8/10  White line over dress (Th. G3)
     20/4  Dark diagonal scratch to margin at lower right (Th. F6–G6)

**WITHDRAWN**  No. U298, 6.10.87, No. U299, 11.4.89

# 28p. Ochre   (1988)

**1988 (23 AUGUST).   COLOUR CHANGED. PHOSPHORISED (ADVANCED COATED) PAPER. PVAD GUM**

U300 (=S.G.X974)   Ochre . .    . .    . .    . .    . .    . .    . .    . .    45    50

**Cylinder Number (Blocks of Six)**

Perforation Type RE

| Cyl. No. | | | | | No dot | Dot |
|---|---|---|---|---|---|---|
| 4 | . . | . . | . . | . . | 3·25 | 3·25 |

**CYLINDER VARIETIES**

**Minor Constant Sheet Flaws**

Cyl. 4.   1/5  Small disturbance at top left (Th. B1)
     13/7  Scratch above dress (Th. F4–F5) multipositive flaw (see 20p. turquoise-green and R.13/8 on 22p. orange-red)
     20/7  Random specks on dress and blot on back of neck (Th. E4)

**WITHDRAWN**  25.9.90 but back on sale March 1991

# 29p. Ochre-brown   (1982)

**1982 (27 JANUARY).   PHOSPHORISED (FLUORESCENT COATED) PAPER. PVAD GUM**

| U301 (=S.G.X975) | Ochre-brown . . | | | | | | 2·50 | 1·25 |
|---|---|---|---|---|---|---|---|---|
| | a. Retouch in front of mouth | . . | . . | . . | . . | | 5·50 | |
| | b. Scratch above dress | . . | . . | . . | . . | | 5·50 | |
| | c. Nick in 9 . . | . . | . . | . . | . . | | 5·00 | |

**Cylinder Numbers (Blocks of Six)**

Perforation Type RE

| Cyl. No. | | | | | No dot | Dot |
|---|---|---|---|---|---|---|
| 1 | . . | . . | . . | . . | 15·00 | 18·00* |

**CYLINDER VARIETIES**
**Listed Flaws**

U301*a*
Large retouch to back-
ground in front of mouth
(Cyl. 1 no dot, R. 5/3)

U301*b*
Long diagonal scratch similar
to an identical flaw on Pane UMFB8
(Cyl. 1 no dot, R. 12/4)

Nick in 9
(Cyl. 1 dot, R. 18/1)

U301*c*

**Minor Constant Sheet Flaws**

Cyl. 1   1/1  White spot below Queen's eye (Th. C2–C3 intersection)
   1/4  Weak spot in background in front of Queen's mouth (Th. D1)
   2/1  Short diagonal scratch at upper left (Th. B1)
   3/5  White nick at the top of 9
   5/2  Pale spot on Queen's eyelid (Th. C3)
   8/3  Pale spot on jawline (Th. E3) and spot in front of lip (Th. D2)
   17/10  Hairline scratch through dress into background at lower left (Th. G4–G5)
   18/1  Small retouch below bust (Th. H5)
Cyl. 1.   10/7  Blemish in background below (Th. G1)

**WITHDRAWN**   29.4.84

# 29p. Deep Mauve   (1989)

**1989   (26   SEPTEMBER).   COLOUR   CHANGED.   PHOSPHORISED
(ADVANCED COATED) PAPER. PVAD GUM**

U302 (=S.G.X976)   Deep mauve ..    ..    ..    ..    ..    ..    ..    45    50

**Cylinder Numbers (Blocks of Six)**
Perforation Type RE

| Cyl. No. | | | | No dot | Dot |
|---|---|---|---|---|---|
| 4 | .. | .. | .. | .. | 3·25 | 3·25 |

**CYLINDER VARIETIES**
**Minor Constant Sheet Flaws**

Cyl. 4   1/1  Pale speck above dress (Th. F4)
   4/7  Pale shaded patch on cheek (Th. D3) multipositive flaw (see 14p. deep blue on R. 4/8 or
     15p. bright blue, R. 4/7)
   6/2  Heavy dot in 9
   6/3  Pale background in front of Queen's eye (Th. C2)
   6/6  Fine diagonal line across shoulder into dress (Th. F4–G5) multi-positive flaw (see
     footnote below the flaw list of 14p. deep blue)

# 30p. Deep Olive-grey  (1989)

**1989 (26 SEPTEMBER).  PHOSPHORISED (ADVANCED COATED) PAPER.
PVAD GUM**

| U303 (=S.G.X977) | Deep olive-grey | .. | .. | .. | .. | .. | .. | 45 | 50 |
| | b. Large spots on shoulder | | .. | .. | .. | .. | 2·50 | | |

**Cylinder Numbers (Blocks of Six)**
Perforation Type RE

| Cyl. No. | | | | | No dot | Dot |
|---|---|---|---|---|---|---|
| 2 | .. | .. | .. | .. | 3·25 | 3·25 |

**CYLINDER VARIETIES**
**Listed Flaw**

Large spots on
Queen's shoulder
and dress (Cyl. 2 dot,
R. 18/8)

U303b

**Minor Constant Sheet Flaws**

| Cyl. 4. | 2/4 | Spot on dress (Th. G3) |
| | 15/1 | Dark spot in background to right of necklace (Th. E5) |
| | 16/2 | Small disturbance on shoulder (Th. F4) |
| | 17/10 | Speck on shoulder (Th. F3) |

# 31p. Purple  (1983–86)

**1983 (30 MARCH).  PHOSPHORISED PAPER. PVAD GUM**

**A. FLUORESCENT COATED PAPER**

| U304 | Purple | .. | .. | .. | .. | .. | .. | .. | 75 |
| | a. Imperforate (pair) | | .. | .. | .. | .. | £975 | |

**Cylinder Numbers (Blocks of Six)**
Perforation Type RE

| Cyl. No. | | | | No dot | Dot |
|---|---|---|---|---|---|
| 2 | .. | .. | .. | 7·00 | 7·00 |

Perforation variety
The 17 pin variety as described in Appendix I. *Price for marginal block of 6 £2000, cylinder no. 2 dot, block of 6 is rare but has been reported.*

**B. ADVANCED COATED PAPER** (17.9.85)

| U305 (=S.G.X978) | Purple | .. | .. | .. | .. | .. | .. | 1·25 | 80 |
| | a. Imperforate (pair) | | .. | .. | .. | .. | | |

**Cylinder Numbers (Blocks of Six)**
Perforation Type RE

| Cyl. No. | | | | No dot | Dot |
|---|---|---|---|---|---|
| 2 | .. | .. | .. | 7·00 | 7·00 |

Perforation variety
The 17 pin variety as described in Appendix I. *Price for marginal block of 6 £10, cylinder no. 2 dot, block of 6 £20.*

## 1986 (18 MARCH). TWO 9·5 mm. PHOSPHOR BANDS. FLUORESCENT COATED PAPER. PVAD GUM

£5 British Rail booklet *se-tenant* pane UWB27

| | | | | | | | | |
|---|---|---|---|---|---|---|---|---|
| U306 (=S.G.X918) | Purple | .. | .. | .. | .. | .. | 5·50 | 4·50 |
| | *a.* Phosphor omitted | .. | .. | .. | .. | .. | £650 | |

**CYLINDER VARIETIES**

**Minor Constant Sheet Flaws**

Cyl. 2.  1/8  Diagonal scratch behind hair (Th. E6)
          10/3  Diagonal scratch across cheek and background (Th. D2–D3)
          13/7  Small pale blemish in lower curve of 3
          16/7  Short scratch above central cross (Th. A5)
          16/10 Dot on dress (Th. G4)
          17/6  Pale blemish below 3
          17/10 Short horizontal dash above crown (Th. B6) and long diagonal scratch from hair to
                background below dress (Th. D5–H4)
          20/9  Scratch into the forehead (Th. B2–B3)

**WITHDRAWN**  No. U304, 31.10.86, No. U305, 4.9.89

# 31p. Ultramarine  (1990)

## 1900 (4 SEPTEMBER). COLOUR CHANGED. PHOSPHORISED (ADVANCED COATED) PAPER. PVAD GUM

| | | | | | | | | |
|---|---|---|---|---|---|---|---|---|
| U307 (=S.G.X979) | Ultramarine | .. | .. | .. | .. | .. | 50 | 50 |

**Cylinder Numbers (Blocks of Six)**

Perforation Type RE

| Cyl. No. | | | | | No dot | Dot |
|---|---|---|---|---|---|---|
| 8 | .. | .. | .. | .. | 4·50 | 4·50 |

**CYLINDER VARIETIES**

**Minor Constant Sheet Flaws**

Cyl. 8  11/1  Dark spot at the base of dress (Th. G3)
         11/9  White speck in band of crown (Th. B4)
         15/3  Specks on hair (Th. B3) and below necklace (Th. F3)
         16/2  Repair at the back of shoulder (Th. F4)

# 32p. Greenish Blue  (1988)

## 1988 (23 AUGUST). PHOSPHORISED (ADVANCED COATED) PAPER. PVAD GUM

| | | | | | | | | |
|---|---|---|---|---|---|---|---|---|
| U308 (=S.G.X980) | Greenish blue .. | .. | .. | .. | .. | .. | 50 | 55 |
| | *a.* Imperforate (pair) | .. | .. | .. | .. | .. | | |

**Cylinder Numbers (Blocks of Six)**

Perforation Type RE

| Cyl. No. | | | | | No dot | Dot |
|---|---|---|---|---|---|---|
| 1 | .. | .. | .. | .. | 4·00 | 4·00 |

**CYLINDER VARIETIES**

**Minor Constant Sheet Flaws**

Cyl. 1   2/1  Specks on Queen's neck (Th. F4)
          2/5  Hairline from dress on R. 2/5 (Th. F6) to chin of R. 2/6
          6/6  Fine diagonal line across shoulder into dress (Th. F4–G5) multipositive flaw (see
               footnote below the flaw list of 14p. deep blue
         18/5  Retouch in front of eye (Th. C2)
Cyl. 1.  16/6  Small retouch on neck just below the necklace (Th. F4)
         20/7  Oblong dark flaw at the back of shoulder just above the dress (Th. F5)

**WITHDRAWN**  25.9.90 but back on sale March 1991

# 33p. Light Emerald   (1990)

**1990 (4 SEPTEMBER).  PHOSPHORISED (ADVANCED COATED) PAPER.
PVAD GUM**

U309 (=S.G.X981)  Light emerald  ..      ..      ..      ..      ..      ..      ..      50      50

**Cylinder Numbers (Blocks of Six)**

Perforation Type RE

| Cyl. No. | | | | | No dot | Dot |
|---|---|---|---|---|---|---|
| 1 | .. | .. | .. | .. | 4·00 | 4·00 |

**CYLINDER VARIETIES**

**Minor Constant Sheet Flaws**

Cyl. 1    5/7  Thin line from hair to dress (Th. E4–G4)
         6/6  Fine diagonal line across shoulder into dress (Th. F4–G5)
  Both of these flaws are multipositive and are also listed under 17p. deep blue

Cyl. 1.   1/10  Small repair above necklace (Th. E4)
       2/6  Short stroke on shoulder above dress (Th. G4)
     3/10  Slightly curved line of specks from hair to beneath eye (Th. D3)
      7/4  Short vertical scratch on cheek (Th. D3)
    13/7  Scratch above dress (Th. F4–F5) multipositive flaw (see 20p. turquoise-green)
    20/7  Pair of dots at the back of shoulder (Th. F5)

# 34p. Ochre-brown   (1984–86)

**1984 (28 AUGUST).  PHOSPHORISED PAPER. PVAD GUM**

**A. FLUORESCENT COATED PAPER**

U310                 Ochre-brown..      ..      ..      ..      ..      ..      ..      1·10

**Cylinder Numbers (Blocks of Six)**

Perforation Type RE

| Cyl. No. | | | | | No dot | Dot |
|---|---|---|---|---|---|---|
| 1 | .. | .. | .. | .. | 6·00 | 6·00 |

**B. ADVANCED COATED PAPER** (24.6.86)

U311 (=S.G.X982)   Ochre-brown..      ..      ..      ..      ..      ..      1·10      80

**Cylinder Numbers (Blocks of Six)**

Perforation Type RE

| Cyl. No. | | | | | No dot | Dot |
|---|---|---|---|---|---|---|
| 2 | .. | .. | .. | .. | 6·00 | 6·00 |

Perforation variety
  The 17 pin variety as described in Appendix I. *Price for marginal block of* 6 £10, *cylinder no. 2 dot,
block of* 6 £32.

**1985 (8 JANUARY).  TWO 9·5 mm. PHOSPHOR BANDS. FLUORESCENT
COATED PAPER. PVAD GUM**

£5 Story of *The Times* booklet *se-tenant* pane No. UWB23

| U312 (=S.G.X919) | Ochre-brown.. | .. | .. | .. | .. | .. | 5·50 | 4·50 |
|---|---|---|---|---|---|---|---|---|
| | *a.* Phosphor omitted | .. | .. | .. | .. | £750 | |
| | *b.* One broad band .. | .. | .. | .. | .. | | |
| | *c.* Phosphor printed on both sides | | .. | .. | .. | £500 | |

**CYLINDER VARIETIES**
**Minor Constant Sheet Flaws**
Cyl. 1   17/5   Dark spot above ear (Th. C4)
          19/8   Pale flaw on cheek (Th. D3)
Cyl. 1.   4/2   Semi-circular weak patch in background (Th. A1–B1)
          6/3   White speck in front of neck (Th. F3)
          8/6   Spot below ear (Th. E4)
          9/1   Blemish in background above central cross (Th. A5)
          10/3   Pale mark in background opposite Queen's chin (Th. D2)
          10/7   Spot on cheek (Th. D3)
Cyl. 2.   3/8   Pale area below dress at right (Th. G5)
          9/2   Small break in shading below jawline (Th. E2–E3 intersection)
          13/8   Hairline scratch across Queen's shoulder (Th. F4–F5)
   On Cyl. 2 dot most examples from the left of the sheet have screened values.

**WITHDRAWN**   No. U310, 23.6.87, No. U311, 4.9.89

## 34p. Deep Bluish Grey   (1989)
**1989   (26   SEPTEMBER).   COLOUR   CHANGED.   PHOSPHORISED (ADVANCED COATED) PAPER. PVAD GUM**
U313 (=S.G.X983)   Deep bluish grey   ..   ..   ..   ..   ..   ..   55   55

**Cylinder Numbers (Blocks of Six)**
Perforation Type RE
            Cyl. No.                              No dot      Dot
            2   ..   ..   ..   ..   3·75      3·75

**CYLINDER VARIETIES**

**Minor Constant Sheet Flaws**

Cyl. 2   11/7   White flaw on Queen's neck below hair (Th. E4)

Cyl. 2.   13/8   Scratch above dress (Th. F4–F5) multipositive flaw (see 20p. turquoise-green on R. 13/7 and 22p. orange-red)

## 35p. Sepia   (1988)
**1988 (23 AUGUST). PHOSPHORISED (ADVANCED COATED) PAPER. PVAD GUM**
U314 (=S.G.X984)   Sepia ..   ..   ..   ..   ..   ..   ..   ..   1·25   75
            a. Imperforate (pair)   ..   ..   ..   ..   ..

**Cylinder Numbers (Blocks of Six)**
Perforation Type RE
            Cyl. No.                              No dot      Dot
            1   ..   ..   ..   ..   7·00      7·00

**CYLINDER VARIETIES**

**Minor Constant Sheet Flaws**

Cyl. 1   6/6   Fine diagonal line across shoulder into dress (Th. F4–G5) multipositive flaw (see footnote below the flaw list of 14p. deep blue)

Cyl. 1.   3/9   Heavy spot retouch in background at right behind hair (Th. E6)
          12/10   Faint smudge on chin (Th. D3)
          13/7   Scratch above dress (Th. F4–F5) multipositive flaw (see 34p. where this flaw is on R. 13/8)
          15/5   Blemish at the back of shoulder close to dress (Th. F5)
          20/7   Spot on the back of shoulder (Th. F5)

**WITHDRAWN**   25.9.90

# 37p. Rosine   (1989)

**1989 (26 SEPTEMBER).   PHOSPHORISED (ADVANCED COATED) PAPER.
PVAD GUM**

U316 (=S.G.X985)   Rosine   .. .. .. .. .. .. .. 60   65

**Cylinder Numbers (Blocks of Six)**

Perforation Type RE

|  | Cyl. No. |  |  |  |  | No dot | Dot |
|---|---|---|---|---|---|---|---|
|  | 2 | .. | .. | .. | .. | 3·75 | 3·75 |

**CYLINDER VARIETIES**

**Minor Constant Sheet Flaws**

Cyl. 2    2/7   Spot on eyebrow (Th. C3)
3/7   Blemish on forehead (Th. C2)
10/1  Dark spot in front of nose (Th. C1)

Cyl. 2.   13/7   Scratch above dress (Th. F4 very faint) multipositive flaw (see 35p. sepia)
19/7   Faint spot below necklace (Th. F4)
20/7   Spot on the back of shoulder (Th. F5) multipositive flaw (see 35p. sepia)

# 50p. Ochre-brown   (1977–80)

## 1977 (2 FEBRUARY).   TWO 9·5 mm. PHOSPHOR BANDS. FLUORESCENT COATED PAPER. PVAD GUM

| U321 (=S.G.X920) | Ochre-brown.. | | | | | | 1·75 | 40 |
|---|---|---|---|---|---|---|---|---|
| | *a.* With "all-over" phosphor | | | | | | 20·00 | |
| | *b.* Neck scratch | | | | | | 4·25 | |
| | *c.* Retouch above value | | | | | | 4·00 | |
| | *d.* Retouched scratch | | | | | | 4·00 | |

The "all-over" phosphor was applied in error and was a very thick coating with which apparently, the phosphor doctor blade was unable to cope. In some cases whole sheets were affected and in others only some vertical rows.

### Cylinder Numbers (Blocks of Six)
Perforation Type RE

| Cyl. No. | Phos. No. | | | | | No dot | Dot |
|---|---|---|---|---|---|---|---|
| 4 | P21 | | | | | 10·00* | 9·00 |
| 4 | 30 | | | | | 12·00* | 9·00 |
| 4 | 30 | −37 mm. (20) | | | | 20·00* | 18·00 |
| 4 | 30 | −45 mm. (20) | | | | 20·00* | 18·00 |
| 4 | 30 | −56 mm. (bot. mar.) | | | | — | 20·00 |
| 4 | 30 | −60 mm. (bot. mar.) | | | | — | 20·00 |
| 4 | | | | | | 30·00* | 24·00 |

## 1980 (21 MAY).   FLUORESCENT COATED PAPER. PVAD GUM

| U322 (=S.G.X986) | Ochre-brown.. | | | | | | 75 | 45 |
|---|---|---|---|---|---|---|---|---|
| | *a.* Imperforate (pair) | | | | | | £400 | |
| | *d.* Retouched scratch | | | | | | 2·25 | |
| | *e.* Cluster of spots | | | | | | 2·00 | |
| | *f.* Retouches above and below necklace | | | | | 2·00 | | |
| | *g.* Mouth retouch | | | | | | 2·00 | |

### Cylinder Numbers (Blocks of Six)
Perforation Type RE

| Cyl. No. | | | | | No dot | Dot |
|---|---|---|---|---|---|---|
| 4 | | | | | 8·00* | 6·00 |
| 21 | | | | | 8·00* | 6·00 |
| 28 | | | | | 20·00 | 18·00 |
| 31 | without dot | | | | 6·00 | 8·00 |
| 31 | with dot.. | | | | † | 6·00 |
| 34 | | | | | 5·00 | 5·00 |

The dot was at first omitted from cyl. 31 but was inserted later. The first version, without the dot, is distinguished by the thick vertical stroke at the point it joins the bottom side of the cylinder box.

Perforation variety

The 17 pin variety as described in Appendix I. *Price for marginal block of* 6 £130, *cylinder no.* 21 *dot, block of* 6 £450.

Phosphor Cylinder Displacements. Phos. cyl. 30 is known displaced up the margin 393 mm. opposite row 2.

## CYLINDER VARIETIES
### Listed Flaws

| U321*b* | U321*c* |
|---|---|
| White scratch through neck and shoulder (Cyl. 4 no dot, R. 1/4) | Retouches above and below value (Cyl. 4 no dot, R. 8/2) |

**159**

U321*d*/22*d*
Retouched scratch from
eyebrow to hair
(Cyl. 4 no dot, R. 18/1)

U322*e*
Cluster of pale spots
(Cyl. 21 dot, R. 15/1)

U322*f*
Retouches above and below
necklace
(Cyl. 21 dot, R. 20/8)

U322*g*
Retouch at the corner
of Queen's mouth
(Cyl. 21 no dot, R. 13/10)

**Minor Constant Sheet Flaws**

Cyl. 4   1/4   Diagonal line from Queen's upper lip to right corner of dress (Th. D2–F5)
          1/7   Diagonal line from top left corner, through crown to right margin (Th. A2–B6)
          1/8   Diagonal line though Queen's face (Th. C1–D4)
          1/10   Diagonal line passes from right margin through Queen to left margin (Th. C2–F6)
          2/4   Two pale spots on lower part of right margin (Th. G6)
          6/4   Smudge over Queen's eye (Th. C2–C3)
          18/6   Retouch in 0 of 50

Cyl. 21   10/7   White specks on Queen's chin and neck (Th. D3–E3)
          15/1   Group of specks on dress (Th. G3–G4)
          18/4   Pale specks to right of P (Th. F3)
          18/7   Retouch on cheek (Th. D3)
          19/8   Pale patch on necklace (Th. E4)

Cyl. 21.   5/9   Dotted retouch in background behind Queen's necklace (Th. E5)
          11/6   Pale stroke through 0 of value
          11/9   Diagonal scratch from central cross to frame (Th. A4–B6)
          15/3   Pale spot touching bottom of dress (Th. G5)
          17/8   Pale dot on Queen's shoulder (Th. F4)
          18/7   Small retouch on Queen's cheek (Th. D3)
          19/10   Pale patch below foot of P

Cyl. 31   1/8   Blemish on cheek (Th. C3)
          2/5   Dark spot on Queen's eyebrow (Th. C2–3 intersection)
          8/2   Damage appears as pale disturbance on chin (Th. D2–E2)

Cyl. 31.   17/1   White spot appears as a large additional pearl in front of crown (Th. A3)

**WITHDRAWN**   No. U321, 10.81, No. U322, 12.3.91

# 50p. Ochre (1990)

**1990 (13 MARCH). COLOUR CHANGED. FLUORESCENT COATED PAPER. PVAD GUM**

U323 (=S.G.X987)    Ochre.. .. .. .. .. .. .. .. 75    45

**Cylinder Numbers (Blocks of Six)**

Perforation Type RE

| Cyl. No. | | | | | No dot | Dot |
|---|---|---|---|---|---|---|
| 35 | .. | .. | .. | .. | 5·00 | 5·00 |
| 36 | .. | .. | .. | .. | 5·00 | 5·00 |

**1990 (20 MARCH). TWO 9.5 mm. PHOSPHOR BANDS. FLUORESCENT COATED PAPER. PVAD GUM**

£5 London Life booklet *se-tenant* pane UWB33

U324 (=S.G.X921)    Ochre.. .. .. .. .. .. .. .. 3·00    3·00

**CYLINDER VARIETIES**

**Minor Constant Sheet Flaws**

Cyl. 35.    1/2  Large patch of white specks in front of Queen's nose (Th. D1–D2)
13/7  Scratch above dress (Th. F4–F5) multipositive flaw (see note under 34p. where this flaw is on R. 13/8)
14/1  Retouch to background in front of nose (Th. D1)
20/7  Spot on the back of shoulder (Th. F5) multipositive flaw (see 35p. sepia)

# 75p. Grey-black (1988)

**1988 (26 JULY). FLUORESCENT COATED PAPER. PVAD GUM**

U325 (=S.G.X988)    Grey-black .. .. .. .. .. .. .. 1·10    1·25

**Cylinder Numbers (Blocks of Six)**

Perforation Type RE

| Cyl. No. | | | | | No dot | Dot |
|---|---|---|---|---|---|---|
| 1 | .. | .. | .. | .. | 8·00 | 8·00 |

**CYLINDER VARIETIES**

**Minor Constant Sheet Flaws**

Cyl. 1    1/3  Retouched background above forehead (Th. B2)
Cyl. 1.    13/7  Scratch above dress (Th. F4–F5) multipositive flaw (see note under 34p. grey where this flaw is on R. 13/8)
20/7  Spot on back of shoulder (Th. F5) multipositive flaw (see 35p. sepia)

The multipositive used for Cyl. 1 was also employed for the 2p. deep green, 4p. new blue, 5p. dull red-brown, Cyls. 16, 15 and 10.

# High Values

The £1, £1·30, £1·33, £1·41, £1·50, £1·60, £2 and £5 photogravure stamps were printed on the "Jumelle" Press in the same sheet arrangement as the vertical format Special issues. They were issued without phosphor. The head is as Type B2 but larger.

**Sheet Details**

Sheet size: 100 (2 panes of 5 × 10). Double pane reel-fed

Sheet markings:

Cylinder numbers: In top margin above vertical row 2, boxed

Marginal arrows: In centre, opposite rows 5/6 at both sides and at each side of vertical gutter

Colour register marks (crossed lines type):

No dot panes: Above vertical row 4 and above and below vertical row 9. Cross in circle type above vertical row 4 (£1·41, £1·50 £1·60) only

Dot panes: Above and below vertical row 4

Autotron marks: Vertical bars in order of traffic lights above vertical rows 9 and 10 and in bottom margin below vertical row 8 (£1·33) on dot panes only

Perforation register marks: Bottom margin, vertical thick bar opposite left gutter perforation row (£1·41, £1·50) or below vertical row 8 (others) on dot panes only

Quality control mark: None

Sheet values: Opposite rows 2/4 and 7/9 reading up at left and down at right

Traffic lights (boxed): In reverse order of cylinder numbers in bottom margin below vertical row 2; also in same order reading up in gutter margin in row 2

Colour designations seen: "G2 GREY" on dot pane of £1 value under vertical rows 9/10

**U7.** Queen Elizabeth II
(Des. after plaster cast by Arnold Machin)

# 1977–87.   Type U7

## £1 (1977)

### 1977 (2 FEBRUARY).   FLUORESCENT COATED PAPER. PVAD GUM

| | | | | | | |
|---|---|---|---|---|---|---|
| U330 (=S.G.1026) | Bright yellow-green and blackish olive | .. | .. | .. | 2·50 | 20 |
| | a. Imperforate (pair) | .. | .. | .. | £650 | |
| | b. Dark spot in hair | .. | .. | .. | 6·00 | |
| | c. Long white scratch | .. | .. | .. | 7·00 | |
| | d. Mark on dress | .. | .. | .. | 7·00 | |

**Cylinder Numbers (Blocks of Four)**

Perforation Type R* of Special Issues

| Cyl. Nos. | No dot | Dot |
|---|---|---|
| 2A (blackish olive)–1B (bright yellow-green) | 13·00 | 13·00 |
| 2A (blackish olive)–3B (bright yellow-green) | 13·00 | 13·00 |
| 8A (blackish olive)–3B (bright yellow-green) | 10·00 | 10·00 |

**CYLINDER VARIETIES**
**Listed Flaws**

U330*b*
(Cyl. 1B dot, R. 9/8)

U330*c*
(Cyl. 1B dot, R. 5/6)
This long diagonal white scratch (later retouched) is a multipositive flaw which was largely retouched in the £2 value where it is recorded as a minor constant flaw.

Multipositive flaw
No. U330*d* is a multipositive flaw occurring in Cyl. 8A no dot, R. 8/8 see illustration below £1·33 value.

**Minor Constant Flaws**

Blackish olive cyl. 2A in combination with bright yellow-green cyl. 1B dot

    3/6  Horizontal scratch on shoulder (Th. J5–K8)
    4/1  Scratch below necklace (Th. J5–7)
    4/9 to 5/10 Dark curved line from base of bust on 4/9 (Th. L8–10) through corner of 4/10 (Th. L1–M2) to 5/10 (Th. A3–B4)
    6/5  Spot on shoulder (Th. K5)
    7/4  Dot in 1 of £1
    7/10  Blemish below nostril (Th. F3)
    10/10  Retouch on jaw (Th. H5)

Blackish olive cyl. 2A in combination with bright yellow-green cyl. 3B dot

    2/10  Dark specks in £ sign
    3/5  Long diagonal scratch (Th. C6–L7)
    3/10  Two specks in bar of £ sign

**WITHDRAWN**   17.10.89

# £1·30 (1983)

### 1983 (3 AUGUST).   FLUORESCENT COATED PAPER. PVAD GUM

U331 (=S.G.1026b)    Pale drab and deep greenish blue ..    ..    ..    .. 10·00   7·50

**Cylinder Numbers (Blocks of Four)**
Perforation Type R* of Special Issues

|                                          | Cyl. Nos. | No dot | Dot   |
|------------------------------------------|-----------|--------|-------|
| 2A (deep greenish blue)–3B (pale drab)   | ..        | 42·00  | 42·00 |

**WITHDRAWN**   7.9.85

# £1·33 (1984)

### 1984 (28 AUGUST).   FLUORESCENT COATED PAPER. PVAD GUM

U332 (=S.G.1026c)    Pale mauve and grey-black..    ..    ..    ..    .. 8·50   6·00
　　　　　　　　　　*a*. Mark on dress   ..    ..    ..    ..    .. 12·00

**Cylinder Numbers (Blocks of Four)**
Perforation Type R* of Special Issues

|                                  | Cyl. Nos. | No dot | Dot   |
|----------------------------------|-----------|--------|-------|
| 1A (grey-black)–3B (pale mauve)  | ..        | 30·00  | 30·00 |

**CYLINDER VARIETIES**
**Listed Flaw**

This is a multipositive flaw
which occurs on background cylinders of
the £1, £1·41 and £2 values

U332*a*
(Cyl. 1A no dot, R. 8/8)

**Minor Constant Flaws**
Grey-black cyl. 1A in combination with pale mauve cyl. 3B no dot
　　3/10 Diagonal thin scratch through dress (Th. L5–L6) and similar flaw in background at lower
　　　　right (Th. L9)
　　4/8 Pale speck on forehead (Th. D3)

**WITHDRAWN**   16.9.86

# £1·41 (1985)

### 1985 (17 SEPTEMBER). FLUORESCENT COATED PAPER. PVAD GUM

U333 (=S.G.1026*d*)    Pale drab and deep greenish blue . .    . .    . .    . .    9·00    5·00
   *a*. Mark on dress    . .    . .    . .    . .    . .    . .    12·00

This value is known on covers postmarked between 5 and 8 September 1985.

**Cylinder Numbers (Blocks of Four)**
Perforation Type R* of Special Issues

|  | Cyl. Nos. | No dot | Dot |
|---|---|---|---|
| 2A (deep greenish blue)–3B (pale drab) . . | . . | 32·00 | 32·00 |

**CYLINDER VARIETY**
**Listed Flaw**

   No. U333*a* is a multipositive flaw occurring on Cyl. 2A no dot, R. 8/8 see illustration below £1·33 value.

**WITHDRAWN**   16.9.87

# £1·50 (1986)

### 1986 (2 SEPTEMBER). FLUORESCENT COATED PAPER. PVAD GUM

U334 (=S.G.1026*e*)    Pale mauve and grey-black . .    . .    . .    . .    . .    5·50    4·00

   This value is known pre-released on 1 September at Castle Street Head P.O., Canterbury, Kent.

**Cylinder Numbers (Blocks of Four)**
Perforation Type R* of Special Issues

|  | Cyl. Nos. | No dot | Dot |
|---|---|---|---|
| 1A (grey-black)–3B (pale mauve) | . . | . . | 20·00 | 20·00 |

**WITHDRAWN**   17.10.89

# £1·60 (1987)

### 1987 (15 SEPTEMBER). FLUORESCENT COATED PAPER. PVAD GUM

U335 (=S.G.1026*f*)    Pale drab and deep greenish blue . .    . .    . .    . .    5·50    4·00

   A supply of the above was sent to the agency in Switzerland postmarked Edinburgh 26 August 1987, three weeks before the official release.

**Cylinder Numbers (Blocks of Four)**
Perforation Type R* of Special Issues

|  | Cyl. Nos. | No dot | Dot |
|---|---|---|---|
| 1A (deep greenish blue)–3B (pale drab) . . | . . | 20·00 | 20·00 |

**WITHDRAWN**   10.89

# £2 (1977)

**1977 (2 FEBRUARY). FLUORESCENT COATED PAPER. PVAD GUM**

| | | | | | | |
|---|---|---|---|---|---|---|
| U336 (=S.G.1027) | Light emerald and purple-brown .. | .. | .. | .. | 5·00 | 75 |
| | *a.* Mark on dress .. | .. | .. | .. | 8·00 | |

**Cylinder Numbers (Blocks of Four)**

Perforation Type R* of Special Issues

| Cyl. Nos. | | | | No dot | Dot |
|---|---|---|---|---|---|
| 4A (purple-brown)–1B (light emerald) | .. | .. | .. | 25·00 | 22·00 |
| 4A (purple-brown)–3B (light emerald) | .. | .. | .. | 22·00 | 22·00 |
| 10A (purple-brown)–3B (light emerald) | .. | .. | .. | 18·00 | 18·00 |

**CYLINDER VARIETIES**

**Listed Flaw**

No. U336*a* is a multipositive flaw occurring on Cyl. 10A no dot, R. 8/8, see illustration below £1·33 value

**Minor Constant Flaws**

Purple-brown cyl. 4A in combination with light emerald cyl. 1B no dot
    1/1 Dark spot on band of crown (Th. D7

Purple-brown cyl. 4A in combination with light emerald cyl. 1B dot
    1/1 Dark flaw at top right (Th. A8)
    1/3 Dot in band of crown (Th. C5)
    3/1 Small retouch on Queen's shoulder (Th. K5)
    4/1 Dot in band of crown (Th. C5)*
    4/4 Spot on Queen's bust (Th. K4)*
    5/6 Faint diagonal scratch (Th. E3–H4)*
    8/1 Dark spot below necklace (Th. J4–J5)
    9/2 Dark nick in bottom of base of £ at right

Purple-brown cyl. 10A in combination with light emerald cyl. 3B no dot
    6/5 Unshaded pearls (Th. I6–J5)

The flaw on R. 5/6 is evidently a retouched state of the variety on the £1 value, suggesting that the same multipositive was used for the Queen's head.
*Flaws marked with an asterisk also occur on Cyl. 4A, 3B dot.

**WITHDRAWN** 17.10.89

# £5 (1977)

**1977 (2 FEBRUARY). FLUORESCENT COATED PAPER. PVAD GUM**

| | | | | | | |
|---|---|---|---|---|---|---|
| U337 (=S.G.1028) | Salmon and chalky blue .. | .. | .. | .. | 12·00 | 2·00 |
| | *b.* Retouched scratch across cheek | .. | .. | .. | 22·00 | |
| | *c.* Blue streak on £ .. | .. | .. | .. | 15·00 | |
| | *d.* Imperforate (vert pair) .. | .. | .. | .. | | |
| | *e.* Imperf. between stamp and left margin | .. | .. | † | — | |

**Cylinder Numbers (Blocks of Four)**

Perforation Type R* of Special Issues

| Cyl. Nos. | | | | No dot | Dot |
|---|---|---|---|---|---|
| 1A (chalky blue)–1B (salmon) | .. | .. | .. | 48·00 | 50·00 |
| 13A (chalky-blue)–3B (salmon) | .. | .. | .. | 50·00 | 60·00 |
| 14A (chalky-blue)–3B (salmon) | .. | .. | .. | 45·00 | 45·00 |

**CYLINDER VARIETIES**
**Listed Flaws**

U337*b*
(Cyl. 1A dot, R.1/3)

U337*c*
(Cyl. 1B no dot, R. 8/1)

**Minor Constant Flaws**

Chalky blue cyl. 1A in combination with salmon cyl. 1B no dot
    1/1  Dark spot in band of crown (Th. D7)
Chalky blue cyl. 1A in combination with salmon cyl. 1B dot
    1/1  White dot on Queen's forehead (Th. D3)

**WITHDRAWN**    17.10.89

# Presentation Packs

UPP5 No. 26 (15.2.71)                    Twelve values                                    4·00
                                         *a.* "Scandinavia 71" Edition (15.4.71)         32·00

The contents of Nos UPP5 and UPP5*a* were stamps of the original issue with PVA gum, namely ½p., 1p., 1½p., 2p., 2½p. (1 band), 3p., 3½p., 4p., 5p., 6p., 7½p. and 9p.

There was also a cellophane packet of each low value plus an extra 2p. and 2½p. sold for 50p. with a white card reading both sides: "This packet contains a complete set of the new DECIMAL LOW VALUE DEFINITIVE STAMPS issued by the British Post Office. Two additional stamps have been added to bring the value to a round 50p. (10s. 0d)."

The "Scandinavia 71" is a special pack produced for sale during a visit to six cities in Denmark, Sweden and Norway by a mobile display unit between 15 April and 20 May 1971. The pack gives details of this tour and also lists the other stamps which were due to be issued in 1971, the text being in English. A separate insert gives translations in Danish, Swedish, and Norwegian. The pack was also available at the Philatelic Bureau, Edinburgh. A special cover showing the royal coat of arms and listing the cities visited was also issued.

UPP6 No. 37 (25.11.71)                   Eighteen values                                  4·00

The contents of UPP6 varied from time to time, the price being altered when new values were added. It contains one of each value current at the time of making up. In April 1976 when it was withdrawn the make-up consisted of the ½p. to 10p. with the exception of the 8½p. and the 9½p. values.

UPP7 No. 90 (2.2.77)                     Nineteen values                                  5·00

The contents of No. UPP7 were originally the ½p., 1p., 1½p., 2p., 2½p. (centre band), 3p. (centre band), 5p., 6½p. (centre band), 7p. (2 bands), 7½p., 8p., 8½p. (2 bands), 9p. violet, 9½p., 10p. orange-brown, 10½p. yellow, 11p., 20p. and 50p. Later the 7p. with centre band was substituted.

UPP8 No. 91 (2.2.77)                     Three values                                    24·00

The contents of No. UPP8 were the £1, £2 and £5 photogravure values.

UPP9 No. 129*a* (28.10.81)               Eighteen values                                 12·00

The contents of No. UPP9 was 2½p. rose-red, 3p. bright magenta, 4p. greenish blue (2 bands), 10½p. dull blue (2 bands), 11½p. (ochre-brown), 11½p. (centre band), 12p., 13p. olive-grey, 13½p., 14p., 15p., 15½p., 17p. light emerald, 17½p., 18p., 22p., 25p. and 75p. All on phosphorised paper except 4p., 10½p., 11½p. and 75p. All in photogravure except 4p. and 75p. which were printed in lithography.

UPP10 No. 1 (3.8.83)                     Twenty values                                   19·00

The contents of No. UPP10 ½p., 1p., 2p., 3p. bright magenta, 3½p. purple-brown, 4p. greenish blue, 5p. claret, 10p. (centre band), 12½p. (centre band), 16p., 16½p., 17p. grey-blue, 20p., 20½p., 23p., 26p., 28p., 31p., 50p. and 75p. All values were printed in photogravure except the following which were printed in lithography, 2p., 4p., 5p., 20p. and 75p.

UPP11 No. 5 (23.10.84)                   Twenty values                                   15·00

The contents of No. UPP11 were ½p., 1p., 2p., 3p. bright magenta. 4p., 5p., 10p., 13p. (centre band), 16p., 17p. 18p. (olive-grey), 20p., 22p. (bright green), 24p., 26p., 28p., 31p., 34p., 50p. and 75p. All values were printed in photogravure except the following which were printed in lithography, 2p., 4p., 5p., 20p. and 75p.

UPP12 No. 9 (3.3.87)                     Twenty values                                    6·50

The contents of No. UPP12 were, 12p. bright emerald, 13p. pale chestnut (centre band), 1p., 3p., 7p., 10p., 17p., 18p., 22p., 24p., 26p., 28p., 31p., 34p., phosphorised paper and 50p. ordinary paper. The following were printed in lithography on phosphorised paper or ordinary paper (75p.), 2p., 4p., 5p., 20p. and 75p. perforated 15 × 14.

UPP13 No. 13 (3.3.87)                    Three values                                    17·00

The contents of No. UPP13 were the £1, £2 and £5 photogravure values as No. UPP8.

UPP14 No. 14 (15.9.87)                   £1·60                                            6·00

UPP15 No. 15 (23.8.88)                   Eight values                                     4·25

The contents of No. UPP15, all printed in photogravure, were 14p. deep blue (centre band), 19p., 20p. (turquoise-green), 23p. (bright green), 27p., 28p. (ochre), 32p. and 35p. on phosphorised paper.

**168**

UPP16 No. 19 (26.9.89)            Seven values                    3·25
   The contents of No. UPP16, all printed in photogravure, were 15p. bright blue (centre band), 20p. (brownish black), 24p. (Indian red), 29p. (deep mauve), 30p., 34p. (deep bluish grey) and 37p. on phosphorised paper.

UPP17 No. 22 (4.9.90)             Seven values                    3·25
   The contents of No. UPP17, all printed in photogravure, were 17p. deep blue (centre band), 10p. (dull orange), 22p. (bright orange-red), 26p. (drab), 27p. (violet), 31p. (ultramarine) and 33p. on phosphorised paper.

**Withdrawn**   No. UPP5, 24.11.71; No. UPP6, 4.76; Nos. UPP7 and 9, 7.83; No. UPP8, 6.85; No. UPP10, 9.84; No. UPP11, 2.3.87; No. UPP13, 17.10.89; No. UPP14, 10.89; No. UPP15, 25.9.90

**Quantity Sold**   No. UPP5, 66,313

# First Day Covers

On official covers prepared and issued by the Post Office and stamps franked with circular "FIRST DAY OF ISSUE" postmarks.

| | | |
|---|---|---|
| UFD 3 (15.2.71)* | Twelve values as UPP5 | 2·75 |
| UFD 4 (11.8.71) | 10p. bicoloured | 1·00 |
| UFD 5 (24.5.72) | Wedgwood pane stamps | 25·00 |
| UFD 6 (24.10.73) | 4½p., 5½p., 8p. | 1·00 |
| UFD 7 (4.9.74) | 6½p. | 1·40 |
| UFD 8 (15.1.75) | 7p. | 75 |
| UFD 9 (24.9.75) | 6½p. (centre band), 8½p. | 1·25 |
| UFD 10 (25.2.76) | 9p., 9½p., 10p., 10½p., 11p., 20p. | 2·75 |
| UFD 11 (2.2.77) | 50p. | 2·25 |
| UFD 12 (2.2.77) | £1, £2, £5 | 12·00 |
| UFD 13 (26.4.78) | 10½p. deep dull blue | 1·00 |
| UFD 14 (15.8.79) | 11½p. ochre, 13p., 15p. | 2·00 |
| UFD 15 (30.1.80) | 4p. (*litho*), 12p., 13½p., 17p., 17½p., 75p. (*litho*) | 4·50 |
| UFD 16 (16.4.80) | Wedgwood *se-tenant* pane | 4·00 |
| UFD 17 (22.10.80) | 3p., 22p. | 1·00 |
| UFD 18 (14.1.81) | 2½p., 11½p., 14p., 15½p., 18p., 25p. | 2·25 |
| UFD 19 (27.1.82) | 5p., 12½p., 16½p., 19½p., 26p., 29p. | 3·25 |
| UFD 20 (19.5.82) | Stanley Gibbons *se-tenant* pane | 3·50 |
| UFD 21 (30.3.83) | 3½p., 16p., 17p., 20½p., 23p., 28p., 31p. | 6·00 |
| UFD 22 (3.8.83) | £1·30 | 10·00 |
| UFD 23 (14.9.83) | Royal Mint *se-tenant* pane | 5·00 |
| UFD 24 (28.8.84) | 13p., 18p., 22p., 24p., 34p. | 5·00 |
| UFD 25 (28.8.84) | £1·33 | 8·50 |
| UFD 26 (4.9.84) | Christian Heritage *se-tenant* pane | 6·00 |
| UFD 27 (8.1.85) | *The Times se-tenant* pane | 6·00 |
| UFD 28 (17.9.85) | £1·41 | 7·50 |
| UFD 29 (29.10.85) | 7p., 12p. | 2·00 |
| UFD 30 (18.3.86) | British Rail *se-tenant* pane | 8·00 |
| UFD 31 (2.9.86) | £1·50 | 8·00 |
| UFD 32 (3.3.87) | P & O *se-tenant* pane | 8·00 |
| UFD 33 (15.9.87) | £1·60 | 8·00 |
| UFD 34 (9.2.88) | *The Financial Times se-tenant* pane | 8·00 |
| UFD 35 (23.8.88) | 14p., 19p., 20p., 23p., 27p., 28p., 32p., 35p. | 5·00 |
| UFD 36 (26.9.89) | 15p., 20p., 24p., 29p., 30p., 34p., 37p. | 3·75 |
| UFD 37 (20.3.90) | London Life *se-tenant* pane | 7·50 |
| UFD 38 (4.9.90) | 10p., 17p., 22p., 26p., 27p., 31p., 33p. | 2·75 |

*The Post Office issued special covers for use on the first day of issue and announced that mail posted on the 15 February 1971 at post offices where special first day posting boxes are provided would be postmarked "First Day of Issue—15 February 1971".

In the event there was a country-wide postal strike at this time and the Post Office then stated that the postmark would be applied to mail posted in the special boxes on the fourth and fifth days following the resumption of work. The postal service was resumed on 10 March and this policy was put into effect for covers posted on the 13 and 14 March which bore a distinguishing cachet "POSTING DELAYED BY THE POST OFFICE STRIKE 1971" or others with similar wording. Our quotation is for a cover containing the set of twelve values posted on one of these days.

Meanwhile it had been possible for some people to purchase stamps on the 15 February at some of the 23,000 sub-offices and the few Crown offices that were open and to get these stamps used on mail in a few scattered areas where local deliveries were still operating. Generally these did not have the special postmark.

First Day Covers with *se-tenant* panes from prestige booklets are also priced in Appendix J, after the appropriate booklet.

**Dated in Error.** No. UFD19 is known cancelled 27.1.81 at Chelmsford and Dundee due to an incorrect date in the handstamp.

No. UFD29 is recorded with November date instead of October.

No. UFD37 exists from Enfield, Middx with incorrect date(s) plus a correct date.

# SECTION UE

## Machin Decimal Issues

### 1971–90. Booklet Panes in Photogravure

### General Notes

**Introduction.** One innovation introduced in the decimal issues was the use of a wide range of commercial advertising labels in the booklet panes on a much greater scale than ever before. These were in use until 1973 when they were dropped but blank labels were retained in later issues.

There were technical problems over perforating the booklet panes and it was soon realised that the use of labels posed special problems for blind people who could not distinguish them from stamps. To overcome this the panes were perforated in such a way that the labels could not be removed except by tearing them out. To fully understand the booklet pane lists it is necessary to study the notes on the perforators used for booklet panes in Appendix I.

In 1976 what have come to be termed "folded booklets" were introduced. These contain single panes of stamps with one or more values which are affixed to the booklet covers by the gummed selvedge and then folded over instead of being stitched in. These booklet panes are printed on the "Jumelle" and Chambon presses, in many instances employing the same cylinders as used for coil stamps. Examples where the two presses have been employed to print the same pane are few, but an interesting comparison can be made by looking at pane numbers UMFB11 and 12 and UMFB14/17. Both examples show significant variation in the value settings.

The folded booklets first appeared with covers showing the value of the booklet only, but from 1978 short series of pictorial covers were introduced.

On 29 September 1987 50p. and £1 booklets were issued with the long side of each pane deliberately imperforate. This was an attempt to reduce the cause for complaint from collectors against panes with trimmed perforations.

Panes in card covers showing a pictorial design continued with the 50p. and £1 booklets, but other pictorial covers were replaced by the barcode booklets with red, yellow and black laminated covers. Panes from these new, and in many ways experimental, covers are listed in chronological sequence. Initially with margins all round the pane, and later with imperforate edges, these panes were attached to the covers by peelable adhesive. Panes printed in lithography will be found listed in Section UH. Panes containing "2nd" or "1st" class no value indicated stamps are listed under Section UI for panes printed in either photogravure or lithography.

At the time of going to press the life of the present 50p. booklet appears to be near its end with the advance of the postal tariff and the need to fill the booklet with as many useful stamps as possible to make the product an economic proposition.

On stitched booklet panes of 6 cylinder numbers occur in the left-hand pane only of the double pane cylinder opposite Row 19/1 (or Row 18/1 for the *se-tenant* panes).

Booklet Cylinder Number

**BOOKLET CYLINDER NUMBERS.** The ink cylinder numbers bear the prefix letter "B" (except for the "Jumelle" folded booklet panes) but this was always trimmed off until booklet panes were printed by the "Jumelle" press.

On the panes of six they appeared on the left-hand panes only, in the left selvedge opposite row 19 (or 18 for the *se-tenant* panes). In the *se-tenant* panes of four they were engraved opposite row 23 but were always trimmed off, and they were also trimmed off panes from the £1, £3, £4 and £5 sponsored booklets.

Being hand-engraved their position in relation to the stamps varied, so that some cylinder numbers were invariably trimmed off, only the tips of the guide box being visible as a means of identification. These are known as "flash panes" and are described in the lists as "(Box tips only)", with the actual cylinder numbers indicated in brackets. Where the cylinder number is partially visible this is indicated by "(Partially removed)".

The phosphor cylinder numbers used for booklets are also numbered but they were occasionally trimmed off, being placed outside the ink cylinder numbers.

**BOOKLET FLAWS.** Cylinder flaws on booklet stamps are listed under the panes in which they occur. We list only significant flaws on the booklet panes and minor flaws are outside the scope of the Catalogue. When checking varieties on single stamps it will be necessary to look at the lists of the sheet and coil stamps as well as the booklet panes.

When quoting the position on booklet panes no attention is paid to the labels. Thus "R. 2/1" in a pane containing a label means the first *stamp* in the second row, which is actually position 5 in a horizontal pane of six. This applies also when the label is blank.

Since this catalogue is primarily concerned with stamps we do not list flaws which sometimes occur in the wording of the labels on booklet panes.

**BOOKLET PANE PRICES.** The prices quoted are for panes with good perforations all round whereas the prices for complete booklets in Appendix J are for booklets with average perforations.

## Check List of Booklet Panes

### A. Panes from Stitched Booklets

I. Panes of One Value

In the following list the advertisement labels are indicated by the first line of the text.

| Cat. Nos. | Description | No. of stamps | Page |
|---|---|---|---|
| UB21/2 | ½p. B. ALAN LTD. | 5 + 1 label | 175 |
| UB23/24 | ½p. LICK | 5 + 1 label | 175 |
| UB25 | ½p. MAKE YOUR LUCKY | 5 + 1 label | 176 |
| UB26/27 | 2½p. UNIFLO/STICK FIRMLY | 4 + 2 labels | 177 |
| UB28/29 | 2½p. STICK FIRMLY | 5 + 1 label | 177 |
| UN30/31 | 2½p. TEAR OFF | 5 + 1 label | 178 |
| UB32 | 2½p. STAMP COLLECTIONS | 5 + 1 label | 178 |
| UB33 | 2½p. DO YOU COLLECT | 4 + 2 labels | 179 |
| UB34/35 | 2½p. B. ALAN for | 5 + 1 label | 179 |
| UB36/38 | 3p., £4,315 | 5 + 1 label | 182 |
| UB39/40 | 3p. | 6 | 183 |
| UB41/42 | 3p. | 5 + 1 blank | 186 |
| UB43/45 | 3½p. | 5 + 1 blank | 188/9 |
| UB46 | 4½p. | 5 + 1 blank | 190 |

II. *Se-tenant Panes* containing Two Values

| Cat. Nos. | Description | No. of stamps | Page |
|---|---|---|---|
| USB1 | 2p./½p. *se-tenant* vertically | 4 | 191 |
| USB2/4 | 2p./½p. *se-tenant* horizontally | 4 | 191 |
| USB5 | 1p./1½p. *se-tenant* vertically | 4 | 194 |
| USB6/8 | 1½p./1p. *se-tenant* horizontally | 4 | 194 |
| USB9/10 | 3p./2½p. *se-tenant* | 6 | 195 |

III. Panes from Prestige Booklets

| Cat. Nos. | Description | No. of stamps | Page |
|---|---|---|---|
| UWB1 | Wedgwood 3p. | 12 | 197 |
| UWB2 | Wedgwood 2½p./3p. | 12 | 197 |
| UWB3 | Wedgwood 2½p./½p. | 12 | 198 |
| UWB4 | Wedgwood ½p./2½p. | 6 | 198 |
| UWB5 | Wedgwood 12p. | 9 | 200 |
| UWB6 | Wedgwood 10p. | 9 | 200 |
| UWB7 | Wedgwood 2p. | 6 | 201 |
| UWB8 | Wedgwood 12p./10p./2p. | 9 | 201 |
| UWB9 | Stanley Gibbons 15½p. | 6 | 202 |
| UWB10 | Stanley Gibbons 12½p. | 6 | 202 |
| UWB11 | Stanley Gibbons 12½p./3p./2p. | 9 | 203 |
| UWB12 | Stanley Gibbons 15½p. | 9 | 203 |
| UWB13 | Royal Mint 12½p. | 6 | 204 |
| UWB14 | Royal Mint 12½p. | 6 | 204 |
| UWB15 | Royal Mint 16p./3½p./3p. | 9 | 205 |
| UWB16 | Royal Mint 16p. | 9 | 205 |

| Cat. Nos. | Description | No. of stamps | Page |
|---|---|---|---|
| UWB17 | Christian Heritage 17p. | 6 | 206 |
| UWB18 | Christian Heritage 13p. | 6 | 206 |
| UWB19 | Christian Heritage 17p./10p./13p. | 9 | 207 |
| UWB20 | Christian Heritage 13p. | 6 | 207 |
| UWB21 | *The Times* 17p. | 6 | 208 |
| UWB22 | *The Times* 13p. | 9 | 208 |
| UWB23 | *The Times* 13p./17p./4p./34p. | 9 | 209 |
| UWB24 | *The Times* 17p. | 9 | 209 |
| UWB25 | British Rail 17p. | 9 | 210 |
| UWB26 | British Rail 12p. | 9 | 210 |
| UWB27 | British Rail 12p./17p./31p. | 9 | 211 |
| UWB28 | British Rail 17p. | 6 | 211 |
| UWB29 | P & O 18p. | 9 | 212 |
| UWB30 | P & O 13p. | 9 | 212 |
| UWB31 | P & O 1p./13p./18p./26p. | 9 | 213 |
| UWB32 | P & O 13p. | 6 | 213 |
| UWB33 | London Life 2nd./50p./1st./15p./20p./15p./29p./20p. | 8 + 1 label | 214 |

No. UWB33 contains no value indicated and Penny Black Anniversary values in addition to normal definitives.

## B. Folded Booklet Panes

I. Multi-value Folded Booklet Panes

| Cat. Nos. | Description | No. of stamps | Page |
|---|---|---|---|
| UMFB1/2 | ½p./6p./1p. | 6 | 217 |
| UMFB3 | ½p./1p./8½p./6½p./ with 6½p. at left | 10 | 219 |
| UMFB4 | ½p./8½p./1p./6½p. with 6½p. at right | 10 | 220 |
| UMFB5 | 1p./7p./9p. with 7p. at left | 8 | 222 |
| UMFB6 | 1p./9p./7p. with 7p. at right | 8 | 222 |
| UMFB7 | ½p./postcode label/1p./7p. | 5 + 1 label | 223 |
| UMFB8 | 9p./7p | 20 | 225 |
| UMFB9 | postcode label/2p./10p./8p. with 8p. at left | 7 + 1 label | 226 |
| UMFB10 | 2p./postcode label/10p./8p. with 8p. at right | 7 + 1 label | 226 |
| UMFB11/12 | postcode label/1p./8p. | 3 + 1 label | 227 |
| UMFB13 | 10p./8p. | 20 | 229 |
| UMFB14 and 16 | postcode label/2p./10p./12p. with 10p. at left | 7 + 1 label | 230/1 |
| UMFB15 and 17 | 2p./postcode label/12p./10p. with 10p. at right | 7 + 1 label | 230/1 |
| UMFB18 | 12p./10p. | 20 | 232 |
| UMFB19 | 11½p./½p./1p./14p. with 11½p. at left | 6 | 233 |
| UMFB20 | ½p./11½p./1p./14p. with 11½p. at right | 6 | 233 |
| UMFB21 | 14p./11½p. with selvedge at left | 10 | 235 |
| UMFB22 | 14p./11½p. with selvedge at right | 10 | 235 |
| UMFB23 | 4p./11½p./2½p. with 11½p. at left | 8 | 236 |
| UMFB24 | 4p./2½p./11½p. with 11½p. at right | 8 | 236 |
| UMFB25 | 14p./11½p. | 20 | 237 |
| UMFB26 | ½p./3p./12½p. with 12½p. at left | 8 | 238 |
| UMFB27 | 3p./½p./12½p. with 12½p. at right | 8 | 238 |
| UMFB28 | 15½p./12½p. with selvedge at left | 10 | 239 |
| UMFB29 | 15½p./12½p. with selvedge at right | 10 | 240 |
| UMFB30 | 15½p./12½p. with underprint | 20 | 240 |
| UMFB31 | 1p./3½p./12½p. | 8 | 241 |
| UMFB32 | 16p./12½p. with 12½p. and selvedge at left | 10 | 242 |
| UMFB33 | 16p./12½p. with 12½p. and selvedge at right | 10 | 242 |
| UMFB34 | 1p./13p./4p. | 8 | 244 |
| UMFB35 | 17p./13p. with 13p. and selvedge at left | 10 | 245 |
| UMFB36 | 17p./13p. with 13p. and selvedge at right | 10 | 245 |
| UMFB37 | 17p./12p. with 12p. and selvedge at left | 10 | 246 |
| UMFB38 | 17p./12p. with 12p. and selvedge at right | 10 | 246 |
| UMFB39 | 1p./12p. | 6 | 247 |
| UMFB40/41 | 1p./13p./5p. | 6 | 248 |
| UMFB42 | 1p./13p./18p. | 4 | 250 |
| UMFB43/44 | 13p./18p. | 6 | 251 |
| UMFB45 | postcode label/19p./14p. | 3 + 1 label | 252 |
| UMFB46 | 14p./19p. imperf. vertically | 6 | 253 |
| UMFB47 | postcode label/15p./20p. | 3 + 1 label | 254 |
| UMFB48 | postcode label/22p./17p. imperf. vertically | 5 + 3 labels | 255 |

II. Panes of One Value

| Cat. Nos. | Description | No. of stamps | Page |
|---|---|---|---|
| UFB1 | 6½p. with selvedge at left | 10 | 256 |
| UFB2 | 6½p. with selvedge at right | 10 | 257 |
| UFB3 | 8½p. with selvedge at left | 10 | 258 |
| UFB4 | 8½p. with selvedge at right | 10 | 258 |
| UFB5 | 7p. with selvedge at left | 10 | 259 |
| UFB6 | 7p. with selvedge at right | 10 | 259 |
| UFB7 | 9p. with selvedge at left | 10 | 260 |
| UFB8 | 9p. with selvedge at right | 10 | 260 |
| UFB9 | 8p. with selvedge at left | 10 | 261 |
| UFB10 | 8p. with selvedge at right | 10 | 261 |
| UFB11 | 10p. "all over" phosphor with selvedge at left | 10 | 262 |
| UFB12 | 10p. "all over" phosphor with selvedge at right | 10 | 262 |
| UFB13 | 10p. one centre band with selvedge at left | 10 | 262 |
| UFB14 | 10p. one centre band with selvedge at right | 10 | 262 |
| UFB15 | 12p. (yellowish green) with selvedge at left | 10 | 263 |
| UFB16 | 12p. (yellowish green) with selvedge at right | 10 | 263 |
| UFB17 | 11½p. with selvedge at left | 10 | 264 |
| UFB18 | 11½p. with selvedge at right | 10 | 264 |
| UFB19 | 14p. (grey-blue) with selvedge at left | 10 | 265 |
| UFB20 | 14p. (grey-blue) with selvedge at right | 10 | 265 |
| UFB21 | 12½p. with selvedge at left | 10 | 267 |
| UFB22 | 12½p. with selvedge at right | 10 | 267 |
| UFB23 | 15½p. with selvedge at left | 10 | 268 |
| UFB24 | 15½p. with selvedge at right | 10 | 268 |
| UFB25 | 16p. with selvedge at left | 10 | 269 |
| UFB26 | 16p. with selvedge at right | 10 | 269 |
| UFB27/28 | 16p. with underprint and selvedge at left or right | 10 | 269/70 |
| UFB29 | 12½p. with underprint | 20 | 270 |
| UFB30 | 13p. with selvedge at left | 10 | 271 |
| UFB31 | 13p. with selvedge at right | 10 | 271 |
| UFB32/33 | 13p. with underprint and selvedge at left or right | 6 | 272 |
| UFB34 | 17p. with selvedge at left | 10 | 273 |
| UFB35 | 17p. with selvedge at right | 10 | 273 |
| UFB36/37 | 17p. with underprint and selvedge at left or right | 6 | 273 |
| UFB38/39 | postcode label/17p. with or without underprint | 3 | 274/5 |
| UFB40 | 12p. (bright emerald) with selvedge at left | 10 | 275 |
| UFB41 | 12p. (bright emerald) with selvedge at right | 10 | 275 |
| UFB42 | 17p. | 6 | 276 |
| UFB43 and 45 | 18p. with selvedge at left | 10 | 277 |
| UFB44 and 46 | 18p. with selvedge at right | 10 | 277 |
| UFB47 | 13p. with margins all round | 4 | 278 |
| UFB48 | 18p. with margins all round | 4 | 278 |
| UFB49 | 26p. with margins all round | 4 | 279 |
| UFB50 | 13p. with margins all round | 10 | 280 |
| UFB51 | 18p. with margins all round | 10 | 281 |
| UFB52 | 14p. with margins all round | 4 | 281 |
| UFB53 | 19p. with margins all round | 4 | 281 |
| UFB54 | 27p. with margins all round | 4 | 282 |
| UFB55 | 14p. with margins all round | 10 | 282 |
| UFB56 | 19p. with margins all round | 10 | 283 |
| UFB57 | 14p. (deep blue) with selvedge at left | 10 | 284 |
| UFB58 | 14p. (deep blue) with selvedge at right | 10 | 284 |
| UFB59 | 19p. with selvedge at left | 10 | 285 |
| UFB60 | 19p. with selvedge at right | 10 | 285 |
| UFB61 | 14p. imperforate horizontally | 4 | 286 |
| UFB62 | 19p. imperforate horizontally | 4 | 286 |
| UFB63 | 27p. imperforate horizontally | 4 | 287 |
| UFB64 | 14p. imperforate horizontally | 10 | 287 |
| UFB65 | 19p. imperforate horizontally | 10 | 288 |
| UFB66 | 14p. imperforate on 3 sides | 4 | 289 |
| UFB67 | 19p. imperforate on 3 sides | 4 | 289 |
| UFB68 | postcode label/20p. imperforate vertically | 5 | 290 |
| UFB69 | postcode label/17p. (deep blue) | 3 | 291 |

# A.   Panes from Stitched Booklets (1971–90)

## I.   PANES OF ONE VALUE

½p.   **Panes. Two 9·5 mm. Phosphor Bands (including label)**

UB21 Type P (UB22 similar)

From 25p. Booklets Nos. DH39/43

|  | | Perf. Type | | |
|---|---|---|---|---|
|  | AP | P | APP | APPa |
| UB21 (containing No. U46 × 5) (15.2.71) | 5·50 | 5·00 | 40·00 | 5·50 |
| a. Phosphor omitted  .. .. .. .. .. £275 | — | — | — | |
|  | APL | PL | APPL | |
| UB22 (containing No. U46 × 5) (17.9.71) .. .. .. 6·50 | 6·00 | 6·50 | | |

UB24 Type PL (UB23 similar)

From 50p. Booklets Nos. DT1/4

|  | | Perf. Type | | |
|---|---|---|---|---|
|  | AP | P | APP | APPa |
| UB23 (containing No. U46 × 5) (15.2.71) | 6·00 | 5·00 | 25·00 | 20·00 |
| a. Phosphor omitted  .. .. ..· .. | — | 90·00 | — | — |
| b. Retouch below diadem at right (R. 2/2) .. .. | † | 6·50 | † | † |
| c. Damage right of central cross (R. 2/2) .. .. | † | 6·50 | † | † |
|  | APL | PL | APPL | |
| UB24 (containing No. U48 × 5) (17.9.71) .. .. .. | 8·50 | 8·00 | 9·00 | |

The price for UB24 PL is for a pane with smooth binding edge; for rough edge the price is £25.

UB25 Type PL

From 25p. Booklets Nos. DH44/52 and 50p. Booklets Nos. DT5/12

| | Perf. Type | | |
|---|---|---|---|
| | APL | PL | APPL |
| UB25 (containing No U48 × 5) (23.12.71) | 2·75 | 2·25 | 3·00 |
| a. Phosphor omitted .. .. .. .. .. | — | — | £550 |
| b. Dark flaw in hair at front (R. 1/1)* .. .. .. | — | † | — |

For flaw on the cylinder pane see footnote under Booklet Cylinder Numbers

**Listed Booklet Cylinder Flaws**

UB23b

UB23c

*Multipositive Flaw. No. UB25b occurs on cylinder panes B17 and B18 and also on 2½p. Panes UB32, 34 and 35 and on 3½p. pane where it is illustrated as Nos. UB43/4b.

**Booklet Cylinder Numbers**

Panes of 6

| | | | | | | Perf. Type | | |
|---|---|---|---|---|---|---|---|---|
| Pane | Cyl. No. | | | | | AP | APL | |
| UB21 | (B8) | .. | .. | .. | .. | 8·00 | † | (Box tips only) |
| UB22 | (B8) | .. | .. | .. | .. | † | 14·00 | (Box tips only) |
| UB23 | B3 | .. | .. | .. | .. | 40·00 | † | (1st printing)† |
| UB23 | B3 | .. | .. | .. | .. | 9·00 | † | (2nd printing) |
| UB24 | B3 | .. | .. | .. | .. | † | 11·00 | |
| | | | | | | APL | APPL | |
| UB25 | B17 | .. | .. | .. | .. | 6·50* | 11·00* | |
| UB25 | B18 | .. | .. | .. | .. | 9·00* | 55·00* | |

†The first printing UB23 appeared without the vertical hand-engraved cut-line.

*Both cylinder panes of No. UB25 contain a multipositive flaw: dark flaw in hair at front (R. 1/1) illustrated as Nos. UB43/4b under the 3½p. panes and it also occurs on the 2½p. panes UB32, 34 and 35.

The phosphor cylinder number was always trimmed off but it is known that for panes UB21/25 phosphor cylinder B2 was employed.

**2½p. Panes. One Centre Phosphor Band (including labels)**

UB26 Type P (UB27 similar)

From 25p. Booklets Nos. DH39/43

|  | | Perf. Type | | |
|---|---|---|---|---|
|  | AP | P | APP | APPa |
| UB26 (containing No. U86e × 4) (15.2.71) | 6·00 | 4·50 | 42·00 | 6·50 |
| a. Phosphor omitted       ..     ..     ..     .. | 75·00 | £300 | — | — |
| b. Missing serif to small 2 (R. 1/1)     ..     .. | 9·00 | † | † | † |
| c. Corner patch (R. 1/2) ..     ..     ..     .. | † | 7·00 | † | † |
|  | APLL | PLL | APPLL | |
| UB27 (containing No. U86e × 4) (17.9.71) | 7·00 | 6·00 | 7·00 | |
| a. Phosphor omitted       ..     ..     .. | — | £300 | † | |
| b. Missing serif to small 2 (R. 1/1)     ..     .. | 10·00 | † | † | |
| c. Corner patch (R. 1/2) ..     ..     ..     .. | † | 8·50 | † | |

UB28 Type P (UB29 similar)

From 25p. Booklets Nos. DH39/43

|  | | Perf. Type | | |
|---|---|---|---|---|
|  | AP | P | APP | APPa |
| UB28 (containing No. U86e × 5) (15.2.71) | 6·00 | 5·00 | 40·00 | 7·00 |
| a. Missing serif to large 2 (R. 1/2)     ..     .. | † | 8·00 | † | † |
| b. Background disturbance behind neck (R. 2/1)     .. | † | 7·50 | † | † |
| c. Short curve to large 2 (R. 2/2)..     ..     .. | † | 8·00 | † | † |
|  | APL | PL | APPL | |
| UB29 (containing No. U86e × 5) (17.9.71) | 7·00 | 6·00 | 7·00 | |
| a. Missing serif to large 2 (R. 1/2)     ..     .. | † | 9·00 | † | |
| ba. State 2 of UB28b (R. 2/1)     ..     ..     .. | † | 9·00 | † | |
| c. Short curve to large 2 (R. 2/2)..     ..     .. | † | 9·00 | † | |
| d. Diagonal scratch behind hair (R. 2/1)     ..     .. | † | 9·00 | † | |

**177**

UB30 Type P (UB31 similar)

From 50p. Booklets Nos. DT1/4

| | | Perf. Type | | |
| --- | --- | --- | --- | --- |
| | AP | P | APP | APPa |
| UB30 (containing No. U86e × 5) (15.2.71) | 6·50 | 5·50 | 35·00 | 30·00 |
| a. Very short curve to large 2 (R. 2/2) .. .. .. | † | 8·50 | † | † |
| b. Short curve to large 2 (R. 2/2).. .. .. .. | † | 8·50 | † | † |
| c. Missing top serif to 1 (R. 1/2) .. .. .. .. | † | 8·50 | † | † |
| d. Phosphor omitted .. .. .. .. | — | — | — | † |

| | APL | PL | APPL | |
| --- | --- | --- | --- | --- |
| UB31 (containing No. U87f × 5) (17.9.71) | 7·50 | 7·00 | 7·50 | |
| a. Very short curve to large 2 (R. 2/2) .. .. .. | † | 9·50 | † | |
| b. Short curve to large 2 (R. 2/2).. .. .. .. | † | 9·50 | † | |
| c. Missing top serif to 1 (R. 1/2) .. .. .. .. | † | 9·50 | † | |

The price for UB31 PL is for pane with smooth binding edge; for rough edge the price is £35.

UB32 Type APPL

From 50p. Booklets Nos. DT5/12

| | | Perf. Type | |
| --- | --- | --- | --- |
| | APL | PL | APPL |
| UB32 (containing No. U87f × 5) (23.12.71) | 4·25 | 3·50 | 4·00 |
| a. Very short curve to large 2 (R. 2/2) .. .. .. | † | 6·00 | † |
| b. Short curve to large 2 (R. 2/2).. .. .. | † | 6·00 | † |
| c. White patch on bottom frame (R. 2/1) .. .. | † | † | 7·00 |
| d. Dark flaw in hair at front (R. 1/1)* .. .. .. | † | † | — |
| e. Phosphor omitted .. .. .. .. .. | † | £160 | — |

UB33 Type PLL

From 25p. Booklets Nos. DH44/52

| | Perf. Type | | |
|---|---|---|---|
| | APLL | PLL | APPLL |
| UB33 (containing No. U87f × 4) (23.12.71) | 5·00 | 4·00 | 5·00 |
| a. Phosphor omitted .. .. .. .. .. | — | £200 | — |
| b. Missing serif to small 2 (R. 1/1) .. .. .. | 7·50 | † | 7·50 |

UB34 Type PL (UB35 similar)

From 25p. Booklets Nos. DH44/52

| | Perf. Type | | |
|---|---|---|---|
| | APL | PL | APPL |
| UB34 (containing No. U87f × 5) (Cyl. B17) (23.12.71) | 4·50 | 4·00 | 5·00 |
| a. Phosphor omitted .. .. .. .. | — | 35·00 | 40·00 |
| b. Large white spot under necklace (R. 1/3) .. .. | † | 6·00 | † |
| ba. Retouched, just visible .. .. .. .. | † | 6·00 | † |
| c. Missing serif to large 2 (R. 1/2) .. .. .. | † | 7·00 | † |
| d. Diagonal scratch (R. 1/3 & 2/2) .. .. .. | 8·50 | 7·00 | 9·00 |
| e. Short curve to large 2 (R. 2/2) .. .. .. | † | 7·00 | — |
| f. Dark flaw in hair at front (R. 1/1)* .. .. .. | — | † | — |

| | PL | APPL |
|---|---|---|
| UB35 (containing No. U87 × 5) (Cyl. B29) | £100 | £120 |
| a. Short curve to small 2 (R. 2/2) .. .. .. | £110 | † |
| b. White patch in dress (R. 2/1) .. .. .. | £110 | † |
| c. Extra curve to large 2 (R. 2/1) .. .. .. | † | £130 |
| d. Dark flaw in hair at front (R. 1/1) .. .. .. | † | — |

No. UB35 does not have the minute scratch in base of small 2.

**Listed Booklet Cylinder Flaws**

UB26/27b, UB33b
Multipositive Flaw

UB26/27c
Unscreened patch
in corner

UB28/29a, UB34c
Multipositive Flaw

UB28b
State 1

UB29ba
State 2 (whiter)

UB29d

UB30/31c

UB28/29c, UB30/32b, UB34e
Short curve to large 2

UB30/32a
Very short curve to large 2

UB32c
Later retouched

Multipositive Flaws

The short curve flaw should not be confused with another multipositive flaw consisting of a slightly short curve which occurs in position 3 of panes UB26/33, and is only a minor flaw.

*R. 1/1 see also the multipositive flaw which occurs on the cylinder panes referred to in the footnote under 2½p. Booklet Cylinder Numbers.

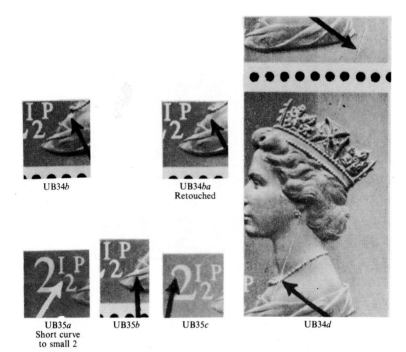

UB34*b*

UB34*ba*
Retouched

UB35*a*
Short curve
to small 2

UB35*b*

UB35*c*

UB34*d*

No. UB34*d*. The illustration is taken from pane R. 9/2 but the scratch starts from the cylinder pane (R. 10/1) perf. Type APL, APLL or APPL and continues through several upper panes with perf. Type PL.

**Booklet Cylinder Numbers**

| Pane | Cyl. No. | | | | AP | Perf. Type APL | APLL | |
|---|---|---|---|---|---|---|---|---|
| UB26 | B4 | .. | .. | .. | .. | 8·00 | † | † | |
| UB27 | B4 | .. | .. | .. | .. | † | † | 14·00 | |
| UB28 | (B6) | .. | .. | .. | .. | 9·00 | † | † | (Box tips only) |
| UB29 | (B6) | .. | .. | .. | .. | † | 14·00 | † | (Box tips only) |
| UB30 | B1 | .. | .. | .. | .. | 45·00 | † | † | (1st printing)* |
| UB30 | B1 | .. | .. | .. | .. | 10·00 | † | † | (2nd printing) |
| UB31 | B1 | .. | .. | .. | .. | † | 14·00 | † | |

*The first printing of UB30 appeared without the vertical etched cut-line.

| | | | | | APL | APPL | APLL | APPLL |
|---|---|---|---|---|---|---|---|---|
| UB32 | B19 | .. | .. | .. | 9·00* | 12·00* | † | † |
| UB33 | B15 | .. | .. | .. | † | † | 8·00 | 18·00 |
| UB34 | B17 | .. | .. | .. | 7·00* | 14·00* | † | † |
| UB35 | B29 | .. | .. | .. | † | £150 | † | † |

On cylinders B4 and B29 guide boxes were engraved opposite row 18 in error and were not removed. These therefore exist for panes UB26AP, UB27APLL and UB35APPL.

The cylinder panes of Nos. UB32, UB34 and UB35 contain a multipositive flaw: dark flaw in hair at front (R. 1/1) illustrated as Nos. UB43/4*b* under the 3½p. pane and it also occurs on the ½p. pane UB25.

The phosphor cylinder number was always trimmed off but it is known that for panes UB26/35 phosphor cylinder B4 was employed.

**181**

## 3p. Panes

### I. Two 9·5 mm. Phosphor Bands (including label)

UB36 Type P (UB37/38 similar)

From 30p. Booklets Nos. DQ56/72

| | I | I(½v) | AP | P | APP | APPa |
|---|---|---|---|---|---|---|
| UB36 (containing No. U101 × 5) (15.2.71) | 11·00 | £100 | 6·50 | 2·25 | £150 | 6·50 |
| a. Dark blue spots on neck (R. 1/1)   ..   .. | † | £110 | † | † | £160 | † |
| aa. State 2. Whitish smear ..   ..   ..   .. | † | † | † | † | £160 | 8·50 |
| ab. State 3. Small pale blue spots ..   ..   .. | † | † | † | † | † | 8·00 |
| b. Scratch on dress (R. 1/1)   ..   ..   .. | 15·00 | † | † | † | £160 | † |
| ba. Partly whitened ..   ..   ..   .. | † | † | † | † | † | 8·50 |
| c. Large retouch on shoulder and dress (R. 2/1) | † | † | † | 7·50 | † | † |
| d. Top serif of 3 missing (R. 1/2)..   ..   .. | † | † | † | 4·75 | † | † |
| e. Phosphor omitted   ..   ..   .. | † | † | — | £250 | — | — |
| f. One broad band ..   ..   ..   .. | — | — | — | — | — | † |

| | APL | PL | APPL |
|---|---|---|---|
| UB37 (containing No. U101 × 5) (23.7.71) | 8·50 | 6·50 | 7·50 |
| ac. Small blue spots on neck and triangular patch at lower right corner (R. 1/1) ..   ..   ..   ..   .. | † | † | 9·50 |
| ba. Scratch on dress whitened (R. 1/1)   ..   .. | † | † | 9·50 |
| c. Large retouch on shoulder and dress (R. 2/1)   .. | † | 14·00 | † |
| d. Top serif of 3 missing (R. 1/1)..   ..   .. | † | 11·00 | † |

| | APL | PL | APPL |
|---|---|---|---|
| UB38 (containing No. U103 × 5) (1.10.71) | 4·00 | 3·50 | 4·00 |
| a. Phosphor omitted   ..   ..   ..   .. | — | — | £350 |
| ac. Small blue spots on neck and triangular patch at lower right corner (R. 1/1) ..   ..   ..   .. | † | † | 9·00 |
| ba. Scratch on dress whitened (R. 1/1)   ..   .. | † | † | 7·50 |
| c. Large retouch on shoulder and dress (R. 2/1)   _ .. | † | 10·00 | † |
| d. Top serif of 3 missing (R. 1/2)..   ..   .. | † | 6·50 | † |
| e. Large repair at base of neck (R. 2/1) ..   .. | † | † | 5·50 |
| f. Pale patch between 3 and P (R. 1/3) ..   .. | † | 5·50 | † |
| g. White gash on mouth (R. 1/2) ..   ..   .. | † | † | 5·50 |
| h. Blue marks on shoulder and in bottom margin (R. 2/1) ..   ..   ..   ..   ..   .. | † | † | 8·00 |
| i. Thin paper   ..   ..   ..   ..   .. | † | 11·00 | 12·00 |
| ia. Phosphor omitted   ..   ..   ..   .. | † | — | £250 |

UB39 Type P (UB40 similar)

From 50p. Booklets Nos. DT1/12

|  | Perf. Type | | | |
|---|---|---|---|---|
|  | AP | P | APP | APPa |
| UB39 (containing No U101 × 6) (15.2.71) | 6·00 | 5·00 | 32·00 | 13·00 |
| *a.* Phosphor omitted | — | £150 | — | — |
| *b.* No serif to top of 3 (R. 1/2) | † | 6·50 | † | † |
| *c.* Spots on neck. State 2. Smeared appearance (R. 1/1) | † | † | 35·00 | — |
| *ca.* State 3. Scratched appearance | † | † | † | 15·00 |
| *d.* Scratch on dress (R. 1/1) | † | † | 35·00 | — |
| *e.* One broad band | † | £550 | † | † |

|  | AP | P | APPa |
|---|---|---|---|
| UB40 (containing No. U103 × 6) (17.9.71) | 2·25 | 2·25 | 5·50 |
| *b.* No serif to top of 3 (R. 1/2) | † | 6·00 | † |
| *c.* Spots on neck (State 2) (R. 1/1) | † | † | 7·50 |
| *ca.* State 3. Scratched appearance | † | † | 7·50 |
| *d.* Scratch on dress (R. 1/1) | † | † | 6·50 |
| *da.* State 2. Clear line, no repair | † | † | 7·50 |

**Listed Booklet Cylinder Flaws**
Multipositive Flaws
(a) Spots on neck flaw

State 1. Dark blue spots

State 2. Smeared appearance

**183**

State 3
Scratched appearance
(3p. pane of 6)

State 3. Small pale blue spots, together
with triangular patch at lower right
(3p. and £4,315 label)

3p. and £4,315 label.   Cylinder B1
  State 1. Dark blue spots                            -      UB36*a*
  State 2. Whitish smear                                UB36*aa*
  State 3. Small pale blue spots                     UB36*ab*
  State 3. As above but with triangular patch at lower right
          corner on same stamp               UB37*ac*, UB38*ac*

3p./2½p. *se-tenant*.   Cylinder B9
  State 1. Dark blue spots                                USB9*b*
  State 2. Smeared appearance                   USB9*ba*, USB10*ba*

3p. pane of 6.   Cylinder B6
  State 2. Smeared appearance                   UB39*c*, UB40*c*
  State 3. Scratched appearance                 UB39*ca*, UB40*ca*
  For panes USB9/10 see under *Se-tenant* Panes.

(b)  Scratch on dress flaw

State 1                   State 2 (3p. pane of 6)

3p. and £4,315 label.
  State 1. Deep blue spots (Cyl. B1)          UB36*b*
          Spots partly whitened on PAP2 and PAP3 and   UB36*ba*
          further whitened on PAP3 (Cyls. B18 and B27)  UB37/38*ba*

3p./2½p. *se-tenant*.
  State 1. Deep blue spots (Cyl. B9)          USB9/10*c*
  State 2. Smudge of pale dots (Cyl. B12)     USB10*ca*

3p. pane of 6.
  State 1. Deep blue spots (Cyl. B6)          UB39*d*, UB40*d*
  State 2. Clear line.   No repair (Cyl. B14)    UB40*da*

3p. and blank label.
  Spots whitened (Cyls. B28 and B35)       UB41/2*d*, UB42*eb*
  For panes USB9/10 see under *Se-tenant* Panes.

3p. and £4,315 label pane. Flaws

UB36/38*d*
Top of serif 3 missing

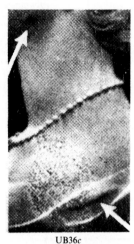

UB36*c*
Large retouch on shoulder and dress with
coloured spot on jaw (on UB37/38*c* spot
has been removed)

UB38*e*
Large repair to base of neck

UB38*f*
Pale patch
between 3 and P

UB38*g*
White gash on mouth
(Later repaired showing
white traces and then
almost completely removed)

UB38*h*
Blue spots on shoulder
and bottom margin

3p. pane of 6. Flaw

Normal      UB39/40*b*
No serif to
top of 3

**Booklet Cylinder Numbers**

|  |  |  |  |  | Perf. Types |  |  |  |  |  |
| --- | --- | --- | --- | --- | --- | --- | --- | --- | --- | --- |
| Pane | Cyl. No. |  |  | I(½v) | AP | APL | APPa | APPL |  |
| UB36 | (B1) | .. | .. | ..、£110 | 10·00 | † | † | † | (Box tips only) |
| UB37 | (B1) | .. | .. | .. † | † | 17·00 | † | † | (Box tips only) |
| UB38 | (B1) | .. | .. | .. † | † | 7·50 | † | 20·00 | (Box tips only) |
| UB38 | B18 | .. | .. | .. † | † | † | † | 18·00 | (Partly removed) |
| UB38 | B27 | .. | .. | .. † | † | † | † | 10·00 | (Partly removed) |
| UB38*i* | B27 | .. | .. | .. † | † | † | † | 20·00 | (Thin paper) |
| UB39 | B6 | .. | .. | .. † | 10·00 | † | † | † | (Partly removed) |
| UB40 | B6 | .. | .. | .. † | 7·50 | † | 18·00 | † | (Partly removed) |
| UB40 | B14 | .. | .. | .. † | † | † | 18·00 | † |  |

The phosphor cylinder number was always trimmed off but it is known that for panes UB36/40 phosphor cylinder B2 was employed.

## II. One Centre Phosphor Band (including label)

UB41 Type PL (UB42 similar)

From 30p. Booklets Nos. DQ73/74 and 50p. Booklets Nos. DT13/14

|  | Perf. Type | |
| --- | --- | --- |
|  | APPL | PL |
| UB41 (containing No. U109 × 5) (14.11.73) | 10·00 | 10·00 |
| *b.* Blue spots on neck (R. 1/2)   ..   ..   ..   .. | 13·00 | † |
| *c.* No serif to top of 3 (R. 1/2)   ..   ..   .. | † | 12·00 |
| *d.* Scratch on dress whitened (R. 1/1)   ..   .. | 13·00 | † |
|  |  |  |
| UB42 (containing No. U108 × 5) (14.11.73) | 5·50 | 4·50 |
| *b.* Blue spots on neck (R. 1/2)   ..   ..   .. | 7·50 | † |
| *c.* No serif to top of 3 (R. 1/2)   ..   ..   .. | † | 6·50 |
| *d.* Scratch on dress whitened (R. 1/1)   ..   .. | 7·50 | † |
| *e.* Thick P (Cyl. B35)   ..   ..   ..   ..   .. | 5·50 | 4·50 |
| *ea.* Blue shoulder scratch (R. 2/2) ..   ..   .. | † | 6·50 |
| *eb.* Scratch on dress whitened R. (1/1)   ..   .. | 7·50 | † |

Stamps from cylinder B35 can be distinguished from those from cylinder B28 as they have a thicker "P".

**Listed Booklet Cylinder Flaws**

UB41/2*b*

Rash of blue spots on neck
(Cyl. B28)
(Later retouched, less intense
but stronger on UB42)

UB42*ea*

Long blue scratch across shoulder
(Cyl. B35)

Multipositive Flaws

The flaw represented by Nos. UB41/2*c* is as UB39/40*b* on 3p. panes of six but "3" is slightly shorter.

The scratch on dress multipositive flaw which occurs in various states on panes UB36/40 and USB9/10 shows a whitened state in panes UB41/42 on cylinders B28 and B35.

**Booklet Cylinder Numbers**

| Pane | Cyl. No. | | | | Perf. Type APPL | |
|------|----------|--|--|--|------|---|
| UB41 | (B28) | .. | .. | .. | .. 27·00 | (Box tips only) Thin P |
| UB42 | (B28) | .. | .. | .. | .. 22·00 | (Box tips only) Thin P |
| UB42*e* | (B35) | .. | .. | .. | .. 22·00 | (Box tips only) Thick P |

Apart from the fact that the box tips on cylinder B35 are etched further to the left than on cylinder B28, cylinder panes of the former can be distinguished by a constant blue mark on the Queen's shoulder on R. 2/1. Part numbers of both cylinders are sometimes visible.

The phosphor cylinder number was always trimmed off but it is known that for panes UB41/42 phosphor cylinder B4 was employed.

---

## 3½p. Panes

### I. Two 9·5 mm. Phosphor Bands (including label)

UB43 Type PL (UB44/45 similar)

From 35p. Booklets Nos. DP1/3 and 50p. Booklets Nos. DT13/14

|  | Perf. Type | |
|---|:---:|:---:|
|  | APPL | PL |
| UB43 (containing No. U115 × 5) (14.11.73) | 8·00 | 6·50 |
| *b.* Dark flaw in hair at front (R. 1/1)* .. .. | — | † |
| *c.* White scratch below collar of dress (R. 1/3) .. .. | † | 8·00 |
| *d.* White vert. scratch at lower right (R. 2/2) .. .. | † | 8·00 |
| *e.* Large weakness above central cross (R. 2/1) .. .. | † | 8·00 |
| *f.* White patch left of central cross (R. 1/3) .. .. | † | 7·50 |
| *g.* Weak patch left of diadem (R. 2/2) .. .. .. | † | 7·50 |
| *h.* White flaw in hair (R. 1/1) .. .. .. .. | † | 8·00 |
| *i.* Extra pearl in necklace and 3 white spots above (R. 1/1) | 10·00 | † |
| *j.* Prominent horiz. line at top right (R. 1/2) .. .. | † | 9·00 |
| *k.* Sliced P (R. 1/3) .. .. .. .. .. .. | † | 8·00 |
| | | |
| UB44 (containing No. U116 × 5) (14.11.73) | 3·00 | 2·25 |
| *a.* Phosphor omitted .. .. .. .. .. | — | 35·00 |
| *b.* Dark flaw in hair at front (R. 1/1)* .. .. .. | — | † |
| *c.* White scratch below collar of dress (R. 1/3) .. .. | † | 4·50 |
| *d.* White vert. scratch at lower right (R. 2/2) .. .. | † | 4·50 |
| *e.* Large weakness above central cross (R. 2/1) .. .. | † | 4·50 |
| *f.* White patch left of central cross (R. 1/3) .. .. | † | 4·00 |
| *g.* Weak patch left of diadem (R. 2/2) .. .. | † | 4·00 |
| *h.* White flaw in hair (R. 1/1) .. .. .. .. | † | 4·50 |
| *i.* Extra pearl in necklace and 3 white spots above (R.1/1) | 5·00 | † |
| *j.* Prominent horiz. line at top right (R. 1/2) .. .. | † | 5·00 |
| *k.* Sliced P (R. 1/3) .. .. .. .. .. .. | † | 4·50 |

*See footnote under Booklet Cylinder Numbers.

**Listed Booklet Cylinder Flaws**

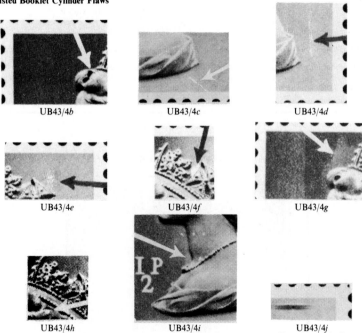

UB43/4*b*    UB43/4*c*    UB43/4*d*

UB43/4*e*    UB43/4*f*    UB43/4*g*

UB43/4*h*    UB43/4*i*    UB43/4*j*
(Later retouched)

Nos. UB43/4*k*. Sliced P flaw. This is exactly the same as the flaw listed on the 7½p. sheet stamps, Nos. U159*b* and U160*ca* and illustrated under that value. It was possibly taken from the same multipositive.

**Booklet Cylinder Numbers**

| Pane | Cyl. No. | | | | Perf. Type APPL | |
|------|----------|--|--|--|------|--|
| UB43 | (B1) | .. | .. | .. | 18·00 | (Box tips only) |
| UB44 | (B1) | .. | .. | .. | 9·00 | (Box tips only) |

The cylinder panes of Nos. UB43/4 contain the flaw Nos. UB43/4b. This is a multipositive flaw which occurs on the ½p. pane containing MAKE YOUR LUCKY label and the 2½p. panes containing STAMP COLLECTIONS and B. ALAN labels.

The phosphor cylinder number was always trimmed off but it is known that for panes UB43/44 phosphor cylinder B2 was employed.

### 3½p. Panes continued

### II.   One Centre Phosphor Band (including label)

From 35p. Booklet No. DP4 and 85p. Booklet No. DW1

| | Perf. Type | |
|--|------|------|
| | IL | ILa |
| UB45 (containing No. U118 × 5) (23.10.74) | 3·00 | 25·00 |
| b. White spot to left of P (R. 1/1) .. .. .. | 4·50 | 28·00 |
| c. White spot on bottom right of P (R. 2/1) .. .. | 4·50 | 28·00 |
| d. White spot on left of P (R. 1/1) .. .. .. | 4·50 | 28·00 |
| UB45A Miscut. Label at top* | 15·00 | £110 |

*Part of the printing of the 35p. Booklets had the sheets wrongly cut so that the label appeared at the top of the pane.

Prices are the same for miscut panes showing the extension hole opposite either the top or bottom perforation row.

**Listed Booklet Cylinder Flaws**

UB45b
(Quickly retouched)

UB45c

UB45d

**Booklet Cylinder Numbers**

| Pane | Cyl. No. | | | | Perf. Type IL | ILa |
|------|----------|--|--|--|------|------|
| UB45 | B2 | .. | .. | .. | 7·50 | 38·00 |
| UB45A | B2 | .. | .. | .. | £100 | £300* |

The phosphor cylinder number was always trimmed off but it is known that for panes UB45/5A phosphor cylinder P24 was employed.

*Examples of No. UB45A with cylinder number occur only with the extra extension hole at the bottom.

**4½p. Pane. Two 9·5 mm. Phosphor Bands (including label)**

UB46 Type IL

From 45p. Booklets Nos. DS1/2 and 85p. Booklet No. DW1

|  | IL | Perf. Type<br>ILa | IL(½v) | ILa(½v) |
|---|---|---|---|---|
| UB46 (containing No. U133 × 5) (9.10.74) | 2·75 | 25·00 | £200 | £500 |
| a. Cream-tinted phosphor .. .. .. .. .. | 75·00 | £400 | † | † |
| b. Extra "pearls" on necklace (R. 1/2) .. .. .. | 5·50 | 27·00 | † | † |
| c. White flaw on nose (R. 2/1) .. .. .. | 5·00 | 27·00 | † | † |
| d. Irregular vertical white scratch (R. 1/1) .. .. | 5·50 | † | † | † |
| e. Blue line over top band of diadem (R. 1/1) .. .. | 5·50 | † | † | † |
| f. Phosphor omitted .. .. .. .. .. | £600 | † | † | † |

Some early sheets only from an inverted printing, had defective top and bottom rows which were torn off and slanting cuts made into the new corners at bottom on panes 9/1 and 2/4 and at top on panes 2/1 and 9/4. Thus they cannot appear on the cylinder pane (10/1). Faked examples of (½v) panes are known but these are from upright printings.

**Listed Booklet Cylinder Flaws**

UB46b

UB46c

UB46e

UB46d

**Booklet Cylinder Number**

| Pane | Cyl. No. | Perf. Type<br>IL | ILa |
|---|---|---|---|
| UB46 | B7 .. .. .. .. | 7·50 | 35·00 |

The phosphor cylinder P25 was used for pane UB46.

## II.  SE-TENANT PANES CONTAINING TWO VALUES

USB1 Type P
*Se-tenant* vertically

USB2 Type P (USB3/4 similar)
*Se-tenant* horizontally

*Se-tenant* vertically. ½p. Type I. From 10p. Booklets Nos. DN46/48

| | Perf. Type | | |
|---|---|---|---|
| | I | I(½v) | P |
| USB1 (containing Nos. U46 × 2, U76 × 2) (15.2.71) | 8·00 | 32·00 | 5·50 |
| *a.* One broad band .. .. .. .. .. | 75·00 | £170 | 70·00 |
| *b.* Two heavy lines below chin (R. 2/1) .. .. | † | † | 25·00 |
| *c.* As last, retouched .. .. .. .. | † | † | 7·00 |
| *d.* Phosphor omitted .. .. .. .. .. | — | — | £150 |

*Se-tenant* horizontally. ½p. Type II. From 10p. Booklets Nos. DN49/75

| | | | |
|---|---|---|---|
| USB2 (containing Nos. 46c × 2, U76 × 2) (14.7.71) | 12·00 | 24·00 | 9·00 |
| *a.* Phosphor omitted .. .. .. .. | — | — | £350 |
| *b.* One broad band .. .. .. .. | £400 | — | £375 |
| *d.* Forehead retouch (R. 1/1) .. .. | † | † | 11·00 |
| | | | |
| USB3 (containing Nos. U48c × 2, U78 × 2) (6.10.71) | 3·75 | 12·00 | 2·50 |
| *a.* Phosphor omitted .. .. .. .. | £600 | — | £550 |
| *b.* One broad band .. .. .. .. | £100 | — | £100 |
| *c.* Gash over eye (R. 2/2) .. .. .. | † | † | 4·50 |
| *d.* Forehead retouch (R. 1/1) .. .. | † | † | 4·50 |
| *e.* Repairs on jawline and necklace (R. 1/1) .. | † | 20·00 | † |
| *f.* Background disturbance left of face (R. 1/1).. | 12·00 | † | † |
| *g.* White dot in diadem (R. 1/1) .. .. .. | 5·50 | † | † |
| | | | |
| USB4 (containing Nos. U50d × 2, U80 × 2) (12.11.73) | 2·75 | 12·00 | 75 |
| *a.* Phosphor omitted .. .. .. .. | — | — | — |
| *b.* One broad band .. .. .. .. | 60·00 | † | 35·00 |
| *c.* Gash over eye (R. 2/2) .. .. .. | † | † | 2·00 |
| *d.* Background disturbance left of face (R. 1/1).. | 14·00 | † | † |
| *e.* White dot in diadem (R. 1/1) .. .. | 7·00 | — | † |
| *f.* Dark patch on cheek (R. 1/1) .. .. | † | † | 3·00 |
| *g.* Shoulder scratch (R. 1/1) .. .. | 5·00 | † | † |
| *h.* White flaw over mouth (R. 2/1) .. .. | † | † | 2·75 |
| *i.* Extra pearl at back of neck (2/2) .. .. | † | † | 2·75 |
| *j.* White patch right of eye (R. 2/1) .. .. | † | † | 2·75 |
| *k.* White patch left of eye (R. 1/1) .. .. | † | † | 3·00 |
| *l.* Pale gash above central cross (R. 2/1) .. | 5·00 | † | † |
| *m.* Flaw on eye, appearing sightless (R. 1/1) .. .. | † | † | 3·50 |

**Listed Booklet Cylinder Flaws**

USB1*b*
1st State

USB1*c*
Partly retouched

USB3/4*c* (½p.)
(Exists partly repaired on USB4)

USB4*i* (½p.)

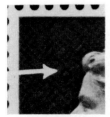

USB2/3*d* (2p.)
(Cyl. B6)

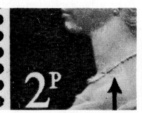

USB3*e*
(Cyl. B6)

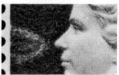

USB3*f*, USB4*d* (2p.)
(Cyl. B7)

USB3*g*, USB4*e* (2p.)
(Cyls. B6, B7 and faint on B9)

USB4*f* (2p.)
1st state
This exists partly removed

192

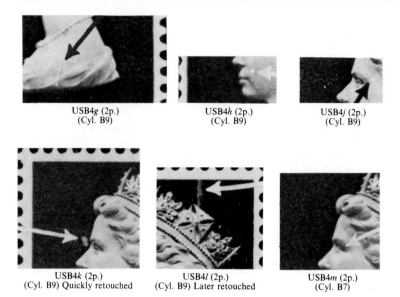

USB4*g* (2p.)
(Cyl. B9)

USB4*h* (2p.)
(Cyl. B9)

USB4*j* (2p.)
(Cyl. B9)

USB4*k* (2p.)
(Cyl. B9) Quickly retouched

USB4*l* (2p.)
(Cyl. B9) Later retouched

USB4*m* (2p.)
(Cyl. B7)

**Se-tenant Booklet Pane Cylinder Numbers**

These are 24-row single-pane cylinders but the cylinder numbers are always trimmed off. Those employed were:—

| | | |
|---|---|---|
| USB1 | B6 (½p.), B2 (2p.) and B1 (phos) | |
| | B7 (½p.), B2 (2p.) and B1 (phos) | |
| | B9 (½p.), B2 (2p.) and B1 (phos) | |
| USB2 | B13 (½p.), B6 (2p.) and B1 (phos) | |
| | B13 (½p.), B6 (2p.) and B5 (phos) | |

| | |
|---|---|
| USB3 | B13 (½p.), B6 (2p.) and B1 (phos) |
| | B13 (½p.), B6 (2p.) and B5 (phos) |
| | B13 (½p.), B7 (2p.) and B5 (phos) |
| USB4 | B13 (½p.), B7 (2p.) and B5 (phos) |
| | B13 (½p.), B9 (2p.) and B5 (phos) |

USB5 Type P
*Se-tenant* vertically

USB6 Type P (USB7/8 similar)
*Se-tenant* horizontally

**193**

*Se-tenant* vertically. From 10p. Booklets Nos. DN46/48

| | I | Perf. Type I(½v) | P |
|---|---|---|---|
| USB5 (containing Nos. U55 × 2, U71 × 2) (15.2.71) | 8·50 | 32·00 | 5·50 |
|   *a.* One broad band ..    ..    ..    ..    .. | £140 | £300 | £100 |

*Se-tenant* horizontally. From 10p. Booklets Nos. DN49/75

| | I | I(½v) | P |
|---|---|---|---|
| USB6 (containing Nos. U55 × 2, U71 × 2) (14.7.71) | 4·50 | 15·00 | 4·00 |
|   *a.* One broad band ..    ..    ..    ..    .. | £200 | — | £180 |
| USB7 (containing Nos. U57 × 2, U72 × 2) (6.10.71) | 3·25 | 12·00 | 2·50 |
|   *a.* 250 phosphor screen    ..    ..    ..    .. | £140 | — | 70·00 |
|   *b.* Phosphor omitted    ..    ..    ..    .. | £120 | £160 | 80·00 |
|   *c.* One broad band ..    ..    ..    ..    .. | £300 | — | £300 |
|   *d.* White patch on collar (R. 1/1)..    ..    .. | 9·00 | † | † |
|   *da.* State 2. Partially repaired (R. 1/1)    ..    .. | 4·25 | † | † |
| USB8 (containing Nos. U59 × 2, U73 × 2) (12.11.73) | 3·00 | 12·00 | 75 |
|   *a.* Phosphor omitted    ..    ..    ..    .. | — | — | £500 |
|   *b.* One broad band ..    ..    ..    ..    .. | £150 | — | 90·00 |
|   *d.* Broken P (R. 1/2)    ..    ..    ..    .. | † | † | 2·00 |
|   *e.* Crimson spot on 2 (R. 2/1)    ..    ..    .. | 3·50 | † | † |
|   *f.* Patch on collar. State 2 (R. 1/1)    ..    .. | 4·00 | † | † |

No. USB7*a* is the only example of the use of a 250 screen in booklets and the panes come from the February and April 1973 issues of the 10p. booklets. The phosphor cylinder was B6 as examples of USB7*a* (1½v) exist with part of the number visible.

**Listed Booklet Cylinder Flaws**

USB8*d*
Broken P

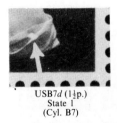  

| USB7*d* (1½p.) | USB7*da*, USB8*f* (1½p.) | USB8*e* |
|---|---|---|
| State 1 | State 2 | Crimson spot on 2 |
| (Cyl. B7) | (Cyl. B7) | |

**Se-tenant Booklet Pane Cylinder Numbers**
    These are 24-row single-pane cylinders but the cylinder numbers are always trimmed off. Those employed were:—

| USB5 | B1 (1p.), B2 (1½p.) and B1 (phosphor) |
|---|---|
| USB6 | B5 (1p.), B6 (1½p.) and B1 (phosphor) |
| USB7 | B5 (1p.), B6 (1½p.) and B1 (phosphor) |
| | B5 (1p.), B6 (1½p.) and B5 (phosphor) |
| USB8 | B5 (1p.), B6 (1½p.) and B5 (phosphor) |
| | B5 (1p.), B7 (1½p.) and B5 (phosphor) |

USB9 Type P (USB10 similar)
3p. with two phosphor bands. 2½p. with phosphor band at left

2½p. Type II.   From 50p. Booklets Nos. DT1/12

| | AP | P | APP | APPa |
|---|---|---|---|---|
| | | Perf. Type | | |
| USB9 (containing Nos. U91 × 2, U101 × 4) (15.2.71) | 11·00 | 11·00 | 30·00 | 14·00 |
|   *a.* Phosphor omitted   ..    ..    ..    .. | £350 | — | † | — |
|   *b.* Dark blue spots on neck (R. 1/1)    ..    ..    .. | † | † | 35·00 | † |
| *ba.* State 2.   Smeared appearance ..    ..    .. | † | † | † | 18·00 |
|   *c.* Scratch on dress (R. 1/1)    ..    ..    .. | † | † | 35·00 | † |
|   *d.* Forehead retouch (R. 1/1)    ..    ..    .. | 14·00 | † | † | † |
|   *e.* Short bottom curve to 3 (R. 1/2)    ..    .. | † | 14·00 | † | † |
|   *f.* Scratch through hair (R. 1/2) ..    ..    .. | † | 14·00 | † | † |
|   *g.* Long vert. scratch (R. 2/1) ..    ..    .. | † | 17·00 | † | † |
|   *h.* Missing serif to small 2 (R. 1/3)    ..    .. | † | 14·00 | † | † |

| | AP | P | APPa |
|---|---|---|---|
| USB10 (containing Nos. U92 × 2, U103 × 4) (17.9.71) | 5·00 | 4·50 | 5·00 |
|   *a.* Phosphor omitted    ..    ..    ..    .. | — | £120 | 90·00 |
| *aa.* First phosphor band at left omitted    ..    .. | — | — | — |
| *ab.* Third phosphor from left omitted    ..    .. | — | — | — |
| *ba.* Blue spots on neck, state 2. Smeared appearance (R. 1/1) | † | † | 7·50 |
|   *c.* Scratch on dress (R. 1/1)    ..    ..    .. | † | † | 8·50 |
| *ca.* State 2.   Pale dots only    ..    ..    .. | † | † | 7·50 |
|   *d.* Forehead retouch (R. 1/1)    ..    ..    .. | 7·50 | † | — |
|   *e.* Short bottom curve to 3 (R. 1/2)    ..    .. | † | 7·00 | † |
|   *f.* Scratch through hair (R. 1/2) ..    ..    .. | † | 9·00 | † |
|   *h.* Missing serif to small 2 (R. 1/3)    ..    .. | † | 7·00 | † |

**Listed Booklet Cylinder Flaws**

Multipositive Flaws

    Nos. USB9*b*/*c* and USB10*ba*/*ca* are multipositive flaws which are illustrated and described in relation to 3p. panes containing £4,315 label.

    Nos. USB9/10*h* are as the illustration of Nos. UB26/27*b* and UB33*b* but are presumably not the same multipositive flaw as they are on a different position in the pane.

**195**

USB9/10*d* (3p.)

USB9/10*e*
For normal 3 see illustration of UB39/40*b*

USB9/10*f* (3p.)

USB9*g* (3p.)
Scratch extends to lower part
of the stamp above

**Se-tenant Booklet Pane Cylinder Numbers**

Panes of 6

(a) Normal Cylinder Pane (Pane R. 10/1)

| Pane | Cyl. Nos. | | | Perf. Type AP | APPa |
|---|---|---|---|---|---|
| USB9 | (B9) (3p.) and B2 (2½p.) | .. | .. | 18·00 | † |
| USB10 | (B9) (3p.) and B2 (2½p.) | .. | .. | 9·00 | 12·00 |
| | (B12) (3p.) and B2 (2½p.) | .. | .. | † | £140 |

The 3p. cylinder numbers are always trimmed off. However cylinder B9 can be distinguished by the vertical blue single stippled cutting line in the margin which is 24 mm. long and extends through the red bar and cylinder 2. Cylinder B12 has a straight ruled line lower down the margin and stopping short of the red bar. The shade is deeper and the paper thinner. Phosphor cylinder B3 was used for both USB9/10.

(b) Pane above the Cylinder Pane (Pane R. 9/1)

| USB9 | (B9) (3p.) | .. | .. | .. | 12·00 | † | (box tips near bottom margin) |
|---|---|---|---|---|---|---|---|
| USB10 | (B9) (3p.)* | .. | .. | .. | † | 10·00 | (box tips near bottom margin) |
| | (B12) (3p.)* | .. | .. | .. | † | 40·00 | (box tips near bottom margin) |

*These can be distinguished in that the B9 pane has a small diagonal slightly curved blue line between the upper 3p. stamps and near the base and this is absent from B12. The shades differ as indicated above.

**196**

## III.   PANES FROM PRESTIGE BOOKLETS

From £1 Wedgwood Booklet No. DX1

The illustrations are reduced, the actual size being 150 × 72 mm. On *se-tenant* panes the arrows indicate the positions of the phosphor bands.

First pane comprising 12 × 3p. Type I two bands

UWB1

|  | Perf. Type I |
|---|---|
| UWB1 (containing No. U103 × 12) (24.5.72) | 5·50 |
|   *a.* One broad band on each stamp .. .. .. .. .. | £200 |
|   *b.* Phosphor omitted .. .. .. .. .. .. .. | £170 |

Second pane comprising 3 × 2½p. Type I centre band; 3 × 2½p. Type I band at right; 6 × 3p. two bands

UWB2

|  | Perf Type I |
|---|---|
| UWB2 (containing Nos. U87 × 3, U94 × 3, U103 × 6) (24.5.72) | 10·00 |
|   *a.* Phosphor omitted .. .. .. .. .. .. | — |
|   *b.* Inverted V scratch (R. 2/1) .. .. .. .. .. .. | 55·00 |
|   *c.* Phosphor bands displaced to right .. .. .. .. .. .. | £350 |

No. UWB2*c* includes 2½p. right band (1st row), 2½p. missing phosphor (2nd row) and all 3p. with broad band at left.

Third pane comprising $3 \times 2\frac{1}{2}$p. Type III band at right; $3 \times \frac{1}{2}$p. Type I two bands; $3 \times 2\frac{1}{2}$p. Type III band at left; $3 \times 2\frac{1}{2}$p. Type III centre band

UWB3

| | Perf. Type I |
|---|---|
| UWB3 (containing Nos. U48 × 3, U87g × 3, U93 × 3, U95 × 3) (24.5.72) | 10·00 |
|    *a.* Shoulder scratch (R. 2/1) | 22·00 |
|    *b.* Shortened P in value (R. 3/4) | 22·00 |
|    *c.* Phosphor omitted | £1500 |
|    *d.* Phosphor bands displaced 19 mm. to right | — |
|    *e.* Phosphor bands displaced 10 mm. to right | — |
|    *s.* Overprinted "Specimen" 14 × 2 mm. | — |

No. UWB3*d* includes three examples of the following: $2\frac{1}{2}$p. missing phosphor (1st row), $\frac{1}{2}$p. broad band right (2nd row), $2\frac{1}{2}$p. 2 bands (3rd row) and $2\frac{1}{2}$p. narrow left side band (4th row).

No. UWB3*e* include the following: $2\frac{1}{2}$p. missing phosphor (1st row), $\frac{1}{2}$p. broad band centre (2nd row), $2\frac{1}{2}$p. broad band centre (3rd row), $2\frac{1}{2}$p. narrow right side band (4th row).

Fourth pane comprising $3 \times \frac{1}{2}$p. Type I two bands; $2 \times 2\frac{1}{2}$p. Type III band at left; $1 \times \frac{1}{2}$p. Type I band at left

UWB4

| | Perf. Type I |
|---|---|
| UWB4 (containing Nos. U48 × 3, U51, U93 × 2) (24.5.72) | 70·00 |
|    *a.* One broad band on each stamp | |
|    *b.* Nose and eye variety (R. 1/1) | 80·00 |
|    *c.* $2\frac{1}{2}$p. Type I (Cyl. B22) | £100 |
|    *cb.* As *c* but with nose and eye variety (R. 1/1) | £110 |
|    *d.* Phosphor omitted | |
|    *s.* Overprinted "Specimen" 14 × 2 mm. | — |

No. UWB4*c* contains the $\frac{1}{2}$p. stamps in a very pale shade.

**Listed Wedgwood Booklet Cylinder Flaws**

UWB2*b* (2½p.)
Large scratch in form of inverted V across shoulder up to
back of hair and extending below hair at right

| UWB3*a* (2½p.) | UWB3*b* (2½p.) | UWB4*b* (½p.) |
|:---:|:---:|:---:|
| Scratch across shoulder Later retouched | Screened leg of P in value | Scratch over Queen's nose and repair below eye |

**Cylinder Numbers**

The cylinders printed three rows of four panes of stamps with space for advertisements, or postage rates in the case of the fourth pane. There were wide margins but the cylinder numbers were always trimmed off. Those employed were:-

UWB1    B25 (3p.) and B11 (phosphor)
UWB2    B14 (2½p.), B21 (3p.) and B8 (phosphor)
UWB3    B23 (½p.), B20 (2½p.) and B10 (phosphor)
UWB4    B14 (½p.), B25 (2½p.) and B9 (phosphor)
UWB4*c*    B14 (½p.), B22 (2½p.) and B9 (phosphor)

NOTE. The phosphor bands on these panes stop short in the horizontal margins at top and bottom. Panes listed with broad bands are the result of sideways displacement.

From £3 Wedgwood Booklet No. DX2

The illustrations are reduced, the actual size being 163 × 97 mm.

First pane comprising 9 × 12p. two 9·5 mm. bands. The first band at left of the pane is 6·5 mm. wide and is placed over the first vertical row of perforations.

UWB5

UWB5 (containing No. U206 × 9) (16.4.80)                                3·50
  *a*. Phosphor omitted      ..      ..      ..      ..      ..      ..    40·00
  *b*. Phosphor printed on both sides      ..      ..      ..      ..    £500
  *c*. One band (6·5 mm. first vert. row and 9·5 mm. others) ..      ..    £100
  *d*. Blemish in front of nose (R. 3/1)      ..      ..      ..      ..    5·00
  *e*. Phosphor omitted from front but printed on the back of stamps ..   ..    £600

**Listed Booklet Cylinder Flaw**

No. UWB5*d* is a multipositive flaw which comes from no dot panes from Cylinders 2, 4 and 6. It is listed as a single stamp under No. U204*c* from sheets and also the DL vertical coil where it occurs on Roll 2.

Second pane comprising 9 × 10p. centre band.

UWB6

UWB6 (containing No. U190 × 9) (16.4.80)                                2·75
  *a*. Phosphor omitted      ..      ..      ..      ..      ..      ..    40·00
  *b*. Phosphor printed on both sides      ..      ..      ..      ..    £500
  *c*. Phosphor omitted from front but printed on the back of stamps ..   ..    £600

Third pane comprising 6 × 2p. Type I with 6·5 and two 9·5 mm. bands.

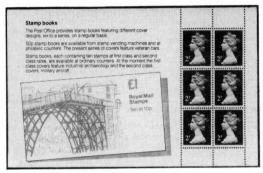

**UWB7**

UWB7 (containing No. U80 × 6) (16.4.80) .. .. 60
   *a.* Phosphor omitted .. .. .. .. .. .. .. .. 50·00
   *b.* One broad band .. .. .. .. .. .. .. .. 75·00
   *c.* Phosphor printed both sides .. .. .. .. .. .. .. £500
   *d.* Red omitted at left (booklet value and inscription omitted) .. .. £1000

Fourth pane comprising 2p. Type I two 9·5 mm. bands; 10p. band at left; 3 × 10p. centre band; 4 × 12p. two 9·5 mm. bands. The first band at left of the pane is 6·5 mm. wide. The 2p. has the right-hand band the height of the stamp and is 4 mm. wide to prevent overlapping onto the 10p. stamps.

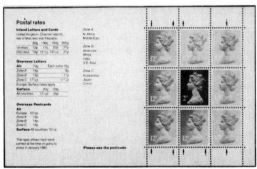

**UWB8**

UWB8 (containing Nos. U80, U191, U190 × 3, U206 × 4) (16.4.80) .. 3·00
   *a.* Phosphor omitted .. .. .. .. .. .. .. .. 50·00
   *b.* One broad band .. .. .. .. .. .. .. .. —
   *c.* Phosphor printed on both sides .. .. .. .. .. .. £850
   *d.* Blemish in front of nose (R. 3/1) .. .. .. .. .. .. 5·00

No. UWB8 exists with the 2p. misplaced 5 mm. to right which leaves a white gap at left, perforations passing through the back of the crown and green background printed over the left-hand side of the 10p.

**Listed Booklet Cylinder Flaw**

No. UWB8*d* is a multipositive flaw which comes from no dot panes from Cylinders 2, 4 and 6. It is listed as a single stamp under No. U204*c* from sheets and also the DL vertical coil where it occurs on Roll 2.

**Cylinder Numbers**

The cylinders printed three rows of four panes similar to the previous Wedgwood Booklet. The cylinder numbers were always trimmed off. Those employed were:—

UWB5   B4 (12p.) and B26 (phosphor)
UWB6   B12 (10p.) and B27 (phosphor)
UWB7   B13 (2p.) and B28 (phosphor)
UWB8   B14 (2p.), B11 (10p.), B2 (12p.) and B29 (phosphor)

From £4 Booklet "Story of Stanley Gibbons" No. DX3.

The illustrations are reduced, the actual size being 163 × 97 mm.

First pane comprising 6 × 15½p. Type I two 9·5 mm. bands. The first band at left of the pane is 6 mm. wide and is placed over the first vertical row of perforations.

UWB9

UWB9 (containing No. U238 × 6) (19.5.82)      3·00
   *a.* Phosphor omitted   ..   ..   ..   ..   ..   ..   ..   75·00
   *b.* One broad band (6·5 mm. first vert. row and 9·5 mm. others)   ..   ..   70·00
   *c.* Phosphor printed on both sides   ..   ..   ..   ..   ..   £400

Second pane comprising 3 × 12½p. band at right; 3 × 12½p. band at left. The pane has one phosphor band 8 mm. wide printed over the second vertical row of perforations.

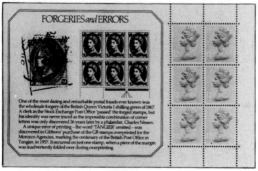

UWB10

UWB10 (containing Nos. U213 × 3, U214 × 3) (19.5.82)      2·25
   *a.* Phosphor omitted   ..   ..   ..   ..   ..   ..   ..   ..   25·00
   *b.* One broad band*   ..   ..   ..   ..   ..   ..   ..   ..   £325
   *c.* Phosphor printed on both sides   ..   ..   ..   ..   ..   £450

*No. UWB10*b* contains the first vertical row without phosphor band and the second row with a broad band.

Third pane comprising 2p. Type I two 9·5 mm. bands; 3p. two 9·5 mm. bands; 3 × 12½p. band at right, 3 × 12½p. band at left and single 12½p. centre band. The 9·5 mm. bands are placed over the second and third vertical rows of perforations and stop short in the horizontal margins except at right where the band stops near the top of the 3p. and 12½p. in the second row. The 12½p. at top right has a 4 mm. centre band which extends from the top margin of the pane to base of the stamp.

UWB11

UWB11 (containing Nos. U80, U113, U212b, U213e, U213 × 2, U214 × 3)
(19.5.82)                                                      6·50
*a*. Phosphor omitted      ..    ..    ..    ..    ..    ..    ..    ..    £100
*b*. One broad band*       ..    ..    ..    ..    ..    ..    ..    ..    £200
*c*. Phosphor printed on both sides    ..    ..    ..    ..    ..    ..    £1500

*No. UWB11b contains stamps with the phosphor bands displaced to the right giving the first vertical row without phosphor and the second and third rows with a broad centre band. The stamp in position R. 1/3 has a narrow band at right which is short at bottom.

Fourth pane comprising 9 × 15½p. Type I two 9·5 mm. bands. The first band at left of the pane is 6 mm. wide and is placed over the first vertical row of perforations.

UWB12

UWB12 (containing No. U238 × 9) (19.5.82)                       4·00
*a*. Phosphor omitted      ..    ..    ..    ..    ..    ..    ..    ..    30·00
*b*. One broad band*       ..    ..    ..    ..    ..    ..    ..    ..    £130
*c*. Phosphor printed on both sides    ..    ..    ..    ..    ..    ..    £750
*ca*. As *c* but two bands on reverse**    ..    ..    ..    ..    ..    ..    £750

*No. UWB12b contains all stamps with a broad 9·5 mm. centre band except the first vertical row in which the stamps each have a 6 mm. band.

**No. UWB12ca contains, three normal, three phosphor both sides and, in the vertical centre row, three examples with 2 bands front and side band left on the gum side.

**203**

**Cylinder Numbers**

The cylinder numbers were always trimmed off. Those employed were:

UWB9   B12 (15½p.) and B45 (phosphor)
UWB10  B12 (12½p.) and B46 (phosphor)
UWB11  B18 (2p.), B42 (3p.), B13 (12½p.) and B48 (phosphor)
UWB12  B10 (15½p.) and B44 (phosphor)

---

From £4 Booklet "Story of the Royal Mint" No. DX4

The illustrations are reduced, the actual size being 163 × 97 mm.

First pane on fluorescent coated paper comprising 3 × 12½p. band at right; 3 × 12½p. band at left. The pane has one phosphor band 9·5 mm. wide placed over the second vertical row of perforations.

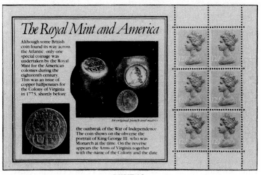

UWB13

| | | | | | | | |
|---|---|---|---|---|---|---|---|
| UWB13 (containing Nos. U213 × 3, U214 × 3) (14.9.83) | | | | | | | 2·25 |
| *a.* Phosphor omitted | | | | | | | £250 |
| *b.* One broad band* | .. | .. | .. | .. | .. | .. | £275 |
| *c.* Phosphor printed on both sides | | .. | .. | .. | .. | .. | £350 |

*No. UWB13*b* contains the first vertical row without phosphor band and the second row with a broad band.

Second pane as No. UWB13 but with counterfoil inscribed "Maundy Money".

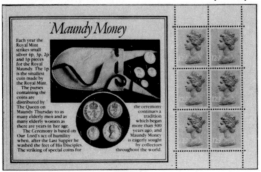

UWB14

| | | | | | | | |
|---|---|---|---|---|---|---|---|
| UWB14 (containing Nos. U213 × 3, U214 × 3) (14.9.83) | | | | | | | 2·25 |
| *a.* Phosphor omitted | .. | .. | .. | .. | .. | .. | £250 |
| *b.* One broad band* | .. | .. | .. | .. | .. | .. | £300 |
| *c.* Phosphor printed on both sides | .. | .. | .. | .. | .. | .. | £400 |

*No. UWB14*b* contains the first vertical row without phosphor band and the second row with a broad band.

**204**

Third pane comprising 3p., 3½p. × 2 and 16p. × 6 phosphorised (advanced coated) paper.

UWB15

UWB15 (containing Nos. U111, U120 × 2, U240 × 6) (14.9.83)              6·00

Fourth pane comprising 9 × 16p. phosphorised (advanced coated) paper.

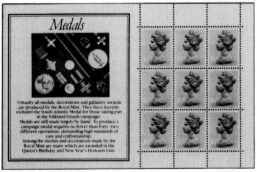

UWB16

UWB16 (containing No. U240 × 9) (14.9.83)              3·75

**Cylinder Numbers**

The cylinder numbers were always trimmed off. Those employed were:—

UWB13    B33 (12½p.) and B59 (phosphor)
              B34 (12½p.) and B59 (phosphor)
UWB14    B33 (12½p.) and B59 (phosphor)
UWB15    B47 (3p.), B10 (3½p.) and B7 (16p.)
UWB16    B6 (16p.)

From £4 Booklet "The Story of our Christian Heritage" No. DX5

The illustrations are reduced, the actual size being 163 × 97 mm.

First pane comprising 6 × 17p. phosphorised (advanced coated) paper.

UWB17

UWB17 (containing No. U247 × 6) (4.9.84)                                      3·00

Second pane on fluorescent coated paper comprising 3 × 13p. band at right; 3 × 13p. band at left. The pane has one phosphor band 9·5 mm. wide placed over the second vertical row of perforations.

UWB18

UWB18 (containing Nos. U219 × 3, U220 × 3) (4.9.84)                2·75
   *a*. Phosphor omitted     ..     ..     ..     ..     ..     ..     ..     £200

Third pane on fluorescent coated paper comprising 10p. Type II two bands (6 mm. at left; 9·5 mm. at right); 13p. band at left; 7 × 17p. The phosphor bands at each side of the pane are 6 mm. wide. At right the band is short on the 17p. values to prevent an overlap on to the 13p. The strip of three 17p. in the centre have two 9·5 mm. bands at each side.

UWB19

UWB19 (containing Nos. U193, U219, U248 × 5, U248c, U248d) (4.9.84)          6·50
   a. Phosphor omitted    ..   ..   ..   ..   ..   ..   ..   ..          —

Fourth pane as No. UWB18 but with counterfoil showing Lillian Baylis and The Old Vic theatre.

UWB20

UWB20 (containing Nos. U219 × 3, U220 × 3) (4.9.84)                           2·75
   a. Phosphor omitted   ..   ..   ..   ..   ..   ..   ..   ..          £225
   b. One broad band*   ..   ..   ..   ..   ..   ..   ..   ..          £350
*No. UWB20b has a broad band on the stamps at right only.

### Cylinder Numbers

The cylinder numbers were always trimmed off. The cylinders printed sheets containing 3 columns each with four panes, on a Rembrandt press. The cylinders known to have been used were:—
UWB17   B6 (17p.)
UWB18   B2 (13p.) and B63 (phosphor)
UWB19   B22 (10p.), B1 (13p.), B1 (17p.) and B64 (phosphor)
UWB20   B2 (13p.) and B63 (phosphor)

From £5 Booklet "The Story of *The Times*" No. DX6

The illustrations are reduced, the actual size being 163 × 95 mm.

First pane comprising 6 × 17p. phosphorised (advanced coated) paper.

UWB21

UWB21 (containing No. U247 × 6) (8.1.85)                    3·00

Second pane on fluorescent coated paper comprising 9 × 13p. with 4·5 mm. centre band.

UWB22

UWB22 (containing No. U221 × 9) (8.1.85)                              4·00
  *a*. Phosphor omitted      ..     ..     ..     ..     ..     ..     ..     £350
  *b*. Phosphor printed on both sides     ..     ..     ..     ..     ..     £550

Third pane on fluorescent coated paper comprising 4p. Type II, band at right and band at left; 2 × 13p. band at right; 2 × 13p. band at left; 2 × 17p. and 34p. with two 9·5 mm. bands.

UWB23

UWB23 (containing Nos. U130/31, U219 × 2, U220 × 2, U248 × 2, U312)
(8.1.85)                                                                                          9·50
*a*. Phosphor omitted        ..        ..        ..        ..        ..        ..        ..        ..    £1000
*b*. One broad band*        ..        ..        ..        ..        ..        ..        ..        ..    £1250
*c*. Phosphor printed both sides  ..        ..        ..        ..        ..        ..        ..        £900
 *No. UWB23*b* contains the first vertical row without phosphor and second and third rows with a broad band on each stamp.

Fourth pane comprising 9 × 17p. phosphorised (advanced coated) paper.

UWB24

UWB24 (containing No. U247 × 9) (8.1.85)                                              4·50

**Cylinder Numbers**
    The printer's sheets contained 3 columns each with four panes which were printed on a Rembrandt press. The cylinder numbers do not occur in the issued booklets but it is known that the following cylinders were used.
UWB21    B6 (17p.)
UWB22    B13 (13p.), B65 (phosphor)
UWB23    B8 (4p.), B15 (13p.), B12 (17p.), B2 (34p.) and B66 (phosphor)
UWB24    B10 (17p.)

From £5 Booklet "The Story of British Rail" No. DX7

The illustrations are reduced, the actual size being 162 × 95 mm.

First pane comprising 9 × 17p. phosphorised (advanced coated) paper.

UWB25

| | | |
|---|---|---|
| UWB25 (containing No. U247 × 9) (18.3.86) | | 4·50 |
| *b*. Vertical smudge below front jewel (R. 1/3) .. .. .. .. .. | | 5·50 |
| *c*. Yellow omitted at left (background and lettering white) .. .. .. | | £1200 |

**Listed Booklet Cylinder Flaw**

UWB25*b*
Dark spot and vertical
smudge below front jewel

Second pane on fluorescent coated paper comprising 9 × 12p. with 4·5 mm. centre band.

UWB26

| | | |
|---|---|---|
| UWB26 (containing No. U211 × 9) (18.3.86) | | 4·50 |
| *a*. Phosphor omitted .. .. .. .. .. .. .. .. | | £160 |
| *b*. Phosphor printed on both sides .. .. .. .. .. .. | | £600 |

Third pane on fluorescent coated paper comprising 3 × 12p. band at right, 3 × 12p. band at left, 2 × 17p. and 31p. with two 9·5 mm. bands.

UWB27

UWB27 (containing Nos. U209 × 3, U210 × 3, U248 × 2, U306) (18.3.86)    8·50
- *a.* Phosphor omitted   ..   ..   ..   ..   ..   ..   ..   ..   £1000
- *b.* One broad band   ..   ..   ..   ..   ..   ..   ..   ..   —
- *c.* Phosphor printed on both sides   ..   ..   ..   ..   ..   ..   —

Fourth pane comprising 6 × 17p. phosphorised (advanced coated) paper.

UWB28

UWB28 (containing No. U247 × 6) (18.3.86)    3·00
- *b.* Yellow omitted at left (background and lettering white) ..   ..   ..   —

**Cylinder Numbers**

The cylinder numbers were always trimmed off but those used were:—
UWB25   B28 (17p.)
UWB26   B15 (12p.), B65 (phosphor)
UWB27   B18 (12p.), B29 (17p.), B1 (31p.) and B66 (phosphor)
UWB28   B32 (17p.)

From £5 Booklet "The Story of P & O 1837–1987" No. DX8

The illustrations are reduced, the actual size being 162 × 95 mm. Phosphor bands continue through pane selvedge at top and bottom.

First pane comprising 9 × 18p. phosphorised (advanced coated) paper.

UWB29

UWB29 (containing No. U256 × 9) (3.3.87)        5·50

Second pane on fluorescent coated paper comprising 9 × 13p. with 4·5 mm. centre band.

UWB30

UWB30 (containing No. U221*b* × 9) (3.3.87)        4·00

Third pane on fluorescent coated paper comprising 1p. and 2 × 13p. band at right; 5 × 18p. and 26p. two 9·5 mm. bands. The band at right is narrow and is placed to avoid the vertical margin.

UWB31

UWB31 (containing Nos. U67, U220d × 2, U258a × 5, U293) (3.3.87)        8·50
  a. Original phosphor ink ..        ..        ..        ..        ..        ..        ..        ..        —

The original phosphor ink appears dark under ultra violet light. It is believed that only 5 panes were found.


Fourth pane a fluorescent coated paper comprising 6 × 13p. with 4·5 mm. centre band.

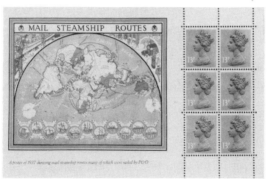

UWB32

UWB32 (containing No. U221b × 6) (3.3.87)        2·50


**Cylinder Numbers**
The cylinder numbers were always trimmed off but those used were:—
UWB29    B8 (18p.)
UWB30    B30 (13p.), B71 (phosphor)
UWB31    B33 (1p.), B29 (13p.), B7 (18p.), B1 (26p.) and B72 (phosphor)
UWB32    B35 (13p.), B73 (phosphor)

From £5 Booklet "London Life" No. DX11

The first pane in the "London Life" booklet contains four 20p. values depicting Alexandra Palace and will be listed in Volume 5. The second and fourth panes contain blocks of six (2 × 3) of the 20p. Penny Black 150th Anniversary issue and both of these panes are listed in the appropriate section in this volume (see Section W).

The illustration is reduced, the actual size being 162 × 95 mm.

Third pane on fluorescent coated paper comprising (2nd), 15p., (1st), 20p., and 50p. Machin with 15p., 20p. and 29p. Penny Black Anniversary stamps in the bottom row. All with two phosphor bands except the three stamps in the first vertical row at left which have a narrow band at right. The other bands are 9·5 and, at left, 4 mm. wide all in new phosphor ink and continuous through top and bottom selvedge.

UWB33

UWB33   (containing Nos. U234, U269, U324, U12, U15, W790/1, W796)
  (20.3.90)                                                            5·00

**Cylinder Numbers**

The cylinder numbers were trimmed off and did not appear in the finished booklets.

# B.    Folded Booklet Panes (1976–90)

## General Notes

**INTRODUCTION.** As mentioned in the Introduction to the General Notes at the beginning of this Section, "Swedish-style" or Folded Booklets were introduced in 1976, printed on the "Jumelle" machine. These have the panes of stamps affixed to the inside of the booklet cover by the selvedge and then folded over to fit the size of the cover. They may contain *se-tenant* panes comprising two, three or four denominations arranged vertically (multi-value panes) or else horizontal panes of ten stamps of the same value or two values *se-tenant*, being the contemporary first and second class letter rates. The Christmas Greetings Booklets which were first issued in 1978 contain a horizontal pane of twenty stamps. These are arranged *se-tenant* vertically with two rows of 10 stamps to cover the first and second class letter rates at the time of issue.

In 1978 several different series of pictorial covers were introduced so that the same panes may be found affixed to different covers.

Unlike the stitched booklets it is inadvisable to remove the folded panes from the covers because if they are separated by the perforations the evidence of perforator type is lost.

We therefore list the folded booklet panes complete with cover. It might be argued that in doing this we are duplicating the listing of the booklets in Appendix J. This is not so because here we list the booklet panes according to perforator type and without necessarily stating with which cover they will be supplied, as some panes are found attached to several different covers.

**BOOKLET CYLINDER NUMBERS.** The printer's booklet sheet contains one or more columns of panes and it became standard practice to place the cylinder number in the margin of one pane in each column. We do not differentiate between the identical numbers and one price is given. By noting cylinder flaws or some distinctive feature in the cylinder number it is possible to identify the column, but this is not attempted here. Detailed information on how to "plate" different columns from booklet sheets is published by the *GB Decimal Study Circle*. After the main listing of cylinder numbers we give a description of the make-up of the booklet sheet in its uncut state and where the cylinder numbers occur. Obviously the quantity ratio between ordinary and cylinder panes is reflected in the prices quoted.

**PHOSPHOR CYLINDER NUMBERS.** The phosphor cylinder numbers are numbered in sequence, but not all are found on the issued panes as some are placed wide and were trimmed away. As in the sheet stamps the phosphor numbers occur displaced, but we only list these when they occur in a separate booklet from the ink cylinder combination. Care should be taken when looking for the phosphor numbers as they can only be identified using an ultra violet lamp and the small numbers in the new phosphor ink are difficult to see due to the type of phosphor employed. The booklets showing ink cylinder in one and phosphor number in another booklet are best collected as a pair of booklets.

**PRICES.** We repeat that prices quoted in this Section are for panes with good perforations whereas the prices for booklets listed in Appendix J according to cover are for those having panes with average perforations. It therefore follows that those who wish to collect booklets primarily for their covers should base their orders on Section J numbers.

**PERFORATORS AND SHEET MAKE-UP.** The perforators used are described in Appendix I where the main types of uncut sheets are illustrated and show the sheet markings.

**MISCUT PANES.** It quite frequently happens that a batch of sheets is miscut but the postal authorities do not regard these as errors as the individual stamps are unaffected. However, they are listed under the catalogue numbers for the normal panes with the addition of an "A" suffix letter.

We do not list cylinder varieties on miscut panes. For one thing they do not necessarily exist as sometimes miscut panes are only known from some, or possibly only one of the columns. Where cylinder varieties do occur they will be found on the adjoining row to that on the normal panes and they will be worth correspondingly more. We do, however, list miscut cylinder panes.

Miscut multi-value panes are obviously identifiable and miscut panes of single values can easily be identified in that instead of having a cutting line at each side of the pane there is a single cutting line at the middle row of perforations.

**SHORT PHOSPHOR BANDS.** In multi-value folded booklet panes where stamps with two phosphor bands are vertically *se-tenant* with stamps having only one band it is important to prevent the spread of phosphor from one stamp to the other and the bands are deliberately made shorter to achieve this. The object is to stop short at the perforations, leaving the *se-tenant* stamp clear of phosphor. Sometimes slight vertical displacement of the phosphor occurs and they are not listed. However, the stamps showing short bands which are consistent and identifiable are listed as varieties of the basic stamp or if the band width has changed, they are recorded as a new basic stamp in Section UD.

Stamps overprinted with the so-called new phosphor ink exist with short bands to avoid encroachment on the next stamp or label. Due to the difficulty of seeing the phosphor cut-off point such stamps are not listed as varieties of the basic stamp. It is recommended that such stamps should be displayed in the pane so that their origin is certain.

**UNDERPRINTS.** Stamps sold at a discount were underprinted with a symbol or letter. Illustrations of the underprints follow the listing of the single stamp in Section UD. The first booklet pane to be issued with an underprint, on Machin issues, was the 1982 Christmas pane with a face value of £2·80 and was sold at £2·50.

**ARRANGEMENT.** The UE section is divided into the following groups:
 UMFB numbers for multi-value booklet panes
 UFB numbers for horizontal and vertical format panes containing stamps of one value
 Panes listed are from plain or pictorial folded booklet covers and barcode style booklets.
 All are listed in date order so as to avoid any need to revise the numbers in the future. This means that a progression of value will be seen but due to the issue of both first and second class panes this is not constant and no attempt to list in value order has been made.

**PANE FACE VALUES.** Panes are described and listed according to the price shown on the booklet cover rather than the total face value of the individual stamps. Slot machine booklets with 50p. and £1 cover prices frequently contained stamps with a total value slightly higher than the booklet cover price.

## I.  Multi-value Folded Booklet Panes

**10p. Pane. Experimental Type Booklets FA1/3**

UMFB1 Type P (UMFB2 has narrow top margin)

Pair of ½p. with 6p. and three 1p. all with two 9·5 mm. phosphor bands. ½p. Type I and 6p. Type II. From Booklets Nos. FA1/2

|  | Perf. Type | |
|---|:---:|:---:|
|  | P | E |
| UMFB1 (containing Nos. U50 × 2, U59 × 3, U146) (10.3.76) | 60 | 1·25 |
|   *a.* One broad band   ..        ..        ..        ..        ..        ..        .. | — | — |
|   *c.* Missing necklace shading (R. 1/2)  ..        ..        ..        ..        .. 2·25 | | † |
|   *d.* Circle between P and chin (R. 2/1) ..        ..        ..        ..        .. 2·75 | | † |
|   *e.* Blue dots on shoulder (R. 2/2)        ..        ..        ..        ..        .. † | | 2·75 |

| | | |
|---|:---:|:---:|
| UMFB1A Miscut. 6p. at right | £750 | † |

Only six examples of No. UMFB1A have been recorded all with trimmed perforations.

As last, narrow margin and affixed to edge. From booklet No. FA3

| | Perf. Type | |
|---|:---:|:---:|
| UMFB2 (containing Nos. U50 × 2, U59 × 3, U146) (13.6.77) | 60 | 1·10 |
|   *a.* One broad band   ..        ..        ..        ..        ..        ..        .. | — | — |
|   *c.* Missing necklace shading (R. 1/2)  ..        ..        ..        ..        .. 1·75 | | † |
|   *d.* Circle between P and chin (R. 2/1) ..        ..        ..        ..        .. 1·75 | | † |
|   *e.* Blue dots on shoulder (R. 2/2)        ..        ..        ..        ..        .. † | | 2·75 |

| | | |
|---|:---:|:---:|
| UMFB2A Miscut. 6p. at right | 5·00 | 6·00 |

Panes UMFB2 have a much narrower selvedge and usually do not show the cutting lines on the panes with margin perforated through. They were affixed to the very edge of the cover so that the fold comes between the second and third rows instead of between the first and second rows. This cover gives revised postal rates and at the bottom there is the slogan: "Please remember to use the postcode—always".

**Listed Booklet Cylinder Flaws**

| UMFB1/2c (½p.) | UMFB1/2d | UMFB1/2e |
|:---:|:---:|:---:|
| Missing shading under necklace | Large circle flaw | Semi-circle of four blue dots on shoulder |

Nos. UMFB1/2d is a multipositive flaw as it recurs on the ½p. value in the same position on pane UMFB7.

**Sheet Make-up**

A reduced sized illustration of an uncut sheet appears in Appendix I. This shows three continuous columns. With the sheet orientated to show the cylinder numbers at left it will be seen that columns 1 and 2 have the margins perforated through and column three has a single extension hole in the margin.

Moreover it is possible to ascribe individual panes to the columns in the sheet through the position of the value in the bottom pair of stamps which consistently varies in each column, as indicated in the following actual size illustrations:

| | | | |
|---|:---:|:---:|:---:|
| Distance between base of value and bottom margin | 2·5 mm. | 2 mm. | 3 mm. |
| Position in relation to base of bust | Above | Level | Well above |
| Perf. Type | P | P | E |

Naturally panes from column 3 are easily distinguished by the perforator type but the above provides a ready distinction between columns 1 and 2. This test applies also to pane UMFB7 containing the *se-tenant* ½, 1, and 7p. values.

**Cylinder Numbers**

36-row single-pane cylinders printed sideways were employed but the cylinder numbers were always trimmed off. Those used were:—

B24 (½p.), B8 (1p.), B5 (6p.) and B15 (phosphor)

**50p. Pane. Plain Cover Booklets FB1A/B**

UMFB3            UMFB4

Pair of ½p. Type I, vertical pairs of 1p. and 6½p. and vertical strip of 4 of 8½p.
½p. 1p., and 8½p., all have two 8 mm. phosphor bands set 12 mm. apart

Pane UMFB3. With 6½p. at left containing narrow phosphor band at right from 50p. Booklet No.
FB1A. The lower 1p. has a short left band at bottom
Pane UMFB4. With 6½p. at right containing narrow phosphor band at left from 50p. Booklet No.
FB1B. The lower 1p. has a short right band at bottom

|  | Perf. Type E |
|---|---|
| UMFB3 (containing Nos. U52 × 2, U60 × 2, U152 × 2, U168 × 4) | |
| (26.1.77) | 2·50 |
|   *c.* Retouch left of chin (R. 1/1)    ..    ..    ..    .. | 5·00 |
|   *d.* Oblong repair in hair (R. 2/1) and three background repairs above | |
|       rear jewels (R. 4/1)    ..    ..    ..    .. | 7·50 |
|   *f.* Pearl on top of central cross (R. 5/1)    ..    ..    .. | 5·00 |
|   *g.* White flaw on front jewel (R. 5/2) ..    ..    ..    .. | 5·00 |

UMFB4 (containing Nos. U52 × 2, U60 × 2, U151 × 2,
U168 × 4) (26.1.77) .. .. .. .. .. 2·00
   *b.* Four background repairs above rear jewels (R. 4/2) .. 5·00
   *c.* Dark green spot left of front curl (R. 5/1) .. .. 4·00

These panes have crimson cutting lines and are folded twice, below the first 1p./8½p. and again below the first 6½p./8½p.

**Listed Booklet Cylinder Flaws**

UMFB3*c*
Retouch left
of chin

UMFB3*d* (1p.)
Oblong repair
in hair

UMFB3*f* (6½p.)
Pearl on top of
central cross
Later retouched

UMFB3*g* (8½p.)
Flaw in front jewel

UMFB4*b* (6½p.)
Four background
repairs above rear
jewels
Later retouched

UMFB4*c* (8½p.)
Green spot

**Sheet Make-up**

A reduced sized illustration of an uncut sheet appears in Appendix I. From this it will be seen that these panes were printed in only two columns with margins on either side of the sheet, both of which have a single extension hole, so that only E perforators exist. Naturally panes UMFB3 and UMFB4 are printed side by side. The stamps are printed sideways.

**Cylinder Numbers**

These appeared in the left margin but they were invariably trimmed off. Those used were:—
B26 (½p.), B10 (1p.), B1 (6½p.), B1 (8½p.) and B16 (phosphor)

**50p. Pane. Plain Cover and Commercial Vehicle Series FB2A/FB8B**

UMFB5                    UMFB6

Pair of 1p. with vertical strips of three of 7p. and 9p.

1p. and 9p. each have two 8 mm. phosphor bands set 12 mm. apart

Pane UMFB5. With 7p. at left containing narrow phosphor band at right from 50p. Pictorial
     Booklets Nos. FB2/8A. The 1p. has a short left band at bottom
Pane UMFB6. With 7p. at right containing narrow phosphor band at left from 50p. Pictorial
     Booklets Nos. FB2/8B. The 1p. has a short right band at bottom

**Thin Value Type of 7p.**

  Normal     Thin value

The marked thin value type occurs only in panes 5 and
6 in column 2, i.e. comprising a block of six in the sheet
of which three stamps have the phosphor band at left and
three with band at right. They can be seen in the illustration
of the complete sheet.

Perf. Type E

UMFB5 (containing Nos. U60 × 2, U156 × 3, U176 × 3) (13.6.77)    4·00
   *c.* Thin value type (R. 2–4/1) and oval repair on dress (R. 2/1)    ..   6·00
   *d.* U-shaped mark on shoulder (R. 1/1)    ..    ..    ..    ..   5·50
   *e.* Mark on back of shoulder (R. 1/2) ..    ..    ..    ..   5·50
   *f.* White dot in corner of 7 (R. 4/1)    ..    ..    ..    ..   5·00

UMFB6 (containing Nos. U60 × 2, U155 × 3, U176 × 3) (13.6.77)    2·50
   *c.* Thin value type (R. 2–4/2)    ..    ..    ..    ..    ..   4·50
   *d.* White scratch across stamp (R. 4/2)    ..    ..    ..   6·50

These panes have purple-brown cutting lines and are folded in the middle.


**Listed Booklet Cylinder Flaws**

UMFB5*c* (7p.)
Prominent repair on dress
combined with thin value

UMFB5*d*
U-shaped mark on dress

UMFB5*e* (1p.)
Mark on back of shoulder
(Later retouched)

UMFB5*f*
Dot in corner of 7

UMFB6*d*
White scratch across stamp


**Sheet Make-up**

   A reduced sized illustration of an uncut sheet appears in Appendix I. These panes were printed in two columns with a single extension hole in the binding margins in the same arrangement as the *se-tenant* ½, 1, 6½ and 8½p. panes except that the spaces used there for the bottom rows of 6½p. and 8½p. stamps are not printed on and the blank margins are trimmed off, leaving a narrow margin at the bottom of the panes which is perforated through.


**Cylinder Numbers**

   These appeared in the left margin but they were invariably trimmed off. Those used were:—
B11 (1p.), B4 (7p.), B1 (9p.) and B18 (phosphor)

**10p. Pane. Farm Buildings Series FA4/9**

UMFB7 Type E

Vertical pairs of ½p. and 1p. with 7p. all with 4 mm. centre phosphor band together with label inscribed "remember the postcode" at top right. On the upper 1p. stamp the phosphor band was short to prevent overlapping on to the label.

½p. Type II. From Pictorial Booklets Nos. FA4/9

|  | Perf. Type | |
|---|---|---|
|  | P | E |
| UMFB7 (containing Nos. U53a × 2, U61 × 2, U154) (8.2.78) | 60 | 75 |
| a. Phosphor omitted* .. .. .. .. .. .. .. | 25·00 | † |
| b. Flaw between cheek and hair (R. 1/1) .. .. .. .. | 1·50 | † |
| c. Dark spot behind hair (R. 1/1) .. .. .. .. | 1·25 | † |
| d. White spot left of central cross (R. 2/1) and circular hole under earring (R. 3/1) .. .. .. .. .. .. .. | † | 3·00 |
| e. Small retouch below value (R. 2/1) .. .. .. .. .. | 1·25 | † |
| f. White scratch from hair to frame (R. 2/1) .. .. .. .. | 1·50 | † |
| g. Circle between P and chin (R. 2/1) .. .. .. .. .. | 1·50 | † |
| h. Lower part of P missing (R. 2/2) .. .. .. .. .. | † | 1·75 |
| i. Small spot on shoulder (R. 2/2) and retouch in bottom left corner (R. 3/2) .. .. .. .. .. .. .. .. | 1·40 | † |
| j. Large scar on cheek and brown spot under earring (R. 3/1) .. | 1·60 | † |
| l. Blue scratch from hair through nose to left margin (R. 3/1) .. | 1·00 | † |

*Price is for pane with phosphor completely omitted. More frequently it occurs on part of the pane only (Perf. Type P). (*Price* £12.50).

| UMFB7A   Miscut.   Postcode label at left | 12·00 | £250 |
|---|---|---|

**Listed Booklet Cylinder Flaws**

Multipositive Flaw

No. UMFB7g is a multipositive flaw which first occurred on the 6p. value in pane UMFB1 where it is illustrated as UMFB1/2d.

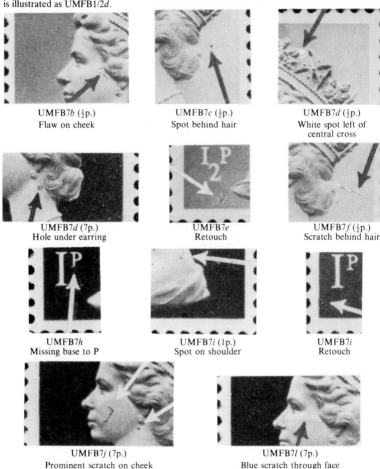

UMFB7b (½p.)
Flaw on cheek

UMFB7c (½p.)
Spot behind hair

UMFB7d (½p.)
White spot left of
central cross

UMFB7d (7p.)
Hole under earring

UMFB7e
Retouch

UMFB7f (½p.)
Scratch behind hair

UMFB7h
Missing base to P

UMFB7i (1p.)
Spot on shoulder

UMFB7i
Retouch

UMFB7j (7p.)
Prominent scratch on cheek
and brown spot under earring

UMFB7l (7p.)
Blue scratch through face

**Sheet Make-up**

A reduced sized illustration of an uncut sheet appears in Appendix I. The layout is exactly the same as that employed for multi-value panes UMFB1/2 containing ½, 1, and 6p. values with three columns of twelve panes, columns 1 and 2 having perforated margins and column 3 with single extension hole in the margin.

Individual panes can be ascribed to the columns using the same test of looking at the positions of the value as described below pane UMFB2.

There are no cutting lines in the margins.

**Cylinder Numbers**

These appeared in the left margin but they were invariably trimmed off. Those used were:—
B28 (½p.), B16 (1p.), B5 (7p.) and B19 (phosphor)

Cylinder B28 is from the same multipositive as was employed for both Cylinder B24 (½p.) and Cylinder B5 (6p.) in pane UMFB1.

**£1·60 Pane. 1978 Christmas Booklet FX1**

UMFB8

*(Illustration reduced to ½ actual size)*

Horizontal strip of ten of 9p. with two 9·5 mm. phosphor bands and similar strip of ten of 7p. with 4 mm. centre phosphor band. In each case the phosphor bands stop short, covering the printed part of the stamps.

The binding margin is always at left as the right-hand margin is guillotined off.

From 1978 Christmas £1·60 Booklet No. FX1

|  | Perf. Type E |
|---|---|
| UMFB8 (containing Nos. U154*m* × 10, U175*n* × 10) (15.11.78) | 4·00 |
| *b.* Scratch above dress (R. 2/4) .. .. .. .. .. .. | 5·50 |

These panes have purple-brown cutting lines and are folded twice, between vertical rows 3/4 and 7/8.

**Booklet Cylinder Numbers**

Perforation as Type RE

|  |  |  | | Perf. Type E | |
|---|---|---|---|---|---|
| Pane No. | Cyl. Nos. | Phos. No. | | No dot | Dot |
| UMFB8 | 9p, B3; 7p, B8 | (B23) .. | .. .. .. | 6·00 | 5·50 |

The dot is omitted after B3 on the dot sheet. The phosphor cylinder number appeared sideways to the left of the ink cylinder numbers.

**Listed Booklet Cylinder Flaw**

UMFB8*b* (7p.)
Scratch above dress
This is a multipositive flaw
which also occurs on pane
No. UMFB13

**Sheet Make-up**

A reduced sized illustration of the uncut dot pane appears in Appendix I. From this it will be seen that the double panes were printed in one column with margins on either side of the sheet. The left-hand side margin has a single extension hole, so that only E perforators exist. The right-hand margin was trimmed away but panes exist with a small margin at right due to bad trimming.

**50p. Pane. Commercial Vehicles and Automobiles Series FB9A/10B**

| UMFB9 | UMFB10 |
|---|---|

Two 2p., vertical pair of 8p. and vertical strip of 3 of 10p. and label inscribed "don't forget the postcode".

2p. and 10p. have two 8 mm. phosphor bands set 12 mm. apart.

Pane UMFB9.    With 8p. at left containing narrow phosphor band at right from 50p. Pictorial Booklet Nos. FB9/10A. On the 2p. below the label the left band is the height of the stamp.

Pane UMFB10.    With 8p. at right containing narrow phosphor band at left from 50p. Pictorial Booklet Nos. FB9/10B. On the 2p. below the label the right band is the height of the stamp.

|  | Perf. Type E |
|---|---|
| UMFB9 (containing Nos. U81 × 2, U164 × 2, U186 × 3) (28.8.79) | 2·00 |
| UMFB9A   Miscut. Face value 36p. (2 × 2p., 4 × 8p.) | £2500 |
| | |
| UMFB10 (containing Nos. U81 × 2, U163 × 2, U186 × 3) (28.8.79) | 2·00 |
| UMFB10A   Miscut. Face value 64p. (2 × 2p., 6 × 10p.) | £2500 |

**Sheet Make-up**

As for panes UMFB5/6. A reduced sized illustration of an uncut sheet appears in Appendix I and shows the stamp and label arrangement.

**Cylinder Numbers**

These appeared in the left margin but were invariably trimmed off. Those used were:—
B11 (2p.), B1 (8p.), B1 (10p.), and B24 (phosphor).

Cylinder B11 is from the same multipositive employed for Cylinder B11 (1p.) in panes UMFB5/6. The 2p. R. 1/1 only, has identical minor flaws seen on 1p. R. 1/1 or R. 1/2 from panes UMFB5/6.

**10p. Pane. "London 1980" Stamp Exhibition Booklets FA10/11**

UMFB11 (1p. Type I, close value)

UMFB12 (1p. Type II, spaced value)

Vertical pair of 1p. with 8p., all with 4 mm. centre phosphor band together with label inscribed "be properly addressed use the postcode" at top left. On the 8p. stamp the phosphor band stops short to prevent overlapping on to the label.

Pane UMFB11.   "JUMELLE". 1p. Type I. From "London 1980" Pictorial Booklets Nos. FA10/11.

|  | Perf. Type P |
|---|---|
| UMFB11 (containing Nos. U61 × 2, U162a) (17.10.79) | 50 |
| b. Large flaw on neck (R. 1/1) .. .. .. .. .. .. | 1·75 |
| c. Mass of white dots (R. 1/1) .. .. .. .. .. .. | 1·75 |
| d. "Beard" flaw (R. 2/2).. .. .. .. .. .. .. | 3·50 |
| e. Diagonal scratch (R. 2/2) .. .. .. .. .. .. | 1·60 |
| f. Retouch inside loop of 8 .. .. .. .. .. .. | 1·60 |
| g. Background repair .. .. .. .. .. .. .. | 1·75 |
| UMFB11A   Miscut. Postcode label at right | 7·00 |

Pane UMFB12.   CHAMBON. 1p. Type II. From "London 1980" Pictorial Booklet No. FA11.

|  | Perf. Type | |
|---|---|---|
|  | P | E |
| UMFB12 (containing U61a × 2, U162a) (4.8.80) | 50 | 50 |
| UMFB12A   Miscut. Postcode label at right | £325 | † |

**Listed Booklet Cylinder Flaws**

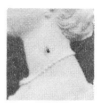

| UMFB11*b* (1p.) | UMFB11*c* (1p.) | UMFB11*d* |
|---|---|---|
| Large flaw on neck | Mass of white dots on chin. | Repair to chin and |
| (Later retouched) | jaw and dress | "beard" flaw |

| UMFB11*e* | UMFB11*f* | UMFB11*g* (8p.) |
|---|---|---|
| Diagonal scratch across dress | Circular retouch | Background repair |
| | inside bottom loop of 8 | |

**Sheet Make-up**

A reduced sized illustration of an uncut sheet appears in Appendix I. This shows four continuous vertical columns which are printed sideways. The sheet illustrated was printed by the "Jumelle" machine and all panes are perf. type P. The Chambon uncut sheet is similar but because of the smaller circumference of the cylinder there are only 16 horizontal stamp rows. Columns 1 and 4 have margins with a single extension hole and these only occur on panes from the Chambon printing. Columns 2 and 3 have margins perforated through.

**Cylinder Numbers**

These appeared in the left margin but were trimmed off. Those used were:—
UMFB11   B1P (9 reversed but later corrected) (1p.), B3 (8p.), B25 (phosphor)
UMFB12   B21 (1p.), B9 (8p.), B32 (phosphor)

---

**£1·80 Pane. 1979 Christmas Booklet FX2**

UMFB13

*(Illustration reduced to ½ actual size)*

228

Horizontal strip of ten of 10p. with two 9·5 mm. phosphor bands and similar strip of ten of 8p. with 4 mm. centre phosphor band. In each case the phosphor bands stop short, covering the printed part of the stamps.

The binding margin is always at left as the right-hand margin is guillotined off.

From 1979 Christmas £1·80 Booklet No. FX2.

|  | Perf. Type E |
|---|---|
| UMFB13 (containing Nos. U162*b* × 10, U184*d* × 10) (14.11.79) | 4·75 |
| *b.* White scratch across stamp (R. 1/7). . | 6·50 |
| *c.* Eye flaw (R. 2/1) . . . . . . . . . . . . | 6·00 |
| *d.* Scratch above dress (R. 2/4) . . . . . . . . . . | 6·50 |

UMFB13A    Miscut. As illustrated but rows transposed    £100

These panes have red cutting lines and are folded twice, between vertical rows 3/4 and 7/8.

**Listed Booklet Cylinder Flaws**

| UMFB13*b* (10p.) | UMFB13*c* (8p.) |
|---|---|
| White scratch across stamp | Flaw masking eye |

No. UMFB13*d* is a multipositive flaw which also occurs on pane UMFB8 where it is illustrated on the 7p. value.

**Booklet Cylinder Numbers**

Perforation as Type RE

|  |  |  |  | Perf. Type E | |
|---|---|---|---|---|---|
| Pane No. | Cyl. Nos. | Phos. No. | | No dot | Dot* |
| UMFB13 | 10p., B5; 8p., B4 | (B23) | . . . . | 7·00 | 7·00 |
| UMFB13 | 10p.; B5 | (B23) | . . . . | £900 | £1500 |
| UMFB13 | 8p., B4 | (—) | . . . . | £900 | £1500 |
| UMFB13A | 10p., B5; 8p., B4 | (B23) | . . . . | £400 | £150 |

*The dot was not engraved but cylinder panes from the dot sheet can be identified by the dot after the phosphor number B23.

During printing the "Jumelle" press was stopped and the ink cylinders B5 and B4 were unsynchronised by two stamp rows. These booklets showing the unsynchronised ink cylinder numbers are rare and when available are usually sold in matched dot or no dot pairs. Except by noting minor flaws the non-cylinder panes cannot be distinguished.

**Sheet Make-up**

As for 1978 Christmas booklet pane UMFB8.

**50p. Pane. Automobiles Series FB11A/13B**

| UMFB16 | UMFB17 |

Panes UMFB14/15 are similar to the above but the value on the 12p. is placed higher and to the left. See illustration under the 12p. listing in Section UD.

Three 2p., vertical pairs of 10p. and 12p. and label inscribed "don't forget the postcode".

2p. and 12p. have two 8 mm. phosphor bands set 12 mm. apart.

Panes UMFB14 and 16.   With 10p. at left containing narrow phosphor band at right. On the 2p. *below* the label the band at left is the height of the stamp.
Panes UMFB15 and 17.   With 10p. at right containing narrow phosphor band at left. On the 2p. *below* the label the band at right is the height of the stamp.

Pane UMFB14.   "JUMELLE". From 50p. Pictorial Booklet No. FB11A

Perf. Type E
UMFB14 (containing Nos. U81 × 3, U192 × 2, U205 × 2) (4.2.80)    2·00

Pane UMFB15.   "JUMELLE". From 50p. Pictorial Booklet No. FB11B

| UMFB15 (containing Nos. U81 × 3, U191 × 2, U205 × 2) (4.2.80) | 2·00 |
| *a.* White nick on frame (R. 3/2) .. .. .. .. .. | 3·00 |
| *b.* Long horizontal line (R. 3/1–2) .. .. .. .. .. | 4·00 |

Pane UMFB16. CHAMBON. From 50p. Pictorial Booklets Nos. FB12/13A
Perf. Type E
UMFB16 (containing Nos. U81 × 3, U192 × 2, U205a × 2) (25.6.80)   2·00
   *a.* Phosphor omitted   ..   ..   ..   ..   ..   ..   ..   30·00
   *b.* Phosphor omitted on 10p. stamps, one broad band on each 2p. and
      12p.   ..   ..   ..   ..   ..   ..   ..   ..   30·00
   *c.* Repair to cheek and shoulder (R. 2/2)   ..   ..   ..   3·75

Pane UMFB17. CHAMBON. From 50p. Pictorial Booklets Nos. FB12/13B
UMFB17 (containing Nos. U81 × 3, U191 × 2, U205a × 2) (25.6.80)   2·00
   *a.* Phosphor omitted   ..   ..   ..   ..   ..   ..   30·00
   *b.* One broad band on each stamp   ..   ..   ..   ..   25·00
   *c.* Damage in Queen's hair (R. 1/1)   ..   ..   ..   ..   3·75

**Listed Booklet Cylinder Flaws**

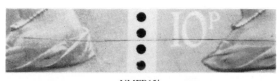

UMFB15*a* (10p.)
White nick in frame

UMFB15*b*
White scratch through bust of 12p. extending as green
hairline through background and across value of 10p.

UMFB16*c* (2p.)
Repair to cheek and shoulder

UMFB17*c* (2p.)
Damage in Queen's hair

**Sheet Make-up**
   Panes UMFB14/5 were as panes UMFB9/10 printed on the "Jumelle" press. The panes UMFB
16/17 were printed on the Chambon press and a reduced sized illustration of an uncut sheet
containing two vertical columns, each with 16 horizontal rows, appears in Appendix I.

**Cylinder Numbers**
   These appeared in the left margin but were invariably trimmed off. Those used were:—
UMFB14/15   B15 (2p.), B10 (10p.), B3 (12p.) and B24 (phosphor)
UMFB16/17   B17 (2p.), B14 (10p.), B6 (12p.) and B31 (phosphor)

**£2·20 Pane. 1980 Christmas Booklet FX3**

UMFB18
*(Illustration reduced to ½ actual size)*

Horizontal strip of ten of 12p. with two 9·5 mm. phosphor bands and similar strip of ten 10p. with 4 mm. centre phosphor band. In each case the phosphor bands stop short, covering the printed part of the stamps.

The binding margin is always at left as the right-hand margin is guillotined off.

From 1980 Christmas £2·20 Booklet No. FX3

UMFB18 (containing Nos. U190c × 10, U206a × 10) (12.11.80)

Perf. Type E
6·00

These panes have green cutting lines and are folded twice, between vertical rows 3/4 and 7/8.

**Listed Booklet Cylinder Flaw**

UMFB18 cylinder pane
Repair across two stamps
(R. 2 stamps 3 and 4)

**Booklet Cylinder Numbers**

Perforation as Type RE. Single pane cylinders

| Pane No. | Cyl. Nos. | Phos No. | Perf. Type E No dot | Phosphor Cyl. Displacement |
|---|---|---|---|---|
| UMFB18 | 12p., B8; 10p., B18 | (B34) | 8·50 | |
| UMFB18 | 12p., B8; 10p., B18 | (—) | 12·00 | B34 |
| UMFB18 | — | (B34) | 14·00 | |

**Sheet Make-up**

A reduced sized illustration of an uncut sheet appears in Appendix I. The sheet contained one column of 12 rows upright printed by a single pane cylinder on the Chambon press. The left-hand margin had a single extension hole. Opposite rows 6/7 in the left-hand margin there is a marginal arrow with vertical cutting line above opposite rows 5/6. The cylinder numbers are sideways reading down in an open box facing right.

**50p. Pane. Automobiles and Follies Series FB14A/16B**

UMFB19 Type P        UMFB20 Type P

Single ½p., 1p., 14p. and vertical strip of 3 of 11½p.

½p., 1p. and 14p. all have two 8 mm. phosphor bands set 12 mm. apart.

Pane UMFB19. With 11½p. at left containing narrow phosphor band at right from 50p. Pictorial Booklets Nos. FB14/16A.
Pane UMFB20. With 11½p. at right containing narrow phosphor band at left from 50p. Pictorial Booklets Nos. FB14/16B.

|  | Perf. Type | |
|---|---|---|
|  | P | E |
| UMFB19 (containing Nos. U52, U60, U203 × 3, U226) (26.1.81) | 2·25 | 3·00 |
| a. Phosphor omitted .. .. .. .. .. .. | 35·00 | † |
| b. "Scar" on cheek (R. 3/1) .. .. .. .. .. | 3·00 | † |
| c. Scratch in hair and back of crown (R. 3/2) .. .. | 3·00 | † |
| UMFB19A    Miscut. Face value 31p. (2 × ½p., 2 × 1p., 2 × 14p.) | £3000* | † |
| UMFB20 (containing Nos. U52, U60, U202 × 3, U226) (26.1.81) | 2·50 | 3·00 |
| a. Phosphor omitted .. .. .. .. .. .. | 35·00 | † |
| b. Dark spot on eyebrow (R. 3/2) .. .. .. .. | 3·00 | † |
| UMFB20A    Miscut. Face value 69p. (6 × 11½p.) | £3500 | † |

*Only seven examples and all with trimmed perforations are known.

233

**Listed Booklet Cylinder Flaws**

| UMFB19*b* (11½p.) | UMFB19*c* (14p.) | UMFB20*b* (11½p.) |
|---|---|---|
| Blemish in hair extending as a "scar" across cheek | Scratch through hair and back of crown | Dark spot on eyebrow |

**Sheet Make-up**

The sheets were printed on the Chambon press.

A reduced sized illustration of an uncut sheet appears in Appendix I. Looking at the sheet from the left columns I and II have the Queen's head facing left and column II has the head facing right. The selvedge at top had a single extension hole and other binding margins of the columns II and III were perforated through.

**Cylinder Numbers**

These were trimmed off but those used were:—
B31 (½p.), B22 (1p.), B2 (11½p.), B7 (14p.) and B37 (phosphor)
B31 (½p.), B22 (1p.), B2 (11½p.), B8 (14p.) and B37 (phosphor)
B31 (½p.), B23 (1p.), B2 (11½p.), B8 (14p.) and B37 (phosphor)
B32 (½p.), B22 (1p.), B2 (11½p.), B8 (14p.) and B37 (phosphor)
B32 (½p.), B22 (1p.), B2 (11½p.), B10 (14p.) and B37 (phosphor)

**£1·30 Pane. Postal History Series FL1A/2B**

UMFB22

Pane of ten containing six 14p. with two 8mm. phosphor bands set 12mm. apart and a horizontal strip of four 11½p. each with one narrow phosphor band at left or right from £1·30 Pictorial Booklet Nos. FL1A/2B.

In the first row the phosphor bands on the 14p. stop short of the upper and lower margins between 2/3 and 4/5. This gives, in the second row, 11½p. band left, right, left and right. The 14p. stamps with short side bands are listed under No. U226.

Pane UMFB21.  Selvedge at left

                                                Perf. Type E
UMFB21 (containing Nos. U202 × 2, U203 × 2, U226 × 2, U226a × 2,
    U226b × 2) (6.5.81)                                   7·00
    *a.* Spot on chin (R. 1/5) ..    ..    ..    ..    ..    ..    9·00

Pane UMFB22.  Selvedge at right

UMFB22 (containing Nos. U202 × 2, U203 × 2, U226 × 2, U226a × 2,
    U226b × 2) (6.5.81)                                   7·00
    *a.* Diagonal scratch above dress (R. 1/1)    ..    ..    ..    9·00
    *b.* Blemish from crown to margin (R. 1/5)    ..    ..    ..    9·00
    *c.* Solid spot on dress at left (R. 1/5) ..    ..    ..    ..    8·00
    *d.* White scratch through necklace (R. 2/5) ..    ..    ..    9·00

**Listed Booklet Cylinder Flaws**
Multipositive Flaw

Nos. UMFB21/22a were multipositive flaws which first occurred on the 14p. value in panes of ten where they are illustrated as Nos. UFB19/20a.

       UMFB22*b* (14p.)                    UMFB22*c*                   UMFB22*d* (11½p.)
     Blemish from crown             Solid spot on dress         White scratch through
        to margin                      at left                       necklace

**Sheet Details**

A reduced sized illustration of an uncut sheet appears in Appendix I. The cylinder numbers were printed in the right-hand margin and were trimmed off. Those used were:—

    B6 (11½p.), B9 (14p.) and B39 (phosphor)

Cylinder B9 is from the same multipositive as Cylinder B3 which was employed for the 14p. in panes of ten.

**235**

**50p. Pane. Follies Series FB17A/18B**

UMFB23 Type E                    UMFB24 Type E

Pair of 4p. with vertical strips of three 2½p. and 11½p.
2½p. and 4p. have two 8 mm. phosphor bands set 12 mm. apart.

Pane UMFB23.    With 11½p. at left containing narrow phosphor band at right from 50p. Pictorial
                Booklets Nos. FB17/18A.
Pane UMFB24.    With 11½p. at right containing narrow phosphor band at left from 50p. Pictorial
                Booklets Nos. FB17/18B.

The 4p. above the 11½p. has a short phosphor band at left in pane UMFB23 and at right in pane
UMFB24. These are listed after No. U126 in Section UD.

|  | Perf. Type | |
|---|---|---|
|  | P | E |
| UMFB23 (containing Nos. U98 × 3, U126, U126b, U203 × 3) (26.8.81) | 15·00 | 6·00 |
| a. Broken serif at base of large 2 (R. 4/2)    ..    ..    .. | 20·00 | 7·50 |
| b. White flaws across shoulder (R. 4/1)    ..    ..    .. | 20·00 | 8·00 |
| UMFB24 (containing Nos. U98 × 3, U126, U126c, U202 × 3) (26.8.81) | 15·00 | 6·50 |
| a. Missing serif at foot of large 1 (R. 4/2)    ..    ..    .. | 20·00 | 8·00 |

**Listed Booklet Cylinder Flaws**

| UMFB23a | UMFB23b | UMFB24a |
|---|---|---|
| Diagonal break to serif of large 2 | White flaw across shoulder and into background | Broken foot to large 1 |

**Sheet Make-up**

A reduced sized illustration of an uncut sheet appears in Appendix I. The sheet contained two vertical columns with 16 horizontal rows arranged sideways.

**Cylinder Numbers**

These appeared in the left margin but were trimmed off; those used were:—
B30 (2½p.), B2 (4p.), B11 (11½p.), B40 (phosphor)

---

**£2·55 Pane. 1981 Christmas Booklet FX4**

UMFB25

Horizontal strip of ten of 14p. with two 9·5 mm. phosphor bands and a similar strip of ten 11½p. with 4 mm. centre phosphor band. In each case the phosphor bands stop short, covering the printed part of the stamps.

The binding margin is always at left as the right-hand margin is guillotined off.

Pane UMFB25.    From 1981 Christmas £2·55 Booklet No. FX4

|  | Perf. Type E |
|---|---|
| UMFB25 (containing Nos. U201b × 10, U227 × 10) (11.11.81) | 8·00 |
| a. Spot on chin (R. 1/5) .. .. .. .. .. .. | 10·00 |
| b. Diagonal scratch above dress (R. 1/6) .. .. .. | 10·00 |
| | |
| UMFB25A Miscut | £800 |

These panes have grey-blue cutting lines and are folded twice, between vertical rows 3/4 and 7/8.

**Listed Booklet Cylinder Flaws**

Nos. UMFB25a and 25b are multipositive flaws and are illustrated as UFB19a and 20a.

**Cylinder Numbers**

These appeared in the right margin but were trimmed off; those used were:—
B12 (11½p.), B13 (14p.), B41 (phosphor)
The dot after B13 was probably not intentional.

**Sheet Make-up**

As for 1980 Christmas Booklet pane UMFB18.

**50p. Pane. Follies and Rare Farm Animals Series FB19A/23B**

UMFB26                                    UMFB27

Single ½p. with vertical strips of four of 3p. and three of 12½p.
½p. and 3p. have two 8 mm. phosphor bands set 12 mm. apart.

Pane UMFB26.    With 12½p. at left containing narrow phosphor band at right from 50p. Pictorial
                Booklets Nos. FB19/23A. The ½p. has a short left band at bottom.
Pane UMFB27.    With 12½p. at right containing narrow phosphor band at left from 50p. Pictorial
                Booklets Nos. FB19/23B. The ½p. has a short right band at bottom.

|  | Perf. Type E |
|---|---|
| UMFB26 (containing Nos. U52*b*, U112 × 4, U214 × 3) (1.2.82) | 2·75 |
| UMFB26A Miscut. Face value 24p. (8 × 3p.) | £500 |
| UMFB27 (containing Nos. U52*c*, U112 × 4, U213 × 3) (1.2.82) | 2·75 |
|    *a*. Retouched background above value (3p.) ..    ..    ..    .. | 5·00 |
| UMFB27A Miscut. Face value 76p. (2 × ½p., 6 × 12½p.) | £500 |

238

**Listed Booklet Cylinder Flaw**

Retouched background
above value

UMFB27*a*

**Cylinder Numbers**

These appeared in the left margin but were trimmed off; those used were:—
B33 (½p.), B39 (3p.) and B9 (12½p.)
B34 (½p.), B39 (3p.) and B9 (12½p.)
B34 (½p.), B40 (3p.) and B9 (12½p.)
B34 (½p.), B39 (3p.) and B11 (12½p.)
B34 (½p.), B40 (3p.) and B17 (12½p.)
B35 (½p.), B40 (3p.) and B17 (12½p.)

The phosphor cylinder was B42.

**Sheet Make-up**

As for panes UMFB23/24. The binding margins at the top have a single extension hole.

---

**£1·43 Pane. Postal History Series and *Golden Hinde* Booklet FN1A/6B**

UMFB28

Pane of ten containing six 15½p. with two 8 mm. phosphor bands set 12 mm. apart and a horizontal strip of four 12½p. each with one narrow phosphor band at left or right from £1·43 Pictorial Booklet Nos. FN1A/6B.

In the first row the phosphor bands on the 15½p. stop short of the upper and lower margins between 2/3 and 4/5. This gives, in the second row, 12½p. band left, right, left and right. The 15½p. stamps with short side bands are listed under No. U237.

Pane UMFB28.   Selvedge at left

Perf. Type E

UMFB28 (containing Nos. U213 × 2, U214 × 2, U237 × 2, U237*a* × 2,
    U237*b* × 2) (1.2.82)                                                5·50
    *a*. Error. Phosphor bands transposed ..    ..    ..    ..    ..    £160

UMFB28A Miscut

**Pane UMFB29.** Selvedge at right

UMFB29 (containing Nos. U213 × 2, U214 × 2, U237 × 2, U237*a* × 2,
U237*b* × 2) (1.2.82)                                                                              5·50

No. UMFB28*a* contains the 12½p. with two bands and 15½p. with one band and as single examples
are listed below Nos. U213 and U237.

**Booklet Cylinder Numbers**
Perforation as Type RE. Single pane cylinders

|             |                    |            | Perf. Type E |                  |
| Pane No.    | Cyl. Nos.          | Phos. No.  | No dot       |                  |
|-------------|--------------------|------------|--------------|------------------|
| UMFB28      | 12½p., B4; 15½p., B2 | (B50)      | 7·50         |                  |
| UMFB28*a*   | 12½p., B4; 15½p., B2 | (B50)      | £225         | Bands transposed |
| UMFB29      | 12½p., B4; 15½p., B2 | (B50)      | 7·50         |                  |

The cylinder numbers were trimmed off on the £1·43 panes in the James Chalmers booklet but
those used were: 12½p., B4; 15½p., B2; (B43) phosphor.

**Sheet Details**
As for £1·25 panes. Panes exist without the hand engraved arrows between rows 6/7.

**£2·80 Pane. 1982 Christmas Booklet FX5**

UMFB30

Horizontal strip of ten of 15½p. with two 9·5 mm. phosphor bands and a similar strip of ten 12½p.
with 4 mm. centre phosphor band.
In each case the phosphor bands stop short, covering the printed part of the stamps.
Each stamp in the pane No. UMFB30 was underprinted with a blue star. This is illustrated in
Section UD above 12½p. No. U215.
The binding margin is always at left as the right-hand margin is guillotined off.

**Pane UMFB30.** From 1982 Christmas £2·80 Booklet No. FX5 (sold at a discount rate of £2.50)

|                                                            | Perf. Type E |
| UMFB30 (containing Nos. U215 × 10, U239 × 10) (10.11.82)   | 12·00        |

These have pale violet cutting lines and are folded twice, between vertical rows 3/4 and 7/8.
Panes without phosphor bands have not been seen but both values exist missing phosphor.

**Booklet Cylinder Numbers**
Perforation as Type RE. Single pane cylinders

|          |                        |           | Perf. Type E |
| Pane No. | Cyl. Nos.              | Phos. No. | No dot |
|----------|------------------------|-----------|--------|
| UMFB30   | 12½p., B20; 15½p., B18 | (B51)     | 15·00  |
|          | 12½p., B22; 15½p., B21 | (B51)     | £180   |
|          | 12½p., B20; 15½p., B18 | (B52)     | 15·00  |
|          | 12½p., B22; 15½p., B21 | (B52)     | 11·00  |
|          | 12½p., B23; 15½p., B21 | (B52)     | £100   |
|          | 12½p., B20; 15½p., B18 | (B53)     | 10·00  |
|          | 12½p., B22; 15½p., B21 | (B54)     | £750   |
|          | 12½p., B22; 15½p., B21 | —         | £900   |
|          | —                      | (B54)     | £700   |
|          | 12½p., B23; 15½p., B21 | (B54)     | £140   |

**Sheet Make-up**
As for pane UMFB18 except for a larger arrow printed in the margin opposite rows 6/7.

**50p. Pane. Rare Farm Animals Series FB24/26**

UMFB31

Pair of 1p. with vertical strips of three of 3½p. and 12½p.

Pane UMFB31.  With 1p., 3½p. and 12½p. each with 4 mm. centre band from 50p. Pictorial Booklet Nos. FB24/26.

Perf. Type E

UMFB31 (containing Nos. U61 × 2, U121 × 3, U212 × 3) (5.4.83)     6·50
  *a.* Phosphor omitted    ..    ..    ..    ..    ..    16·00

UMFB31A    Miscut. 3½p. at right, 12½p. at left      £170

**Sheet Make-up**

    The sheet make-up was changed from the previous 50p. booklet issues. A reduced sized illustration of an uncut sheet appears in Appendix I. This shows that the rows of 3½p. and 12½p. alternate so that in the event of miscutting the face value of the pane would remain the same.

**Cylinder Numbers**

    These appeared in the left margin but were trimmed off; those used were:—

B24 (1p.), B8 (3½p.), 12½p. (B31)      B25 (1p.), B8 (3½p.), 12½p. (B31)
B24 (1p.), B9 (3½p.), 12½p. (B31)      B25 (1p.), B9 (3½p.), 12½p. (B37)
B24 (1p.), B9 (3½p.), 12½p. (B37)      B25 (1p.), B9 (3½p.), 12½p. (B48)
B24 (1p.), B8 (3½p.), 12½p. (B37)      B25 (1p.), B8 (3½p.), 12½p. (B48)

    The phosphor number was B57 in each printing.

**£1·46 Pane. Postal History Series FO1A/3B**

UMFB32
(UMFB33 similar but 12½p. values at right)

Pane of ten containing six 16p. with to 9·5 mm. phosphor bands set 10·5 mm. apart and a horizontal strip of four 12½p. each with one narrow phosphor band at left or right from £1·46 Pictorial Booklet Nos. FO1A/FO3B

Pane UMFB32.   In the first row the phosphor bands on the 16p. stop short of the upper and lower margins between 1/2 and 3/4. This gives, in the second row, 12½p. band left, right, left and right. The 16p. stamps with short side bands are listed under No. U242.

Pane UMFB33.   In the first row the phosphor bands on the 16p. stop short of the upper and lower margins between 2/3 and 4/5. The 12½p. stamps each have a side phosphor band arranged in the same order as pane No. UMFB32.

Pane UMFB32.   Selvedge at left

Perf. Type E

UMFB32 (containing Nos. U213 × 2, U214 × 2, U242 × 2, U242a × 2,
  U242b × 2) (5.4.83)                                                                           10·00
  *a.* Spot in 6 (R. 1/5)   ..   ..   ..   ..   ..   ..   .. 13·00

Pane UMFB33.   Selvedge at right

UMFB33 (containing Nos. U213 × 2, U214 × 2, U242 × 2, U242a × 2,
  U242b × 2) (5.4.83)                                                                           10·00

**Listed Booklet Cylinder Flaw**

Spot in 6
(Cyl. B5)

UMFB32*a*

**Booklet Cylinder Numbers**

Perforation as Type RE. Single pane cylinders

| Pane No. | Cyl. Nos. | Phos. No. | | | | | Perf. Type E No dot |
|---|---|---|---|---|---|---|---|
| UMFB32 | 12½p., B26; 16p., B1 | (B55) | .. | .. | .. | .. | 12·00 |
| UMFB33 | 12½p., B26; 16p., B1 | (B55) | .. | .. | .. | .. | 12·00 |
| UMFB32 | 12½p., B26; 16p., B5 | (B55) | .. | .. | .. | .. | 12·00 |
| UMFB33 | 12½p., B26; 16p., B5 | (B55) | .. | .. | .. | .. | 12·00 |
| UMFB32 | 12½p., B39; 16p., B5 | (B55) | .. | .. | .. | .. | 85·00 |

**Sheet Make-up**

A reduced sized illustration of an uncut sheet appears in Appendix I and shows the stamp arrangement. The cylinder was continuous and the booklet sheet had no horizontal margins.

Sheet size: 120 (10 × 12). Single pane reel-fed on the Chambon press

Sheet markings:
Cylinder numbers: Opposite row 7, at both sides, reading downwards at left and upwards at right. The numbers are printed in open boxes and placed so that they appear in the finished booklets
Marginal arrows: Opposite the "W" shaped arrows at each corner of the sheet
Vertical cutting line: Opposite rows 11/12 at both sides
Horizontal cutting line: In alternate rows 2/3, etc.

---

**50p. Pane. Orchid Series FB27/30**

UMFB34

Three 1p., vertical pair of 4p. and vertical strip of three 13p.

Pane UMFB34.   With 1p., 4p. and 13p. each with 4 mm. centre band from 50p. Pictorial Booklet No. FB27/30

|  |  |  |  |  |  |  | Perf. Type E |
|---|---|---|---|---|---|---|---|
| UMFB34 (containing Nos. U61 × 3, U129 × 2, U218 × 3) (3.9.84) |  |  |  |  |  |  | 4·00 |
| *a.* Phosphor omitted | .. | .. | .. | .. | .. | .. | £180 |
| *b.* Large white spot (R. 2/1) | .. | .. | .. | .. | .. | .. | 9·00 |
| *ba.* Retouched state (R. 2/1) | .. | .. | .. | .. | .. | .. | 5·50 |
| *c.* Vertical scratch (R. 2/2) | .. | .. | .. | .. | .. | .. | 6·00 |

**243**

**Listed Booklet Cylinder Flaw**

| UMFB34*b* | UMFB34*c* |
|---|---|
| Large white spot after P | Vertical scratch on necklace |
| This was quickly retouched with | (Cyl. B8) |
| screening dots leaving the spot | |
| just visible against the solid | |
| background (Cyl. B26) | |

**Booklet Cylinder Numbers**

|  |  |  |  |  |  |  | Perf. Type E | |
|---|---|---|---|---|---|---|---|---|
|  |  |  |  |  |  |  | Top | Bottom |
| Pane No. | Cyl. Nos. (all No dot) | Phos. No. |  |  |  |  | margin | margin · |
| UMFB34 | 1p., B26; 4p., B7; 13p., B8 | (B57) | .. | .. | .. | .. | 6·00 | 5·00 |
|  | 1p., B26; 4p., B7; 13p., B8 | (—) | .. | .. | .. | .. | 15·00 | 18·00 |
|  | — | (B57) | .. | .. | .. | .. | 7·00 | 10·00 |
|  | 1p., B26; 4p., B7; 13p., B9 | (B57) | .. | .. | .. | .. | 9·00 | 12·00 |
|  | 1p., B26; 4p., B7 | (B57)† | .. | .. | .. | .. | £700 | £110 |
|  | 13p., B8 | (—) | .. | .. | .. | .. | £700 | £110 |
|  | 1p., B27; 4p., B6; 13p., B8 | (B57) | .. | .. | .. | .. | 6·00 | 6·00 |
|  | 1p., B27; 4p., B7; 13p., B8 | (B57) | .. | .. | .. | .. | 6·00 | 6·00 |
|  | 1p., B27; 4p., B8; 13p., B8 | (—) | .. | .. | .. | .. | 20·00 | 20·00 |

During printing the phosphor cylinder was displaced and has been found on ordinary panes as well as printed on the 1p. value in the pane.

† The pane with B8 displaced and showing B26, B7 and phos(B57) is rare and collectors should be careful when purchasing as similar panes exist with B9 omitted due to a dry print. The price in the catalogue is for the upper margin pane which shows the 13p. R.4/2 with a white retouch to the right of the Queen's hairbun. This flaw on the B8 (13p.) cylinder does not occur with B9.

The 4p. cylinder number was originally shown as B6. In most examples a "6" shows as a blemish beneath the "7" (state 1), "6" over heavy "7" (state 2) and later the "6" was re-engraved.

**Sheet Make-up**

As for No. UMFB31 but with the stamps upright the cylinder number appears in the top margin of the fourth booklet from the left and the cylinder number in the bottom margin is on the booklet pane below. A gutter margin separates the two columns and marginal arrows appear at each corner of the uncut sheet.

**£1·54 Pane. Postal History Series FQ1A/4B**

UMFB35
(UMFB36 similar but 13p. values at right)

Pane of ten containing six 17p. with two 9·5 mm. phosphor bands set 10·5 mm. apart and a horizontal strip of four 13p. each with one narrow phosphor band at left or right from £1·54 Pictorial Booklet No. FQ1A/4B.

Pane UMFB35.    In the first row the phosphor bands on the 17p. stop short of the upper and lower margins between 1/2 and 3/4. This gives, in the second row, 13p. band left, right, left and right. The 17p. stamps with short side bands are listed under No. U248.

Pane UMFB36.    In the first row the phosphor bands on the 17p. stop short of the upper and lower margins between 2/3 and 4/5. The 13p. stamps each have a side phosphor band arranged in the same order as pane No. UMFB35.

Pane UMFB35.    Selvedge at left

Perf. Type E

UMFB35 (containing Nos. U219 × 2, U220 × 2, U248 × 2, U248*a* × 2,
U248*b* × 2) (3.9.84)        7·00
*a.* Error. Phosphor bands transposed ..    ..    ..    ..    60·00
*b.* Retouch in front of dress (R. 1/4) ..    ..    ..    ..    10·00

Pane UMFB36.    Selvedge at right

UMFB36 (containing Nos. U219 × 2, U220 × 2, U248 × 2, U248*a* × 2,
U248*b* × 2) (3.9.84)        7·00
*a.* Error. Phosphor bands transposed ..    ..    ..    ..    80·00
*b.* Diagonal scratch (R. 2/5) ..    ..    ..    ..    11·00
*c.* Scratches opposite P (R. 1/4)    ..    ..    ..    ..    10·00
Panes with phosphor bands transposed contain the 13p. with two bands and 17p. with one band.

**Listed Booklet Cylinder Flaws**

| UMFB35*b*, UMFB37*b* | UMFB36*b* | UMFB36*c*, UMFB38*b* |
|---|---|---|
| Retouch in front of dress | Diagonal scratch from | Scratches opposite P |
| (Several states exist) (Cyl. B8) | hair to frame (Cyl. B4) | and necklace (Cyl. B8) |

**Booklet Cylinder Numbers**

Perforation as Type RE. Single pane cylinders

| | | | Perf. Type E |
|---|---|---|---|
| Pane No. | Cyl. Nos. | Phos. No | No dot |
| UMFB35 | 13p., B4; 17p., B5 | (B55) | 9·00 |
| UMFB36 | 13p., B4; 17p., B5 | (B55) | 9·00 |
| UMFB35 | 13p., B4; 17p., B5 | (—) | 80·00 |
| UMFB36 | 13p., B4; 17p., B5 | (—) | 80·00 |
| UMFB35 | — | (B55) | 70·00 |
| UMFB36 | — | (B55) | 70·00 |
| UMFB35*a* | 13p., B4; 17p., B5 | (—) | 65·00 |
| UMFB35*a* | — | (B55) | 60·00 |
| UMFB36*a* | 13p., B4; 17p., B5 | (—) | 90·00 |
| UMFB36*a* | — | (B55) | 85·00 |
| UMFB35 | 13p., B4; 17p., B5 | (B56) | 9·00 |
| UMFB36 | 13p., B4; 17p., B5 | (B56) | 9·00 |
| UMFB35 | 13p., B4; 17p., B8 | (B56) | 9·00 |
| UMFB36 | 13p., B4; 17p., B8 | (B56) | 9·00 |

**Sheet Make-up**

As £1·46 panes UMFB32/33

**£1·50 Pane. "Write Now", National Gallery and Handwriting Booklets FP1A/3B**

UMFB37
(UMFB38 similar but 12p. values at right)

Pane of ten containing six 17p. with two 9·5 mm. phosphor bands set 10·5 mm. apart and a horizontal strip of four 12p. each with one narrow phosphor band at left or right from £1·50 Pictorial Booklet Nos. FP1A/3B.

Pane UMFB37.   In the first row the phosphor bands on the 17p. stop short of the upper and lower margins between 1/2 and 3/4. This gives, in the second row, 12p. band at left, right, left and right. The 17p. stamps with short side bands are listed under No. U248.

Pane UMFB38.   In the first row the phosphor bands on the 17p. stop short of the upper and lower margins between 2/3 and 4/5. The 12p. stamps each have a side phosphor band arranged in the same order as pane No. UMFB37.

Pane UMFB37.   Selvedge at left.

|  | Perf. Type E |
|---|---|
| UMFB37 (containing Nos. U209 × 2, U210 × 2, U248 × 2, U248*a* × 2, U248*b* × 2) (14.1.86) | 5·50 |
| *b*. Retouch in front of dress (R. 1/4)   ..    ..    ..    ..    .. | 7·50 |

Pane UMFB38. Selvedge at right

| | |
|---|---|
| UMFB38 (containing Nos. U209 × 2, U210 × 2, U248 × 2, U248*a* × 2, U248*b* × 2) (14.1.86) | 5·50 |
| *b*. Scratches opposite P (R. 1/4)    ..    ..    ..    ..    .. | 7·50 |
| *c*. Retouch to right of nose (R. 2/5)   ..    ..    ..    ..    .. | 8·00 |

**Listed Booklet Cylinder Flaws**

UMFB38*c* (12p.)
Retouch to right of nose
(Cyl. B17)

For illustration of No. UMFB37*b*, see No. UMFB35*b* and for No. UMFB38*b*, see No. UMFB36*c*.

**Booklet Cylinder Numbers**

Perforation as Type RE. Single pane cylinders

| Pane No. | Cyl. Nos. | Phos. No. | | | | Perf. Type E<br>No dot |
|---|---|---|---|---|---|---|
| UMFB37 | 12p., B14; 17p., B8 | (B55) | .. | .. | .. | 7·50 |
| UMFB38 | 12p., B14. 17p., B8 | (B55) | .. | .. | .. | 7·50 |
| UMFB37 | 12p., B17. 17p., B8 | (B55) | .. | .. | .. | 7·50 |
| UMFB38 | 12p., B17. 17p., B8 | (B55) | .. | .. | .. | 7·50 |

**Sheet Make-up**

As for £1·46 panes UMFB32/33.

---

**50p. Pane. Roman Britain Series FB34**

UMFB39

Pair of 1p. and block of four of 12p.

Pane UMFB39. With 1p. and 12p. each with 4·5 mm. centre band from 50p. Booklet, No. FB34.

| | Perf. Type E<br>7·00 |
|---|---|
| UMFB39 (containing Nos. U65 × 2, U211 × 4) (29.7.86) | |

**Booklet Cylinder Numbers**

Perforation as Type RE. Single pane cylinder

| Pane No. | Cyl. Nos. | Phos. No. | | | | Perf. Type E<br>No dot |
|---|---|---|---|---|---|---|
| UMFB39 | 1p., B29; 12p., B21 | (B68) | .. | .. | .. | 10·00 |

**Sheet Make-up**

As Pane UMFB31 but with cylinder numbers added in both columns above the second 1p. value of the fourth pane from left. Each column contains eight panes including one showing the cylinder number. The cutting lines and arrows at each corner of the sheet were printed in crimson.

**50p. Pane. Pond Life and Botanical Gardens Series FB35/36 and FB43/44**

UMFB40                                      UMFB41 (cyl. pane)

Single 1p. with pair of 5p. and vertical strip of 3 of 13p.

Pane UMFB40.    With 1p., 5p. and 13p. each with 4·5 mm. centre band from 50p. Pictorial
Booklet Nos. FB35/36 and FB43/44.

|  |  | Perf. Type E |
|---|---|---|
| UMFB40 (containing Nos. U65, U139 × 2, U221 × 3) (20.10.86) | | 3·25 |
| *b.* New phosphor ink (27.1.87) ..   ..   ..   ..   .. | | 3·25 |
| *c.* Diagonal lines across dress (*cyl. pane* R. 2/1)   ..   ..   .. | | 6·00 |
| *d.* Repair on eye and forehead (R. 2/2)   ..   ..   ..   .. | | 7·50 |

**50p. Pane with imperforate vertical sides. Botanical Gardens, London Zoo and Marine Life Series
FB45/46, FB48 and FB50**

Pane UMFB41.    With 1p., 5p., and 13p. each with 4·5 mm. centre band in new phosphor ink and the
pane with vertical sides imperforate. From 50p. Pictorial Booklet Nos. FB45/46,
FB48 and FB50.

|  |  | Perf. Type IEI |
|---|---|---|
| UMFB41 (containing Nos. U65*b*, U139*b* × 2, U221*b* × 3) (29.9.87) | | 2·50 |
| *a.* 4 mm. centre phosphor bands (30.10.87) ..   ..   ..   .. | | 3·00 |
| *b.* Phosphor omitted   ..   ..   ..   ..   ..   ..   .. | | £200 |
| *c.* Diagonal lines across dress (*cyl. pane* R. 2/1)   ..   ..   .. | | 6·00 |

Pane UMFB41*a* derives from the booklet FB45*a* showing "Mount Stewart" spelt correctly. The
5p. value from this pane is listed as No. U139*c* in Section ŪD.

**Listed Booklet Cylinder Flaws**

UMFB40/1c
Diagonal lines on dress
(Cyl. B1 on the cyl. no
pane from Col. 2)

UMFB40d (13p.)
Repair on Queen's eye and
forehead
(Cyl. B27)

**Booklet Cylinder Numbers**
Perforation as Type RE. Single pane cylinders

| Pane No. | Cyl. Nos. (No dot) | Phos. No. | | | | | Perf. Types | |
|---|---|---|---|---|---|---|---|---|
| | | | | | | | E | IEI |
| UMFB40 | 5p., B1; 13p., B24; 1p., B32 | (B68) | .. | .. | .. | .. | 5·00 | † |
| UMFB40b | 5p., B1; 13p., B24; 1p., B32 | (B68) | .. | .. | .. | .. | £275 | † |
| UMFB40b | 5p., B1; 13p., B27; 1p., B32 | (B68) | .. | .. | .. | .. | 4·50 | † |
| UMFB40b | 5p., B1; 13p., B27; 1p., B32 | (B68 over B32) | | | | | 32·00 | † |
| UMFB41 | 5p., B1; 13p., B43; 1p., B32 | (B68) | (4·5 mm. bands) | | .. | | † | 4·00 |
| UMFB41a | 5p., B1; 13p., B24; 1p., B32 | (B68)* | (4 mm. bands) | | .. | | † | 6·00 |

*Although the phosphor cylinder number is the same the band width measures 4 mm. instead of 4·5 mm.

**Sheet Make-up**
As Pane UMFB39 but cylinder numbers above 1p. and phosphor number above first 13p. when synchronised. Each column contained eight panes including one with a cylinder number.

---

**50p. Pane. Roman Britain, MCC and London Zoo Series FB37/42, FB47 and FB49**

UMFB42

Single 1p. and 13p. with pair of 18p.

Pane UMFB42.    With 1p. left and 13p. right phosphor bands and two 18p. with two 9·5 mm. bands. Between the bottom pair of stamps (18p.) the phosphor band is the height of the stamp and stops at, or when misplaced, just below the horizontal perforations. From 50p. Pictorial Booklet, Nos. FB37/42, FB47 and FB49.

| | Perf. Type E |
|---|---|
| UMFB42 (containing Nos. U66, U220, U258 × 2) (20.10.86) | 2·50 |
| a. Error. Phosphor bands transposed ..   ..   ..   ..   .. | 20·00 |
| b. Phosphor omitted   ..   ..   ..   ..   ..   .. | 90·00 |
| c. New phosphor ink (27.1.87) ..   ..   ..   ..   .. | 2·50 |
| ca. Error. Phosphor bands transposed ..   ..   ..   .. | 75·00 |
| e. Thick bottom lip (R. 2/2)   ..   ..   ..   ..   .. | 3·00 |

Panes with transposed bands contain 1p. band at right, 13p. band at left and 18p. *pair* with short bands at extreme left and right instead of between the pair. The 1p. with phosphor band at right in original phosphor ink is listed below No. U67 and UMFB42*a* was the only source.

An example of No. UMFB42 from FB37 was found which contained broad bands in the original phosphor ink on the 1p. and 18p. This was subsequently separated and the singles are listed. The 13p. was a missing phosphor example. See UD section Nos. U66*a* and U258*d*.

**Listed Booklet Cylinder Flaw**

UMFB42*e* (18p.)
Retouch to Queen's lower lip
(Cyl. B4)
(Later retouched)

**Booklet Cylinder Numbers**

Perforation as Type RE. Single pane cylinders

| | | | Perf. Type E | | | |
|---|---|---|---|---|---|---|
| Pane No. | Cyl. Nos. | Phos. No. | | | | |
| UMFB42 | 13p., B21; 18p., B4; 1p., B30 | (B69) | .. | .. | .. | 5·00 |
| UMFB42 | 13p., B21; 18p., B4; 1p., B31 | (B69) | .. | .. | .. | 10·00 |
| UMFB42*a* | 13p., B21; 18p., B4; 1p., B30 | (B69) | .. | .. | .. | 40·00 |
| UMFB42*a* | 13p., B21; 18p., B4; 1p., B30 | (—) | .. | .. | .. | £180 |
| UMFB42*a* | — | (B69) | .. | .. | .. | £180 |
| UMFB42*c* | 13p., B21; 18p., B4; 1p., B30 | (B69) | .. | .. | .. | 5·00 |
| UMFB42*c* | 13p., B21; 18p., B6; 1p., B30 | (B69) | .. | .. | .. | 5·00 |
| UMFB42*c* | 13p., B21; 18p., B4; 1p., B31 | (B69) | .. | .. | .. | 40·00 |
| UMFB42*ca* | 13p., B21; 18p., B4; 1p., B31 | (B69) | .. | .. | .. | £100 |

**Sheet Make-up**

As Pane UFB36. The printer's sheet contained three columns of eight panes each including one showing a cylinder number. When synchronised the ink number appears above the 1p. and the phosphor number is above the 13p.

**£1 Pane. Musical Instruments and Sherlock Holmes Series FH6/9**

UMFB43                          UMFB44 (cyl. pane)

Single 13p. and five 18p.

Pane UMFB43.   The 13p. with left phosphor band *se-tenant* with 18p. two bands but at left the band is 3·5 mm. wide. Also four 18p. each with two 9·5 mm. bands. From £1 Pictorial Booklets, Nos. FH6/9.

|  | Perf. Type E |
|---|---|
| UMFB43 (containing Nos. U219, U258 × 4, U258*b*) (20.10.86) | 4·75 |
| *b.* New phosphor ink (27.1.87) ..    ..    ..    ..    ..    .. | 4·75 |

**£1 Pane with imperforate vertical sides. Sherlock Holmes, London Zoo and Charles Dickens Series FH10/13**

Pane UMFB44.   With 13p. left phosphor band *se-tenant* with 18p. two bands in new phosphor ink. As UMFB43 but vertical sides imperforate. From £1 Pictorial Booklet, Nos. FH10/13

|  | Perf. Type IEI |
|---|---|
| UMFB44 (containing Nos. U219*d*, U258*a* × 4, U258*ba*) (29.9.87) | 4·75 |

**Booklet Cylinder Numbers**

Perforation as Type RE. Single pane cylinders

| Pane No. | Cyl. Nos. (Not dot) | Phos. No. |  |  |  | Perf. Types E | IEI |
|---|---|---|---|---|---|---|---|
| UMFB43 | 18p., B5; 13p., B26 | (B70) | .. | .. | .. | 6·00 | † |
| UMFB43*b* | 18p., B5; 13p., B26 | (B70) | .. | .. | .. | 6·00 | † |
| UMFB44 | 18p., B5; 13p., B41 | (B70) | .. | .. | .. | † | 6·00 |

**Sheet Make-up**

As Pane UMFB40 with two columns of eight panes in each including one pane showing a cylinder number. This was printed above 13p. and the phosphor number was above the 18p. in row 1.

**251**

**50p. Pane. Gilbert and Sullivan Operas and Marine Life Series FB51/54**

UMFB45

Single 14p. (deep blue), pair of 19p. (bright orange-red) with postcode label

Pane UMFB45.   With 14p. right phosphor band and pair of 19p. with two phosphor bands 3 mm. wide except on stamp 3 where the band is 9·5 mm. between the 14p. and 19p. stamps. The label is inscribed "Please use the postcode" in deep blue and is without phosphor bands. From 50p. Pictorial Booklets, FB51/54

| | Perf. Type | |
| --- | :---: | :---: |
| | P | E |
| UMFB45 (containing Nos. U229, U260, U260c) (5.9.88) | 2·75 | 2·75 |
|   *a* Phosphor omitted   ..   ..   ..   ..   ..   ..   .. 10·00 | 10·00 | — |
| | | |
| UMFB45A Miscut. Label at right | — | † |

**Booklet Cylinder Numbers**

| | | | Perf. Type | |
| --- | --- | --- | :---: | :---: |
| Pane No. | Cyl. Nos. (No dot) | Phos. No. | P | E |
| UMFB45 | 19p., B1; 14p., B16 | (B76)   ..   ..   .. | 4·50 | 5·00 |
| UMFB45 | 19p., B1; 14p., B17 | (B76)   ..   ..   .. | 7·00 | 10·00 |
| UMFB45 | 19p., B2; 14p., B16 | (B76)   ..   ..   .. | † | 5·00 |
| UMFB45A | 19p., B1; 14p., B16 | (—)   ..   ..   .. | — | † |
| UMFB45A | — | (B76)   ..   ..   .. | — | † |

**Sheet Make-up**
    As Pane UMFB42. The printer's sheet contained three columns of eight panes each including one showing a cylinder number. For the first time the Chambon press was used with the APS rotary perforator. This replaced the Grover type perforator described in Appendix I.

**£1 Pane with imperforate vertical sides. Charles Dickens and Marine Life Series FH14/15 and FH17**

UMFB46

Vertical pair 14p. (deep blue) and four 19p. (bright orange-red)

Pane UMFB46.    Pair of 14p. with narrow phosphor band at right *se-tenant* with 19p. two bands. At the right the band is 3 mm. wide on the vertical strip of three stamps. The 19p. at left, below the 14p., has a left band the height of the stamp and a continuous band at right. From £1 Pictorial Booklets, Nos. FH14/15 and FH17

|  | Perf. Type IEI |
|---|---|
| UMFB46 (containing Nos. U229 × 2, U260 × 3, U260*b*) (5.9.88) | 4·00 |

**Booklet Cylinder Numbers**

| Pane No. | Cyl. Nos. | Phos. No. |  |  |  | Perf. Type IEI |
|---|---|---|---|---|---|---|
| UMFB46 | 19p., B6; 14p., B21 | (B78) | .. | .. | .. | 6·50 |
| UMFB46 | 19p., B6; 14p., B21 | (—) | .. | .. | .. |  |
| UMFB46 | — | (B78) | .. | .. | .. |  |

**Sheet Make-up**
   As Pane UMFB43/4 with two columns of eight panes in each including one pane showing a cylinder number.

**50p. Pane. Aircraft Series FB55**

UMFB47

Vertical pair 15p. (bright blue) and 20p. (brownish black)

Pane UMFB47.    Vertical pair of 15p. with left phosphor band 3 mm. wide on top 15p. On the bottom row the band is 9·5 mm. wide between 20p. and 15p. The postcode label has no bands as the left narrow band on the 20p. is the height of the stamp. From 50p. Pictorial Booklet, No. FB55

Perf. Type E

UMFB47 (containing Nos. U233, U233*a*, U269) (2.10.89)                    2·25
   *a*. Phosphor omitted    ..    ..    ..    ..    ..    ..    ..

**Booklet Cylinder Numbers**

| | | | Perf. Type E |
| Pane No. | Cyl. Nos. | Phos. No. | No dot |
|---|---|---|---|
| UMFB47 | 15p., B1; 20p., B3 | (B85)    ..    ..    .. | 4·25 |

**Sheet Make-up**
   As Pane UMFB42 but printed on the Chambon press with the APS rotary perforator.

**£1 Pane with imperforate vertical sides. Mills Series FH21**

UMFB48

Vertical pair 17p. (deep blue) and three 22p. (bright orange-red)

Pane UMFB48.    Pair of 17p. with right phosphor band and vertical strip of three 22p. two bands.
The 22p. below the postcode label has two 3 mm. bands which are clear of the
vertical sides and the other two have a side band at left over the perforations and a
3 mm. wide band at right clear of the vertical edge. There are no bands on the
three postcode labels. From £1 Pictorial Booklet, No. FH21

|  | Perf. Type IEI |
|---|---|
| UMFB48 (containing Nos. U253 × 2, U282 × 2, U282a) (4.9.90) | 1·50 |

**Booklet Cylinder Numbers**

| Pane No. | Cyl. Nos. | Phos. No. |  |  |  | Perf. Type IEI No dot |
|---|---|---|---|---|---|---|
| UMFB48 | 17p., B45; 22p., B1 | (B88) | .. | .. | .. | 3·50 |

**Sheet Make-up**
Printed on the Chambon press and perforated by the APS rotary perforator. The sheet contained
two vertical columns of eight panes arranged sideways. Each column of eight included one cylinder
number pane.

## II.  Panes of One Value

**Horizontal Panes of Ten.** It was intended that these sheets, with various marginal marks and inscriptions, should have the dual purpose of serving both for booklet panes and as sheets for issuing over the Post Office counters. This last has not yet happened, but some of the booklet stamps have been printed from cylinders which were also used for vertical delivery coils. Thus the same cylinder flaws can be found on coil stamps and on booklet panes.

Since panes are affixed by the left and right selvedge, the marginal markings assist greatly in establishing the positions of the panes on the cylinder and thus for plating flaws.

The stamps were printed in double panes from no dot and dot cylinders. In 1981 the £1·15 and £1·40 booklets were issued and these panes are printed from single pane cylinders. In each instance we illustrate only one of the panes, i.e. with selvedge at left or right. Reduced sized illustrations of uncut sheets will be found in Appendix I and should be studied to note the positions of the sheet markings. Miscut panes also occur and are listed under the same catalogue numbers but with an "A" suffix letter.

**Horizontal Pane of Twenty.** In 1983 it was decided to issue the Christmas Booklet with Machin stamps in the form of a pane of twenty 12½p. at a special discount rate of £2.20, a saving of 30p. on the total face value. The double lined star was printed on the reverse of each stamp to act as an accountancy measure. This was to show that these stamps had been sold to the public below their face value and could not be redeemed for the higher figure. The experiment was not repeated and UFB29 and the miscut variety remain the only panes of twenty in the section.

**Other Formats.** Single value panes of four and six stamps or labels are included from the automatic slot-machine series.

**Barcode Booklet Panes.** The first issue appeared on 4 August 1987. They were distinctive as they had a margin all round the pane. In the listings they are included in chronological order with the original folded booklets. The sheet make-up of these booklets is different from the original concept of a continuous reel of stamps and details will be found in Appendix I. Later booklets show the panes with an imperforate edge replacing the margin. This reduced the overall size of the booklet and panes continue to appear with either three or two opposite sides imperforate.

**ILLUSTRATIONS.** Panes from counter and slot-machines are shown full size but Barcode booklet panes are shown ¾ size.

---

**65p. Pane. Plain Cover Booklets FC1A/B**

UFB2 Type P

Pane of ten 6½p. stamps with centre phosphor band from 65p. Booklet No. FC1A/B
Pane UFB1.   Selvedge at left

| | Perf. Type | |
| --- | --- | --- |
| | E | P |
| UFB1 (containing No. U149 × 10) (14.7.76) | 10·00 | 12·00 |
| UFB1A Miscut | 12·00 | 13·00 |

Pane UFB2.   Selvedge at right

| | Perf. Type | |
|---|---|---|
| | E | P |
| UFB2 (containing No. U149 × 10) (14.7.76) | 8·00 | 15·00 |
| a. Vertical repair above dress (R. 1/2) .. .. .. .. | — | 17·00 |
| b. Repair on throat (R. 2/3) .. .. .. .. .. .. | — | 17·00 |
| c. White spot on 6 (R. 2/3) .. .. .. .. .. .. | 10·00 | † |
| UFB2A Miscut | 10·00 | 10·00 |

**Listed Booklet Cylinder Flaws**

| UFB2a | UFB2b | UFB2c |
|---|---|---|
| Repair above dress and another below necklace at right (Cyl. 7 dot) | Repair on throat and scratches across face and neck (Cyl. 7 dot) | White spot at bottom of 6 (Cyl. 7 no dot) |

**Booklet Cylinder Numbers**

Perforation as Type R

| | | | | | | Perf. Type | |
|---|---|---|---|---|---|---|---|
| | | | | | | No dot | Dot |
| Pane No. | Cyl. No. | Phos. No. | | | | E | P |
| UFB1 | 7 | 27 | .. | .. | .. | 14·00 | 18·00 |
| UFB1A | 7 | 27 | .. | .. | .. | 42·00 | 42·00 |

Perforation as Type RE

| | | | | | | Perf. Type E | |
|---|---|---|---|---|---|---|---|
| | | | | | | No dot | Dot |
| UFB1 | 7 | 27 | .. | .. | .. | —* | 15·00 |
| UFB1A | 7 | 27 | .. | .. | .. | —* | 50·00 |
| UFB1 | 8 | 27 | .. | .. | .. | £200 | £225 |

*No dot panes with the single extension hole (perf. type E) produced by perforators type R and RE are identical and are worth the same.

Cylinder 7 was also used for the 6½p. R.L. coil.

**Sheet Details**

Sheet size: 200 (10 × 20). Double pane reel-fed

Sheet markings:

Cylinder numbers: Opposite row 18, left margin, boxed

Triangles: Solid right-angle triangles at each side on both panes pointing down at row 1 and up at row 20. On the left-hand pane (cols. 1 and 2) the vertical side of the triangle is on the right but it is at left on the right-hand pane (cols. 3 and 4). Two triangles appear on the miscut pane.

Marginal arrows: Opposite rows 10/11 at each side on both panes

Total sheet values: Opposite rows 5/6 and 15/16 at each side on both panes

Vertical cutting line: Opposite rows 3/4 at each side on both panes; also opposite rows 19/20, left margin on no dot pane and opposite rows 17/18, right margin on dot pane and on interpane gutters opposite rows 13/14

Horizontal cutting line: In alternate rows, 2/3, etc.

On no dot pane with selvedge at right, part of the dot cylinder box appears on row 18.

As the cylinders are continuous the sheets have no horizontal selvedge and the triangles (illustrated on panes UFB2 and UFB3) were introduced to indicate where the sheets have to be divided. The 6½p. pane comes from rows 19/20 and the 8½p. from rows 1/2.

**85p. Pane. Plain Cover Booklets FF1A/B**

UFB3 Type E

Pane of ten 8½p. stamps with two 9·5 mm. phosphor bands from 85p. Booklet No. FF1A/B
Pane UFB3.   Selvedge at left

|  | Perf. Type | |
|---|---|---|
|  | E | P |
| UFB3 (containing No. U166 × 10) (14.7.76) | 6·00 | 9·00 |
|   *a.* Damaged loop to 8 (R. 1/1) .. .. .. .. .. .. | 7·50 | 11·00 |
|   *b.* Deformed bottom loop to 8 (R. 2/1) .. .. .. .. | 7·50 | 12·00 |
| UFB3A Miscut | 10·00 | £200 |

Pane UFB4.   Selvedge at right

| | | |
|---|---|---|
| UFB4 (containing No. U166 × 10) (14.7.76) | 6·00. | 18·00 |
| UFB4A Miscut | 32·00 | £450 |

Nos. UFB3*a*/*b* also occur on vertical coils and sheets printed from the same cylinder and as singles are listed under Nos. U166*e* and U166*i*.

**Booklet Cylinder Numbers**

Perforation as Type R

| | | | | | | Perf. Type | |
|---|---|---|---|---|---|---|---|
| | | | | | | No dot | Dot |
| Pane No. | Cyl. No. | Phos. No. | | | | E | P |
| UFB3 | 3 | 28 | .. | .. | .. | 10·00 | 11·00 |
| UFB3A | 3 | 28 | .. | .. | .. | 60·00 | £450 |

Perforation as Type RE

| | | | | | | Perf Type E | |
|---|---|---|---|---|---|---|---|
| | | | | | | No dot | Dot |
| UFB3 | 3 | 28 | .. | .. | .. | —* | 10·00 |
| UFB3A | 3 | 28 | .. | .. | .. | —* | 60·00 |

*No dot panes with the single extension hole (perf. type E) produced by perforators type R and RE are identical and are worth the same.
Cylinder 3 was also used for the 8½p. TL coil.

**Sheet Details**

As for 65p. panes.

**70p. Pane. Plain, Derby and Country Crafts Series FD1A/8B**

UFB6

Pane of ten 7p. stamps with one 4 mm. centre phosphor band from 70p. Booklets Nos. FD1A/8B.

Pane UFB5.  Selvedge at left

|  | Perf. Type E |
|---|---|
| UFB5 (containing No. U154 × 10) (13.6.77) | 6·00 |
| UFB5A Miscut | 8·00 |

Pane UFB6.  Selvedge at right

|  | Perf. Type E |
|---|---|
| UFB6 (containing No. U154 × 10) (13.6.77) | 6·00 |
| *a.* Flaw on front jewel (R. 1/4) . . . . . . . . | 7·50 |
| UFB6A Miscut | 8·00 |

**Listed Booklet Cylinder Flaw**

No. UFB6*a* comes from Cylinder 11 which was also used for the vertical XL coil. It is listed with illustration under No. U154*n*.

**Booklet Cylinder Numbers**

Perforation as Type RE

|  |  |  |  | Perf. Type E | |
|---|---|---|---|---|---|
| Pane No. | Cyl. No. | Phos. No. |  | No dot | Dot |
| UFB5 | 11 | 27 | . . . . . . | 10·00 | 10·00 |
| UFB5A | 11 | 27 | . . . . . . | 18·00 | 18·00 |

**Sheet Details**

As for 65p. panes

**90p. Pane. Plain, Derby and British Canals Series FG1A/8B**

UFB7

Pane of ten 9p. stamps with two 9·5 mm. phosphor bands from 90p. Booklets Nos. FG1A/8B
Pane UFB7. Selvedge at left

| | | | | | | Perf. Type E |
|---|---|---|---|---|---|---|
| UFB7 (containing No. U175 × 10) (13.6.77) | | | | | | 6·00 |
| b. Extra phosphor band* | .. | .. | .. | .. | .. | 40·00 |
| c. White blob on 9 (R. 2/4) | .. | .. | .. | .. | .. | 7·50 |
| d. Dark spot below hair bun (R. 1/5) | .. | .. | .. | .. | 7·50 |
| UFB7A Miscut | | | | | | 15·00 |

Pane UFB8. Selvedge at right

| | | | | | | Perf. Type E |
|---|---|---|---|---|---|---|
| UFB8 (containing No. U175 × 10) (13.6.77) | | | | | | 6·00 |
| c. Dark scratch on crown (R. 1/5) | .. | .. | .. | .. | 7·50 |
| UFB8A Miscut | | | | | | 10·00 |

*This extra band of about 7 mm. wide has been found between the normal bands on stamps in the 5th vertical row from column 1, i.e. no dot panes with selvedge at left.

**Listed Booklet Cylinder Flaws**

No. UFB7c comes from no dot panes from Cylinder 24 which was also used for the vertical YL coils where it occurs on Roll 4. It is listed as a single under U175l. Similarly No. UFB8c also comes from the YL coils Roll 6 and is listed under No. U175m.

Dark spot below hair bun
(Cyl. 25 dot)

UFB7d

**Booklet Cylinder Numbers**

Perforation as Type RE

| | | | | | | Perf. Type E | |
|---|---|---|---|---|---|---|---|
| Pane No. | Cyl. No. | Phos No. | | | | No dot | Dot |
| UFB7 | 24 | 28 | .. | .. | .. | 10·00 | 10·00 |
| UFB7 | 25 | 28 | .. | .. | .. | 10·00 | 10·00 |
| UFB7A | 24 | 28 | .. | .. | .. | † | 75·00 |
| UFB7A | 25 | 28 | .. | .. | .. | £140 | — |

The phosphor cylinder number 28 occurs displaced +25 mm. and appears at the top of the margin on some panes showing ink cylinder 25. This cylinder pane also occurs with the experimental fold listed as booklet FG6a in Appendix J. (*Price* £60 *each, No dot;* £50 *each, dot*).

**Sheet Details**

As for 65p. panes

**80p. Pane. Military Aircraft Series FE1A/B**

UFB10

Pane of ten 8p. stamps with one 4 mm. centre phosphor band from 80p. Pictorial Booklet No. FE1A/B

Pane UFB9. Selvedge at left

|  | Perf. Type E |
|---|---|
| UFB9 (containing No. U162 × 10) (3.10.79) | 4·00 |
| *a.* Dark spot in band (R. 2/1) .. .. .. .. .. .. | 6·00 |

Pane UFB10. Selvedge at right
| UFB10 (containing No. U162 × 10) (3.10.79) | 4·00 |

**Listed Booklet Cylinder Flaw**

No. UFB9*a* comes from no dot panes from Cylinder 8 which was also used for the vertical AL coils where it occurs on Roll 1. It is listed as a single under No. U162*i*.

**Booklet Cylinder Numbers**

Perforation as Type RE

|  |  |  | Perf. Type E | |
|---|---|---|---|---|
| Pane No. | Cyl. No. | Phos. No. | No dot | Dot |
| UFB9 | 8 | 27 .. .. | 6·50 | 6·50 |

**Sheet Details**

As for 65p. panes

---

**£1 Pane. Industrial Archaeology Series FH1A/B**

UFB11, UFB13

Pane of ten 10p. stamps with "All over" phosphor from £1 Pictorial Booklet No. FH1A/B

Pane UFB11. Selvedge at left

|  | Perf. Type E |
|---|---|
| UFB11 (containing No. U187 × 10) (3.10.79) | 5·00 |
|   *a*. Horizontal blemish from lower lip (*cyl. pane* R. 2/4) .. | 7·50 |
| UFB11A Miscut | 12·00 |

Pane UFB12. Selvedge at right

| UFB12 (containing No. U187 × 10) (3.10.79) | 5·00 |
|---|---|
|   *a*. Dark line in background behind Queen (R. 2/5) ..    .. | 7·00 |
|   *b*. Diagonal line (R. 2/2)..    ..    ..    ..    ..    .. | 7·00 |
| UFB12A Miscut | 7·00 |

**Booklet Cylinder Numbers**

Perforation as Type RE

|  |  |  |  | Perf. Type E | |
|---|---|---|---|---|---|
| Pane No. | Cyl. No. | Phos. No. |  | No dot | Dot |
| UFB11 | 5 | (—)* | ..    ..    .. | 8·00 | 8·00 |
| UFB11A | 5 | (—)* | ..    ..    .. | 60·00 | † |

*The phosphor cylinder employed was P37. The number is inverted and unsynchronised and is found in the right-hand margin only. *Price* £8 UFB12. Ditto but miscut pane UFB11A with phosphor cylinder P37, *price* £15.

---

**£1 Pane. Military Aircraft Series FH2A/4B**

Pane of ten 10p. stamps with one 4 mm. centre phosphor band from £1 Booklet Nos. FH2A/4B

Pane UFB13. Selvedge at left

|  | Perf. Type E |
|---|---|
| UFB13 (containing No. U190 × 10) (4.2.80) | 5·00 |
|   *a*. Horizontal blemish from lower lip (*cyl. pane* R. 2/4) ..    .. | 10·00 |
| UFB13A Miscut | 26·00 |

Pane UFB14. Selvedge at right

| UFB14 (containing No. U190 × 10) (4.2.80) | 5·00 |
|---|---|
|   *a*. Dark line in background behind Queen (R. 2/5) ..    .. | 7·50 |
|   *b*. Diagonal line (R. 2/2)..    ..    ..    ..    ..    .. | 7·50 |
| UFB14A Miscut | 24·00 |

**Listed Booklet Cylinder Flaws**

| UFB11*a*, UFB13*a* | UFB12*a*, UFB14*a* | UFB12*b*, UFB14*b* |
|---|---|---|
| Short horizontal blemish | Diagonal line (R. 2/5) | Diagonal line |
| from Queen's lower lip | extends to stamp above in | (Cyl. 5 no dot) |
| (Only on the Cyl. 5 dot | the pane | |
| pane, R. 2/4) | (Cyl. 5 dot) | |

**Booklet Cylinder Numbers**

Perforation as Type RE

| Pane No. | Cyl. No. | Phos. No. | | | | Perf. Type E No dot | Dot |
|---|---|---|---|---|---|---|---|
| UFB13 | 5 | 27 | .. | .. | .. | 7·50 | 7·50 |
| UFB13 | (—) | 27 | .. | .. | .. | 7·00 | 7·00 |
| UFB13A | 5 | 27 | .. | .. | .. | † | 65·00 |

Cylinder 5 was also used for the 10p. CL coil.

**Sheet Details**

As for 65p. panes

---

**£1·20 Pane. Industrial Archaeology Series FJ1A/3B**

UFB15

Pane of 12p. stamps on phosphorised (fluorescent coated) paper from £1·20 Pictorial Booklets Nos. FJ1A/3B

Pane UFB15. Selvedge at left

| | Perf. Type E |
|---|---|
| UFB15 (containing No. U204 × 10) (4.2.80) | 5·00 |
|   *a.* Heavy dash below bust (R. 1/1) .. .. .. .. .. | 7·00 |
|   *b.* "Rivet" in band of crown and white spot below eye (R. 2/1), also dark spot behind hair (R. 2/5) .. .. .. .. | 7·50 |
|   *c.* White dots above ear and behind hair (R. 2/4) .. .. .. | 7·00 |
| UFB15A Miscut | 11·00 |

Pane UFB16. Selvedge at right

| | |
|---|---|
| UFB16 (containing No. U204 × 10) (4.2.80) | 5·00 |
|   *a.* Long white scratch (R. 1/1) .. .. .. .. .. .. | 7·50 |
| UFB16A   Miscut | 10·00 |

The flaws listed above all occur on Cylinder 4 no dot.

**Listed Booklet Cylinder Flaws**

UFB15*a*
Heavy dash below
bust

UFB15*b*
"Rivet" in band and
white spot below eye

UFB15*b*
Dark spot behind hair

**263**

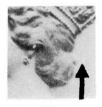

White dot above ear
and behind hair

UFB15c

UFB16a
Long white scratch

**Booklet Cylinder Numbers**
Perforation as Type RE

| Pane No. | Cyl. No. | | | | Perf. Type E No dot | Dot* |
|----------|----------|---|---|---|---------------------|------|
| UFB15    | 4        | .. | .. | .. | 8·00 | 8·00 |
| UFB15A   | 4        | .. | .. | .. | 15·00 | 12·00 |

*The dot was not engraved but the no dot pane may be identified by a circular flaw in the background between the Queen's hair and right border (R. 1/1). Cylinder 4 was also used for the 12p. DL coil.

**Sheet Details**
As for 65p. panes

---

**£1·15 Pane. Military Aircraft and Museums Series FI1A/4B**

UFB17
Pane of ten 11½p. stamps with one 4 mm. centre phosphor band from £1·15 Booklets Nos. FI1A/4B

Pane UFB17. Selvedge at left

UFB17 (containing No. U201 × 10) (26.1.81)

Perf. Type E
5·00

**264**

Pane UFB18. Selvedge at right                                                       Perf. Type E
UFB18 (containing No. U201 × 10) (26.1.81)                                          5·00

**Booklet Cylinder Numbers**
Perforation as Type RE

| Pane No. | Cyl. No. | Phos. No. | | | | Perf. Type E<br>No dot |
|----------|----------|-----------|--|--|--|--------------|
| UFB17 | B5 | B36 | .. | .. | .. | 8·00 |
| UFB17 | B5 | (—)* | .. | .. | .. | 8·00 |

\* Copies of No. UFB17 exist with displaced phosphor cylinder No. B36. *Price* £10 *mint.*
The cylinder B5 (B36) was also used for the 11½p. EL coil.

**Sheet Details**
Sheet size: 120 (10 × 12). Single pane reel-fed on the Chambon press
Sheet markings:
Cylinder numbers: Opposite row 3, left margin, reading downwards in open box facing left
Vertical cutting line: Opposite row 12 on both sides of the pane
Horizontal cutting line: In alternate rows 2/3, etc.
   The cylinder is continuous and the sheets have no horizontal margins.

---

**£1·40 Pane. Industrial Archaeology and 19th Cent. Women's Costume Series FM1A/4B**

UFB19

Pane of ten 14p. stamps on phosphorised (fluorescent coated) paper from £1·40 Pictorial Booklet
Nos. FM1A/4B.

Pane UFB19. Selvedge at left

| | Perf. Type E |
|--|--------------|
| UFB19 (containing No. U225 × 10) (26.1.81) | 6·50 |
| *a.* Spot on chin (R. 1/5) .. .. .. .. .. | 8·00 |

Pane UFB20. Selvedge at right

| UFB20 (containing No. U225 × 10) (26.1.81) | 6·50 |
|--|--|
| *a.* Fluorescent brightener omitted .. .. .. .. | 15·00 |
| *b.* Diagonal scratch above dress (R. 1/1) .. .. .. | 8·00 |
| *c.* Oval blemish between 4 and P (R. 1/1) .. .. .. | 8·00 |
| *d.* White scratch through dress (R. 2/3) .. .. .. | 8·00 |
| *e.* Long diagonal line (R. 1/3) .. .. .. .. .. | 9·00 |
| UFB20A   Miscut | £700 |

Pane UFB20*a* derives from Booklet Nos. FM3B and FM4B.

   Both panes are known on phosphorised paper with either a shiny ink surface which gives a
photo-negative reflection or a matt surface without the negative effect.
   The flaws listed above all occur on Cylinder B3.

**Listed Booklet Cylinder Flaws**

UFB19a
Dark spot on chin

UFB20b
Diagonal scratch
above dress

No. UFB19a is a multipositive flaw which occurs on Cyl. Nos. B3 and B6.

UFB20c
Oval blemish between
4 and P
(Later retouched appearing
as a white mark)

UFB20d
White scratch through dress

Long diagonal scratch
across stamp

UFB20e

**Booklet Cylinder Numbers**
Perforation as Type RE

| Pane No. | Cyl. No. | | | | | Perf. Type E No dot |
|----------|----------|--|--|--|--|---------------------|
| UFB19 | B3 | .. | .. | .. | .. | 10·00 |
| UFB19 | B6 | .. | .. | .. | .. | 10·00 |

Two additional cylinders (B11 and B14) were used for printings of the Booklet No. FM4. Both numbers were placed so that they did not appear in the issued booklets.

The cylinder B3 was also used for the 14p. FL coil.

**Sheet Details**

As for £1·15 panes except the cylinder number is between rows 3/4 with the open box facing right.

**£1·25 Pane. Museums and Railway Engines Series FK1A/8B**

UFB22

Pane of ten 12½p. stamps with one 4 mm. centre phosphor band from £1·25 Pictorial Booklet Nos. FK1A/8B

Pane UFB21. Selvedge at left

|  | Perf. Type E |
|---|---|
| UFB21 (containing No. U212 × 10) (1.2.82) | 4·50 |

Pane UFB22. Selvedge at right

| UFB22 (containing No. U212 × 10) (1.2.82) | 4·50 |
|---|---|
|     *a.* Diagonal scratch above dress (R. 2/1)    ..    ..    ..    .. | 6·00 |

**Listed Booklet Cylinder Flaw**

No. UFB22*a* is a multipositive flaw which first occurred on the 14p. value in pane UFB20 where it is illustrated as UFB20*a*.

**Booklet Cylinder Numbers**

No cylinder numbers appeared in the booklet Nos. FK1/2. The cylinder numbers appeared in the right margin but were trimmed off but those used were:—

B1 (12½p.) and B36 (phosphor). This combination was used for the 12½p. GL coil.

Perforation as type RE. Single pane cylinders

| Pane No. | Cyl. Nos. | Phos. No. |  |  |  |  | Perf. Type E No dot | Phosphor Cyl. Displacement |
|---|---|---|---|---|---|---|---|---|
| UFB22 | 12½p., B1 | (—) | .. | .. | .. | .. | 7·00 | B36*, B49 |
| UFB21 | 12½p., B1 | (B49) | .. | .. | .. | .. | 7·00 | |
| UFB22 | 12½p., B1 | (B49) | .. | .. | .. | .. | 7·00 | |
| UFB21 | 12½p., B8 | (B49) | .. | .. | .. | .. | 7·00 | |
| UFB22 | 12½p., B8 | (B49) | .. | .. | .. | .. | 7·00 | |
| UFB21 | 12½p., B8 | (—) | .. | .. | .. | .. | 9·00 | B49 |
| UFB22 | 12½p., B8 | (—) | .. | .. | .. | .. | 9·00 | B49 |
| UFB21 | 12½p., B36 | (B49) | .. | .. | .. | .. | 7·00 | |
| UFB22 | 12½p., B36 | (B49) | .. | .. | .. | .. | 7·00 | |
| UFB21 | 12½p., B36 | (B36) | .. | .. | .. | .. | 75·00 | |
| UFB22 | 12½p., B36 | (B36) | ·· | ·· | ·· | ·· | £500 | |
| UFB21 | 12½p., B36 | (—) | .. | .. | .. | .. | 50·00 | B36 |
| UFB22 | 12½p., B36 | (—) | .. | .. | .. | .. | £500 | B36 |

*The phosphor cylinder B36 did not appear in booklet Nos. FK4/6. Ink cylinder B1 was placed in the right margin and appears on pane UFB22 and the phosphor cylinder was probably placed wide so that it was always trimmed off. Panes from booklet No. FK8 show phosphor cylinder B36 engraved twice, but this was probably an error for B63.

Nos. UFB21 or 22 with phosphor cylinder number only. *Price for* UFB21 (B36) £32, UFB22 (B36) £500, UFB21 *or* 22 (B49) £9.

**Sheet Make-up**

Sheet size: 120 (10 × 12). Single pane reel-fed on the Chambon press

Sheet markings:
 Cylinder numbers: Opposite row 5 at each side, boxed. Initially the cylinder number was engraved
  in the right margin but was trimmed off
 Horizontal cutting line: In alternate rows, 2/3, etc.
 Marginal arrows: At each corner of the sheet

**£1·55 Pane. 19th Cent. Women's Costume Series FR1A/4B**

UFB24

Pane of ten 15½p. stamps on phosphorised (fluorescent coated) paper from £1·55 Pictorial Booklet Nos. FR1A/4B

Pane UFB23. 15½p. Type II. Selvedge at left

|  | Perf. Type E |
|---|---|
| UFB23 (containing No. U235*b* × 10) (1.2.82) | 5·50 |

Pane UFB24. 15½p. Type II. Selvedge at right

| UFB24 (containing No. U235*b* × 10) (1.2.82) | 5·50 |
|---|---|
|   *a.* White scratch between 1 and P (R. 2/5) .. .. .. .. | 7·00 |

Both panes are known on phosphorised paper with either a shiny ink surface which gives a photo-negative reflection or a matt surface without the negative effect.

**Listed Booklet Cylinder Flaw**

White scratch between 1 and P

UFB24*a*

No. UFB24*a* comes from cylinder B7 which was also used for the vertical HL coil where it occurs on Roll No. 10 and is listed as a single under No. U235*ba*.

**Booklet Cylinder Numbers**

No cylinder numbers appeared in the booklet No. FR1. The cylinder used was B7 and engraved in the right margin so that it was always trimmed off.

Perforation as Type RE. Single pane cylinder

| Pane No. | Cyl. No. | | | | | Perf. Type E No dot |
|----------|----------|---|---|---|---|---------------------|
| UFB23 | B7 | .. | .. | .. | .. | 8·00 |
| UFB24 | B7 | .. | .. | .. | .. | 8·00 |

**Sheet Make-up**

As for £1·25 panes except for hand-engraved arrows between rows 6/7 at both sides.

**£1·60 Pane. "Birthday Box", British Countryside and "Write it" Booklets FS1A/B and FS3A/4B**

UFB26 (UFB28 similar with underprint)

Pane of ten 16p. stamps on phosphorised (fluorescent coated) paper from £1·60 Pictorial Booklet Nos. FS1A/B and FS3A/4B

Pane UFB25. Selvedge at left

| | Perf. Type E |
|--|--------------|
| UFB25 (containing No. U241 × 10) (5.4.83) | 6·00 |
| a. Circular retouch on back above dress (R. 1/1) .. .. .. | 7·50 |

Pane UFB26. Selvedge at right

| | Perf. Type E |
|--|--------------|
| UFB26 (containing No. U241 × 10) (5.4.83) | 6·00 |
| a. Diagonal scratch above dress (R. 2/1) .. .. .. .. | 8·00 |

**Booklet Cylinder Numbers**

Perforation as Type RE. Single pane cylinders

| Pane No. | Cyl. No. | | | | Perf. Type E No dot |
|----------|----------|---|---|---|---------------------|
| UFB25 | B3 | .. | .. | .. | 8·00 |
| UFB26 | B3 | .. | .. | .. | 8·00 |
| UFB25 | B10 | .. | .. | .. | 10·00 |
| UFB26 | B10 | .. | .. | .. | 9·00 |

**£1.60 Pane. British Countryside Booklet FS2A/B**

Pane of ten 16p. stamps with double lined "D" underprint in blue. Printed on phosphorised (fluorescent coated) paper from £1·60 Pictorial Booklet No. FS2A/B (sold at a discount rate of £1·45)

Pane UFB27. Selvedge at left

| | Perf. Type E |
|--|--------------|
| UFB27 (containing No. U243 × 10) (10.8.83) | 7·00 |
| a. Circular retouch on back above dress (R. 1/1) .. .. .. | 10·00 |
| UFB27A Miscut. | £1800 |

Pane UFB28. Selvedge at right

UFB28 (containing No. U243 × 10) (10.8.83)      7·00
  *a.* Diagonal scratch above dress (R. 2/1)    ..    ..    ..    .. 11·00

**Listed Booklet Cylinder Flaws**

UFB26*a* and 28*a* is a multipositive flaw which first occurred on the 14p. value in pane UFB20 where it is illustrated as UFB20*b*.

Circular retouch on back
above dress (Cyl. B3)

UFB25*a*, UFB27*a*

**Booklet Cylinder Numbers**

Perforation as Type RE. Single pane cylinders

|  |  |  |  |  |  | Perf. Type E No dot |
|---|---|---|---|---|---|---|
| Pane No. | Cyl. No. |  |  |  |  |  |
| UFB27 | B3 | .. | .. | .. | .. | 10·00 |
| UFB27A | B3 | .. | .. | .. | .. | £2000 |
| UFB28 | B3 | .. | .. | .. | .. | 10·00 |

The cylinder B3 was also used for the 16p. JL coil.

**Sheet Make-up**

As for £1·25 panes

**£2.50 Pane. 1983 Christmas Booklet FX6**

UFB29
(*Illustration reduced to ½ actual size*)

Pane of twenty 12½p. stamps with one 4 mm. centre phosphor band from 1983 £2·50 Christmas Booklet No. FX6 (sold at a discount rate of £2.20)

In each case the stamps were printed with a double lined star in blue over the gummed side. This is illustrated as Type (2) above the listing of No. U216 in Section UD.

The binding margin is always at left as the right-hand margin is guillotined off.

|  | Perf. Type E |
|---|---|
| UFB29 (containing No. U216 × 20) (9.11.83) | 10·00 |
| UFB29A Miscut. (ex. Cyl. B44) | £1800 |

This was the only Christmas booklet to contain stamps of a single denomination for the second-class postage rate. Each pane was folded twice, between vertical rows 3/4 and 7/8.

**270**

**Booklet Cylinder Numbers**

Perforation as Type RE. Single pane cylinders

| Pane No. | Cyl. No. | Phos. No. | | | | | Perf. Type E No dot |
|---|---|---|---|---|---|---|---|
| UFB29 | B36 | (B49) | .. | .. | .. | .. | 12·00 |
| UFB29 | B36 | (B62) | .. | .. | .. | .. | 14·00 |
| UFB29 | B40 | (B36) | .. | .. | .. | .. | 32·00 |
| UFB29 | B40 | (—) | .. | .. | .. | .. | £200 |
| UFB29 | — | (B36) | .. | .. | .. | .. | — |
| UFB29 | B40 | (B49) | .. | .. | .. | .. | 14·00 |
| UFB29 | B42 | (B49) | .. | .. | .. | .. | £180 |
| UFB29 | B44 | (B36) | .. | .. | .. | .. | 18·00 |
| UFB29 | B46 | (B36) | .. | .. | .. | .. | 24·00 |
| UFB29A | B44 | (B36) | .. | .. | .. | .. | — |

The B36 (B62) cylinder pane exists with the phosphor figure 2 on a separate booklet.

**Sheet Make-up**

As for 1980 Christmas pane UMFB18 except for a larger arrow opposite rows 6/7.

---

**£1·30 Pane. Trams Series, Books for Children, "Keep in Touch", "Ideas for Your Garden", "Brighter Writer", "Jolly Postman", Linnean Society, Recipe Cards and "Children's Parties" Booklets FL3A/14B**

UFB30 (UFB32 similar with underprint)

Pane of ten 13p. stamps with one 4 mm. centre phosphor band from £1·30 Pictorial Booklet Nos. FL3A/14B

Pane UFB30. Selvedge at left

| | Perf. Type E |
|---|---|
| UFB30 (containing No. U218 × 10) (3.9.84) | 5·00 |
| a. Phosphor omitted .. .. .. .. .. .. .. | 60·00 |
| b. New phosphor ink .. .. ... .. .. .. | 5·00 |

Pane UFB31. Selvedge at right

| | Perf. Type E |
|---|---|
| UFB31 (containing No. U218 × 10) (3.9.84) | 5·00 |
| a. Phosphor omitted .. .. .. .. .. .. | 75·00 |
| b. New phosphor ink .. .. .. .. .. .. | 5·00 |

**Booklet Cylinder Numbers**

Perforation as Type RE. Single pane cylinders

| Pane No. | Cyl. No. | | Phos. No. | | | | | Perf. Type E No dot |
|---|---|---|---|---|---|---|---|---|
| UFB30 | B7 | | (B62) | .. | .. | .. | .. | 7·50 |
| UFB31 | B7 | | (B62) | .. | .. | .. | .. | 7·50 |
| UFB30 | B12 | ' | (B49) | .. | .. | .. | .. | 10·00 |
| UFB31 | B12 | | (B49) | .. | .. | .. | .. | 9·00 |

**271**

| Pane No. | Cyl. No. | Phos. No. | | | | Perf. Type E No dot |
|---|---|---|---|---|---|---|
| UFB30 | B12 | (B62) | .. | .. | .. .. | 7·50 |
| UFB31 | B12 | (B62) | .. | .. | .. .. | 7·50 |

The following cylinder booklet panes all have the new phosphor ink

| Pane No. | Cyl. No. | Phos. No. | | | | Perf. Type E No dot |
|---|---|---|---|---|---|---|
| UFB30*b* | B12 | (B62) | .. | .. | .. | 6·00 |
| UFB31*b* | B12 | (B62) | .. | .. | .. | 6·00 |
| UFB30*b* | B36 | (B62) | .. | .. | .. | 12·00 |
| UFB31*b* | B36 | (B62) | .. | .. | .. | 12·00 |
| UFB30*b* | B37 | (B62) | .. | .. | .. | 6·00 |
| UFB31*b* | B37 | (B62) | .. | .. | .. | 6·00 |
| UFB30*b* | B37 | (—) | .. | .. | .. | 7·00 |
| UFB30*b* | — | (B49) | .. | .. | .. | 7·00 |
| UFB31*b* | B37 | (—) | .. | .. | .. | 10·00 |
| UFB31*b* | — | (B49) | .. | .. | .. | 10·00 |
| UFB30*b* | — | (B62) | .. | .. | .. | 30·00 |
| UFB31*b* | — | (B62) | .. | .. | .. | 10·00 |

**£1·30 Pane. 1986 Christmas Booklet FX9**

Pane of ten 13p. stamps with one 4 mm. centre phosphor band and a single double lined star underprint in blue. From 1986 Christmas Booklet No. FX9 (face value £1·30 and sold at a discount rate of £1·20).

Pane UFB32. Selvedge at left

| | Perf. Type E |
|---|---|
| UFB32 (containing No. U222 × 10) (2.12.86) | 12·00 |

Pane UFB33. Selvedge at right

| | |
|---|---|
| UFB33 (containing No. U222 × 10) (2.12.86) | 8·00 |

**Booklet Cylinder Numbers**

Perforation as Type RE. Single pane cylinder

| Pane No. | Cyl. No. | Phos. No. | | | | | Perf. Type E No dot |
|---|---|---|---|---|---|---|---|
| UFB32 | 13p., B12 | (B62) | .. | .. | .. | .. | 15·00 |
| UFB33 | 13p., B12 | (B62) | .. | .. | .. | .. | 20·00 |

**Sheet Make-up**

As for £1·25 panes

**£1·70 Pane. Social Letter Writing, Pillar Box, National Gallery and Handwriting, "Yes" Booklets FT1A/B, FT3A/B and FT5A/7B**

UFB35 (UFB37 similar with underprint)

Pane of ten 17p. stamps on phosphorised (fluorescent coated) paper from £1·70 Pictorial Booklet Nos. FT1A/B, FT3A/B and FT5A/7B.

Pane UFB34. Selvedge at left

|  | Perf. Type E |
|---|---|
| UFB34 (containing No. U246 × 10) (3.9.84) | 7·00 |
|    *a.* Background repair (R. 1/5). .    ..    ..    ..    ..    .. | 9·00 |

Pane UFB35. Selvedge at right

| | |
|---|---|
| UFB35 (containing No. U246 × 10) (3.9.84) | 7·00 |

**Listed Booklet Cylinder Flaw**

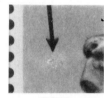

Background repair between forehead and left frame (Cyl. B18)

UFB34*a*

**Booklet Cylinder Numbers**

Perforation as Type RE. Single pane cylinders

| Pane No. | Cyl. No. | | | | | Perf. Type E<br>No dot |
|---|---|---|---|---|---|---|
| UFB34 | B7 | .. | .. | .. | .. | 10·00 |
| UFB35 | B7 | .. | .. | .. | .. | 10·00 |
| UFB34 | B9 | .. | .. | .. | .. | 12·00 |
| UFB35 | B9 | .. | .. | .. | .. | 15·00 |
| UFB34 | B18 | .. | .. | .. | .. | 12·00 |
| UFB35 | B18 | .. | .. | .. | .. | 12·00 |
| UFB34 | B19 | .. | .. | .. | .. | £300 |
| UFB35 | B19 | .. | .. | .. | .. | 55·00 |
| UFB34 | B20 | .. | .. | .. | .. | 12·00 |
| UFB35 | B20 | .. | .. | .. | .. | 12·00 |
| UFB34 | B21 | .. | .. | .. | .. | 10·00 |
| UFB35 | B21 | .. | .. | .. | .. | 10·00 |
| UFB34 | B22 | .. | .. | .. | .. | 10·00 |
| UFB35 | B22 | .. | .. | .. | .. | 10·00 |

The cylinder B7 was also used for the 17p. LL coil.

**£1·70 Pane. Social Letter Writing Series FT2A/B**

Pane of ten 17p. stamps with a single double lined "D" underprint in blue. Printed on phosphorised (fluorescent coated) paper. From £1·70 Pictorial Booklet, Letters Abroad, Nos. FT2A/B (sold at a discount rate of £1·55).

Pane UFB36. Selvedge at left

| | Perf. Type E |
|---|---|
| UFB36 (containing No. U249 × 10) (5.3.85) | 7·50 |

Pane UFB37. Selvedge at right

| | |
|---|---|
| UFB37 (containing No. U249 × 10) (5.3.85) | 7·50 |

**Booklet Cylinder Numbers**

Perforation as Type RE. Single pane cylinders

| Pane No. | Cyl. No. | | | | | Perf. Type E<br>No dot |
|---|---|---|---|---|---|---|
| UFB36 | B7 | .. | .. | .. | .. | 10·00 |
| UFB37 | B7 | .. | .. | .. | .. | 10·00 |
| UFB36 | B9 | .. | .. | .. | .. | 10·00 |
| UFB37 | B9 | .. | .. | .. | .. | 12·00 |
| UFB36 | B14 | .. | .. | .. | .. | £200 |
| UFB37 | B14 | .. | .. | .. | .. | £1400 |

**Sheet Make-up**

As for £1·25 panes

**50p. Pane. Pillar Box and Pond Life Series FB31/33**

UFB38

(UFB39 similar without underprint)

Three 17p. with two 9·5 mm. phosphor bands and label (without bands) inscribed "Please use the postcode". Multiple double lined star underprint type (4) in blue printed over the gum. For identical pane but without underprint see Pane UFB39.

The stamp below the label has short phosphor bands at top on both sides and is listed under No. U250.

Pane UFB38. From 50p. Booklet showing Pillar box, No. FB31 and Pond Life series, Nos. FB32/33. Face value 51p. but all sold at 50p.

| | Perf. Type E |
|---|---|
| UFB38 (containing Nos. U250 × 2, U250a) (4.11.85) | 2·75 |
| a. Phosphor omitted  ..   ..   ..   ..   ..   ..   .. | 50·00 |
| b. Heavy line opposite eyebrow (R. 2/2)   ..   ..   ..   .. | 3·50 |

**Booklet Cylinder Numbers**

Perforation as Type RE. Single pane cylinders

| | | | | | | | Perf. Type E |
|---|---|---|---|---|---|---|---|
| Pane No. | Cyl. No. | Phos. No. | | | | | No dot |
| UFB38 | B25 | (B67) | .. | .. | .. | .. | 4·00 |
| UFB38 | B25 | (—) | .. | .. | .. | .. | 4·00 |
| UFB38 | — | (B67) | .. | .. | .. | .. | 4·00 |
| UFB38 | B26 | (B67) | .. | .. | .. | .. | 5·50 |
| UFB38 | B36 | (B67) | .. | .. | .. | .. | 6·00 |
| UFB38 | B43 | (B67) | .. | .. | .. | .. | 6·00 |

**Listed Booklet Cylinder Flaw**

Heavy line from eyebrow
(Cyl. B25)

UFB38b

**50p. Pane. Pond Life Series FB33a**

Three 17p. with two 9·5 mm. phosphor bands and label inscribed "Please use the postcode". The stamp below the label has short phosphor bands at top and is listed below No. U248. Pane UFB39. From 50p. Pond Life No. 2 Booklet No. FB33a.

| | Perf. Type E |
|---|---|
| | 2·75 |
| UFB39 (containing Nos. U248 × 2, U248g) (12.8.86) | |
| a. Error. Phosphorised paper  .. .. .. .. .. .. | £200 |

Pane No. UFB39a is printed on phosphorised (fluorescent coated) paper with two phosphor bands. It is probable that paper intended for UFB42 was used in error.

**Booklet Cylinder Numbers**

Perforation as Type RE. Single pane cylinders

| | | | | Perf. Type E No dot |
|---|---|---|---|---|
| Pane No. | Cyl. No. | Phos. No. | | |
| UFB39 | B43 | (B67) | .. .. .. .. | 3·50 |
| UFB39a | B43 | (B67) | Phosphorised paper  .. | £400 |

**Sheet Make-up**

The printer's uncut sheet contained three columns of 8 panes each including one with a cylinder number. With the Queen's head upright and printed arrows at each corner the cylinder numbers were engraved above the printed label of the fifth pane from left in each of the three columns. Stamp width gutter margins formed the binding selvedge for panes in the second and third columns.

---

**£1.20 Pane. Pillar Box, National Gallery and Handwriting, "Maybe" Booklets FJ4A/6B**

UFB40

Pane of ten 12p. stamps with one 4 mm. centre band from £1·20 Pictorial Booklet Nos. FJ4/6B. Pane UFB40. Selvedge at left

| | Perf. Type E |
|---|---|
| | 7·00 |
| UFB40 (containing No. U207 × 10) (14.1.86) | |
| a. Phosphor omitted  .. .. .. .. .. .. .. | 75·00 |

Pane UFB41. Selvedge at right

| | |
|---|---|
| UFB41 (containing No. U207 × 10) (14.1.86) | 7·00 |
| a. Phosphor omitted  .. .. .. .. .. .. | £150 |
| b. Weak screening at base with retouches (R. 1/1) .. .. .. | 9·00 |
| UFB41A Miscut  .. .. .. .. .. .. .. .. | £300 |

**Listed Booklet Cylinder Flaw**

UFB41*b*
Weak screening at base with
extra retouches
(Cyl. B10)

**Booklet Cylinder Numbers**

Perforation as Type RE. Single pane cylinders

| Pane No. | Cyl. Nos. | Phos. No. | | | | | Perf. Type E No Dot |
|----------|-----------|-----------|---|---|---|---|---------------------|
| UFB40 | B10 | (B62) | .. | .. | .. | .. | 8·00 |
| UFB40 | B10 | (—) | .. | .. | .. | .. | £300 |
| UFB40 | — | (B62) | .. | .. | .. | .. | £250 |
| UFB41 | B10 | (B62) | .. | .. | .. | .. | 8·00 |
| UFB41 | B10 | (—) | .. | .. | .. | .. | £600 |
| UFB41 | — | (B62) | .. | .. | .. | .. | — |
| UFB40 | B12 | (B62) | .. | .. | .. | .. | 8·00 |
| UFB41 | B12 | (B62) | .. | .. | .. | .. | 8·00 |
| UFB41A | B12 | (B62) | .. | .. | .. | .. | £750 |

**Sheet Make-up**

As for £1·25 panes

**£1 Pane. Musical Instruments Series FH5**

UFB42

Pane of six 17p. stamps on phosphorised (fluorescent coated) paper from £1 Pictorial Booklet, Musical Instruments, No. 1, Booklet No. FH5.

UFB42 (containing No. U246 × 6) (29.7.86)                Perf. Type E
                                                          5·50

**Booklet Cylinder Numbers**

Perforation as Type RE. Single pane cylinder.

|          |         |    |    |    |    | Perf. Type E<br>No dot |
|----------|---------|----|----|----|----|------------------------|
| Pane No. | Cyl. No. | .. | .. | .. | .. |                        |
| UFB42    | B42     | .. | .. | .. | .. | 7·00                   |

**Sheet Make-up**

As for pane UMFB31 but with two columns of eight panes each. With Queen's head upright the cylinder number is above R. 1/1 of the fifth pane from the left side of the sheet.

---

**£1·80 Pane. Books for Children and "Keep in Touch" Booklets FU1A/2B**

UFB43, UFB45

Pane of ten 18p. stamps on phosphorised (fluorescent coated) paper from £1·80 Pictorial Booklet Nos. FU1A/2B

Pane UFB43. Selvedge at left

|                                               | Perf. Type E |
|-----------------------------------------------|--------------|
| UFB43 (containing No. U257 × 10) (20.10.86)   | 7·00         |

Pane UFB44. Selvedge at right

|                                               |      |
|-----------------------------------------------|------|
| UFB44 (containing No. U257 × 10) (20.10.86)   | 7·00 |

**Booklet Cylinder Numbers**

Perforation as Type RE. Single pane cylinders

| Pane No. | Cyl. No. |    |    |    | Perf. Type E<br>No dot |
|----------|----------|----|----|----|------------------------|
| UFB43    | B1       | .. | .. | .. | 11·00                  |
| UFB44    | B1       | .. | .. | .. | 11·00                  |
| UFB43    | B2       | .. | .. | .. | 10·00                  |
| UFB44    | B2       | .. | .. | .. | 10·00                  |

---

**£1·80 Pane. "Ideas for your Garden", "Brighter Writer", "Jolly Postman", Linnean Society, Recipe Cards and "Children's Parties" Booklets FU3A/8B**

Pane of ten 18p. stamps on phosphorised (advanced coated) paper from £1·80 Pictorial Booklet Nos. FU3A/8B

Pane UFB45. Selvedge at left

|                                               | Perf. Type E |
|-----------------------------------------------|--------------|
| UFB45 (containing No. U256 × 10) (14.4.87)    | 7·00         |
| UFB45A Miscut  ..   ..   ..   ..   ..   ..   ..   .. | £110   |

Pane UFB46. Selvedge at right

|  | Perf. Type E |
|---|---|
| UFB46 (containing No. U256 × 10) (14.4.87) | 7·00 |
| UFB46A Miscut    ..    ..    ..    ..    ..    ..    ..    .. | £110 |

**Booklet Cylinder Numbers**

Perforation as Type RE. Single pane cylinder

| Pane No. | Cyl. No. | | | | Perf. Type E<br>No dot |
|---|---|---|---|---|---|
| UFB45 | B1 | .. | .. | .. | 9·00 |
| UFB46 | B1 | .. | .. | .. | 9·00 |
| UFB45 | B2 | .. | .. | .. | 9·00 |
| UFB46 | B2 | .. | .. | .. | 9·00 |
| UFB46A | B2 | .. | .. | .. | £500 |
| UFB45 | B13 | .. | .. | .. | 10·00 |
| UFB45A | B13 | .. | .. | .. | £375 |
| UFB46 | B13 | .. | .. | .. | 10·00 |

**Sheet Make-up**

As for £1·25 panes

---

**52p. Pane. Barcode Booklets GA1A/B**

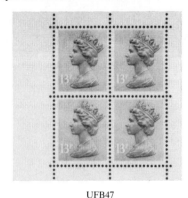    

UFB47                              UFB48

Pane of four 13p. stamps with one 4·5 mm. centre phosphor band from 52p. Barcode Booklet Nos. GA1A/B

|  | Perf. Type EP3 |
|---|---|
| UFB47 (containing No. U221*b* × 4) (4.8.87) | 2·25 |

**Booklet Cylinder Numbers**

Single pane cylinder

| Pane No. | Cyl. No. | Phos. No. | | | | Perf. Type EP3<br>No dot |
|---|---|---|---|---|---|---|
| UFB47 | B40 | (B75) | .. | .. | .. | 4·00 |

**Sheet Make-up**

Single pane and continuous with margins round each pane of four stamps. The uncut sheet contained 20 panes made-up of four vertical columns each with five panes. Cylinder numbers were opposite R. 1/1 of each pane in the second horizontal row. Vertical selvedges at both sides contained sprocket holes and photo-etched arrows at top and bottom, right margin only. Vertical positioning lines were placed between margins of the fifth horizontal row of the sheet.

**72p. Pane. Barcode Booklets GC1A/B**

Pane of four 18p. stamps on phosphorised (advanced coated) paper from 72p. Barcode Booklet Nos. GC1A/B

|  | Perf. Type EP3 |
|---|---|
| UFB48 (containing No. U256 × 4) (4.8.87) | 3·00 |

**Booklet Cylinder Number**
Single pane cylinder

| | | | | | Perf. Type EP3 |
|---|---|---|---|---|---|
| Pane No. | Cyl. No. | | | | No dot |
| UFB48 | B10 | .. | .. | .. | 5·00 |

**Sheet Make-up**
As for 52p. panes

---

**£1·04 Pane. Barcode Booklets GE1A/B**

UFB49

Pane of four 26p. stamps on phosphorised (advanced coated) paper from £1·04 Barcode Booklet Nos. GE1A/B

26p. Type II

|  | Perf. Type EP3 |
|---|---|
| UFB49 (containing No. U294 × 4) (4.8.87) | 18·00 |

**Booklet Cylinder Number**
Single pane cylinder

| | | | | | Perf. Type EP3 |
|---|---|---|---|---|---|
| Pane No. | Cyl. No. | | | | No dot |
| UFB49 | B2 | .. | .. | .. | 32·00 |

**Sheet Make-up**
As for 52p. panes

**£1·30 Pane. Barcode Booklets GI1A/B**

UFB50

Pane of ten 13p. stamps with one 4·5 mm. centre phosphor band from £1·30 Barcode Booklet Nos. GI1A/B

|  | Perf. Type EP3 |
|---|---|
| UFB50 (containing No. U221*b* × 10) (4.8.87) | 4·50 |

**Booklet Cylinder Numbers**

Single pane cylinder

| | | | | | | Perf. Type EP3 |
|---|---|---|---|---|---|---|
| Pane No. | Cyl. No. | Phos. No. | | | | No dot |
| UFB50 | B39 | (B74) | .. | .. | .. | 9·00 |
| UFB50 | B39 | — | .. | .. | .. | 10·00 |
| UFB50 | — | (B74) | .. | .. | .. | 15·00 |

**Sheet Make-up**

Single pane and continuous with margins round each pane of ten stamps. The uncut sheet contained 10 panes made-up of two vertical columns each with five panes. Cylinder numbers were opposite R. 1/1 of both panes in the second horizontal row. Vertical selvedges at both sides contained sprocket holes and photo-etched arrows at top and bottom, right margin only. Vertical positioning lines were placed between and at the sides of the two panes in the bottom row. The sheets were printed and perforated on a Chambon press.

---

**£1·80 Pane. Barcode Booklets GK1A/B**

UFB51

Pane of ten 18p. stamps on phosphorised (advanced coated) paper from £1·80 Barcode Booklets Nos. GK1A/B

UFB51 (containing No. U256 × 10) (4.8.87)

Perf. Type EP3
6·50

**Booklet Cylinder Number**

Single pane cylinder

| Pane No. | Cyl. No. | | | Perf. Type EP3 No dot |
|---|---|---|---|---|
| UFB51 | B9 | .. | .. .. | 12·00 |

**Sheet Make-up**

As for £1·30 pane UFB50

---

**56p. Pane. Barcode Booklets GB1A/2B**

UFB52                     UFB53

Pane of four 14p. deep blue stamps with one 4·5 mm. centre phosphor band from 56p. Barcode Booklet Nos. GB1A/2B

UFB52 (containing No. U230 × 4) (23.8.88)
*a*. Phosphor omitted .. .. .. .. .. .. .. .. .. ..

Perf. Type EP3
2·50

**Booklet Cylinder Number**

Single pane cylinder

| Pane No. | Cyl. No. | Phos. No. | | | Perf. Type EP3 No dot |
|---|---|---|---|---|---|
| UFB52 | B23 | (B80) | .. | .. .. | 5·00 |

**Sheet Make-up**

As for 52p. pane in Booklet No. GA1.

---

**76p. Pane. Barcode Booklets GD1A/2B**

Pane of four 19p. stamps on phosphorised (advanced coated) paper from 76p. Barcode Booklet Nos. GD1A/2B.

UFB53 (containing No. U259 × 4) (23.8.88)

Perf. Type EP3
3·50

**Booklet Cylinder Number**

Single pane cylinder

| Pane No. | Cyl. No. | | | Perf. Type EP3 No dot |
|---|---|---|---|---|
| UFB53 | B8 | .. | .. .. | 7·00 |

**Sheet Make-up**

As for 52p. pane in Booklet No. GA1.

**£1·08 Pane. Barcode Booklets GF1A/B**

UFB54

Pane of four 27p. chestnut stamps on phosphorised (advanced coated) paper from £1·08 Barcode Booklet Nos. GF1A/B.

|  | Perf. Type EP3 |
|---|---|
| UFB54 (containing No. U296 × 4) (23.8.88) | 4·00 |

**Booklet Cylinder Number**

Single pane cylinder

| Pane No. | Cyl. No. | | | | Perf. Type EP3 No dot |
|---|---|---|---|---|---|
| UFB54 | B1 | .. | .. | .. | 9·00 |

**Sheet Make-up**

As for 52p. pane in Booklet No. GA1.

**£1·40 Pane. Barcode Booklets GJ1A/B**

UFB55

Pane of ten 14p. stamps with one 4 mm. centre phosphor band from £1·40 Barcode Booklet Nos. GJ1A/B.

|  | Perf. Type EP3 |
|---|---|
| UFB55 (containing No. U228 × 10) (23.8.88) | 6·00 |

**Booklet Cylinder Numbers**

Single pane cylinder

| Pane No. | Cyl. No. | Phos. No. | | | | Perf. Type EP3 No dot |
|---|---|---|---|---|---|---|
| UFB55 | B22 | (B74) | .. | .. | .. | 12·00 |

**Sheet Make-up**

As for £1.30 pane in Booklet No. GI1.

---

**£1·90 Pane. Barcode Booklets GL1A/B**

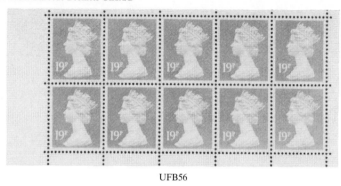

UFB56

Pane of ten 19p. stamps on phosphorised (advanced coated) paper from £1·90 Barcode Booklet Nos. GL1A/B.

| | Perf. Type EP3 |
|---|---|
| UFB56 (containing No. U259 × 10) (23.8.88) | 7·00 |

No. UFB56 exists printed on paper giving a dull reaction under ultra violet light. This was due to a reduction in the brightening agent of the paper coating.

**Booklet Cylinder Number**

Single pane cylinder

| Pane No. | Cyl. No. | | | | Perf. Type EP3 No dot |
|---|---|---|---|---|---|
| UFB56 | B7 | .. | .. | .. | 14·00 |

**Sheet Make-up**

As for £1·30 pane in Booklet No. GI1.

**£1·40 Pane. "Pocket Planner" and William Henry Fox Talbot Booklets FM5/6**

UFB57

Pane of ten 14p. deep blue stamps with one 4 mm. centre phosphor band from £1·40 Pictorial Booklet, Nos. FM5/6

Pane UFB57. Selvedge at left

|  | Perf. Type E |
|---|---|
| UFB57 (containing No. U228 × 10) (5.9.88) | 5·50 |
|   *a*. Phosphor omitted    ..      ..     ..     ..     ..   ..   .. | |

Pane UFB58. Selvedge at right

| UFB58 (containing No. U228 × 10) (5.9.88) | 5·50 |
|---|---|

**Booklet Cylinder Numbers**

Perforation as Type RE. Single pane cylinders

|  |  |  |  |  |  | Perf. Type E |
|---|---|---|---|---|---|---|
| Pane No. | Cyl. No. | Phos. No. |  |  |  | No dot |
| UFB57 | B18 | (B49) | .. | .. | .. | 8·00 |
| UFB58 | B18 | (B49) | .. | .. | .. | 8·00 |
| UFB57 | B18 | (B62) | .. | .. | .. | 8·00 |
| UFB58 | B18 | (B62) | .. | .. | .. | 8·00 |
| UFB57 | B19 | (B62) | .. | .. | .. | 9·00 |
| UFB58 | B19 | (B62) | .. | .. | .. | 9·00 |

**Sheet Make-up**

As for £1·25 panes.

**£1·90 Pane. "Pocket Planner" and William Henry Fox Talbot Booklets FV1/2**

UFB59

Pane of ten 19p. stamps on phosphorised (advanced coated) paper from £1·90 Pictorial Booklet, Nos. FV1/2

Pane UFB59. Selvedge at left

Perf. Type E

UFB59 (containing No. U259 × 10) (5.9.88)                           6·50

Pane UFB60. Selvedge at right

UFB60 (containing No. U259 × 10) (5.9.88)                                    6·50

**Booklet Cylinder Numbers**

Perforation as Type RE. Single pane cylinder

| Pane No. | Cyl. No. | | | | Perf. Type E<br>No dot |
|----------|----------|----|----|----|---------|
| UFB59 | B3 | .. | .. | .. | 10·00 |
| UFB60 | B3 | .. | .. | .. | 10·00 |

**Sheet Make-up**

As for £1·25 panes

**56p. Pane. Barcode Booklet GB3**

UFB61                                    UFB62

Pane of four 14p. stamps with one 4 mm. centre phosphor band from 56p. Barcode Booklet No. GB3. Pane has imperforate horizontal edges

|  |  |  |
|---|---|---|
|  | Perf. Type IEI |  |
| UFB61 (containing No. U228 × 4) (11.10.88) | 3·00 |  |

**Booklet Cylinder Numbers**

| Pane No. | Cyl. Nos. | Phos. No. | | | | Perf. Type IEI No dot |
|---|---|---|---|---|---|---|
| UFB61 | B26 | (B82) | .. | .. | .. | 5·50 |

**Sheet Make-up**

As for 52p. pane in Booklet No. GA1

---

**76p. Pane. Barcode Booklet GD3**

Pane of four 19p. stamps on phosphorised (advanced coated) paper from 76p. Barcode Booklet No. GD3. Pane has imperforate horizontal edges.

|  |  |
|---|---|
|  | Perf. Type IEI |
| UFB62 (containing No. U259 × 4) (11.10.88) | 4·00 |

**Booklet Cylinder Number**

| Pane No. | Cyl. No. | | | | Perf. Type IEI No dot |
|---|---|---|---|---|---|
| UFB62 | B16 | .. | .. | .. | 8·00 |

**Sheet Make-up**

As for 52p. pane in Booklet No. GA1

**£1·08 Pane. Barcode Booklet GF2**

UFB63

Pane of four 27p. chestnut stamps on phosphorised (advanced coated) paper from £1·08 Barcode Booklet No. GF2. Pane has imperforate horizontal edges.

Perf. Type IEI

UFB63 (containing No. U271 × 4) (11.10.88)    4·75

**Booklet Cylinder Number**

| Pane. No. | Cyl. No. | | | | Perf. Type IEI<br>No dot |
|-----------|----------|--|--|--|------------------------|
| UFB63 | B2 | .. | .. | .. | 8·50 |

**Sheet Make-up**
  As for 52p. pane in Booklet No. GA1

**£1·40 Pane. Barcode Booklet GJ3**

UFB64

Pane of ten 14p. deep blue stamps with one 4 mm. centre phosphor band from £1·40 Barcode Booklet No. GJ3. The panes were printed on the Chambon, and later, the Jumelle press. Pane has imperforate horizontal edges.

Perf. Type IEI

UFB64 (containing No. U228 × 10) (11.10.88)    6·00
  *a.* Phosphor omitted    ..    ..    ..    ..    ..    ..    ..    £100

**Booklet Cylinder Numbers**

Single pane cylinders. Chambon printing

|  |  |  |  |  |  | Perf. Type IEI |
|---|---|---|---|---|---|---|
| Pane No. | Cyl. Nos. | Phos. No. |  |  |  | No dot |
| UFB64 | B27 | (B81) | .. | .. | .. | 12·00 |
| UFB64 | B29 | (B81) | .. | .. | .. | 12·00 |
| UFB64 | B30 | (B81) | .. | .. | .. | 12·00 |

Single pane cylinder. Jumelle printing (26.6.89)

| UFB64 | B31 | (B84) | .. | .. | .. | 12·00 |
|---|---|---|---|---|---|---|

**Sheet Make-up**

Chambon press. As for £1·30 pane UFB50.

Jumelle press. Similar to the Chambon printing, but with four vertical columns separated by gutter margins which have short horizontal cutting lines above and below each individual pane. The narrow horizontal gutters between the rows of panes have no extension holes; the only ones seen occur on the panes at the selvedge. Cylinder numbers (boxed) were opposite stamp row one at the ratio of one in five in each of the four vertical columns of the primary sheet.

---

**£1·90 Pane. Barcode Booklet GL3**

UFB65

Pane of ten 19p. stamps on phosphorised (advanced coated) paper from £1·90 Barcode Booklet No. GL3. The panes were printed on the Chambon, and later, the Jumelle press. Pane has imperforate horizontal edges.

|  | Perf. Type IEI |
|---|---|
| UFB65 (containing No. U259 × 10) (11.10.88) | 7·00 |

**Booklet Cylinder Numbers**

Single pane cylinders. Chambon printing

|  |  |  |  |  | Perf. Type IEI |
|---|---|---|---|---|---|
| Pane No. | Cyl. Nos. |  |  |  | No dot |
| UFB65 | B12 | .. | .. | .. | 14·00 |
| UFB65 | B17 | .. | .. | .. | 14·00 |
| UFB65 | B17 | bar | .. | .. | 17·00 |

Single pane cylinder. Jumelle printing (26.6.89)

| UFB65 | B19 | .. | .. | .. | 15·00 |
|---|---|---|---|---|---|

**Sheet Make-up**

Chambon press. As for £1·30 pane UFB50
Jumelle press. As for £1·40 pane UFB64

**56p. Pane. Barcode Booklet GB4**

UFB66                                        UFB67

Pane of four 14p. stamps with one 4 mm. centre phosphor band from 56p. Barcode Booklet No. GB4. Pane has three edges imperforate

|  | Perf. Type IEI |
|---|---|
| UFB66 (containing No. U228 × 4) (24.1.89) | 3·00 |
| a. Phosphor omitted .. .. .. .. .. .. .. | 16·00 |

**Cylinder Numbers and Sheet Make-up**

Cylinder numbers appeared in the bottom margin below the second and third columns. There were six vertical columns each separated by a gutter margin used for the binding selvedge. Each vertical column contained 3 panes but the cylinder number was placed well below the stamps and was trimmed off. Those used were:
B28 and B33, the phosphor cylinder was B83.

**76p. Pane. Barcode Booklet GD4**

Pane of four 19p. stamps on phosphorised (advanced coated) paper from 76p. Barcode Booklet No. GD4. Pane has three edges imperforate.

|  | Perf. Type IEI |
|---|---|
| UFB67 (containing No. U255 × 4) (24.1.89) | 4·00 |

**Cylinder Numbers and Sheet Make-up**

The cylinder numbers were placed in the bottom margin between vertical columns 2/3 but they do not appear in the finished booklets. Those used were:
B13, B20 and B21.
The sheet layout is as described below pane No. UFB66.

**£1 Pane with imperforate vertical sides. Mills Series FH18**

UFB68

Pane of five 20p. (brownish black) stamps on phosphorised (advanced coated) paper and postcode label from £1 Pictorial Booklet No. FH18

| | | Perf. Type IEI |
|---|---|---|
| UFB68 (containing No. U268 × 5) (2.10.89) | | 3·25 |

**Booklet Cylinder Numbers**

| | | | | | Perf. Type IEI |
|---|---|---|---|---|---|
| Pane No. | Cyl. No. | | | | No dot |
| UFB68 | B8 | .. | .. | .. | 6·00 |
| UFB68 | B9 | .. | .. | .. | 7·00 |

**Sheet Make-up**

As Panes UMFB43/4. The primary sheet contained two columns of eight panes with the cylinder pane opposite booklet pane 4 in each column printed on the Chambon press.

**50p. Pane. Aircraft Series FB57**

UFB69

Three 17p. (deep blue) with narrow 3 mm. left band on upper stamp *se-tenant* with label without bands inscribed "Please use the postcode". Between the horizontal pair of 17p. there is a 9·5 mm, wide band to give band at right and band at left. From 50p. Pictorial Booklet, FB57.

|  | Perf. Type E |
|---|---|
| UFB69 (containing Nos. U252, U252*a*, U253) (4.9.90) | 75 |
|   *a*. Phosphor omitted  ..  ..  ..  ..  ..  ..  .. | 30·00 |

**Booklet Cylinder Numbers**

Perforation as Type RE. Single pane cylinders

| | | | | | | Perf. Type E |
|---|---|---|---|---|---|---|
| Pane No. | Cyl. Nos. | Phos. No. | | | | No dot |
| UFB69 | B46 | (B87) | .. | .. | .. | 2·50 |
| UFB69 | B46 | (—) | .. | .. | .. | 10·00 |
| UFB69 | B48 | (—) | .. | .. | .. | 2·50 |

**Sheet Make-up**

As Pane UMFB42 but printed on the Chambon press with the APS rotary perforator. The primary sheet contained three vertical columns of eight panes including a cylinder pane in position four giving a ratio of one in eight.

# SECTION UF

## Machin Decimal Issues

### 1971–90.   Multi-value Coil Strips in Photogravure

#### General Notes

**INTRODUCTION.**   With the introduction of decimal postage stamps it was decided to discontinue issuing single values through automatic coil machines, partly no doubt because of the problems of adapting them when postal rates changed, as was already happening with growing frequency in the pre-decimal period. Naturally the old pre-decimal machines were useless as they could not take the new coinage and they were gradually adapted to take a new 5p. piece and to issue multi-value coil stamps in strips of five low values which could be used in combination to meet the current rates.

After the end of 1975 following substantial increases in postal rates the machines were altered again to take a 10p. piece and the composition of the strip was changed to include at least one copy of the value (or stamps which together make up the value) required to meet the current second class letter rate. The machines issuing the 10p. coil strips were gradually withdrawn and converted for use with the 50p. booklets during 1980.

**CYLINDER VARIETIES.**   Cylinder varieties on multi-value coil stamps will be found listed under the basic sheet stamps.

**SHEET ARRANGEMENT.**   This is as described for the ordinary sideways delivery coils as explained in the General Notes to Section UD.

**CYLINDER NUMBERS.**   The cylinder numbers employed have an R prefix letter and can be identified by reference to the uncut registration sheets in the National Postal Museum.

**PRICES.**   Multi-value coil strips are priced in unmounted mint condition only.

5p. G1/2 Coils

---

#### 1971 (15 FEBRUARY).   STRIP OF FIVE (2p. + ½p. + ½p. + 1p. + 1p.), EACH WITH TWO 9·5 mm. PHOSPHOR BANDS

**A.   ORIGINAL COATED PAPER. GUM ARABIC**

| | | | | | |
|---|---|---|---|---|---|
| UMC1 | ½p. (U47), 1p. (U56) and 2p. (U77) | .. | .. | .. | 2·00 |
| | *a.* Phosphor omitted | .. | .. | .. | .. 30·00 |
| | *b.* One broad band .. | .. | .. | .. | — |

This is also known with silicone coating. These can be faked but genuine strips will show a photogravure screen. *Price* £250.

No. UMC1*a* normally shows the phosphor screen but it also exists with the screen completely omitted. *Price* £350.

**B.   FLUORESCENT COATED PAPER. GUM ARABIC with Silicone Coating** (9.72)

UMC2 (=S.G.X841n)   ½p. (U49), 1p. (U58) and 2p. (U79   ..   ..   .. 2·00

No. UMC2 is known without the silicone coating which was applied as an experiment to counter-act dampness in wet weather affecting coil machines and causing the stamps to stick together.

**C.   FLUORESCENT COATED PAPER. PVAD GUM. Thin Paper** (4.74)

UMC3   ½p. (U50c), 1p. (U59c) and 2p. (U80c)   ..   ..   .. 40·00

**D.   FLUORESCENT COATED PAPER. PVAD GUM. Normal Paper** (4.74)

| | | | | | |
|---|---|---|---|---|---|
| UMC4 | ½p. (U50), 1p. (U59) and 2p. (U80) | .. | .. | .. | 35 |
| (=S.G.X841nEv) | *a.* Phosphor omitted | .. | .. | .. | 9·00 |
| | *b.* One broad band .. | .. | .. | .. | 50·00 |

**Coils**

Sideways delivery and printed in continuous reels

| Code No. | Issued | Number in roll | Face value | Paper/gum | Screen | Perf. Type |
|---|---|---|---|---|---|---|
| G1 | 15.2.71 | 1500 (300 strips) | £15 | OCP/GA | 150 | R(S) |
| G2 | 15.2.71 | 3000 (600 strips) | £30 | OCP/GA | 150 | R(S) |
| G1 | 9.72 | 1500 (300 strips) | £15 | FCP/GA | 150 | R(S) |
| G2 | 9.72 | 3000 (600 strips) | £30 | FCP/GA | 150 | R(S) |
| G2 | 4.74 | 3000 (600 strips) | £30 | FCP/PVAD* | 150 | R(S) |
| G1 | 4.74 | 1500 (300 strips) | £15 | FCP/PVAD | 150 | R |
| G2 | 5.74 | 3000 (600 strips) | £30 | FCP/PVAD | 150 | R |

Coils with the R(S) perforator were printed on the Thrissell press and those with the R perforator were made on the "Jumelle" press. The PVAD stamps on thin paper came from the Thrissell and those on the ordinary paper were from the "Jumelle" press.

*The Thrissell printing on the thinner paper with dextrin gum only occurred on a few coils of G2, presumably due to a shortage of gum arabic paper to complete the old contract, and had the usual "GA" orange-coloured wrappers. The main printing of the G1 and G2 coils on the normal paper with dextrin gum were being printed concurrently and appeared with new buff-coloured wrappers.

**Cylinders Numbers**

½p. R1, R2, R4, R5, R6, R8
1p. R1, R4, R6, R7, R21
2p. R1, R2, R4, R6, R8, R10, R12

It has not been possible to ascribe the above to particular papers and gums with certainty except that it is known that ½p. R6, 1p. R21, 2p. R10 together with phosphor R10 were used with FCP/PVAD. Presumably the ½p. R8 and 2p. R12 were later used with the same paper and gum.

10p. G3 Coil

**1975 (3 DECEMBER).   STRIP OF FIVE (6p. + 2p. + 1p. + ½p. + ½p.), EACH WITH TWO 9·5 mm. PHOSPHOR BANDS**

**A.   FLUORESCENT COATED PAPER. PVAD GUM**

| UMC5 (=S.G.X841q) | ½p. (U50), 1p. (U59), 2p. (U80) and 6p. (U146d) | .. | 80 |
|---|---|---|---|
| | b. One broad band .. | .. .. .. .. .. | 2·50 |

**B.   ORIGINAL COATED PAPER. PVA GUM (3.77)**

| UMC6 | ½p. (U46), 1p. (U55), 2p. (U76) and 6p. (U143c) | .. | 3·50 |
|---|---|---|---|

**Coils**

Sideways delivery and printed in continuous reels on the "Jumelle" press

| Code No. | Issued | Number in roll | Face value | Paper/gum | Screen | Perf. Type |
|---|---|---|---|---|---|---|
| G3 | 3.12.75 | 2500 (500 strips) | £50 | FCP/PVAD | 150 | R |
| G3 | 3.77 | 2500 (500 strips) | £50 | OCP/PVA | 150 | R |

**Cylinder Numbers**

| ½p. | R6 |
|---|---|
| 1p. | R27 |
| 2p. | R10 |
| 6p. | R1 |
| Phosphor | R10 |

10p. G4 Coil

## 1977 (14 DECEMBER). STRIP OF FIVE (7p. + 1p. + 1p. + ½p. + ½p.), EACH WITH ONE 4 mm. PHOSPHOR BAND AT CENTRE. FLUORESCENT COATED PAPER. PVAD GUM

UMC7 (=S.G.X843l) ½p. (U53), 1p. (U61) and 7p. (U154)    ..    ..    ..    55

**Coils**

Sideways delivery and printed in continuous reels

| Code No. | Issued | Number in roll | Face value | Paper/gum | Screen | Perf. Type |
|---|---|---|---|---|---|---|
| G4 | 14.12.77 | 2500 (500 strips) | £50 | FCP/PVAD | 150 | R |

**Cylinder Numbers**

| | 1st ptg. | 2nd ptg. |
|---|---|---|
| ½p. | R9 | R10 |
| 1p. | R31 | R32 |
| 7p. | R7 | R8 |
| Phosphor | R11 | R11 |

10p. G5 Coil

## 1980 (16 JANUARY). STRIP OF FIVE (8p. + 1p. + 1p. + 2 LABELS), THE STAMPS WITH ONE 4 mm. PHOSPHOR BAND AT CENTRE. FLUORESCENT COATED PAPER. PVAD GUM

UMC8 (=S.G.X845m) 1p. (U61) and 8p. (U162) ..    ..    ..    ..    ..    45

**Coils**

Sideways delivery and printed in continuous reels

| Code No. | Issued | Number in roll | Face value | Paper/Gum | Screen | Perf. Type |
|---|---|---|---|---|---|---|
| G5 | 16.1.80 | 1500 (500 strips) | £50 | FCP/PVAD | 150 | R |

**Cylinder Numbers**

| | |
|---|---|
| 1p. | R31 |
| 8p. | R 1 |

**294**

11½p. Reader's Digest first coil

## 1981 (JUNE). STRIP OF FOUR (2½p.+3p.+3p.+3p.) PHOSPHORISED (FLUORESCENT COATED) PAPER. PVAD GUM

UMC9 (=S.G.X929l)   2½p. (U97) and 3p. (U110) ..      ..        ..       ..       ..      75
　　　　　　　*a*. Fluorescent brightener omitted　　..       ..   .. 20·00

　　Coil strip No. UMC9 was produced by the Post Office for the use of a large direct mail marketing firm. Stocks were delivered from 28 May 1981 and a few examples are known postmarked on 22 June 1981. From 2 September 1981 No. UMC9 was available from the Philatelic Bureau. Edinburgh and subsequently, from other Post Office philatelic counters.

　　Nos. UMC9*a* and 10*a* were printed on chalk-surfaced paper without the fluorescent additive which was probably omitted in error.

### Coils

Sideways delivery and printed in continuous reels on the Chambon press

| Code No. | Issued | Number in roll | Face value | Paper/gum | Screen | Perf. Type |
|---|---|---|---|---|---|---|
| Unprinted leader | 2.9.81 | 2800 (700 strips) | £80·50 | Phos. paper | 150 | Comb. |

### Cylinder Numbers

|  | 1st ptg. | 2nd ptg. |
|---|---|---|
| 2½p. | R5 | R6 |
| 3p. | R19 | R19 |

12½p. Reader's Digest second coil

## 1981 (30 DECEMBER). STRIP OF FOUR (½p.+4p.+4p.+4p.) PHOSPHORISED (FLUORESCENT COATED) PAPER. PVAD GUM

UMC10 (=S.G.X924l) ½p. (U54) and 4p. (U127(1))      ..       ..       ..       ..      45
　　　　　　　*a*. Fluorescent brightener omitted　　..       ..       ..

　　Coil strip No. UMC10 was produced by the Post Office for the use of a large direct mail marketing firm and was issued and sold at the Philatelic Bureau and Post Office philatelic counters on 30 December 1981.

　　No. UMC10*a* was printed on chalk-surfaced paper without the fluorescent additive which was probably omitted in error. Perfect unmounted examples are rare (*price* £1800) and care should be exercised when buying. The strips were usually mounted by waxed strips on Reader's Digest promotional cards. The gummed sides show disturbance to some degree (*price* £150).

**Coils**

Sideways delivery and printed in continuous reels on the Chambon press

| Code No. | Issued | Number in roll | Face value | Paper/gum | Perf. Type |
|---|---|---|---|---|---|
| Unprinted leader | 30.12.81 | 2800 (700 strips) | £87·50 | Phos. paper | Comb. |

**Cylinder Numbers**

| | 1st ptg. | 2nd ptg. |
|---|---|---|
| ½p. | R11 | R12 |
| 4p. | R1 | R2 |

13p. Reader's Digest third coil

## 1984 (14 AUGUST).　STRIP OF FOUR (1p.+4p.+4p.+4p.)

**A. PHOSPHORISED (FLUORESCENT COATED) PAPER. PVAD GUM**

| UMC11 | 1p. (U63) and 4p. (U127) (2) | .. | .. | .. | .. | 40 |
|---|---|---|---|---|---|---|

**B. PHOSPHORISED (ADVANCED COATED) PAPER. (3.88)**

| UMC12 (=S.G.X925l) | 1p. (U64) and 4p. (U128).. | .. | .. | .. | .. | 20 |
|---|---|---|---|---|---|---|

**Coils**

Sideways delivery and printed in continuous reels on the Halley press

| Code No. | Issued | Number in roll | Face value | Paper/gum | Perf. Type |
|---|---|---|---|---|---|
| Unprinted leader | 14.8.84 | 2800 (700 strips) | £91 | Phos. paper | Comb. |
| Unprinted leader | 3.88 | 2800 (700 strips) | £91 | ACP/PVAD | Comb. |

**Cylinder Numbers**

Both printings

| 1p. | R35 |
|---|---|
| 4p. | R4 |

14p. Reader's Digest fourth coil

## 1988 (5 SEPTEMBER).  STRIP OF FOUR (2p.+4p.+4p.+4p.)
## PHOSPHORISED (ADVANCED COATED) PAPER. PVAD GUM

UMC13 (=S.G.X928l) 2p. (U84) and 4p. (U128) ..    ..    ..    ..    ..    90

**Coils**

Sideways delivery and printed in continuous reels

| Code No. | Issued | Number in roll | Face value | Paper/gum | Perf. Type |
|---|---|---|---|---|---|
| Unprinted leader | 5.9.88 | 2800 (700 strips) | £98 | Phos. paper | Comb. |

**Cylinder Numbers**

2p.  R1
4p.  R4

15p. Reader's Digest fifth coil

## 1989 (10 OCTOBER).  STRIP OF FOUR (4p.+4p.+4p.+3p.)
## PHOSPHORISED (ADVANCED COATED) PAPER. PVAD GUM

UMC14 (=S.G.X930cl)3p. (U111b) and 4p. (U132)    ..    ..    ..    ..    25

**Coils**

Sideways delivery and printed in continuous reels

| Code No. | Issued | Number in roll | Face value | Paper/Gum | Perf. Type |
|---|---|---|---|---|---|
| — | 10.10.89 | 2800 (700 strips) | £105 | Phos. paper | Comb. |

**Cylinder Numbers**

3p.  R21
4p.  R5

17p. Reader's Digest sixth coil

---

## 1990 (27 NOVEMBER). STRIP OF FOUR (4p.+4p.+4p.+5p.) PHOSPHORISED (ADVANCED COATED) PAPER. PVAD GUM

UMC15 (=S.G.X933l) 4p. (U132) and 5p. (U140)..    ..    ..    ..    ..    25

**Coils**

Sideways delivery and printed in continuous reels on the Chambon press

| Code No. | Issued | Number in roll | Face value | Paper/Gum | Perf. Type |
|---|---|---|---|---|---|
| — | 27.11.90 | 2800 (700 strips) | £119 | Phos. paper | Comb. |

**Cylinder Numbers**

4p.   R5
5p.   R1

# SECTION UG

# Machin Decimal Issues

## 1980–90. Printed by Lithography

## General Notes

**INTRODUCTION.** Following a decision by the Post Office to extend the range of definitive stamps, contracts were placed with John Waddington Ltd. and The House of Questa to print sheet stamps in the Machin design using the lithographic process. The 4p. and 75p. values were issued on 30 January 1980 and these were followed by the 2p., 5p. and 20p. issued on 21 May.

The third printer, Walsall Security Printers Ltd., were chosen by the British Post Office to supply booklet stamps printed by lithography. On 25 April 1988 a £1 booklet was issued containing 14p. and 19p. values with phosphor bands. These differ from the similar Questa values by having a horizontal perforation of 14 instead of Questa's 15. Further new values from Walsall followed in 1989 (29p.) and 1990 (31p.), both for the overseas postcard rate.

**ARRANGEMENT.** Following the style of the Machin photogravure section, each value is dealt with in turn irrespective of the printer concerned. The present value range is 2p. to 75p. from sheets and booklets only. No stamps in this section come from coils. Withdrawal dates are stated where known.

**PRINTING PROCESS.** The method is based on the fact that grease repels water but will accept printer's ink. A camera is used to separate the colours of the artwork. In order to achieve the necessary dot make-up of the printed image the colour(s) need to be screened to 300 dots in every linear inch, or 90,000 dots in each square inch. The next stage in the process involves the use of a step-and-repeat camera to photograph the image into a flexible zinc or aluminium plate which, after processing, is curved around a cylinder for use in a rotary press. The revolving, inked plate is brought in close contact with a "blanket" roller which receives a reversed impression of the original plate of stamp images. These are transferred in turn by "offset" contact with the paper which is fed by the "impression" cylinder.

**PRINTERS AND SHEET ARRANGEMENTS.** The stamps were printed in double pane sheets, i.e. 400 stamps consisting of two panes each of 200 stamps (20 horizontal rows of ten stamps). The two panes were guillotined before issue. Waddington printings followed a similar style to the photogravure issues by adopting the no dot and dot marking after plate numbers. The left pane was the dot and right-hand pane no dot. Questa plate numbers are in chronological order with odd numbers representing the left-hand pane and even numbers the right.

**PERFORATION.** Initially the stamps were perforated 14 but during 1984 Questa changed the gauge to 15 × 14. The 4p. and 20p. printed by Waddington remained 14, so that these values perforated 15 × 14 are Questa printings. Initial printings were perforation Type L and details are given in Appendix I. Direction of the feed was from the left giving plate blocks with odd numbers an imperforate left margin. Later the direction of feed changed to the right side and this gave both even and odd numbered plate blocks with a side margin perforated through. This is described as Type L(P) in the listings.

The issues from Walsall have come only from booklets and these are perforated 14. They have one or two adjacent sides imperforate as shown in the illustrations of the litho-printed booklet panes. The price quoted covers any combination of imperforate side(s).

**PHOSPHORISED PAPER.** This paper can usually be defined as fluorescent coated and advanced coated by the use of an ultra-violet lamp. The fluorescent coated paper has a dull appearance and the advanced coated paper is rather brighter. It is helpful to look at the unprinted area or sheet margin when trying to assess brightness. We use the description original coated paper to describe the 5p. light violet where the response to u.v. is very dull. This stamp does not exist on advanced coated paper and therefore this is helpful in establishing the difference between original and fluorescent coated papers. The 5p. claret perforated 15 × 14 only exists on the fluorescent and advanced coated paper. Used examples cannot be accurately identified as water on the printed surface of the stamp destroys the fluorescent property in the coating.

**MACHIN HEAD.** The head types used in this section have a clear similarity to those on the photogravure stamps. The process of lithography is, however, very different from photogravure and, although some details agree on certain values, it is clear that as each issue appears the printers have employed their skills to improve on their original attempts to obtain some visual parity with stamps printed using the photogravure process. It must be emphasised that the photogravure types have been adapted for lithography and are not exact replicas in every detail.

The following list shows that only head type F1 has been employed for both solid and light backgrounds.

**Check List of Machin Issues Printed in Lithography**

| Value | Spec. Number | Head Type | Background | Printer | Source |
|---|---|---|---|---|---|
| 2p. | UG1/3 | B | Solid | Questa | Sheets |
| 2p. | UG4 | F1 | Solid | Questa | Sheets |
| 4p. | UG5/6 | B | Solid | Waddington | Sheets |
| 4p. | UG7 | F1 | Solid | Questa | Sheets |
| 5p. | UG8/12 | C | Gradated | Questa | Sheets |
| 13p. | UG13/15 | G | Light | Questa | Booklet (DX9) |
| 14p. | UG16 | F1 | Solid | Questa | Booklets (GJ2, 4) |
| 14p. | UG17 | F2 | Solid | Walsall | Booklet (FH16) |
| 18p. | UG21/2 | F1 | Solid | Questa | Booklet (DX9) |
| 19p. | UG23 | F1 | Solid | Questa | Booklets (GL2, 4) |
| 19p. | UG24 | F2 | Solid | Walsall | Booklet (FH16) |
| 20p. | UG25/6 | E | Light | Waddington | Sheets |
| 20p. | UG27 | F1 | Light | Questa | Sheets |
| 22p. | UG28 | F1 | Solid | Questa | Booklet (DX9) |
| 29p. | UG32/3 | F2 | Solid | Walsall | Booklets (GG1/2) |
| 31p. | UG34 | F2 | Solid | Walsall | Booklet (GH1) |
| 34p. | UG35 | F1 | Solid | Questa | Booklet (DX9) |
| 75p. | UG41/4 | B | Solid | Questa | Sheets |
| 75p. | UG45 | F1 | Solid | Questa | Sheets |

**Value Types.** It is interesting to note that, as in the case of the stamps printed in photogravure, the litho stamps continue to evolve with first wide and then narrower figures of value. These are clearly different and are allocated basic numbers in the listings. The values which occur with both wide and narrow figures are 2p., 4p., 20p. and 75p.

**PLATE BLOCKS.** We give one entry and price for even numbered plate number blocks with perforated left margin. A full width row of ten stamps would be required to establish whether it was from perforator L or the later, perforator L(P). The right-hand selvedge would be perforated through, or in the case of perforator L(P), imperforate.

| Head B | Head C |
|---|---|

| Two curved shadows in hair and pearls irregular (one missing) | One curved shadow in hair and pearls regular |
|---|---|

Head E

One curved shadow in hair, white pearls and jewels. The nose outline curved

Head F1

Head F1 on light background. Two curved shadows in hair and pearls are shaded. The nose outline pointed with less shading under the nostril

Head F1

Head F1 on solid background used by Questa

Head F2

Used by Walsall. Distinct separation to the jewels on the back of the crown

**301**

Head G

Head Type G was used by Questa in the £5
Story of the Financial Times booklet.
Strengthened outline at back of hair, collar and
front of dress

**SHEET MARKINGS.**

Waddington Plate Number          Plate Number and Questa Logo

**Plate Number.** Sheet plate numbers on the 4p. and 20p. printed by Waddington occurred first above vertical row 8 in the top margin so that listing blocks of 8 was necessary. Later the numbers were placed in the left margin opposite R. 18/1, similar to Harrison cylinder blocks. The blocks of 8 included the Waddington logo above row 7. The first plate number at left relates to the Machin head and the second to the background. The first empty box contained the phosphor number which was synchronised. The change to phosphorised paper in November 1981 ended the brief period of phosphor bands on Waddington printings and no stamp printed by Questa had phosphor bands. Late in 1983 Waddington changed the position of the plate numbers to the left margin opposite R. 18/1. Questa did the same, changing from the original arrangement of placing the numbers in the right-hand margin opposite rows 1/10 and 20/10.

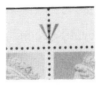

Waddington marginal rules and arrow at foot        Questa arrow at top

**Marginal Arrows.** Marginal rules set above the arrow are illustrated and they occur only on Waddington sheets. Questa sheets show a vertical band, in the colour of the stamp, between the double pane sheet which acts as a guide when the sheet is cut into Post Office size sheets of 200 stamps. The arrows are placed four times in the margin of each sheet in the same position as the Harrison printings. The arrows indicate the division when the sheet is separated into blocks of 50 (5 × 10).

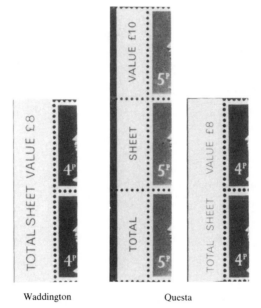

Waddington        Questa

**Total Sheet Values.** These are similar to Harrison and as described in the Notes in Section UD. The inscription reads up at left and down at right being opposite rows 5/6 and 15/16 at both sides of the sheet. The original position of this inscription on Questa printings was opposite rows 6/8 and 16/18 but this was changed when the plate numbers were placed opposite R. 18/1 at left instead of the right-hand margin.

**MINOR CONSTANT FLAWS.** Numerous minor flaws caused by specks of dust settling on the printing plate and preventing the ink from reaching the area appear as white inkless rings and are known as litho "ring" flaws. Minor flecks of colour are similarly caused. As such flaws only affect part of a printing and cannot be regarded as constant we have decided not to record them.

# Type U6 as illustrated in Section UD

## 2p. Emerald-green   (1980–86)

**Two Value Types**

Type I.  Wide figure (Nos. UG1/3)
Type II. Narrow figure

I       II

**Printed by Questa**

**1980 (21 MAY).   PERF. 14. PHOSPHORISED (FLUORESCENT COATED) PAPER. TYPE I. PVAD GUM**

UG1 (=S.G.X1000)   Emerald-green   ..    ..    ..    ..    ..    ..    20    20

**Plate Numbers (Blocks of Six)**
Double Pane Plates
Perforation Type L

A. Plate Nos. in right margin

| Pl. No. | | | | Row 1 | Row 20 | Pl. No. | | | | Row 1 | Row 20 |
|---|---|---|---|---|---|---|---|---|---|---|---|
| 1 | .. | .. | .. | 1·10 | 1·10 | 4 | .. | .. | ... | 2·25 | 2·25 |
| 2 | .. | .. | .. | 1·10 | 1·10 | 5 | .. | .. | .. | 1·50 | 1·50 |
| 3 | .. | .. | .. | 2·00 | 3·00 | 6 | .. | .. | .. | 1·25 | 1·25 |

Printings from plates 1 and 2 occur with a wide bottom margin showing 8 extension holes. *Prices for plate blocks of 6 from Plate 1 £50, Plate 2 £30.*
Printings from plates 5 and 6 are found perforated from the gummed side. *Prices for plate blocks of 6, Plate 5 £5, Plate 6 £8.*

Perforation Type L

B. Plate Nos. in left margin

| Pl. No. | | | | Row 18 |
|---|---|---|---|---|
| 7 | .. | .. | .. | 1·75 |
| 8 | .. | .. | .. | 1·75 |

**1984 (10 JULY).   PERF. 15 × 14. PHOSPHORISED PAPER. TYPE I. PVAD GUM**
**A. FLUORESCENT COATED PAPER.**
UG2         Emerald-green   ..    ..    ..    ..    ..    ..    30

**Plate Numbers (Blocks of Six)**
Double Pane Plates
Perforation Type L

| Pl. No. | | | (I) | Pl. No. | | | (P) |
|---|---|---|---|---|---|---|---|
| 7 | .. | .. | 1·50 | 8 | .. | .. | 1·50 |
| 9 | .. | .. | 1·50 | 10 | .. | .. | 2·00 |
| 11 | .. | .. | 1·50 | 12 | .. | .. | 1·60 |

**B. ADVANCED COATED PAPER** (25.2.86)
UG3 (=S.G.X1000a)   Emerald-green   ..    ..    ..    ..    ..    ..    30    20

**304**

**Plate Numbers (Blocks of Six)**
Double Pane Plates
Perforation Type L

| Pl. No. | | | (I) | Pl. No. | | | (P) |
|---|---|---|---|---|---|---|---|
| 11 | .. | .. | 1·50 | 12 | .. | .. | 1·50 |
| 13 | .. | .. | 1·50 | 14 | .. | .. | 1·50 |
| 15 | .. | .. | 1·50 | 16 | .. | .. | 1·50 |
| 17 | .. | .. | 40·00 | 18 | .. | .. | 90·00 |
| 19 | .. | .. | 1·75 | 20 | .. | .. | 1·75 |

Printings from plates 15 and 16 are found perforated from the gummed side. *Prices for plate blocks of 6, Plate 15 £8, Plate 16 £8.*

# 2p. Bright Green and Deep Green   (1988)
**Printed by Questa**

**1988 (23 FEBRUARY). COLOUR CHANGED. PERF. 15 × 14. PHOS-PHORISED (ADVANCED COATED) PAPER. TYPE II. PVAD (CLEAR) GUM**
UG4 (=S.G.X1001)    Bright green and deep green    ..    ..    ..    ..    25    25

This stamp was printed on paper supplied by Henry Leigh Slater which had PVAD dextrin gum with the greenish dye omitted.

**Plate Numbers (Blocks of Six)**
Double Pane Plates
Perforation Type L

| Pl. No. | | | (I) |
|---|---|---|---|
| 1, 1 | .. | .. | 3·00 |

Perforation Type L(P)

| Pl. No. | | | (P) | Pl. No. | | | (P) |
|---|---|---|---|---|---|---|---|
| 1, 1 | .. | .. | 4·25 | 2, 2 | .. | .. | 3·00 |

**WITHDRAWN.** No. UG1, 11.81 but put on sale again at the Philatelic Bureau in May 1983 and sold out or withdrawn April 1985. No. UG2 withdrawn 24.2.87; No. UG3, 22.2.89 and No. UG4, 11.4.89.

# 4p. Greenish Blue   (1980–86)

**Two Value Types**

Type I. Waddington. Wide figure with long thin crossbar
Type II. Questa. Redrawn figure with short crossbar

I         II

## Printed by Waddington

**1980 (30 JANUARY).   PERF. 14. TWO 9·5 mm. PHOSPHOR BANDS (applied typo). TYPE I. FLUORESCENT COATED PAPER. PVA GUM**

UG5 (=S.G.X996)     Greenish blue     ..    ..    ..    ..    ..    ..    20    25
                   *a.* Imperforate between stamp and right margin    ..
                   *b.* Phosphor omitted    ..    ..    ..    ..    ..

**Plate Numbers (Blocks of Eight)**

Double Pane Plates
Perforation Type L
Plate Nos. in top margin

| Pl. Nos. | Phos. No. | | | | Pl. Nos. | Phos. No. | | | |
|---|---|---|---|---|---|---|---|---|---|
| 1, 1* | 1 | .. | .. | 1·50 | 4A, 3B No dot | 4 | .. | .. | 2·25 |
| 1, 1 No dot | 2 | .. | .. | 1·50 | 4A, 4B Dot | 3 | .. | .. | 4·00 |
| 2, 1* | 1 | .. | .. | 3·50 | 4A, 4B No dot | 4 | .. | .. | 4·00 |
| 2, 1 No dot | 2 | .. | .. | 10·00 | 5A, 4B Dot | 3 | .. | .. | 2·00 |
| 3A, 3B Dot | 3 | .. | .. | 2·50 | 5A, 4B No dot | 4 | .. | .. | 2·00 |
| 3A, 3B No dot | 4 | .. | .. | 2·50 | 6A, 4B Dot | 3 | .. | .. | 22·00 |
| 4A, 3B Dot | 3 | .. | .. | 2·25 | 6A, 4B No dot | 4 | .. | .. | 12·00 |

*The dot was not engraved but the different phosphor number distinguishes the printing.

**1981   (NOVEMBER).   PERF.   14.   PHOSPHORISED   (FLUORESCENT COATED) PAPER. TYPE I. PVAD GUM**

UG6 (=S.G.X997)     Greenish blue     ..    ..    ..    ..    ..    ..    25    20

**Plate Numbers (Blocks of Eight)**

Double Pane Plates
Perforation Type L

A. Plate Nos. in top margin

| Pl. Nos. | | | | No dot | Dot |
|---|---|---|---|---|---|
| 7A, 6B | .. | .. | .. | £850 | £300 |
| 8A, 6B | .. | .. | .. | 2·00 | 2·00 |
| 8A, 7B | .. | .. | .. | 55·00 | 55·00 |
| 9A, 7B | .. | .. | .. | 2·00 | 2·00 |
| 10A, 8B | .. | .. | .. | 2·25 | 2·00 |
| 10A, 9B | .. | .. | .. | 5·50 | 4·25 |
| 11A, 9B | .. | .. | .. | 2·00 | 2·00 |

**Plate Numbers (Blocks of Six)**

B. Plate Nos. in left margin opposite row 18

| Pl. Nos. | | | | No dot | Dot |
|---|---|---|---|---|---|
| 12A, 10B | .. | .. | .. | 2·25 | 1·75 |
| 13A, 11B | .. | .. | .. | 8·00 | 8·00 |
| 14A, 11B | .. | .. | .. | 2·00 | 2·00 |
| 15A, 11B | .. | .. | .. | 1·75 | 1·75 |
| 16A, 12B | .. | .. | .. | 2·00 | 2·00 |

**Printed by Questa**

**1986 (13 MAY).   PERF. 15 × 14. PHOSPHORISED (ADVANCED COATED) PAPER. TYPE II. PVAD GUM**

UG7 (=S.G.X1002)   Greenish blue   ..   ..   ..   ..   ..   ..   30   20

**Plate Numbers (Blocks of Six)**

Double Pane Plates
Perforation Type L

| Pl. No. | | | (I) | Pl. No. | | | (P) |
|---|---|---|---|---|---|---|---|
| 1 | .. | .. | 1·75 | 2 | .. | .. | 1·75 |
| 3 | .. | .. | 1·75 | 4 | .. | .. | 1·75 |
| 5 | .. | .. | 1·75 | 6 | .. | .. | 1·75 |

Perforation Type L(P)

| Pl. No. | | | (P) |
|---|---|---|---|
| 7 | .. | .. | 1·60 |
| 8 | .. | .. | 1·60 |

**WITHDRAWN**   No. UG5, 31.12.82; No. UG6, 12.5.87 and No. UG7, 11.4.89

# 5p. Light Violet   (1980–81)

**Printed by Questa**

**1980 (21 MAY).   PERF. 14. PHOSPHORISED PAPER**

**A. FLUORESCENT COATED PAPER. PVAD GUM**

UG8 (=S.G.X1003)  Light violet  .. .. .. .. .. .. .. 40   20
              *a*. Imperforate between stamp and right margin  .. .. £400

**Plate Numbers (Blocks of Six)**

Double Pane Plates
Perforation Type L
Plate Nos. in right margin

| Pl. No. | | | | Row 1 | Row 20 | Pl. No. | | | | Row 1 | Row 20 |
|---|---|---|---|---|---|---|---|---|---|---|---|
| 1 | .. | .. | .. | 5·00 | 5·00 | 3 | .. | .. | .. | 2·25 | 2·25 |
| 2 | .. | .. | .. | 18·00 | 18·00 | 4 | .. | .. | .. | 2·50 | 2·50 |

**B. ORIGINAL COATED PAPER. PVA GUM** (10.81)

UG9 .. Light violet .. .. .. .. .. .. .. 55

**Plate Numbers (Blocks of Six)**

Double Pane Plates
Perforation Type L
Plate Nos. in right margin

| Pl. No. | | | | Row 1 | Row 20 |
|---|---|---|---|---|---|
| 5 | .. | .. | .. | 3·00 | 3·00 |
| 6 | .. | .. | .. | 3·00 | 3·00 |

**WITHDRAWN**  Nos. UG8/9, 26.1.83

# 5p. Claret   (1982–86)

**Printed by Questa**

**1982 (27 JANUARY).   COLOUR CHANGED. PERF. 14. PHOSPHORISED (FLUORESCENT COATED) PAPER. PVAD GUM**

UG10 (=S.G.X1004)  Claret.. .. .. .. .. .. .. .. 40   20

**Plate Numbers (Blocks of Six)**

Double Pane Plates
Perforation Type L

A. Plate Nos. in right margin

| Pl. No. | | | | Row 1 | Row 20 | Pl. No. | | | | Row 1 | Row 20 |
|---|---|---|---|---|---|---|---|---|---|---|---|
| 1 | .. | .. | .. | 2·50 | 2·50 | 3 | .. | .. | .. | 2·75 | 2·75 |
| 2 | .. | .. | .. | 2·50 | 2·50 | 4 | .. | .. | .. | 4·25 | 4·25 |

B. Plate Nos. in left margin opposite row 18

| Pl. No. | | | | (I) | | Pl. No. | | | | (P) | |
|---|---|---|---|---|---|---|---|---|---|---|---|
| 1 | .. | .. | .. | 3·00 | | 2 | .. | .. | .. | 2·25 | |
| 3 | .. | .. | .. | 3·00 | | 4 | .. | .. | .. | 2·25 | |

**1984 (21 FEBRUARY).   PERF. 15 × 14. PHOSPHORISED PAPER. PVAD GUM**

**A. FLUORESCENT COATED PAPER**

UG11 .. Claret.. .. .. .. .. .. .. .. 25

**Plate Numbers (Blocks of Six)**

Double Pane Plates
Perforation Type L

| Pl. No. | | | (I) | Pl. No. | | | (P) |
|---|---|---|---|---|---|---|---|
| 5 | .. | .. | 1·75 | 6 | .. | .. | 1·75 |
| 7 | .. | .. | 3·00 | 8 | .. | .. | 1·75 |
| 9 | .. | .. | 1·75 | 10 | .. | .. | 3·00 |
| 11 | .. | .. | 1·75 | 12 | .. | .. | 1·75 |
| 13 | .. | .. | 10·00 | 14 | .. | .. | 10·00 |

Perforation Type L(P)

| Pl. No. | | | (P) | Pl. No. | | | (P) |
|---|---|---|---|---|---|---|---|
| 25 | .. | .. | 5·00 | 26 | .. | .. | 5·00 |

**B. ADVANCED COATED PAPER** (25.2.86)

UG12 (=S.G.X1004a) Claret..    ..   ..   ..   ..   ..   ..   ..    25    25

**Plate Numbers (Blocks of Six)**

Double Pane Plates
Perforation Type L

| Pl. No. | | | (I) | Pl. No. | | | (P) |
|---|---|---|---|---|---|---|---|
| 13 | .. | .. | 1·75 | 14 | .. | .. | 1·75 |
| 15 | .. | .. | 1·75 | 16 | .. | .. | 1·75 |
| 17 | .. | .. | 1·75 | 18 | .. | .. | 1·75 |
| 21 | .. | .. | — | | | | |
| 23 | .. | .. | — | | | | |

Perforation Type L(P)

| Pl. No. | | | (P) | Pl. No. | | | (P) |
|---|---|---|---|---|---|---|---|
| 19 | .. | .. | 4·00 | 24 | .. | .. | 5·00 |
| 20 | .. | .. | 5·50 | 25 | .. | .. | 1·60 |
| 21 | .. | .. | 1·75 | 26 | .. | .. | 1·60 |
| 22 | .. | .. | 1·75 | 27 | .. | .. | 2·00 |
| 23 | .. | .. | 1·75 | 28 | .. | .. | 2·00 |

**WITHDRAWN**   No. UG10, 21.2.85; No. UG11, 24.2.87 and No. UG12, 11.4.89

# 13p. Pale Chestnut   (1988)

**Printed by Questa**

**1988 (9 FEBRUARY). PERF. 15 × 14. ONE 4 mm. CENTRE BAND. FLUORESCENT COATED PAPER. PVA GUM**

£5 Story of *The Financial Times* booklet pane UHP2
UG13 (=S.G.X1005) Pale chestnut..   ..   ..   ..   ..   ..   ..    70    70

**1988 (9 FEBRUARY). PERF. 15 × 14. ONE NARROW BAND AT LEFT. FLUORESCENT COATED PAPER. PVA GUM**

£5 Story of *The Financial Times* booklet *se-tenant* pane UHP3
UG14 (=S.G.X1006Ea) Pale chestnut   ..   ..   ..   ..   ..    60    60

**1988 (9 FEBRUARY). PERF. 15 × 14. ONE NARROW BAND AT RIGHT. FLUORESCENT COATED PAPER. PVA GUM**

£5 Story of *The Financial Times* booklet *se-tenant* pane UHP3
UG15 (=S.G.X1006) Pale chestnut..   ..   ..   ..   ..   ..    60    60

# 14p. Deep Blue   (1988–89)

**Printed by Questa**

**1988 (11 OCTOBER).   PERF. 15 × 14.  ONE 4 mm. CENTRE PHOSPHOR BAND SHORT AT TOP AND BOTTOM. FLUORESCENT COATED PAPER. PVA GUM**

£1·40 booklet pane ULP1
UG16 (=S.G.X1007)   Deep blue   ..      ..      ..      ..      ..      ..      ..      60      50

**Printed by Walsall**

**1989 (25 APRIL).   PERF. 14.   ONE NARROW BAND AT RIGHT. FLUORESCENT COATED PAPER. PVA GUM**

£1 booklet pane UMLP1
UG17 (=S.G.X1019)   Deep blue   ..      ..      ..      ..      ..      ..      ..      1·00    1·00
                    *a*. Phosphor omitted      ..      ..      ..      ..      ..      £200
                    *b*. Error. Two bands      ..      ..      ..      ..      ..      4·00
                    *c*. Error. Band at right short at top      ..      ..      ..      3·00
  No. UG17 is imperforate at left.

# 18p. Deep Olive-grey   (1988)

**Printed by Questa**

**1988 (9 FEBRUARY).   PERF. 15 × 14.  PHOSPHORISED (ADVANCED COATED) PAPER. PVAD GUM**

£5 Story of *The Financial Times* booklet panes UHP1 and UHP4
UG21 (=S.G.X1009)   Deep olive-grey   ..      ..      ..      ..      ..      ..      60      60

**1988 (9 FEBRUARY).   PERF. 15 × 14.  TWO 9·5 mm. PHOSPHOR BANDS. FLUORESCENT COATED PAPER. PVA GUM**

£5 Story of *The Financial Times* booklet *se-tenant* pane UHP3
UG22 (=S.G.X1010)   Deep olive-grey   ..      ..      ..      ..      ..      ..      3·00    2·00

# 19p. Bright Orange-red    (1988–89)

### Printed by Questa

**1988 (11 OCTOBER). PERF. 15 × 14. PHOSPHORISED (ADVANCED COATED) PAPER. PVA GUM**

£1·90 booklet pane ULP2
UG23 (=S.G.X1011)   Bright orange-red   ..      ..      ..      ..      ..      ..      90      75


### Printed by Walsall

**1989 (25 APRIL). PERF. 14. TWO 9.5 mm. PHOSPHOR BANDS. FLUORESCENT COATED PAPER. PVA GUM**

£1·00 booklet pane UMLP1
UG24 (=S.G.X1020)   Bright orange-red   ..      ..      ..      ..      ..      ..      1·00      1·00
                    *a*. Left band short at top (R. 3/1)..      ..      ..      ..      1·00
                    *b*. Phosphor omitted      ..      ..      ..      ..      ..      £150
                    *c*. Error. Two bands short at bottom      ..      ..      ..      2·50

No. UG24 is imperforate at right and No. UG24*a* imperforate at left. No. UG24 with right band clear of the imperforate edge was due to wide trimming.

No. UG24*b* (phosphor omitted) is known imperforate at left or right and our price is for the cheapest version. The imperf at left with phosphor omitted is very scarce and is worth twice the amount quoted.

# 20p. Dull Purple    (1980–86)

**Two Value Types**

Type I.  Waddington. Broad 0.
Type II.  Questa. Narrow 0 and thinned at top and
bottom.

I                II

**Printed by Waddington**

**1980 (21 MAY).   PERF. 14. TWO 9·5 mm. PHOSPHOR BANDS (applied typo).
FLUORESCENT COATED PAPER. TYPE I. PVA GUM**

UG25 (=S.G.X998)    Dull purple  ..     ..     ..     ..     ..     ..     .. 1·00     40

**Plate Numbers (Blocks of Eight)**

Double Pane Plates
Perforation Type L
Plate Nos. in top margin

| Pl. Nos. | Phos. No. | | |
|---|---|---|---|
| 1A, 1B Dot | 1 | .. | .. 7·00 |
| 1A, 1B No dot | 2 | .. | .. 7·00 |
| 2A, 2B Dot | 1 | .. | .. 12·00 |
| 2A, 2B No dot | 2 | .. | .. 12·00 |
| 3A, 2B Dot | 1 | .. | .. 7·50 |
| 3A, 2B No dot | 2 | .. | .. 7·50 |
| 4A, 3B Dot | 5 | .. | .. £1500 |
| 4A, 3B No dot | 6 | .. | .. — |
| 4A, 4B Dot | 5 | .. | .. 7·00 |
| 4A, 4B No dot | 6 | .. | .. 7·00 |
| 4A, 5B Dot | 5 | .. | .. 6·50 |
| 4A, 5B No dot | 6 | .. | .. 6·50 |
| 4A, 6B Dot | 5 | .. | .. 75·00 |
| 4A, 6B No dot | 6 | .. | .. 75·00 |

**1981   (NOVEMBER).   PERF.   14.   PHOSPHORISED   (FLUORESCENT
COATED) PAPER. TYPE I. PVAD GUM**

UG26
(=S.G.X999)    (1)  Dull purple  ..     ..     ..     ..     ..     ..     .. 1·00     40
                (2)  Blackish brown and dull purple (Pls. 22A, 14B; 23A, 15B)   1·25

**Plate Numbers (Blocks of Eight)**

Double Pane Plates
Perforation Type L
Plate Nos. in top margin

| Pl. Nos. | | | No dot | Dot |
|---|---|---|---|---|
| 5A, 6B | .. | .. | .. 7·00 | 7·00 |
| 6A, 6B | .. | .. | .. 7·00 | 7·00 |
| 6A, 7B | .. | .. | .. 9·00 | 55·00 |
| 7A, 7B | .. | .. | .. 75·00 | 70·00 |
| 8A, 8B | .. | .. | .. 10·00 | 10·00 |
| 9A, 8B | .. | .. | .. 80·00 | 42·00 |
| 10A, 9B | .. | .. | .. 7·00 | 7·00 |
| 11A, 9B | .. | .. | .. 7·00 | 7·00 |
| 12A, 9B | .. | .. | .. 27·00 | 12·00 |
| 13A, 10B | .. | .. | .. 6·50 | 6·50 |
| 14A, 10B | .. | .. | .. 6·50 | 6·50 |
| 15A, 10B | .. | .. | .. 20·00 | 30·00 |

**Plate Numbers (Blocks of Six)**

Double Pane Plates
Plate Nos. in left margin opposite row 18

| Pl. Nos. | | | | No dot | Dot |
|---|---|---|---|---|---|
| 16A, 11B | .. | .. | .. | 5·50 | 5·50 |
| 17A, 11B | .. | .. | .. | 16·00 | 5·50 |
| 18A, 12B | .. | .. | .. | 5·50 | 5·50 |
| 19A, 12B | .. | .. | .. | 16·00 | 9·00 |
| 20A, 12B | .. | .. | .. | 5·50 | 5·50 |
| 20A, 13B | .. | .. | .. | 6·50 | 6·50 |
| 21A, 13B | .. | .. | .. | 8·50 | 6·50 |
| 22A, 13B | .. | .. | .. | 6·00 | 6·00 |
| 22A, 14B (Shade 1) | | .. | .. | 7·00 | 7·00 |
| 22A, 14B (Shade 2) | | .. | .. | 8·00 | 8·00 |
| 23A, 15B | .. | .. | .. | 8·00 | 8·00 |

Although there are a range of minor shades in the above printings, shades (1) and (2) were a deliberate attempt to improve contrast between the Machin head and background. The stamps printed from plates 23A, 15B are all shade (2) but plates 22A, 14B exist in both the listed shades.

**Printed by Questa**

**1986 (13 MAY). PERF. 15 × 14. PHOSPHORISED (ADVANCED COATED) PAPER. TYPE II. PVAD GUM**
UG27 (=S.G.X1012)   Dull purple ..    ..    ..    ..    ..    ..    ..   1·00   70

**Plate Numbers (Blocks of Six)**

Double Pane Plates
Perforation Type L

| Pl. No. | | | (I) | Pl. No. | | | (P) |
|---|---|---|---|---|---|---|---|
| 1, 1 | .. | .. | 5·00 | 9, 9 | .. | .. | 40·00 |
| 3, 3 | .. | .. | 40·00 | 2, 2 | .. | .. | 5·00 |
| 5, 5 | .. | .. | 5·00 | 4, 4 | .. | .. | 28·00 |
| 7, 7 | .. | .. | 6·00 | 6, 6 | .. | .. | 5·00 |

Perforation Type L(P)

| Pl. No. | | | (P) | Pl. No. | | | (P) |
|---|---|---|---|---|---|---|---|
| 7, 7 | .. | .. | 18·00 | 13, 13 | .. | .. | 6·00 |
| 8, 8 | .. | .. | 5·00 | 14, 14 | .. | .. | 7·50 |
| 9, 9 | .. | .. | 7·00 | 15, 15 | .. | .. | 5·00 |
| 10, 10 | .. | .. | 7·00 | 16, 16 | .. | .. | 5·00 |
| 11, 11 | .. | .. | 5·00 | 17, 17 | .. | .. | 20·00 |
| 12, 12 | .. | .. | 5·00 | 18, 18 | .. | .. | 7·00 |

Plate Nos. 13 and 14 exist with 8 pin spur in bottom margin instead of being perforated through to the edge of the sheet. *Plate* 13 *or* 14, *block of six, £6 each.*

**WITHDRAWN**   No. UG25, 31.12.82; No. UG26, 12.5.87; No. UG27, 11.4.89

# 22p. Bright Green   (1988)

**Printed by Questa**

**1988 (9 FEBRUARY). PERF. 15 × 14. TWO 9·5 mm. PHOSPHOR BANDS. FLUORESCENT COATED PAPER. PVA GUM**
£5 Story of *The Financial Times* booklet *se-tenant* pane UHP3
UG28 (=S.G.X1013)   Bright green ..    ..    ..    ..    ..    ..    ..   3·00   2·00

# 29p. Deep Mauve    (1989)

**Printed by Walsall**

**1989 (2 OCTOBER).   PERF. 14. TWO PHOSPHOR BANDS. FLUORESCENT COATED PAPER. PVAD (clear) GUM**

£1·16 booklet pane ULP3
UG32 (=S.G.X1021)   Deep mauve ..      ..      ..      ..      ..      ..      ..      1·10   1·00
 No. UG32 came from barcode booklet No. GG1 in which the pane of four stamps was imperforate at top, bottom and at right.

**1990 (17 APRIL).   PERF. 14. PHOSPHORISED (ADVANCED COATED) PAPER. PVAD (clear) GUM**

£1·16 booklet pane ULP4
UG33 (=S.G.X1022)   Deep mauve ..      ..      ..      ..      ..      ..      ..      45      50
 No. UG33 came from barcode booklet No. GG2 in which the pane of four stamps was imperforate at top, bottom and at right.
 The booklet was prereleased in various areas from late February and the earliest reported date of use is 28 February 1990.

# 31p. Ultramarine    (1990)

**Printed by Walsall**

**1990 (17 SEPTEMBER).   PERF. 14. PHOSPHORISED (ADVANCED COATED) PAPER. PVAD (clear) GUM**

£1·24 booklet pane ULP5
UG34 (=S.G.X1020)   Ultramarine ..      ..      ..      ..      ..      ..      ..      50      50
 No. UG34 came from barcode booklet No. GH1 in which the pane of four stamps was imperforate at top and bottom.

# 34p. Ochre-brown    (1988)

**Printed by Questa**

**1988 (9 FEBRUARY).   PERF. 15 × 14. TWO 9·5 mm. PHOSPHOR BANDS. FLUORESCENT COATED PAPER. PVA GUM**

£5 Story of *The Financial Times* booklet *se-tenant* pane UPH3
UG35 (=S.G.X1016)   Ochre-brown..      ..      ..      ..      ..      ..      ..      3·00   2·00

# 75p. Black    (1980–86)

**Two Value Types**

Type I.  Wide figures (Nos. UG41/44)

Type II.  Narrow figures

I           II

**Printed by Questa**

**1980 (30 JANUARY).   PERF. 14. FLUORESCENT COATED PAPER. TYPE I. PVAD GUM**

UG41 (=S.G.X1017)    Black .. .. .. .. .. .. .. .. 2·75  1·50
    *a*. Imperforate between stamp and right margin   .. £250

**Plate Numbers (Blocks of Six)**
Double Pane Plates
Perforation Type L
Plate Nos. in right margin

| Pl. No. | | | | Row 1 | Row 20 | Pl. No. | | | | Row 1 | Row 20 |
|---|---|---|---|---|---|---|---|---|---|---|---|
| 1 | .. | .. | .. | 15·00 | 15·00 | 7 | .. | .. | .. | 14·00 | 14·00 |
| 2 | .. | .. | .. | 14·00 | 14·00 | 8 | .. | .. | .. | 16·00 | 20·00 |
| 3 | .. | .. | .. | 14·00 | 14·00 | 9 | .. | .. | .. | 14·00 | 14·00 |
| 4 | .. | .. | .. | 14·00 | 14·00 | 10 | .. | .. | .. | 14·00 | 14·00 |
| 5 | .. | .. | .. | 24·00 | 24·00 | 11 | .. | .. | .. | 14·00 | 14·00 |
| 6 | .. | .. | .. | 28·00 | 28·00 | 12 | .. | .. | .. | 14·00 | 14·00 |

**1984 (21 FEBRUARY).   PERF. 15 × 14. TYPE I**
**A. ORIGINAL COATED PAPER. PVA GUM**

UG42                    Black .. .. .. .. .. .. .. .. 3·25

**Plate Numbers (Blocks of Six)**
Double Pane Plates
Perforation Type L
Plate Nos. in left margin

| Pl. No. | | | (I) | Pl. No. | | | (P) |
|---|---|---|---|---|---|---|---|
| 1 | .. | .. | 18·00 | 2 | .. | .. | 25·00 |

**B. FLUORESCENT COATED PAPER. PVAD GUM** (19.2.85)

UG43                    Black .. .. .. .. .. .. .. .. 3·00

**Plate Numbers (Blocks of Six)**
Double Pane Plates
Plate Nos. in left margin

| Pl. No. | | | (I) | Pl. No. | | | (P) |
|---|---|---|---|---|---|---|---|
| 1 | .. | .. | 16·00 | 2 | .. | .. | 28·00 |
| 3 | .. | .. | 16·00 | 4 | .. | .. | 16·00 |

**C. FLUORESCENT COATED PAPER. PVA GUM** (7.10.86)

UG44 (=S.G.X1017a) Black .. .. .. .. .. .. .. .. 2·75  1·50

**Plate Numbers (Blocks of Six)**
Double Pane Plates
Plate Nos. in left margin

| Pl. No. | | | (I) | Pl. No. | | | (P) |
|---|---|---|---|---|---|---|---|
| 5 | .. | .. | 14·00 | 6 | .. | .. | 14·00 |
| 7 | .. | .. | £190 | 8 | .. | .. | £350 |

**WITHDRAWN**   No. UG41, 21.2.85; Nos. UG42/3, 6.10.87 and UG44, 22.2.89

# 75p. Brownish Grey and Black    (1988)

**Printed by Questa**

**1988 (23 FEBRUARY). COLOUR CHANGED. PERF. 15 × 14. FLUORESCENT COATED PAPER. TYPE II. PVA GUM**
UG45 (=S.G.X1018)   Brownish grey and black   ..      ..      ..      ..      ..    7·50    3·50

**Plate Numbers (Blocks of Six)**
Double Pane Plates
Perforation Type L(P)

| Pl. No. | | (P) |
|---|---|---|
| 1, 1 | .. | 45·00 |
| 2, 2 | .. | 40·00 |

**WITHDRAWN**   11.4.89

# SECTION UH

## Machin Decimal Issues

### 1989–90. Booklet Panes in Lithography

#### I. Multi-value Folded Booklet Panes

**Printed by Walsall**

**£1 Pane with imperforate vertical sides. Charles Dickens Series FH16**

UMLP1 (cyl. pane)

Vertical pair 14p. (deep blue) and four 19p. (bright orange-red)

Pane UMLP1. Pair of 14p. with narrow phosphor band at right *se-tenant* with 19p. two bands. At the right the band ends at the edge of the vertical strip of three 19p. Below the 14p. the 19p. has a left band short at top left and a continuous band at right. From £1 Pictorial Booklet, No. FH16

Pane UMLP1. Lithographed, selvedge at top

|  |  | Perf. Type IPI |
| --- | --- | --- |
| UMLP1 (containing Nos. UG17 × 2, UG24 × 3, UG24*a*) (25.4.89) | | 4·00 |
| *a*. Phosphor omitted   ..     ..     ..     ..     ..     ..     .. | | £950 |

For short phosphor band errors from this pane see section UG under basic stamp numbers.

**Booklet Plate Numbers**
Single Pane Plates

| Pane No. | Plate Nos. (No dot) | | | | Perf. Type IPI |
| --- | --- | --- | --- | --- | --- |
| UMLP1 | 19p., W2, W1; 14p., W2, W1 | .. | .. | .. | 6·00 |
| UMLP1 | 19p., W3, W1; 14p., W2, W1 | .. | .. | .. | 6·00 |

The phosphor was printed at a separate operation and phosphor numbers do not appear on the panes.

**Sheet Make-up**
   The uncut printer's sheet contained 45 booklet panes arranged in 15 (3 × 5) blocks each containing three blocks side by side. The blocks were surrounded by vertical and horizontal gutters with the first pane in each block from the first three horizontal rows showing the plate numbers in the upper margin. The uncut sheet contains a total of 9 plate number panes and 36 ordinary panes.
   Colour control dabs placed in the bottom margin did not appear on the issued panes.
   This was a sheet-fed printing on a four colour Roland "Favorit" machine which required two plates to achieve the Jeffery Matthews colour standards for photogravure stamps.
   The sheets were perforated and trimmed on a Bickel machine. The vertical sides of each pane are imperforate and the central row of perforations runs vertically through the binding margin to give perforation Type IPI.


## II. Panes of One Value

## Printed by Questa

**£1·40 Pane. Barcode Booklets GJ2 and GJ4**

ULP1

   Pane of ten 14p. stamps with 4 mm. centre phosphor band from £1·40 Booklets Nos. GJ2 and 4. The phosphor band was the height of the stamp

Pane ULP1. Lithographed, selvedge at left

|  | Perf. Type P |
|---|---|
| ULP1 (containing No. UG16 × 10) (11.10.88) | 6·00 |

   No. ULP1 exists with either guillotined or torn edges.


**Booklet Plate Numbers**
   There were no plate numbers on these panes.

**Sheet Make-up**
   The primary sheet contained 16 booklet panes arranged in four vertical columns of four panes in each. The panes were perforated all round and across the selvedge to give perforation Type P. They were printed on a Heidelberg press.

## Printed by Questa

**£1·90 Pane. Barcode Booklets GL2 and GL4**

ULP2

Pane of ten 19p. stamps on phosphorised (advanced coated) paper from £1·90 Barcode Booklets Nos. GL2 and 4

Pane ULP2. Lithographed, selvedge at left

Perf. Type P

ULP2 (containing No. UG23 × 10) (11.10.88)     7·00

No. ULP2 exists with either guillotined or torn edges.

**Booklet Plate Numbers**
There were no plate numbers on these panes.

**Sheet Make-up**
As Pane ULP1.

---

## Printed by Walsall

**£1·16 Pane. Barcode Booklets GG1 and GG2**

ULP3, ULP4            ULP5

Pane of four 29p. (deep mauve) stamps with two phosphor bands from Barcode Booklet No. GG1. The band between the stamps is 9·5 mm. wide and the pane has three edges imperforate

Pane ULP3. Lithographed, selvedge at left

Perf. Type
IEI   IEIb

ULP3 (containing No. UG32 × 4) (2.10.89)     3·50   7·00

**319**

**Booklet Plate Numbers**

| Pane No. | Pl. Nos. (No dot) | | | | | | | Perf. Type IEI | IEIb |
|----------|-------------------|---|---|---|---|---|---|-----|------|
| ULP3 | W1, W1 | .. | .. | .. | .. | .. | .. | 5·00 | 12·00 |
| | W1, W1 bar | .. | .. | .. | .. | .. | 18·00 | † |

For note on primary sheet format see below No. ULP4.

Pane of four 29p. (deep mauve) stamps on phosphorised (advanced coated) paper from Barcode Booklet No. GG2. The pane has three edges imperforate

Pane ULP4. Lithographed, selvedge at left

| | | Perf. Type |
|---|---|---|
| | | IEI  IEIb |
| ULP4 (containing No. UG33 × 4) (17.4.90*) | | 3·50  7·00 |

* Earliest reported prerelease date is 28 February 1990.

**Booklet Plate Numbers**

| Pane No. | Pl. Nos. (No dot) | | | | | | | Perf. Type IEI | IEIb |
|----------|-------------------|---|---|---|---|---|---|-----|------|
| ULP4 | W2, W2 | .. | .. | .. | .. | .. | .. | 5·00 | 12·00 |
| | W2, W2 bar | .. | .. | .. | .. | .. | 15·00 | † |

**Sheet Make-up**

The uncut sheet contained 72 panes made up of 8 vertical columns of 9 panes each. The top selvedge was perforated through, but the bottom of the sheet was not and this gives a blind perforation to 8 panes across the bottom of the sheet (perf. type IEIb). Plate number panes were in the first vertical column in positions 1/3 and 7/9 and this format was repeated in vertical column 8. A further 3 plate number panes were in the fifth column in positions 4/6 giving a total of 15 plate number panes. The pane in position 7 in column 1 had a plate number plus the trace of a bar on left edge depending on the extent of the trim.

## Printed by Walsall

### £1·24 Pane. Barcode Booklet GH1

Pane of four 31p. (ultramarine) stamps on phosphorised (advanced coated) paper from Barcode Booklet No. GH1. The pane has imperforate horizontal edges

Pane ULP5. Lithographed, selvedge at left

| | | Perf. Type |
|---|---|---|
| | | IEI  IEIb |
| ULP5 (containing No. UG34 × 4) (17.9.90) | | 1·90  3·50 |

**Booklet Plate Numbers**

| Pane No. | Pl. Nos. (No dot) | | | | | | | Perf. Type IEI | IEIb |
|----------|-------------------|---|---|---|---|---|---|-----|------|
| ULP5 | W2, W1, W1 | .. | .. | .. | .. | .. | .. | 2·75 | 7·00 |
| | W2, W1, W1 bar | .. | .. | .. | .. | .. | 10·00 | † |

**Sheet Make-up**

As for £1·16 panes.

## III. PANES FROM PRESTIGE BOOKLETS
### Printed by Questa

From £5 Booklet "The Story of *The Financial Times*" No. DX9

The illustrations are reduced, the actual size being 162 × 97 mm.

First pane comprising 9 × 18p. phosphorised (advanced coated) paper.

UHP1

UHP1 (containing No. UG21 × 9) (9.2.88)      4·50

Second pane comprising 6 × 13p. with 4 mm. centre band.

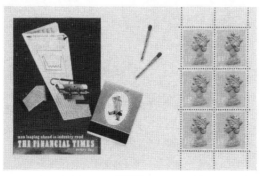

UHP2

UHP2 (containing No. UG13 × 6) (9.2.88)      3·00

Third pane comprising 3 × 13p. band at right; 3 × 13p. band at left; 18p, 22p. and 34p. two 9·5 mm. bands.

UHP3

UHP3 (containing Nos. UG14 × 3, UG15 × 3, UG22, UG28, UG35) (9.2.88)                                      11·00
  *a*. Blanket offset of grey-green on 18p.    ..   ..   ..   ..

Fourth pane comprising 6 × 18p. phosphorised (advanced coated) paper.

UHP4

UHP4 (containing No. UG21 × 6) (9.2.88)                                       3·00

**Plate Numbers**
  No plate numbers were printed on the sheets. The marginal markings, colour bars along the lower edge, traffic lights towards the top of the left side, and various cutting lines and trimming instructions, occurring on the sheets, interleaves and covers were all trimmed off and do not appear on the issued books.

# SECTION UI

# Machin No Value Indicated Issues

## 1989–90. Stamps Printed in Lithography and Photogravure from Booklets

### General Notes

**INTRODUCTION.** The stamps in this Section are all inscribed "2nd" or "1st" instead of numeral face values. They only came from barcoded booklets with the binding margin at left. This was the first occasion that the Royal Mail issued adhesive stamps without a specific face value. Similar indicators had been employed on postal stationery for a number of years.

**ARRANGEMENT.** In effect many of the panes have two important dates and values. This information is given in the booklet pane section so that dates of first issue are followed by the change of tariff value when the new, and increased postal charge came into effect. Three printers are involved—Harrisons (photogravure printings), Questa and Walsall (both lithography printing). The stamps and panes are arranged by printer and then divided between the 2nd and 1st class issues. Each class is listed in chronological order.

**PRINTERS AND PRIMARY SHEET ARRANGEMENTS.** The essential information on the printer's uncut booklet sheet, known as the primary sheet, is given after the pane listing. The work of each of the three printers is different and the lithographed issues can be easily identified as Questa use 15 × 14 perforations and Walsall 14.

**PHOSPHORISED PAPER.** After the introduction of advanced coated paper the amount of optical brightening agent varied with the result that some panes give a markedly dull response under ultra-violet light. These should not be confused with the original phosphorised paper.

**IMPERFORATE EDGES.** Stamps with imperforate edges are not listed separately but are covered by footnotes. It is helpful to note that the Questa printings are perforated on all sides and that those stamps imperforate on adjacent sides only come from the panes of four.

Straight edges could be manufactured, but only by reducing the size of the stamp so that careful comparison with a normal example would reveal if a stamp had been trimmed.

### Check List of Machin No Value Indicated Issues

(L) = litho, (P) = photo

| Spec. Number | S.G. Standard Number | Description | Printer/Method | Booklet Source |
|---|---|---|---|---|
| **(2nd) Class. 15p. Bright Blue** | | | | |
| UIH 1 | 1445 | Centre band | Harrison (P) | 60p. HB1, £1·40 HE1/a |
| UIH 2 | 1446 | Right band | Harrison (P) | £5 London Life |
| UIQ1 | 1451 | 15 × 14 | Questa (L) | £1·40 HE2 |
| UIW1 | 1449 | 14 | Walsall (L) | 56p. HA1 |
| **(2nd) Class. 17p. Deep Blue** | | | | |
| UIH3 | 1511 | Centre band | Harrison (P) | £1·50 HF1 |
| UIQ2 | 1513 | 15 × 14 | Questa (L) | £1·50 HF2 |
| UIW2 | 1515 | 14 | Walsall (L) | 60p. HB2, £1·50 HF3 |
| **(1st) Class. 20p. Black** | | | | |
| UIH4 | 1447 | 15 × 14 | Harrison (P) | 80p. HB2, £1·90 HG1/a |
| UIH5 | 1448 | 2 bands | Harrison (P) | £5 London Life |
| UIQ3 | 1452 | 15 × 14 | Questa (L) | £1·90 HG2 |
| UIW3 | 1450 | 14 | Walsall (L) | 76p. HC1 |
| **(1st) Class. 22p. Orange-red** | | | | |
| UIH6 | 1512 | 15 × 14 | Harrison (P) | £2 HH1 |
| UIQ4 | 1514 | 15 × 14 | Questa (L) | £2 HH2 |
| UIW4 | 1516 | 14 | Walsall (L) | 80p. HD2, £2 HH3 |

**U7** Queen Elizabeth II
(Des. after plaster cast by Arnold Machin)

# Type U7

### I. Printed by Harrison in Photogravure

All stamps are perforated 15 × 14

## (2nd) Bright Blue   (1989)

**1989 (22 AUGUST).   ONE 4 mm. CENTRE BAND. FLUORESCENT COATED PAPER. PVAD GUM**

£1·40 and 60p. Barcode booklet panes UIP1/2
UIH1 (=S.G.1445)      Bright blue  ..     ..     ..     ..     ..     ..     45     45
   Imperforate edges: No. UIH1 exists with imperforate edges at top or bottom from pane UIP1 or at top, top and right, bottom, bottom and right from pane UIP2

## (2nd) Bright Blue   (1990)

**1990 (20 MARCH).   ONE NARROW BAND AT RIGHT. FLUORESCENT COATED PAPER. PVAD GUM**

£5 London Life booklet *se-tenant* pane UWB33
UIH2 (=S.G.1446)      Bright blue  ..     ..     ..     ..     ..     ..     2·75   2·75

## (2nd) Deep Blue   (1990)

**1990 (7 AUGUST).   ONE 4 mm. CENTRE BAND. FLUORESCENT COATED PAPER. PVAD GUM**

£1·50 Barcode booklet pane UIP3
UIH3 (=S.G.1511)      Deep blue  ..     ..     ..     ..     ..     ..     25     30
   Imperforate edges: No. UIH3 exists with imperforate edges at top or bottom

## (1st) Brownish Black   (1989)

**1989 (22 AUGUST).   PHOSPHORISED (ADVANCED COATED) PAPER. PVAD GUM**

£1·90 and 80p. Barcode booklet panes UIP4/5
UIH4 (=S.G.1447)      Brownish black     ..     ..     ..     ..     ..     75     75
   Imperforate edges: No. UIH4 exists with imperforate edges at top or bottom from pane UIP4 or at top, top and right, bottom, bottom and right from pane UIP5

## (1st) Brownish Black   (1990)

**1990 (20 MARCH).   TWO 9·5 mm. PHOSPHOR BANDS. FLUORESCENT COATED PAPER. PVAD GUM**

£5 London Life booklet *se-tenant* pane UWB33
UIH5 (=S.G.1448)      Brownish black     ..     ..     ..     ..     ..     2·75   2·75

# (1st) Bright Orange-red  (1990)
**1990 (7 AUGUST).  PHOSPHORISED (ADVANCED COATED) PAPER. PVAD GUM**

£2 Barcode booklet pane UIP6
UIH6 (=S.G.1512)    Bright orange-red  ..    ..    ..    ..    ..    ..    30    35
  Imperforate edges: No. UIH6 comes with imperforate edges at top or bottom

---

### II. Printed by Questa in Lithography

All stamps are perforated 15 × 14.

**NOTE.** Under ultra violet light the phosphor band can be found short at the top or bottom of the stamp due to fractional misplacement, but such variations are outside the scope of the catalogue.

# (2nd) Bright Blue  (1989)
**1989 (19 SEPTEMBER).  ONE CENTRE 4 mm. SHORT PHOSPHOR BAND. FLUORESCENT COATED PAPER. PVA GUM**

£1·40 Barcode booklet pane UIP13
UIQ1 (=S.G.1451)    Bright blue ..    ..    ..    ..    ..    ..    ..    45    45

# (2nd) Deep Blue  (1990)
**1990 (7 AUGUST).  ONE CENTRE 4 mm. SHORT PHOSPHOR BAND. FLUORESCENT COATED PAPER. PVAD (clear) GUM**

£1·50 Barcode booklet pane UIP14
UIQ2 (=S.G.1513)    Deep blue  ..    ..    ..    ..    ..    ..    ..    25    30

# (1st) Brownish Black  (1989)
**1989 (19 SEPTEMBER).  PHOSPHORISED (ADVANCED COATED) PAPER. PVA GUM**

£1·90 Barcode booklet pane UIP15
UIQ3 (=S.G.1452)    Brownish black    ..    ..    ..    ..    ..    75    75

# (1st) Bright Orange-red  (1990)
**1990 (7 AUGUST).  PHOSPHORISED (ADVANCED COATED) PAPER. PVAD GUM**

£2 Barcode booklet pane UIP16
UIQ4 (=S.G.1514)    Bright orange-red  ..    ..    ..    ..    ..    ..    30    35

### III. Printed by Walsall in Lithography

All stamps are perforated 14 *unless otherwise stated*

## (2nd) Bright Blue   (1989)

**1989 (22 AUGUST). ONE 4 mm. CENTRE BAND. FLUORESCENT COATED PAPER. PVA GUM**

56p. Barcode booklet pane UIP7

| | | | | | | | |
|---|---|---|---|---|---|---|---|
| UIW1 (=S.G.1449) | Bright blue | .. | .. | .. | .. | 45 | 45 |

Imperforate edges: No. UIW1 comes with imperforate edges at top, top and right, bottom, bottom and right

## (2nd) Deep Blue   (1990)

**1990 (7 AUGUST). ONE 4mm. CENTRE BAND. FLUORESCENT COATED PAPER. PVA GUM**

60p. and £1·50 Barcode booklet pane UIP8/9

| | | | | | | | |
|---|---|---|---|---|---|---|---|
| UIW2 (=S.G.1515) | Deep blue | .. | .. | .. | .. | 25 | 30 |

Imperforate edges: No. UIW2 comes with imperforate edges at top or bottom from both panes

## (1st) Blackish Brown   (1989)

**1989 (22 AUGUST). TWO PHOSPHOR BANDS. FLUORESCENT COATED PAPER. PVA GUM**

76p. Barcode booklet pane UIP10

| | | | | | | | |
|---|---|---|---|---|---|---|---|
| UIW3 (=S.G.1450) | Blackish brown | .. | .. | .. | .. | 75 | 75 |
| | *a.* Phosphor omitted | | .. | .. | .. | | |

Imperforate edges: No. UIW3 comes with imperforate edges at top, top and right, bottom, bottom and right

Complete panes of four of pane UIP10 without phosphor have not been seen.

Examples of No. UIW3 exist showing a clear edge of the phosphor band on one side due to slight misplacement. The side bands were 5 mm. but between the horizontal pair the band was 9·5 mm. wide.

## (1st) Bright Orange-red   (1990)

**1990 (7 AUGUST). PHOSPHORISED (ADVANCED COATED) PAPER. PVA GUM**

80p. and £2 Barcode booklet pane Nos. UIP11/12

| | | | | | | | |
|---|---|---|---|---|---|---|---|
| UIW4 (=S.G.1516) | Bright orange-red | .. | .. | .. | .. | 30 | 35 |
| | *a.* Error. Perf. 13 (10.90) | .. | .. | .. | .. | 2·50 | 2·00 |

Imperforate edges: No. UIW4 comes with imperforate edges at top or bottom from both panes

No. UIW4*a* was first reported in October 1990 and was caused by the use, in error, of a smaller gauge comb perforator.

## Check List of Machin No Value Indicated Booklet Panes

The check list gives a description of the pane content and booklet source. Printing process is indicated by (P) for photogravure and (L) for lithography.

**Booklet Panes containing Machin No Value Indicated stamps**

## I. Printed by Harrison in Photogravure

**(2nd) £1·40 Pane (£1·50 from 2.10.89). Barcode Booklet HE1/a**

UIP1, UIP3, UIP9

Pane of ten (2nd) class stamps (bright blue) with one 4 mm. centre phosphor band from £1·40 Barcode Booklet Nos. HE1/a. Pane has imperforate horizontal edges.

Pane UIP1. Photogravure, selvedge at left

|  | Perf. Type IEI |
|---|---|
| UIP1 (containing No. UIH1 × 10) (22.8.89) | 5·00 |

**Booklet Cylinder Numbers**

| Pane No. | Cyl. No. | Phos. No. |  |  |  | Perf. Type IEI<br>No dot |
|---|---|---|---|---|---|---|
| UIP1 | B1 | (B84) | .. | .. | .. | 7·00 |

**Sheet Make-up**

The printer's sheet from the Jumelle press was single pane containing four columns of ten booklet panes each. Gutter margins between vertical columns 2, 3 and 4 were trimmed to provide the binding margin at left. The right side margin was trimmed to the perforation edge, but the extent of trim varies. The columns were continuous and contained a cylinder pane every fifth pane. There were 8 cylinder and 32 ordinary panes in the printer's sheet. Horizontal trimming lines in the vertical margins at left indicated the cutting lines with cylinder numbers placed opposite row 1 in the pane.

**(2nd) 60p Pane. Barcode Booklet HB1**

UIP2, UIP7

UIP5, UIP10

Pane of four (2nd) class stamps (bright blue) with one 4 mm. centre phosphor band from 60p. Barcode Booklet No. HB1. Pane has three edges imperforate.

Pane UIP2. Photogravure, selvedge at left

UIP2 (containing No. UIH1 ×4) ( 28.11.89)

Perf. Type IEI
3·50

**Cylinder Numbers and Sheet Make-up**
    The primary sheet contained a total of eighteen booklet panes of four arranged in six vertical columns of three panes. Each pane was perforated across its centre, but otherwise left imperforate horizontally. Each pane was also imperforate vertically at right and each of the six columns was separated by a vertical gutter margin just over 15 mm. wide. A single cylinder number in L right-angle was placed in the bottom margin but this was wide and always trimmed off.
    Those used were: B2, (B83).

---

**(2nd) £1·50 Pane (£1·70 from 17.9.90). Barcode Booklet HF1**

As pane No. UIP1

    Pane of ten (2nd) class stamps (deep blue) with one 4 mm. centre phosphor band from £1·50 Barcode Booklet No. HF1. Pane has imperforate horizontal edges.

Pane UIP3. Photogravure, selvedge at left

UIP3 (containing No. UIH3 × 10) (7.8.90)

Perf. Type IEI
2·25

**Booklet Cylinder Numbers**

| Pane No. | Cyl. No. | Phos. No. | | | | Perf. Type IEI No dot |
|----------|----------|-----------|---|---|---|-----------------------|
| UIP3 | B1 | (B84) | .. | .. | .. | 4·50 |

**Sheet Make-up**
    As Pane UIP1.

---

**(1st) £1·90 Pane (£2 from 2.10.89). Barcode Booklet HG1/a**

UIP4, UIP6, UIP12

    Pane of ten (1st) class stamps (brownish black) on phosphorised (advanced coated) paper from £1·90 Barcode Booklet Nos. HG1/a. Pane has imperforate horizontal edges.

Pane UIP4. Photogravure, selvedge at left

UIP4 (containing No. UIH4 × 10) (22.8.89)

Perf. Type IEI
7·00

**Booklet Cylinder Number**

| Pane No. | Cyl. No. | | | | | | Perf. Type IEI<br>No dot |
|---|---|---|---|---|---|---|---|
| UIP4 | B3 | .. | .. | .. | .. | .. | 10·00 |

**Sheet Make-up**
As Pane UIP1

---

**(1st) 80p. Pane. Barcode Booklet HD1**

Pane of four (1st) class stamps (brownish black) on phosphorised (advanced coated) paper from 80p. Barcode Booklet No. HD1. Pane has three edges imperforate.

Pane UIP5. Photogravure, selvedge at left

| | Perf. Type IEI |
|---|---|
| UIP5 (containing No. UIH4 × 4) (5.12.89) | 5·00 |

**Cylinder Number and Sheet Make-up**
As UIP2. It is believed that B2 was the cylinder number.

---

**(1st) £2 Pane (£2·20 from 17.9.90). Barcode Booklet HH1**

As pane No. UIP4

Pane of ten (1st) class stamps (bright orange-red) on phosphorised (advanced coated) paper from £2 Barcode Booklet No. HH1. Pane has imperforate horizontal edges.

Pane UIP6. Photogravure, selvedge at left

| | Perf. Type IEI |
|---|---|
| UIP6 (containing No. UIH6 × 10) (7.8.90) | 3·00 |

**Booklet Cylinder Number**

| Pane No. | Cyl. No. | | | | | | Perf. Type IEI<br>No dot |
|---|---|---|---|---|---|---|---|
| UIP6 | B3 | .. | .. | .. | .. | .. | 6·00 |

**Sheet Make-up**
As Pane UIP1.

---

## II.    Printed by Walsall in Lithography

All stamps are perforated 14, except pane no. UIP11a.

**(2nd) 56p. Pane (60p. from 2.10.89). Barcode Booklet HA1**

As pane No. UIP2

Pane of four (2nd) class stamps (bright blue) with one 4 mm. centre phosphor band from 56p. Barcode Booklet No. HA1. Pane has three edges imperforate.

**330**

Pane UIP7. Lithographed, selvedge at left

|  | Perf. Type | |
|---|---|---|
|  | IEI | IEIb |
| UIP7 (containing No. UIW1 × 4) (22.8.89) | 3·00 | 10·00 |

**Booklet Plate Numbers**

| Pane No. | Pl. Nos. (No dot) | | | | | | | Perf. Type | |
|---|---|---|---|---|---|---|---|---|---|
|  |  |  |  |  |  |  |  | IEI | IEIb |
| UIP7 | W1, W1 | .. | .. | .. | .. | .. | .. | 4·50 | 22·00 |
| UIP7 | W1, W1 bar | .. | .. | .. | .. | .. | .. | 8·00 | † |

**Sheet Make-up**

The uncut sheet contained 72 panes made up of 8 vertical columns of 9 panes each. The top selvedge was perforated through, but the bottom of the sheet was not and this gives a blind perforation to 8 panes across the bottom of the sheet (perf. type IEIb). Plate number panes were in the first vertical column in positions 1/3 and 7/9 and this format was repeated in vertical column 8. A further 3 plate number panes were in the fifth column in positions 4/6 giving a total of 15 plate number panes. The pane in position 7 in column 1 had a plate number plus the trace of a bar on left edge depending on the extent of the trim.

---

**(2nd) 60p. Pane (68p. from 17.9.90). Barcode Booklet HB2**

UIP8 (Cyl. pane)

Pane of four (2nd) class stamps (deep blue) with one 4 mm. centre phosphor band from 60p. Barcode Booklet No. HB2. The pane has imperforate horizontal edges.

Pane UIP8. Lithographed, selvedge at left

|  | Perf. Type | |
|---|---|---|
|  | IEI | IEIb |
| UIP8 (containing No. UIW2 × 4) (7.8.90) | 90 | 3·00 |

**Booklet Plate Numbers**

| Pane No. | Pl. Nos. (No dot) | | | | | | | Perf. Type | |
|---|---|---|---|---|---|---|---|---|---|
|  |  |  |  |  |  |  |  | IEI | IEIb |
| UIP8 | W1, W1, W1 | .. | .. | .. | .. | .. | .. | 3·00 | 6·00 |
| UIP8 | W1, W1, W1 bar | .. | .. | .. | .. | .. | .. | 8·00 | † |
| UIP8 | W2, W1, W2 | .. | .. | .. | .. | .. | .. | 8·00 | 6·00 |
| UIP8 | W2, W1, W2 bar | .. | .. | .. | .. | .. | .. | 10·00 | † |
| UIP8 | W2, W2, W2 | .. | .. | .. | .. | .. | .. | 3·00 | 5·00 |
| UIP8 | W2, W2, W2 bar | .. | .. | .. | .. | .. | .. | 8·00 | † |

**Sheet Make-up**

As Pane UIP7.

**(2nd) £1·50 Pane (£1·70 from 17.9.90). Barcode Booklet HF3**

As pane No. UIP1

Pane of ten (2nd) class stamps (deep blue) with one 4 mm. centre phosphor band from £1·50 Barcode Booklet No. HF3. Pane has imperforate horizontal edges.

Pane UIP9. Lithographed, selvedge at left

|  | Perf. Type | |
|---|---|---|
|  | IEI | IEIb |
| UIP9 (containing No. UIW2 × 10) (7.8.90) | 2·25 | 4·00 |

**Booklet Plate Numbers**

| | | Perf. Type | |
|---|---|---|---|
| Pane No. | Pl. Nos. (No dot) | IEI | IEIb |
| UIP9 | W1, W1, W1 | 6·00 | 7·50 |
| UIP9 | W1, W1, W1 bar | 10·00 | † |
| UIP9 | W2, W1, W1 | 8·00 | 7·00 |
| UIP9 | W2, W1, W1 bar | 15·00 | † |
| UIP9 | W2, W1, W2 | 10·00 | 15·00 |
| UIP9 | W2, W1, W2 bar | 30·00 | † |
| UIP9 | W2, W2 | 8·00 | 12·00 |
| UIP9 | W2, W2 bar | 15·00 | † |
| UIP9 | W3, W3, W3 | 8·00 | 10·00 |
| UIP9 | W3, W3, W3 bar | 10·00 | † |
| UIP9 | W4, W3, W3 | 6·00 | 10·00 |
| UIP9 | W4, W3, W3 bar | 15·00 | † |
| UIP9 | W4, W3, W4 | 4·00 | 8·00 |
| UIP9 | W4, W3, W4 bar | 10·00 | † |

The W2, W2 printing had the third plate number (W3) trimmed off.

**Sheet Make-up**

The uncut sheet contained 36 panes in a similar format to the panes of four stamps printed by Walsall. The sheet was made up of 4 vertical columns with 9 panes in each. As in the panes of four the top selvedge was perforated through and the bottom of the sheet gave perf. type IEIb. Plate number panes were in the first vertical column in positions 1/3 and 7/9 and this was repeated in the last column in the sheet. In addition there were a further three plate number panes in the third column in positions 4/6. The plate number bar booklet was again in the first column, position 7. The length of the bar varied according to the trim.

**(1st) 76p. Pane (80p. from 2.10.89). Barcode Booklet HC1**

As pane No. UIP5

Pane of four (1st) class stamps (blackish brown) with 2 phosphor bands from 76p. Barcode Booklet No. HC1. Pane has three edges imperforate.

Pane UIP10. Lithographed, selvedge at left

|  | Perf. Type | |
|---|---|---|
|  | IEI | IEIb |
| UIP10 (containing No. UIW3 × 4) (22.8.89) | 3·50 | 10·00 |

**Booklet Plate Numbers**

| | | Perf. Type | |
|---|---|---|---|
| Pane No. | Pl. Nos. (No dot) | IEI | IEIb |
| UIP10 | W1, W1 | 6·00 | — |
| UIP10 | W1, W1 bar | 60·00 | † |
| UIP10 | W1, W2 | 5·00 | 15·00 |
| UIP10 | W1, W2 bar | 18·00 | † |
| UIP10 | W1, W3 | 5·50 | 15·00 |
| UIP10 | W1, W3 bar | 55·00 | † |
| UIP10 | W2, W4 | 7·00 | 20·00 |
| UIP10 | W2, W4 bar | 65·00 | † |

**Sheet Make-up**

As Pane UIP7.

**(1st) 80p. Pane (88p. from 17.9.90). Barcode Booklet HD2**

UIP11

Pane of four (1st) class stamps (bright orange-red) on phosphorised (advanced coated) paper from 80p. Barcode Booklet No. HD2. The pane has imperforate horizontal edges.

Pane UIP11. Lithographed, selvedge at left

| | Perf. Type | | |
|---|---|---|---|
| | IEI | IEIb | I |
| UIP11 (containing No. UIW4 × 4) (7.8.90) | 1·25 | 3·50 | † |
| a. Error. Perf. 13 (containing No. UIW4a × 4) (10.90) .. .. | † | † | 7·00 |

Pane UIP11 also exists with low optical brightening property in the coating.

**Booklet Plate Numbers**

| | | | | | | | Perf. Type | | |
|---|---|---|---|---|---|---|---|---|---|
| Pane No. | Pl. Nos. (No dot) | | | | | | IEI | IEIb | I |
| UIP11 | W1, W1, W1 | .. | .. | .. | .. | .. | 4·00 | 10·00 | † |
| UIP11 | W1, W1, W1 bar | .. | .. | .. | .. | .. | 8·00 | † | † |
| UIP11a | W1, W1, W1 | .. | .. | .. | .. | .. | † | † | 10·00 |
| UIP11a | W1, W1, W1 bar | .. | .. | .. | .. | .. | † | † | 30·00 |
| UIP11 | W1, W2, W2 | .. | .. | .. | .. | .. | 8·00 | 10·00 | † |
| UIP11 | W1, W2, W2 bar | .. | .. | .. | .. | .. | 15·00 | † | † |
| UIP11 | W2, W3, W3 | .. | .. | .. | .. | .. | 5·00 | 8·00 | † |

Perforation 13 (Type I) is without the central extension hole in the binding margin.

**Sheet Make-up**
As Pane UIP7.

---

**(1st) £2 Pane (£2·20 from 17.9.90). Barcode Booklet HH3**

As pane No. UIP4

Pane of ten (1st) class stamps (bright orange-red) on phosphorised (advanced coated) paper from £2 Barcode Booklet No. HH3. Pane has imperforate horizontal edges.

Pane UIP12. Lithographed, selvedge at left

| | Perf. Type | |
|---|---|---|
| | IEI | IEIb |
| UIP12 (containing No. UIW4 × 10) (7.8.90) | 3·00 | 4·00 |

Pane UIP12 also exists with low optical brightening property in the coating.

**Booklet Plate Numbers**

|  |  | Perf. Type | |
|---|---|---|---|
| Pane No. | Pl. Nos. (No dot) | IEI | IEIb |
| UIP12 | W1, W1 .. .. .. .. .. .. | 5·00 | 8·00 |
| UIP12 | W1, W1 bar .. .. .. .. .. | 15·00 | † |
| UIP12 | W1, W1, W1 .. .. .. .. .. | 10·00 | 8·00 |
| UIP12 | W1, W1, W1 bar .. .. .. .. .. | 14·00 | † |
| UIP12 | W3, W3, W3 .. .. .. .. .. | 10·00 | 12·00 |
| UIP12 | W3, W3, W3 bar .. .. .. .. .. | 10·00 | † |
| UIP12 | W4, W4, W4 .. .. .. .. .. | 5·00 | 8·00 |
| UIP12 | W4, W4, W4 bar .. .. .. .. .. | 10·00 | † |

**Sheet Make-up**
  As Pane UIP9.

---

## III.   Printed by Questa in Lithography

All stamps are perforated 15 × 14

**(2nd) £1·40 Pane (£1·50 from 2.10.89). Barcode Booklet HE2**

UIP13, UIP14

  Pane of ten (2nd) class stamps (bright blue) with one centre 4 mm. short phosphor band from £1·40 Barcode Booklet No. HE2.

Pane UIP13. Lithographed, selvedge at left

|  | Perf. Type | |
|---|---|---|
|  | P | I |
| UIP13 (containing No. UIQ1 × 10) (19.9.89) | 5·00 | 40·00 |

**Sheet Make-up**
  The uncut printer's sheet contained 16 booklet panes arranged in four vertical columns of four panes in each. The panes were perforated all round and across the selvedge to give perf. Type P. Panes with perf. Type I came from a small part of the printing towards the end of November 1989. These were not distributed through the Philatelic Bureau but were available from some post offices and other retail outlets. Plate numbers do not appear on these panes as none were printed on the primary sheets. They were printed on a Heidelberg press.

---

**(2nd) £1·50 Pane (£1·70 from 17.9.90). Barcode Booklet HF2**

As pane No. UIP13

  Pane of ten (2nd) class stamps (deep blue) with one centre 4 mm. short phosphor band from £1·50 Barcode Booklet No. HF2.

Pane UIP14. Lithographed, selvedge at left

|  | Perf. Type P |
|---|---|
| UIP14 (containing No. UIQ2 × 10) (7.8.90) | 2·25 |

    No. UIP14 exists with either guillotined or torn edges.

**Sheet Make-up**
    As Pane UIP13 but only perf. Type P.

---

**(1st) £1·90 Pane (£2 from 2.10.89). Barcode Booklet HG2**

UIP15, UIP16

    Pane of ten (1st) class stamps (brownish black) on phosphorised (advanced coated) paper from £1·90 Barcode Booklet No. HG2.

Pane UIP15. Lithographed, selvedge at left

|  | Perf. Type | |
|---|---|---|
|  | P | I |
| UIP15 (containing No. UIQ3 × 10) (19.9.89) | 7·00 | 7·00 |

    Pane UIP15 also exists with low optical brightening property in the coating.

**Sheet Make-up**
    As Pane UIP13.

---

**(1st) £2 Pane (£2·20 from 17.9.90). Barcode Booklet HH2**

As pane No. UIP15.

    Pane of ten (1st) class stamps (bright orange-red) on phosphorised (advanced coated) paper from £2 Barcode Booklet No. HH2.

Pane UIP16. Lithographed, selvedge at left

|  | Perf. Type P |
|---|---|
| UIP16 (containing No. UIQ4 × 10) (7.8.90) | 3·00 |

    No. UIP16 exists with either guillotined or torn edges.

**Sheet Make-up**
    As Pane UIP13 but only perf. Type P.

# SECTION UJ

# Decimal Castles Issue

## 1988–90.  High Values.  Recess-printed

### General Notes

**INTRODUCTION.**  This issue was adapted from photographs taken by H.R.H. The Duke of York. The dies were engraved by Chris Matthews and the stamps were printed by Harrison & Sons Limited on their Giori press.

**PAPER.**  The stamps are all on fluorescent coated paper without watermark. Variations in the amount of fluorescent or brightening agent is apparent, but this is within standards and varieties of this kind are not listed. A glossy surface on printings of the £1·50 and £2 values has been recorded in combination with weak fluorescent reaction.

**PERFORATION.**  All stamps in this Section are perforated 15 × 14. Top and bottom margins are perforated through and side margins have a single extension hole opposite each horizontal row. The vertical and horizontal gutter margins separating the four panes of 25 stamps are perforated across their width.

**GUM.**  Only PVAD with greenish dye additive was used.

**SHEET LAYOUT.**  All values were issued in sheets of 100 (4 panes of 5 × 5) with 'TOTAL SHEET VALUE' inscriptions repeated four times in the horizontal margins reading left to right at top and right to left (upside down) at base. A colour band printed in the colour of the stamp is printed horizontally on the central gutter as these are stamp-size. A boxed guide hole which is unpunched appears opposite row 2, in the right-hand vertical margin.

**PLATES.**  A master die is used to make a 5 × 5 pane of 25 impressions. This is then used to produce a master sheet plate of 100. Any flaws and retouch marks introduced on the pane of 25 will be repeated in identical positions on all four panes. Printing plates are made from it and each is lettered sequentially. Any re-entries or flaws made on the master plate sheet will therefore only be found once in the printed sheet of 100 impressions. Plate numbers missing from the issued series were probably prepared but were found unsuitable for printing and rejected. Plate numbers are added to the plates and this explains the positional variations and the different style from solid colour to a dot pattern. Plate number blocks of four including the Harrison logo are from the bottom left-hand corner of the sheet.

UJ1. Carrickfergus Castle

UJ2. Caernarfon Castle

UJ3. Edinburgh Castle

UJ4. Windsor Castle

(Des. from photographs by Prince Andrew, Duke of York. Eng. Chris Matthews and recess-printed by Harrison)

# £1 Type UJ1   (1988)

### 1988 (18 OCTOBER).   FLUORESCENT COATED PAPER. PVAD GUM

UJ1 (=S.G.1410)     Deep green  ..     ..     ..     ..     ..     ..     ..   1·50     50

#### Plate Numbers (Blocks of Four)

| Pl. No. | | Pl. No. | | Pl. No. | |
|---|---|---|---|---|---|
| 1B .. | .. 12·00 | 1F .. | .. 10·00 | 1J .. | .. 10·00 |
| 1C .. | .. 12·00 | 1G .. | .. 10·00 | 1K .. | .. 10·00 |
| 1D .. | .. 12·00 | 1H .. | .. 10·00 | 1M .. | .. 10·00 |
| 1E .. | .. 10·00 | 1I .. | .. 10·00 | 1N .. | .. 10·00 |

#### Minor Constant Flaws

Some of the following varieties are repeated within the sheet of 100 impressions. The same flaw may also occur on succeeding plates but the list is not complete and we have noted only those varieties which appear to be constant.

£1 Plate 1C

3/3  Diagonal scratch above third R in CARRICKFERGUS
3/8  As R. 3/3
8/3  As R. 3/3
8/8  As R. 3/3
5/4  Thin vertical scratch above T in CASTLE
5/9  As R. 5/4
10/4  As R. 5/4

Plates 1C, 1D, 1E
9/2  Small thickness at the inner centre of C of CASTLE

**337**

# £1·50 Type UJ2   (1988)

**1988 (18 OCTOBER).   FLUORESCENT COATED PAPER. PVAD GUM**

UJ2 (=S.G.1411)    Maroon    ..    ..    ..    ..    ..    ..    ..    2·25   1·00

Examples of No. UJ2 from plates 2F and 2G exist on paper with a glossy or glazed surface. *Price £5, mint.*

**Plate Numbers (Blocks of Four)**

| Pl. No. | | Pl. No. | | Pl. No. | |
|---|---|---|---|---|---|
| 2A .. | .. 12·00 | 2E .. | .. 14·00 | 2H .. | .. 12·00 |
| 2B .. | .. 15·00 | 2F .. | .. 14·00 | | |
| 2D .. | .. 14·00 | 2G .. | .. 14·00 | | |

# £2 Type UJ3   (1988)

**1988 (18 OCTOBER).   FLUORESCENT COATED PAPER. PVAD GUM**

UJ3 (=S.G.1412)    Steel blue    ..    ..    ..    ..    ..    ..    ..    3·00   1·50

Examples of No. UJ3 from plate 1G exist with a weak fluorescent reaction and a glossy surface to the paper. *Price £18, mint.*

**Plate Numbers (Blocks of Four)**

| Pl. No. | | Pl. No. | | Pl. No. | |
|---|---|---|---|---|---|
| 1C .. | .. 18·00 | 1H .. | .. 20·00 | 2P .. | .. 18·00 |
| 1D .. | .. 18·00 | 1I .. | .. 50·00 | 2Q .. | .. 18·00 |
| 1E .. | .. 18·00 | 2M .. | .. 18·00 | 2R .. | .. 18·00 |
| 1F .. | .. 20·00 | 2N .. | .. 18·00 | | |
| 1G .. | .. 20·00 | 2O .. | .. 18·00 | | |

# £5 Type UJ4   (1988)

**1988 (18 OCTOBER).   FLUORESCENT COATED PAPER. PVAD GUM**

UJ4 (=S.G.1413)    Deep brown ..    ..    ..    ..    ..    ..    ..    7·50   3·00

**Plate Numbers (Blocks of Four)**

| Pl. No. | | Pl. No. | | Pl. No. | |
|---|---|---|---|---|---|
| 1C .. | .. 35·00 | 1E .. | .. 35·00 | 1G .. | .. 35·00 |
| 1D .. | .. 35·00 | 1F .. | .. 35·00 | | |

# Presentation Pack

UJPP1 No. 17 (18.10.88)   £1., £1·50., £2., £5                                    14·00

# First Day Cover

On official cover prepared and issued by the Post Office and stamps franked with a commemorative postmark.

UJFD1 (18.10.88)   £1., £1·50., £2., £5                                    40·00

# SECTION UK

## Greetings Stamps from Booklets

### 1989–90.  Printed in Photogravure

### General Notes
**INTRODUCTION.**  The basic idea of these issues is that stamp and the label should complement the card or letter. The labels were selected after consultation with greeting card producers; the subjects chosen being the most popular designs for greetings cards.

The first issue on 31 January 1989 was in the form of a folded booklet with label panel attached to the stamp pane. The second issue was completely different with the pane and labels produced separately with the stamps in photogravure and the labels in lithography.

---

**£1·90 Pane.   1989 Greetings Booklet FX10**

UK1 Rose                                    UK2 Cupid

UK3 Yachts                                  UK4 Fruit

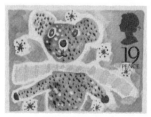

UK5 Teddy Bear

Types **UK1/5** were printed horizontally *se-tenant* within the booklet pane

(Des. Philip Sutton)

## 1989 (31 JANUARY). Types UK1/5. PHOSPHORISED (ADVANCED COATED) PAPER. PVAD GUM

Printed in photogravure by Harrison. Perf. 15 × 14, reel-fed

| | | | |
|---|---|---|---|
| UK1 (=S.G.1423) **UK1** 19p. | black, greenish yellow, bright rose, red, new blue, light green and gold | 3·00 | 1·50 |
| | *a.* Strip of 5. Nos. UK1/5 .. | 15·00 | |
| UK2 (=S.G.1424) **UK2** 19p. | black, greenish yellow, bright rose, red, new blue, light green and gold | 3·00 | 1·50 |
| UK3 (=S.G.1425) **UK3** 19p. | black, greenish yellow, bright rose, red, new blue, light green and gold | 3·00 | 1·50 |
| UK4 (=S.G.1426) **UK4** 19p. | black, greenish yellow, bright rose, red, new blue, light green and gold | 3·00 | 1·50 |
| UK5 (=S.G.1427) **UK5** 19p. | black, greenish yellow, bright rose, red, new blue, light green and gold | 3·00 | 1·50 |

| | |
|---|---|
| First Day Cover (UK1/5) .. | 9·00 |

## FOLDED SE-TENANT BOOKLET PANE OF TEN

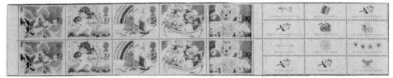

UKP6 *Se-tenant* pane of 10 with binding margin at left and 12 labels at right

(*Actual size* 331 × 60 *mm.*)

Pane UKP6. From £1·90 Greetings Stamp Booklet No. FX10

Perforation Type E

| | | |
|---|---|---|
| UKP6   (containing Nos. UK1/5 × 2) (31.1.89) .. | 28·00 |
| UKP6A   Gutter perforated as illustrated | 35·00 |

    These panes have black cutting lines and are folded three times between vertical rows 3/4, 5/6 and 7/8.

    No. UKP6 includes the label panel with a gutter margin perforated horizontally at the top and bottom and not across the centre as in the case of No. UKP6A. Both panes are perf. type E with an extension hole in the binding margin opposite each row of stamps.

    No. UKP6 exists with half of each design above and below a centre row of complete stamps due to cutting a half stamp width below the trim line.

### Booklet Cylinder Numbers

Perforation Type E

| Pane No. | Cyl. Nos. (No dot) | |
|---|---|---|
| UKP6 | B1A (black)-B1B (greenish yellow)-B1C (bright rose)-B1D (red)-B1E (new blue)-B1F (light green)-B1G (gold) .. | 40·00 |
| UKP6A | Gutter perforated as illustrated .. | 50·00 |

### Booklet Cylinder Numbers and Sheet Make-up

    The stamps and labels were printed by Harrison on the Jumelle press. The printer's uncut sheet contained 11 booklet panes with labels. There were two cylinder numbers (upright) in the left margin opposite panes 5 and 11. The pane opposite position 5 had a short "1" in "B1D". This figure is normal height opposite pane 11.

**WITHDRAWN** 30.1.90

**£2 Pane.   1990 Greetings Booklet KX1**

**UK7** Teddy Bear

**UK8** Dennis the Menace

**UK9** Punch

**UK10** Cheshire Cat

**UK11** Man in the Moon

**UK12** Laughing Policeman

**UK13** Clown

**UK14** Mona Lisa

**341**

**UK15** Queen of Hearts          **UK16** Stan Laurel (comedian)

Types **UK7/16** were printed *se-tenant* in a booklet pane with margins all round. The designs of Type Nos. **UK7, 9/11, 13** and **16** extend onto the pane margin.

(Des. Michael Peters and Partners Ltd.)

---

**1990 (6 FEBRUARY). Types UK7/16. TWO 4 mm. PHOSPHOR BANDS. FLUORESCENT COATED PAPER. PVAD GUM**

Printed in photogravure by Harrison. Perf. 15 × 14, reel-fed

| | | | | |
|---|---|---|---|---|
| UK7 (=S.G.1483) **UK7** | 20p. gold, greenish yellow, bright rose-red, new blue and grey-black | | 55 | 60 |
| UK8 (=S.G.1484) **UK8** | 20p. gold, greenish yellow, bright rose-red, new blue, deep blue and grey-black | | 55 | 60 |
| UK9 (=S.G.1485) **UK9** | 20p. gold, greenish yellow, bright rose-red, new blue, deep blue and grey-black | | 55 | 60 |
| UK10 (=S.G.1486) **UK10** | 20p. gold, greenish yellow, bright rose-red, new blue and grey-black | | 55 | 60 |
| UK11 (=S.G.1487) **UK11** | 20p. gold, greenish yellow, bright rose-red, new blue and grey-black | | 55 | 60 |
| UK12 (=S.G.1488) **UK12** | 20p. gold, greenish yellow, bright rose-red, new blue and grey-black | | 55 | 60 |
| UK13 (=S.G.1489) **UK13** | 20p. gold, greenish yellow, bright rose-red, new blue and grey-black | | 55 | 60 |
| UK14 (=S.G.1490) **UK14** | 20p. gold, greenish yellow, bright rose-red and grey-black | | 55 | 60 |
| UK15 (=S.G.1491) **UK15** | 20p. gold, greenish yellow, bright rose-red, new blue and grey-black | | 55 | 60 |
| UK16 (=S.G.1492) **UK16** | 20p. gold and grey-black | | 55 | 60 |

First Day Cover (UK7/16) .. .. .. .. .. 6·00

---

**FOLDED SE-TENANT BOOKLET PANE OF TEN**

UKP17 *Se-tenant* pane of 10 with margins all round
(*Actual size* 223 × 80 *mm.*)

Pane UKP17. From £2 Greetings Barcode Booklet No. KX1

Perforation Type P

UKP17 (containing Nos. UK7/16) (6.2.90)  ..  ..  ..  ..  5·00

These panes are folded once between rows 3/4 in order that they would fit inside the booklet.

### Booklet Cylinder Numbers and Sheet Make-up

There were no markings on the margins of the pane. The printer's sheet contained two columns of six panes with cylinder numbers in the left-hand vertical margin opposite pane 4. Crossed lines were set below opposite panes 4/6 which were repeated in the right-hand vertical margin of the sheet. The central gutter margin had traffic light markings between horizontal rows 1 and 4. All markings were placed so that they were removed when the individual panes were guillotined. The traffic light colour dabs were (from top to bottom) greenish yellow, bright rose-red, new blue, deep blue, grey-black and gold. The cylinder numbers were upright in the vertical margin opposite the third pane in the first of the two columns of the sheet. It is understood that those used were: 2A (gold), 1B (greenish yellow), 1C (bright rose-red), 1D (new blue), 1E (deep blue), 1F (grey-black), P93 (phosphor). These numbers were trimmed off in production and do not appear on the issued panes.

### THE LABELS

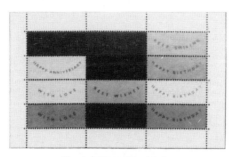

Sheet of 12 greetings labels
(*Actual size* 132 × 80 *mm.*)

The labels were printed by offset-lithography and were loose in the folder. Instances are known where more than one of these sheets were supplied in error. The paper used was Harrison's HS8 clay-coated litho paper with PVAD gum on reverse. Printed on the Roland sheet-fed machine the uncut printer's sheet contained sixteen panes (4 × 4). Each pane of 12 labels (4 rows of 3) is inscribed in gold which on pale colours is very distinct; less so on the darker backgrounds. Perforation was by a sheet-fed Grover machine with margins fully perforated through at top and bottom and single extension holes at each side. There were no marginal markings.

### WITHDRAWN  5.2.91

# SECTION W

## 150th Anniversary of the Penny Black

This listing will be repeated in the 2nd edition of Volume 5, *G.B. Specialised Catalogue, Q.E. II Decimal Special Issues*.

**ILLUSTRATIONS.** Unless otherwise stated the illustrations of the panes are ¾ size.

**W751**
Queen Victoria and Queen Elizabeth II

(Des. Jeffery Matthews (after Wyon and Machin))

## 1990 (10 JANUARY–12 JUNE). 150th ANNIVERSARY OF THE PENNY BLACK

Rowland Hill inaugurated the Uniform Penny Postage on 10 January 1840. This major postal reform was the culmination of years of persuasion and preparation. The rate was 1d. per ½ ounce anywhere in the British Isles if prepaid, or 2d. if unpaid. The new charge was an immediate success, the number of letters carried in 1840 being more than double that of 1839 and by 1850 the number had increased more than fourfold.

### I. Type W751. Printed in photogravure by Harrison

Perforation 15 × 14

ONE 4 mm. CENTRE BAND. FLUORESCENT COATED PAPER
Sheets and £1.50 booklet pane No. WP799

| | | | | | | | | |
|---|---|---|---|---|---|---|---|---|
| W788 (=S.G.1467) | 15p. bright blue | .. | .. | .. | .. | .. | 25 | 30 |
| | *a*. Imperforate (pair) (Cyl. 3) | .. | .. | .. | .. | | | |

Imperforate edges: No. W788 exists with imperforate edges at top or bottom from pane WP799. This stamp exists with a screened value from sheets.

ONE NARROW BAND AT LEFT. FLUORESCENT COATED PAPER
50p. booklet pane No. WP797

| | | | | | | | | |
|---|---|---|---|---|---|---|---|---|
| W789 (=S.G.1468) | 15p. bright blue (30.1.90) .. | .. | .. | .. | .. | 50 | 50 |
| | *a*. One 3 mm. band at left | .. | .. | .. | .. | 50 | |
| | *b*. Error. Two narrow bands (right short at top) | | .. | 12·00 | | |

ONE NARROW BAND AT RIGHT. FLUORESCENT COATED PAPER
£5 London Life *se-tenant* booklet pane No. UWB33

| | | | | | | | |
|---|---|---|---|---|---|---|---|
| W790 (=S.G.1468Ea) | 15p. bright blue (20.3.90) .. | .. | .. | .. | .. | 4·50 | 4·50 |

PHOSPHORISED (ADVANCED COATED) PAPER
Sheets and £1 booklet pane No. WP798, £2 Barcode booklet pane No. WP800, £5 London Life booklet panes Nos. WP801/2, 80p. Barcode booklet pane No. WP803, £1 "Stamp World 90" WMS815

| | | | | | | | |
|---|---|---|---|---|---|---|---|
| W791 (=S.G.1469) | 20p. brownish black and cream | .. | .. | .. | .. | 30 | 35 |

Imperforate edges: No. W791 exists imperforate at left (WP798); right (WP798); top (WP800, 803); bottom (WP800, 803); top and right (WP803); bottom and right (WP803). This stamp exists with a screened value from sheets.

TWO PHOSPHOR BANDS. FLUORESCENT COATED PAPER
50p. booklet pane No. WP797, £5 London Life *se-tenant* booklet pane No. UWB33

| | | | | | | | |
|---|---|---|---|---|---|---|---|
| W792 (=S.G.1470) | 20p. brownish black and cream (30.1.90) | .. | .. | 1·00 | 1·00 |
| | *b*. Error. Two bands short at top | .. | .. | .. | 3·00 | |

PHOSPHORISED (ADVANCED COATED) PAPER
Sheets

| | | | | | | | | | |
|---|---|---|---|---|---|---|---|---|---|
| W793 (=S.G.1471) | 29p. deep mauve | .. | .. | .. | .. | .. | .. | 45 | 50 |
| W794 (=S.G.1473) | 34p. deep bluish grey | .. | .. | .. | .. | .. | 55 | 55 |
| W795 (=S.G.1474) | 37p. rosine .. | .. | .. | .. | .. | .. | .. | 60 | 65 |

Nos. W793/5 exist with a screened value.

TWO PHOSPHOR BANDS. FLUORESCENT COATED PAPER
£5 London Life *se-tenant* booklet pane No. UWB33
W796 (=S.G.1472)   29p. deep mauve (20.3.90).. .. .. .. .. 2·75 2·75

| | | | |
|---|---|---|---|
| First Day Cover (W788, 791, 793/95) .. .. | † | 5·00 | |
| Presentation Pack (W788, 791, 793/95) .. .. 2·40 | † | | |

**Cylinder Numbers (Blocks of Six)**

| | Perforation Type RE | |
|---|---|---|
| | No dot | Dot |
| One 4 mm. centre phosphor band (No. W788) | | |
| 15p. 3 (bright blue)–41 (phosphor)–41 mm. (20).. .. .. .. .. 1·75 | 1·75 |

Phosphorised (advanced coated) paper (Nos. W791, W793/5)

| | No dot | Dot |
|---|---|---|
| 20p. 1A (brownish black)–1B (cream) .. .. .. .. .. .. 2·10 | 2·10 |
| 29p. 1 (deep mauve).. .. .. .. .. .. .. .. .. 3·25 | 3·25 |
| 34p. 1 (deep bluish grey) .. .. .. .. .. .. .. .. 4·00 | 4·00 |
| 37p. 1 (rosine) .. .. .. .. .. .. .. .. .. 4·25 | 4·25 |

**Cylinder Varieties**

The following is a faint multipositive flaw which occurs on 29, 34 and 37p. dot cylinders.

1/10   Curved hairline scratch across shoulder (Th.F4–F5)

For a flaw on 20p. see pane Nos. WP801/2.

**Sheet Details**

Sheet size: 200 (20 horizontal rows of ten stamps). Double pane (no dot and dot) reel-fed on the Jumelle press
Sheet markings:
    Cylinder numbers: Opposite row 18, left margin (20p. vertical (H), 1A (top) and 1B (bottom); normal sideways box (others)
    Marginal arrows: Between vertical rows 5/6 and horizontal rows 10/11 at both sides
    Colour register marks:
        Cross in circle opposite row 2, left margin of 20p. no dot pane. This may occur on the dot right margin and confirmation is needed
    Autotron marks: Thick bar opposite rows 8/9, left margin on no dot panes only. It is printed in brownish black (1A) on 20p.
    Perforation guide marks: Opposite rows 14/15, left margin on no dot and right margin on dot panes. This is the "S O N" marking with "S" for "Selvedge", "N" for "near-side" and "O" for "off-side". They appear in reverse order on the other side of the double-pane sheet. Since the printing was reel-fed the boxes were not punched through as they would have been if a sheet-fed perforator had been used
    Positioning lines: Horizontal lines at top left corner (no dot) and at top right (dot) pane. Vertical line opposite rows 11/13, left margin on no dot panes only
    Extra extension holes: The extra marker pin exists on the 15p., 20p. no dot, left margin. It probably occurs also on other values in the left margin on no dot and in right margin on dot panes
    Total Sheet Values: Repeated four times on each pane opposite rows 5/7 and 15/17 reading up at left and down at right

For illustrations of sheet markings see under the notes in Section UD.

## II. Type W751. Printed in Lithography by Walsall

Perforation 14

ONE 4 mm. CENTRE BAND. FLUORESCENT COATED PAPER
60p. Barcode booklet pane No. WP808, £1·50 Barcode booklet pane No. WP811
W804 (=S.G.1475)     15p. bright blue (30.1.90) ..     ..     ..     ..     ..     50     60
    Imperforate edges: No. W804 exists imperforate at top (WP808, WP811); bottom (WP808, WP811); top and right (WP808, WP811); bottom and right (WP808, WP811)

PHOSPHORISED (ADVANCED COATED) PAPER
80p. Barcode booklet pane No. WP809, £1 booklet pane No. WP810, £2 Barcode booklet pane No. WP812
W805 (=S.G.1476)     20p. brownish black and cream (30.1.90)     ..     ..     60     70
    Imperforate edges: No. W805 exists imperforate at left (WP810); right (WP810); top (WP809, WP812); bottom (WP809, WP812); top and right (WP809, WP812); bottom and right (WP809, WP812)

## III. Type W751. Printed in Lithography by Questa

Perforation 15 × 14

ONE SHORT 4 mm. CENTRE BAND. FLUORESCENT COATED PAPER
£1·50 Barcode booklet pane No. WP813
W806 (=S.G.1477)     15p. bright blue (17.4.90) ..     ..     ..     ..     ..     50     60

PHOSPHORISED (ADVANCED COATED) PAPER
£2 Barcode booklet pane No. WP814
W807 (=S.G.1478)     20p. brownish black (17.4.90)     ..     ..     ..     ..     65     70

## Booklet Panes containing Machin Penny Black Anniversary stamps

## I. Printed by Harrison in Photogravure

**50p. Pane. Aircraft Series FB56**

WP797

Vertical pair 15p. (bright blue) and 20p. (brownish black and cream)

Pane WP797. Pair of 15p. with left phosphor band 3 mm. wide on 15p. top row and below the band is 9.5 mm. wide between 20p. and 15p. The postcode label has no bands as the left narrow band on the 20p. is the height of the stamp. From 50p. Pictorial Booklet, No. FB56

Pane WP797. Photogravure, selvedge at top

|  |  | Perf. Type E |
|---|---|---|
| WP797 (containing Nos. W789, W789a, W792) (30.1.90) | | 2·25 |

**Booklet Cylinder Numbers**

| Pane No. | Cyl. Nos. | Phos. No. | | | Perf. Type E<br>No dot |
|---|---|---|---|---|---|
| WP797 | 15p., B3; 20p., B2A, B2B (cream) | (B85) | .. | .. | 4·00 |
| WP797 | 15p., B3; 20p., B2A, B2B (cream) | (—) | .. | .. | 10·00 |
| WP797 | — | (B85) | .. | .. | 10·00 |

**Sheet Make-up**

The printer's sheet contained three columns of eight panes each including one with cylinder numbers. New phosphor ink was used and this is not easy to see under ultra violet light. The stamps were printed on the Chambon press and perforated by an APS rotary type perforator.

**£1 Pane with imperforate vertical sides. Mills Series FH20**

WP798, WP810

Pane of five 20p. (brownish black and cream) stamps on phosphorised (advanced coated) paper and postcode label from £1 Pictorial Booklet No. FH20. Pane imperforate on vertical sides

Pane WP798. Photogravure, selvedge at top

|  | Perf. Type IEI |
|---|---|
| WP798 (containing No. W791 × 5) (30.1.90) | 3·25 |

**Booklet Cylinder Numbers**

| | | Perf. Type IEI |
|---|---|---|
| Pane No. | Cyl. No. | No dot |
| WP798 | B3A, B3B (cream)    ..    ..    ..    ..    ..    .. | 5·00 |

Various omissions affecting the cylinder number letters are due to dry prints.

**Sheet Make-up**

The printer's sheet contained two columns of eight panes including one pane showing a cylinder number. The stamps were printed on the Chambon press and perforated by an APS rotary type perforator.

---

**£1.50 Pane. Barcode Booklet JC1**

WP799

Pane of ten 15p. stamps with one 4 mm. centre phosphor band from £1.50 Barcode Booklet No. JC1. Pane has imperforate horizontal edges.

Pane WP799. Photogravure, selvedge at left

WP799 (containing No. W788 × 10) (30.1.90)

Perf. Type IEI
4·50

**Booklet Cylinder Numbers**

| Pane No. | Cyl. Nos. | Phos. No. | | | | Perf. Type IEI<br>No dot |
|---|---|---|---|---|---|---|
| WP799 | B6 | (B84) | .. | .. | .. | 7·00 |

**Sheet Make-up**

The printer's sheet was single pane containing four columns of ten panes each. Gutter margins between vertical columns 2, 3 and 4 were trimmed to provide the binding margin at left. The right side margin was trimmed to the perforation edge. The columns were continuous and contained a cylinder pane every fifth pane. There were 8 cylinder and 32 ordinary panes in the printer's sheet. Horizontal trimming lines in the vertical margins at left indicated the cutting lines with cylinder numbers placed opposite row 1 in the pane.

---

**£2 Pane. Barcode Booklet JD1**

WP800

Pane of ten 20p. (brownish black and cream) stamps on phosphorised (advanced coated) paper from £2 Barcode Booklet No. JD1. Pane has imperforate horizontal edges.

Pane WP800. Photogravure, selvedge at left

WP800 (containing No. W791 × 10) (30.1.90)

Perf. Type IEI
6·00

**Booklet Cylinder Numbers**

| Pane No. | Cyl. Nos. | | | | | Perf. Type IEI<br>No dot |
|---|---|---|---|---|---|---|
| WP800 | B1A, B1B (cream) | .. | .. | .. | .. | ..   8·00 |

**Sheet Make-up**
As for £1·50 pane No. WP799.

From £5 Booklet "London Life" No. DX11

Second pane comprising 6 × 20p. in photogravure on phosphorised (advanced coated) paper.

WP801

(*Actual size* 163 × 97 *mm.*)

| | | |
|---|---|---|
| WP801 (containing No. W791 × 6) (20.3.90) | | 2·50 |
| *b.* Diagonal scratch (R. 1/2) | .. .. .. .. .. .. | 5·00 |

Third pane on fluorescent coated paper comprising: top horizontal row, (2nd) bright blue, band at right, 50p. ochre, two 9·5 mm. bands, (1st) brownish black, two 9·5 mm. bands; second horizontal row containing, 15p. Machin bright blue, band at right, Stamp World London '90 label, 20p. Machin brownish black, two bands, third horizontal row containing, Penny Black Anniversary Nos. W790 (15p.), W796 (29p.), W792 (20p.). The band at right is narrow to avoid the vertical margin.

This pane is listed and illustrated in Section UE under "III. Panes from Prestige Booklets"—see pane No. UWB33 from the £5 London Life Booklet.

Fourth pane comprising 6 × 20p. in photogravure on phosphorised (advanced coated) paper.

WP802

(*Actual size* 163 × 97 *mm.*)

| | | |
|---|---|---|
| WP802 (containing No. W791 × 6) (20.3.90) | | 2·50 |
| *b.* Diagonal scratch (R. 1/2) | .. .. .. .. .. .. .. | 5·00 |

**Listed London Life Booklet Cylinder Flaws**

This scratch is a multipositive flaw occurring on both panes (R. 1/2)

WP801*b*, WP802*b*

**Booklet Cylinder Numbers**
The cylinder numbers did not occur in the finished booklets.

---

**80p. Pane. Barcode Booklet JB2**

WP803, WP809

Pane of four 20p. stamps on phosphorised (advanced coated) paper from 80p. Barcode Booklet No. JB2. Pane has three edges imperforate

Pane WP803. Photogravure, selvedge at left

Perf. Type IEI

WP803 (containing No. W791 × 4) (17.4.90)     1·25

**Booklet Cylinder Numbers**
The cylinder numbers were trimmed off and do not occur on the finished booklet panes. Those used were: B6A, B4A and B7A, B4B (cream).

## II. Printed in Lithography by Walsall

Perforation 14

**60p. Pane. Barcode Booklet JA1**

WP808

Pane of four 15p. stamps with one 4 mm. centre phosphor band from 60p. Barcode Booklet No. JA1. Pane has three edges imperforate

Pane WP808. Lithographed, selvedge at left

| | Perf. Type | |
|---|---|---|
| | IEI | IEIb |
| WP808 (containing No. W804 × 4) (30.1.90) | 3·00 | 7·00 |

The prices quoted are for panes in booklets showing Queen Victoria's face in blue. Card covers showing Queen Victoria's face in cream were from a later printing and corresponding panes from this cover variety are worth more.

**Booklet Plate Numbers**

| Pane No. | Pl. Nos. (No dot) | | | | | | Perf. Type | |
|---|---|---|---|---|---|---|---|---|
| | | | | | | | IEI | IEIb |
| WP808 | W1, W1, W1 | | | | | | 6·00 | — |
| WP808 | W2, W1 | .. | .. | .. | .. | .. | 6·50 | 10·00 |
| WP808 | W2, W1 bar | .. | .. | .. | .. | .. | 15·00 | † |
| WP808 | W2, W2 | .. | .. | .. | .. | .. | 8·00 | 30·00 |
| WP808 | W2, W2 bar | .. | .. | .. | .. | .. | 45·00 | † |

**Sheet Make-up**

The uncut sheet contained 72 panes made up of 8 vertical columns of 9 panes each. The top selvedge was perforated through but the bottom of the sheet was not and this gives a blind perforation to 8 panes across the bottom of the sheet (perf. type IEIb). Plate number panes were in the first and eighth vertical columns in positions 1/3 and 7/9. A further 3 plate number panes were in the fifth column in positions 4/6 giving a total of 15 plate number panes. The pane in position 7 in column 1 shows a plate number plus the trace of a bar depending on the extent of the trim.

**80p. Pane. Barcode Booklet JB1**

As pane No. WP803

Pane of four 20p. (brownish black and cream) stamps on phosphorised (advanced coated) paper from 80p. Barcode Booklet No. JB1. Pane has three edges imperforate

Pane WP809. Lithographed, selvedge at left

| | Perf. Type | |
|---|---|---|
| | IEI | IEIb |
| WP809 (containing No. W805 × 4) (30.1.90) | 4·00 | 8·00 |

**Booklet Plate Numbers**

| | | | | | | | Perf. Type | |
|---|---|---|---|---|---|---|---|---|
| Pane No. | Pl. Nos. (No dot) | | | | | | IEI | IEIb |
| WP809 | W1, W1, W1 | .. | .. | .. | .. | .. | 7·00 | 12·00 |
| WP809 | W1, W1, W1 bar | .. | .. | .. | .. | .. | 12·00 | † |

**Sheet Make-up**
As for 60p. pane No. WP808.

---

**£1 Pane with imperforate vertical sides. Mills Series FH19 (Experimental glossy card cover)**

As pane No. WP798

Pane of five 20p. (brownish black and cream) stamps on phosphorised (advanced coated) paper and postcode label from £1 Pictorial Booklet No. FH19. Pane imperforate on vertical sides

Pane WP810. Lithographed, selvedge at top

| | Perf. Type IPI |
|---|---|
| WP810 (containing No. W805 × 5) (30.1.90) | 3·25 |

**Booklet Plate Numbers**

| Pane No. | Pl. Nos. (No dot) | | | | | | Perf. Type IPI |
|---|---|---|---|---|---|---|---|
| WP810 | W1, W1, W1 | .. | .. | .. | .. | .. | 6·00 |

**Sheet Make-up**
It is believed that the sheet format was similar to the 14p./19p. multi-value £1 pane in Booklet No. FH16.

---

**£1·50 Pane. Barcode Booklet JC3**

WP811 (Perf. Type IEIb)

Pane of ten 15p. stamps with one 4 mm. centre phosphor band from £1·50 Barcode Booklet No. JC3. Pane has three edges imperforate.

Pane WP811. Lithographed, selvedge at left

|  | Perf. Type | |
| --- | --- | --- |
|  | IEI | IEIb |
| WP811 (containing No. W804 × 10) (12.6.90) | 2·25 | 3·50 |

**Booklet Plate Numbers**

| | | Perf. Type | |
| --- | --- | --- | --- |
| Pane No. | Pl. Nos. (No dot) | IEI | IEIb |
| WP811 | W1, W1 .. .. .. .. .. .. .. | 6·00 | 8·00 |
| WP811 | W1, W1 bar .. .. .. .. .. .. | 12·00 | † |

**Sheet Make-up**
  The uncut sheet contained 36 panes in a similar format to the panes of four stamps printed by Walsall. The sheet was made up of 4 vertical columns with 9 panes in each. As in the panes of four the top selvedge was perforated through and the bottom of the sheet perf. type IEIb. Plate number panes were in the first and last vertical columns in positions 1/3 and 7/9. In addition there were a further three plate number panes in the third column in positions 4/6. The plate number bar booklet was again in the first column, position 7. The length of the bar varies according to the trim.

---

**£2 Pane. Barcode Booklet JD3**

WP812

  Pane of ten 20p. (brownish black and cream) stamps on phosphorised (advanced coated) paper from Barcode Booklet No. JD3. Pane has three edges imperforate.

Pane WP812. Lithographed, selvedge at left

|  | Perf. Type | |
| --- | --- | --- |
|  | IEI | IEIb |
| WP812 (containing No. W805 × 10) (12.6.90) | 3·00 | 4·25 |

**Booklet Plate Numbers**

| | | Perf. Type | |
| --- | --- | --- | --- |
| Pane No. | Pl. Nos. (No dot) | IEI | IEIb |
| WP812 | W1, W1, W1 .. .. .. .. .. .. | 6·00 | 10·00 |
| WP812 | W1, W1, W1 bar .. .. .. .. .. .. | 15·00 | † |
| WP812 | W1, W2, W1 .. .. .. .. .. .. | 10·00 | 15·00 |
| WP812 | W1, W2, W1 bar .. .. .. .. .. .. | 20·00 | † |
| WP812 | W1, W2, W2 .. .. .. .. .. .. | 8·00 | 10·00 |
| WP812 | W1, W2, W2 bar .. .. .. .. .. .. | 12·00 | † |

**Sheet Make-up**
  As for £1·50 pane No. WP811.

## III. Printed in Lithography by Questa

Perforation 15 × 14

**£1·50 Pane. Barcode Booklet JC2**

WP813

Pane of ten 15p. stamps with one centre 4 mm. short phosphor band from £1·50 Barcode Booklet
No. JC2

Pane WP813. Lithographed, selvedge at left

| | Perf. Type P |
|---|---|
| WP813 (containing No. W806 × 10) (17.4.90) | 2·25 |

**Sheet Make-up**
The uncut printer's sheet contained 16 booklet panes arranged in four vertical columns of four
panes in each. The panes were perforated all round to give Perf. Type P and there were no plate
numbers in the issued booklets.

**£2 Pane. Barcode Booklet JD2**

WP814

Pane of ten 20p. stamps on phosphorised (advanced coated) paper from £2 Barcode Booklet No.
JD2

Pane WP814. Lithographed, selvedge at left

| | Perf. Type P |
|---|---|
| WP814 (containing No. W807 × 10) (17.4.90) | 3·00 |

**Sheet Make-up**
As Pane WP813.

**W760** Miniature Sheet

(*Illustration reduced to three quarters actual size*)

(Des. Sedley Place Design Ltd. Recess and photogravure Harrison)

## 1990 (3 MAY). "STAMP WORLD 90" INTERNATIONAL STAMP EXHIBITION, LONDON

The miniature sheet was sold with a premium of 80p. for the benefit of the "Stamp World 90" exhibition funds. In No. WMS815 *only* the 20p. No. W792, is perforated 15 × 14.

Phosphorised (advanced coated) paper

WMS815
    (=S.G.**MS**1501) **W760** Sheet size 122 × 89 mm. issued in pack with printed

| | | | | | | | |
|---|---|---|---|---|---|---|---|
| card (sold at £1) | .. | .. | .. | .. | .. | 2·25 | 2·25 |
|   *a*. Imperforate sheet | .. | .. | .. | .. | .. | | |
|   *b*. Black (recess printing) omitted | .. | .. | .. | | | |
|   *c*. Black (recess printing) inverted | .. | .. | .. | | | |

No. WMS815*b* shows an albino impression on the gummed side. The 1d. black (recess printing) and Seahorse background are omitted on the front due to one sheet becoming attached to the underside of another just prior to recess-printing.

| | | | | | | | |
|---|---|---|---|---|---|---|---|
| First Day Cover (WMS815) | .. | .. | .. | .. | .. | .. † | 5·00 |
| Souvenir Book (Nos. W788, 791, 793/5, WMS815) | | .. | .. | .. 10·50 | † |

**Miniature Sheet**
    The printer's uncut sheet comprised two panes (no dot and dot) of eight miniature sheets (2 × 4). The cylinder and plate numbers were trimmed off. It is believed that the cylinder numbers were 2C, 1A (photo) and 1E, 1G (recess).

**Withdrawn**   2.5.91

# SECTION XB
# Regional Decimal Issues

## 1971–81. Photogravure

### General Notes

As from a press notice dated 3 December 1973 the Post Office has designated these stamps as Country issues but this term has not generally been adopted in philatelic literature and we continue to describe them as Regional issues.

**INTRODUCTION.** On 7 July 1971 new stamps appeared in decimal currency showing a reduced size Machin head accompanied by emblems representing the Isle of Man, Northern Ireland, Scotland and Wales and Monmouthshire. They were all designed by Jeffery Matthews.

The ordinary postage stamps of Great Britain in the same values are not on sale at post offices in these regions except at the Philatelic Counters in Belfast, Cardiff, Edinburgh and Glasgow, apart from Monmouthshire where the Welsh Regionals and Great Britain stamps were on sale concurrently (see notes at the beginning of Wales). All regional stamps are valid for use throughout Great Britain with the exception of the Channel Islands and also the Isle of Man from 5 July 1973.

**PRINTERS.** All were printed in photogravure by Harrison & Sons. As with the ordinary decimal Machin issues they were printed in double pane width, i.e. 400 stamps consisting of two panes (no dot and dot) each of 200 stamps arranged in twenty rows of ten stamps, the panes being guillotined before issue. All the 5½p. and the 8p. values were printed in single panes but from double pane cylinders. The 5p. and 7½p. were sheet-fed but all the rest were reel-fed.

**MACHIN PORTRAIT.** The original Head A with the flatter bust was used for the 3½p., 4½p., 6½p., 7p., 8½p., 10½p., 12p., 13½p. and 15p. values. Head B with the curved "shadow" was employed for the 2½p., 3p., 5p., 5½p., 7½p. and 8p. values. Head C was used for the 9p., 10p. and 11p. values. The following illustrations are reproduced from Vol. 3—

Head A
Flatter Base

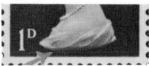

Head B
Curved Shadow

Head C
Three-dimensional effect with light background

**MULTIPOSITIVES.** It is believed that two multipositives are used for each of the Regional issues—one for the head and background and the other for the country symbol and value.

**PAPER AND GUM.** The same unwatermarked papers and gums have been used as for the ordinary Machin decimal stamps and for explanation of the terms OCP, FCP, GA, PVA and PVAD see the General Notes for Section UD.

**PERFORATION.** All stamps are perforated 15 × 14 as before. Cylinder numbers are listed according to the perforation types used and these are illustrated in Appendix I.

**PHOSPHOR BANDS.** The remarks under this heading in the General Notes to Section UD also apply to the regional stamps.

**YELLOW PHOSPHOR.**  The yellowish afterglow after exposure to longwave ultraviolet light caused by contamination in 1973 of the normal "violet" phosphor with zinc oxide, which is described more fully in the General Notes to Section UD, is also found on certain regional issues. These are:—

| Region | Value | Cat. No. | Paper/gum | Cyl. No. | Phos. No. |
|---|---|---|---|---|---|
| Northern Ireland | 3p. | XN21 | FCP/PVA | 1 | 7 |
| Scotland | 3p. | XS33 | FCP/GA | 8 | 7 |
|  | 5p. | XS42 | FCP/PVA | 7 | 11 |
| Wales | 3p. | XW23 | FCP/GA | 1 | 7 |

They are recorded in footnotes below the catalogue numbers

**PHOSPHOR SCREENS.**  See General Notes for Section UD. In the regional issues the 250 screen was used for the 3p. 2 bands, 5½p. 2 bands and 8p. All the remainder have 150 screen.

**PHOSPHOR CYLINDER NUMBERS.**  See the General Notes for Section UD. They normally appear synchronised in the box to the left of the cylinder number in the form illustrated in Section UD and on both panes. In the case of double figure numbers in the dot pane the margins are often narrow so that the first figure is liable to be trimmed off. They also occur synchronised but displaced.

**CYLINDER VARIETIES.**  We have only listed those that we have actually seen and know to be constant in the position given. Some of these may exist on other papers or with other gums and these will be added as they are brought to our attention. Other varieties have been reported and may be added in future editions as specimens become available for illustration. For further information see the General Notes to Section UD under "Varieties in Sheets".

**MINOR CONSTANT FLAWS.**  The notes under these headings in the General Notes to Section UD also apply to regional issues.

**DATES OF ISSUE.**  Earliest known dates of issue are given for changes of paper and gum.

**SHEET MARKINGS**

**Cylinder Numbers.**  Boxed opposite R. 18/1 (Section UD).

**Marginal Arrows.**  Exactly as for Section UD.

**Perforation Guide Holes**

Punched Perforation Guide Hole Box

**Perforation Guide Holes.**  There are none on the 5p. and 7½p. On the 5½p. and 8p. a three-sided box as illustrated above appears in the left-hand margin of the no dot pane and in the right-hand margin of the dot pane it faces the other way. On the 5½p. for Northern Ireland and Scotland these occur opposite rows 13/14 and for Wales, together with all the 8p. values, they occur opposite row 14. They are punched through on the 5½p. two bands and the 8p. but were not used on the 5½p. centre band. All the remaining values have the usual " S O N " box at rows 14/15 as illustrated in the notes for Section UD.

**Marginal Rules.**  Wide co-extensive rule below the bottom row (Section UD).

**Coloured Cross.**  A single cross as illustrated in Section W appears above and below vertical row 5 next to the marginal arrow on the no dot panes of the 5p. and 7½p.

**Autotron Mark.**  This occurs in the colour of the stamp opposite rows 8/9 in the left-hand margin of no dot panes printed by the "Jumelle" press (Perforation Type R). Illustrated in Section UD.

**Total Sheet Values.**  These are preceded by "I O MAN", "N. IRELAND", "SCOTLAND" or "WALES" and occur four times on each pane opposite rows 5/7 and 15/17, reading up at left and down at right (Section UD).
  Exceptionally the inscription on the 5½p. and 8p. Northern Ireland stamps is larger so that it appears opposite rows 4/7 and 15/18 and on the 6½p. and 8½p. values it reads "NORTHERN IRELAND" in full and appears in the same position as the 5½p. and 8p. On the 7p., 9p., 10p., 10½p., 11p., 12p., 13½p. and 15p. the inscription is the same except that in the upper half of the sheet it appears opposite rows 5/7 instead of 4/7.

# A.   Isle of Man

**XM3**

(Des. Jeffery Matthews)

# Type XM3

## $2\frac{1}{2}$p.   (1971–73)

### 1971 (7 JULY).   ONE 4 mm. CENTRE PHOSPHOR BAND

#### A. ORIGINAL COATED PAPER. PVA GUM

| | | | | | | | | |
|---|---|---|---|---|---|---|---|---|
| XM12 ( = S.G.8) | Bright magenta | .. | .. | .. | .. | .. | .. | 20 | 15 |
| | a. Phosphor omitted | | .. | .. | .. | .. | .. | £900 |
| | b. Ankle flaw | .. | .. | .. | .. | .. | .. | 2·25 |

**Cylinder Numbers (Blocks of Six)**

Perforation Type A

| Cyl. No. | Phos. No. | | | | | No dot | Dot |
|---|---|---|---|---|---|---|---|
| 3 | 5 | .. | .. | .. | .. | 2·50 | 2·50 |

#### B. FLUORESCENT COATED PAPER. PVA GUM

| | | | | | | | | |
|---|---|---|---|---|---|---|---|---|
| XM13 | Bright magenta | .. | .. | .. | .. | .. | .. | 70 | 70 |

**Cylinder Numbers (Blocks of Six)**

Perforation Type A

| Cyl. No. | Phos. No. | | | | | No dot | Dot |
|---|---|---|---|---|---|---|---|
| 3 | 9 | .. | .. | .. | .. | 8·50 | 8·50 |

#### CYLINDER VARIETY
**Listed Flaw**

**XM12***b*

White projection in ankle of bottom leg
(Cyl. 3 no dot, R. 15/1)

**WITHDRAWN**   4.7.74

## 3p.   (1971–73)

### 1971 (7 JULY).   TWO 9·5 mm. PHOSPHOR BANDS

#### A. ORIGINAL COATED PAPER. PVA GUM

| | | | | | | | | |
|---|---|---|---|---|---|---|---|---|
| XM14 ( = S.G.9) | Ultramarine | .. | .. | .. | .. | .. | .. | 20 | 15 |
| | a. Blurred emblem | .. | .. | .. | .. | .. | 2·50 |

**Cylinder Numbers (Blocks of Six)**

Perforation Type A

| Cyl. No. | Phos. No. | | | | | No dot | Dot |
|---|---|---|---|---|---|---|---|
| 1 | 4 | .. | .. | .. | .. | 2·50 | 2·50 |

**359**

**B. FLUORESCENT COATED PAPER. PVA GUM** (7.73)

XM15                    Ultramarine  ..    ..    ..    ..    ..    ..    ..    1·60    1·60
                        a. Blurred emblem  ..    ..    ..    ..    ..    ..    4·50

**Cylinder Numbers (Blocks of Six unless otherwise stated)**
Perforation Type A

| Cyl. No. | Phos. No. | | | | | No dot | Dot | |
|---|---|---|---|---|---|---|---|---|
| 1 | — |  .. | .. | .. | .. | 22·00 | 22·00 | |
| 1 | — | 7 + 35 mm. (17) | | | .. | 30·00 | † | Block of eight |
| 1 | — | 7 + 37 mm. (17) | | | .. | † | 32·00 | Block of eight |

**CYLINDER VARIETIES**
**Listed Flaw**

XM14a, XM15a
Design at top of emblem very blurred
(No dot, R. 1/9)

**Minor Constant Flaw**

Cyl. 1    12/2  White line below right leg of emblem (Th. B2–B3)

**WITHDRAWN**   Nos. XM14/5, 4.7.74

---

# 5p.   (1971)

**1971 (7 JULY).   TWO 9·5 mm. PHOSPHOR BANDS. ORIGINAL COATED PAPER. PVA GUM**

XM16 ( = S.G.10)        Reddish violet..    ..    ..    ..    ..    ..    ..    70    75
                        a. Phosphor omitted..    ..    ..    ..    ..    ..    £200

**Cylinder Numbers (Blocks of Six)**
Perforation Type F*

| Cyl. No. | Phos. No. | | | | No dot | Dot |
|---|---|---|---|---|---|---|
| 4 | 12 | .. | .. | .. | 5·00 | 5·00 |

**WITHDRAWN**   4.7.74

---

# 7½p.   (1971)

**1971 (7 JULY).   TWO 9·5 mm. PHOSPHOR BANDS. ORIGINAL COATED PAPER. PVA GUM**

XM17 ( = S.G.11)        Chestnut    ..    ..    ..    ..    ..    ..    ..    70    90
                        a. White flaw on 7  ..    ..    ..    ..    ..    ..    3·75

**Cylinder Numbers (Blocks of Six)**
Perforation Type F*

| Cyl. No. | Phos. No. | | | | No dot | Dot |
|---|---|---|---|---|---|---|
| 4 | 10 | .. | .. | .. | 6·50 | 6·50 |

**CYLINDER VARIETIES**
Listed Flaw

XM17*a*
(Cyl. 4 dot, R. 12/7)

**Minor Constant Flaws**
Cyl. 4.   10/10 Vertical scratch from cross on crown to back of collar (Th. B5–F5)
        10/11 Extension of above scratch in background to cross on crown (Th. A5/6–B5/6)

**WITHDRAWN**   4.7.74

## Presentation Pack

XMPP2 No. 30 (7.7.71)                     2½p., 3p., 5p., 7½p.                2·00
  Comprises Nos. XM12, 14 and 16/17

**WITHDRAWN**   4.7.74

## First Day Cover

XMFD1 (7.7.71)                .              2½p., 3p., 5p., 7½p.        †    3·50

# B. Northern Ireland

**XN4**
(Des. Jeffery Matthews)

## Type XN4

### 2½p. (1971–73)

#### 1971 (7 JULY). ONE 4 mm. CENTRE PHOSPHOR BAND

**A. ORIGINAL COATED PAPER. PVA GUM**

| | | | | | | | | |
|---|---|---|---|---|---|---|---|---|
| XN18 (=S.G.NI12) | Bright magenta | .. | .. | .. | .. | .. | .. | 90 | 25 |
| | a. Missing pearls on crown.. | | .. | .. | .. | .. | 3·75 | |
| | b. White patch on shoulder.. | | .. | .. | .. | .. | 3·50 | |

**Cylinder Numbers (Blocks of Six)**
Perforation Type A

| Cyl. No. | Phos. No. | | | | No dot | Dot |
|---|---|---|---|---|---|---|
| 4 | 5 | .. | .. | .. | 6·50 | 6·50 |

**B. FLUORESCENT COATED PAPER. PVA GUM**

| | | | | | | | | |
|---|---|---|---|---|---|---|---|---|
| XN19 | Bright magenta | .. | .. | .. | .. | .. | .. | 3·00 | 3·00 |

**Cylinder Numbers (Blocks of Six)**
Perforation Type A

| Cyl. No. | Phos. No. | | | | No dot | Dot |
|---|---|---|---|---|---|---|
| 4 | 8 | .. | .. | .. | 24·00 | 30·00 |
| 4 | 9 | .. | .. | .. | 50·00 | 50·00 |
| 4 | 9 | −21 mm. (19) | | .. | 30·00 | 25·00 |

**CYLINDER VARIETIES**
**Listed Flaws**

XN18a          Normal
Last two pearls at right of
crown in emblem almost missing
(Cyl. 4 dot, R. 3/6)

XN18b
White patch on Queen's
shoulder
(Cyl. 4 dot, R. 6/10)

**WITHDRAWN** Nos. XN18/9, 22.1.75

362

# 3p.   (1971–74)

**1971 (7 JULY).   TWO 9·5 mm. PHOSPHOR BANDS**
**A. ORIGINAL COATED PAPER. PVA GUM**

| | | | | | | | | | |
|---|---|---|---|---|---|---|---|---|---|
| XN20 (=S.G.N113) | Ultramarine | .. | .. | .. | .. | .. | .. | 40 | 15 |
| | a. Phosphor omitted.. | | .. | .. | .. | .. | .. | 20·00 | |

**Cylinder Numbers (Blocks of Six)**
Perforation Type A

| Cyl. No. | Phos. No. | | | | | No dot | Dot |
|---|---|---|---|---|---|---|---|
| 1 | 4 | .. | .. | .. | .. | 4·00 | 4·00 |

**B. FLUORESCENT COATED PAPER. PVA GUM** (4.73)

| | | | | | | | | | |
|---|---|---|---|---|---|---|---|---|---|
| XN21 | Ultramarine | .. | .. | .. | .. | .. | .. | 10·00 | 5·00 |

Examples of No. XN21 exist with contaminated "yellow phosphor". *Price £5 mint.*

**Cylinder Numbers (Blocks of Six)**
Perforation Type A

| Cyl. No. | Phos. No. | | | | | No dot | Dot |
|---|---|---|---|---|---|---|---|
| 1 | — | .. | .. | .. | .. | 70·00 | 85·00 |
| 1 | 7 | .. | .. | .. | .. | 80·00 | 85·00 |

Phosphor Cylinder Displacement. With ink cyl. 1, phos. cyl. 7 is known displaced up the margin 185 mm. opposite row 11.

**1974 (23 JANUARY).   CHANGE TO ONE 4 mm. CENTRE BAND**
**A. FLUORESCENT COATED PAPER. PVAD GUM**

| | | | | | | | | |
|---|---|---|---|---|---|---|---|---|
| XN22 | Ultramarine | .. | .. | .. | .. | .. | .. | 70 |

**Cylinder Numbers (Blocks of Six)**
Perforation Type A

| Cyl. No. | Phos. No. | | | | | No dot | Dot |
|---|---|---|---|---|---|---|---|
| 1 | 8 | .. | .. | .. | .. | 6·50 | 6·50 |

**B. FLUORESCENT COATED PAPER. PVA GUM** (4.74)

| | | | | | | | | | |
|---|---|---|---|---|---|---|---|---|---|
| XN23 (=S.G.N114) | Ultramarine | .. | .. | .. | .. | .. | .. | 20 | 15 |

**Cylinder Numbers (Blocks of Six)**
Perforation Type A

| Cyl. No. | Phos. No. | | | | | No dot | Dot |
|---|---|---|---|---|---|---|---|
| 1 | 8 | .. | .. | .. | .. | 1·60 | 1·60 |

**WITHDRAWN**   Nos. XN20/1, 22.1.75
Nos. XN22/3, 8.4.78

# 3½p.   (1974)

**1974 (23 JANUARY).   TWO 9·5 mm. PHOSPHOR BANDS. FLUORESCENT COATED PAPER. PVAD GUM**

| | | | | | | | | | |
|---|---|---|---|---|---|---|---|---|---|
| XN24 (=S.G.N115) | Olive-grey | .. | .. | .. | .. | .. | .. | 20 | 20 |

**Cylinder Numbers (Blocks of Six)**
Perforation Type R

| Cyl. No. | Phos. No. | | | | | No dot | Dot |
|---|---|---|---|---|---|---|---|
| 1 | 17 | .. | .. | .. | .. | 2·40 | 2·40 |

## 1974 (6 NOVEMBER). CHANGE TO ONE 4 mm. CENTRE BAND. FLUORESCENT COATED PAPER. PVAD GUM

XN25 (= S.G. N16)    Olive-grey    ..    ..    ..    ..    ..    ..    ..    20    25
　　　　　　　　　　*a.* White dots under chin    ..    ..    ..    ..    ..    2·75

**Cylinder Numbers (Blocks of Six)**
Perforation Type R
　　　Cyl. No.  Phos. No.　　　　　　　　　　　　No dot　　Dot
　　　　1　　　　20    ..    ..    ..    ..    2·75    2·40

**CYLINDER VARIETIES**
**Listed Flaws**

Rectangle of white dots over phosphor
band below chin
(Cyl. 1 no dot, R. 4/10)

XN25*a*

**Minor Constant Flaws**
Cyl. 1    2/2  One missing screening dot at edge of design over cross on crown (Th. A2)
　　　　　9/3  Vertical scratch marks on Queen's cheek (Th. D4–D5)
　　　　11/2  As on 2/2

**WITHDRAWN**   Nos. XN24/5, 9.76

# 4½p.   (1974)
## 1974 (6 NOVEMBER).   TWO 9·5 mm. PHOSPHOR BANDS. FLUORESCENT COATED PAPER. PVAD GUM

XN26 (= S.G. N17)    Grey-blue    ..    ..    ..    ..    ..    ..    25    25

**Cylinder Numbers (Blocks of Six)**
Perforation Type R
　　　Cyl. No.  Phos. No.　　　　　　　　　　　　No dot　　Dot
　　　　1　　　　17    ..    ..    ..    ..    2·75    2·75

**CYLINDER VARIETIES**
**Minor Constant Flaws**

Cyl. 1    3/8  White spot above necklace (Th. F4)
　　　　　9/2  White speck over pearls on right of crown in emblem (Th. A2)
　　　　18/2  White speck in Queen's hair (Th. D5)

**WITHDRAWN**   9.76

# 5p.   (1971)
## 1971 (7 JULY).   TWO 9·5 mm. PHOSPHOR BANDS. ORIGINAL COATED PAPER. PVA GUM

XN27 (= S.G. N18)    Reddish violet..    ..    ..    ..    ..    ..    1·50    1·50

**Cylinder Numbers (Blocks of Six)**
Perforation Type F*
　　　Cyl. No.  Phos. No.　　　　　　　　　　　　No dot　　Dot
　　　　4　　　　10    ..    ..    ..    ..    11·00    11·00

**WITHDRAWN**   22.1.75

**364**

# 5½p.   (1974–75)

## 1974 (23 JANUARY).   TWO 9·5 mm. PHOSPHOR BANDS. FLUORESCENT COATED PAPER. PVAD GUM

| | | | | |
|---|---|---|---|---|
| XN28 (= S.G.NI19) | Violet .. .. .. .. .. .. .. .. | 20 | 20 |
| | a. Phosphor omitted.. .. .. .. .. | £225 | |
| | b. Cylinder scratch (in block of 40) .. .. .. | 25·00 | |
| | c. No top to cross on crown .. .. .. .. | 2·40 | |

**Cylinder Numbers (Blocks of Six)**

Perforation Type A.   Single pane cylinder

| Cyl. No. | Phos. No. | | | | No dot | Dot |
|---|---|---|---|---|---|---|
| 1 | 22* | .. | .. | .. | 3·00 | † |

*The phosphor 22 is shown upright but superimposed over inverted figures.

## 1975 (21 MAY).   CHANGE TO ONE 4 mm. CENTRE BAND. FLUORESCENT COATED PAPER. PVAD GUM

| | | | | |
|---|---|---|---|---|
| XN29 (= S.G.NI20) | Violet .. .. .. .. .. .. .. .. | 20 | 20 |
| | b. No top to cross on crown .. .. .. .. | 2·40 | |

**Cylinder Numbers (Blocks of Six)**

Perforation Type R(S).

| Cyl. No. | Phos. No. | | | | No dot | Dot |
|---|---|---|---|---|---|---|
| 1 | 19 | .. | .. | .. | 2·50 | † |

Normally the Swedish rotary perforator produces a single extension hole in the left-hand margin on no dot panes. Sheets from cylinder 1 have been seen with the left-hand margin fully perforated through and also with two extension holes. *Price for cylinder block of 6 £5 mint.*

**CYLINDER VARIETIES**

**Listed Flaws**

| (R. 1/6)   XN28b   (R. 20/7) | XN28c, XN29b |
|---|---|
| Scratch extends diagonally from R. 1/6 to R. 20/7, Cyl. 1 no dot | Missing top to cross on crown (Cyl. 1 no dot, R. 11/10) |

**Minor Constant Flaw**

Cyl. 1   1/10 Diagonal hairline scratch across Queen's shoulders (Th. G3–F6)

**WITHDRAWN** Nos. XN28/9, 31.5.77

# 6½p.   (1976)

## 1976 (14 JANUARY).   ONE 4 mm. CENTRE PHOSPHOR BAND. FLUORESCENT COATED PAPER. PVAD GUM

| | | | | | | | | |
|---|---|---|---|---|---|---|---|---|
| XN30 (= S.G.N121) | Greenish blue .. | .. | .. | .. | .. | .. | .. | 20   20 |
| | b. Blue shoulder scratch | .. | .. | .. | .. | .. | 1·75 |
| | c. Dark spot in hair .. | .. | .. | .. | .. | .. | 2·00 |
| | d. Collar scratch | .. | .. | .. | .. | .. | 1·75 |
| | e. White spot over small crown | .. | .. | .. | .. | 2·00 |
| | f. Dark spot in band | .. | .. | .. | .. | .. | 1·75 |

**Cylinder Numbers (Blocks of Six)**

Perforation Type R

| Cyl. No. | Phos. No. | | | | | No dot | Dot |
|---|---|---|---|---|---|---|---|
| 1 | 18 | .. | .. | .. | .. | 2·00 | 2·00 |
| 2 | 18 | .. | .. | .. | .. | 50·00 | 5·00 |
| 2 | 20 | .. | .. | .. | .. | 2·50 | 3·25 |

Perforation Type RE

| | | | | | | | |
|---|---|---|---|---|---|---|---|
| 2 | 20 | .. | .. | .. | .. | —* | 2·50 |

*Same price as perforation type R with single extension holes in left margin.

**CYLINDER VARIETIES**

**Listed Flaws**

| X N30b | XN30d | XN30e |
|---|---|---|
| Small blue scratch on back of shoulder (Cyl. 1 dot, R. 1/4) | Scratch from collar into background (Cyl. 1 dot, R. 13/9) | White spot over small crown (Cyl. 1 dot, R. 15/3) |

Multipositive Flaws

The following also occur on 6½p. Scotland cyl. 1 dot and Wales cyl. 1 dot as well as on 4½p. Wales cyl. 1 dot.

| XN30c | XN30f |
|---|---|
| Dark spot in hair (Cyl. 1 dot, R. 12/8) | Dark spot in band of crown (Cyl. 1 dot, R. 16/6) |

See also Northern Ireland 12p. cyl. 1 dot, 13½p. cyl. 2 dot, 15p. cyl. 1 dot and Wales 12p. cyl. 2 dot where these flaws are listed in positions R. 12/10 and R. 16/8. Both flaws were retouched on the Wales 15p. cyl. 1 dot.

**Minor Constant Flaws**

Cyl. 1.   6/2  Small retouch at back of collar (Th. G5). Original flaw on Wales 4½p.
6/4  Blue speck on Queen's forehead (Th. C4–D4)
6/5  Blue blemish on Queen's cheek (Th. E4)
9/3  Blue spot on Queen's neck (Th. F5)
14/10  Small retouch under necklace (Th. F4)
20/2  Small speck under necklace (Th. F4–5)

Some of the above are multipositive flaws which occur to a greater or less extent on the 6½p. Scotland and 4½p. and 6½p. Wales from Cyl. 1 dot.

**WITHDRAWN**   3.79

# 7p.   (1978)
### 1978 (18 JANUARY).   ONE 4 mm. CENTRE PHOSPHOR BAND. FLUORESCENT COATED PAPER. PVAD GUM

| XN31 (=S.G.NI22) | Purple-brown | .. | .. | .. | .. | .. | .. | 25 | 25 |
|---|---|---|---|---|---|---|---|---|---|
| | b. White dots left of crown | | .. | .. | .. | .. | .. | 1·75 | |
| | c. Dark spot in band of crown | | .. | .. | .. | .. | 1·75 | |
| | d. Missing pearls | .. | .. | .. | .. | .. | .. | 2·00 | |

**Cylinder Numbers (Blocks of Six)**
Perforation Type RE

| Cyl. No. | Phos. No. | | | | No dot | Dot |
|---|---|---|---|---|---|---|
| 1 | 20 | .. | .. | .. | .. 22·00 | 28·00 |
| 1 | 31· | .. | .. | .. | .. 2·25 | 2·25 |

**CYLINDER VARIETIES**
**Listed Flaws**

XN31*b*
White dots left of crown
(Cyl. 1 no dot, R. 1/8)

XN31*c*
Dark spot in band of crown
(Cyl. 1 no dot, R. 6/3)

XN31*d*
Missing pearls at left of crown
(Cyl. 1. no dot, R. 20/7)

**Minor Constant Flaws**

Cyl. 1   1/7 Two dark spots on Queen's neck (Th. F5)
3/10 Dark speck on collar (Th. G5)
4/6 White scratch touching P
14/7 Dark spot over necklace (Th. F4)

**WITHDRAWN**   3.81

---

# 7½p.   (1971)
### 1971 (7 JULY).   TWO 9·5 mm. PHOSPHOR BANDS. ORIGINAL COATED PAPER. PVA GUM

| XN32 (=S.G.NI23) | Chestnut | .. | .. | .. | .. | .. | .. | 2·50 | 2·50 |
|---|---|---|---|---|---|---|---|---|---|
| | a. Phosphor omitted | .. | .. | .. | .. | .. | 55·00 | |

**Cylinder Numbers (Blocks of Six)**
Perforation Type F*

| Cyl. No. | Phos. No. | | | | No dot | Dot |
|---|---|---|---|---|---|---|
| 6 | 12 | .. | .. | .. | .. 18·00 | 18·00 |

**CYLINDER VARIETY**
**Minor Constant Flaw**

Cyl. 6   20/8 Background retouch left of Queen's eye (Th. D4)

**WITHDRAWN**   22.1.75

# 8p. (1974)

## 1974 (23 JANUARY).   TWO 9·5 mm. PHOSPHOR BANDS. FLUORESCENT COATED PAPER. PVAD GUM

| | | | | | | | | | |
|---|---|---|---|---|---|---|---|---|---|
| XN33 (=S.G.NI24) | Rosine .. | .. | .. | .. | .. | .. | .. | 30 | 30 |
| | a. Phosphor omitted.. | .. | .. | .. | .. | .. | 45·00 | |
| | b. Lip flaw | .. | .. | .. | .. | .. | .. | 3·00 | |

**Cylinder Numbers (Blocks of Six)**

Perforation Type A. Single pane cylinder

| Cyl. No. | Phos. No. | | | | No dot | Dot |
|---|---|---|---|---|---|---|
| 1 | 22* | .. | .. | .. | 2·25 | † |

*The phosphor 22 is shown upright but superimposed over inverted figures.

**CYLINDER VARIETIES**

**Listed Flaw**

Dark spot over Queen's upper lip
(Cyl. 1 no dot, R. 3/7)

XN33b

**Minor Constant Flaws**

Cyl. 1   15/4  Dark blemish on Queen's jaw (Th. F3)
16/9  Coloured line below necklace (Th. F4)

**WITHDRAWN**   3.79

---

# 8½p. (1976)

## 1976 (14 JANUARY).   TWO 9·5 mm. PHOSPHOR BANDS. FLUORESCENT COATED PAPER. PVAD GUM

| | | | | | | | | | |
|---|---|---|---|---|---|---|---|---|---|
| XN34 (=S.G.NI25) | Yellow-green .. | .. | .. | .. | .. | .. | .. | 30 | 30 |
| | a. Missing cross on crown | .. | .. | .. | .. | .. | 2·25 | |

**Cylinder Numbers (Blocks of Six)**

Perforation Type R

| Cyl. No. | Phos. No. | | | | No dot | Dot |
|---|---|---|---|---|---|---|
| 1 | 17 | .. | .. | .. | 2·50 | 2·50 |

Perforation Type RE

| | | | | | | |
|---|---|---|---|---|---|---|
| 1 | 17 | .. | .. | .. | —* | 3·50 |
| 1 | P21 | .. | .. | .. | 6·00 | 18·00 |

*Same price as perforation type R with single extension holes in left margin.

**CYLINDER VARIETIES**

**Listed Flaw**

Missing cross in crown
(Cyl. 1 no dot, R. 9/1)

XN34a

**Minor Constant Flaw**

Cyl. 1.  20/3  Blemishes on Queen's forehead (Th. C3–C4)

**WITHDRAWN**   11.79

# 9p.  (1978)

**1978 (18 JANUARY).    TWO 9·5 mm. PHOSPHOR BANDS.**
**FLUORESCENT COATED PAPER. PVAD GUM**

| XN35 (=S.G.NI26) | Deep violet .. | | | | | | | 30 | 30 |
|---|---|---|---|---|---|---|---|---|---|
| | a. Phosphor omitted | | | | | | | 25·00 | |
| | b. Curved white flaw over jewel of crown | | | | | | | 2·25 | |
| | c. Missing cross on crown .. | | | | | | | 2·50 | |
| | d. Sliced 9 .. | | | | | | | 2·25 | |
| | e. Phosphor band at left omitted .. | | | | | | | 55·00 | |
| | f. Phosphor band at right omitted | | | | | | | 25·00 | |

**Cylinder Numbers (Blocks of Six)**
Perforation Type RE

| Cyl. No. | Phos. No. | | | | No dot | Dot |
|---|---|---|---|---|---|---|
| 1 | P21 | .. | .. | .. | 7·00 | 14·00 |
| 1 | 30 | .. | .. | .. | 2·50 | 2·50 |

**CYLINDER VARIETIES**
**Listed Flaws**

XN35*b*
Curved white flaw over jewel
(Cyl. 1 no dot, R. 16/10)

XN35*c*
Missing cross on crown
(Cyl. 1 no dot, R. 17/4)
(Later retouched)

XN35*d*
Sliced 9
(Cyl. 1 dot, R. 9/10)

**Minor Constant Flaws**

Cyl. 1    10/9 Small retouch under hand (Th. D2)
          19/4 Cross on crown partly omitted (Th.A2)
Cyl. 1.    1/9 White speck under P
           6/7 Dark blemish above back of crown (Th. C6)
           6/8 Dark speck on Queen's bust (Th. G4)
           8/2 White specks under 9
           8/10 Horizontal dark scratch under Queen's bust at right (Th. G6)
           12/2 Dark speck at upper right (Th. A6)
           16/2 White cut in second finger of hand
           20/7 Dark blemish under Queen's bust (Th. G4)

**WITHDRAWN**   30.4.82

# 10p.  (1976–80)

**1976 (20 OCTOBER).    TWO 9·5 mm. PHOSPHOR BANDS.**
**FLUORESCENT COATED PAPER. PVAD GUM**

| XN36 (=S.G.NI27) | Orange-brown.. | | | | | | | 35 | 35 |
|---|---|---|---|---|---|---|---|---|---|
| | b. Right cross in crown partly missing | | | | | | | 2·50 | |

**Cylinder Numbers (Blocks of Six)**
Perforation Type RE

| Cyl. No. | Phos. No. | | | | No dot | Dot |
|---|---|---|---|---|---|---|
| 1 | 17 | .. | .. | .. | 2·50 | 2·50 |
| 1 | 30 | .. | .. | .. | 18·00 | £350 |

## 1980 (23 JULY).    CHANGE TO ONE 4 mm. CENTRE BAND. FLUORESCENT COATED PAPER. PVAD GUM

XN37 (=S.G.NI28)    Orange-brown . .    . .    . .    . .    . .    . .    . .    35    35
                    *b*. Right cross in crown partly missing    . .    . .    . .    1·75

**Cylinder Numbers (Blocks of Six)**
Perforation Type RE

| Cyl. No. | Phos. No. | | | | No dot | Dot |
|---|---|---|---|---|---|---|
| 1 | 20 | . . | . . | . . | 2·50 | 2·50 |

**CYLINDER VARIETIES**
**Listed Flaw**

Right cross in crown partly missing
(Cyl. 1 dot, R. 8/3)

XN36/7*b*

**Minor Constant Flaws**
Cyl. 1.   13/7  Small retouch at upper centre (Th. A4)
         19/6  Missing screening dots in right frame (Th. G6)

**WITHDRAWN**    No. XN36, 11.82; No. XN37, sold out 10.87

# 10½p. (1978)

## 1978 (18 JANUARY).    TWO 9·5 mm. PHOSPHOR BANDS. FLUORESCENT COATED PAPER. PVAD GUM

XN38 (=S.G.NI29)    Steel-blue    . .    . .    . .    . .    . .    . .    . .    40    40
                    *b*. Missing cross to crown    . .    . .    . .    . .    . .    3·50
                    *c*. Heavy line under bust    . .    . .    . .    . .    . .    2·25
                    *d*. White blob over crown    . .    . .    . .    . .    . .    2·75

**Cylinder Numbers (Blocks of Six)**
Perforation Type RE

| Cyl. No. | Phos. No. | | | | No dot | Dot |
|---|---|---|---|---|---|---|
| 3 | 30 | . . | . . | . . | 4·00* | 3·00 |

**CYLINDER VARIETIES**
**Listed Flaws**

| XN38*b* | XN38*c* | XN38*d* |
|---|---|---|
| Missing cross to crown | Heavy line under bust | White blob over crown |
| (Cyl. 3 no dot, R. 4/3) | (Cyl. 3 no dot, R. 18/2) | (Cyl. 3 no dot, R. 20/8) |
| | (Later retouched) | (Later retouched) |

**Minor Constant Flaws**
Cyl. 3   2/3  Retouch in top right corner (Th. A6)
       3/8  Cross in crown partly omitted
       6/7  Dark speck left of emblem (Th. B1)
     12/6  Dark speck left of 2
     17/1  Dark speck under Queen's bust (Th. G4)

**WITHDRAWN**    30.4.82

# 11p. (1976)
## 1976 (20 OCTOBER).   TWO 9·5 mm. PHOSPHOR BANDS. FLUORESCENT COATED PAPER. PVAD GUM

| | | | | | | | |
|---|---|---|---|---|---|---|---|
| XN39 (=S.G.NI30) | Scarlet | .. | .. | .. | .. | .. | .. | 40 | 40 |
| | *a.* Phosphor omitted | | .. | .. | .. | .. | .. | 4·50 |
| | *b.* Phosphor band at left omitted .. | | .. | .. | .. | 12·00 |
| | *c.* Phosphor band at right omitted | | .. | .. | .. | 15·00 |

**Cylinder Numbers (Blocks of Six)**
Perforation Type RE

| Cyl. No. | Phos. No. | | | | No dot | Dot |
|---|---|---|---|---|---|---|
| 1 | 17 | .. | .. | .. | .. | 3·00 | 3·00 |

**CYLINDER VARIETIES**

**Minor Constant Flaws**

Cyl. 3   1/7   White flaw in band of crown (Th. B4)
13/2   Red speck on Queen's forehead (Th. C4)
15/2   Small retouch under Queen's chin (Th. E3)
15/3   Retouch behind and below Queen's hair (Th. E5–E6)
20/8   Vertical scratch from back of Queen's hair to collar (Th. E6–F6)

The flaw on R. 20/8 also occurs on the 11p. for Scotland and for Wales.

**WITHDRAWN**   30.4.82

---

# 12p. (1980)
## 1980 (23 JULY).   PHOSPHORISED (FLUORESCENT COATED) PAPER. PVAD GUM

| | | | | | | | | |
|---|---|---|---|---|---|---|---|---|
| XN41 (=S.G.NI31) | Yellowish green | .. | .. | .. | .. | .. | .. | 40 | 45 |
| | *a.* Dark spot in hair .. | | .. | .. | .. | .. | .. | 2·75 |

**Cylinder Numbers (Blocks of Six)**
Perforation Type RE

| Cyl. No. | | | | No dot | Dot |
|---|---|---|---|---|---|
| 1 | .. | .. | .. | .. | 3·00 | 3·00 |

**CYLINDER VARIETIES**

**Listed Flaw**
Multipositive Flaw
XN41*a.* Cyl. 1 dot, R. 12/10. See XN30*c* of Northern Ireland

**Minor Constant Flaws**

Cyl. 1.   4/5   Nick in frame bottom right (Th. G6–7)
4/10   Spot in band of crown (Th. C6)
6/6   Spot above Queen's eyebrow (Th. D4)
7/3   Dark blemish top left of 1 (Th. E1)
15/3   Retouch above Queen's eyebrow (Th. D4)
16/8   Small speck in band of crown (Th. C5)
17/3   Dark spot in hair (Th. E5)
17/5   Dark speck on bust (Th. G4)
19/3   Small dark spot on Queen's forehead (Th. C4)
20/6   Pale blemish behind Queen's neck (Th. F5)

Most of the above are multipositive flaws which occur to a greater or less extent on the Northern Ireland 13½p. cyl. 2 dot, 15p. cyl. 1 dot and Scotland 13½p. cyl. 1 dot as well as on Wales 12p. cyl. 2 dot and 15p. cyl. 1 dot.

**WITHDRAWN**   9.82

# 13½p. (1980)

## 1980 (23 JULY).   PHOSPHORISED (FLUORESCENT COATED) PAPER. PVAD GUM.

| | | | | |
|---|---|---|---|---|
| XN42 (=S.G.NI32) | Purple-brown .. .. .. .. .. .. .. | 60 | 70 |
| | *a.* Dark spot in hair .. .. .. .. .. .. | 3·00 | |
| | *b.* Dark spot in band of crown .. .. .. .. | 3·00 | |

**Cylinder Numbers (Blocks of Six)**

Perforation Type RE

| Cyl. No. | | | | | No dot | Dot |
|---|---|---|---|---|---|---|
| 2 | .. | .. | .. | .. | 4·50 | 4·50 |

## CYLINDER VARIETIES

**Listed Flaws**

Multipositive Flaws
XN42*a*. Cyl. 2 dot, R. 12/10.   See XN30*c* of Northern Ireland.
XN42*b*. Cyl. 2 dot, R. 16/8.   See XN30*f* of Northern Ireland.

**Minor Constant Flaws**

Cyl. 2.   4/10 Spot in band of crown (Th. C5)
6/6 Spot above Queen's eyebrow (Th. D4)
9/5 Dark spot below necklace (Th. F5)
15/3 Dark spot above Queen's eyebrow (Th. C4)
17/5 Dark speck on bust (Th. G4)
19/3 Small dark spot on Queen's forehead (Th. C4)
20/3 Dark speck on Queen's temple (Th. D4)

Most of the above are multipositive flaws which occur to a greater or less extent on the Northern Ireland 12p. cyl. 1 dot, 15p. cyl. 1 dot and Scotland 13½p. cyl. 1 dot as well as on Wales 12p. cyl. 2 dot and 15p. cyl. 1 dot.

**WITHDRAWN**   8.82

---

# 15p (1980)

## 1980 (23 JULY).   PHOSPHORISED (FLUORESCENT COATED) PAPER. PVAD GUM.

| | | | | |
|---|---|---|---|---|
| XN44 (=S.G.NI33) | Ultramarine .. .. .. .. .. .. .. | 45 | 50 |
| | *a.* Dark spot in hair .. .. .. .. .. .. | 2·25 | |
| | *b.* Dark spot in band of crown .. .. .. .. | 2·25 | |

**Cylinder Numbers (Blocks of Six)**

Perforation Type RE

| Cyl. No. | | | | | No dot | Dot |
|---|---|---|---|---|---|---|
| 1 | .. | .. | .. | .. | 3·25 | 3·25 |

## CYLINDER VARIETIES

**Listed Flaws**

Multipositive Flaws
XN44*a*. Cyl. 1 dot, R. 12/10.   See XN30*c* of Northern Ireland.
XN44*b*. Cyl. 1 dot, R. 16/8.   See XN30*f* of Northern Ireland.

**Minor Constant Flaws**

Cyl. 1.   4/10 Spot in band of crown (Th. C5)
6/6 Spot above Queen's eyebrow (Th. D4)
15/3 Dark spot above Queen's eyebrow (Th. C4)

The above are multipositive flaws which occur to a greater or less extent on the 12p. cyl. 1 dot, 13½p. cyl. 2 dot and Scotland 13½p. 1 dot as well as on Wales 12p. cyl. 2 dot and 15p. cyl. 1 dot.

**WITHDRAWN**   14.1.84

# Presentation Packs

XNPP2 No. 30 (7.7.71)                                     2½p., 3p., 5p., 7½p.                          4·00
  Comprises Nos. XN18, 20, 27 and 32
XNPP3 No. 61 (29.5.74)                                   3p., 3½p., 5½p., 8p.                          3·00
  Comprises Nos. XN22 or 23, 24, 28 and 33
XNPP4 No. 61 (6.11.74)                                   3p., 3½p., 4½p., 5½p., 8p.               3·50
  As last but with No. XN26 added
  Presumably No. XNPP4 had the 3½p. with centre band instead of two bands and no doubt
it was later issued under the same stock number with the 5½p. centre band instead of two bands.
XNPP5 No. 84 (20.10.76)                                 6½p., 8½p., 10p., 11p.                       1·75
  Comprising Nos. XN30, 34, 36 and 39

**WITHDRAWN**  No. XNPP2, 22.1.75; No. XNPP3, 1974?; No. XNPP4, 9.76; XNPP5, 8.83

---

# First Day Covers

XNFD1 (7.7.71)                                 2½p., 3p., (2 bands), 5p., 7½p.        †  4·00

XNFD2 (23.1.74)                                3p. (1 band), 3½p. (2 bands),
                                                       5½p. (2 bands), 8p.                       †  1·50

XNFD3 (6.11.74)                                4½p.                                                     †  1·00

XNFD4 (14.1.76)                                6½p., 8½p.                                           †    60

XNFD5 (20.10.76)                              10p. (2 bands), 11p.                          †  1·00

XNFD6 (18.1.78)                                7p., 9p., 10½p.                                    †  1·00

XNFD7 (23.7.80)                                12p., 13½p., 15p.                              †  2·00

  No special provision was made for first day covers for the 3½p. centre band also issued on
the same day as the 4½p., but of course first day covers exist with both values.
  No special covers were issued for the 5½p. change to one centre band issued on 21 May 1975.
  No special provision was made for first day covers for the 10p. centre band also issued on
the same day as the 12p., 13½p. and 15p., but first day covers exist franked with all values.

## C. Scotland

**XS4**

(Des. Jeffery Matthews)

# Type XS4
## 2½p. (1971–73)
### 1971 (7 JULY). ONE 4 mm. CENTRE PHOSPHOR BAND
**A. ORIGINAL COATED PAPER. PVA GUM**

| | | | | | | | | |
|---|---|---|---|---|---|---|---|---|
| XS29 (=S.G.S14) | Bright magenta | .. | .. | .. | .. | .. | .. | 20 | 15 |
| | *a.* Phosphor omitted.. | .. | .. | .. | .. | .. | 3·50 | |

**Cylinder Numbers (Blocks of Six)**

Perforation Type A

| Cyl. No. | Phos. No. | | | | No dot | Dot |
|---|---|---|---|---|---|---|
| 2 | 5 | .. | .. | .. | 3·25 | 3·25 |

**B. FLUORESCENT COATED PAPER. GUM ARABIC** (22.9.72)

| | | | | | | | |
|---|---|---|---|---|---|---|---|
| XS30 (=S.G.S14Eg) | Bright magenta | .. | .. | .. | .. | .. | 20 | 25 |

**Cylinder Numbers (Blocks of Six)**

Perforation Type R(S)

| Cyl. No. | Phos. No. | | | | No dot | Dot |
|---|---|---|---|---|---|---|
| 2 | 9 | .. | .. | .. | 3·25 | 3·25 |
| 2 | 9 | —34 mm. (20) | .. | 12·00 | 26·00 |

**C. FLUORESCENT COATED PAPER. PVA GUM** (6.73)

| | | | | | | | |
|---|---|---|---|---|---|---|---|
| XS31 | Bright magenta | .. | .. | .. | .. | .. | 2·00 |
| | *a.* Phosphor omitted.. | .. | .. | .. | .. | 7·00 |

**Cylinder Numbers (Blocks of Six)**

Perforation Type A

| Cyl. No. | Phos. No. | | | | No dot | Dot |
|---|---|---|---|---|---|---|
| 2 | 5 | .. | .. | .. | 20·00 | 20·00 |
| 2 | 8 | .. | .. | .. | 15·00 | 15·00 |

**WITHDRAWN** Nos. XS29/31, 22.1.75

---

## 3p. (1971–74)
### 1971 (7 JULY). TWO 9·5 mm. PHOSPHOR BANDS
**A. ORIGINAL COATED PAPER. PVA GUM**

| | | | | | | | | |
|---|---|---|---|---|---|---|---|---|
| XS32 (=S.G.S15) | Ultramarine | .. | .. | .. | .. | .. | .. | 30 | 15 |
| | *a.* Phosphor omitted.. | .. | .. | .. | .. | 14·00 | |

**Cylinder Numbers (Blocks of Six)**

Perforation Type A

| Cyl. No. | Phos. No. | | | | No dot | Dot |
|---|---|---|---|---|---|---|
| 1 | 4 | .. | .. | .. | 3·75 | 3·75 |

**B. FLUORESCENT COATED PAPER. GUM ARABIC** (14.12.72)

XS33 (=S.G.S15Eg)  Ultramarine .. .. .. .. .. .. .. 30 40
            *a.* Imperforate (pair) .. .. .. .. .. £400
            *b.* Top margin imperforate .. .. .. .. ¬ ₁ £250
  Examples of No. XS33 from Cyl. 8 exist with contaminated "yellow phosphor". *Price £2 mint.*

**Cylinder Numbers (Blocks of Six)**

Perforation Type R(S)

| Cyl. No. | Phos. No. | | | | No dot | Dot |
|---|---|---|---|---|---|---|
| 4 | 7 | .. | .. | .. | 3·75 | 3·75 |
| 8 | 7 | .. | .. | .. | 20·00 | 30·00 |

**C. FLUORESCENT COATED PAPER. PVA GUM** (1.73)

XS34           Ultramarine .. .. .. .. .. .. .. 2·50
            *a.* Phosphor omitted .. .. .. .. .. .. 5·50

**Cylinder Numbers (Blocks of Six)**

Perforation Type A

| Cyl. No. | Phos. No. | | | | No dot | Dot |
|---|---|---|---|---|---|---|
| 1 | 7 | .. | .. | .. | 35·00 | 35·00 |
| 1 | — | .. | .. | .. | 30·00 | 30·00 |

  Phosphor Cylinder Displacement. Phosphor cylinder 7 is known displaced up the margin 185 mm. opposite row 10.

## 1974 (23 JANUARY).  CHANGE TO ONE 4 mm. CENTRE BAND

**A. FLUORESCENT COATED PAPER. PVA GUM**

XS35 (=S.G.S16)  Ultramarine .. .. .. .. .. .. 15 15

**Cylinder Numbers (Blocks of Six unless otherwise stated)**

Perforation Type A

| Cyl. No. | Phos. No. | | | | No dot | Dot |
|---|---|---|---|---|---|---|
| 8 | 8 | .. | .. | .. | 1·50 | 1·75 |
| 8 | — | 8 + 34 mm. (17) | | .. | 8·50 | 15·00 Block of eight |

Dot panes from cylinder 8 have the dot at top right of 8.

**B. FLUORESCENT COATED PAPER. PVAD GUM** (9.74)

XS36           Ultramarine .. .. .. .. .. .. 50
            *a.* Deformed tongue .. .. .. .. .. 3·00

**Cylinder Numbers (Blocks of Six unless otherwise stated)**

Perforation Type A

| Cyl. No. | Phos. No. | | | | No dot | Dot |
|---|---|---|---|---|---|---|
| 8 | 8 | .. | .. | .. | 6·50 | 6·50 |
| 8 | — | 8 + 32 mm. (17) | | .. | 45·00 | 45·00 Block of eight |

Dot panes from cylinder 8 have the dot at top right of 8.

**CYLINDER VARIETIES**

**Listed Flaw**

Deformed tongue
(Cyl. 8 no dot, R. 19/7)

XS36*a*

**Minor Constant Flaws**

Cyl. 1.  18/1 Pale patch at lower right of value (Th. G2)
Cyl. 4.   2/9 Pale patch in background at top (Th. A5)
        13/3 White speck in Queen's shoulder (Th. G4)
        18/7 Dark spot in Queen's forehead (Th. C3) and small retouch on cheek (Th. D4)
        19/2 White speck on top of P
Cyl. 8    4/1 Dark spot on Queen's shoulder (Th. F4–5)
         4/3 Weak letter P
       10/6 White blemish on Queen's shoulder (Th. F5)

**375**

**WITHDRAWN**   Nos. XS32/4, 22.1.75; Nos. XS35/6, 8.4.78

# 3½p.  (1974)
## 1974 (23 JANUARY).   TWO 9·5 mm. PHOSPHOR BANDS
### A. FLUORESCENT COATED PAPER. PVA GUM
XS37                      Olive-grey    ..     ..     ..     ..     ..     ..     .. 8·00

**Cylinder Numbers (Blocks of Six)**
Perforation Type A

| Cyl. No. | Phos. No. | | | | | No dot | Dot |
|---|---|---|---|---|---|---|---|
| 1 | 17 | .. | .. | .. | .. | £200 | £150 |

The dot was not inserted on the dot cylinder and the no dot cylinder box shows line breaks.

### B. FLUORESCENT COATED PAPER. PVAD GUM. (23.1.74)
XS38 (= S.G.S17)         Olive-grey    ..     ..     ..     ..     ..     ..     ..   20     20
                         a. Phosphor omitted..     ..     ..     ..     ..     .. 20·00

**Cylinder Numbers (Blocks of Six)**
Perforation Type A

| Cyl. No. | Phos. No. | | | | | No dot | Dot |
|---|---|---|---|---|---|---|---|
| 1 | 17 | .. | .. | .. | .. | 2·00 | 2·50 |

## 1974 (6 NOVEMBER).   CHANGE TO ONE 4 mm. CENTRE BAND. FLUORESCENT COATED PAPER. PVAD GUM

XS39 (= S.G.S18)         Olive-grey    ..     ..     ..     ..     ..     ..     ..   20     20

**Cylinder Numbers (Blocks of Six)**
Perforation Type R

| Cyl. No. | Phos. No. | | | | | No dot | Dot |
|---|---|---|---|---|---|---|---|
| 1 | 20 | .. | .. | .. | .. | 2·00 | 2·50 |

**CYLINDER VARIETY**
**Minor Constant Flaws**
Cyl. 1   11/7   White scratch behind Queen's hair (Th. D6) (centre band only)

**WITHDRAWN**   Nos. XS37/9, 9.76

# 4½p.  (1974)
## 1974 (6 NOVEMBER).   TWO 9·5 mm. PHOSPHOR BANDS. FLUORESCENT COATED PAPER. PVAD GUM

XS40 (= S.G.S19)         Grey-blue    ..     ..     ..     ..     ..     ..     ..   25     20
                         b. White spot in 4   ..     ..     ..     ..     ..     .. 2·50
                         c. Blob joining hind legs    ..     ..     ..     ..     .. 2·75
                         d. Large white stop after P ..     ..     ..     ..     .. 5·00

**Cylinder Numbers (Blocks of Six)**
Perforation Type R

| Cyl. No. | Phos. No. | | | | | No dot | Dot |
|---|---|---|---|---|---|---|---|
| 1 | 17 | .. | .. | .. | .. | 5·00 | 5·00 |
| 1 | — | .. | .. | .. | .. | 3·50 | 4·50 |

\*The phosphor cylinder was unnumbered and inverted so that the no dot cylinder block is without phosphor number and the dot cylinder block has part of an inverted phosphor box only. The inverted cylinder box occurs in the right-hand selvedge.
   Phosphor Cylinder Displacement. With ink cyl. 1, the unnumbered phos. cyl. box is known displaced up the margin 102 mm. opposite row 14.

**CYLINDER VARIETIES**
**Listed Flaws**

XS40*b*
White spot in figure 4
(Cyl. 1 no dot, R. 2/7)

XS40*c*
Large white blob joining
lion's hind legs
(Cyl. 1 no dot, R. 3/5)

XS40*d*
Large white spot after P
(Cyl. 1 no dot, R. 5/1)
(Believed later retouched)

**WITHDRAWN** 9.76

# 5p. (1971–73)

### 1971 (7 JULY).   TWO 9·5 mm. PHOSPHOR BANDS
#### A. ORIGINAL COATED PAPER. PVA GUM
XS41 (=S.G.S20)     Reddish violet..     ..     ..     ..     ..     ..     .. 1·50    1·50

**Cylinder Numbers (Blocks of Six)**
Perforation Type F*
| Cyl. No. | Phos. No. |  |  |  | No dot | Dot |
|---|---|---|---|---|---|---|
| 3 | 12 | .. | .. | .. | 11·00 | 11·00 |

#### B. FLUORESCENT COATED PAPER. PVA GUM (6.73)

XS42     Reddish violet     ..     ..     ..     ..     ..     .. 14·00   2·50
    *a*. One broad band ..     ..     ..     ..     ..     .. £100
All examples of No. XS42 from cyl. 7 exist with contaminated "yellow phosphor". *Price* £4 *mint*.

**Cylinder Numbers (Blocks of Six)**
Perforation Type F(L)*
| Cyl. No. | Phos. No. |  |  |  | No dot | Dot |
|---|---|---|---|---|---|---|
| 3 | 11 | .. | .. | .. | 90·00 | £100 |
| 7 | 11 | .. | .. | .. | 30·00 | 40·00 |

**WITHDRAWN** Nos. XS41/2, 22.1.75

# 5½p.  (1974–5)

### 1974 (23 JANUARY).   TWO 9·5 mm. PHOSPHOR BANDS.
### FLUORESCENT COATED PAPER. PVAD GUM

XS43 (=S.G.S21)     Violet ..     ..     ..     ..     ..     ..     .. 20    20
    *b*. Hair flaw ..     ..     ..     ..     ..     ..     .. 2·25
    *c*. Spot in 5 ..     ..     ..     ..     ..     ..     .. 2·40

**Cylinder Numbers (Blocks of Six)**
Perforation Type A. Single pane cylinder
| Cyl. No. | Phos. No. |  |  |  | No dot | Dot |
|---|---|---|---|---|---|---|
| 1 | 22* | .. | .. | .. | 2·00 | † |

*The phosphor 22 is known upright but superimposed over inverted figures.

### 1975 (21 MAY).   CHANGE TO ONE 4 mm. CENTRE BAND.
### FLUORESCENT COATED PAPER. PVAD GUM

XS44 (=S.G.S22)     Violet ..     ..     ..     ..     ..     ..     .. 20    20
    *a*. Imperforate (pair)..     ..     ..     ..     .. £350
    *c*. Hair flaw ..     ..     ..     ..     ..     .. 2·25
    *d*. Spot in 5 ..     ..     ..     ..     ..     .. 2·40

**Cylinder Numbers (Blocks of Six)**
Perforation Type R(S). Single pane cylinder

| Cyl. No. | Phos. No. | | | | | No dot | Dot |
|---|---|---|---|---|---|---|---|
| 1 | 19 | .. | .. | .. | .. | 3·00 | † |

Perforation Type A

| | | | | | | | |
|---|---|---|---|---|---|---|---|
| 1 | 19 | .. | .. | .. | .. | 10·00 | † |

Normally the Swedish rotary perforator produces a single extension hole in the left-hand margin on no dot panes. The above has been seen with the left-hand margin fully perforated through and also with anything between this and a single perforation hole, sometimes with blind perforations.

**CYLINDER VARIETIES**
**Listed Flaws**

| XS43b, XS44c | XS43c, XS44d |
|---|---|
| Dark squiggle in hair below band | Coloured spot in 5 |
| (Cyl. 1 no dot, R. 2/10) | (Cyl. 1 no dot, R. 11/10) |

**WITHDRAWN**   31.5.77

---

# 6½p.   (1976)

## 1976 (14 JANUARY).   ONE 4 mm. CENTRE PHOSPHOR BAND. FLUORESCENT COATED PAPER. PVAD GUM

| | | | | | | | | | |
|---|---|---|---|---|---|---|---|---|---|
| XS45 (= S.G.S23) | Greenish blue .. | .. | .. | .. | .. | .. | .. | 20 | 20 |
| | *a.* Top margin imperforate .. | | .. | .. | .. | .. | .. | | |
| | *b.* Dark spot in hair .. | .. | | .. | .. | .. | .. | 1·50 | |
| | *c.* Dark spot in band | .. | .. | .. | .. | .. | .. | 1·50 | |
| | *d.* Break in lion's tail | .. | .. | .. | .. | .. | .. | 1·50 | |
| | *e.* Missing claw to lower fore paw .. | | .. | .. | .. | .. | | 2·00 | |
| | *f.* Extra claw to hind leg | .. | .. | .. | .. | .. | | 1·75 | |

No. XS45 exists in a range of shades the most marked being dull greenish blue.

**Cylinder Numbers (Blocks of Six unless otherwise stated)**
Perforation Type R

| Cyl. No. | Phos. No. | | | | | No dot | Dot | |
|---|---|---|---|---|---|---|---|---|
| 1 | 18 | .. | .. | .. | .. | 2·00 | 2·00 | |
| 1 | 18 | +20 mm. (18) | .. | | .. | 12·00 | 12·00 | |
| 1 | 18 | +35 mm. (17) | .. | | .. | 6·00 | 6·00 | Block of ten |
| 1 | 18 | +47 mm. (16) | .. | | .. | 6·00 | 6·00 | Block of ten |
| 1 | — | .. | .. | .. | .. | 5·00 | 5·00 | |

Perforation Type RE

| | | | | | | | | |
|---|---|---|---|---|---|---|---|---|
| 1 | 18 | .. | .. | .. | .. | —* | 40·00 | |
| 1 | 20 | .. | .. | .. | .. | 2·00 | 2·00 | |
| 1 | 20 | +54 mm. (16) | .. | | .. | 5·00 | 12·00 | Block of ten |

On the dot panes the dot appears before the ink cylinder 1.

*Same price as perforation type R with single extension holes in left margin.

Phosphor Cylinder Displacement. With ink cyl. 1, phos. cyl. 18 is known displaced up the margin 137 mm. opposite row 13.

**CYLINDER VARIETIES**
Listed Flaws

| XS45d | XS45e | XS45f |
|---|---|---|
| Break in lion's tail | Missing claw to | Extra claw to upper |
| (Cyl. 1 no dot, R. 1/4) | lower fore paw | hind leg |
|  | (Cyl. 1 no dot. R. 2/6) | (Cyl. 1 no dot, R. 4/3) |

Multipositive Flaws
XS45b.  Cyl. 1 dot, R. 12/8.  See XN30c of Northern Ireland.
XS45c.  Cyl. 1 dot, R. 16/6.  See XN30f of Northern Ireland.

**Minor Constant Flaws**
Cyl. 1.  6/2  Small retouch at back of collar (Th. G5). Original flaw on Wales 4½p.
        9/3  Dark spot on Queen's neck (Th. F5)
        20/2  Small speck under necklace (Th. F4–5)
    The above are multipositive flaws which also occur on 6½p. Northern Ireland cyl. 1 dot and Wales cyl. 1 dot and 20/2 also on Wales 4½p. cyl. 1 dot.

**WITHDRAWN**   3.79

---

# 7p. (1978)

**1978 (18 JANUARY).   ONE 4 mm. CENTRE PHOSPHOR BAND. FLUORESCENT COATED PAPER. PVAD GUM**

| | | | | | | | | | |
|---|---|---|---|---|---|---|---|---|---|
| XS46 (=S.G.S24) | Purple-brown | .. | .. | .. | .. | .. | .. | 25 | 25 |
| | b. White spot on P | .. | .. | .. | .. | .. | .. | 1·50 | |
| | c. Tail flaw | .. | .. | .. | .. | .. | .. | 1·75 | |

**Cylinder Numbers (Blocks of Six)**
Perforation Type RE

| Cyl. No. | Phos. No. | | | | No dot | Dot |
|---|---|---|---|---|---|---|
| 1 | 20 | .. | .. | .. | 20·00 | 20·00 |
| 1 | 31 | .. | .. | .. | 2·25 | 2·25 |

**CYLINDER VARIETIES**
Listed Flaw

| XS46b | XS46c |
|---|---|
| White spot on P | Truncated prong to tail |
| (Cyl. 1 no dot, R. 8/5) | (Cyl. 1 dot, R. 7/4) |

**Minor Constant Flaw**
Cyl. 1  9/9 Cluster of white specks between crown and lion (Th. A-B/4-5)

**WITHDRAWN**   1.81

# 7½p.   (1971–73)

## 1971 (7 JULY).   TWO 9·5 mm. PHOSPHOR BANDS

### A. ORIGINAL COATED PAPER. PVA GUM

| | | | | | | | | | |
|---|---|---|---|---|---|---|---|---|---|
| XS47 (=S.G.S25) | Chestnut | .. | .. | .. | .. | .. | .. | 2·00 | 2·00 |
| | *a.* Phosphor omitted | | .. | .. | .. | .. | .. | 4·50 | |
| | *b.* One broad band .. | | .. | .. | .. | .. | .. | 20·00 | |

**Cylinder Numbers (Blocks of Six)**

Perforation Type F*

| Cyl. No. | Phos. No. | | | | No dot | Dot |
|---|---|---|---|---|---|---|
| 6 | 10 | .. | .. | .. | 18·00 | 18·00 |

### B. FLUORESCENT COATED PAPER. PVA GUM (11.73)

| | | | | | | | | |
|---|---|---|---|---|---|---|---|---|
| XS48 | Chestnut | .. | .. | .. | .. | .. | 45·00 | 15·00 |

**Cylinder Numbers (Blocks of Six)**

Perforation Type F*

| Cyl. No. | Phos. No. | | | | No dot | Dot |
|---|---|---|---|---|---|---|
| 6 | 11 | .. | .. | .. | £250 | £300 |

**CYLINDER VARIETY**

**Minor Constant Flaw**

Cyl. 6.   4/1 Background retouch below emblem (Th. C1)

**WITHDRAWN**   Nos. XS47/8, 22.1.75

# 8p. (1974)

## 1974 (23 JANUARY).   TWO 9·5 mm. PHOSPHOR BANDS. FLUORESCENT COATED PAPER. PVAD GUM

| | | | | | | | | |
|---|---|---|---|---|---|---|---|---|
| XS49 (=S.G.S26) | Rosine .. | .. | .. | .. | .. | .. | 30 | 40 |

**Cylinder Numbers (Blocks of Six)**

Perforation Type A. Single pane cylinder

| Cyl. No. | Phos. No. | | | | No dot | Dot |
|---|---|---|---|---|---|---|
| 1 | 22 | .. | .. | .. | 2·50 | † |

**CYLINDER VARIETY**

**Minor Constant Flaw**

Cyl. 1   20/2 White speck on lion's tongue

**SOLD OUT**   1.79

# 8½p.   (1976)

## 1976 (14 JANUARY).   TWO 9·5 mm. PHOSPHOR BANDS. FLUORESCENT COATED PAPER. PVAD GUM

| | | | | | | | | |
|---|---|---|---|---|---|---|---|---|
| XS50 (=S.G.S27) | Yellow-green .. | .. | .. | .. | .. | .. | 30 | 30 |
| | *b.* White flaw on toes | .. | .. | .. | .. | .. | 2·00 | |
| | *c.* Scratch by lion's mane | .. | .. | .. | .. | .. | 2·25 | |

**Cylinder Numbers (Blocks of Six)**
Perforation Type R

| Cyl. No. | Phos. No. | | | | | No dot | Dot |
|---|---|---|---|---|---|---|---|
| 2 | 17 | .. | .. | .. | .. | 2·00 | 2·50 |

Perforation Type RE

| | | | | | | | |
|---|---|---|---|---|---|---|---|
| 1 | P21 | .. | .. | .. | .. | 4·00 | 2·50 |
| 2 | 17 | .. | .. | .. | .. | —* | 3·00 |
| 2 | P21 | .. | .. | .. | .. | 22·00 | 15·00 |

*Same price as perforation type R with single extension holes in left margin.

**CYLINDER VARIETIES**
**Listed Flaws**

| XS50*b* | XS50*c* |
|---|---|
| White flaw joining toe to lion's hind paw (Cyl. 2 dot, R. 8/10) | White scratch from mane to right fore paw (Cyl. 2 dot, R. 11/1) |

**WITHDRAWN** 11.79

## 9p. (1978)

### 1978 (18 JANUARY). TWO 9·5 mm. PHOSPHOR BANDS. FLUORESCENT COATED PAPER. PVAD GUM

| XS51 (=S.G.S28) | Deep violet | .. | .. | .. | .. | .. | .. | .. | 30 | 30 |
|---|---|---|---|---|---|---|---|---|---|---|

**Cylinder Numbers (Blocks of Six)**
Perforation Type RE

| Cyl. No. | Phos. No. | | | | | No dot | Dot |
|---|---|---|---|---|---|---|---|
| 1 | P21 | .. | .. | .. | .. | 3·50 | 3·50 |
| 1 | 30 | .. | .. | .. | .. | 2·50 | 2·50 |

**CYLINDER VARIETIES**
**Minor Constant Flaws**
Cyl. 1. 6/7 Blemish in background behind Queen's neck (Th. F6)
       7/7 Damaged claw on lion's right hind paw (Th. C1)
     10/3 Pale blemish at lower right edge (Th. G6)
     11/7 Dark scratch over crown (Th. B5–A6)
     12/7 Diagonal dark scratch over crown (Th. A5–B6)
     17/2 Dark speck on Queen's shoulder (Th. F4–F5)
     20/2 Dark spot over crown (Th. B5)
**WITHDRAWN** 30.4.82

## 10p. (1976–80)

### 1976 (20 OCTOBER). TWO 9·5 mm. PHOSPHOR BANDS. FLUORESCENT COATED PAPER. PVAD GUM

| XS52 (=S.G.S29) | Orange-brown.. | .. | .. | .. | .. | .. | 35 | 30 |
|---|---|---|---|---|---|---|---|---|
| | *b.* Dark spot on lion's thigh .. | .. | .. | .. | .. | 2·50 | | |

**Cylinder Numbers (Blocks of Six)**
Perforation Type RE

| Cyl. No. | Phos. No. | | | | | No dot | Dot |
|---|---|---|---|---|---|---|---|
| 4 | 17 | .. | .. | .. | .. | 2·50 | 2·50 |
| 4 | 30 | .. | .. | .. | .. | 3·50 | 3·50 |

**381**

### 1980 (23 JULY).   CHANGE TO ONE 4 mm. CENTRE BAND. FLUORESCENT COATED PAPER. PVAD GUM

XS53 ( = S.G.S30)      Orange-brown ..    ..    ..    ..    ..    ..    ..      35      35

**Cylinder Numbers (Blocks of Six)**
Perforation Type RE

| Cyl. No. | Phos. No. | | | | No dot | Dot |
|---|---|---|---|---|---|---|
| 4 | 20 | .. | .. | .. | 2·50 | 2·50 |

**CYLINDER VARIETIES**
**Listed Flaw**

Dark spot on lion's thigh
(Cyl. 4 dot, R. 18/3)
Retouched on No. XS53

XS52*b*

**Minor Constant Flaws**

Cyl. 4.   3/5  Pale blemish on jaw line (Th. E4)
        3/9  Pale spot on bust (Th. G4)
     13/7  Pale blemish in upper background (Th. A4)
     19/6  Brown mark touching front of Queen's neck (Th. E4–F4)

**WITHDRAWN**   No. XS52, 1.81; XS53 sold out, 2.87

---

## 10½p.   (1978)

### 1978 (18 JANUARY).   TWO 9·5 mm. PHOSPHOR BANDS. FLUORESCENT COATED PAPER. PVAD GUM

XS54 ( = S.G.S31)      Steel-blue    ..    ..    ..    ..    ..    ..    ..      40      35

**Cylinder Numbers (Blocks of Six)**
Perforation Type RE

| Cyl. No. | Phos. No. | | | | No dot | Dot |
|---|---|---|---|---|---|---|
| 1 | 30 | .. | .. | .. | 3·00 | 3·00 |

**CYLINDER VARIETIES**
**Minor Constant Flaws**

Cyl. 1   5/3  White speck under lion (Th. D2)
      5/9  Dark speck on Queen's cheek (Th. D3)
      8/5  White speck to right of small figure 1 (Th. F4)
   15/7  Dark speck in Queen's hair (Th. D4)
   18/1  Dark dot in front of necklace (Th. F4)

Cyl. 1.   2/1  White dot over P

**WITHDRAWN**   2.82

---

## 11p.   (1976)

### 1976 (20 OCTOBER).   TWO 9·5 mm. PHOSPHOR BANDS. FLUORESCENT COATED PAPER. PVAD GUM

| | | | | | | | |
|---|---|---|---|---|---|---|---|
| XS55 ( = S.G.S32) | Scarlet ..   ..   .. | .. | .. | .. | .. | 40 | 35 |
| | *a.* Phosphor omitted .. | .. | .. | .. | .. | 1·75 | |
| | *b.* Left-hand band omitted .. | .. | .. | .. | .. | 15·00 | |
| | *c.* Right-hand band omitted | .. | .. | .. | .. | 15·00 | |

**Cylinder Numbers (Blocks of Six)**
Perforation Type RE

| Cyl. No. | Phos. No. | | | | No dot | Dot |
|---|---|---|---|---|---|---|
| 1 | 17 | .. | .. | .. | 2·75 | 2·75 |
| 1 | 17 | —30 mm. (20) | | .. | 30·00 | † |
| 1 | 30 | .. | .. | .. | 3·75 | 3·75 |

**CYLINDER VARIETIES**
**Minor Constant Flaws**

Cyl. 1    10/2  Red spot in background (Th. A5)
        11/7  White speck on collar (Th. G4)
        20/8  Vertical scratch from back of Queen's hair to collar (Th. E6–F6) (less pronounced than on 11p. Northern Ireland)

**WITHDRAWN**    2.82

---

# 12p. (1980)

**1980 (23 JULY).    PHOSPHORISED (FLUORESCENT COATED) PAPER. PVAD GUM**

| XS57 (=S.G.S33) | Yellowish green | .. | .. | .. | .. | .. | .. | 40 | 30 |
|---|---|---|---|---|---|---|---|---|---|

**Cylinder Numbers (Blocks of Six)**
Perforation Type RE

| Cyl. No. | | | | No dot | Dot |
|---|---|---|---|---|---|
| 2 | .. | .. | .. | 2·75 | 2·75 |

**CYLINDER VARIETIES**
**Minor Constant Flaws**

Cyl. 2.    2/3  Pale blemish in background touching Queen's lips (Th. E3)
        4/3  Retouch to necklace (Th. F4)
        10/6  Pale patch in background upper right (Th. A5)

**WITHDRAWN**    9.82

---

# 13½p.  (1980)

**1980 (23 JULY).    PHOSPHORISED (FLUORESCENT COATED) PAPER. PVAD GUM**

| XS58 (=S.G.S34) | Purple-brown .. | .. | .. | .. | .. | .. | 60 | 65 |
|---|---|---|---|---|---|---|---|---|
| | *a.* Pale spot on dress | .. | .. | .. | .. | .. | 2·75 | |

**Cylinder Numbers (Blocks of Six)**
Perforation Type RE

| Cyl. No. | | | | No dot | Dot |
|---|---|---|---|---|---|
| 1 | .. | .. | .. | 4·50 | 4·50 |

**CYLINDER VARIETIES**
**Listed Flaw**

XS58*a*
Pale spot on dress
(Cyl. 1 dot, R. 6/4)

**Minor Constant Flaws**

Cyl. 1. 4/10  Spot in band of crown (Th. C6)
　　　　6/6  Spot above Queen's eyebrow (Th. D4)
　　　　9/5  Dark spot below necklace (Th. F5)
　　　　15/3  Retouch above Queen's eyebrow (Th. D4)
　　　　17/1  Pale blemishes touching lion's head
　　　　17/5  Dark speck on bust (Th. G4) and retouch in front of Queen's lips (Th. D3)
　　　　18/1  Pale blemish on shoulder (Th. G4)
　　　　20/3  Dark speck on Queen's temple Th. D4)

　　Most of the above multipositive flaws which occur to a greater or less extent on the Northern Ireland 12p. cyl 1 dot, 13½p. cyl. 2 dot and 15p. cyl. 1 dot as well as on Wales 12p. cyl. 2 dot and 15p. cyl. 1 dot.

**WITHDRAWN**  8.82

# 15p. (1980)

**1980 (23 JULY).    PHOSPHORISED (FLUORESCENT COATED) PAPER. PVAD GUM**

XS60 (= S.G.S35)　　　Ultramarine  ..　　..　　..　　..　　..　　..　　..　　45　　　45

**Cylinder Numbers (Blocks of Six)**

Perforation Type RE

| Cyl. No. | | | | No dot | Dot |
|---|---|---|---|---|---|
| 1 | .. | .. | .. | .. 3·25 | 3·25 |

**CYLINDER VARIETIES**

**Minor Constant Flaws**

Cyl. 1　3/2  White specks in front of eye (Th. D3)
　　　10/3  Retouch in background opposite Queen's lips (Th. D2–E2)
　　　10/4  Diagonal white scratch touches lower lip (Th. D3)
　　　20/5  Diagonal line of dots across lion's left hind leg (Th. B2–C2)
　　　20/8  Small retouch above lip (Th. D3)

**WITHDRAWN**  14.1.84

# Presentation Packs

| | | |
|---|---|---|
| XSPP2 No. 27 (7.7.71) | 2½p., 3p., 5p., 7½p. | 4·00 |
| Comprises Nos. XS29, 32, 41 and 47 | | |
| XSPP3 No. 62 (29.5.74) | 3p., 3½p., 5½p., 8p. | 3·00 |
| Comprises Nos. XS35, 38, 43 and 49 | | |
| XSPP4 No. 62 (6.11.74) | 3p., 3½p., 4½p., 5½p., 8p. | 3·50 |
| As last but with No. XS40 added | | |

Presumably No. XSPP4 had the 3½p. with centre band instead of two bands and no doubt it was later issued under the same stock number with the 5½p. centre band instead of two bands.

| | | |
|---|---|---|
| XSPP5 No. 85 (20.10.76) | 6½p., 8½p., 10p., 11p. | 1·75 |
| Comprises Nos. XS45, 50, 52 and 55 | | |

**WITHDRAWN** No. XSPP2, 22.1.75; No. XSPP3, 1974?; No. XSPP4, 9.76; No. XSPP5, 8.83

# First Day Covers

| | | | |
|---|---|---|---|
| XSFD1 (7.7.71) | 2½p., 3p. (2 bands), 5p., 7½p. | † | 4·00 |
| XSFD2 (23.1.74) | 3p. (1 band), 3½p. (2 bands), 5½p. (2 bands), 8p. | † | 1·50 |
| XSFD3 (6.11.74) | 4½p. | † | 1·00 |
| XSFD4 (14.1.76) | 6½p., 8½p., | † | 60 |
| XSFD5 (20.10.76) | 10p. (2 bands), 11p. | † | 1·00 |
| XSFD6 (18.1.78) | 7p., 9p., 10½p. | † | 1·00 |
| XSFD7 (23.7.80) | 12p., 13½p., 15p. | † | 2·00 |

No special provision was made for first day covers for the 3½p. centre band also issued on the same day as the 4½p., but of course first day covers exist with both values.

No special covers were issued for the 5½p., change to one centre band issued on 21 May 1975.

No special provision was made for first day covers for the 10p. centre band also issued on the same day as the 12p., 13½p., and 15p., but first day covers exist franked with all values.

### Scottish Experimental Machine Packets

These are small cartons containing loose stamps for sale in vending machines. The experiment was confined to the Scottish Postal Board area, where six vending machines were installed, the first becoming operational in Dundee about February 1977.

The cartons contain labels inscribed "ROYAL MAIL STAMPS", their total face value (30p. or 60p.) and their contents. There are several versions of the labels and styles of packets.

At first the 30p. packet contained two 6½p. and two 8½p. Scottish Regional stamps and the 60p. packet had one of each. The stamps could be in pairs or blocks but also in strips or singles.

With the change in postal rates on 13 June 1977 these packets were withdrawn on 11 June and on the 13 the contents were changed, giving three 7p. and one 9p. for the 30p. packet and double this for the 60p. packet. However, this time ordinary British Machin stamps were used. Moreover the Edinburgh machine, situated in an automatic sorting area, was supplied with 7p. stamps with two phosphor bands instead of the new centre band 7p. stamps, despite instructions having been given to withdraw the two band stamps. However, the demand for these packets was too great to be filled and by 27 June the machine was closed down. It was brought back into use on 16 August 1977, supplying 7p. stamps with the centre band.

The 6½p. and 8½p. Scottish Regional packets were put on sale at the Edinburgh Philatelic Bureau in June 1977 and withdrawn in April 1978. The packets with the 7p. and 9p. Machin stamps were put on sale at the Bureau in June 1977 and withdrawn in December 1978. This suggests that these machines were withdrawn once the 50p. coin machines dispensing 50p. folded booklets were operational in Scotland.

These can make a very interesting study but owing to the ephemeral nature of their contents it is not practical to list them in detail. More information will be found in study papers by Mr. M. A. M. Imrie in the May and October 1977 issues of *Guidec*, published by the British Decimal Stamps Study Circle.

## D.  Wales

From the inception of the Regional stamps, the Welsh versions were tendered to members of the public at all Post Offices within the former County of Monmouthshire but the English alternatives were available on request. Offices with a Monmouthshire address but situated outside the County, namely Beachley, Brockweir, Redbrook, Sedbury, Tutshill, Welsh Newton and Woocroft, were not supplied with the Welsh Regional stamps.

With the re-formation of Counties, Monmouthshire became known as Gwent and was also declared to be part of Wales. From 1 July 1974, therefore, except for the offices mentioned above, only Welsh Regional stamps were available at the offices under the jurisdiction of Newport, Gwent.

**XW4**
(Des. Jeffery Matthews)

## Type XW4
## 2½p.   (1971–73)
### 1971 (7 JULY).   ONE 4 mm. CENTRE PHOSPHOR BAND
#### A. ORIGINAL COATED PAPER. PVA GUM

| | | | | | | | | |
|---|---|---|---|---|---|---|---|---|
| XW18 (= S.G.W13) | Bright magenta | .. | .. | .. | .. | .. | 20 | 15 |
| | a. Imperf. top margin | .. | .. | .. | .. | .. | £325 | |
| | b. Phosphor omitted.. | .. | .. | .. | .. | .. | 5·50 | |
| | c. Extra line in dragon | .. | .. | .. | .. | .. | 3·00 | |
| | d. Extra hind leg claw | .. | .. | .. | .. | .. | 2·00 | |
| | e. Severed snout | .. | .. | .. | .. | .. | 4·00 | |
| | f. Spur to hindmost foot | .. | .. | .. | .. | .. | 2·00 | |
| | g. Weak tips to wings | .. | .. | .. | .. | .. | 2·00 | |
| | h. Extra line in wing.. | .. | .. | .. | .. | .. | 2·25 | |
| | i. White flaw by tip of dragon's tongue | .. | | .. | .. | .. | 2·00 | |

**Cylinder Numbers (Blocks of Six)**
Perforation Type A

| Cyl. No. | Phos. No. | | | | No dot | Dot |
|---|---|---|---|---|---|---|
| 3 | 5 | .. | .. | .. | 2·75 | 3·75* |

#### B. FLUORESCENT COATED PAPER. GUM ARABIC (22.9.72)

| | | | | | | | | |
|---|---|---|---|---|---|---|---|---|
| XW19 (= S.G.W13Eg) | Bright magenta | .. | .. | .. | .. | .. | 20 | 20 |
| | a. Imperforate (pair).. | .. | .. | .. | .. | .. | £350 | |
| | d. Weak tips to wing | .. | .. | .. | .. | .. | 2·25 | |
| | e. Extra line in wing.. | .. | .. | .. | .. | .. | 2·50 | |

**Cylinder Numbers (Blocks of Six)**
Perforation Type R(S)

| Cyl. No. | Phos. No. | | | | No dot | Dot |
|---|---|---|---|---|---|---|
| 3 | 9 | .. | .. | .. | 3·00 | 3·50 |

#### C. FLUORESCENT COATED PAPER. PVA GUM (1973)

| | | | | | | | |
|---|---|---|---|---|---|---|---|
| XW20 | Bright magenta | .. | .. | .. | .. | .. | 90 |
| | a. Spur to hindmost foot | .. | .. | .. | .. | .. | 4·00 |
| | b. Weak tips to wings | .. | .. | .. | .. | .. | 4·50 |
| | c. Extra line in wing.. | .. | .. | .. | .. | .. | 4·75 |
| | d. White flaw by arrow from dragon's mouth | .. | | .. | .. | 4·50 |

**Cylinder Numbers (Blocks of Six)**

Perforation Type A

| Cyl. No. | Phos. No. | | | | | No dot | Dot |
|---|---|---|---|---|---|---|---|
| 3 | 9 | .. | .. | .. | .. | 20·00 | 15·00 |

**CYLINDER VARIETIES**

**Listed Flaws**

XW18c

Extra curved line from top
of dragon's head to bottom
of central leg
(No dot, R. 4/6)

XW18d

Extra claw to hind leg
(No dot, R 18/6)

XW18e

Snout completely
severed
(Dot, R. 3/1)
(Later retouched)

XW18f, 20a

Spur to hindmost
foot
(Dot, R. 3/5)

XW18g, 19d, 20b

Weak tips to wings
(Dot, R. 15/2)

XW18h, 19e, 20c

Extra line in wing
(Dot, R. 18/8)

XW18i, 20d

White flaw by
dragon's mouth
(Dot, R. 19/1)

**Minor Constant Flaws**

Cyl. 3.   2/9   Retouch on Queen's shoulder (Th. F4–5)
       14/5   Pink marks in dragon's foreleg (Th. B1)

**WITHDRAWN**   Nos. XW18/20, 22.1.75

# 3p.   (1971–74)

## 1971 (7 JULY)   TWO 9·5 mm. PHOSPHOR BANDS

**A. ORIGINAL COATED PAPER. PVA GUM**

| | | | | | | | | |
|---|---|---|---|---|---|---|---|---|
| XW21 (=S.G.W14) | Ultramarine | .. | .. | .. | .. | .. | 25 | 15 |
| | a. Phosphor omitted.. | .. | .. | .. | .. | 15·00 | |
| | b. Break in line in dragon by head | | .. | .. | 2·50 | |
| | c. Similar break and forelegs joined by white flaw | | .. | 2·50 | |
| | d. Break in line in dragon by foot .. | .. | .. | .. | 2·75 | |
| | e. "v" flaw by claw on hindmost leg | .. | .. | .. | 2·50 | |

**Cylinder Numbers (Blocks of Six)**
Perforation Type A

| Cyl. No. | Phos. No. | | | | | No dot | Dot |
|---|---|---|---|---|---|---|---|
| 1 | 4 | .. | .. | .. | .. | 5·00* | 3·00 |

**B. FLUORESCENT COATED PAPER. PVA GUM** (2.73)

| XW22 | Ultramarine .. | .. | .. | .. | .. | .. | .. | 3·50 | 1·00 |
|---|---|---|---|---|---|---|---|---|---|
| | *a.* One broad band .. | .. | .. | .. | .. | .. | 75·00 | |
| | *b.* Break in line in dragon by head | | | .. | .. | .. | 8·00 | |
| | *c.* Similar break and forelegs joined by white flaw | | | | .. | 8·00 | |
| | *d.* Break in line in dragon by foot .. | | .. | .. | .. | 8·00 | |
| | *e.* "v" flaw by claw on hindmost leg | | .. | .. | .. | 8·00 | |

**Cylinder Numbers (Blocks of Six)**
Perforation Type A

| Cyl. No. | Phos. No. | | | | | No dot | Dot |
|---|---|---|---|---|---|---|---|
| 1 | 7 | .. | .. | .. | .. | 30·00* | 25·00 |

**C. FLUORESCENT COATED PAPER. GUM ARABIC** (6.6.73)

| XW23 (= S.G.W14Eg) | Ultramarine .. | .. | .. | .. | .. | .. | .. | 30 |
|---|---|---|---|---|---|---|---|---|
| | *a.* Phosphor omitted.. | .. | .. | .. | .. | .. | 3·50 |
| | *b.* Break in line in dragon by head | | .. | .. | .. | 3·50 |
| | *c.* Similar break and forelegs joined by white flaw | | | | .. | 3·50 |
| | *d.* Break in line in dragon by foot .. | | .. | .. | .. | 3·75 |
| | *e.* "v" flaw by claw on hindmost leg | | .. | .. | .. | 3·50 |
| | *f.* Phosphor band at left omitted .. | | .. | .. | .. | 38·00 |
| | *g.* Phosphor band at right omitted | | .. | .. | .. | 35·00 |

Examples of No. XW23 only exist with contaminated "yellow phosphor".

**Cylinder Numbers (Blocks of Six)**
Perforation Type R(S)

| Cyl. No. | Phos. No. | | | | | No dot | Dot |
|---|---|---|---|---|---|---|---|
| 1 | 7 | .. | .. | .. | .. | 12·00 | 14·00 |

## 1974 (23 JANUARY).　CHANGE TO ONE 4 mm. CENTRE BAND. FLUORESCENT COATED PAPER. PVA GUM

| XW24 (= S.G.W15) | Ultramarine .. | .. | .. | .. | .. | .. | 20 | 20 |
|---|---|---|---|---|---|---|---|---|
| | *b.* Break in line in dragon by head | .. | .. | .. | .. | 2·25 | |
| | *c.* Broken body line and forelegs joined by white flaw | | | .. | 1·75 | |
| | *d.* Break in line in dragon by foot | .. | .. | .. | .. | 1·75 | |
| | *e.* "v" flaw by claw of hindmost leg | .. | .. | .. | .. | 1·75 | |

**Cylinder Numbers (Blocks of Six)**
Perforation Type A

| Cyl. No. | Phos. No. | | | | No dot | Dot |
|---|---|---|---|---|---|---|
| 1 | 8* | .. | .. | .. | 2·75* | 1·50 |

*Exists without phosphor number showing due to a dry print.

**CYLINDER VARIETIES**
**Listed Flaws**

| XW21/4*b* | XW21/4*c* | XW21/4*d* |
|---|---|---|
| Broken body line near head (No dot, R. 2/1) | Broken body line and forelegs joined (No dot, R. 6/10) | Broken body line near foot (Dot, R. 10/10) |

XW21/4e
"v" flaw appearing as extra
claw to hind leg
(No dot, R. 18/1)

**Minor Constant Flaws**

Cyl. 1   8/1   Missing tips to dragon's nose and arrow from mouth (Th. A1)
8/9   Small coloured spot in fork of dragon's tongue (Th. A1) and three white dots at
back of Queen's hair (Th. E6)

**WITHDRAWN**   Nos. XW21/3, 22.1.75
No. XW24, 8.4.78

# $3\frac{1}{2}$p.   (1974)

## 1974 (23 JANUARY).   TWO 9·5 mm. PHOSPHOR BANDS. FLUORESCENT COATED PAPER. PVAD GUM

XW26 (= S.G.W16)   Olive-grey    ..        ..     ..      ..      ..      ..     20      25
b. Break in line in dragon ..     ..     ..      ..      ..     2·25
c. White spot in value     ..      ..      ..      ..     3·00

**Cylinder Numbers (Blocks of Six)**

Perforation Type R

| Cyl. No. | Phos. No. | | | | No dot | Dot |
|---|---|---|---|---|---|---|
| 2 | 17 | .. | .. | .. .. | 2·25 | 2·25 |

**CYLINDER VARIETIES**
**Listed Flaws**

XW26/7b
Broken body line
(Cyl. 2 dot, R. 3/7)

XW26/7c
Large white spot before P of value
(Cyl. 2 dot, R. 17/5)

**Minor Constant Flaws**

Cyl. 2.   6/5   Dark scratch across Queen's jaw (Th. E4)
11/2   Disturbance between figure 1 and P in value

## 1974 (6 NOVEMBER).   CHANGE TO ONE 4 mm. CENTRE BAND. FLUORESCENT COATED PAPER. PVAD GUM

XW27 (= S.G.W17)   Olive-grey    ..      ..        ..      ..      ..      ..     20      25
b. Break in line in dragon ..     ..     ..      ..      ..     2·25
c. White spot in value     ..      ..      ..      ..     3·00

**Cylinder Numbers (Blocks of Six)**

Perforation Type R

| Cyl. No. | Phos. No. | | | | No dot | Dot |
|---|---|---|---|---|---|---|
| 2 | 20 | .. | .. | .. .. | 2·25 | 2·25 |

A no dot cylinder block of 6 has been seen without a phosphor cylinder number.

**389**

**CYLINDER VARIETIES**

**Minor Constant Flaws**

Cyl. 2.  6/5  Dark scratch across Queen's jaw (Th. E4)
         11/2  Disturbance between figure 1 and P in value

**WITHDRAWN**   Nos. XW26/7, 9.76

---

# 4½p.   (1974)

## 1974 (6 NOVEMBER).   TWO 9·5 mm. PHOSPHOR BANDS. FLUORESCENT COATED PAPER. PVAD GUM

| | | | | | | | | | |
|---|---|---|---|---|---|---|---|---|---|
| XW28 (= S.G.W18) | Grey-blue | .. | .. | .. | .. | .. | .. | .. | 25 | 20 |
| | *b.* Scratch below eye.. | .. | .. | .. | .. | .. | 2·00 | |
| | *c.* Dark spot in hair .. | .. | .. | .. | .. | .. | 2·00 | |
| | *d.* Spot in crown | .. | .. | .. | .. | .. | 2·00 | |

**Cylinder Numbers (Blocks of Six)**

Perforation Type R

| Cyl. No. | Phos. No. | | | | No dot | Dot |
|---|---|---|---|---|---|---|
| 1 | 17 | .. | .. | .. | 2·50 | 2·50 |

**CYLINDER VARIETIES**

**Listed Flaws**

Vertical scratch below
Queen's eye
(Cyl. 1 dot, R. 5/4)

XW28*b*

Multipositive Flaws
XW28*c*. Cyl. 1 dot, R. 12/8. See XN30*c* of Northern Ireland.
XW28*d*. Cyl. 1 dot, R. 16/6. See XN30*f* of Northern Ireland.

**Minor Constant Flaws**

Cyl. 1.  3/7  Scratch through dragon's wing extending through head into left margin on stamp
              (Th. A2-B1)
         6/2  White patch at back of collar (Th. G5)
         6/4  Small retouch on Queen's forehead (Th. C4-D4)
         6/5  Dotted line on Queen's cheek (Th. E4)
         7/7  Dark speck in front of Queen's hair (Th. B3)
        14/10 Small retouch under necklace (Th. F4)
        16/8  Dark speck on Queen's cheek (Th.D4)
        17/1  White speck in hair below band of diadem (Th. D5)
        20/2  Small speck under necklace (Th. F4-5)
     Some of the above are multipositive flaws which occur to a greater or less extent on the 6½p.
Northern Ireland, Scotland and Wales from Cyl. 1 dot.

**WITHDRAWN**  9.76

---

# 5p.   (1971–73)

## 1971 (7 JULY).   TWO 9·5 mm. PHOSPHOR BANDS.

### A. ORIGINAL COATED PAPER. PVA GUM

| | | | | | | | | | |
|---|---|---|---|---|---|---|---|---|---|
| XW29 (= S.G.W19) | Reddish violet.. | .. | .. | .. | .. | .. | .. | 1·50 | 1·50 |
| | *a.* Phosphor omitted.. | .. | .. | .. | .. | .. | 11·00 | |
| | *b.* One broad band .. | .. | .. | .. | .. | .. | 60·00 | |
| | *c.* Extra claw .. | .. | .. | .. | .. | .. | 5·00 | |

**Cylinder Numbers (Blocks of Six)**

Perforation Type F*

| Cyl. No. | Phos. No. | | | | No dot | Dot |
|---|---|---|---|---|---|---|
| 3 | 12 | .. | .. | .. | 11·00 | 11·00 |

**B. FLUORESCENT COATED PAPER. PVA GUM** (6.73)

XW30       Reddish violet..    ..    ..    ..    ..    ..    ..   14·00   3·50
                *a.* Phosphor omitted..    ..    ..    ..    ..    ..   30·00

**Cylinder Numbers (Blocks of Six)**
Perforation Type F(L)*

| Cyl. No. | Phos. No. | | | | No dot | Dot |
|---|---|---|---|---|---|---|
| 3 | 11 | .. | .. | .. | £100 | £100 |

**CYLINDER VARIETIES**
**Listed Flaws**

Normal

Extra claw on dragon's hind foot
(Cyl. 3 dot, R. 17/2)

XW29*c*

**Minor Constant Flaw**
Cyl. 3    18/1   Extensive retouching above Queen's head (Th. A3–5)

**WITHDRAWN**   Nos. XW29/30, 22.1.75.

---

# 5½p.   (1974–75)

**1974 (23 JANUARY).   TWO 9·5 mm. PHOSPHOR BANDS.
FLUORESCENT COATED PAPER. PVAD GUM**

XW31 ( = S.G.W20)    Violet ..    ..    ..    ..    ..    ..    ..    20    25
                    *a.* Phosphor omitted..    ..    ..    ..    ..    ..   £160
                    *b.* Spot on forehead ..    ..    ..    ..    ..    ..   2·00

**Cylinder Numbers (Blocks of Six)**
Perforation Type A.   Single pane cylinder

| Cyl. No. | Phos. No. | | | | No dot | Dot |
|---|---|---|---|---|---|---|
| 1 | 22* | .. | .. | .. | 2·25 | † |

*The phosphor 22 is shown upright but superimposed over inverted figures.

**1975 (21 MAY).   CHANGE TO 4 mm. CENTRE BAND. FLUORESCENT
COATED PAPER. PVAD GUM**

XW32 ( = S.G.W21)    Violet ..    ..    ..    ..    ..    ..    ..    20    25
                    *a.* Imperforate (pair)..    ..    ..    ..    ..   £400
                    *b.* Top margin imperforate ..    ..    ..    ..
                    *c.* Spot on forehead ..    ..    ..    ..    ..   2·00

**Cylinder Numbers (Blocks of Six)**
Perforation Type R(S).   Single pane only

| Cyl. No. | Phos. No. | | | | No dot | Dot |
|---|---|---|---|---|---|---|
| 1 | 19 | .. | .. | .. | 2·40 | † |

Perforation Type A.   Single pane only

| 2 | 19 | .. | .. | .. | £300 | † |
|---|---|---|---|---|---|---|

    Normally the Swedish rotary perforator produces a single extension hole in the left-hand margin
on no dot panes. Sheets from cylinder 1 have been seen with the left-hand margin fully perforated
through or else with four to six extension holes, the rest being blind perforations.

**CYLINDER VARIETIES**
Listed Flaw

Dark spot on forehead
(Cyl. 1 no dot, R. 15/9)

XW31*b*, 32*c*

**Minor Constant Flaws**
Cyl. 1    2/1  Vertical scratch on Queen's cheek (Th. D4)
            10/4  Vertical scratch on Queen's neck (Th. E4–D4)

**WITHDRAWN**    Nos. XW31/2, 31.5.77

---

# 6½p.    (1976)

## 1976 (14 JANUARY).    ONE 4 mm. CENTRE PHOSPHOR BAND. FLUORESCENT COATED PAPER. PVAD GUM

| XW33 (= S.G.W22) | Greenish blue .. | .. | .. | .. | .. | .. | 20 | 20 |
|---|---|---|---|---|---|---|---|---|
| | *a.* Dark blob in diadem | .. | .. | .. | .. | .. | 2·50 | |
| | *b.* Blue mark on wing | .. | .. | .. | .. | .. | 2·25 | |
| | *c.* White spot by arrow | .. | .. | .. | .. | .. | 1·75 | |
| | *d.* Blue spot in hair .. | .. | .. | .. | .. | .. | 1·50 | |
| | *e.* Blue spot in band.. | .. | .. | .. | .. | .. | 1·50 | |
| | *f.* Missing tip to dragon's wing | .. | .. | .. | .. | 1·50 | |
| | *g.* Blunted arrow | .. | .. | .. | .. | .. | 2·25 | |

**Cylinder Numbers (Blocks of Six unless otherwise stated)**
Perforation Type R

| Cyl. No. | Phos. No. | | | | No dot | Dot | |
|---|---|---|---|---|---|---|---|
| 1 | 18 | .. | .. | .. | 2·00 | 2·00 | |

Perforation Type RE

| | 1 | 20 | .. | .. | .. | 35·00 | 30·00 | |
|---|---|---|---|---|---|---|---|---|
| | 1 | — | .. | .. | .. | 9·00 | 6·00 | |
| | 2 | 20 | .. | .. | .. | 6·50 | 6·50 | |
| | 2 | 20 | +65 mm. (16).. | .. | 22·00 | 25·00 | Block of ten |

On the dot panes the dot appears before the ink cylinder 1.
Phosphor Cylinder Displacement. With ink cyl. 1, phos. cyl. 20 is known displaced up the margin 433 mm. opposite row 1.

**CYLINDER VARIETIES**
Listed Flaws

| XW33*a* | XW33*b* | XW33*c* |
|---|---|---|
| Dark blob on central cross (Cyl. 1 no dot, R. 14/9) | Blue mark on dragon's wing (Cyl. 1 dot, R. 4/8) | White spot by arrow (Cyl. 1 dot, R. 11/9) |

XW33*f*
Missing tip to dragon's wing
(Cyl. 1 dot, R. 20/7)

XW33*g*
Blunted arrow behind wing
(Cyl. 1 dot, R. 4/6)

Multipositive Flaws

XW33*d*. Cyl. 1 dot, R. 12/8. See XN30*c* of Northern Ireland.
XW33*e*. Cyl. 1 dot, R. 16/6. See XN30*f* of Northern Ireland.

**Minor Constant Flaws**

Cyl. 1.  6/2 Small retouch on back of collar (Th. G5).  Original flaw on Wales 4½p.
     6/4 Blue speck on Queen's forehead (Th. C4–D4)
     6/5 Blue blemish on Queen's cheek (Th. E4)
     9/3 Blue spot on Queen's neck (Th. F5)
    14/6 White flaw under band of crown (Th. D5) and missing cylinder dots in bottom frame (Th. H6)
   14/10 Small retouch under necklace (Th. F4)
    16/8 Dark spot on Queen's cheek (Th. D4)
    17/2 White speck in fold of collar (Th. G5)
    19/3 Dark speck in Queen's shoulder (Th. G4)
    19/5 Small retouch on Queen's shoulder adjoining back of collar (Th. F5)
    20/2 Small speck under necklace (Th. F4–5)
    20/8 Two white spots in Queen's hair (Th. D5)

Some of the above are multipositive flaws which occur to a greater or less extent on the 6½p. Northern Ireland and Scotland and 4½p. Wales from Cyl. 1 dot.

**WITHDRAWN**  4.79

# 7p.  (1978)

**1978 (18 JANUARY).  ONE 4 mm. CENTRE PHOSPHOR BAND. FLUORESCENT COATED PAPER. PVAD GUM**

XW34 ( = S.G.W23)   Purple-brown .. .. .. .. .. .. 25  25

**Cylinder Numbers (Blocks of Six)**

Perforation Type RE

| Cyl. No. | Phos. No. | | | | | No dot | Dot |
|---|---|---|---|---|---|---|---|
| 1 | 18 | .. | .. | .. | .. | 8·00 | 5·00 |
| 1 | 31 | .. | .. | .. | .. | 3·50 | 3·50 |

Perforation Type A

| | | | | | | | |
|---|---|---|---|---|---|---|---|
| 1 | 20 | .. | .. | .. | .. | 15·00 | 20·00 |

**CYLINDER VARIETIES**

**Minor Constant Flaws**

Cyl. 1.  4/6 Dark spot below back of Queen's hair (Th. E6)
     5/5 White scratch from top of design through crown and hair to dress (Th. A5–G5)
    15/6 Dark spot on Queen's bust (Th. G6)
    16/4 Curved scratch from Queen's neck to ear (Th. F4–E4)
    20/8 Three white spots on Queen's neck (Th. E4)

**WITHDRAWN**  5.80

# 7½p.  (1971)

**1971 (7 JULY).  TWO 9·5 mm. PHOSPHOR BANDS. ORIGINAL COATED PAPER. PVA GUM**

XW35 ( = S.G.W24)   Chestnut .. .. .. .. .. .. .. 2·00  2·25
                *a.* Phosphor omitted.. .. .. .. .. .. 75·00

**393**

**Cylinder Numbers (Blocks of Six)**
Perforation Type F*

| Cyl. No. | Phos. No. | | | | | No dot | Dot |
|---|---|---|---|---|---|---|---|
| 7 | 10 | .. | .. | .. | .. | 15·00 | 15·00 |

**WITHDRAWN**  22.1.75

# 8p.  (1974)
## 1974 (23 JANUARY).   TWO 9·5 mm. PHOSPHOR BANDS. FLUORESCENT COATED PAPER. PVAD GUM

| XW36 (= S.G.W25) | Rosine | .. | .. | .. | .. | .. | .. | .. | 30 | 30 |
|---|---|---|---|---|---|---|---|---|---|---|
| | *a.* Two wing-tips missing | .. | | .. | .. | .. | .. | .. | 3·50 | |
| | *b.* Phosphor omitted | | .. | .. | .. | .. | .. | £450 | |

**Cylinder Numbers (Blocks of Six)**
Perforation Type A.   Single pane cylinder

| Cyl. No. | Phos. No. | | | | | No dot | Dot |
|---|---|---|---|---|---|---|---|
| 1 | 22 | .. | .. | .. | .. | 2·25 | † |

**CYLINDER VARIETIES**
**Listed Flaw**

Two wing-tips missing
(Cyl. 1, R. 12/3)

XW36*a*

**Minor Constant Flaw**
Cyl. 1   2/8  White spot on Queen's temple (Th. D4)
**WITHDRAWN**  3.79

# 8½p.  (1976)
## 1976 (14 JANUARY).   TWO 9·5 mm. PHOSPHOR BANDS. FLUORESCENT COATED PAPER. PVAD GUM

| XW37 (= S.G.W26) | Yellow-green | .. | .. | .. | .. | .. | .. | .. | 30 | 30 |
|---|---|---|---|---|---|---|---|---|---|---|
| | *b.* White spot over crown | .. | | .. | .. | .. | .. | .. | 2·25 | |

**Cylinder Numbers (Blocks of Six)**
Perforation Type R

| Cyl. No. | Phos. No. | | | | | No dot | Dot |
|---|---|---|---|---|---|---|---|
| 1 | 17 | .. | .. | .. | .. | 3·00 | 3·00 |

Perforation Type RE

| | | | | | | | |
|---|---|---|---|---|---|---|---|
| 1 | 17 | .. | .. | .. | .. | —* | 4·00 |
| 1 | 17 | −30 mm. (20) | | .. | | 30·00 | † |
| 1 | P21 | .. | .. | .. | .. | 3·00 | 3·00 |
| 1 | P21 | −29 mm. (20) | | .. | | 50·00 | 50·00 |

*Same price as perforation type R with single extension holes in left margin.

**CYLINDER VARIETIES**
**Listed Flaw**

White spot over crown
(Cyl. 1 no dot, R. 8/1)

XW37*b*

**Minor Constant Flaw**

Cyl. 1    17/2   Small white line between claws of dragon's hind foot (Th. C2)

**WITHDRAWN**   April 1979 but put on sale again at the Philatelic Bureau in June and finally withdrawn in October 1979.

# 9p. (1978)

**1978 (18 JANUARY).   TWO 9·5 mm. PHOSPHOR BANDS. FLUORESCENT COATED PAPER. PVAD GUM**

XW38 ( = S.G.W27)    Deep violet   ..    ..    ..    ..    ..    ..    ..    30     30

**Cylinder Numbers (Blocks of Six)**

Perforation Type RE

| Cyl. No. | Phos. No. | | | | | No dot | Dot |
|----------|-----------|--|--|--|--|--------|-----|
| 2 | P21 | .. | .. | .. | .. | 3·25 | 3·25 |
| 2 | 30 | .. | .. | .. | .. | 2·50 | 2·50 |

**CYLINDER VARIETIES**

**Minor Constant Flaws**

Cyl. 2   2/4   Dark blemish touching back of collar (Th. F6–G6)

        7/1   Dark speck in background near back of crown (Th. D6)

        7/4   Dark blemish touching back of Queen's neck (Th. F5)

        9/5   Dark specks above crown (Th. B5–B6)

        9/8   Dark specks on Queen's neck (Th. E4)

      15/8   Dark speck above crown (Th. A5)

      20/8   Vertical scratch at upper right extending into margin (Th. A5)

**WITHDRAWN**   30.4.82

# 10p. (1976)

**1976 (20 OCTOBER).   TWO 9.5 mm. PHOSPHOR BANDS. FLUORESCENT COATED PAPER. PVAD GUM**

XW39 ( = S.G.W28)    Orange-brown..    ..    ..    ..    ..    ..    ..    35     30

**Cylinder Numbers (Blocks of Six)**

Perforation Type RE

| Cyl. No. | Phos. No. | | | | | No dot | Dot |
|----------|-----------|--|--|--|--|--------|-----|
| 2 | P21 | .. | .. | .. | .. | 2·50 | 2·50 |
| 2 | 30 | .. | .. | .. | .. | £225 | £300 |

**1980 (23 JULY).   CHANGE TO ONE 4 mm. CENTRE BAND. FLUORESCENT COATED PAPER. PVAD GUM**

XW40 ( = S.G.W29)    Orange-brown..    ..    ..    ..    ..    ..    ..    35     30

                    *a.* Two white dots on tongue    ..    ..    ..    ..    2·25

                    *b.* Extra claw ..    ..    ..    ..    ..    ..    2·25

**Cylinder Numbers (Blocks of Six)**

Perforation Type RE

| Cyl. No. | Phos. No. | | | | | No dot | Dot |
|----------|-----------|--|--|--|--|--------|-----|
| 2 | 20 | .. | .. | .. | .. | 2·50 | 2·50 |

**CYLINDER VARIETIES**
**Listed Flaws**

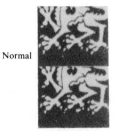

Normal

XW40*a*
Two white dots above
dragon's tongue
(Cyl. 2 no dot, R. 3/10)

XW40*b*
Extra claw on dragon's
hind foot
(Cyl. 2 no dot, R. 20/10)

**Minor Constant Flaws**

Cyl. 2  8/4  White spot below dragon's wing tip (Th. A3)
        13/5  Dark speck on Queen's neck (Th. F5)
        15/4  Dark speck behind Queen's neck under hair (Th. E5)
        18/9  Disturbance on Queen's cheek (Th. D4)
        19/2  White speck on Queen's forehead (Th. C4)
        19/4  Dark spot on Queen's forehead (Th. C3)

**WITHDRAWN**  No. XW39, 1.81; No. XW40, sold out 2.87

# 10½p.  (1978)

**1978 (18 JANUARY).  TWO 9·5 mm. PHOSPHOR BANDS.
FLUORESCENT COATED PAPER. PVAD GUM**

XW41 (=S.G.W30)    Steel-blue    ..    ..    ..    ..    ..    ..    ..    40    35

**Cylinder Numbers (Blocks of Six)**
Perforation Type RE

| Cyl. No. | Phos. No. | | | | No dot | Dot |
|---|---|---|---|---|---|---|
| 3 | 30 | .. | .. | .. | 3·00 | 3·00 |

**CYLINDER VARIETIES**
**Minor Constant Flaws**

Cyl. 3  3/10  Background blemish behind Queen's hair (Th. E6)
        9/5  Blemish on Queen's cheek (Th. D-E/3–4)

**WITHDRAWN**  30.4.82

# 11p.  (1976)

**1976 (20 OCTOBER).  TWO 9·5 mm. PHOSPHOR BANDS.
FLUORESCENT COATED PAPER. PVAD GUM**

| | | | | | | | | | |
|---|---|---|---|---|---|---|---|---|---|
| XW42 (=S.G.W31) | Scarlet .. | .. | .. | .. | .. | .. | .. | 40 | 45 |
| | *b.* Front wing-tip missing | .. | .. | .. | .. | .. | 2·50 | |
| | *c.* Two wing-tips missing | .. | .. | .. | .. | .. | 2·75 | |

**Cylinder Numbers (Blocks of Six)**
Perforation Type RE

| Cyl. No. | Phos. No. | | | | No dot | Dot |
|---|---|---|---|---|---|---|
| 1 | 17 | .. | .. | .. | 4·50* | 3·00 |
| 1 | 30 | .. | .. | .. | — | £750 |

CYLINDER VARIETIES
Listed Flaws

XW42*b*
Front wing-tip missing
(Cyl. 1 no dot, R. 15/7)

XW42*c*
Two wing-tips missing
(Cyl. 1 no dot, R. 16/9 and 20/1)

**Minor Constant Flaws**

Cyl. 1.　13/2　Two dark specks on Queen's cheek (Th. D4)
　　　　19/6　Pale blemish on Queen's neck above necklace (Th. F4)
　　　　20/8　Vertical scratch from back of Queen's hair to collar (Th. E6–F6) (as on 11p. Northern
　　　　　　　Ireland)

**WITHDRAWN**　30.4.82

# 12p. (1980)

**1980 (23 JULY).　PHOSPHORISED (FLUORESCENT COATED) PAPER.
PVAD GUM**

XW44 ( = S.G.W32)　Yellowish green　　..　　..　　..　　..　　..　　..　　40　　45
　　　　　　　　　　　*a*. Dark spot in hair ..　　..　　..　　..　　..　　..　　2·50

**Cylinder Numbers (Blocks of Six)**

Perforation Type RE
　　　　　　　Cyl. No.　　　　　　　　　No dot　　Dot
　　　　　　　2　　..　　..　　..　　..　　3·00　　3·00

**CYLINDER VARIETIES**

**Listed Flaw**
Multipositive Flaw
XW44*a*. Cyl. 2 dot, R. 12/10. See XN30*c* of Northern Ireland.

**Minor Constant Flaws**

Cyl. 2.　6/6　Spot above Queen's eyebrow (Th. D4)
　　　　10/6　Dark spot in background above crown (Th. A5)
　　　　15/3　Retouch above Queen's eyebrow (Th. C4)
　　　　16/8　Retouch in band of crown (Th. C5)
　　　　17/5　Dark speck on bust (Th. G4)
　　　　20/6　Pale blemish behind Queen's neck (Th. F5)

　　Most of the above are multipositive flaws which occur to a greater or less extent on the 15p.
cyl. 1 dot and Northern Ireland 12p. cyl. 1 dot, 13½p. cyl. 2 dot and 15p. cyl. 1 dot as well
as on Scotland 13½p. cyl. 1 dot.

**WITHDRAWN**　9.82

# 13½p. (1980)

**1980 (23 JULY).　PHOSPHORISED (FLUORESCENT COATED) PAPER.
PVAD GUM**

XW45 ( = S.G.W33)　Purple-brown ..　　..　　..　　..　　..　　..　　60　　70

**Cylinder Numbers (Blocks of Six)**

Perforation Type RE
　　　　　　　Cyl. No.　　　　　　　　　No dot　　Dot
　　　　　　　2　　..　　..　　..　　..　　4·50　　4·50

**CYLINDER VARIETIES**

**Minor Constant Flaws**

Cyl. 2   10/2   Short scratch on Queen's dress (Th. G6)
           12/1   Distorted lower curve to figure 3
           18/1   Retouch left of Queen's ear-ring (Th. D/E4)

**WITHDRAWN**   8.82

# 15p.   (1980)

**1980 (23 JULY).   PHOSPHORISED (FLUORESCENT COATED) PAPER. PVAD GUM.**

XW47 ( = S.G.W34)     Ultramarine   ..     ..     ..     ..     ..     ..     ..     45      50

**Cylinder Numbers (Blocks of Six)**

Perforation Type RE

| Cyl. No. | | | | | No dot | Dot |
|---|---|---|---|---|---|---|
| 1 | .. | .. | .. | .. | 3·25 | 3·25 |

**CYLINDER VARIETIES**

**Minor Constant Flaws**

Cyl. 1.   4/10   Spot in band of crown (Th. C5) and spot on Queen's neck (Th. E4)
         6/6   White spot above Queen's eyebrow (Th. D4)
         9/5   Dark spot below necklace (Th. F5)
      12/10   Retouch in hair (Th. D5)
      15/2   Blemishes in background behind portrait (Th. F6-G6)
      15/3   Retouch on Queen's hairline above eyebrow (Th. C4)
      16/8   Retouch in band of crown (Th. C5)
      17/7   Retouch to Queen's upper lip (Th. D3)

    Most of the above are multipositive flaws which occur to a greater or less extent on the 12p. cyl. 2 dot and Northern Ireland 12p. cyl. 1 dot, 13½p. cyl. 2 dot and 15p. cyl. 1 dot as well as on Scotland 13½p. cyl. 1 dot.

**WITHDRAWN**   14.1.84

# Presentation Packs

XWPP2 No. 28 (7.7.71)      2½p., 3p., 5p., 7½p.      4·00
  Comprises Nos. XW18, 21, 29 and 35

XWPP3 No. 63 (29.5.74)      3p., 3½p., 5½p., 8p.      3·00
  Comprises Nos. XW24, 26, 31 and 36

XWPP4 No. 63 (6.11.74)      3p., 3½p., 4½p., 5½p., 8p.      3·50
  As last but with No. XW28 added
  Presumably No. XWPP4 had the 3½p. with centre band instead of two bands and no doubt
it was later issued under the same stock number with the 5½p. centre band instead of two bands.

XWPP5 No. 86 (20.10.76)      6½p., 8½p., 10p., 11p.      1·75
  Comprises Nos. XW33, 37, 39 and 42

**WITHDRAWN**   No. XWPP2, 22.1.75; No. XWPP3, 1974?; No. XWPP4, 9.76; No. XWPP5, 8.83

# First Day Covers

XWFD1 (7.7.71)      2½p., 3p. (2 bands), 5p., 7½p.  ✝  4·00

XWFD2 (23.1.74)      3p. (1 band), 3½p., (2 bands),
                5½p. (2 bands), 8p.  ✝  1·50

XWFD3 (6.11.74)      4½p.  ✝  1·00

XWFD4 (14.1.76)      6½p, 8½p.  ✝  60

XWFD5 (20.10.76)      10p. (2 bands), 11p.  ✝  '1·00

XWFD6 (18.1.78)      7p., 9p., 10½p.  ✝  1·00

XWFD7 (23.7.80)      12p., 13½p., 15p.  ✝  2·00

  No special provision was made for first day covers for the 3½p. centre band also issued on
the same day as the 4½p., but of course first day covers exist with both values.
  No special covers were issued for the 5½p. change to one centre band issued on 21 May 1975.
  No special provision was made for first day covers for the 10p. centre band also issued on
the same day as the 12p., 13½p. and 15p., but first day covers exist franked with all values.

# SECTION XC

## Regional Decimal Issues

### 1981–90.   Printed by Lithography

---

### General Notes

**INTRODUCTION.** Following the decision to employ the lithographic process to print five denominations of the Machin issues in 1980 the Post Office placed further contracts with John Waddington Ltd., for Scottish issues and The House of Questa for the Northern Ireland and Welsh Regional stamps issued on 8 April 1981. In April 1986 Questa took over from Waddington the work of printing Scottish regional issues.

**PRINTING PROCESS.** Details are given under this heading in the General Notes to Section UG.

**MACHIN PORTRAIT.** Reduced size Machin head portraits have been used but none of the basic listings occur with more than one type and it is not necessary to include head types in the descriptions of each stamp. For collectors requiring further information on the head types see an article by Don Staddon in Volume 26, No. 6, February 1989 issue of *British Philatelic Bulletin*.

**PLATES.** Most printings are recorded with two plates, one in a deeper shade than the other. As an exception the 13p. printed by Questa in 1984 for Northern Ireland and Wales had grey as the second plate.

**MINOR CONSTANT FLAWS.** The remarks under this heading in the General Notes to Section UG also apply to the Regional stamps listed here.

## Regional issues for Northern Ireland, Scotland and Wales printed by The House of Questa

**SHEET ARRANGEMENT AND MARKINGS.** The sheet make-up and markings are as described in Section UG. Unlike the photogravure printings the "Total Sheet Value" inscription was not preceded by the country name until 1986. The value of the sheet is shown with a decimal point placed at the centre between the figures for all values except the 22p. where it is placed between the figures in the full stop position.

**PERFORATION.** All values are comb perforated 14 or 15 × 14 with perforation Type L and later, Type L(P) as described in Appendix I. On plate blocks (I) indicates an imperf. left margin and (P) is perforated. Plate blocks Type L(P) from the *right feed* have margins perforated through.

**PAPER AND GUM.** Original coated paper was used for the 11½p. value and one printing of the Northern Ireland 12½p. Thereafter fluorescent coated paper with PVAD gum was used for the 12½p. and 13p. values. Other values were printed on phosphorised paper with the fluorescent additive in the coating. On the 22p. value, printed in yellow-green phosphorised (advanced coated) paper was employed and this was later used for other values. PVA gum was replaced by PVAD gum for issues from 1982 except for the Northern Ireland 12½p. No. XNL5. From April 1987 values for second class mail were issued with PVA gum and a 4 mm. phosphor band printed at the left-hand side or right of centre.
   In 1988 paper supplied to Questa for the 19, 23 and 32p. issued on 8 November had PVAD gum without the greenish dye additive. In the lists such stamps are described as having PVAD (clear) gum.

**PHOSPHOR BANDS.** Values for second class mail have been issued with a phosphor band which gives a violet after-glow following irradiation by shortwave ultra violet light. The bands, which are continuous, are probably applied using a litho process.
   In 1986 the 12p. second class mail value was printed with a short phosphor band on each stamp in the sheet. This was to reduce wear on the perforator pins and the measure was continued with the 13, 14, 15 and 17p. values.

For General Notes describing the issues printed by John Waddington Ltd., see Section XC under Scotland.

# A. Northern Ireland

## Type XN4 as illustrated in Section XB printed by Questa

**Redrawn Crown**

I            II

**Type I.** Crown with all pearls individually drawn. Screened background.
**Type II.** Crown with clear outlines, large pearls and strong white line below them. First 3 pearls at left are joined. Solid background.

## 11½p. Drab (1981)

**1981 (8 APRIL). PERF. 14. ONE 4 mm. PHOSPHOR BAND AT LEFT. ORIGINAL COATED PAPER. PVA GUM**

XNL1 (=S.G.N134)   Drab  ..    ..    ..    ..    ..    ..    ..    ..    1·00   60

**Plate Numbers (Blocks of Six)**

Double Pane Plates
Plate Nos. in right margin

|  | Pl. Nos. |  |  | Row 1 | Row 20 |
|---|---|---|---|---|---|
|  | 1, 1 | .. | .. | .. 5·50 | 5·50 |
|  | 2, 2 | .. | .. | .. 6·00 | 6·00 |

**WITHDRAWN** 26.2.83

## 12p. Bright Emerald (1986)

**1986 (7 JANUARY). PERF. 15 × 14. ONE 4 mm. PHOSPHOR BAND AT LEFT. FLUORESCENT COATED PAPER. PVAD GUM**

XNL2 (= S.G.NI35)   Bright emerald    ..    ..    ..    ..    ..    ..    50   50

**Plate Numbers (Blocks of Six)**

Double Pane Plates
Plate Nos. in left margin

| Pl. Nos. | (I) | Pl. Nos. | (P) |
|---|---|---|---|
| 1, 1   ..  ..  .. | 2·50 | 2, 2   ..  ..  .. | 3·00 |

**1986 (JULY). PERF. 15 × 14. ONE SHORT PHOSPHOR BAND AT LEFT. FLUORESCENT COATED PAPER. PVAD GUM**

XNL3           Bright emerald    ..    ..    ..    ..    ..    ..    70   70

**Plate Numbers (Blocks of Six)**

Double Pane Plates
Plate Nos. in left margin

| Pl. Nos. | (I) | Pl. Nos. | (P) |
|---|---|---|---|
| 3, 3   ..  ..  .. | 5·00 | 4, 4   ..  ..  .. | 5·50 |

No. XNL3 was printed with the 4 mm. wide phosphor band at left cut short opposite the perforations at the top and bottom.

**SOLD OUT** Nos. XNL 2/3, 10.87

# 12½p. Light Emerald (1982–84)

**1982 (24 FEBRUARY). PERF. 14. ONE 4 mm. PHOSPHOR BAND AT LEFT. FLUORESCENT COATED PAPER. PVAD GUM**

XNL4 (=S.G.NI36)    Light emerald ..    ..    ..    ..    ..    ..    ..    50    40

**Plate Numbers (Blocks of Six)**

Double Pane Plates
Plate Nos. in right margin

| Pl. Nos. | | | | Row 1 | Row 20 |
|---|---|---|---|---|---|
| 1, 1 | .. | .. | .. | 10·00 | 15·00 |
| 2, 2 | .. | .. | .. | 4·50 | 5·00 |
| 1, 3 | .. | .. | .. | — | — |
| 2, 4 | .. | .. | .. | — | — |
| 3, 3 | .. | .. | .. | 3·25 | 3·25 |
| 4, 4 | .. | .. | .. | 4·50 | 4·50 |

Plate Nos. in left margin

| Pl. Nos. | | | (I) | Pl. Nos. | | | (P) |
|---|---|---|---|---|---|---|---|
| 1,1 | .. | .. | 12·00 | 2,2 | .. | .. | 12·00 |

## 1984 (28 FEBRUARY). PERF. 15 × 14. ONE 4 mm. PHOSPHOR BAND AT LEFT

**A. ORIGINAL COATED PAPER. PVA GUM**

XNL5    Light emerald ..    ..    ..    ..    ..    ..    ..    4·00    4·00

**Plate Numbers (Blocks of Six)**

Double Pane Plates
Plate Nos. in left margin

| Pl. Nos. | | | (I) | Pl. Nos. | | | (P) |
|---|---|---|---|---|---|---|---|
| 1,1 | .. | .. | 40·00 | 2,2 | .. | .. | £190 |

**B. FLUORESCENT COATED PAPER. PVAD GUM** (6.84)

XNL6 (=S.G.NI36a)    Light emerald ..    ..    ..    ..    ..    ..    ..    4·00    4·00

**Plate Numbers (Blocks of Six)**

Double Pane Plates
Plate Nos. in left margin

| Pl. Nos. | | | (I) | Pl. Nos. | | | (P) |
|---|---|---|---|---|---|---|---|
| 1, 3 | .. | .. | 30·00 | 2, 4 | .. | .. | 20·00 |

**WITHDRAWN**    No. XNL4, 28.2.85; Nos. XNL5/6, 28.6.85

# 13p. Pale Chestnut (1984–87)

**1984 (23 OCTOBER). PERF. 15 × 14. ONE 4 mm. PHOSPHOR BAND AT LEFT. FLUORESCENT COATED PAPER. TYPE I. PVAD GUM**

XNL7 (=S.G.NI37)    Pale chestnut..    ..    ..    ..    ..    ..    ..    50    35
                    *a.* Phosphor omitted    ..    ..    ..    ..    ..

**Plate Numbers (Blocks of Six)**

Double Pane Plates (Second plate number is grey)
Plate Nos. in left margin

| Pl. Nos. | | | (I) | Pl. Nos. | | | (P) |
|---|---|---|---|---|---|---|---|
| 1, 1 | .. | .. | 2·75 | 2, 2 | .. | .. | 2·75 |
| 3, 3 | .. | .. | 7·00 | 4, 4 | .. | .. | 5·50 |
| 5, 5 | .. | .. | 2·75 | 6, 6 | .. | .. | 2·75 |

**1986 (11 DECEMBER). PERF. 15 × 14. ONE SHORT PHOSPHOR BAND AT LEFT. FLUORESCENT COATED PAPER. TYPE II**

**A. PVAD GUM**

XNL8                 Pale chestnut..    ..    ..    ..    ..    ..    ..    50    30

**Plate Numbers (Blocks of Six)**

Double Pane Plates (Second plate number is chestnut)
Plate Nos. in left margin

| Pl. Nos. | (I) | Pl. Nos. | (P) |
|---|---|---|---|
| 1, 1    ..    ..    .. | 4·50 | 2, 2    ..    ..    .. | 18·00 |

**B. PVA GUM** (14.4.87)

XNL9 (=S.G.Ni37Ea) Pale chestnut    ..    ..    ..    ..    ..    ..    ..    ..    50    30

**Plate Numbers (Blocks of Six)**

Double Pane Plates (Second plate number is chestnut)
Plate Nos. in left margin

| Pl. Nos. | (I) | Pl. Nos. | (P) |
|---|---|---|---|
| 1, 1    ..    ..    .. | 3·00 | 1, 1    ..    ..    .. | 3·50 |
| | | 2, 2    ..    ..    .. | 3·50 |
| | | 3, 3    ..    ..    .. | — |
| | | 4, 4    ..    ..    .. | 4·50 |

Plate Nos. 1, 1 and 2, 2 also exist with a short imperforate section at base below the 8th perforation. *Price for plate* 1, 1, £25 *and* 2, 2 £20.

**WITHDRAWN** No. XNL7, 14.4.88; Nos. XNL 8/9, 4.9.89

---

# 14p. Grey-blue (1981)

**1981 (8 APRIL). PERF. 14. PHOSPHORISED (FLUORESCENT COATED) PAPER. PVA GUM**

XNL10 (=S.G.NI38)  Grey-blue    ..    ..    ..    ..    ..    ..    ..    60    50

**Plate Numbers (Blocks of Six)**

Double Pane Plates
Plate Nos. in right margin

| Pl. Nos | | | | Row 1 | Row 20 |
|---|---|---|---|---|---|
| 1, 1    .. | .. | .. | | 4·00 | 4·00 |
| 2, 2    .. | .. | .. | | 4·00 | 4·00 |

**WITHDRAWN**    14.1.84

---

# 14p. Deep Blue (1988)

**1988 (8 NOVEMBER). PERF. 15 × 14. ONE 4 mm. SHORT PHOSPHOR BAND (RIGHT OF CENTRE). FLUORESCENT COATED PAPER. PVA GUM**

XNL11 (=S.G.NI39)  Deep blue    ..    ..    ..    ..    ..    ..    ..    35    35

**Plate Numbers (Blocks of Six)**

Double Pane Plates
Plate Nos. in left margin

| Pl. Nos. | | | (P) |
|---|---|---|---|
| 1, 1    .. | .. | .. | 2·25 |
| 2, 2    .. | .. | .. | 2·25 |
| 3, 3    .. | .. | .. | 8·50 |
| 4, 4    .. | .. | .. | 8·50 |

**WITHDRAWN**    27.11.90

## 15p. Bright Blue (1989)

**1989 (28 NOVEMBER). PERF. 15 × 14. ONE 4 mm. SHORT PHOSPHOR BAND (RIGHT OF CENTRE). FLUORESCENT COATED PAPER. PVA GUM**

XNL12 (=S.G.NI40)   Bright blue   ..      ..      ..      ..      ..      ..      25      30

**Plate Numbers (Blocks of Six)**
Double Pane Plates
Plate Nos. in left margin

| Pl. Nos. | | | | (P) |
|---|---|---|---|---|
| 1, 1 | .. | .. | .. | 1·90 |
| 2, 2 | .. | .. | .. | 1·90 |
| 3, 3 | .. | .. | .. | 3·00 |
| 4, 4 | .. | .. | .. | 3·00 |

Plate Nos. 3, 3 and 4, 4 also exist with a short imperforate section at base below the 8th perforation. *Price for plate* 3, 3 *and* 4, 4 £8 *each*.

## 15½p. Pale Violet (1982)

**1982 (24 FEBRUARY). PERF. 14. PHOSPHORISED (FLUORESCENT COATED) PAPER. PVAD GUM**

XNL13 (=S.G.NI41)   Pale violet   ..      ..      ..      ..      ..      ..      60      65

**Plate Numbers (Blocks of Six)**
Double Pane Plates
Plate Nos. in right margin

| Pl. No. | | | Row 1 | Row 20 |
|---|---|---|---|---|
| 1 | .. | .. | 4·00 | 4·00 |
| 2 | .. | .. | 4·00 | 4·00 |

**WITHDRAWN**   29.4.84

## 16p. Drab (1983–84)

**1983 (27 APRIL). PERF. 14. PHOSPHORISED (FLUORESCENT COATED) PAPER. PVAD GUM**

XNL15 (=S.G.NI42)   Drab ..      ..      ..      ..      ..      ..      ..      1·00      1·00

**Plate Numbers (Blocks of Six)**
Double Pane Plates
Plate Nos. in left margin

| Pl. No. | | | (I) | Pl. No. | | | (P) |
|---|---|---|---|---|---|---|---|
| 1 | .. | .. | 14·00 | 2 | .. | .. | 6·00 |

**1984 (28 FEBRUARY). PERF. 15 × 14. PHOSPHORISED (FLUORESCENT COATED) PAPER. PVAD GUM**

XNL16 (=S.G.NI42a) Drab   ..      ..      ..      ..      ..      ..      ..      3·50      1·00

**Plate Numbers (Blocks of Six)**
Double Pane Plates
Plate Nos. in left margin

| Pl. No. | | | (I) | Pl. No. | | | (P) |
|---|---|---|---|---|---|---|---|
| 3 | .. | .. | 17·00 | 4 | .. | .. | 17·00 |

**WITHDRAWN**   No. XNL15, 28.2.85; No. XNL16, 7.2.87

## 17p. Grey-blue (1984–86)

**1984 (23 OCTOBER). PERF. 15 × 14. PHOSPHORISED PAPER. TYPE I. PVAD GUM**

**A. FLUORESCENT COATED PAPER**

XNL17 (=S.G.NI43)  Grey-blue  ..  ..  ..  ..  ..  ..  ..  60    40

**Plate Numbers (Blocks of Six)**
Double Pane Plates
Plate Nos. in left margin

| Pl. No. | | (I) | Pl. No. | | | (P) |
|---|---|---|---|---|---|---|
| 1 | .. .. .. | 10·00 | 2 | .. .. | .. | 8·00 |

**B. ADVANCED COATED PAPER** (25.2.86)

XNL18          Grey-blue  ..  ..  ..  ..  ..  ..  ..  60    40

**Plate Numbers (Blocks of Six)**
Double Pane Plates
Plate Nos. in left margin

| Pl. No. | | (I) | Pl. No. | | | (P) |
|---|---|---|---|---|---|---|
| 3 | .. .. .. | 4·00 | 4 | .. .. | .. | 4·00 |

**1986 (10 SEPTEMBER). PERF. 15 × 14. PHOSPHORISED (ADVANCED COATED) PAPER. TYPE II. PVAD GUM**

XNL19 (=S.G.NI43Ea) Grey-blue  ..  ..  ..  ..  ..  ..  .. 13·00  15·00

**Plate Numbers (Blocks of Six)**
Double Pane Plates
Plate Nos. in left margin

| Pl. Nos. | | (I) | Pl. Nos. | | | (P) |
|---|---|---|---|---|---|---|
| 1, 1 | .. .. | 70·00 | 2, 2 | .. | .. | 70·00 |

**WITHDRAWN**  No. XNL17, 24.2.87; No. XNL18/19, sold out 10.87

## 17p. Deep Blue (1990)

**1990 (4 DECEMBER). PERF. 15 × 14. ONE 4 mm. SHORT PHOSPHOR BAND (RIGHT OF CENTRE). FLUORESCENT COATED PAPER. PVA GUM**

XNL20 (=S.G.NI44)  Deep blue  ..  ..  ..  ..  ..  ..  ..  30    35

**Plate Numbers (Blocks of Six**
Double Pane Plates
Plate Nos. in left margin

| Pl. Nos. | | | (P) |
|---|---|---|---|
| 1, 1 | .. | .. .. | 2·40 |
| 2, 2 | .. | .. .. | 2·40 |

## 18p. Deep Violet (1981)

**1981 (8 APRIL). PERF. 14. PHOSPHORISED (FLUORESCENT COATED) PAPER. PVA GUM**

XNL21 (=S.G.NI45)  Deep violet  ..  ..  ..  ..  ..  ..  ..  80    80

**Plate Numbers (Blocks of Six)**
Double Pane Plates
Plate Nos. in right margin

| Pl. Nos. | | | Row 1 | Row 20 |
|---|---|---|---|---|
| 1, 1 | .. | .. .. | 5·00 | 5·00 |
| 2, 2 | .. | .. .. | 5·00 | 5·00 |

**WITHDRAWN**  14.1.84

## 18p. Deep Olive-grey (1987)

**1987 (6 JANUARY). PERF. 15 × 14. PHOSPHORISED (ADVANCED COATED) PAPER. PVAD GUM**

XNL22 (S.G.NI46)    Olive-grey   ..    ..    ..    ..    ..    ..    ..    60    45

**Plate Numbers (Blocks of Six)**
Double Pane Plates
Plate Nos. in left margin

| Pl. Nos. | | | | (I) | | Pl. Nos. | | | | (P) |
|---|---|---|---|---|---|---|---|---|---|---|
| 1, 1 | .. | .. | .. | 2·75 | | 2, 2 | .. | .. | .. | 3·25 |
| | | | | | | 3, 3 | .. | .. | .. | £120 |
| | | | | | | 4, 4 | .. | .. | .. | £180 |

**WITHDRAWN**   4.9.89

## 19p. Bright Orange-red (1988)

**1988 (8 NOVEMBER). PERF. 15 × 14. PHOSPHORISED (ADVANCED COATED) PAPER. PVAD (clear) GUM**

XNL23 (S.G.NI47)    Bright orange-red   ..    ..    ..    ..    ..    ..    50    50

**Plate Numbers (Blocks of Six)**
Double Pane Plates
Plate Nos. in left margin

| Pl. Nos. | | | | (P) |
|---|---|---|---|---|
| 1, 1 | .. | .. | .. | 3·00 |
| 2, 2 | .. | .. | .. | 3·00 |
| 3, 3 | .. | .. | .. | 5·50 |
| 4, 4 | .. | .. | .. | 5·50 |

**WITHDRAWN**   27.11.90

## 19½p. Olive-grey (1982)

**1982 (24 FEBRUARY). PERF. 14. PHOSPHORISED (FLUORESCENT COATED) PAPER. PVAD GUM**

XNL24 (=S.G.NI48)   Olive-grey    ..    ..    ..    ..    ..    ..    ..    2·00    2·00

**Plate Numbers (Blocks of Six)**
Double Pane Plates
Plate Nos. in right margin

| Pl. No. | | | | Row 1 | Row 20 |
|---|---|---|---|---|---|
| 1 | .. | .. | .. | 12·00 | 12·00 |
| 2 | .. | .. | .. | 13·00 | 13·00 |

**WITHDRAWN**   29.4.84

## 20p. Brownish Black (1989)

**1989 (28 NOVEMBER). PERF. 15 × 14. PHOSPHORISED (ADVANCED COATED) PAPER. PVAD (clear) GUM**

XNL25 (=S.G.NI49)   Brownish black    ..    ..    ..    ..    ..    ..    30    30

**Plate Numbers (Blocks of Six)**
Double Pane Plates
Plate Nos. in left margin

| Pl. Nos. | | | | (P) |
|---|---|---|---|---|
| 1, 1 | .. | .. | .. | 2·40 |
| 2, 2 | .. | .. | .. | 7·50 |
| 3, 3 | .. | .. | .. | 3·00 |
| 4, 4 | .. | .. | .. | 3·00 |

## 20½p. Ultramarine (1983)
**1983 (27 APRIL). PERF. 14. PHOSPHORISED (FLUORESCENT COATED) PAPER. PVAD GUM**

XNL26 (=S.G.NI50)   Ultramarine ..    ..    ..    ..    ..    ..    ..   1·60   1·50

**Plate Numbers (Blocks of Six)**
Double Pane Plates
Plate Nos. in left margin

| Pl. No. | | | | (I) | Pl. No. | | | (P) |
|---|---|---|---|---|---|---|---|---|
| 1 | .. | .. | .. | 10·00 | 2 | .. | .. | 10·00 |

**WITHDRAWN**   28.6.65

## 22p. Blue (1981)
**1981 (8 APRIL). PERF. 14. PHOSPHORISED (FLUORESCENT COATED) PAPER. PVA GUM**

XNL27 (=S.G.NI51)   Blue   ..    ..    ..    ..    ..    ..    ..    ..    90   1·10

**Plate Numbers (Blocks of Six)**
Double Pane Plates
Plate Nos. in right margin

| Pl. Nos. | | | | Row 1 | Row 20 |
|---|---|---|---|---|---|
| 1, 1 | .. | .. | .. | 6·50 | 5·50 |
| 2, 2 | .. | .. | .. | 6·00 | 6·00 |

**WITHDRAWN**   29.4.84

## 22p. Yellow-green (1984)
**1984 (23 OCTOBER). PERF. 15 × 14. PHOSPHORISED (ADVANCED COATED) PAPER. PVAD GUM**

XNL28 (=S.G.NI52)   Yellow-green ..    ..    ..    ..    ..    ..    ..   55    55

**Plate Numbers (Blocks of Six)**
Double Pane Plates
Plate Nos. in left margin

| Pl. Nos. | | | (I) | Pl. Nos. | | | (P) |
|---|---|---|---|---|---|---|---|
| 1, 1 | .. | .. | 3·25 | 2, 2 | .. | .. | 3·25 |

**WITHDRAWN**   27.11.90

## 22p. Bright Orange-red (1990)
**1990 (4 DECEMBER). PERF. 15 × 14. PHOSPHORISED (ADVANCED COATED) PAPER. PVAD GUM**

XNL29 (=S.G.NI53)   Bright orange-red   ..    ..    ..    ..    ..    ..   35    40

**Plate Numbers (Blocks of Six)**
Double Pane Plates
Plate Nos. in left margin

| Pl. Nos. | | | | (P) |
|---|---|---|---|---|
| 1, 1 | .. | .. | .. | 2·75 |
| 2, 2 | .. | .. | .. | 2·75 |

## 23p. Bright Green (1988)

**1988 (8 NOVEMBER). PERF. 15 × 14. PHOSPHORISED (ADVANCED COATED) PAPER. PVAD (clear) GUM**

XNL30 (=S.G.NI54)   Bright green ..    ..    ..    ..    ..    ..    ..    55    50

**Plate Numbers (Blocks of Six)**
Double Pane Plates
Plate Nos. in left margin

| Pl. Nos. | | | | (P) |
|---|---|---|---|---|
| 1, 1 | .. | .. | .. | 2·75 |
| 2, 2 | .. | .. | .. | 2·75 |

**WITHDRAWN**   27.11.90

## 24p. Indian Red (1989)

**1989 (28 NOVEMBER). PERF. 15 × 14. PHOSPHORISED (ADVANCED COATED) PAPER. PVAD (clear) GUM**

XNL31 (=S.G.NI55)   Indian red    ..    ..    ..    ..    ..    ..    ..    40    45

**Plate Numbers (Blocks of Six)**
Double Pane Plates
Plate Nos. in left margin

| Pl. Nos. | | | | (P) |
|---|---|---|---|---|
| 1, 1 | .. | .. | .. | 2·75 |
| 2, 2 | .. | .. | .. | 2·75 |

## 26p. Rosine (1982–87)

**1982 (24 FEBRUARY). PERF. 14. PHOSPHORISED (ADVANCED COATED) PAPER. TYPE I. PVAD GUM**

XNL32 (=S.G.NI56)   Rosine ..    ..    ..    ..    ..    ..    ..    ..    90    90

**Plate Numbers (Blocks of Six)**
Double Pane Plates
Plate Nos. in right margin

| Pl. No. | | | | Row 1 | Row 20 |
|---|---|---|---|---|---|
| 1 | .. | .. | .. | 6·00 | 6·00 |
| 2 | .. | .. | .. | 20·00 | 20·00 |
| 3 | .. | .. | .. | 5·00 | 5·00 |
| 4 | .. | .. | .. | 5·00 | 5·00 |

**1987 (27 JANUARY). PERF. 15 × 14. PHOSPHORISED (ADVANCED COATED) PAPER. TYPE II. PVAD GUM**

XNL33 (=S.G.NI56a)   Rosine    ..    ..    ..    ..    ..    ..    1·25    1·25

**Plate Numbers (Blocks of Six)**
Double Pane Plates
Plate Nos. in left margin

| Pl. No. | | | (I) | Pl. No. | | | (P) |
|---|---|---|---|---|---|---|---|
| 1 | .. | .. | 7·00 | 2 | .. | .. | 7·00 |

**WITHDRAWN**   No. XNL32, 26.1.88; No. XNL33, 4.9.89

## 26p. Drab (1990)

**1990 (4 DECEMBER). PERF. 15 × 14. PHOSPHORISED (ADVANCED COATED) PAPER. PVAD GUM**

XNL34 (=S.G.NI57)   Drab  ..    ..    ..    ..    ..    ..    ..    ..    40    45

**Plate Numbers (Blocks of Six)**
Double Pane Plates
Plate Nos. in left margin

|  | Pl. Nos. |  |  | (P) |
|---|---|---|---|---|
|  | 1, 1 | .. | .. | .. 3·00 |
|  | 2, 2 | .. | .. | .. 3·00 |

## 28p. Deep Violet-blue (1983–87)

**1983 (27 APRIL). PERF. 14. PHOSPHORISED (FLUORESCENT COATED) PAPER. TYPE I. PVAD GUM**

XNL35 (=S.G.NI58)   Deep violet-blue    ..    ..    ..    ..    ..    ..    1·00    1·00

**Plate Numbers (Blocks of Six)**
Double Pane Plates
Plate Nos. in left margin

| Pl. No. |  |  | (I) | Pl. No. |  |  | (P) |
|---|---|---|---|---|---|---|---|
| 1 | .. | .. | .. 5·50 | 2 | .. | .. | .. 5·50 |

**1987 (27 JANUARY). PERF. 15 × 14. PHOSPHORISED (ADVANCED COATED) PAPER. TYPE II. PVAD GUM**

XNL36 (=S.G.NI58a)  Deep violet-blue    ..    ..    ..    ..    ..    ..    45    45

**Plate Numbers (Blocks of Six)**
Double Pane Plates
Plate Nos. in left margin

| Pl. No. |  |  | (I) | Pl. No. |  |  | (P) |
|---|---|---|---|---|---|---|---|
| 1 | .. | .. | .. 3·25 | 2 | .. | .. | .. 3·25 |

**WITHDRAWN**   No. XNL35, 26.1.88

## 31p. Bright Purple (1984–87)

**1984 (23 OCTOBER). PERF. 15 × 14. PHOSPHORISED (FLUORESCENT COATED) PAPER. TYPE I. PVAD GUM**

XNL37 (=S.G.NI59)   Bright purple ..    ..    ..    ..    ..    ..    ..    1·00    90

**Plate Numbers (Blocks of Six)**
Double Pane Plates
Plate Nos. in left margin

| Pl. No. |  |  | (I) | Pl. No. |  |  | (P) |
|---|---|---|---|---|---|---|---|
| 3 | .. | .. | .. 5·50 | 2 | .. | .. | .. 5·50 |

**1987 (14 APRIL).   PERF. 15 × 14. PHOSPHORISED (ADVANCED COATED) PAPER. TYPE II. PVAD GUM**

XNL38 (=S.G.NI59Ea)  Bright purple    ..    ..    ..    ..    ..    ..    1·00    90

**Plate Numbers (Block of Six)**
Double Pane Plates
Plate Nos. in left margin

| Pl. No. |  |  | (I) | Pl. No. |  |  | (P) |
|---|---|---|---|---|---|---|---|
| 5 | .. | .. | .. 5·50 | 6 | .. | .. | .. 5·50 |

**WITHDRAWN**   No. XNL37, 14.4.88; No. XNL38, 4.9.89

## 32p. Greenish Blue (1988)

**1988 (8 NOVEMBER). PERF. 15 × 14. PHOSPHORISED (ADVANCED COATED) PAPER. PVAD (clear) GUM**

XNL39 (=S.G.NI60)   Greenish blue    ..    ..    ..    ..    ..    ..    75    60

**Plate Numbers (Blocks of Six)**

Double Pane Plates
Plate Nos. in left margin

| Pl. Nos. | | | | (P) |
|---|---|---|---|---|
| 1, 1 | .. | .. | .. | 5·00 |
| 2, 2 | .. | .. | .. | 5·00 |

**WITHDRAWN**   27.11.90

## 34p. Deep Bluish Grey (1989)

**1989 (28 NOVEMBER). PERF 15 × 14. PHOSPHORISED (ADVANCED COATED) PAPER. PVAD (clear) GUM**

XNL40 (=S.G.NI61)   Deep bluish grey   ..    ..    ..    ..    ..    ..    55    55

**Plate Numbers (Blocks of Six)**

Double Pane Plates
Plate Nos. in left margin

| Pl. Nos. | | | | (P) |
|---|---|---|---|---|
| 1, 1 | .. | .. | .. | 3·75 |
| 2, 2 | .. | .. | .. | 3·75 |

## 37p. Rosine (1990)

**1990 (4 DECEMBER). PERF. 15 × 14. PHOSPHORISED (ADVANCED COATED) PAPER. PVAD GUM**

XNL43 (=S.G.NI62)   Rosine    ..    ..    ..    ..    ..    ..    ..    60    65

**Plate Numbers (Blocks of Six)**

Double Pane Plates
Plate Nos. in left margin

| Pl. Nos. | | | | (P) |
|---|---|---|---|---|
| 1, 1 | .. | .. | .. | 4·25 |
| 2, 2 | .. | .. | .. | 4·25 |

# Presentation Packs

XNPP6 No. 129*d* (28.10.81)                  7p., 9p., 10½p., 11½p., 12p.,
                                             13½p., 14p., 15p., 18p., 22p.    6·00
   Comprises Nos XN31, 35, 38, 41/2, 44, XNL1, 10, 21 and 27.

XNPP7 No. 4 (3.8.83)                         10p., 12½p., 16p., 20½p., 26p.,
                                             28p.                            5·00
   Comprises Nos. XN37, XNL4, 12, 26, 32 and 35.

XNPP8 No. 8 (23.10.84)                       10p., 13p., 16p., 17p., 22p.,
                                             26p., 28p., 31p.                8·00
   Comprises Nos. XN37, XNL7, 13, 14, 28, 32, 35 and 37.

XNPP9 No. 12 (3.3.87)                        12p., 13p., 17p., 18p., 22p.,
                                             26p., 28p., 31p.                3·50
   Comprises Nos. XNL3, 8, 18, 22, 28, 33, 36 and 37.

**WITHDRAWN**    No. XNPP6, 8.83; No. XNPP7, 10.84; No. XNPP8, 2.3.87

# Presentation Packs (Three Regions)

XPP2 No. 17 (8.11.88)                        Twelve values                   4·25
   The issued pack contained one each of the 14p., 19p., 23p., and 32p. stamps from Northern
Ireland, Scotland and Wales. Nos. XNL11, 23, 30, 39; XSL10, 24, 35, 46; XWL10, 22, 30 and 39.
For No. XPP1 see the Wilding Section XA in Volume 3 of this catalogue.

XPP3 No. 20 (28.11.89)                       Twelve values                   5·00
   The issued pack contained one each of the 15p., 20p., 24p. and 34p. stamps from Northern
Ireland, Scotland and Wales. Nos. XNL12, 25, 31, 40; XSL13, 28, 37, 47; XWL11, 25, 31 and 40.

XPP4 No. 23 (4.12.90)                        Twelve values                   5·00
   The issued pack contained one each of the 17p., 22p., 26p. and 37p. stamps from Northern
Ireland, Scotland and Wales. Nos. XNL20, 29, 34, 43; XSL20, 34, 40, 50; XWL18, 29, 34 and 43.

**WITHDRAWN**    No. XPP2, 27.11.90

# First Day Covers

| | | | |
|---|---|---|---|
| XNLFD1 (8.4.81) | 11½p., 14p., 18p., 22p. | † | 2·00 |
| XNLFD2 (24.2.82) | 12½p., 15½p., 19½p., 26p. | † | 3·00 |
| XNLFD3 (27.4.83) | 16p., 20½p., 28p. | † | 3·00 |
| XNLFD4 (23.10.84) | 13p., 17p., 22p., 31p. | † | 4·50 |
| XNLFD5 (7.1.86) | 12p. | † | 1·25 |
| XNLFD6 (6.1.87) | 18p. | † | 1·75 |
| XNLFD7 (8.11.88) | 14p., 19p., 23p., 32p. | † | 3·00 |
| XNLFD8 (28.11.89) | 15p., 20p., 24p., 34p. | † | 2·25 |
| XNLFD9 (4.12.90) | 17p., 22p., 26p., 37p. | † | 2·00 |

# B. Scotland

### John Waddington Printings

**SHEET ARRANGEMENT AND MARKINGS.** The sheet make-up and markings are as described in Section UG except that the sheets were serially numbered in black after printing for checking purposes.

**PERFORATION.** All Waddington printings were comb perforated 14 with perforation Type L which is described in Appendix I. Questa printings are perforated 15 × 14.

**PAPER AND GUM.** Fluorescent coated paper was used for the 11½p., 12½p. and 13p. values and phosphorised paper with fluorescent additive was employed for other values. The phosphorised (advanced) coated paper gives a stronger reaction to ultra violet on the 22p. printed in yellow-green and this paper was employed for other values. The gum was PVAD except for the 11½p., 12½p. and 13p. which have PVA.

**PHOSPHOR BANDS.** The 11½p., 12½p. and 13p. have a 4 mm. phosphor band printed at the left-hand side. This reacts violet after irradiation by shortwave ultra violet light. The phosphor band was applied by typography and a phosphor cylinder number appears synchronised in the printed box. The bands stop short in the top and bottom sheet margins.

For details of Questa printings see page 400.

## Type XS4 as illustrated in Section XB

Printed by Waddington (1981–86) or Questa (1986–90)

Redrawn Lion

I         II

**Type I.** The eye and jaw appear larger and there is no line across the bridge of the nose.
**Type II.** The tongue is thick at the point of entry to the mouth and the eye is linked to the background by a solid line.

## 11½p. Drab (1981)

Printed by Waddington

**1981 (8 APRIL). PERF. 14. ONE 4 mm. PHOSPHOR BAND AT LEFT. FLUORESCENT COATED PAPER. PVA GUM**

| XSL1 (=S.G.S36) | Drab .. | .. | .. | .. | .. | .. | .. | .. | 75 | 60 |
|---|---|---|---|---|---|---|---|---|---|---|
| | a. Imperforate between stamp and right margin | | | | | | | .. | 75·00 | |
| | b. Phosphor omitted | | .. | .. | .. | .. | .. | £700 | | |

### Plate Numbers (Blocks of Eight)

Double Pane Plates
Plate Nos. in top margin

| Pl. Nos. | Phos. No. | | | No dot | Dot | Pl. Nos. | Phos. No. | | | No dot | Dot |
|---|---|---|---|---|---|---|---|---|---|---|---|
| 1A, 1B | 1A | .. | .. | 90·00 | 20·00 | 5A, 4B | 1A | .. | .. | 18·00 | 7·00 |
| 1A, 2B | 1A | .. | .. | £110 | £110 | 6A, 4B | 1A | .. | .. | 50·00 | 50·00 |
| 2A, 2B | 1A | .. | .. | 6·00 | 6·00 | 6A, 5B | 1A | .. | .. | 70·00 | 70·00 |
| 3A, 3B | 1A | .. | .. | 45·00 | 45·00 | 7A, 6B | 1A | .. | .. | £500 | £600 |
| 4A, 4B | 1A | .. | .. | 8·00 | 28·00 | | | | | | |

WITHDRAWN 26.2.83

# 12p. Bright Emerald (1986)

**Printed by Waddington**

**1986 (7 JANUARY). PERF. 14. ONE 4 mm. PHOSPHOR BAND AT LEFT. FLUORESCENT COATED PAPER. PVA GUM**

XSL2 (=S.G.S37)    Bright emerald    ..    ..    ..    ..    ..    ..    60    70

**Plate Numbers (Blocks of Six)**
Double Pane Plates
Plate Nos. in left margin

| Pl. Nos. | Phos. No. | | | | No dot (P) | Dot (I) |
|---|---|---|---|---|---|---|
| 1A, 1B | 1A | .. | .. | .. | 4·00 | 4·00 |

**Printed by Questa**

**1986 (29 APRIL). PERF. 15 × 14. ONE SHORT PHOSPHOR BAND AT LEFT. FLUORESCENT COATED PAPER. PVAD GUM**

XSL3 (=S.G.S52)    Bright emerald    ..    ..    ..    ..    ..    ..    60    60

**Plate Numbers (Blocks of Six)**
Double Pane Plates
Plate Nos. in left margin

| Pl. Nos. | | | (I) | Pl. Nos. | | | (P) |
|---|---|---|---|---|---|---|---|
| 1, 1 | .. | .. | 4·00 | 2, 2 | .. | .. | 4·00 |

No. XSL3 was printed with the 4 mm. wide phosphor band at left cut short opposite the perforations at the top and bottom of each stamp in the sheet.

**WITHDRAWN**    No. XSL2, 28.4.87; No. XSL3, sold out 10.87

# 12½p. Light Emerald (1982)

**Printed by Waddington**

**1982 (24 FEBRUARY). PERF. 14. ONE 4 mm. PHOSPHOR BAND AT LEFT. FLUORESCENT COATED PAPER. PVA GUM**

| XSL4 (=S.G.S38) | Light emerald    ..    ..    ..    ..    ..    .. | 40 | 40 |
|---|---|---|---|
| | *b.* With varnish coating (12.83)  ..    ..    ..    .. | 20·00 | |

**Plate Numbers (Blocks of Eight)**

Double Pane Plates
Plate Nos. in top margin

| Pl. Nos. | Phos. Nos. | | | No dot | Dot | Pl. Nos. | Phos. Nos. | | | No dot | Dot |
|---|---|---|---|---|---|---|---|---|---|---|---|
| 1A, 1B | 1B/1A | .. | .. | 4·25 | 4·25 | 4A, 4B | 2B/2A | .. | .. | 45·00 | £170 |
| 2A, 2B | 1B/1A | .. | .. | 3·75 | 3·75 | 5A, 4B | 2B/2A | .. | .. | 50·00 | 35·00 |
| 3A, 3B | 1B/1A | .. | .. | 4·75 | 18·00 | 5A, 5B | 2B/2A | .. | .. | 50·00 | 28·00 |
| 4A, 4B | 1B/1A | .. | .. | 9·00 | 9·00 | | | | | | |

**Plate Numbers (Blocks of Six)**

Double Pane Plates
Plate Nos. in left margin

| Pl. Nos. | Phos. Nos. | | | | No dot (P) | Dot (I) |
|---|---|---|---|---|---|---|
| 6A, 6B | 2B/2A | .. | .. | .. | 3·50 | 3·50 |
| 7A, 7B | 2B/2A With varnish coating | | .. | | £120 | £140 |
| 8A, 8B | 2B/2A | .. | .. | .. | 3·00 | 3·00 |

The phosphor number is "A" on dot or "B" on no dot plate blocks.
On No. XSL4*b* the varnish coating completely covers the stamp but the phosphor band is visible under u.v. light.

**WITHDRAWN**    28.6.85

# 13p. Pale Chestnut (1984–87)

**Printed by Waddington**

**1984 (23 OCTOBER). PERF. 14. ONE 4 mm. PHOSPHOR BAND AT LEFT. FLUORESCENT COATED PAPER. TYPE I. PVA GUM**

**A. TYPE I**

XSL5 (=S.G.S39)    Pale chestnut. .    . .    . .    . .    . .    . .    . .    40    30

**Plate Numbers (Blocks of Six)**

Double Pane Plates
Plate Nos. in left margin

| Pl. Nos. | Phos. Nos. | | | | | No dot (P) | Dot (I) |
|----------|-----------|---|---|---|---|-----------|---------|
| 1A, 1B | 1A | . . | . . | . . | . . | 3·00 | 4·50 |

**B. TYPE II** (1.85)

XSL6 (=S.G.S39Ea)    Pale chestnut. .    . .    . .    . .    . .    . .    . .    60    50

**Plate Numbers (Blocks of Six)**

Double Pane Plates
Plate Nos. in left margin

| Pl. Nos. | Phos. Nos. | | | | | No dot (P) | Dot (I) |
|----------|-----------|---|---|---|---|-----------|---------|
| 2A, 2B | 1A | . . | . . | . . | . . | 4·00 | 5·00 |
| 3A, 3B | 1A | . . | . . | . . | . . | 3·00 | 4·25 |
| 3A, 4B | 1A | . . | . . | . . | . . | 4·50 | 4·50 |

**Printed by Questa**

**1986 (4 NOVEMBER).   PERF. 15 × 14. ONE 4 mm. SHORT PHOSPHOR BAND AT LEFT. FLUORESCENT COATED PAPER. TYPE II**

**A. PVAD GUM**

XSL7 (=S.G.S53)    Pale chestnut. .    . .    . .    . .    . .    . .    . .    50    30

**Plate Numbers (Blocks of Six)**

Double Pane Plates
Plate Nos. in left margin

| Pl. Nos. | | | (I) | Pl. Nos. | | | (P) |
|----------|---|---|-----|----------|---|---|-----|
| 1, 1 | . . | . . | . . 3·25 | 2, 2 | . . | . . | . . 3·25 |

**B. PVA GUM** (14.4.87)

XSL8    Pale chestnut. .    . .    . .    . .    . .    . .    . .    50

**Plate Numbers (Blocks of Six)**

Double Pane Plates
Plate Nos. in left margin

| Pl. Nos. | | | (I) | (P) | Pl. Nos. | | | (I) | (P) |
|----------|---|---|-----|-----|----------|---|---|-----|-----|
| 3, 3 | . . | . . | . . 4·00 | 10·00 | 7, 7 | . . | . . | . . † | 16·00 |
| 4, 4 | . . | . . | . . † | 2·75 | 8, 8 | . . | . . | . . † | 28·00 |
| 5, 5 | . . | . . | . . † | 2·75 | 9, 9 | . . | . . | . . † | 20·00 |
| 6, 6 | . . | . . | . . † | 3·00 | 10, 10 | . . | . . | . . † | 5·00 |

Plate Nos. 5, 5 and 6, 6 also exist with a short imperforate section at base below 8th perforation. *Price for plate* 5, 5, £18 *and* 6, 6, £8.

**WITHDRAWN**   Nos. XSL5/6, 3.11.87; No. XSL7, 14.4.88; No. XSL8, 4.9.89

# 14p. Grey-blue (1981)

**Printed by Waddington**

**1981 (8 .APRIL). PERF. 14. PHOSPHORISED (FLUORESCENT COATED) PAPER. PVAD GUM**

XSL9 (=S.G.S40)  Grey-blue  ..  ..  ..  ..  ..  ..  ..  55  50

**Plate Numbers (Blocks of Eight)**
Double Pane Plates
Plate Nos. in top margin

| Pl. Nos. | | | | | No dot | Dot |
|---|---|---|---|---|---|---|
| 2A, 1B | .. | .. | .. | .. | 4·50 | 4·50 |
| 2A, 2B | .. | .. | .. | .. | 10·00 | 18·00 |
| 3A, 3B | .. | .. | .. | .. | 7·50 | 35·00 |
| 4A, 3B | .. | .. | .. | .. | 70·00 | 70·00 |
| 4A, 4B | .. | .. | .. | .. | 10·00 | 5·50 |

**WITHDRAWN**  14.1.84

# 14p. Deep Blue (1988–89)

**Printed by Questa**

**1988 (8 NOVEMBER). PERF. 15 × 14. ONE 4 mm. SHORT PHOSPHOR BAND (RIGHT OF CENTRE). FLUORESCENT COATED PAPER. PVA GUM**

XSL10 (=S.G.S54)  Deep blue  ..  ..  ..  ..  ..  ..  ..  40  30

**Plate Numbers (Blocks of Six)**
Double Pane Plates
Plate Nos. in left margin

| Pl. Nos. | | | (P) | Pl. Nos. | | | (P) |
|---|---|---|---|---|---|---|---|
| 1, 1 | .. | .. | .. 2·50 | 6, 6 | .. | .. | .. 3·25 |
| 2, 2 | .. | .. | .. 3·75 | 7, 7 | .. | .. | .. 3·00 |
| 3, 3 | .. | .. | .. 2·50 | 8, 8 ' | .. | .. | .. 4·50 |
| 4, 4 | .. | .. | .. 3·75 | 9, 9 | .. | .. | .. 45·00 |
| 5, 5 | .. | .. | .. 2·50 | 10, 10 | .. | .. | .. 10·00 |

**1989 (21 MARCH). PERF. 15 × 14. ONE 4 mm. PHOSPHOR BAND (RIGHT OF CENTRE). FLUORESCENT COATED PAPER. PVA GUM**

£5 The Scots Connection booklet pane No. XDS2
XSL11  Deep blue  ..  ..  ..  ..  ..  ..  ..  50  50

No. XSL10 shows the phosphor band short at top or bottom of the stamp whereas on No. XSL11 the band is continuous.

**1989 (21 MARCH). PERF. 15 × 14. ONE 4 mm. PHOSPHOR BAND AT LEFT. FLUORESCENT COATED PAPER. PVA GUM**

£5 The Scots Connection booklet *se-tenant* pane No. XDS3
XSL12 (=S.G.S55)  Deep blue  ..  ..  ..  ..  ..  ..  ..  50  50

**WITHDRAWN**  No. XSL10, 27.11.90

## 15p. Bright Blue (1989)

Printed by Questa

**1989 (28 NOVEMBER). PERF. 15 × 14. ONE 4 mm. SHORT PHOSPHOR BAND (RIGHT OF CENTRE). FLUORESCENT COATED PAPER. PVA GUM**

| | | | |
|---|---|---|---|
| XSL13 (=S.G.S56) | Bright blue .. .. .. .. .. .. .. .. | 25 | 30 |
| | *a.* Imperforate (3 sides) (*block of four*) .. .. .. £275 | | |

No. XSL13*a* occurred in the second vertical row of two sheets. The price is for a block of four including the left-hand vertical pair imperforate on three sides.

**Plate Numbers (Blocks of Six)**

Double Pane Plates
Plate Nos. in left margin

| Pl. Nos. | | | (P) | Pl. Nos. | | | (P) |
|---|---|---|---|---|---|---|---|
| 1, 1 | .. | .. | .. 1·90 | 5, 5 | .. | .. | .. 6·00 |
| 2, 2 | .. | .. | .. 1·90 | 6, 6 | .. | .. | .. 6·00 |
| 3, 3 | .. | .. | .. 14·00 | 7, 7 | .. | .. | .. 4·00 |
| 4, 4 | .. | .. | .. 4·50 | 8, 8 | .. | .. | .. 4·00 |

Plate Nos. 3, 3 and 4, 4 also exist with a short imperforate section at base below the 8th perforation.

## 15½p. Pale Violet (1982)

Printed by Waddington

**1982 (24 FEBRUARY). PERF. 14. PHOSPHORISED (FLUORESCENT COATED) PAPER. PVAD GUM**

| | | | | | |
|---|---|---|---|---|---|
| XSL14 (=S.G.S41) | Pale violet .. | .. | .. .. .. .. .. | 60 | 65 |

**Plate Numbers (Blocks of Eight)**

Double Pane Plates
Plate Nos. in top margin

| Pl. Nos. | | | | No dot | Dot | Pl. Nos. | | | | No dot | Dot |
|---|---|---|---|---|---|---|---|---|---|---|---|
| 1A, 1B | .. | .. | .. | 15·00 | 7·00 | 4A, 3B | .. | .. | .. | 60·00 | 15·00 |
| 2A, 1B | .. | .. | .. | 12·00 | 15·00 | 5A, 3B | .. | .. | .. | 32·00 | 32·00 |
| 3A, 1B | .. | .. | .. | £350 | £350 | 6A, 4B | .. | .. | .. | 10·00 | 5·50 |
| 3A, 2B | .. | .. | .. | 5·50 | 5·50 | | | | | | |

**WITHDRAWN** 29.4.84

## 16p. Drab (1983)

Printed by Waddington

**1983 (27 APRIL). PERF. 14. PHOSPHORISED (FLUORESCENT COATED) PAPER. PVAD GUM**

| | | | | | |
|---|---|---|---|---|---|
| XSL15 (=S.G.S42) | Drab .. | .. .. | .. .. .. .. .. | 55 | 45 |

**Plate Numbers (Blocks of Six)**

Double Pane Plates
Plate Nos. in left margin

| Pl. Nos. | | | | No dot (P) | Dot (I) |
|---|---|---|---|---|---|
| 1A, 1B | .. | .. | .. | 4·00 | 4·00 |
| 2A, 2B* | .. | .. | .. | 4·00 | 3·75 |
| 3A, 3B | .. | .. | .. | 20·00 | 18·00 |
| 4A, 4B | .. | .. | .. | 30·00 | 22·00 |
| 5A, 4B | .. | .. | .. | 30·00 | 7·00 |

*This printing was on paper produced by Harrisons for print quality trials by Waddingtons. Under both ordinary and ultraviolet light this paper appeared similar to the paper it replaced.

**WITHDRAWN** 31.10.86

# 17p. Grey-blue (1984–86)

Printed by Waddington

**1984 (23 OCTOBER). PERF. 14. PHOSPHORISED (FLUORESCENT COATED) PAPER. TYPE I. PVAD GUM**

XSL16 (=S.G.S43)    Grey-blue    ..    ..    ..    ..    ..    ..    ..    3·25    2·00

**Plate Numbers (Blocks of Six)**

Double Pane Plates
Plate Nos. in left margin

| Pl. Nos. | | | No dot (P) | Dot (I) |
|---|---|---|---|---|
| 1A, 1B  .. | .. | .. | 18·00 | 18·00 |
| 1A, 2B  .. | .. | .. | 20·00 | 20·00 |

**1985 (JANUARY).   PERF. 14. PHOSPHORISED (FLUORESCENT COATED) PAPER. TYPE II.**

**A. PVAD GUM**

XSL17    Grey-blue    ..    ..    ..    ..    ..    ..    ..    1·00    1·10

**Plate Numbers (Blocks of Six)**

Double Pane Plates
Plate Nos. in left margin

| Pl. Nos. | | | No dot (P) | Dot (I) | Pl. Nos. | | | No dot (P) | Dot (I) |
|---|---|---|---|---|---|---|---|---|---|
| 2A, 3B  .. | .. | .. | 5·50 | 5·50 | 2A, 5B  .. | .. | .. | 5·50 | 5·50 |
| 2A, 4B  .. | .. | .. | 6·00 | 5·50 | 3A, 5B  .. | .. | .. | 15·00 | 15·00 |

**B. PVA GUM** (25.6.85)

XSL18 (=S.G.S43Ea) Grey-blue    ..    ..    ..    ..    ..    ..    ..    1·00    1·00

**Plate Numbers (Blocks of Six)**

Double Pane Plates
Plate Nos. in left margin

| Pl. Nos. | | | No dot (P) | Dot (I) |
|---|---|---|---|---|
| 2A, 4B  .. | .. | .. | † | 5·50 |

No. XSL18 was an experimental issue printed on paper made by Henry & Leigh Slater Ltd.

Printed by Questa

**1986 (29 APRIL).   PERF. 15 × 14. PHOSPHORISED (ADVANCED COATED) PAPER. TYPE II. PVAD GUM**

XSL19 (S.G.S57)    Grey-blue    ..    ..    ..    ..    ..    ..    ..    3·25    2·00

**Plate Numbers (Blocks of Six)**

Double Pane Plates
Plate Nos. in left margin

| Pl. Nos. | | | (I) | Pl. Nos. | | | (P) |
|---|---|---|---|---|---|---|---|
| 1, 1  .. | .. | .. | 18·00 | 2, 2  .. | .. | .. | 18·00 |

**SOLD OUT**   Nos. XSL16/18, 5.86; No. XSL19, 10.87

# 17p. Deep Blue (1990)
**Printed by Questa**

**1990 (4 DECEMBER). PERF. 15 × 14. ONE 4 mm. SHORT PHOSPHOR BAND (RIGHT OF CENTRE). FLUORESCENT COATED PAPER. PVA GUM**

XSL20 (=S.G.S58)    Deep blue  ..    ..    ..    ..    ..    ..    ..    30    35

**Plate Numbers (Blocks of Six)**
Double Pane Plates
Plate Nos. in left margin

| Pl. Nos. | | | (P) |
|---|---|---|---|
| 1, 1 .. | .. | .. | 2·40 |
| 2, 2 .. | .. | .. | 2·40 |

# 18p. Deep Violet (1981)
**Printed by Waddington**

**1981 (8 APRIL). PERF. 14. PHOSPHORISED (FLUORESCENT COATED) PAPER. PVAD GUM**

XSL21 (=S.G.S44)    Deep violet ..    ..    ..    ..    ..    ..    ..    70    65

**Plate Numbers (Blocks of Eight)**
Double Pane Plates
Plate Nos. in top margin

| Pl. Nos. | | | No dot | Dot |
|---|---|---|---|---|
| 1A, 1B .. | .. | .. | 5·50 | 5·50 |

**WITHDRAWN**  14.1.84

# 18p. Deep Olive-grey (1987–88)
**Printed by Questa**

**1987 (6 JANUARY). PERF. 15 × 14. PHOSPHORISED (ADVANCED COATED) PAPER**

**A. PVAD GUM**

XSL22 (S.G.S59)    Deep olive-grey    ..    ..    ..    ..    ..    ..    ..    60    45

**Plate Numbers (Blocks of Six)**
Double Pane Plates
Plate Nos. in left margin

| Pl. Nos. | | | (I) | (P) |
|---|---|---|---|---|
| 1, 1 .. | .. | .. | 3·50 | † |
| 2, 2 .. | .. | .. | † | 3·50 |
| 3, 3 .. | .. | .. | 10·00 | 5·00 |
| 4, 4 .. | .. | .. | † | 3·50 |
| 5, 5 .. | .. | .. | † | 6·00 |
| 6, 6 .. | .. | .. | † | 6·00 |
| 7, 7 .. | .. | .. | † | 16·00 |
| 8, 8 .. | .. | .. | † | 16·00 |

Plate Nos. 3, 3 and 4, 4 also exist with a short imperforate section at base below the 8th perforation. *Price for plate* 3, 3, £30 *and* 4, 4 £15.

**B. PVAD (clear) GUM** (29.3.88)

XSL23    Deep olive-grey    ..    ..    ..    ..    ..    ..    ..    60
This printing was on phosphorised (advanced coated) paper supplied to Questa by Henry & Leigh Slater Ltd. The PVAD gum does not have the green dye additive.

**Plate Numbers (Blocks of Six)**
Double Pane Plates
Plate Nos. in left margin

| Pl. Nos. | | | (P) |
|---|---|---|---|
| 5, 5 .. | .. | .. | 3·50 |
| 6, 6 .. | .. | .. | 3·50 |

**WITHDRAWN**  4.9.89

**418**

# 19p. Bright Orange-red (1988–89)

**Printed by Questa**

## 1988 (8 NOVEMBER). PERF. 15 × 14. PHOSPHORISED (ADVANCED COATED) PAPER

**A. PVAD (clear) GUM**
XSL24 (=S.G.S60)    Bright orange-red  ..    ..    ..    ..    ..    ..    60    45

No. XSL24 is known pre-released on 4 November at Edinburgh. The same note below No. XSL23 applies here.

**Plate Numbers (Blocks of Six)**

Double Pane Plates
Plate Nos. in left margin

|  | Pl. Nos. |  |  | (P) |
|---|---|---|---|---|
|  | 1, 1 | .. | .. | 3·75 |
|  | 2, 2 | .. | .. | 3·75 |

**B. PVA GUM** (white back) (25.4.89)
XSL25    Bright orange-red  ..    ..    ..    ..    ..    ..    60
This paper was supplied by Coated Papers Limited of Leek, Staffordshire. It can be distinguished by the whiter gummed side from No. XSL24 which is cream. Both are similar under ultra violet.

~ **Plate Numbers (Blocks of Six)**

Double Pane Plates
Plate Nos. in left margin

|  | Pl. Nos. |  |  | (P) |
|---|---|---|---|---|
|  | 3, 3 | .. | .. | 3·75 |
|  | 4, 4 | .. | .. | 3·75 |

## 1989 (21 MARCH). PERF. 15 × 14. TWO PHOSPHOR BANDS. FLUORESCENT COATED PAPER. PVA GUM

£5 The Scots Connection booklet *se-tenant* pane No. XDS3
XSL26 (=S.G.S61)    Bright orange-red  ..    ..    ..    ..    ..    ..    1·00    1·00

**WITHDRAWN**  No. XSL24, 24.4.90; No. XSL25, 27.11.90

# 19½p. Olive-grey (1982)

**Printed by Waddington**

## 1982 (24 FEBRUARY). PERF. 14. PHOSPHORISED (FLUORESCENT COATED) PAPER. PVAD GUM

XSL27 (=S.G.S45)    Olive-grey  ..    ..    ..    ..    ..    ..    ..    2·00    2·25

**Plate Numbers (Blocks of Eight)**

Double Pane Plates
Plate Nos. in top margin

|  | Pl. Nos. |  |  | No dot | Dot |
|---|---|---|---|---|---|
|  | 1A, 1B | .. | .. | 15·00 | 15·00 |

**WITHDRAWN**  29.4.84

## 20p. Brownish Black (1989)

Printed by Questa

**1989 (28 NOVEMBER). PERF. 15 × 14. PHOSPHORISED (ADVANCED COATED) PAPER. PVAD (clear) GUM**

XSL28 (=S.G.S62)    Brownish black    ..    ..    ..    ..    ..    ..    30    30

**Plate Numbers (Blocks of Six)**

Double Pane Plates
Plate Nos. in left margin

|   | Pl. Nos. |   |   |   | (P) |
|---|---|---|---|---|---|
|   | 1, 1 | .. | .. | .. | 3·50 |
|   | 2, 2 | .. | .. | .. | 2·50 |
|   | 3, 3 | .. | .. | .. | 2·50 |
|   | 4, 4 | .. | .. | .. | 3·50 |
|   | 5, 5 | .. | .. | .. | 5·00 |
|   | 6, 6 | .. | .. | .. | 5·00 |

## 20½p. Ultramarine (1983)

Printed by Waddington

**1983 (27 APRIL). PERF. 14. PHOSPHORISED (FLUORESCENT COATED) PAPER. PVAD GUM**

XSL29 (=S.G.S46)    Ultramarine ..    ..    ..    ..    ..    ..    ..    2·00    1·50

**Plate Numbers (Blocks of Six)**

Double Pane Plates
Plate Nos. in left margin

|   | Pl. Nos. | | No dot (P) | Dot (I) |
|---|---|---|---|---|
|   | 1A, 1B .. | .. | .. 12·00 | 14·00 |

**WITHDRAWN**    28.6.85

## 22p. Blue (1981)

Printed by Waddington

**1981 (8 APRIL). PERF. 14. PHOSPHORISED (FLUORESCENT COATED) PAPER. PVAD GUM**

XSL30 (=S.G.S47)    Blue  ..    ..    ..    ..    ..    ..    ..    ..    80    1·10

**Plate Numbers (Blocks of Eight)**

Double Pane Plates
Plate Nos. in top margin

|   | Pl. Nos. | | No dot | Dot |
|---|---|---|---|---|
|   | 4A, 1B .. | .. | .. 6·50 | 6·50 |

**WITHDRAWN**    29.4.84

## 22p. Yellow-green (1984–87)

Printed by Waddington

**1984 (23 OCTOBER).   PERF. 14. PHOSPHORISED (ADVANCED COATED) PAPER. TYPE I. PVAD GUM**

XSL31 (=S.G.S48)    Yellow-green    ..    ..    ..    ..    ..    ..    1·00    80

**Plate Numbers (Blocks of Six)**

Double Pane Plates
Plate Nos. in left margin

|   | Pl. Nos. | | No dot (P) | Dot (I) |
|---|---|---|---|---|
|   | 1A, 1B .. | .. | .. 5·50 | 5·50 |

**1986 (JANUARY). PERF. 14. PHOSPHORISED (ADVANCED COATED) PAPER. TYPE II. PVAD GUM**

XSL32 (S.G.S48Ea)    Yellow-green    .. .. .. .. .. ..    80    1·00

**Plate Numbers (Blocks of Six)**
Double Pane Plates
Plate Nos. in left margin

| Pl. Nos. | | | | No dot (P) | Dot (I) |
|---|---|---|---|---|---|
| 2A, 2B | .. | .. | .. | 8·00 | 8·00 |
| 3A, 2B | .. | .. | .. | 5·00 | 16·00 |

**Printed by Questa**

**1987 (27 JANUARY). PERF. 15 × 14. PHOSPHORISED (ADVANCED COATED) PAPER. TYPE II. PVAD GUM**

XSL33 (=S.G.S63)    Yellow-green    .. .. .. .. .. ..    55    50

**Plate Numbers (Blocks of Six)**
Double Pane Plates
Plate Nos. in left margin

| Pl. Nos. | | | (I) | Pl. Nos. | | | (P) |
|---|---|---|---|---|---|---|---|
| 1, 1 | .. | .. | 3·50 | 2, 2 | .. | .. | 3·50 |

**WITHDRAWN** Nos. XSL31/32, 26.1.88; No. XSL33, 27.11.90

# 22p. Bright Orange-red (1990)
**Printed by Questa**

**1990 (4 DECEMBER). PERF. 15 × 14. PHOSPHORISED (ADVANCED COATED) PAPER. PVAD GUM**

XSL34 (=S.G.S64)    Bright orange-red .. .. .. .. .. ..    35    40

**Plate Numbers (Blocks of Six)**
Double Pane Plates
Plate Nos. in left margin

| Pl. Nos. | | | (P) |
|---|---|---|---|
| 1, 1 | .. | .. | 2·75 |
| 2, 2 | .. | .. | 2·75 |
| 3, 3 | .. | .. | 3·50 |
| 4, 4 | .. | .. | 3·50 |

# 23p. Bright Green (1988–89)
**Printed by Questa**

**1988 (8 NOVEMBER). PERF. 15 × 14. PHOSPHORISED (ADVANCED COATED) PAPER. PVAD (clear) GUM**

XSL35 (=S.G.S65)    Bright green .. .. .. .. .. .. ..    55    40

**Plate Numbers (Blocks of Six)**
Double Pane Plates
Plate Nos. in left margin

| Pl. Nos. | | | (P) |
|---|---|---|---|
| 1, 1 | .. | .. | 3·50 |
| 2, 2 | .. | .. | 3·50 |

**1989 (21 MARCH). PERF. 15 × 14. TWO PHOSPHOR BANDS. FLUORESCENT COATED PAPER. PVA GUM**

£5 The Scots Connection booklet *se-tenant* pane No. XDS3
XSL36 (=S.G.S66)    Bright green .. .. .. .. .. .. ..    3·00    3·00

**WITHDRAWN** No. XSL35, 27.11.90

## 24p. Indian Red (1989)

**Printed by Questa**

**1989 (28 NOVEMBER). PERF. 15 × 14. PHOSPHORISED (ADVANCED COATED) PAPER. PVAD (clear) GUM**

XSL37 (=S.G.S67)    Indian red   ..     ..     ..     ..     ..     ..     ..     40     45

**Plate Numbers (Blocks of Six)**

Double Pane Plates
Plate Nos. in left margin

| Pl. Nos. | | | (P) |
|---|---|---|---|
| 1, 1 | .. | .. | .. 2·75 |
| 2, 2 | .. | .. | .. 2·75 |

## 26p. Rosine (1982–87)

**Printed by Waddington**

**1982 (24 FEBRUARY). PERF. 14. PHOSPHORISED (FLUORESCENT COATED) PAPER. TYPE I. PVAD GUM**

XSL38 (=S.G.S49)    Rosine     ..     ..     ..     ..     ..     ..     ..     90     80

**Plate Numbers (Blocks of Eight)**

Double Pane Plates
Plate Nos. in top margin

| Pl. Nos. | | No dot | Dot |
|---|---|---|---|
| 1A, 1B | .. | .. 7·00 | 7·00 |

**Printed by Questa**

**1987 (27 JANUARY). PERF. 15 × 14. PHOSPHORISED (ADVANCED COATED) PAPER. TYPE II. PVAD GUM**

XSL39 (=S.G.S68)    Rosine     ..     ..     ..     ..     ..     ..     ..     1·25     1·10

**Plate Numbers (Blocks of Six)**

Double Pane Plates
Plate Nos. in left margin

| Pl. No. | | | (I) | Pl. No. | | | (P) |
|---|---|---|---|---|---|---|---|
| 1 | .. | .. | .. 7·00 | 2 | .. | .. | .. 7·00 |

**WITHDRAWN**  4.9.89

## 26p. Drab (1990)

**Printed by Questa**

**1990 (4 DECEMBER). PERF. 15 × 14. PHOSPHORISED (ADVANCED COATED) PAPER. PVAD GUM**

XSL40 (=S.G.S69)    Drab ..     ..     ..     ..     ..     ..     ..     ..     40     45

**Plate Numbers (Blocks of Six)**

Double Pane Plates
Plate Nos. in left margin

| Pl. Nos. | | | (P) |
|---|---|---|---|
| 1, 1 | .. | .. | .. 2·75 |
| 2, 2 | .. | .. | .. 2·75 |

## 28p. Deep Violet-blue (1983–87)

**Printed by Waddington**

**1983 (27 APRIL). PERF. 14. PHOSPHORISED (FLUORESCENT COATED) PAPER. PVAD GUM**

XSL41 (=S.G.S50)    Deep violet-blue    ..    ..    ..    ..    ..    ..    1·00    80

**Plate Numbers (Blocks of Six)**

Double Pane Plates
Plate Nos. in left margin

|  | Pl. Nos. | No dot (P) | Dot (I) |
|---|---|---|---|
|  | 1A, 1B .. .. .. | 6·00 | 6·00 |

**Printed by Questa**

**1987 (27 JANUARY). PERF. 15 × 14. PHOSPHORISED (ADVANCED COATED) PAPER. PVAD GUM**

XSL42 (=S.G.S70)    Deep violet-blue    ..    ..    ..    ..    ..    ..    45    65

**Plate Numbers (Blocks of Six)**

Double Pane Plates
Plate Nos. in left margin

| Pl. No. |  | (I) | Pl. No. |  | (P) |
|---|---|---|---|---|---|
| 1 .. .. | .. | 3·25 | 2 .. | .. .. | 3·25 |

**WITHDRAWN**   No. XSL41, 26.1.88; No. XSL42, 27.11.90

## 31p. Bright Purple (1984–86)

**Printed by Waddington**

**1984 (23 OCTOBER). PERF. 14. PHOSPHORISED (FLUORESCENT COATED) PAPER. PVAD GUM**

**A. TYPE I**

XSL43 (=S.G.S51)    Bright purple ..    ..    ..    ..    ..    ..    ..    1·25    90

**Plate Numbers (Blocks of Six)**

Double Pane Plates
Plate Nos. in left margin

|  | Pl. Nos. | No dot (P) | Dot (I) |
|---|---|---|---|
|  | 1A, 1B .. .. | 7·00 | 7·00 |

**B. TYPE II** (1.86)

XSL44 (=S.G.S51Ea)  Bright purple    ..    ..    ..    ..    ..    ..    45·00  20·00

**Plate Numbers (Blocks of Six)**

Double Pane Plates
Plate Nos. in left margin

|  | Pl. Nos. | No dot (P) | Dot (I) |
|---|---|---|---|
|  | 2A, 2B .. .. | £400 | £250 |

**Printed by Questa**

**1986 (29 APRIL). PERF. 15 × 14. PHOSPHORISED (ADVANCED COATED) PAPER. TYPE II. PVAD GUM**

XSL45 (=S.G.S71)    Bright purple    ..    ..    ..    ..    ..    ..    1·25    70

**Plate Numbers (Blocks of Six)**

Double Pane Plates
Plate Nos. in left margin

| Pl. No. | (I) | Pl. Nos. | (P) |
|---|---|---|---|
| 1 | .. .. .. 7·00 | 2, 2 | .. .. .. 7·00 |

**SOLD OUT**   Nos. XSL43/44, 12.86

**WITHDRAWN**   No. XSL45, 4.9.89

## 32p. Greenish Blue (1988)

**Printed by Questa**

**1988 (8 NOVEMBER). PERF. 15 × 14. PHOSPHORISED (ADVANCED COATED) PAPER. PVAD (clear) GUM**

XSL46 (=S.G.72)      Greenish blue      ..      ..      ..      ..      ..      ..      75      60

**Plate Numbers (Blocks of Six)**

Double Pane Plates
Plate Nos. in left margin

| Pl. Nos. | (P) |
|---|---|
| 1, 1   ..      ..      .. | 4·25 |
| 2, 2   ..      ..      .. | 4·25 |

**WITHDRAWN**   27.11.90

## 34p. Deep Bluish Grey (1989)

**Printed by Questa**

**1989 (28 NOVEMBER). PERF. 15 × 14. PHOSPHORISED (ADVANCED COATED) PAPER. PVAD (clear) GUM**

XSL47 (=S.G.S73)      Deep bluish grey   ..      ..      ..      ..      ..      ..      55      55

**Plate Numbers (Blocks of Six)**

Double Pane Plates
Plate Nos. in left margin

| Pl. Nos. | (P) |
|---|---|
| 1, 1   ..      ..      .. | 3·50 |
| 2, 2   ..      ..      .. | 3·50 |

## 37p. Rosine (1990)

**Printed by Questa**

**1990 (4 DECEMBER). PERF. 15 × 14. PHOSPHORISED (ADVANCED COATED) PAPER. PVAD GUM**

XSL50 (=S.G.S74)      Rosine      ..      ..      ..      ..      ..      ..      ..      60      65

**Plate Numbers (Blocks of Six)**

Double Pane Plates
Plate Nos. in left margin

| Pl. Nos. | (P) |
|---|---|
| 1, 1   ..      .. | 3·75 |
| 2, 2   ..      .. | 3·75 |

# Presentation Packs

Presentation Packs containing stamps of Northern Ireland, Scotland and Wales are listed after those of Northern Ireland.

XSPP6 No. 129*b* (28.10.81)  7p., 9p., 10½p., 11½p., 12p.,
13½p., 14p., 15p., 18p., 22p.  6·00
  Comprises Nos. XS46, 51, 54, 57/8, 60, XSL9, 21 and 30.

XSPP7 No. 2 (3.8.83)  10p., 12½p., 16p., 20½p., 26p.,
28p.  5·00
  Comprises Nos. XS52, XSL4, 15, 29, 38 and 41.

XSPP8 No. 6 (23.10.84)  10p., 13p., 16p., 17p., 22p.,
26p., 28p., 31p.  8·00
  Comprises Nos. XS53, XSL5, 15, 16, 31, 38, 41 and 43.

XSPP9 No. 10 (3.3.87)  12p., 13p., 17p., 18p., 22p.,
26p., 28p., 31p.  3·00
  Comprises Nos. XSL3, 7, 19, 22, 33, 39, 42, and 45.

**WITHDRAWN**   No. XSPP6, 8.83; No. XSPP7, 10.84; No. XSPP8, 2.3.87

---

# First Day Covers

| | | | |
|---|---|---|---|
| XSLFD1 (8.4.81) | 11½p., 14p., 18p., 22p. | † | 2·00 |
| XSLFD2 (24.2.82) | 12½p., 15½p., 19½p., 26p. | † | 3·00 |
| XSLFD3 (27.4.83) | 16p., 20½p., 28p. | † | 3·00 |
| XSLFD4 (23.10.84) | 13p., 17p., 22p., 31p. | † | 5·00 |
| XSLFD5 (7.1.86) | 12p. | † | 1·25 |
| XSLFD6 (6.1.87)* | 18p. | † | 1·75 |
| XSLFD7 (8.11.88) | 14p., 19p., 23p., 32p. | † | 3·00 |
| XSLFD8 (21.3.89) | Scots Connection *se-tenant* pane | † | 7·50 |
| XSLFD9 (28.11.89) | 15p., 20p., 24p., 34p. | † | 2·25 |
| XSLFD10 (4.12.90) | 17p., 22p., 26p., 37p. | † | 2·00 |

*The Questa printings issued on 27 January 1987 for 22p., 26p. and 28p. were affixed to No. XSLFD6 in error by the Edinburgh Philatelic Bureau; three weeks earlier than the official date of release.

# C. Wales

## Type XW4 as illustrated in Section XB printed by Questa

**Redrawn Dragon**

I          II

**Type I.** The eye is complete with white dot in the centre. Wing-tips, tail and tongue are thin.
**Type II.** The eye is joined to the nose by a solid line. Tail, wing-tips, claws and tongue are wider than in Type I.

## 11½p. Drab (1981)

**1981 (8 APRIL). PERF. 14. ONE 4 mm. PHOSPHOR BAND AT LEFT. ORIGINAL COATED PAPER. PVA GUM**

XWL1 (=S.G.W35)   Drab   ..     ..     ..   ..    ..    ..    ..     ..     75     60

**Plate Numbers (Blocks of Six)**

Double Pane Plates
Plate Nos. in right margin

| Pl. Nos. | | | | Row 1 | Row 20 |
|---|---|---|---|---|---|
| 1, 1 | .. | .. | .. | 4·75 | 4·75 |
| 2, 2 | .. | .. | .. | 4·75 | 4·75 |

**WITHDRAWN**   26.2.83

## 12p. Bright Emerald (1986)

**1986 (7 JANUARY). PERF. 15 × 14. ONE 4 mm. PHOSPHOR BAND AT LEFT. FLUORESCENT COATED PAPER. PVAD GUM**

XWL2 (=S.G.W36)   Bright emerald   ..     ..    ..    ..    ..    ..    1·40    1·10

**Plate Numbers (Blocks of Six)**

Double Pane Plates
Plate Nos. in left margin

| Pl. Nos. | | | (I) | Pl. Nos. | | | (P) |
|---|---|---|---|---|---|---|---|
| 1, 1 | .. | .. | 7·50 | 2, 2 | .. | .. | 7·50 |

**1986 (JULY). PERF. 15 × 14. ONE SHORT PHOSPHOR BAND AT LEFT. FLUORESCENT COATED PAPER. PVAD GUM**

XWL3          Bright emerald   ..     ..    ..    ..    ..    ..    3·75    2·75

No. XWL3 was printed with the 4 mm. wide phosphor band at left cut short opposite the perforations at the top and bottom of each stamp in the sheet.

**Plate Numbers (Blocks of Six)**

Double Pane Plates
Plate Nos. in left margin

| Pl. Nos. | | | (I) | Pl. Nos. | | | (P) |
|---|---|---|---|---|---|---|---|
| 3, 3 | .. | .. | 22·00 | 4, 4 | .. | .. | 22·00 |

**SOLD OUT**   Nos. XWL2/3, 10.87

# 12½p. Light Emerald (1982–84)

**1982 (24 FEBRUARY). PERF. 14. ONE 4 mm. PHOSPHOR BAND AT LEFT. FLUORESCENT COATED PAPER. PVAD GUM**

XWL4 (=S.G.W37)  Light emerald ..    ..    ..    ..    ..    ..    ..    60    60

**Plate Numbers (Blocks of Six)**

Double Pane Plates
Plate Nos. in right margin

| Pl. Nos. | | | | Row 1 | Row 20 |
|---|---|---|---|---|---|
| 1, 1 | .. | .. | .. | 3·75 | 3·75 |
| 2, 2 | .. | .. | .. | 3·50 | 3·50 |
| 3, 1 | .. | .. | .. | 3·75 | 3·75 |
| 4, 2 | .. | .. | .. | 26·00 | 26·00 |

Plate Nos. in left margin

| Pl. Nos. | | | (I) | Pl. Nos. | | | (P) |
|---|---|---|---|---|---|---|---|
| 1, 1 | .. | .. | .. 12·00 | 2, 2 | .. | .. | .. 28·00 |

**1984 (10 JANUARY). PERF. 15 × 14. ONE 4 mm. PHOSPHOR BAND AT LEFT. FLUORESCENT COATED PAPER. PVAD GUM**

XWL5 (=S.G.W37a)  Light emerald ..    ..    ..    ..    ..    ..    ..    5·50    4·50

**Plate Numbers (Blocks of Six)**

Double Pane Plates
Plate Nos. in left margin

| Pl. Nos. | | | (I) | Pl. Nos. | | | (P) |
|---|---|---|---|---|---|---|---|
| 1, 1 | .. | .. | .. 30·00 | 2, 2 | .. | .. | .. 30·00 |
| 1, 3 | .. | .. | .. 30·00 | 2, 4 | .. | .. | .. £275 |

**WITHDRAWN**  No. XWL4, 28.2.85; No. XWL5, 28.6.85

# 13p. Pale Chestnut (1984–87)

**1984 (23 OCTOBER). PERF. 15 × 14. ONE 4 mm. PHOSPHOR BAND AT LEFT. FLUORESCENT COATED PAPER. TYPE I. PVAD GUM**

XWL6 (=S.G.W38)    Pale chestnut ..    ..    ..    ..    ..    ..    ..    40    35

**Plate Numbers (Blocks of Six)**

Double Pane Plates (Second plate number is grey)
Plate Nos. in left margin

| Pl. Nos. | | | (I) | Pl. Nos. | | | (P) |
|---|---|---|---|---|---|---|---|
| 1, 1 | .. | .. | .. 3·75 | 2, 2 | .. | .. | .. 3·75 |
| 1, 3 | .. | .. | .. 7·50 | 2, 4 | .. | .. | .. £180 |
| 3, 3 | .. | .. | .. 20·00 | 4, 4 | .. | .. | .. 20·00 |
| 5, 3 | .. | .. | .. 2·75 | 6, 4 | .. | .. | .. 2·75 |
| 7, 5 | .. | .. | .. 3·25 | 8, 6 | .. | .. | .. 3·25 |

**1987 (JANUARY). PERF. 15 × 14. ONE SHORT PHOSPHOR BAND AT LEFT. FLUORESCENT COATED PAPER. TYPE II**

**A. PVAD GUM**

XWL7                Pale chestnut ..    ..    ..    ..    ..    ..    ..    2·50

Examples of No. XWL7 showing a "continuous" phosphor band similar to No. XWL6, but Type II, were from an overinked printing.

**427**

**Plate Numbers (Blocks of Six)**

Double Pane Plates (Second plate number is chestnut)
Plate Nos. in left margin

| Pl. Nos. | | | (I) | Pl. Nos. | | | (P) |
|---|---|---|---|---|---|---|---|
| 1, 1 | .. | .. | .. 24·00 | 2, 2 | .. | .. | .. 25·00 |

**B. PVA GUM** (14.4.87)

XWL8 (=S.G.W38Ea) Pale chestnut..    ..    ..    ..    ..    ..    ..    40    35

**Plate Numbers (Blocks of Six)**

Double Pane Plates (Second plate number is chestnut)
Plate Nos. in left margin

| Pl. Nos. | | | (I) | Pl. Nos. | | | (P) |
|---|---|---|---|---|---|---|---|
| 1, 1 | .. | .. | .. 3·25 | 2, 2 | .. | .. | .. 9·00 |
| 3, 3 | .. | .. | .. 2·50 | 4, 4 | .. | .. | .. 2·50 |

**WITHDRAWN**  No. XWL6, 14.4.88: Nos. XWL7/8, 4.9.89

---

# 14p. Grey-blue (1981)

### 1981 (8 APRIL). PERF. 14. PHOSPHORISED (FLUORESCENT COATED) PAPER. PVA GUM

XWL9 (=S.G.W39)    Grey-blue    ..    ..    ..    ..    ..    ..    ..    55    50

**Plate Numbers (Blocks of Six)**

Double Pane Plates
Plate Nos. in right margin

| Pl. Nos. | | | | Row 1 | Row 20 |
|---|---|---|---|---|---|
| 1, 1 | .. | .. | .. | 3·50 | 3·50 |
| 2, 2 | .. | .. | .. | 4·75 | 4·75 |
| 1, 3 | .. | .. | .. | 3·50 | 3·50 |
| 2, 4 | .. | .. | .. | 12·00 | 18·00 |

**WITHDRAWN**  14.1.84

---

# 14p. Deep Blue (1988)

### 1988 (8 NOVEMBER). PERF. 15 × 14. ONE 4 mm. SHORT PHOSPHOR BAND (RIGHT OF CENTRE). FLUORESCENT COATED PAPER. PVA GUM

XWL10 (=S.G.W40)    Deep blue    ..    ..    ..    ..    ..    ..    ..    35    30

**Plate Numbers (Blocks of Six)**

Double Pane Plates
Plate Nos. in left margin

| Pl. Nos. | | | (P) |
|---|---|---|---|
| 1, 1 | .. | .. | .. 2·75 |
| 2, 2 | .. | .. | .. 2·75 |
| 3, 3 | .. | .. | .. 5·50 |
| 4, 4 | .. | .. | .. 5·50 |
| 5, 5 | .. | .. | .. 2·40 |
| 6, 6 | .. | .. | .. 2·40 |

**WITHDRAWN**  27.11.90

## 15p. Bright Blue (1989)

1989 (28 NOVEMBER). PERF. 15 × 14. ONE 4 mm. SHORT PHOSPHOR BAND (RIGHT OF CENTRE). FLUORESCENT COATED PAPER. PVA GUM

XWL11 (=S.G.W41)    Bright blue    .. .. .. .. .. .. .. ..    25    30
                    a. Phosphor omitted ..    .. .. .. .. .. ..

**Plate Numbers (Blocks of Six)**
Double Pane Plates
Plate Nos. in left margin

| Pl. Nos. | | | (P) |
|---|---|---|---|
| 1, 1 | .. | .. | .. 2·00 |
| 2, 2 | .. | .. | .. 2·00 |
| 3, 3 | .. | .. | .. 45·00 |
| 4, 4 | .. | .. | .. 50·00 |
| 5, 5 | .. | .. | .. 4·00 |
| 6, 6 | .. | .. | .. 4·00 |

Plate Nos. 5, 5 and 6, 6 also exist with a short imperforate section at base below the 8th perforation. *Price for plate* 5, 5 £9 *and* 6, 6 £12.

## 15½p. Pale Violet (1982)

1982 (24 FEBRUARY). PERF. 14. PHOSPHORISED (FLUORESCENT COATED) PAPER. PVAD GUM

XWL12 (=S.G.W42)    Pale violet    .. .. .. .. .. .. ..    60    65

**Plate Numbers (Blocks of Six)**
Double Pane Plates
Plate Nos. in right margin

| Pl. Nos. | | | Row 1 | Row 20 |
|---|---|---|---|---|
| 1 | .. | .. | .. 3·75 | 3·75 |
| 2 | .. | .. | .. 4·00 | 4·00 |
| 3 | .. | .. | .. 24·00 | 24·00 |
| 4 | .. | .. | .. 14·00 | 14·00 |
| 5 | .. | .. | .. £200 | £200 |
| 6 | .. | .. | .. £200 | £200 |

**WITHDRAWN** 29.4.84

## 16p. Drab (1983–84)

1983 (27 APRIL). PERF. 14. PHOSPHORISED (FLUORESCENT COATED) PAPER. PVAD GUM

XWL13 (=S.G.W43)    Drab ..    .. .. .. .. .. .. ..    1·50    1·25

**Plate Numbers (Blocks of Six)**
Double Pane Plates
Plate Nos. in left margin

| Pl. Nos. | | | (I) | Pl. Nos. | | | (P) |
|---|---|---|---|---|---|---|---|
| 1 | .. | .. | .. 8·00 | 2 | .. | .. | .. 14·00 |
| 3 | .. | .. | .. 60·00 | 4 | .. | .. | .. 18·00 |

## 1984 (10 JANUARY). PERF. 15 × 14. PHOSPHORISED (FLUORESCENT COATED) PAPER. PVAD GUM

XWL14 (=S.G.W43a)  Drab ..     ..     ..     ..     ..     ..     ..     .. 1·25   1·10

**Plate Numbers (Blocks of Six)**
Double Pane Plates
Plate Nos. in left margin

| Pl. Nos. | | | (I) | Pl. Nos. | | | (P) |
|---|---|---|---|---|---|---|---|
| 3 | .. | .. | .. 20·00 | 4 | .. | .. | .. 7·00 |
| 5 | .. | .. | .. 6·50 | 6 | .. | .. | .. 6·50 |

**WITHDRAWN**   No. XWL13, 10.1.85; No. XWL14, 7.2.87

# 17p. Grey-blue (1984–86)

## 1984 (23 OCTOBER). PERF. 15 × 14. PHOSPHORISED PAPER. TYPE I. PVAD GUM

**A. FLUORESCENT COATED PAPER**
XWL15 (=S.G.W44)  Grey-blue  ..     ..     ..     ..     ..     ..     .. 70     55

**Plate Numbers (Blocks of Six)**
Double Pane Plates
Plate Nos. in left margin

| Pl. Nos. | | | (I) | Pl. Nos. | | | (P) |
|---|---|---|---|---|---|---|---|
| 1 | .. | .. | .. 5·50 | 2 | .. | .. | .. 10·00 |
| 3 | .. | .. | .. 4·75 | 4 | .. | .. | .. 4·75 |

The following plate number blocks are on paper of intermediate brightness and were issued with those listed above. The paper used was a forerunner to the brighter advanced coated paper of February 1986.

| Pl. Nos. | | | (I) | Pl. Nos. | | | (P) |
|---|---|---|---|---|---|---|---|
| 3 | .. | .. | .. £175 | 4 | .. | .. | .. 38·00 |
| 5 | .. | .. | .. 4·75 | 6 | .. | .. | .. 4·75 |
| 7 | .. | .. | .. 12·00 | 8 | .. | .. | .. 6·00 |

**B. ADVANCED COATED PAPER** (25.2.86)

XWL16            Grey-blue  ..     ..     ..     ..     ..     ..     .. 90

**Plate Numbers (Blocks of Six)**
Double Pane Plates
Plate Nos. in left margin

| Pl. Nos. | | | (I) | Pl. Nos. | | | (P) |
|---|---|---|---|---|---|---|---|
| 7 | .. | .. | .. 5·50 | 8 | .. | .. | .. 5·50 |

## 1986 (18 AUGUST). PERF. 15 × 14. PHOSPHORISED (FLUORESCENT COATED) PAPER. TYPE II. PVAD GUM

XWL17 (=S.G.W44Ea)  Grey-blue ..     ..     ..     ..     ..     ..     .. 8·00   8·00

**Plate Numbers (Blocks of Six)**
Double Pane Plates
Plate Nos. in left margin

| Pl. Nos. | | | (I) | Pl. Nos. | | | (P) |
|---|---|---|---|---|---|---|---|
| 1, 1 | .. | .. | .. 48·00 | 2, 2 | .. | .. | .. 48·00 |

**WITHDRAWN**   No. XWL15, 24.2.87; No. XWL16/17, sold out 10.87

# 17p. Deep Blue (1990)

**1990 (4 DECEMBER). PERF. 15 × 14. ONE 4 mm. SHORT PHOSPHOR BAND (RIGHT OF CENTRE). FLUORESCENT COATED PAPER. PVA GUM**

XWL18 (=S.G.W45)  Deep blue  .. .. .. .. .. .. ..   30   35

**Plate Numbers (Blocks of Six)**

Double Pane Plates
Plate Nos. in left margin

| Pl. Nos. | | | | (P) |
|---|---|---|---|---|
| 1, 1 | .. | .. | .. | 2·40 |
| 2, 2 | .. | .. | .. | 2·40 |

# 18p. Deep Violet (1981)

**1981 (8 APRIL). PERF. 14. PHOSPHORISED (FLUORESCENT COATED) PAPER. PVA GUM**

XWL19 (=S.G. W46)  Deep violet  .. .. .. .. .. .. ..   70   75

**Plate Numbers (Blocks of Six)**

Double Pane Plates
Plate Nos. in right margin

| Pl. Nos. | | | | Row 1 | Row 20 |
|---|---|---|---|---|---|
| 1, 1 | .. | .. | .. | 4·50 | 4·50 |
| 2, 2 | .. | .. | .. | 4·50 | 4·50 |

**WITHDRAWN** 14.1.84

# 18p. Deep Olive-grey (1987)

**1987 (6 JANUARY). PERF. 15 × 14. PHOSPHORISED (ADVANCED COATED) PAPER.**

**A. PVAD GUM**

XWL20 (S.G.W47)  Deep olive-grey  .. .. .. .. .. .. ..   60   45

**Plate Numbers (Blocks of Six)**

Double Pane Plates
Plate Nos. in left margin

| Pl. Nos. | | | | (I) | | Pl. Nos. | | | | (P) |
|---|---|---|---|---|---|---|---|---|---|---|
| 1, 1 | .. | .. | .. | 3·75 | | 2, 2 | .. | .. | .. | 3·75 |
| 3, 3 | .. | .. | .. | 4·50 | | 3, 3 | .. | .. | .. | 6·00 |
| | | | | | | 4, 4 | .. | .. | .. | 3·75 |
| | | | | | | 5, 5 | .. | .. | .. | 10·00 |
| | | | | | | 6, 6 | .. | .. | .. | 16·00 |

Plate Nos. 3, 3 and 4, 4 also exist with a short imperforate section at base below the 8th perforation. *Price for plate* 3, 3 £35 *and* 4, 4 £30.

**B. PVAD (clear) GUM** (29.3.88)
XWL21   Deep olive-grey  .. .. .. .. .. .. ..   60
This printing was on paper supplied to Questa by Henry & Leigh Slater Ltd. The PVAD gum does not have the green dye additive.

**Plate Numbers (Blocks of Six)**

Double Pane Plates
Plate Nos. in left margin

| Pl. Nos. | | | | (P) |
|---|---|---|---|---|
| 5, 5 | .. | .. | .. | 3·50 |
| 6, 6 | .. | .. | .. | 3·50 |

**WITHDRAWN** 4.9.89

## 19p. Bright Orange-red (1988)

**1988 (8 NOVEMBER). PERF. 15 × 14. PHOSPHORISED (ADVANCED COATED) PAPER**

**A. PVAD (clear) GUM**

XWL22 (=S.G.W48)   Bright orange-red  ..   ..   ..   ..   ..   ..   50   45

**Plate Numbers (Blocks of Six)**

Double Pane Plates
Plate Nos. in left margin

| Pl. Nos. | | | (P) |
|---|---|---|---|
| 1, 1 | .. | .. | .. 3·25 |
| 2, 2 | .. | .. | .. 3·25 |
| 3, 3 | .. | .. | .. 25·00 |
| 4, 4 | .. | .. | .. 25·00 |

**B. PVA GUM** (white back) (20.6.89)

XWL23                  Bright orange-red  ..   ..   ..   ..   ..   ..   60

The note below Scotland No. XSL25 also applies here.

**Plate Numbers (Blocks of Six)**

Double Pane Plates
Plate Nos. in left margin

| Pl. Nos. | | | (P) |
|---|---|---|---|
| 3, 3 | .. | .. | .. 3·75 |
| 4, 4 | .. | .. | .. 3·75 |

**WITHDRAWN**   No. XWL22, 19.6.90; No. XWL23, 27.11.90

## 19½p. Olive-grey (1982)

**1982 (24 FEBRUARY). PERF. 14. PHOSPHORISED (FLUORESCENT COATED) PAPER. PVAD GUM**

XWL24 (=S.G.W49)   Olive-grey   ..   ..   ..   ..   ..   ..   ..   2·00   2·00

**Plate Numbers (Blocks of Six)**

Double Pane Plates
Plate Nos. in right margin

| Pl. Nos. | | | Row 1 | Row 20 |
|---|---|---|---|---|
| 1 | .. | .. | .. 12·00 | 12·00 |
| 2 | .. | .. | .. 14·00 | 14·00 |

**WITHDRAWN**   29.4.84

## 20p. Brownish Black (1989)

**1989 (28 NOVEMBER). PERF. 15 × 14. PHOSPHORISED (ADVANCED COATED) PAPER. PVAD (clear) GUM**

XWL25 (=S.G.W50)   Brownish black   ..   ..   ..   ..   ..   ..   30   30

**Plate Numbers (Blocks of Six)**

Double Pane Plates
Plate Nos. in left margin

| Pl. Nos. | | | (P) |
|---|---|---|---|
| 1, 1 | .. | .. | .. 2·25 |
| 2, 2 | .. | .. | .. 2·25 |
| 3, 3 | .. | .. | .. 4·75 |
| 4, 4 | .. | .. | .. 7·00 |
| 5, 5 | .. | .. | .. 6·50 |
| 6, 6 | .. | .. | .. 6·50 |

Plate Nos. 3, 3 and 4, 4 also exist with a short imperforate section at base below the 8th perforation. *Price for plate* 3, 3 £5 *and* 4, 4 £7.

## 20½p. Ultramarine (1983)

1983 (27 APRIL). PERF. 14. PHOSPHORISED (FLUORESCENT COATED) PAPER. PVAD GUM

XWL26 (=S.G.W51)   Ultramarine  ..      ..     ..     ..     ..     ..     ..     2·00   1·50

**Plate Numbers (Blocks of Six)**
Double Pane Plates
Plate Nos. in left margin

| Pl. No. | | (I) | | Pl. No. | | | (P) |
|---|---|---|---|---|---|---|---|
| 1 | .. .. | .. 12·00 | | 2 | .. | .. | .. 12·00 |

**WITHDRAWN** 28.6.85

## 22p. Blue (1981)

1981 (8 APRIL). PERF. 14. PHOSPHORISED (FLUORESCENT COATED) PAPER. PVA GUM

XWL27 (=S.G.W52) - Blue  ..      ..     ..     ..     ..     ..     ..     80   1·10

**Plate Numbers (Blocks of Six)**
Double Pane Plates
Plate Nos. in right margin

| Pl. Nos. | | | Row 1 | Row 20 |
|---|---|---|---|---|
| 1, 1 | .. | .. .. | 5·00 | 5·00 |
| 2, 2 | .. | .. .. | 5·00 | 5·00 |

**WITHDRAWN** 29.4.84

## 22p. Yellow-green (1984)

1984 (23 OCTOBER). PERF. 15 × 14. PHOSPHORISED (ADVANCED COATED) PAPER. PVAD GUM

XWL28 (=S.G.W53)   Yellow-green ..      ..     ..     ..     ..     ..     ..     55   50

**Plate Numbers (Blocks of Six)**
Double Pane Plates
Plate Nos. in left margin

| Pl. Nos. | | | (I) | Pl. Nos. | | | (P) |
|---|---|---|---|---|---|---|---|
| 1,1 | .. | .. | .. 4·25 | 2,2 | .. | .. .. | 3·50 |
| 1,3 | .. | .. | .. 3·50 | 2,4 | .. | .. .. | 3·50 |

**WITHDRAWN** 27.11.90

## 22p. Bright Orange-red (1990)

1990 (4 DECEMBER). PERF. 15 × 14. PHOSPHORISED (ADVANCED COATED) PAPER. PVAD GUM

XWL29 (=S.G.W54)   Bright orange-red  ..      ..     ..     ..     ..     ..     35   40

**Plate Numbers (Blocks of Six)**
Double Pane Plates
Plate Nos. in left margin

| Pl. Nos. | | | (P) |
|---|---|---|---|
| 1, 1 | .. | .. | .. 2·75 |
| 2, 2 | .. | .. | .. 2·75 |

## 23p. Bright Green (1988)

**1988 (8 NOVEMBER). PERF. 15 × 14. PHOSPHORISED (ADVANCED COATED) PAPER. PVAD (clear) GUM**

XWL30 (=S.G.W55)   Bright green ..    ..    ..    ..    ..    ..    ..    55    50

**Plate Numbers (Blocks of Six)**

Double Pane Plates
Plate Nos. in left margin

| Pl. Nos. | | | (P) |
|---|---|---|---|
| 1, 1 | .. | .. | .. 2·75 |
| 2, 2 | .. | .. | .. 2·75 |

**WITHDRAWN**   27.11.90

## 24p. Indian Red (1989)

**1989 (28 NOVEMBER). PERF. 15 × 14. PHOSPHORISED (ADVANCED COATED) PAPER. PVAD (clear) GUM**

XWL31 (=S.G.W56)   Indian red   ..    ..    ..    ..    ..    ..    ..    40    45

**Plate Numbers (Blocks of Six)**

Double Pane Plates
Plate Nos in left margin

| Pl. Nos. | | | (P) |
|---|---|---|---|
| 1, 1 | .. | .. | .. 2·75 |
| 2, 2 | .. | .. | .. 2·75 |

## 26p. Rosine (1982–87)

**1982 (24 FEBRUARY). PERF. 14. PHOSPHORISED (FLUORESCENT COATED) PAPER. TYPE I. PVAD GUM**

XWL32 (=S.G.W57)   Rosine ..    ..    ..    ..    ..    ..    ..    ..    90    80

**Plate Numbers (Blocks of Six)**

Double Pane Plates
Plate Nos. in right margin

| Pl. No. | | | | Row 1 | Row 20 |
|---|---|---|---|---|---|
| 1 | .. | .. | .. | 5·00 | 5·00 |
| 2 | .. | .. | .. | 5·00 | 5·00 |

**1987 (27 JANUARY). PERF. 15 × 14. PHOSPHORISED (ADVANCED COATED) PAPER. TYPE II. PVAD GUM**

XWL33 (=S.G.W57a)   Rosine   ..    ..    ..    ..    ..    ..    ..    ..    2·50    1·75

**Plate Numbers (Blocks of Six)**

Double Pane Plates
Plate Nos. in left margin

| Pl. No. | | | (I) | Pl. No. | | | (P) |
|---|---|---|---|---|---|---|---|
| 1 | .. | .. | .. 15·00 | 2 | .. | .. | .. 15·00 |

**WITHDRAWN**   No. XWL32, 26.1.88; No. XWL33, 4.9.89

**434**

# 26p. Drab (1990)

**1990 (4 DECEMBER). PERF. 15 × 14. PHOSPHORISED (ADVANCED COATED) PAPER. PVAD GUM**

XWL34 (=S.G.W58)  Drab ..    ..    ..    ..    ..    ..    ..    ..    40    45

**Plate Numbers (Blocks of Six)**

Double Pane Plates
Plate Nos. in left margin

| Pl. Nos. | | | (P) |
|---|---|---|---|
| 1, 1 | .. | .. | .. 3·00 |
| 2, 2 | .. | .. | .. 3·00 |

# 28p. Deep Violet-blue (1983–87)

**1983 (27 APRIL). PERF. 14. PHOSPHORISED (FLUORESCENT COATED) PAPER. TYPE I. PVAD GUM**

XWL35 (=S.G.W59)  Deep violet-blue    ..    ..    ..    ..    ..    ..    1·00    80

**Plate Numbers (Blocks of Six)**

Double Pane Plates
Plate Nos. in left margin

| Pl. No. | | (I) | Pl. No. | | | (P) |
|---|---|---|---|---|---|---|
| 1 | .. .. | .. 5·50 | 2 | .. | .. | .. 5·50 |

**1987 (27 JANUARY). PERF. 15 × 14. PHOSPHORISED (ADVANCED COATED) PAPER. TYPE II. PVAD GUM**

XWL36 (=S.G.W59a)  Deep violet-blue    ..    ..    ..    ..    ..    ..    ..    45    65

**Plate Numbers (Blocks of Six)**

Double Pane Plates
Plate Nos. in left margin

| Pl. No. | | | (I) | Pl. No. | | | (P) |
|---|---|---|---|---|---|---|---|
| 1 | .. | .. | .. 3·25 | 2 | .. | .. | .. 3·25 |

**WITHDRAWN**  No. XWL35 26.1.88

# 31p. Bright Purple (1984–87)

**1984 (23 OCTOBER). PERF. 15 × 14. PHOSPHORISED PAPER. PVAD GUM**

**A. FLUORESCENT COATED PAPER**

XWL37              Bright purple  ..    ..    ..    ..    ..    ..    ..    ..    1·00    90

**Plate Numbers (Blocks of Six)**

Double Pane Plates
Plate Nos. in left margin

| Pl. No. | | | (I) | Pl. No. | | | (P) |
|---|---|---|---|---|---|---|---|
| 3 | .. | .. | .. 5·50 | 4 | .. | .. | .. 9·00 |
| 5 | .. | .. | .. 6·00 | 6 | .. | .. | .. 5·50 |

**B. ADVANCED COATED PAPER** (27.1.87)

XWL38 (=S.G.W60)  Bright purple    ..    ..    ..    ..    ..    ..    ..    1·00    70

**Plate Numbers (Blocks of Six)**

Double Pane Plates
Plate Nos. in left margin

| Pl. No. | | | (I) | Pl. No. | | | (P) |
|---|---|---|---|---|---|---|---|
| 5 | .. | .. | .. 5·50 | 6 | .. | .. | .. 5·50 |

**WITHDRAWN**  No. XWL37 26.1.88; No. XWL38, 4.9.89

## 32p. Greenish Blue (1988)

**1988 (8 NOVEMBER). PERF. 15 × 14. PHOSPHORISED (ADVANCED COATED) PAPER. PVAD (clear) GUM**

XWL39 (=S.G.W61)   Greenish blue   ..   ..   ..   ..   ..   ..   75   60

**Plate Numbers (Blocks of Six)**

Double Pane Plates
Plate Nos. in left margin

| Pl. Nos. | | | (P) |
|---|---|---|---|
| 1, 1 | .. | .. | .. 5·00 |
| 2, 2 | .. | .. | .. 5·00 |

**WITHDRAWN**   27.11.90

## 34p. Deep Bluish Grey (1989)

**1989 (28 NOVEMBER). PERF. 15 × 14. PHOSPHORISED (ADVANCED COATED) PAPER. PVAD (clear) GUM**

XWL40 (=S.G.W62)   Deep bluish grey   ..   ..   ..   ..   ..   ..   55   55

**Plate Numbers (Blocks of Six)**

Double Pane Plates
Plate Nos. in left margin

| Pl. Nos. | | | (P) |
|---|---|---|---|
| 1, 1 | .. | .. | .. 3·75 |
| 2, 2 | .. | .. | .. 3·75 |

## 37p. Rosine (1990)

**1990 (4 DECEMBER). PERF. 15 × 14. PHOSPHORISED (ADVANCED COATED) PAPER. PVAD GUM**

XWL43 (=S.G.W63)   Rosine   ..   ..   ..   ..   ..   ..   ..   60   65

**Plate Numbers (Blocks of Six)**

Double Pane Plates
Plate Nos. in left margin

| Pl. Nos. | | | (P) |
|---|---|---|---|
| 1, 1 | .. | .. | .. 4·25 |
| 2, 2 | .. | .. | .. 4·25 |

# Presentation Packs

Presentation Packs containing stamps of Northern Ireland, Scotland and Wales are listed after those of Northern Ireland.

| | | |
|---|---|---|
| XWPP6 No. 129c (28.10.81) | 7p., 9p., 10½p., 11½p., 12p., 13½p., 14p., 15p., 18p., 22p. | 6·00 |
| Comprises Nos. XW34, 38, 41, 44/5, 47, XWL1, 9, 19 and 27. | | |
| XWPP7 No. 3 (3.8.83) | 10p., 12½p., 16p., 20½p., 26p., 28p. | 5·00 |
| Comprises Nos. XW40, XWL4, 13, 26, 32 and 35. | | |
| XWPP8 No. 7 (23.10.84) | 10p., 13p., 16p., 17p., 22p., 26p., 28p., 31p. | 8·50 |
| Comprises Nos. XW40, XWL6, 14, 15, 28, 32, 35 and 37. | | |
| XWPP9 No. 11 (3.3.87) | 12p., 13p., 17p., 18p., 22p., 26p., 28p., 31p. | 3·00 |
| Comprises Nos. XWL2, 6, 16, 20, 28, 33, 36 and 38. | | |

**WITHDRAWN**   No. XWPP6, 8.83; No. XWPP7, 10.84; No. XWPP8, sold out 10.86

---

# First Day Covers

| | | | |
|---|---|---|---|
| XWLFD1 (8.4.81) | 11½p., 14p., 18p., 22p. | † | 2·00 |
| XWLFD2 (24.2.82) | 12½p., 15½p., 19½p., 26p. | † | 3·00 |
| XWLFD3 (27.4.83) | 16p., 20½p., 28p. | † | 3·00 |
| XWLFD4 (23.10.84) | 13p., 17p., 22p., 31p. | † | 4·50 |
| XWLFD5 (7.1.86) | 12p. | † | 1·25 |
| XWLFD6 (6.1.87) | 18p. | † | 1·75 |
| XWLFD7 (8.11.88) | 14p., 19p., 23p., 32p. | † | 3·00 |
| XWLFD8 (28.11.89) | 15p., 20p., 24p., 34p. | † | 2·25 |
| XWLFD9 (4.12.90) | 17p., 22p., 26p., 37p. | † | 2·00 |

# SECTION XD

## Regional Decimal Booklet Panes

### 1989. Printed in Lithography

---

#### General Notes

The 1989 £5 prestige stamp book was issued on 21 March printed by The House of Questa in lithography. It was the first occasion that Regional stamps had been included in a booklet of this type.

**PAPER AND GUM.** All stamps were printed from two plates in order to provide added depth of tone. The paper used was supplied to Questa from two suppliers, Henry & Leigh Slater Ltd., referred to as HLS paper and Coated Papers Ltd., (CPL). Panes 1 and 4 contained 19p. stamps in panes of 9 and 6 which are on HLS paper with PVAD (clear) gum. Panes 2 and 3 containing 14p. and mixed values are on paper produced by CPL and the gum is PVA. Because there is no green additive in the PVAD gum there is only a small difference between the two types of gum. The PVA is white and the surface, when viewed at an angle to a light source, is slightly shiny. The PVAD by comparison is shiny and has a creamy appearance. These stamps are on phosphorised paper and the PVA stamps are on fluorescent coated paper with phosphor bands printed in the original ink. These bands are dull under ultra violet and were continuous on the pane of six but on the *se-tenant* pane the bands stopped short in the pane selvedge.

From £5 Booklet "The Scots Connection" No. DX10

The illustrations are reduced, the actual size being 162 × 97 mm.

First pane comprising 9 × 19p. phosphorised (advanced coated) paper.

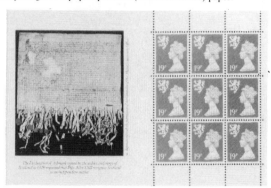

XDS1

XDS1 (containing No. XSL24 × 9) (21.3.89)                2·75

Second pane comprising 6 × 14p. with 4 mm. band to right of centre.

XDS2

XDS2 (containing No. XSL11 × 6) (21.3.89)       1·50

Third pane comprising 5 × 14p. band at left: 2 × 19p. and 23p. two bands.

XDS3

XDS3 (containing Nos. XSL12 × 5, XSL25 × 2, XSL36) (21.3.89)    3·00
   *a*. Error. Imperforate pane    ..   ..   ..   ..   ..
   *b*. First vertical row imperf. on 3 sides (top, left and bottom)    ..
   *c*. Partly imperf. (top row imperf, centre row perf. at left, right and
       bottom, bottom row perf.)    ..   ..   ..   ..   ..
   *d*. Partly imperf. (top two rows imperf., bottom row perf. at left,
       right and bottom sides)    ..   ..   ..   ..   ..   ..

The error No. XDS3*b* was perforated as a normal pane of six.

Fourth pane comprising 6 × 19p. phosphorised (advanced coated) paper.

XDS4

XDS4 (containing No. XSL24 × 6) (21.3.89)                              1·90

**Plate Numbers**
The printer's sheet contained 3 columns each with four panes but none of the plate numbers appeared on the sheets.

# SECTION Y
# Royal Mail Postage Labels

## 1984

### General Note

These imperforate labels were issued as an experiment by the Post Office. Special microprocessor controlled machines were installed at four Post Offices in Cambridge, London. Southampton and Windsor to provide an after-hours sales service to the public. The machines print and dispense the labels according to the coins inserted and the buttons operated by the customer. Values were initially available in ½p. steps to 16p. and in addition, the labels were sold at philatelic counters in two packs containing either 3 values (3½, 12½, 16p.) or 32 values (½p. to 16p.). From 28 August 1984 the machines were adjusted to provide values up to 17p. After 31 December 1984 labels including ½p. values were withdrawn. The machines were taken out of service on 30 April 1985, but the labels remained on sale at the Philatelic Bureau for a further 12 months.

The test was not successful and there are no plans, at present, to repeat the experiment.

The set of seventeen values was available in *black* with specimen imprint from the National Postal Museum to commemorate the Penny Black's 150th anniversary. Black ink was added to red on 23 May 1990 which produced blackish red labels.

**Y1**

(Des. Martin Newton)

Machine postage-paid impression in red on unwatermarked phosphorised paper with grey-green background design.

### Two Value Types (All values)

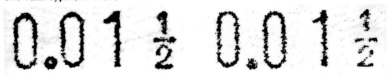

Type I                                    Type II

Type I. The 0 appears broad and the serif to 1 is solid.
Type II. The 0 is less broad and the serif to 1 appears to be curved at the top.

Types I and II came from the packs sold by the Philatelic Bureau and Type II came from the vending machines. Prices are the same for either type.

The following combinations were sold in "packs" (inscribed transparent envelopes) by the Philatelic Bureau and at philatelic counters.

| | | | | |
|---|---|---|---|---|
| YPP1 | Set of 3 values (1.5.84) | 3½p., 12½p., 16p. | 4·00 | 4·50 |
| YPP2 | Set of 32 values (1.5.84) | ½p. to 16p. | 28·00 | 30·00 |
| YPP3 | Set of 2 values (28.8.84) | 16½p., 17p. | 3·00 | 3·50 |

**1984.  IMPERFORATE. PVAD GUM**

| | | | | | | |
|---|---|---|---|---|---|---|
| Y1 | **Y1** | 1.5.84 | ½p. | | 25 | 40 |
| | | | *a.* No value* | | 45·00 | |
| | | | *b.* White paper | | £100 | |
| Y2 | | 1.5.84 | 1p. | | 30 | 45 |
| | | | *a.* White paper | | £100 | |
| Y3 | | 1.5.84 | 1½p. | | 35 | 50 |
| Y4 | | 1.5.84 | 2p. | | 40 | 55 |
| | | | *a.* White paper | | £100 | |
| Y5 | | 1.5.84 | 2½p. | | 45 | 60 |
| Y6 | | 1.5.84 | 3p. | | 50 | 65 |
| | | | *b.* Printed on the gum | | £300 | |
| Y7 | | 1.5.84 | 3½p. | | 55 | 70 |
| Y8 | | 1.5.84 | 4p. | | 60 | 75 |
| Y9 | | 1.5.84 | 4½p. | | 65 | 80 |
| Y10 | | 1.5.84 | 5p. | | 70 | 85 |
| Y11 | | 1.5.84 | 5½p. | | 75 | 90 |
| Y12 | | 1.5.84 | 6p. | | 80 | 95 |
| Y13 | | 1.5.84 | 6½p. | | 85 | 1·00 |
| Y14 | | 1.5.84 | 7p. | | 90 | 1·10 |
| Y15 | | 1.5.84 | 7½p. | | 95 | 1·10 |
| Y16 | | 1.5.84 | 8p. | | 1·00 | 1·25 |
| Y17 | | 1.5.84 | 8½p. | | 1·10 | 1·25 |
| Y18 | | 1.5.84 | 9p. | | 1·10 | 1·25 |
| Y19 | | 1.5.84 | 9½p. | | 1·25 | 1·40 |
| Y20 | | 1.5.84 | 10p. | | 1·25 | 1·40 |
| Y21 | | 1.5.84 | 10½p. | | 1·25 | 1·40 |
| Y22 | | 1.5.84 | 11p. | | 1·40 | 1·50 |
| Y23 | | 1.5.84 | 11½p. | | 1·40 | 1·50 |
| Y24 | | 1.5.84 | 12p. | | 1·40 | 1·60 |
| Y25 | | 1.5.84 | 12½p. | | 1·50 | 1·60 |
| | | | *a.* White paper | | £100 | |
| | | | *b.* Printed on the gum | | £225 | |
| Y26 | | 1.5.84 | 13p. | | 1·50 | 1·60 |
| | | | *b.* Printed on the gum | | £300 | |
| Y27 | | 1.5.84 | 13½p. | | 1·50 | 1·60 |
| Y28 | | 1.5.84 | 14p. | | 1·50 | 1·60 |
| Y29 | | 1.5.84 | 14½p. | | 1·60 | 1·75 |
| Y30 | | 1.5.84 | 15p. | | 1·60 | 1·75 |
| Y31 | | 1.5.84 | 15½p. | | 1·60 | 1·75 |
| Y32 | | 1.5.84 | 16p. | | 1·75 | 1·90 |
| | | | *a.* White paper | | | |
| | | | *b.* Printed on the gum | | £225 | |
| Y33 | | 28.8.84 | 16½p. | | 1·75 | 2·00 |
| | | | *b.* Printed on the gum | | £300 | |
| Y34 | | 28.8.84 | 17p. | | 1·75 | 2·00 |
| | | | *b.* Printed on the gum | | £300 | |

*Instead of a printed value No. Y1*a* shows "0·00" in error.

The labels printed on plain white paper came from a machine in which an engineer had left this paper in the machine by mistake. The error was quickly discovered but not before a quantity of labels were sold.

The labels printed on the gum side only came from a roll of paper which was placed in a machine incorrectly.

**WITHDRAWN**   No. YPP1, 28.6.85, Nos. YPP2/3, April 1986

# First Day Cover

YFD1 (1.5.84)        3½p., 12½p., 16p.        6·50

The Philatelic Bureau only serviced first day covers bearing the 3½p., 12½p. and 16p. labels on 1 May 1984 although first day boxes were provided for collectors to post covers with all values. No first day cover facilities were available for the 16½p. and 17p. values on 28 August 1984.

# SECTION ZB
## Postage Due Stamps

### 1970–84. Photogravure

## General Notes

**INTRODUCTION.** These stamps fulfil two functions: to collect amounts payable to the postman by the addressee on mail which is unstamped or under franked and for the collection of customs charges (including purchase tax or value added tax) on mail from abroad. For this reason the old inscription "POSTAGE DUE" has been superseded by "TO PAY".

This accounts for the need for a £5 value (introduced in 1973) but it is understood that this is also needed for the collection of postage due from time to time when incoming overseas parcels have unwittingly been underpaid as a result of the wrong setting of a meter franking machine in a business firm and is probably more frequently used to collect postage due on parcels returned to sender from abroad, often at air mail rates.

**PRINTERS.** All the decimal Postage Due stamps were printed in photogravure by Harrison & Sons.

**PAPER AND GUM.** As with the Machin definitive issues original printings were on ordinary coated paper with PVA gum followed in 1973/74 by fluorescent coated paper with PVA gum and from 1974 on the same paper but with PVAD gum. In June/August 1980 the 10p. and 20p. values were issued, on phosphorised (fluorescent coated) paper with PVAD gum, which had been used in error. For further particulars see the General Notes to Section UD.

**PERFORATION.** All stamps are perforated 14 × 15. Perforation Types A (T) and RE have been used (see Appendix I).

**DATES OF ISSUE.** Actual dates of issue are quoted for each value on its first appearance but as no official dates were announced for the changes in paper and gum the earliest reported dates to the nearest month are given.

**SHEET MARKINGS.** These are described at the end of each issue and illustrations of them are shown at the end of the General Notes to Section UD.

Z3

Z4

(Des. Jeffery Matthews)

### 1970–76. CHALKY PAPER. PERF. 14 × 15
#### A. ORIGINAL COATED PAPER. PVA GUM

| | | | | | | | | | | | |
|---|---|---|---|---|---|---|---|---|---|---|---|
| Z48 | D77 | **Z3** | 15.2.71 | ½p. turquoise-blue.. | .. | .. | .. | .. | .. | 10 | 20 |
| Z49 | — | | 15.2.71 | 1p. deep reddish purple | .. | .. | .. | .. | .. | 20 | 15 |
| Z50 | — | | 15.2.71 | 2p. myrtle-green | .. | .. | .. | .. | .. | 20 | 15 |
| Z51 | — | | 15.2.71 | 3p. ultramarine | .. | .. | .. | .. | .. | 40 | 25 |
| Z52 | D81 | | 15.2.71 | 4p. yellow-brown .. | .. | .. | .. | .. | .. | 15 | 15 |
| Z53 | — | | 15.2.71 | 5p. violet .. | .. | .. | .. | .. | .. | 60 | 25 |
| Z54 | — | **Z4** | 17.6.70 | 10p. carmine | .. | .. | .. | .. | .. | 80 | 30 |
| Z55 | – | | 17.6.70 | 20p. olive-brown | .. | .. | .. | .. | .. | 1·25 | 50 |
| Z56 | — | | 17.6.70 | 50p. ultramarine | .. | .. | .. | .. | .. | 2·50 | 40 |
| Z57 | — | | 17.6.70 | £1 black .. | .. | .. | .. | .. | .. | 4·00 | 60 |

**Cylinder Numbers (Blocks of Six)**
Perforation Type A (T)

| Value | Cyl. No. | | | | No dot | Value | Cyl. No. | | | | No dot |
|---|---|---|---|---|---|---|---|---|---|---|---|
| ½p. | 2 | .. | .. | .. | 75 | 5p. | 8 | .. | .. | .. | 9·00 |
| 1p. | 1 | .. | .. | .. | 1·50 | 10p. | 2 | .. | .. | .. | 6·00 |
| 2p. | 1 | .. | .. | .. | 1·50 | 20p. | 2 | .. | .. | .. | 10·00 |
| 3p. | 2 | .. | .. | .. | 3·00 | 50p. | 1 | .. | .. | .. | 20·00 |
| 4p. | 3 | .. | .. | .. | 1·25 | £1 | 2 | .. | .. | .. | 30·00 |
| 5p. | 4 | .. | .. | .. | £400 | | | | | | |

## B. FLUORESCENT COATED PAPER. PVA GUM

| | | | | | | | | | | |
|---|---|---|---|---|---|---|---|---|---|---|
| Z58 | — | **Z3** | 10.74 | 1p. deep reddish purple | .. | .. | .. | .. | .. | 40 |
| Z59 | — | | 10.74 | 3p. ultramarine | .. | .. | .. | .. | .. | 2·10 |
| Z60 | — | | 2.74 | 5p. violet .. | .. | .. | .. | .. | .. | 2·10 |
| Z61 | — | **Z4** | 12.74 | 10p. carmine | .. | .. | .. | .. | .. | 55·00 |
| Z62 | — | | 10.74 | 20p. olive-brown | .. | .. | .. | .. | .. | 60·00 |
| | | | | a. Bent frame | .. | .. | | .. | .. | 70·00 |
| Z63 | D89 | | 2.4.73 | £5 orange-yellow and black | | .. | | .. | .. | 20·00 |

**Cylinder Numbers (Blocks of Six)**
Perforation Type A (T)

| Value | Cyl. No. | | | | No dot | Value | Cyl. No. | | | | No dot |
|---|---|---|---|---|---|---|---|---|---|---|---|
| 1p. | 1 | .. | .. | .. | 4·00 | 10p. | 2 | .. | .. | .. | £450 |
| 3p. | 2 | .. | .. | .. | 18·00 | 20p. | 1 | .. | .. | .. | £600* |
| 5p. | 8 | .. | .. | .. | 18·00 | £5 | 1A (black) –2B (orange-yellow) | | | | £100 |

## C. FLUORESCENT COATED PAPER. PVAD GUM

| | | | | | | | | | | | No dot | |
|---|---|---|---|---|---|---|---|---|---|---|---|---|
| Z64 | D78 | **Z3** | 12.74 | 1p. deep reddish purple | .. | .. | .. | .. | .. | 10 | 15 | |
| Z65 | D79 | | 12.74 | 2p. myrtle-green | .. | .. | .. | .. | .. | 10 | 15 | |
| Z66 | D80 | | 6.75 | 3p. ultramarine | .. | .. | .. | .. | .. | 15 | 10 | |
| Z67 | — | | 1.78 | 4p. yellow-brown .. | .. | .. | .. | .. | .. | 30 | 30 | |
| Z68 | D82 | | 1.76 | 5p. violet .. | .. | .. | .. | .. | .. | 20 | 20 | |
| Z69 | D83 | | 21.8.74 | 7p. red-brown | .. | .. | .. | .. | .. | 35 | 45 | |
| Z70 | D84 | **Z4** | 3.75 | 10p. carmine | .. | .. | .. | .. | .. | 30 | 20 | |
| | | | | a. Cylinder crack (*horiz. pair*) | .. | | .. | .. | .. | 5·00 | | |
| Z71 | D85 | | 18.6.75 | 11p. slate-green | .. | .. | .. | .. | .. | 50 | 60 | |
| Z72 | D86 | | 2.5.74 | 20p. olive-brown | .. | .. | .. | .. | .. | 60 | 50 | |
| | | | | a. Bent frame | .. | .. | | .. | .. | 3·00 | | |
| Z73 | D87 | | 12.74 | 50p. ultramarine | .. | .. | .. | .. | .. | 1·50 | 40 | |
| Z74 | D88 | | 3.75 | £1 black .. | .. | .. | .. | .. | .. | 2·75 | 60 | |
| Z75 | — | | 11.78 | £5 orange-yellow and black | .. | | .. | .. | .. | 25·00 | 2·00 | |

**Cylinder Numbers (Blocks of Six)**
Perforation Type A (T)

| Value | Cyl. No. | | | | No dot | Value | Cyl. No. | | | | No dot |
|---|---|---|---|---|---|---|---|---|---|---|---|
| 1p. | 1 | .. | .. | .. | 1·50 | 7p. | 1A | .. | .. | .. | 2·50 |
| | 2 | .. | .. | .. | 1·40 | 10p. | 2 | .. | .. | .. | 10·00* |
| 2p. | 1 | .. | .. | .. | 1·60 | 11p. | 1A | .. | .. | .. | 4·00 |
| | 2 | .. | .. | .. | 1·75 | 20p. | 1 | .. | .. | .. | 7·00 |
| 3p. | 2 | .. | .. | .. | 1·00 | | 2 | .. | .. | .. | 5·00 |
| | 3 | .. | .. | .. | 15·00 | 50p. | 1 | .. | .. | .. | 12·00 |
| 4p. | 3 | .. | .. | .. | 12·00 | | 2 | .. | .. | .. | 18·00† |
| | 4 | .. | .. | .. | 2·50 | £1 | 1 | .. | .. | .. | 20·00 |
| 5p. | 8 | .. | .. | .. | 1·75 | | 2 | .. | .. | .. | 25·00 |
| | | | | | | £5 | 1A (black)–2B (orange-yellow) | | | | £150 |

Perforation as Type A (T) but with left margin perforated through

| 1p. | 2 | .. | .. | .. | 1·00 | 7p. | 1A | .. | .. | .. | 4·50 |
|---|---|---|---|---|---|---|---|---|---|---|---|
| 2p. | 1 | .. | .. | .. | 1·50 | 10p. | 2 | .. | .. | .. | £150 |
| 4p. | 3 | .. | .. | .. | 5·00 | £1 | 2 | .. | .. | .. | 20·00 |
| 5p. | 4 | .. | .. | .. | 3·50 | £5 | 1A (black)–2B (orange-yellow) | | | | £180 |

The 10p. Cyl. 2, 20p. Cyl. 1 and 50p. Cyl. 1 also exist Perf. as Type A (T) but with right margin perforated through.

† There are two separate cylinder numbers and the price quoted is for a block from the upper or lower left of the sheet.

## D. PHOSPHORISED (FLUORESCENT COATED) PAPER. PVAD GUM.

| | | | | | | | | | | |
|---|---|---|---|---|---|---|---|---|---|---|
| Z76 | — | **Z4** | 6.80 | 10p. carmine | .. | .. | .. | .. | .. | 30 |
| Z77 | — | | 6.80 | 20p. olive-brown | .. | .. | .. | .. | .. | 1·25 |

**Cylinder Numbers (Blocks of Six)**

Perforation Type A (T)

| Value | Cyl. No. | | | | No dot |
|-------|----------|--|--|--|--------|
| 10p. | 1 .. | .. | .. | .. | 3·50 |
| 20p. | 2 .. | .. | .. | .. | 15·00 |

Nos. Z76/7 occurred as a result of the use of the wrong paper. The phosphor additive is the "yellow" type which gives a response under short and long-wave ultra violet light.

**CYLINDER VARIETIES**
**Listed Flaws**

|  |  |
|---|---|
| Z62*a*, Z72*a* | Z70*a* |
| Frame bent at upper left | Cylinder crack |
| (Cyl. 1, R. 2/3) | (Cyl. 2, R. 1/2–3) |

**Sheet Details**

Sheet sizes: 200 (20 × 10). Single pane sheet-fed

Sheet markings:
  Cylinder numbers:
    7p. and 11p. In top margin above vertical row 2, unboxed
    £5. In top margin above vertical rows 2/3, boxed
    Others: In top margin above vertical row 3, unboxed (10p. has an additional fainter cyl. No. 2 above vertical row 4) and the 50p. cyl. No. 2 has an additional cyl. number in the left margin opposite row 8)
  Guide holes: None
  Marginal arrows: At top, bottom and sides
  Colour register marks:
    £5. Crossed circle type in each corner of the sheet
    Others: None
  Coloured crosses:
    £5. Opposite rows 5/6, at both sides
    Others: Opposite rows 6/7, at both sides
  Additional coloured crosses: Additional temporary crosses were engraved on the cylinders and used for PVAD printings made on narrower paper to assist in trimming as follows:
    10p. Opposite rows 6/7 at both sides and nearer to stamps and another additional cross opposite row 3 at right
    20p. Opposite row 7 at left and rows 6/7 at right
    50p. As 10p. but without the cross opposite row 3 at right
  Sheet values: Above and below vertical rows 5/6 and 15/16 reading from left to right in top margin and from right to left (upside down) in bottom margin

**SOLD OUT**   ½p. 7.83; 1p. 1.83; 2p. and 3p. 6.84; 5p. 11.82; 11p. 11.83; £1 1.84

**WITHDRAWN**   4p., 7p., 10p., 20p., 50p., £5, 20.8.84

Z5                                          Z6
(Des. Sedley Place Design Limited)

## 1982 (9 JUNE). CHALKY PAPER. PERF. 14 × 15. FLUORESCENT COATED PAPER. PVAD GUM

| | | | | | | | | | | | | |
|---|---|---|---|---|---|---|---|---|---|---|---|---|
| Z78 | D90 | Z5 | 1p. lake .. | .. | .. | .. | .. | .. | .. | .. | 10 | 10 |
| Z79 | D91 | | 2p. bright blue .. | .. | .. | .. | .. | .. | .. | .. | 10 | 10 |
| | | | *a.* Retouched frame | .. | .. | .. | .. | .. | .. | .. | 2·00 | |
| Z80 | D92 | | 3p. deep mauve .. | .. | .. | .. | .. | .. | .. | .. | 10 | 15 |
| Z81 | D93 | | 4p. deep blue .. | .. | .. | .. | .. | .. | .. | .. | 10 | 20 |
| Z82 | D94 | | 5p. sepia .. | .. | .. | .. | .. | .. | .. | .. | 10 | 20 |
| Z83 | D95 | Z6 | 10p. light brown .. | .. | .. | .. | .. | .. | .. | .. | 15 | 25 |
| Z84 | D96 | | 20p. olive-green .. | .. | .. | .. | .. | .. | .. | .. | 30 | 30 |
| Z85 | D97 | | 25p. deep greenish blue .. | .. | .. | .. | .. | .. | .. | 40 | 70 |
| Z86 | D98 | | 50p. grey-black .. | .. | .. | .. | .. | .. | .. | 75 | 1·00 |
| | | | *a.* Retouch to top of Y | .. | .. | .. | .. | .. | .. | 3·00 | |
| Z87 | D99 | | £1 red .. | .. | .. | .. | .. | .. | .. | .. | 1·50 | 80 |
| Z88 | D100 | | £2 turquoise-blue | .. | .. | .. | .. | .. | .. | .. | 3·00 | 2·00 |
| Z89 | D101 | | £5 dull orange .. | .. | .. | .. | .. | .. | .. | 7·50 | 1·50 |

**Cylinder Numbers (Blocks of Six)**
Perforation Type RE
Single pane cylinders. Chambon press
(No dot panes only)

| Value | Cyl. No. | | Block of 8 | Block of 6 | Value | Cyl. No. | | Block of 8 | Block of 6 |
|---|---|---|---|---|---|---|---|---|---|
| 1p. | 4 | .. | 60 | 50 | 20p. | 3 | .. | 3·25 | 2·10 |
| 2p. | 4 | .. | 60 | 50 | 25p. | 1 | .. | 4·25 | 2·75 |
| 3p. | 4 | .. | 60 | 50 | 50p. | 3 | .. | 7·50 | 5·50 |
| 4p. | 5 | .. | 80 | 60 | £1 | 3 | .. | 15·00 | 11·00 |
| 5p. | 9 | .. | 80 | 60 | £2 | 1 | .. | 30·00 | 22·00 |
| 10p. | 4 | .. | 1·75 | 1·25 | £5 | 3 | .. | 70·00 | 50·00 |

The above are with sheets orientated with "To Pay" reading from left to right (1p. to 5p.) or at left reading down (others).

The 10p. value exists with a 3 hole extension in the left margin with the stamp orientated to left and "To Pay" reading down. The cylinder was 4 and it is believed that a reserve perforator comb was used on the Chambon press. *Price for upper block of 8 with gutter £275 and lower block of 6, £120.*

**CYLINDER VARIETIES**

**Listed Flaws**

Z79a                                    Z86a
Retouched frame at upper left        Retouch to top of Y
(Cyl. 4, pane position R. 1/7)       (Cyl. 3, pane position R. 6/10)

**Sheet Details**

Sheet sizes: 200 (2 identical panes 10 × 10 separated by a gutter margin). Single pane reel-fed
Sheet markings:
    Cylinder numbers: Bottom margin below R. 10/9 and R. 10/19, boxed
    Marginal arrows: At each corner of pane and central between horizontal rows 5/6 at both sides
    Sheet values: Above and below vertical rows 5/6 and 15/16 reading from left to right in top margin
        and from right to left (upside down) in bottom margin
    Trimming line: In the colour of the stamp between each pane

# Presentation Packs

ZPP1 No. 36 (3.11.71) (Sold at £2.00, later at
  £2.01½)                                    Nos. Z48/57   ..    ..    .. 10·00
  In September 1974 the 7p. was added to this pack and the price increased to £2·08½.

ZPP2 No. 93 (30.3.77) (Sold at £2·23½)       With 11p. added      ..    .. . 6·00
  The text was revised on Pack No. 93. As fresh supplies of the above packs were made up,
stamps on FCP/PVA and FCP/PVAD were included as available.
  For Postage Due stamps sold in slip-in wallet at foreign Philatelic Exhibitions, see note after
No. UPP3 at the end of Section UC.

ZPP3 No. 135 (9.6.82) (Sold at £9·40)        Nos. Z78/89   ..    ..    .. 14·00
  The presentation pack contains an illustrated brochure describing the history of the usage of
postage due stamps in Britain and abroad.

  Nos. Z54/7 also exist on black card printed in white: "The British Post Office/Special Labels to be
issued/17 June 1970/Decimal Currency To Pay Labels—Four values/10p. 20p. 50p. and £1/Designed
by/Jeffery Matthews MSIA/Printed by Harrison & Sons Ltd". The actual stamps were affixed and
embedded in plastic on both sides.
  The card was supplied with press releases to certain national newspapers but not to the philatelic
press. This practice was not repeated because the colours did not remain fast under the plastic.

**WITHDRAWN**   No. ZPP1, 9.76; No. ZPP2, 9.83

# APPENDIX I

## Perforators

### General Notes

**INTRODUCTION.** Basically, six kinds of perforating machines have been used for the decimal issues:—

(a) Grover sheet-fed machines employing a two-row comb (Types A, A(T), F* and F (L)*) or a single-row comb in the case of the high values (Type K). A few sheets are fed at a time so that the rate of output is comparatively low.

(b) A Swedish rotary cylinder machine known as the "lawnmower" perforator (Type R(S)). This is reel-fed by a separate operation.

(c) A German Kampf machine which is also a rotary cylinder and later became an integral part of the "Jumelle" press (Types R and RE). This perforates in the reel as fast as the stamps are printed.

(d) Bickel and German Gammerler sheet-fed machines employing a single-row comb (Type L).

(e) A two-row comb of single pane width used for sheets printed on the Chambon press. This perforates the sheets in the reel (Type RE).

(f) Replacement for the German Kampf machine known as the APS perforator after the name of the makers (Ab Produktion Services—the Swedish company which originally made this perforator). This is a rotary type perforator with pins which are designed to pierce the paper from the printed side. Surplus paper is removed from the gummed side by blades which are set in rollers. This perforates stamps in the reel (Type RE).

All, except (e) are able to perforate two panes side by side.

**GUIDE HOLES.** Perforation guide holes can be an indication of the type of perforator used and these are recorded, where known, following the sheet perforation characteristics for each type. For reasons unknown these may not always appear in the sheet margins.

**ORDER.** This Appendix is divided into five sections:

1. Low Value Definitive Stamps (including Coils, Regionals and Postage Due Stamps)
2. High Value Definitive Stamps
3. Stitched Booklet Panes
4. Folded Booklet Panes
5. Barcode Booklet Panes

### 1. Low Value Definitive Stamps

This section deals with the Machin small format definitives (including the coils), the Regionals and the Postage Due stamps.

**Type A.** Horizontal two-row comb. Sheet-fed.

| No dot and dot panes— | Top margin | Perforated through |
|---|---|---|
| | Bottom margin | Imperforate |
| | Left margin | A single extension hole |
| | Right margin | A single extension hole |
| | Guide holes | Opposite rows 14/15, at left (no dot panes) or right (dot panes) |

In this machine an appropriate number of sheets (usually six to eight) are impaled through the guide holes and they go forward together under the comb. The imperf. margin (at the bottom) indicates the point of entry.

**Type A (T).** Horizontal two-row comb. Sheet-fed.

| Single pane printing— | Top margin | Imperforate |
|---|---|---|
| | Bottom margin | Perforated through |
| | Left margin | A single extension hole |
| | Right margin | A single extension hole |
| | Guide holes | None |

This is simply a top (T) instead of a bottom feed of Type A. In the definitive issues it occurs only in the first issue of the Postage Due stamps.

Variations of this perforator with the left or right margin perforated through and the opposite margin with a single extension hole occur. The printers state that to save making new perforator heads they have sometimes employed those previously used for perforating definitive stamps. We are not sure whether these constitute variants of Type A (T) but have listed them without allocating a Perforator Type.

**448**

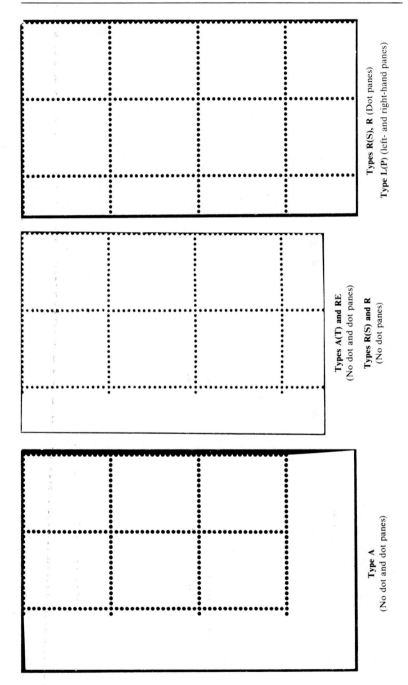

Types **R(S)**, **R** (Dot panes)
Type **L(P)** (left- and right-hand panes)

Types **A(T)** and **RE**
(No dot and dot panes)
Types **R(S)** and **R**
(No dot panes)

Type **A**
(No dot and dot panes)

# APPENDIX I  Perforators—Low Values

**Type R(S).** Horizontal rotary cylinder. Reel-fed.

| No dot panes— | | |
|---|---|---|
| | Top margin | Perforated through |
| | Bottom margin | Perforated through |
| | Left margin | A single extension hole |
| | Right margin | Perforated through |
| | Guide holes | None |

| Dot panes— | | |
|---|---|---|
| | Top margin | Perforated through |
| | Bottom margin | Perforated through |
| | Left margin | Perforated through |
| | Right margin | A single extension hole |
| | Guide holes | None |

Sheets in the reel are drawn over a cylinder containing short pins which push up pimples from the undersurface which are then shaved off, hence the nickname "lawnmower". It did not work satisfactorily with stamps with PVA gum and was at first used only for the £.s.d. and decimal ordinary and multi-value coils, which have gum arabic.

Later it was pressed into use for decimal sheet issues in order to cope with the demand and for these gum arabic had to be brought back into use. Occasionally rows of stamps went through without being perforated which accounts for the imperforate stamps listed. Moreover the pins frequently broke off or became worn and had to be replaced. Thus blind perforations are common from this perforator. An additional part, extension hole ("¼ Moon") can sometimes be found in the left or right margin.

**Type R.** Horizontal rotary cylinder. Reel-fed.

This produces the same perforation types as Type R(S).

It is an integral part of the "Jumelle" (or twin) press introduced by Harrisons in 1972 and so called because it can print stamps in a combination of the recess and photogravure processes. This German Kampf perforator consists of a large cylinder which perforates the sheets in the reel as soon as they are printed.

Different sized perforating cylinders are used according to the sheet size and format etc., including Special issues and sheets for booklets and ordinary and multi-value coils.

The Machin sheet stamps are printed from double-pane cylinders of 20 rows, each sheet being separated in the reel by a stamp-size gutter. The sheets were divided by a rotary knife. Occasionally a sheet missed the rotary knife and had to be guillotined along the perforations, giving rise to stamps *se-tenant* vertically with blank labels but containing the marginal bars.

For sheet stamps the perforating cylinder, or drum, has 48 rows of pins. On its introduction in 1973 one of the rows of pins had an extra pin on each side giving an extra extension hole in the left margin of the no dot sheets and in the right margin of the dot sheets. The purpose is to make it easier to locate faulty pins, hence it is called a marker pin. The pin on the left side disappeared late in 1975, reappeared early 1977 and disappeared again in the autumn of 1978. It is assumed there are two drums, one without the left marker pin, and that each is periodically taken out of service for repair. Early in 1980 two further pins were added to a drum to give a single extension hole in both sides of the no dot and dot panes.

With each revolution of the perforating drum the extra extension holes appear in a different position in the second or third sheet in the sequence and as there can be either two or three stamp-sized gutters within a single revolution the extension holes occur under both even and odd numbered rows. There are three possible sequences (or Setting) depending upon the starting position of the drum, as follows:—

| Sheet No. | 1 | 2 | 3 | 4 | 5 | 6 | 7 | 8 | 9 | 10 | 11 | 12 | 13 | 14 | 15 | 16 | 17 |
|---|---|---|---|---|---|---|---|---|---|---|---|---|---|---|---|---|---|
| Setting 1: Ext. hole in Row | 1 | – | 7 | – | 13 | – | 19 | – | – | 4 | – | 10 | – | 16 | – | – | 1 |
| Setting 2: Ext. hole in Row | 2 | – | 8 | – | 14 | – | 20 | – | – | 5 | – | 11 | – | 17 | – | – | 2 |
| Setting 3: Ext. hole in Row | 3 | – | 9 | – | 15 | – | 21 | – | – | 6 | – | 12 | – | 18 | – | – | 3 |

Thus if all the settings are used the extra extension holes can be found in every row of the sheet, but the three settings are not always used for every listed stamp.

So far as cylinder blocks are concerned, Setting 1 gives the extra hole on no dot blocks in row 19, Setting 2 in row 20 and Setting 3 in rows 18 or 21. These are, of course, collectable items and worth a premium but since they are not representative of a different perforator we do not list them.

Further information on this subject can be found in articles by Mr. F. D. Wild and Dr. C. Pennington in the January and December 1977 issues of *Guidec*, published by The British Decimal Stamps Study Circle.

## Type RE

In 1976 the horizontal pins across the interpane margin on the rotary cylinder were removed giving a single extension hole in the right margin of the no dot pane and the same in the left margin of the dot pane. Hence the perforations of the no dot and dot panes are the same. This was done as an economy measure to reduce the total number of pins which are liable to become bent or broken.

As the Type RE no dot cylinder number blocks have the same perforations as the Type R no dot cylinder blocks it follows that where printings exist of the same cylinder numbers in Types R and RE prices for each are identical.

In 1982 a Swedish style rotary perforator was introduced which eventually replaced the German Kampf machine. Known as the APS machine this is an improved "lawnmower" type perforator which has blades in a cylinder to shave surplus perforation matter from the gummed side of the reel. The perforator has 26 rows with extension pins at each side of the pane. The perforator type remained the same as previously (Type RE). This machine originally did not have the extension marker pins but they were introduced early in 1989.

(ii)  Chambon printings.

Horizontal two-row comb. Reel-fed.

This perforator was used for the 10p. orange-brown and 1982 postage due issues, printed by the Chambon press. In this machine the continuous web of paper advances under the comb in a single thickness and without interruption, hence both top and bottom margins are perforated through. The perforation characteristics are identical to those produced by the rotary perforator except there are no marker pins.

**Type F\*.** Vertical two-row comb. Sheet-fed.

| No dot panes— | Top margin | A single extension hole |
|---|---|---|
| | Bottom margin | A single extension hole |
| | Left margin | Perforated through |
| | Right margin | Perforated through |
| | Guide holes | None |
| Dot panes— | Top margin | A single extension hole |
| | Bottom margin | A single extension hole |
| | Left margin | Perforated through |
| | Right margin | Imperforate |
| | Guide holes | None |

This perforator has only been used for the 5p. and 7½p. Regional issues.

**Type F (L)\*.** Vertical two-row comb. Sheet-fed.

| No dot panes— | Top margin | A single extension hole |
|---|---|---|
| | Bottom margin | A single extension hole |
| | Left margin | Imperforate |
| | Right margin | Perforated through |
| | Guide holes | Above and below eighth vertical row |
| Dot panes— | Top margin | A single extension hole |
| | Bottom margin | A single extension hole |
| | Left margin | Perforated through |
| | Right margin | Perforated through |
| | Guide holes | None (occur on no dot panes *only*) |

This perforator has only been used for 5p. Scottish and Welsh Regional stamps.

The 8p printed by Enschedé was perforated in the reel by a perforator producing the characteristics Type F(L)\* but without guide holes.

**Type L(I) and L(P).** Vertical comb. Sheet-fed. Left feed.

| Left-hand panes— | Top margin | Perforated through |
|---|---|---|
| | Bottom margin | Perforated through |
| | Left margin | Imperforate |
| | Right margin | Perforated through |
| | Guide holes | None |
| Right-hand panes— | Top margin | Perforated through |
| | Bottom margin | Perforated through |
| | Left margin | Perforated through |
| | Right margin | Perforated through |
| | Guide holes | None |

This perforator has only been used for the Machin stamps printed by lithography (Sections UG and XC).

**Type L(I)** (*right feed*)

During 1987 the sheets were perforated from the right which gave identical perforation characteristics except the left margin is perforated through (P) and the right margin of a double pane printing was imperforate (I). This change only applies to the ordinary and regional stamps printed by Questa and makes all plate blocks perf. type (P).

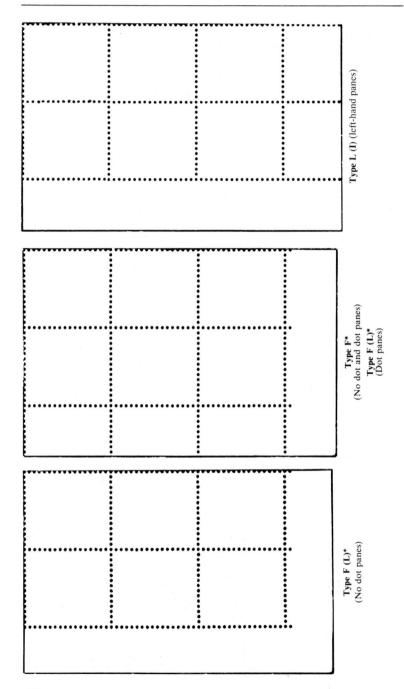

# APPENDIX I   Perforators—Table of Types for Low Values

## TABLE OF LOW VALUE PERFORATION TYPES

For ease of reference the perforation types described on the previous pages are shown here in tabular form.

| Perforation Type | Top margin | Bottom margin | Left margin | Right margin |
|---|---|---|---|---|
| **Type A** (*bottom feed*) | Perforated through | Imperforate | Single extension hole | Single extension hole |
| **Type A (T)** (*top feed*) | Imperforate | Perforated through | Single extension hole | Single extension hole |
| **Types R(S) and R** | | | | |
| No dot | Perforated through | Perforated through | Single extension hole | Perforated through |
| Dot | Perforated through | Perforated through | Perforated through | Single extension hole |
| **Type RE** No dot and dot | Perforated through | Perforated through | Single extension hole | Single extension hole |
| **Type F\*** (*right feed*) | | | | |
| No dot | Single extension hole | Single extension hole | Perforated through | Perforated through |
| Dot | Single extension hole | Single extension hole | Perforated through | Imperforate |
| **Type F (L)\*** (*left feed*) | | | | |
| No dot | Single extension hole | Single extension hole | Imperforate | Perforated through |
| Dot | Single extension hole | Single extension hole | Perforated through | Perforated through |
| **Type L** | | | | |
| Left-hand pane | Perforated through | Perforated through | Imperforate | Perforated through |
| Right-hand pane | Perforated through | Perforated through | Perforated through | Perforated through |

\*The asterisks are retained in the above Types to distinguish them from Types F and F (L) which are used only in Vol. 3.

Postage Due stamps. See also the variants of Type A (T) described under that Type.

### Perforation Type RE

**Perforation Variety.** A single additional pin was inserted on one APS perforation drum by Harrisons. It is probable that this was an error and does not have any operating function nor can it be identified as a marker pin. *The variety does not occur on every sheet and only one drum was responsible.* The extra pin occurs once every 26 rows between columns 1 and 2 on the dot panes only. It produces a stamp with 17 perfs instead of the normal 16. Since the variety was probably due to a repair to the drum we list both ordinary and cylinder blocks of six since these are the block sizes most frequently offered.

The broken pins or blocks showing the marker pin described below types R and RE are outside the scope of this Catalogue.

## 2. High Value Definitive Stamps

### Recess-printed Issues  1970–74

The following type applies to the recess-printed 10p., 20p., 50p. and £1 stamps listed in Section UC.

**Type K.** Horizontal single-row comb. Sheet-fed.

Single pane printings—

| | |
|---|---|
| Top margin | Perforated through |
| Bottom margin | Imperforate |
| Left margin | Perforated through |
| Right margin | Perforated through |
| Guide holes | None |

Double pane printings—    As above except that where a single width comb head has been used guide holes are found opposite row 6

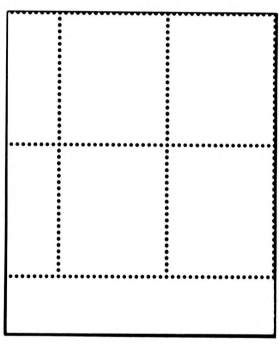

**Type K**

The illustration is taken from the bottom-left corner of the sheet although the plate number appears in the bottom-right corner.

### Photogravure Issues 1977–87

The £1 to £5 photogravure stamps were perforated as Type R* which was an adaptation of the rotary perforator used for the low value definitive issues.

**Type R\***. Horizontal rotary cylinder. Reel-fed.

No dot and dot panes (with stamps sideways, Crown to left)

| | |
|---|---|
| Top margin | Perforated through |
| Inter-pane gutter | Perforated through |
| Bottom margin | Perforated through |
| Left margin | A single extension hole |
| Right margin | A single extension hole |
| Guide holes | None |

Machin high value stamps were printed sideways with the head to left and at first were perforated by a German Kampf machine. This had a rotary cylinder which later became an integral part of the "Jumelle" press. This perforated in the reel as fast as the stamps were printed. Until 1982 it was the standard perforator used for all the Special issues and high value Machin photogravure stamps which appeared in Post Office sheets containing two panes of 50 stamps separated by an inter-pane gutter margin.

The Kampf and the later APS rotary machines produced perforation type R\*. Additional high values between £1·30 and £1·60 were perforated on the APS perforator.

**INTER-PANE GUTTER MARGINS.** The reason for the gutter margins arises from the need to relate the circumference of the perforating drum to that of the printing cylinders. Since the stamp size of the special issues had already been standardised to meet the requirements of the designers this could not be varied.

The circumference of the perforating drum for special issues was fixed at 45·15″. If it were to be any smaller the pins would enter the mating holes at an acute angle which would cause them to be bent or possibly broken. The ratio of the circumference of the perforating drum to that of the printing cylinders was fixed at 4 : 7 so that the circumference of the printing cylinders had to be 45·15″ × 4/7 = 25·8″.

With standard-sized horizontal format special issues the vertical measurement of complete sheets of 200 would be 23·6″, leaving a gap of 2·2″. Therefore the stamp images had to be spaced evenly round the cylinders in four panels of 50 stamps separated by gutter margins to take account of the 2·2″ gap (Machin vertical format stamps were printed sideways).

Thus with each revolution of the perforating drum seven panes of 50 stamps are perforated in precise register with the printed design. The reel is then guillotined to produce counter sheets of 100 stamps in two panes of 50. Further information is contained in the *Philatelic Bulletin* for April 1978, from which this information was drawn.

Gutter margin pairs, like other multiples from special positions in the sheet, are outside the scope of this catalogue. We list the cylinder blocks because of the information they give and for identifying the perforators.

**Extension or Marker Pins.** As with Type R for the Machin issues, extra pins were introduced on the perforating drum to help with the location of damaged pins and, whilst the extra holes are in theory liable to occur anywhere in the sheet margins, they are in practice to be found only at the corners or gutter margins. They are collectable items and worth a premium but are outside the scope of this catalogue since they are not representative of a different perforator.

Unlike the Machin definitives, where the intersheet gutter is the height of one stamp and the no dot and dot sheets are printed side by side, in the high value Machin photogravure stamps the gutter margins were not the height of a stamp, and the no dot and dot cylinders were placed one below the other.

Thus if an extra extension pin exists on the perforation drum on "perforation" pane 1 and this coincides with printed pane 1 at the start of a run, the extra extension hole will reappear seven panes later at pane 8, 15 etc. As the ratio of the perforating drum to the ink cylinders is seven panes to four, the exact sequence will recommence at sheet 15 with pane 29. This is demonstrated by the following diagram:—

Pane No.          Layout          Position of
                                  extra holes

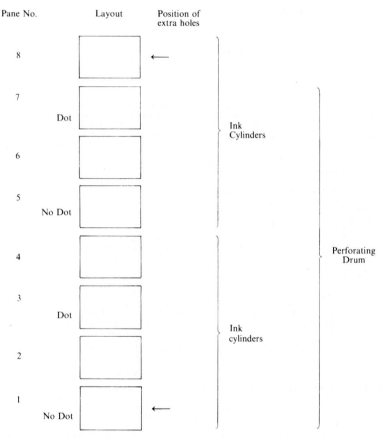

| Pane No. | | |
|---|---|---|
| 8 | | ⟵ |
| 7 | Dot | |
| 6 | | |
| 5 | No Dot | |
| 4 | | |
| 3 | Dot | |
| 2 | | |
| 1 | No Dot | ⟵ |

Ink Cylinders

Ink cylinders

Perforating Drum

Taking this a stage further it will be seen that the positions of the extra extension holes will be as follows:—

| No dot | Lower pane | Pane 1 |
| Dot | Upper pane | Pane 8 |
| Dot | Lower pane | Pane 15 |
| No dot | Upper pane | Pane 22 |
| No dot | Lower pane | Pane 29 etc. |

The same sequence of occurrence may be applied for the repetition of such other perforating irregularities as bent or broken pins.

For this information we are indebted to a further article by Mr. F. D. Wild and one by Mr. P. Daniels, in the May 1978 issue of *Guidec*, published by The British Decimal stamps Study Circle.

### Castles Recess-printed Issue 1988–90
Plate blocks from the bottom left corner of the sheet are as Type RE and horizontal and vertical gutter margins are perforated through.

## 3.   Stitched Booklet Panes

**(a) Se-tenant Panes of Four**

These were continuously printed in the reel in single-pane sheets of 240. The cylinders were laid down sideways to produce 24 rows of 10 stamps with a blank gutter every 25th row. The sheet of the ½p./2p. panes *se-tenant* vertically which is illustrated on the next page has had the selvedge at left trimmed to margin width, the top selvedge has been cut off and the right and bottom selvedge torn off.

In order to facilitate access to the bottom selvedge, which has to be torn off by hand a slanting scissor cut is made in the left-hand trimmed margin. This pane is termed "I(½v)". A few 1p./1½p. panes *se-tenant* horizontally are known with slanting cut at right.

The P panes can be further sub-divided into those cut by guillotine which produce a smooth edge (Ps) and those cut by rotary knife which have a rough edge (Pr) and these are illustrated below. Since these are methods of cutting and not different forms of perforation we do not list them separately (and this also applies to the panes of six). Moreover Pr panes can easily be converted to Ps panes by trimming but the converse is not possible.

The comb produces 1 I(½v) pane, 11 I panes and 48 P panes.

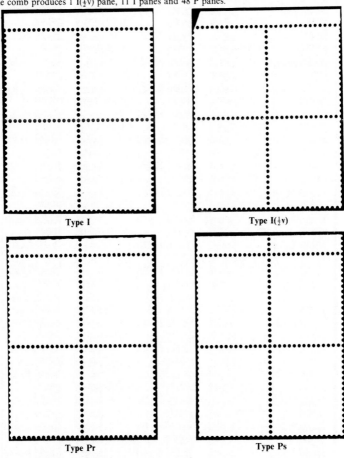

| | |
|---|---|
| **Type I** | **Type I(½v)** |
| **Type Pr** | **Type Ps** |

| | |
|---|---|
| **Type I** | Margin imperforate. Always cut smooth |
| **Type I(½v)** | Ditto but with slanting cut |
| **Type Pr** | Margin fully perforated through. Rough cut |
| **Type Ps** | Ditto but with smooth cut |

457

*Photo:* National Postal Museum.

A sheet of the ½p./2p. pane from 10p. Booklets with values arranged *se-tenant* vertically. The selvedge has been removed and the slanting cut can be seen at bottom left.

**(b) Panes of Six**

These were continuously printed in the reel in sheets of 480 images comprising two panes of 240 with a transverse gutter equal to one stamp in height. The right-hand pane with selvedge intact of the 2½p. with Esso/Stick label is illustrated.

The cylinder number occurs only in the left-hand pane against stamp R. 19/1.

As with the panes of four, the P panes occur with rough and smooth edges. We only quote separately for rough edges where they are worth more than smooth edges; otherwise prices are the same for each.

**First Perforator**

State 1 (I/P/I)

This was only for part of the printing of the 30p. Booklet of February 1971 (3p. with £4,315 For You label), producing I and P panes. Again it was necessary to make a slanting cut in the left and right margins of the sheet of 480 in order to tear off the bottom margin. The result is an I(½v) pane with cut at bottom from the left of the sheet and another with cut at top (since the pane is inverted) from the right of the sheet. This comb produced 2 I(½v) panes, 18 I panes and 60 P panes (40 rough and 20 smooth).

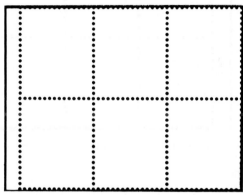

Type I

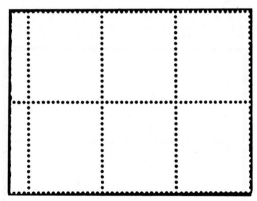

Type P

| | |
|---|---|
| **Type I** | Margin imperforate. Always cut smooth |
| **Type I(½v)** | Ditto with slanting cut at bottom or top. |
| **Type P** | Margin fully perforated through. Rough or smooth cut. |

**459**

State 2 (AP/P/AP)

To eliminate the need to make a slanting cut to facilitate tearing off the bottom selvedge, the comb was amended by adding three extra pins to extend the perforations in alternate rows (AP) into the left margin of the left-hand pane and the right margin of the right-hand pane.

It was used for part of the first printing of the 50p. Booklets and accounts for the existence of the very few reported AP panes of ½p. with Lick label and 2½p. with Tear Off label from the inverted position in the right sheet pane. One possible inverted 3p. with £4,315 For You label pane has also been reported AP so this amended perforator may have been used on part of the 30p. Booklets. The comb produced 20 AP panes and 60 P panes (40 rough and 20 smooth).

The 1st Perforator states were experimental in nature and occurred prior to the main perforation of the decimal booklet panes. State 2 had a very short life before being superseded by the main Second Perforator.

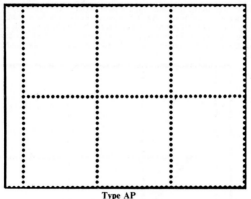

**Type AP**

**Type AP**   Margin fully perforated through in alternate rows. Always cut smooth

**Second Perforator**

State 1 (AP/P/APP)

A second perforator was brought into use which not only eliminated the slanting cut but also made it possible to remove the *right-hand* selvedge by tearing and also leave a binding margin. This had an AP perforation in the left-hand margin but the AP perforation in the right-hand margin was converted into a APP perforation by adding an extra vertical row of pins. To maintain the correct size of pane, the vertical perforations had to be misaligned half a perforation hole to the right and this made tearing difficult and trimming had to be resumed.

This perforator was used for the greater part of the initial editions of the 25p., 30p. and 50p. Booklets and for some later editions. It produced 10 AP panes, 60 P panes and 10 APP panes.

One of the heads suffered a broken pin in the extra row of vertical perforations opposite the imperf. row of horizontal perforations. This was not intentional and we do not list it.

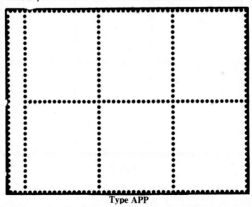

**Type APP**

**Type APP**   Perforated margin with alternate horizontal rows perforated through

*Photo:* National Postal Museum.
A right-hand pane of the 2½p. with Stick Firmly label before removal of selvedge. This shows P panes and APP panes at right.

**461**

State 2 (AP/P/APPa)

To enable tearing to be resumed a modification was made in the right-hand margin by substituting a large pin for a small one at the intersection of the perforated margins. Thus instead of there being three small horizontal holes in the margins there were two small holes and one large one (APPa).

This comb produced 10 AP panes, 60 P panes and 10 APPa panes.

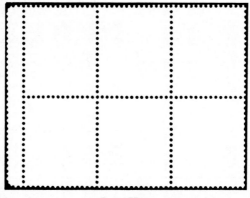

**Type APPa**

**Type APPa**  As Type APP but with two small holes and one large one instead of three small holes in the margin

State 3 (APPa/P/APPa)

Late in 1972 the left-hand comb head was converted from AP to APPa, producing panes exactly the same as those from the right-hand margin, apart from the direction of the printing.* This applies only to panes of six without labels (3p./2½p. *se-tenant* and 3p.) and it was done to make it easier to tear off the left-hand selvedge by leaving a perforated edge to the binding margin which facilitated knocking up the sheets prior to guillotining the assembled mass.

This comb produced 60 P and 20 APPa panes.

*See notes above "Wedgwood Booklet Panes".

**"Blind" Perforators**

In mid-1971 it was decided to modify the perforators used for panes with labels so by removing the vertical perforations between the labels and the binding margins. This was to prevent blind people from confusing labels with stamps.

For ease of reference and to distinguish the panes of the two main perforators the letter L, indicating label, has been incorporated in the perforator type headings.

State 1

(a) Panes with 1 label (APL/PL/APPL)

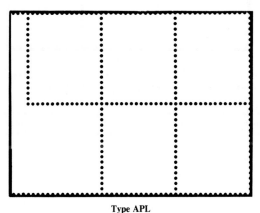

**Type APL**
As Type AP but imperforate between label and binding margin

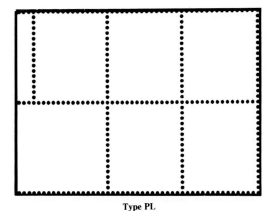

**Type PL**
As Type P but imperforate between label and rough or smooth
(*illustrated*) binding margin

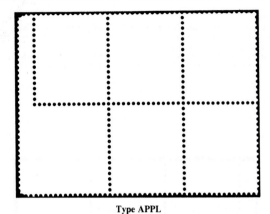

**Type APPL**
As Type APPa but imperforate between label and binding margin
This comb produced 10 APL panes, 60 PL panes and 10 APPL panes.

The small pin next to the large one broke off on one of the comb heads giving a very short imperforate section in the AP part of the APP panes, but this was quickly replaced. They occur on panes 3p. with £4,315 For You label and ½p. with Make Your Lucky label, but we do not list them.

(b) Panes with 2 labels (APLL/PLL/APPLL)

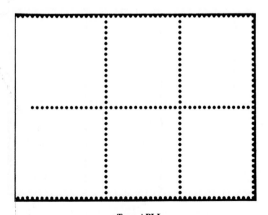

**Type APLL**
As Type AP but imperforate between two labels and binding margin

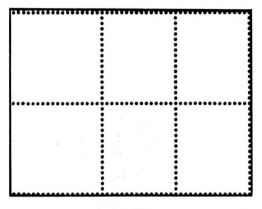

**Type PLL**
As Type P but imperforate between two labels and rough or smooth
(*illustrated*) binding margin

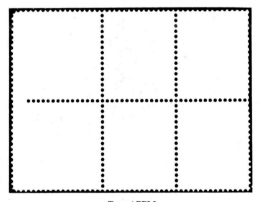

**Type APPLL**
As Type APPa but imperforate between two labels and binding margin
This comb produced 10 APLL panes, 60 PLL panes and 10 APPLL panes.

State 2

(a) Panes with 1 label (APPL/PL/APPL)
(b) Panes with 2 labels (APPLL/PLL/APPLL)

When the third state of the First Perforator was brought into use for the panes without labels (APPa/P/APPa) the "Blind" Perforators for the panes with one or two labels were similarly adapted to make it easier to tear off the left-hand selvedge and leave a perforated edge to the binding margin to facilitate knocking up prior to guillotining the assembled mass.

For the panes with one label the left-hand comb head was converted from APL to APPL producing panes identical with those of the right-hand margin, apart from the direction of the printing* (see next page). This perforator continued to be used for panes with blank labels.

This comb produced 60 PL panes and 20 APPL panes.

For the panes with two labels the left-hand comb head was converted from APLL to APPLL producing panes identical with those of the right-hand margin, apart from the direction of the printing.*

This comb produced 60 PLL panes and 30 APPLL panes.

*Some specialists distinguish between APPa panes from the left and right margins of the third state of the Second Perforator, and between APPL and APPLL panes from the left and right margins of the second state of the "Blind" Perforators. The difference lies in the *direction of the printing*. Left margin panes are described as being upright because they are upright as they move through the press, whilst right margin panes from both states are always inverted as they go through the press.

To determine the difference one has to examine the top and bottom frame lines through a powerful magnifying glass. The Bookmark Catalogue states that one edge will show the serrated edge of the screen reasonably clean while the opposite edge will be relatively blurred, with little "points" of ink spreading into the gutters. These "points" indicate the direction of the printing. If the clear edge of the stamp is at the top of the pane it was inverted in the uncut sheet (State 1). The reverse situation indicates State 2. This difference between upright and inverted panes of the same type is outside the scope of this catalogue; however this information is important in plating the position of panes containing varieties and flaws.

### Prestige Booklet Panes 1972–90

The stamps and stubs in the £1 Wedgwood Booklet were sheet-fed printed on a Linotype and Machinery No. 4 press, the panes being printed in four rows of three columns. They were perforated on the Grover machine with one comb being used for the three panes of 12 stamps and another for the pane of 6 stamps. Both combs produce I panes as can be seen from the reduced size illustrations of the panes in the text. The cylinder numbers appeared in the left selvedge opposite row 11 but were always trimmed off. The stub cylinders had no number.

The panes in the £3 Wedgwood Booklet were printed on a sheet-fed Rembrandt press and perforated on a Grover machine using two combs for the panes of 6 and 9 stamps. The uncut sheets were printed in four rows of three columns. Cylinder numbers were trimmed away but were placed above the first column in the top margin of each sheet.

The panes printed by Harrison in the £4 and £5 prestige booklets, were all printed on a sheet-fed Rembrandt press except the £5 Story of the P & O which was printed and perforated on the Jumelle press. The sheet-fed Grover machine was used to perforate the panes in the Stanley Gibbons booklet. The perforation characteristics on the panes containing 6 or 9 stamps do not differ and each pane is illustrated with the listing.

Panes of 6 or 9 stamps from the prestige £5 and £6 booklets printed in lithography by Questa have the same perforation characteristics as the Harrison panes although they are perforated on sheet-fed comb machines.

### The "Jumelle" Press

In 1974, the Jumelle press was first used for printing and perforating the 4½p. pane with blank label for the 45p. Booklets of September 1974. All previous perforating of booklet sheets had been done a few sheets at a time on Grover machines.

As indicated in the description of the R (Rotary) perforator used for the Machin sheet printings, this is a German Kampf machine which was an integral part of the "Jumelle" press, perforating stamps in the reel as they came off the machine.

The stamps were printed by a single-pane cylinder of 20 rows without any inter-sheet gutter. They were perforated by a cylinder of 32 rows' circumference giving "I" margins in all panes and with imperforate labels. This is described as Type IL.

There is a second extension pin in the left and right margins giving two panes with a single extension hole in every revolution to help in identifying the position of damaged pins. This is known as Type ILa. Although not strictly a different perforation type we list it, even though we do not list the similar extra extension hole found on sheets printed by the "Jumelle" press.

The cylinder thus produces two ILa panes and 62 IL panes in every revolution of sixty-four panes.

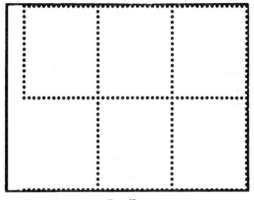

**Type IL**

Rough or smooth (*illustrated*) binding margin

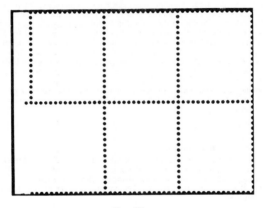

**Type ILa**

**Type IL** Imperforate margin with imperforate label

**Type ILa** As above but with single extension hole in middle row

A few early sheets containing 4½p. × 5 panes had the top and bottom selvedge torn off by hand, giving rise to IL(½v) and ILa(½v) types.

Miscut Panes

Some 3½p. × 5 centre band panes were miscut after perforation, resulting in the label being at the top.

This 32-row perforator drum with the extra marker pin has since come to be known as Perforator 1.

## 4.    Folded Booklet Panes

## A. Multi-value Booklet Panes

### (a) Vertical Panes of Six

For multi-value booklet panes of 6 with imperforate edges see Section 5. Barcode Booklets.

### Panes UMFB1/2 (½p. × 2, 1p. × 3, 6p.)

These panes for the Experimental Booklets were continuously printed in the reel on the "Jumelle" press. An illustration of an uncut sheet appears on the next page. The cylinders produce 36 panes at a single revolution, comprising three columns of twelve panes, printed sideways.

There are no horizontal margins. When looking at the illustration from the left the first column has the head facing left and the top margin perforated through. The second column has the head facing right and the margin is also perforated through. The third column has the head facing left and there is a single extension hole in the margin.

There are cutting lines in crimson at alternate rows and the left margin, containing the cylinder numbers and autotron marks, is trimmed off. The illustration shows a sheet which, if cut as shown with the cutting lines in the centre of the panes, would produce mis-cut panes.

In the issue for the June 1977 booklet the margins were trimmed much closer so that the cutting lines do not show in columns 1 and 2 and in consequence miscut panes are comparatively common.

The stamps were perforated on a perforating drum attached to the "Jumelle" machine in the usual manner. There is an extra pin on the drum for identifying damaged pins and this produces an extra extension hole in the binding margin in every 56th row as described for sheet Perforator Type R. As already indicated these extra extension hole types are outside the scope of this catalogue, although they are collected by specialists and are worth a premium. This has become to be known as Perforator 3 and it has been used, in various settings, for panes **UMFB1/7, 9/10** and **UMFB14/i5**. Further information about the various settings of this perforator is given in the June 1977 and November 1989 issues of *The Bookmark*.

The actual booklets are made on a Goebels machine which slits the reels of cover card and stamp panes and automatically attaches the pane of stamps to the cover, and then folds and cuts the booklet from the strip.

### Pane UMFB7 (½p. × 2, 1p. × 2, 7p., label)

On comparing the illustrations of uncut sheets of this pane and of Panes **UMFB1/2** it will be seen that the arrangement is the same except that there are now no cutting lines. The sheet, if cut as shown, would produce miscut panes with the postcode label on the left.

The perforator is the same and the extra marker pin produces the extra extension hole on the E pane in every 56th row.

### Panes UMFB19/20 (½p., 1p., 11½p. × 3, 14p.)

An illustration of an uncut sheet printed on the Chambon press, is shown on a following page. The stamps are arranged as in Pane **UMFB7** printed on the "Jumelle" press but reversed. The selvedge at both sides with single extension holes and the gutter is perforated through giving Perf. Type P. There is no need for a marker pin on the 2 row perforator attached to the Chambon press.

### Panes UMFB39 (1p. × 2, 12p. × 4), UMFB40/41 (1p., 5p. × 2, 13p. × 3), UMFB43/44 (13p., 18p. × 5) and UMFB46 (14p. × 2, 19p. × 4)

These panes were printed on the Chambon press and the uncut sheet is similar to Pane UMFB31. Each binding margin has a single extension hole giving Perf. Type E. Panes **UMFB41, 44** and **46** have one row of perforations removed at each side of the pane to give Perf. Type IEI.

### Pane UMLP1 (14p. × 2, 19p. × 4)

These panes were printed in lithography by Walsall on the "Favorit" press. For description of sheet make-up see Section UH. All panes were Perf. Type IPI.

## (b) Vertical Panes of Four
### Panes UMFB11/12 (1p. × 2, 8p., label)

These panes were printed on the "Jumelle" and the Chambon presses. An illustration of an uncut sheet printed on the "Jumelle" press is shown on a following page. The cylinders produce 48 panes at a single revolution, comprising four columns of twelve panes, printed sideways. The Chambon uncut sheet has four columns but because of the smaller diameter of the cylinder there are 32 panes in an uncut sheet. The first and third columns have the head facing down and the other columns have the head facing up. The left and right selvedge margins have one extension hole and these form the binding margins. There is a centre gutter margin perforated across which forms the P perf binding margins for panes in columns 2 and 3. The sheets were comb perforated in the reel and extra extension holes do not occur.

### Pane UMFB42 (1p., 13p., 18p. × 2), UMFB45 (19p. × 2, 14p. and label) and UMFB47 (15p. × 2, 20p., and label)

The uncut sheet contains three columns of panes. There is a stamp width margin between columns two and three with trimming lines opposite every second row of stamps. The cylinder numbers occur on the fifth pane from the left in each of the three columns and a single extension hole in the binding margin gives Perf. Type E or perforated through (Perf. Type P) on part of the printing of Pane **UMFB45**.

## (c) Vertical Panes of Ten
### Panes UMFB3/4 (½p. × 2, 1p. × 2, 6½p. × 2, 8½p. × 4)

These panes were continuously printed in the reel in two columns in much the same way as columns 2 and 3 of Panes **UMFB1/2**, as a comparison with the accompanying illustration will show.

Both panes have a single extension hole in the margin with the extra marker pin on the drum giving the extra extension hole every 56th row, so that the extra extension hole recurs every 28th book on sheets printed on the "Jumelle" press.

The only sheet markings which remain after the left selvedge has been trimmed are the cutting lines, which are printed in the colour of the 1p. value.

The phosphor bands are narrower, being 8 mm. wide, and every fourth band is broken at the bottom of the 1p. values so as to avoid the 6½p. values, leaving them with just one narrow band at one side or the other.

Thus this pair of panes provides five new basic stamps, the ½p., 1p. and 8½p. with 8 mm. phosphor bands and the 6½p. with narrow phosphor band at right or left.

## (d) Vertical Panes of Eight
### Panes UMFB5/6 (1p. × 2, 7p. × 3, 9p. × 3)

As will be seen from the illustration of an uncut pane which follows, the same arrangement as was employed for the panes of ten was adapted for these panes of eight stamps. The spaces previously used for the bottom rows of the 6½p./8½p. values were not printed on, leaving a gutter margin between the two columns. This gutter margin was then trimmed off leaving a narrow margin at the bottom of the panes which is perforated through. At one place under the 7p. stamps of each column horizontal cutting lines were printed and were subsequently trimmed off. The only surviving marginal markings are the normal cutting lines which are printed in the colour of the 7p. value.

The remarks above regarding the extra marker pin on the drum also apply here.

The 8 mm. phosphor bands were again applied to the 1p. value and, for the first time, to the 9p., whilst there are narrow phosphor bands on the 7p. at right or at left. Thus three new basic stamps are provided by these panes. As before every fourth phosphor band is broken below the 1p. stamps so as to avoid the 7p. value.

### Panes UMFB9/10 (2p. × 2, 8p. × 2, 10p. × 3, label) and UMFB14/17 (2p. × 3, 10p. × 2, 12p. × 2, label)

An uncut sheet of Panes **UMFB9/10** is illustrated and shows the label arrangement with the 2p. stamps. This sheet and Panes **UMFB14/15** from Booklet No. FB11 were printed on the "Jumelle" press. Both panes have a single extension hole in the margin and panes showing the extra marker pin occur.

The Chambon press was used for Panes **UMFB16/17** from Booklet Nos. FB12/3 and the uncut sheet has 16 rows of stamps arranged in two vertical columns separated by a single vertical gutter margin perforated through. This uncut sheet is illustrated on a following page for comparison with Panes **UMFB9/10** ("Jumelle" printing). Only Perf. Type E exist.

### Panes UMFB23/24 (2½p. × 3, 4p. × 2, 11½p. × 3); UMFB26/27 (½p., 3p. × 4, 12½p. × 3); UMFB31 (1p. × 2, 3½p. × 3, 12½p. × 3) and UMFB34 (1p. × 3, 4p. × 2, 13p. × 3)

An uncut sheet of Panes **UMFB23/24** is illustrated and shows 16 horizontal rows of stamps arranged in two vertical columns. The illustration shows an unprinted row of blanks which is removed to leave the bottom margin perforated through. Early in the printing of Panes **UMFB23/24** the pins in the gutter margin were removed to give Perf. Type E throughout. As will be seen from the illustration the cylinder numbers were printed so that they would be trimmed off. This was changed for Pane **UMFB34** so that the cylinder numbers appeared in either the top or bottom selvedge. An illustration of Pane **UMFB31** is shown on a following page to show the arrangement adopted to avoid the different pane content when, due to error, panes are miscut. It will be seen that both columns are Perf. Type E with cutting lines in alternate rows.

# APPENDIX I    Perforators—Folded Booklet Panes

**Pane UMFB48 (14p. × 2, 19p. × 4, labels (3))**
This pane was printed on the Chambon press and perforated by the APS rotary machine. The uncut sheet contained two vertical columns of eight panes in each including one cylinder pane. The panes had two vertical edges imperforate but the margin showed one extension hole in the centre to give Perf. Type IEI.

**(e) Horizontal Panes of Twenty**
**Panes UMFB8 (7p. × 10, 9p. × 10) and UMFB13 (8p. × 10, 10p. × 10)**
An illustration of the dot pane of **UMFB8** is shown on a following page. The stamps are arranged upright in two panes of 200 stamps (10 panes of 20 stamps) with cutting lines in the margins printed in the colour of the 7p. The 7p./9p. phosphor bands stop short of the edges of the designs in each row. Pane **UMFB13** was also printed by a double pane cylinder with the short bands on the 8p./10p. values.

The sheet size is identical with those for the single value counter books, but the marginal markings, other than the vertical and horizontal cutting lines, have been omitted.

The marker pin did not occur in the left-hand margin and the right-hand margins were removed before assembly.

**Panes UMFB18 (10p. × 10, 12p. × 10); UMFB25 (11½p. × 10, 14p. × 10) and UMFB30 (12½p. × 10, 15½p. × 10)**
An uncut sheet of Pane **UMFB18** is illustrated on a following page. The stamps were printed on the Chambon press in single panes. There were only 6 booklet panes from the uncut sheet. The left-hand margin provided the Perf. Type E the right hand selvedge margin was trimmed away.

**(f) Horizontal Panes of Ten**
**Panes UMFB21/22 (11½p. × 4, 14p. × 6) and UMFB28/29 (12½p. × 4, 15½p. × 6)**
The stamps are arranged upright in a single pane of 10 stamps with cutting lines in the margins printed in the colour of the 14p. On the 14p. the 8 mm. phosphor bands printed over the third and fifth vertical perforation rows in each pane are short at top and bottom. This prevents an overlap on the 11½p. values which have a side phosphor band at left or right.

The stamps were perforated in the reel by a two row horizontal comb. Since there is no need for marker pins only panes with Perf. Type E exist.

**Panes UMFB32/33 (12½p. × 4, 16p. × 6), UMFB35/36 (13p. × 4, 17p. × 6) and UMFB37/38 (12p. × 4, 17p. × 6)**
An illustration of the uncut sheet of Panes **UMFB32/33**, is shown on a following page. This shows a changed stamp arrangement from the previous panes in the series. The vertical margins give Perf. Type E panes throughout and cylinder numbers were engraved at each side of the sheet so that these numbers would appear in the finished booklets.

**Pane UMFB1. Vertical Panes of Six**

Col. 1 (P)          Col. 2 (P)          Col. 3 (E)

*Photo:* National Postal Museum.

**Pane UMFB7. Vertical Panes of Six**

Col. 1 (P)          Col. 2 (P)          Col. 3 (E)

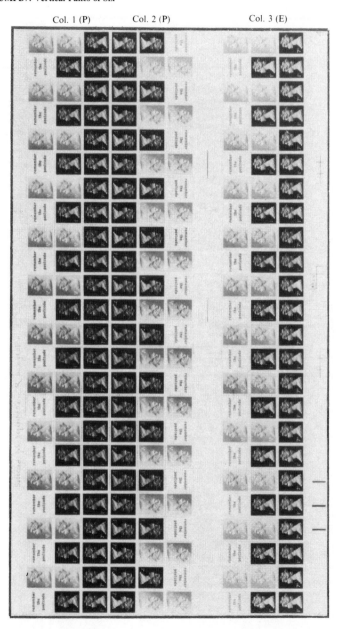

*Photo:* National Postal Museum

**Panes UMFB19 and 20. Vertical Panes of Six (Chambon Printing)**
Col. 1 (E)          Col. 2 (P)                    Col. 3 (P)

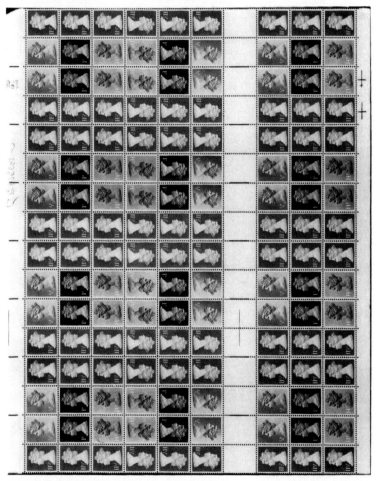

*Photo:* National Postal Museum

**Pane UMFB11. Vertical Panes of Four ("Jumelle" Printing)**

Col. 1 (P)  Col. 2 (P)  Col. 3 (P)  Col. 4 (P)

*Photo:* National Postal Museum

**Panes UMFB3 and 4. Vertical Panes of Ten**

Col. 1 (E)                    Col. 2 (E)

*Photo:* National Postal Museum

**Panes UMFB5 and 6. Vertical Panes of Eight**

Col. 1 (E)                    Col. 2 (E)

*Photo:* National Postal Museum

476

**Panes UMFB9 and 10. Vertical Panes of Eight ("Jumelle" Printing)**

Col. 1 (E)　　　　　　　　　　　Col. 2 (E)

*Photo:* National Postal Museum

**Panes UMFB16 and 17. Vertical Panes of Eight (Chambon Printing)**

Col. 1 (E)                    Col. 2 (E)

*Photo:* National Postal Museum

**Panes UMFB23 and 24. Vertical Panes of Eight (Chambon Printing)**

Col. 1 (E)                    Col. 2 (P)

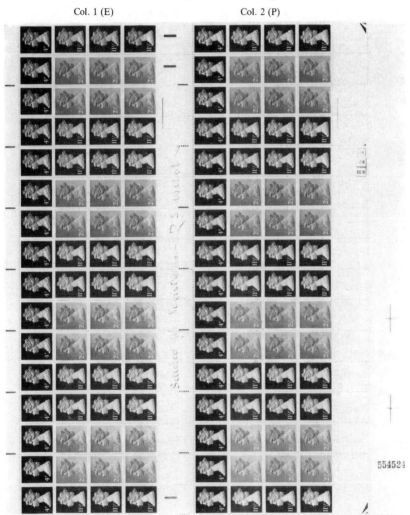

*Photo:* National Postal Museum

**Pane UMFB31. Vertical Panes of Eight (Chambon Printing)**

Col. 1 (E)                                        Col. 2 (E)

*Photo:* National Postal Museum

**Pane UMFB8. Horizontal Panes of Twenty. Dot pane ("Jumelle" Printing)**
(E)

*Photo:* National Postal Museum

**Pane UMFB18. Horizontal Pane of Twenty (Chambon Printing)**

(E)

*Photo:* National Postal Museum

**Panes UMFB21 and 22. Horizontal Panes of Ten (Chambon Printing)**

Col. 1 (E)          Col. 2 (E)

*Photo:* National Postal Museum

**Panes UMFB32 and 33. Horizontal Panes of Ten (Chambon Printing)**

Col. 1 (E)                        Col. 2 (E)

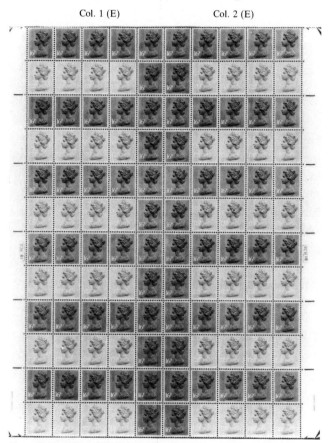

*Photo:* National Postal Museum

## B. Panes of Single Values

### (a) Horizontal Panes of Ten

**Panes UFB1/2 (6½p.), UFB3/4 (8½p.), UFB5/6 (7p.), UFB7/8 (9p.), UFB9/10 (8p.), UFB11/14 (10p.) and UFB15/16 (12p.)**

They are printed by the "Jumelle" press from continuous cylinders with no horizontal margins. The sheet size is the usual two panes, each of 200 stamps arranged in twenty rows of ten stamps. The cylinder numbers, no dot and dot, appear as in normal sheets in row 18 in the left margin with "P" phosphor numbers and not "B" numbers associated with Booklets, although the "P" does not appear.

The markings in the left and right margins are described in the text at the end of the listing of Panes **UFB1/2** and can be seen in the reduced sized illustrations of the uncut sheets. They are the same for all the horizontal panes on ten.

The double pane sheets are broken down into columns 1 to 4, the individual panes with selvedge at left being either from column 1 (no dot) or 3 (dot) and those with selvedge at right being from column 2 (no dot) or 4 (dot).

We show the uncut sheet no dot panes of the 6½p. and 8½p. values. For these two values the perforator was at first an adaptation of Type R giving:—

| | | |
|---|---|---|
| No dot panes— | Left margin | A single extension hole |
| | Right margin | Perforated through |
| Dot panes— | Left margin | Perforated through |
| | Right margin | A single extension hole |

This perforator produced cylinder panes from no dot sheets Type E and from dot sheets Type P.

In later printings an adaptation of Type RE was employed, the horizontal perforations between the no dot and dot panes being removed, leaving a single extension hole in each margin, i.e. there was a single extension hole in both margins of both panes.

Our illustrations show Type R for the no dot 6½p. pane and Type RE for the no dot 8½p. pane.

Only Type RE was employed for panes of ten; 7p., 9p., 8p., 10p. and 12p.

### Perforator 2

The stamps were perforated on a perforating drum attached to the "Jumelle" machine in the usual manner. It perforates 48 rows so that the extra extension hole recurs every 24th book. It is the normal perforating drum used for the sheet stamps as described for Type R under the Low Values in this Appendix. However, the perforator settings are different from those given for the sheets since for the booklets the perforator is used with 20-row cylinders, whilst for the sheets it is used with 21-row cylinders, including the blank gutter margin.

At first the marker pin existed only in the right-hand margin but it also occurred in the left-hand margin towards the end of the printings of panes of 10 6½p. and 8½p. values. It exists on all the early printings of panes of 10 7p. and 9p. values but disappeared during the perforating of the third pictorial editions. The reason for this is suggested under the description of Perf. Type R. Early in 1980 two further pins were added to a drum which gave a single extension hole in both sides of the sheet and this was employed for panes of 10 10p. centre band and 12p. on phosphorised paper.

A full listing of panes showing the extra extension hole is outside the scope of this Catalogue. A detailed listing of the panes reported with the variety appeared in the June 1984 issue of "*The Bookmark*".

Other panes are not illustrated since the arrangement is the same as that for the 6½p. and 8½p. values and, of course, they only exist with the adapted Type RE perforator giving a single extension hole in all side margins.

**Panes UFB17/18 (11½p.), UFB19/20 (14p.), UFB21/22 (12½p.), UFB23/24 (15½p.), UFB25/28 (16p.), UFB30/3 (13p.), UFB34/37 (17p.), UFB40/41 (12p.), UFB43/46 (18p.), UFB57/58 (14p.) and UFB59/60 (19p.)**

These panes were printed from single pane cylinders by the Chambon press. The sheets are arranged in two vertical columns of twelve horizontal rows and were comb perforated in the reel. The comb gives a single extension hole (Perf. Type E) in all side margins.

### (b) Horizontal Panes of Twenty

**Pane UFB29 (12½p. with Multiple Star underprint)**

This pane was perforated by a 2 row comb attached to the Chambon press. This gives only Perf. Type E panes from the left margin. The right-hand margin was trimmed off. See illustration for Pane **UMFB18**.

### (c) Vertical Panes of Four

**Panes UFB38/39 (17p. with and without Multiple Star underprint) and UFB69 (17p. × 3 and label)**

These panes were printed on the Chambon press and the perforator gave Type E. The format of the uncut sheet is as for Pane **UMFB42 (1p., 13p., 18p. × 2).**

**485**

**Panes UFB1 and 2. Horizontal Panes of Ten. No dot. Perf. Type R**

Col. 1 (E)                    Col. 2 (P)

*Photo:* National Postal Museum

# APPENDIX I    Perforators—Folded Booklet Panes

**Panes UFB3 and 4. Horizontal Panes of Ten. No dot. Perf. Type RE**

Col. 1 (E)                Col. 2 (E)

*Photo:* National Postal Museum

**(d) Vertical Panes of Six**
**Pane UFB42 (17p.) and UFB68 (20p. × 5 and label)**

These panes were printed and perforated on the Chambon press. The uncut sheet is identical to Pane **UMFB31** but with cylinder numbers above the fifth pane from the left with the Queen's head facing left. Each column contains eight panes including one with a cylinder number and Perf. Type E.

Pane **UFB68** is similar but with cylinder pane opposite pane 4 and Perf. Type IEI.

---

## 5.    Barcode Booklet Panes

---

### Panes of Single Values
**Horizontal Panes of Four and Ten**

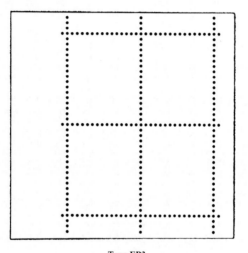

**Type EP3**

**Type EP3** A single extension hole at side with 3 pin extension in top and bottom margins

**(a) Panes of Four**
**Panes UFB47 (13p.), UFB48 (18p.), UFB49 (26p.), UFB52 (14p.), UFB53 (19p.), UFB54 (27p.), UFB61 (14p.), UFB62 (19p.) and UFB63 (27p.)**

**Panes of 4.** The uncut sheet contained five horizontal rows arranged in four columns. Panes in the second row had a cylinder number etched in the left-hand margin opposite stamp 1. The stamps were printed in the reel on a Chambon press and the perforator attached to the press was modified twice so that panes of 10 and then 4 could be produced. After perforating the panes of 10 in two columns some pins were removed in order to perforate the panes of 4 in the four columns.

Panes UFB61/3 have horizontal rows of pins removed to produce Perf. Type IEI.

**(b) Panes of Ten**
**Panes UFB50 (13p.), UFB51 (18p.), UFB55 (14p.), UFB56 (19p.) UFB64 (14p.) and UFB65 (19p.)**

**Panes of 10. Chambon Press.** The same size sheet was used but there were two columns of five panes with cylinder numbers in the second row similar to the panes of 4. The Perf. Type is EP3 since only the pane content differs from the above.

Panes UFB64/5 have horizontal rows of pins removed to produce Perf. Type IEI. In June 1989 the Chambon printed panes were replaced by Jumelle panes but again with Perf. Type IEI as illustrated on a subsequent page.

**Panes with imperforate edges from Barcode and Automatic Machine 50p. and £1 booklets**

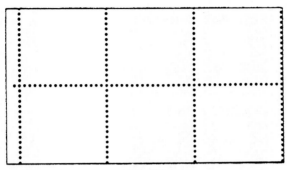

**Type IEI**

Pane orientated to left as Type E but with complete rows of pins removed at each side. Binding margin at top or at left. Panes with perf. Type IEI also occur with three sides imperforate.

We do not list single stamps with a straight edge which is close to the design of the stamp. The exception is where the stamp may have an imperforate side margin and the Queen Victoria line-engraved ½d. listed in Volume 1 of this Catalogue is an example where the margin is deliberately imperforate and there is no problem regarding identification.

**Horizontal Panes of Four (Chambon Printing) with three edges imperforate**
    Machin Panes **UFB66 (14p.)** and **UFB67 (19p.)** were issued with three edges imperforate (perf. type IEI) in January 1989. Similar panes followed for NVI and Penny Black Anniversary issues and an illustration on a subsequent page shows the layout of the primary sheet for photogravure printings.

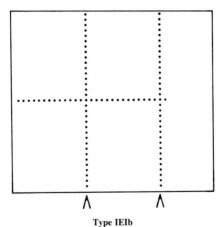

**Type IEIb**

Showing the reverse side of a pane of four with perforations stopped above the bottom edge by just over 1 mm. Such panes derive from the bottom of each row in the Walsall primary sheets. Bar with perf. Type IEIb panes do not occur.

**Perforation Type IEI with Bar**

Walsall Barcode Booklet Pane with Bar                    Harrison Cylinder Number and Bar

**Walsall Panes.** In the illustration we show a pane with plate numbers and the bar at left which has been emphasized in the illustration since it was printed in a pale shade.

**Harrison Pane.** The 19p. in panes of ten UFB65 with horizontal edges imperforate occur with cylinder number with bar as illustrated.

**Panes of Four (Chambon Printing) with three edges imperforate**

*Photo:* National Postal Museum

The panes are printed sideways with the stamps orientated as shown.

**Panes of Ten (Jumelle Printing) with two edges imperforate**

| Col. 1 (IEI) | Col. 2 (IEI) | Col. 3 (IEI) | Col. 4 (IEI) |
|---|---|---|---|

*Photo:* National Postal Museum

492

# APPENDIX J
## Post Office Booklets of Stamps

### General Notes
This appendix is sub-divided into the following sections:
- A. Stitched booklets including prestige booklets (1971–90)
- B. Folded booklets (1976–90)
- C. Barcode booklets containing Machin stamps (1987–90)
- D. Barcode booklets containing Machin NVI stamps (1989–90)
- E. Barcode booklets containing Machin Penny Black Anniversary stamps (1990)
- F. Barcode booklets containing Greetings stamps (1990)
- G. Barcode booklets containing Christmas stamps (1990)

**BOOKLET SHEET ARRANGEMENT.** The arrangement of the primary sheets for making up into booklet panes can be seen by studying the illustrations of the full sheets given in Appendix I.

**Automatic Machine Booklets.** On page 458 we show a primary sheet (10 × 24) of the 2p. and ½p. *se-tenant* vertically pane from 10p. Booklets, the stamps being printed sideways. The sheets for the stamps *se-tenant* horizontally are similar except that they are arranged as follows:

2p. and ½p. *se-tenant* horizontally

The rules indicate where the panes are separated. In these booklets the cylinder numbers were placed sideways in "H" boxes opposite row 23 in the selvedge but they, and other sheet markings, are invariably trimmed off.

**Counter Sale Booklets.** We also illustrate a primary sheet of 2½p. magenta/Stick Firmly label and the other panes of six are similarly arranged. Cylinder numbers occur in the left margin opposite R. 19/1.
The Prestige booklets were printed 12-up with three rows of the four booklet panes. The cylinder numbers were trimmed off before assembly.

**DATES.** The dates quoted on the back covers of the booklets refer to the period of their expected usage and are quoted for identification purposes, but the actual dates of issue are also given in brackets and withdrawal dates are set out at the end of each series.
The folded booklets have dates printed inside the covers which refer to the postal rates quoted to protect the Post Office in case any changes in them should take place between the time of going to press and the period of usage of the booklet.

**PICTORIAL BOOKLETS.** In addition to the pictorial covers, first introduced for the Machin £.s.d. booklets, the decimal series contain descriptive notes on the inside front cover.

**CATALOGUE NUMBERS.** The basic booklet numbers used are the same as those employed in the *Great Britain Concise Catalogue* (1991 Edition).

**ADVERTISEMENT LABELS.** One of the problems of introducing booklets for decimal stamps was that it was necessary to use existing machinery designed for counter booklets in panes of six when panes of four or five were needed to make up convenient selling prices for booklets. This was solved by using the vacant spaces for advertising labels. The advertising contracts were ended in 1973 when blank, and later Postcode, labels were introduced.

**INTERLEAVES.** All stitched booklets contained interleaves with commercial advertising until June 1975 when they ceased. Contemporary information about postal rates appears in all booklets, except the 10p. Nos. DN71/5.

**ADVERTISERS' VOUCHER COPIES.** These dummy booklets were issued during 1971 to June 1975 when commercial advertising ceased. A small quantity of each edition was prepared and supplied to the Advertisement Contractor, Canonsreach Ltd., and some were passed through the agencies as proofs, others being used as samples for selling space in future editions to new clients. The booklets were made up in the same way as the issued booklets, but without the stamps. Where an advertisement appeared on the *se-tenant* labels the advertiser was supplied with a booklet from which the stamps had been torn out, leaving the label in position.

Voucher copies were supplied for the following editions:—

| | | |
|---|---|---|
| 10p. | Feb. 1971 to June 1975 | Nos. DN46/72 |
| 25p. | Feb. 1971 to June 1973 | Nos. DH39/52 |
| 30p. | Spring and June 1974 | Nos. DQ73/74 |
| 35p. | September 1974 | No. DP4 |

Voucher copies of the following are known with the cover handstamped "ADVERTISER VOUCHER COPY/WITH COMPLIMENTS/CANONSREACH LTD.":—

| | | |
|---|---|---|
| 30p. | Feb. 1971 to Aug. 1973 | Nos. DQ56/72 |
| 35p. | Autumn 1973 to June 1974 | Nos. DP1/3 |
| 45p. | Sept. and Dec. 1974 | Nos. DS1/2 |
| 50p. | Feb. 1971 to March 1974 | Nos. DT1/14 |
| 85p. | September 1974 | No. DX1 |
| | December 1974 (unissued) | — |

**DUMMY TESTING BOOKLETS.** 10p. stitched booklets and 10p. and 50p. folded booklets were prepared for the engineers for testing vending machines. They contain testing labels printed in black from printings normally used for testing coil machines. The front cover of the 50p. booklet reads "50p./DUMMY BOOKLET/FOR TESTING PURPOSES ONLY". These are not available to the public.

**ERRORS IN MAKE-UP.** There are two kinds: (*a*) genuine mistakes where wrong panes have been used or the panes are in the wrong order and (*b*) intentional use of a different pane of equal face value (perhaps with a different label) in part of an issue to use up remaining stocks of good stamps. We also list booklets containing miscut panes but these are not regarded as significant errors by Post Office stock controllers.

Stitched booklets were normally assembled by hand in batches of 40. The contents of each batch was checked by a Post Office controller before sewing, but mistakes were sometimes undetected when a simple substitution was made and there was no shortage or surplus of panes in the batch.

Hitherto we have refrained from listing such errors on the grounds that they could easily be faked. Although fakes of known errors were made in the past, we are now satisfied that they can be detected by experts. Caution should be exercised in buying them and an expert in these issues should be consulted if in doubt.

When re-assembling a booklet from other exploded booklets it is extremely doubtful if the stitch holes will match, and so the faked book will have some panes with more stitch holes than the rest. If they *do* match then it is certain that edges which should be flush will be uneven. Moreover, the booklet panes have been so extensively studied by experts that they can be plated for position in the sheet by the direction of the printing, the method of separation of the various edges (rotary cutter or guillotine), the cylinder flaws, cutting lines and cylinder numbers. Hence a faker would have to choose exactly the right panes and search through so many booklets to find them that it would hardly be worth while to make the effort.

**ILLUSTRATIONS.** The illustrations of the covers are $\frac{3}{4}$ size except where otherwise stated.

**STITCHED BOOKLETS.** All covers are printed in black unless otherwise stated and all booklets are stitched in black.

**FOLDED AND BARCODE BOOKLETS.** These are listed under Sections B to G where further General Notes will be found.

---

**BOOKLET PRICES.** Where applicable prices in the Appendix are for booklets containing panes with "average" perforations (i.e. full perforations on two edges of the pane only). Booklets containing panes with complete perforations are worth more.

---

# A. Stitched Booklets (1971–90)

## 10p. Booklets

**For Sale in Automatic Slot Machines**

Type G
Pillar Box Series

Type GA
Postal Uniforms Series

*Cover.* Orange-yellow
*Composition.* Two panes of four: Pane USB1 (pairs of ½p. and 2p. *se-tenant* vertically) and Pane USB5 (pairs of 1p. and 1½p. *se-tenant* vertically)

*British Pillar Box Series as Type G, designed by Ronald Maddox*

| Cat. No. | Date | Paper/Gum | Quantity printed | Price |
|---|---|---|---|---|
| No. 1. Earliest London type, 1855 | | | | |
| DN46 FEBRUARY 1971 (15.2.71) | | OCP/PVA | 2,215,250 | 1·25 |
| DN47 APRIL 1971 (19.3.71) | | OCP/PVA | 2,413,320 | 1·25 |
| In No. DN47 the design was in a reduced size. | | | | |
| No. 2. "Giant" type of 1856 | | | | |
| DN48 JUNE 1971 (1.6.71) | | OCP/PVA | 1,205,690 | 1·25 |
| *New composition.* Panes USB2, 3 or 4 and USB6, 7 or 8 containing same values but *se-tenant* horizontally | | | | |
| DN49 AUGUST 1971 (14.7.71) | | OCP/PVA | 1,880,700 | 2·25 |
| No. 3. Standard type for urban areas, 1857–59 | | | | |
| DN50 OCTOBER 1971 (27.8.71) | | OCP/PVA | 2,605,490 | 2·25 |
| DN51 DECEMBER 1971 (6.10.71) | | FCP/PVA | 4,056,320 | 20·00 |
| *a.* First pane 2p./½p. OCP  .. .. .. .. .. | | | | 32·00 |
| *c.* Both panes OCP  .. .. .. .. .. .. | | | | 2·25 |
| No. 4. Penfold type of 1866–79 | | | | |
| DN52 FEBRUARY 1972 (8.12.71) | | FCP/PVA | 2,084,720 | 2·00 |
| *a.* Second pane 1½p./1p. OCP .. .. .. .. | | | | 20·00 |
| *b.* First pane 2p./½p. OCP  .. .. .. .. .. | | | | 30·00 |
| *c.* Both panes OCP  .. .. .. .. .. | | | | 45·00 |
| DN53 APRIL 1972 (24.2.72) | | FCP/PVA | 2,743,200 | 2·00 |
| *a.* Second pane 1½p./1p. OCP .. .. .. .. | | | | 20·00 |
| No. 5. Double aperture type of 1899 | | | | |
| DN54 JUNE 1972 (12.4.72) | | FCP/PVA | 2,675,520 | 2·00 |
| DN55 AUGUST 1972 (8.6.72) | | FCP/PVA | 2,515,660 | 2·00 |
| No. 6. Mellor design, 1968 | | | | |
| DN56 OCTOBER 1972 (2.8.72) | | FCP/PVA | 5,626,240 | 2·00 |
| DN57 December 1972 Issue (30.10.72) | | FCP/PVA | 3,515,380 | 2·00 |
| In the following issues the value and list of contents on the cover are set in larger type. | | | | |
| No. 7. King Edward VIII type of 1936 | | | | |
| DN58 February 1973 (5.1.73) | | FCP/PVA | 4,098,840 | 2·00 |
| DN59 April 1973 Issue (2.4.73) | | FCP/PVA | 987,690 | 2·50 |
| No. 8. Standard Queen Elizabeth II type of 1952 | | | | |
| DN60 June 1973 Issue (18.4.73) | | FCP/PVA | 4,098,270 | 2·00 |
| DN61 August 1973 Issue (4.7.73) | | FCP/PVA | 2,020,200 | 12·00 |
| No. 9. Double aperture type of 1973 | | | | |
| DN62 October 1973 Issue (16.8.73) | | FCP/PVA | 4,943,530 | 2·25 |

DN63 December 1973 Issue (12.11.73)    FCP/PVA   ⎫    2·25
   *a.* First pane 2p./½p. dextrin    ..    ..    ..    ..    ..   ⎬ 4,101,980    4·00
   *b.* Second pane 1½p./1p. dextrin..    ..    ..    ..   ⎭    4·00
   *c.* Both panes dextrin    ..    ..    ..    ..    ..    5·00
DN64 February 1974 Issue (17.12.73)    FCP/PVA   ⎫    6·00
   *a.* First pane 2p./½p. dextrin    ..    ..    ..    ..    4·00
   *b.* Ditto, but pane in reverse order    ..    ..   ⎬ 2,969.610    £150
   *c.* Second pane 1½p./1p. dextrin..    ..    ..    ..    7·00
   *d.* Both panes dextrin    ..    ..    ..    ..⎭    2·25
No. 10. Philatelic Posting Box of 1974
DN65 April 1974 Issue (22.2.74)    FCP/PVA   ⎫    10·00
   *a.* First pane 2p./½p. dextrin    ..    ..    ..    ..    5·00
   *b.* Second pane 1½p./1p. dextrin..    ..    ..    ..⎬ 3,415,930    7·00
   *c.* Both panes dextrin    ..    ..    ..    ..    1·50
DN66 June 1974 Issue (23.4.74)    FCP/PVAD    4,226,130    1·50
   *a.* Panes in reverse order ..    ..    ..    ..    ..    ..    £110

*Postal Uniforms Series as Type* **GA**, *designed by Clive Abbott*
No. 1. General Post Letter Carrier of 1793
DN67 August 1974 Issue (23.7.74)    FCP/PVAD    5,011,270    1·50
DN68 October 1974 Issue (27.8.74)    FCP/PVAD    4,364,520    1·50
No. 2. Letter Carrier of 1837
DN69 December 1974 Issue (25.10.74)    FCP/PVAD    3,801,980    1·50
   *a.* Panes in reverse order    ..    ..    ..    ..    ...    £150
DN70 February 1975 Issue (12.12.74)    FCP/PVAD    4,294.300    1·50
No. 3. Letter Carrier of 1855
DN71 April 1975 Issue (26.3.75)    FCP/PVAD    4,447,870    1·50
DN72 June 1975 Issue (21.5.75)    FCP/PVAD    3,165,010    1·00
DN73 August 1975 Issue (27.6.75)    FCP/PVAD    6,149,760    1·00
   *a.* Panes in reverse order    ..    ..    ...    
DN74 October 1975 Issue (3.10.75)    FCP/PVAD    8,621,600    55
DN75 January 1976 Issue (16.3.76)    FCP/PVAD    55

*Withdrawn or sold out:*

| DN46 | .. | .. 11.71 | DN56 | .. | 31.10.73 | DN66 | .. | 30.6.75 |
|---|---|---|---|---|---|---|---|---|
| DN47 | .. | .. 3.72 | DN57 | .. | 31.12.73 | DN67 | .. | 30.8.75 |
| DN48 | .. | .. 11.71 | DN58 | .. | 27.2.74 | DN68 | .. | 31.10.75 |
| DN49 | .. | .. 12.71 | DN59 | .. | 30.4.74 | DN69 | .. | 31.12.75 |
| DN50 | .. | 31.10.72 | DN60 | .. | 28.6.74 | DN70 | .. | 28.2.76 |
| DN51 | .. | 30.12.72 | DN61 | .. | 31.8.74 | DN71 | .. | 30.4.76 |
| DN52 | .. | 28.2.73 | DN62 | .. | 31.10.74 | DN72 | .. | .. 4.76 |
| DN53 | .. | 30.4.73 | DN63 | .. | 31.12.74 | DN73 | .. | .. 9.76 |
| DN54 | .. | 30.6.73 | DN64 | .. | 28.2.75 | DN74 | .. | 30.10.76 |
| DN55 | .. | 31.8.73 | DN65 | .. | 30.4.75 | DN75 | .. | 31.12.77 |

## 25p. Booklets

Type I
Pictorial Type

Type J
Issued to publicise the National Postal Museum
Exhibition of 80 Years of British Stamp Books

*Cover.* Dull purple

*Composition.* Three panes of six: Pane UB28 or 29 ( 5 × 2½p. with "STICK" label), Pane UB26 or 27
(4 × 2½p. with "UNIFLO" and "STICK" labels) and Pane UB21 or 22 (5 × ½p. with "ALAN"
label)

*Veteran Transport Series as Type* I, *designed by David Gentleman*

No. 1. Knifeboard Omnibus of the 1850's

| | | | | | |
|---|---|---|---|---|---|
| DH39 FEBRUARY 1971 (15.2.71) | | OCP/PVA | 2,506,568 | 3·75 |
|   *a.* Pane UB23 for UB21 | .. | .. | .. | .. | 50·00 |
|   *b.* Extra Pane UB28 for UB26 | .. | .. | .. | .. | 70·00 |
|   *c.* Extra Pane UB26 for UB28 | .. | .. | .. | .. | £225 |

*Change to Type* J *cover, designed by Stuart Rose*

| | | | | | |
|---|---|---|---|---|---|
| DH40 APRIL 1971 (19.3.71) | | OCP/PVA | 1,389,800 | 5·50 |
|   *a.* Panes UB26 and UB28 reversed | .. | .. | .. | .. | £140 |

*Change back to Veteran Transport Series as Type* I

No. 2. B-type Omnibus of 1910

| | | | | | |
|---|---|---|---|---|---|
| DH41 JUNE 1971 (11.6.71) | | OCP/PVA | 1,350,048 | 5·50 |
| DH42 AUGUST 1971 (17.9.71) | | OCP/PVA | 550,320 | 7·50 |
|   *a.* Pane UB31 for UB29 | .. | .. | .. | .. | 18·00 |

No. 3. Showman's Engine No. 3 of 1886

| | | | | |
|---|---|---|---|---|
| DH43 OCTOBER 1971 (22.11.71) | | OCP/PVA | 616,040 | 7·50 |

*New composition.* Change of advertising labels: Pane UB34 or 35 (5 × 2½p. with "ALAN" label),
Pane UB33 (4 × 2½p. with two "RUSHSTAMPS" labels) and Pane UB25 (5 × ½p. with
"RUSHSTAMPS" label)

No. 4. Royal Mail Van of 1913

| | | | | | |
|---|---|---|---|---|---|
| DH44 FEBRUARY 1972 (23.12.71) | | FCP/PVA | 572,080 | 6·00 |
|   *a.* Extra Pane UB33 for UB25 | .. | .. | .. | .. | 90·00 |
|   *b.* Extra Pane UB25 for UB33 | .. | .. | .. | .. | 90·00 |
|   *c.* Extra Pane UB33 for UB34 | .. | .. | .. | .. | £160 |
|   *d.* Extra Pane UB34 for UB33 | .. | .. | .. | .. | |
| DH45 APRIL 1972 (13.3.72) | | FCP/PVA | 404,080 | 7·50 |

No. 5. Motor Wagonette of 1901

| | | | | | |
|---|---|---|---|---|---|
| DH46 JUNE 1972 (24.4.72) | | FCP/PVA | 509,880 | 6·00 |
|   *a.* Pane UB32 for UB34 | .. | .. | .. | .. | 60·00 |
| DH47 AUGUST 1972 (14.6.72) | | FCP/PVA | 420,640 | 6·00 |
|   *a.* Pane UB32 for UB34 | .. | .. | .. | .. | 60·00 |
|   *b.* Panes UB34 and UB25 transposed | .. | .. | .. | 60·00 |

No. 6. London Taxi Cab of 1913

| | | | | |
|---|---|---|---|---|
| DH48 OCTOBER 1972 (17.7.72) | | FCP/PVA | 1,081,480 | 6·00 |
| DH49 December 1972 Issue (19.10.72) | | FCP/PVA | 503,728 | 6·00 |
| DH50 December 1972 Issue S (6.11.72) | | FCP/PVA | 2,121,188 | 6·00 |

No. 7. Norwich Electric Tramway

| | | | | |
|---|---|---|---|---|
| DH51 February 1973 Issue (26.2.73) | | FCP/PVA | 310,480 | 7·50 |

Type K

*Change to Type K cover advertising the Save the Children Fund*
DH52 June 1973 Issue (7.6.73)                     FCP/PVA              833,560              7·50

*Withdrawn or sold out:*

| | | | | | | | | |
|---|---|---|---|---|---|---|---|---|
| DH39 | .. | 29.2.72 | DH44 | .. | 28.2.73 | DH49 | .. | 31.12.73 |
| DH40 | .. | 28.4.72 | DH45 | .. | 30.4.73 | DH50 | .. | 31.12.73 |
| DH41 | .. | 30.6.72 | DH46 | .. | 30.6.73 | DH51 | .. | 27.2.74 |
| DH42 | .. | 31.8.72 | DH47 | .. | 31.8.73 | DH52 | .. | 28.6.74 |
| DH43 | .. | 31.10.72 | DH48 | .. | 31.10.73 | | | |

## 30p. Booklets

*Cover.*   Bright purple (*shades*)

*Composition.*   Two panes of six: 2 × Pane UB36, 37 or 38 (5 × 3p. with "£4,315" label)

*British Birds Series as Type* I, *designed by Harry Titcombe*
No. 1. Curlew
DQ56 FEBRUARY 1971 (15.2.71)              OCP/PVA            1,991,960            3·50

*Change to Type J cover, designed by Stuart Rose*
DQ57 APRIL 1971 (19.3.71)                  OCP/PVA            1,867,680            3·50

*Change back to British Birds Series as Type* I
No. 2. Lapwing
DQ58 JUNE 1971 (26.5.71)                   OCP/PVA            1,540,080            3·50
DQ59 AUGUST 1971 (23.7.71)                 OCP/PVA            2,237,400            3·50
No. 3. Robin
DQ60 OCTOBER 1971 (1.10.71)                FCP/PVA            2,432,680            4·50
    *a.* Both panes OCP/PVA      ..      ..      ..      ..
DQ61 DECEMBER 1971 (10.11.71)              FCP/PVA            1,785,460            4·50
    *a.* Both panes OCP/PVA      ..      ..      ..      ..      ..                           10·00
No. 4. Pied Wagtail
DQ62 FEBRUARY 1972 (21.12.71)              FCP/PVA            1,734,840            4·00
    *a.* Both panes OCP/PVA      ..      ..      ..      ..      ..
DQ63 APRIL 1972 (9.2.72)                   FCP/PVA            2,045,440            4·00
No. 5. Kestrel
DQ64 JUNE 1972 (12.4.72)                   FCP/PVA            2,136,040            4·00
DQ65 AUGUST 1972 (8.6.72)                  FCP/PVA            2,294,040            4·50
No. 6. Black Grouse
DQ66 OCTOBER 1972 (31.7.72)                FCP/PVA            3,821,240            4·00
DQ67 December 1972 Issue (30.10.72)        FCP/PVA            2,170,080            4·00
DQ68 December 1972 Issue S (6.12.72)       FCP/PVA            1,463,720            4·00
No. 7. Skylark
DQ69 February 1973 Issue (29.1.73)         FCP/PVA            3,335,240            4·00
DQ70 April 1973 Issue (2.4.73)             FCP/PVA            1,084,120            4·50
No. 8. Oyster-catcher
DQ71 June 1973 Issue (8.5.73)              FCP/PVA            1,572,560            4·75
DQ72 August 1973 Issue (7.6.73)            FCP/PVA            2,820,200            5·00
    *a.* Buff cover (10.8.73) ..      ..      ..      ..      ..      ..            804,000            5·00
    The printing on buff cover was made in the absence of supplies of the normal bright purple card.

*Change to red cover as Type* K *but with value at top right*
*New composition.*   Two panes of six: 2 × Pane UB41 or 42 (5 × 3p. centre band with blank label)
DQ73 Spring 1974 Issue (30.1.74)           FCP/PVA ⎤                              7·50
    *a.* First pane dextrin   ..      ..      ..      ..      ..      ..  ⎬  3,649,680        18·00
    *b.* Second pane dextrin ..      ..      ..      ..      ..      ..  ⎬                   24·00
    *c.* Both panes dextrin   ..      ..      ..      ..      ..      ..  ⎦                    3·75

*Change to red cover as Type* M *but with value at top right*
DQ74 JUNE 1974 Issue (21.6.74)             FCP/PVAD           1,662,160            3·75
    It had not been intended to issue this booklet but some were sent to the Sheffield Head Post Office in error on 14 May and issued shortly afterwards. In consequence a philatelic issue was made on 21 June but post offices were asked to withdraw all 30p. booklets on 22 June, although supplies remained on sale at the Philatelic Bureau.

*Withdrawn or sold out:*

| | | | | | | | | |
|---|---|---|---|---|---|---|---|---|
| DQ56 | .. | 1.72 | DQ63 | .. | 30.4.73 | DQ70 | .. | 30.4.74 |
| DQ57 | .. | 28.4.72 | DQ64 | .. | 30.6.73 | DQ71 | .. | 28.6.74 |
| DQ58 | .. | 30.6.72 | DQ65 | .. | 31.8.73 | DQ72 | .. | 31.8.74 |
| DQ59 | .. | 31.8.72 | DQ66 | .. | 31.10.73 | DQ73 | .. | 31.1.75 |
| DQ60 | .. | 31.10.72 | DQ67 | .. | 31.12.73 | DQ74 | .. | 30.6.75 |
| DQ61 | .. | 30.12.72 | DQ68 | .. | 31.12.73 | | | |
| DQ62 | .. | 28.2.73 | DQ69 | .. | 27.2.74 | | | |

## 35p. Booklets

Type L
British Coins Type

*Cover.* Blue

*Composition.* Two panes of six: 2 × Pane UB43 or 44 (5 × 3½p. two bands with blank label)

*British Coins Series as Type L, designed by Peter Gauld*
No. 1. Cuthred Penny, King of Kent, 798–807

| | | | | | | | |
|---|---|---|---|---|---|---|---|
| DP1 | Autumn 1973 Issue (12.12.73) | | FCP/PVA | ⎫ | | | 6·00 |
| a. | First pane dextrin | .. .. .. .. .. | | ⎬ | 4,700,260 | | 7·50 |
| b. | Second pane dextrin | .. .. .. .. .. | | | | | 9·00 |
| c. | Both panes dextrin | .. .. .. .. .. | | ⎭ | | | 2·50 |
| DP2 | April 1974 Issue (10.4.74) | | FCP/PVA | ⎫ | | | 6·00 |
| a. | First pane dextrin | .. .. .. .. .. | | ⎬ | 2,611,560 | | 9·00 |
| b. | Second pane dextrin | .. .. .. .. .. | | | | | 10·00 |
| c. | Both panes dextrin | .. .. .. .. .. | | ⎭ | | | 4·50 |

No. 2. Edward I Silver Groat, 1279

| | | | | | | | |
|---|---|---|---|---|---|---|---|
| DP3 | June 1974 Issue (4.7.74) | | FCP/PVA | ⎫ | | | 12·00 |
| a. | First pane dextrin | .. .. .. .. .. | | ⎬ | 1,395,400 | | 9·00 |
| b. | Second pane dextrin | .. .. .. .. .. | | | | | 8·50 |
| c. | Both panes dextrin | .. .. .. .. .. | | ⎭ | | | 2·50 |

*Change to cover as Type M but with value at top right*
*New composition.* Two panes of six: 2 × Pane UB45 (5 × 3½p. centre band with blank label)

| | | | | | | | |
|---|---|---|---|---|---|---|---|
| DP4 | September 1974 Issue (23.10.74) | | FCP/PVAD | ⎫ | | | 2·50 |
| a. | First pane miscut | .. .. .. .. .. | | ⎬ | 3,017,020 | | 30·00 |
| b. | Second pane miscut | .. .. .. .. .. | | | | | 22·00 |
| c. | Both panes miscut | .. .. .. .. .. | | ⎭ | | | 20·00 |

The miscut panes have the label at the top.

*Withdrawn:*

| | | | | | | |
|---|---|---|---|---|---|---|
| DP1 | .. | .. | 31.12.74 | DP3 | .. | .. | 30. 5.75 |
| DP2 | .. | .. | 30. 4.75 | DP4 | .. | .. | 30. 9.75 |

## 45p. Booklets

*Cover.*   Yellow-brown

*Composition.*   Two panes of six: 2 × Pane UB47 (5 × 4½p. with blank label)

*British Coins Series as Type* L, *designed by Peter Gauld*

No. 3. Elizabeth Gold Crown

| | | | | |
|---|---|---|---|---|
| DS1 September 1974 Issue (9.10.74) | | FCP/PVAD | 2,936,520 | 4·50 |
| DS2 December 1974 Issue (1.11.74) | | FCP/PVAD ⎫ | 3,486,220 | 5·00 |
| a. Orange-brown cover (26.11.74) | .. .. .. .. ⎬ | | | 6·00 |

The printing was completed on the orange-brown cover because of a shortage of the original yellow-brown card.

*Withdrawn:*

| | | | |
|---|---|---|---|
| DS1 | .. | .. | 30. 9.75 |
| DS2 | .. | .. | 31.12.75 |

## 50p. Booklets

*Cover.*   Turquoise-green (*shades*)

*Composition.*   Four panes of six: Pane UB39 or 40 (6 × 3p.), Pane USB9 or 10 (4 × 3p. *se-tenant* horizontally with 2 × 2½p.), Pane UB30 or 31 (5 × 2½p. with "TEAR OFF" label) and Pane UB23 or 24 (5 × ½p. with "LICK" label)

*British Flowers Series as Type* I, *designed by Rosalie Southall*

| | | | |
|---|---|---|---|
| No. 1. Large Bindweed | | | |
| DT1 FEBRUARY 1971 (15.2.71) | OCP/PVA | 1,296,960 | 7·00 |
| No. 2. Primrose | | | |
| DT2 MAY 1971 (24.3.71) | OCP/PVA | 1,226,960 | 7·00 |
| a. Pane UB28 for UB30 .. .. .. .. .. | | | 75·00 |
| No. 3. Honey Suckle | | | |
| DT3 AUGUST 1971 (28.6.71) | OCP/PVA | 1,374,480 | 7·00 |
| No. 4. Hop | | | |
| DT4 NOVEMBER 1971 (17.9.71) | FCP/PVA | 1,923,369 | 8·00 |
| a. Additional Pane UB31 .. .. .. .. .. | | | £100 |
| b. Pane UB23 in place of UB24 (pre-"blind" perf.).. .. | | | |
| c. Panes 3p. and 3p./2½p. OCP .. .. .. .. | | | 15·00 |
| d. Panes 3p. OCP .. .. .. .. .. | | | 35·00 |

*New composition.*   Change of advertising labels: Panes UB39 or 40 and USB9 or 10 as before, Pane UB32 (5 × 2½p. with "RUSHSTAMPS" label) and Pane UB25 (5 × ½p. with "RUSHSTAMPS" label)

| | | | |
|---|---|---|---|
| No. 5. Common Violet | | | |
| DT5 FEBRUARY 1972 (23.12.71)* | FCP/PVA | 1,133,280 | 8·00 |
| No. 6. Lords-and-Ladies | | | |
| DT6 MAY 1972 (13.3.72) | FCP/PVA | 1,316,680 | 7·00 |
| No. 7. Wood Anemone | | | |
| DT7 AUGUST 1972 (31.5.72) | FCP/PVA | 1,506,848 | 7·00 |
| No. 8. Deadly Nightshade | | | |
| DT8 NOVEMBER 1972 (15.9.72) | FCP/PVA | 2,758,560 | 7·00 |

* Although generally released on 24 December, this booklet was put on sale at the London E.C.1 Philatelic Counter and also at one other philatelic counter at least on 23 December.

Type M

---

*Change to Type* **M** *advertising the Canada Life Assurance Group*

| | | | | |
|---|---|---|---|---|
| DT9 | February 1973 Issue (19.1.73) | FCP/PVA | 497,880 | 7·00 |
| DT10 | April 1973 Issue (26.2.73) | FCP/PVA | 753,080 | 7·00 |
| DT11 | May 1973 Issue (2.4.73) | FCP/PVA | 791,307 | 8·00 |
| DT12 | August 1973 Issue (14.6.73) | FCP/PVA | 1,424,267 | 12·00 |

*Change to moss-green covers as Type* **M** *but with value at top right*

*New composition*. Three panes of six: 2 × Pane UB43 or 44 (5 × 3½p. two bands with blank label) and Pane UB41 or 42 (5 × 3p. centre band with blank label)

| | | | | |
|---|---|---|---|---|
| DT13 | Autumn 1973 Issue (14.11.73) | FCP/PVA | | 6·00 |
| | *a.* First 3½p. pane dextrin | | | 20·00 |
| | *b.* Second 3½p. pane dextrin | | | 25·00 |
| | *c.* Both 3½p. panes dextrin | | 2,935,832 | 12·00 |
| | *d.* 3p. pane dextrin | | | 12·00 |
| | *e.* 3p. and first 3½p. panes dextrin | | | 18·00 |
| | *f.* 3p. and second 3½p. panes dextrin | | | 18·00 |
| | *g.* All panes dextrin | | | 12·00 |
| DT14 | March 1974 Issue (18.2.74) | FCP/PVAD | | 4·00 |
| | *a.* First 3½p. pane PVA | | 2,820,292 | 15·00 |
| | *b.* Both 3½p. panes PVA | | | 12·00 |

---

*Withdrawn or sold out:*

| | | | | | | | | |
|---|---|---|---|---|---|---|---|---|
| DT 1.. | .. | 10.71 | DT 6.. | .. | 31. 5.73 | DT11.. | .. | 31. 5.74 |
| DT 2.. | .. | 31. 5.72 | DT 7.. | .. | 31. 8.73 | DT12.. | .. | 31. 8.74 |
| DT 3.. | .. | 31. 8.72 | DT 8.. | .. | 30.11.73 | DT13.. | .. | 10.74 |
| DT 4.. | .. | 30.11.72 | DT 9.. | .. | 27. 2.74 | DT14.. | .. | 31. 3.75 |
| DT 5.. | .. | 28. 2.73 | DT10.. | .. | 30. 4.74 | | | |

---

## 85p. Booklet

*Cover*. Purple as Type **M** but with value at top right

*Composition*. Four panes of six: 3 × Pane UB47 (5 × 4½p. two bands with blank label) and Pane UB45 (5 × 3½p. centre band with blank label)

| | | | | |
|---|---|---|---|---|
| DW1 | Sept. 1974 Issue (13.11.74) | FCP/PVAD | 1,918,355 | 6·50 |

A December 1974 issue was prepared and then cancelled but advertisers' voucher copies were distributed.

*Withdrawn*: 30.9.75

**501**

DX1

*(Illustration reduced actual size* 152 × 72 *mm.)*

This booklet was commissioned by Josiah Wedgwood & Sons Ltd., the pottery firm. The cover, designed by John Wallis, shows the founder and some of his products. All the interleaves were printed in colour by Sir Joseph Causton & Sons Ltd. and show other examples of Wedgwood's wares. The booklets were assembled by Harrisons.

*Composition.* Three panes of twelve stamps and one of six stamps: Pane UWB1 (12 × 3p. two bands); Pane UWB2 (3 × 2½p. centre band with 3 × 2½p. band at right *se-tenant* with 6 × 3p. two bands); Pane UWB3 (3 × 2½p. band at right *se-tenant* with 3 × ½p. two bands *se-tenant* with 3 × 2½p. band at left and 3 × 2½p. centre band); and Pane UWB4 (3 × ½p. two bands *se-tenant* with 2 × 2½p. band at left and 1 × ½p. band at left)

| | | | |
|---|---|---|---|
| DX1  MAY 1972 (24.5.72) | FCP/PVA | 501,734 | 55·00 |

    *a.* Cover without list of contents..    ..    ..    ..    ..

    *s.* Each stamp overprinted "Specimen"..    ..    ..    ..

| | | |
|---|---|---|
| DX1 | First Day Cover | 25·00 |

An official first day cover showing a blue Portland Vase was issued by the Post Office and special First Day postmarks were applied at post offices with special posting facilities. The Philatelic Bureau also applied special handstamps showing Josiah Wedgwood and "FIRST DAY OF ISSUE OF NEW £1 STAMP BOOK 24 MAY 1972", whilst as an alternative or in addition the Philatelic Bureau offered commemorative postmarks for Edinburgh or Barlaston, Stoke-on-Trent. To qualify covers were affixed with a strip of four from Panes UWB2 or UWB3 or the complete block of six from Pane UWB4. In practice stamps from Pane UWB1 were also used. The Philatelic Bureau took their stamps from uncut sheet rather than break up books and be left with some wastage.

25,000 publicity booklets without stamps and with the contents omitted from the cover were produced for Wedgwood to advertise their products. One of these was enclosed in first day covers sent from Barlaston where Wedgwood's own publicity campaign coincided with the Post Office launching of the issue. Two of these booklets (with contents omitted from the cover) were accidentally made up with stamps and issued at Bristol and up to ten more could exist.

*Sold out:* 2.73

DX2

*(Illustration reduced actual size* 163 × 97 *mm.)*

This booklet, promoted by Josiah Wedgwood & Sons Ltd., was issued to commemorate the 250th birth anniversary of Josiah Wedgwood, the founder of the Company. The booklet and the first day cover were both designed by John Wallis. The cover and the interleaves were printed in lithography by Harrison & Sons, who also assembled the booklets.

*Composition.*    Three panes of nine stamps and one of six stamps: Pane UWB5 (9 × 12p. two bands); Pane UWB6 (9 × 10p. centre band); Pane UWB7 (6 × 2p. two bands); Pane UWB8 (4 × 12p. two bands *se-tenant* with 2p. two bands, 10p. band at left and 3 × 10p. centre band)

DX2 January 1980 (16.4.80)            FCP/PVAD            1,269,409            8·00
DX2                                             First Day Cover                                             4·00

The Post Office first day cover was issued with Pane UWB8 cancelled by a special First Day postmark at the Philatelic Bureau, Edinburgh or Barlaston, Stoke-on-Trent.

*Withdrawn:*    30.4.82

DX3

(*Illustration reduced actual size* 163 × 97 *mm.*)

This booklet was commissioned by Stanley Gibbons International Ltd., and marks 125 years of service and tradition in philately. All the interleaves were printed in colour by lithography and give a brief history of the Company. The stamp panes together with the attached counterfoils were printed in photogravure. Brian Dedman was responsible for the design of the booklet and Michael O'Reilly designed the first day cover. The booklet was printed and assembled by Harrison & Sons.

*Composition.*    Two panes each of six and nine stamps: Pane UWB9 (6 × 15½p. two bands); Pane UWB10 (3 × 12½p. band at right with 3 × 12½p. band at left); Pane UWB11 (2p. and 3p. two bands *se-tenant* with 3 × 12½p. band at left and 3 × 12½p. band at right and 12½p. centre band); Pane UWB12 (9 × 15½p. two bands)

DX3 February 1982 (19.5.82)            FCP/PVAD            269,322            13·00
DX3                                             First Day Cover                                             3·50

The Post Office first day cover was issued with Pane UWB11 cancelled by a special First Day postmark at the Philatelic Bureau, Edinburgh or London WC.

*Withdrawn:*    19.5.83

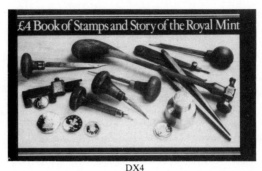

DX4

(*Illustration reduced actual size* 163 × 97 *mm.*)

Issued to mark the 1,000 year history of the Royal Mint, this booklet was printed and assembled entirely by Harrison & Sons. The booklet was sponsored by the Royal Mint and the covers and interleaves give an account of the history of the Mint together with illustrations showing coins and how they are made. The stamps and attached interleaves were printed in photogravure and the cover and the other pages were printed in lithography. The cover depicts coins, hand-tools and a die used to produce the one pound coin. The booklet and the first day cover were designed by Barrie West.

*Composition.*    Two panes each of six and nine stamps: Panes UWB13/14 (3 × 12½p. band at right with 3 × 12½p. band at left); Pane UWB15 (3p. (bright magenta) with 2 × 3½p. (purple-brown) *se-tenant* with 6 × 16p. phosphorised (advanced coated) paper); Pane UWB16 (9 × 16p. phosphorised (advanced coated) paper)

DX4 (14.9.83)           FCP/PVAD or Phosphorised paper              498,225            12·00
    *a.* Additional Pane UWB16    ..      ..    ..    ..
DX4                                        First Day Cover                                      5·00

The Post Office first day cover was issued with Pane UWB15 cancelled by a special First Day postmark at the Philatelic Bureau, Edinburgh or Llantrisant Pontyclun, Mid Glamorgan, the new Mint premises north-west of Cardiff.

*Withdrawn:*   13.9.84

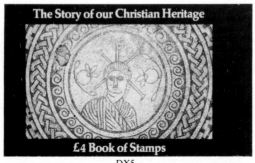

DX5

(*Illustration reduced actual size* 163 × 97 *mm.*)

This booklet was issued to commemorate Christian Heritage Year which began on 7 May 1984. The booklet was sponsored by the *Christian Heritage* organisation, backed by the Trinity Trust which is a registered charity. The booklet contains four panes of stamps with interleaves which are illustrated with an account of the history of Britain's Christian heritage. The text and research was by Murray Watts and Jim Douglas. Philip Miles designed the booklet and the associated first day cover. The cover and interleaves were printed in lithography and the stamps together with attached counterfoils were printed in photogravure by Harrison & Sons, who also assembled the booklets.

*Composition.*    One pane of nine and three panes each of six stamps: Pane UWB17 (6 × 17p. phosphorised (advanced coated) paper); Panes UWB18 and 20 (3 × 13p. band at right with 3 × 13p. band at left); Pane UWB19 (10p. (orange-brown) two bands and 13p. band at left *se-tenant* with 7 × 17p. two bands)

| | | | |
|---|---|---|---|
| DX5 (4.9.84) | FCP/PVAD or Phosphorised paper | 397,350 | 15·00 |
| DX5 | First Day Cover | | 6·00 |

The Post Office first day cover was issued with Pane UWB19 cancelled by a special First Day postmark at the Philatelic Bureau, Edinburgh or Canterbury. It is known pre-released on 28 August 1984, from London, S.E.1.

*Withdrawn:*    2.9.85

Type DX6
(*Illustration reduced actual size* 163 × 95 *mm.*)

This booklet was sponsored by *The Times* and marks the bi-centenary of one of the most famous newspapers in the world. The booklet contains interleaves depicting events in the history of *The Times* which originally appeared under the title of *The Daily Universal Register*. The name was changed to *The Times* three years later. The interleaves were printed in lithography and the stamps with attached counterfoils were printed in photogravure. The booklet text was written by *The Times* Literary Editor, Philip Howard. Another member of the staff, David Driver, Head of Design, was responsible for the graphics. On this occasion the usual front cover with a black background proved unsatisfactory and a white surround was chosen. The booklets were printed and assembled by Harrison & Sons.

*Composition.*    One pane of six and three panes each of nine stamps: Pane UWB21 (6 × 17p. phosphorised (advanced coated) paper); Pane UWB22 (9 × 13p. centre band); Pane UWB23 (4p. band at right and band at left, 2 × 13p. band at right, 2 × 13p. band at left, 2 × 17p. two bands and 34p. two bands arranged *se-tenant* with 34p. in the centre); Pane UWB24 (9 × 17p. phosphorised (advanced coated) paper)

| | | | |
|---|---|---|---|
| DX6 (8.1.85) | FCP/PVAD or Phosphorised paper | 386,700 | 20·00 |
| DX6 | First Day Cover | | 6·00 |

The Post Office first day cover was issued with Pane UWB23 cancelled by a special First Day postmark at the Philatelic Bureau, Edinburgh or London WC.

*Withdrawn:*    7.1.86

Type DX7
(*Illustration reduced actual size 162 × 95 mm.*)

This booklet was produced jointly by the Post Office and British Rail. The booklet contains illustrations of famous locomotives on every page with the story of British Rail from establishment on 31 December 1947. The outer covers and interleaves were printed in lithography except for counterfoils and stamps which were in photogravure. Designed by Trickett and Webb Ltd., the text was by Mike Barden of Woods Barden Associates Ltd., and printing was by Harrison & Sons.

*Composition.* One pane of six and three panes each of nine stamps: Pane UWB25 (9 × 17p. phosphorised (advanced coated) paper); Pane UWB26 (9 × 12p. centre band); Pane UWB27 (3 × 12p. band at right and 3 × 12p. band at left arranged *se-tenant* with 2 × 17p. and 31p. two bands); Pane UWB28 (6 × 17p. phosphorised (advanced coated) paper)

| | | | |
|---|---|---|---|
| DX7 (18.3.86) | FCP/PVAD or Phosphorised paper | 350,325 | 20·00 |
| DX7 | First Day Cover | | 8·00 |

The Post Office first day cover was issued with Pane UWB27 cancelled by a special First Day postmark at the Philatelic Bureau, Edinburgh or Crewe, Cheshire.

*Withdrawn:*   17.3.87

Type DX8
(*Illustration reduced actual size 162 × 95 mm.*)

Issued by the Post Office in conjunction with P & O, this booklet marked the 150th anniversary of the first mail contract with the Peninsular Steam Navigation Co. The story of the Company's history from the early 1800s to the present day is given by Stephen Rabson, the Group Librarian for P & O. The booklet was designed by Aitken Blakeley Designers and printed by Harrison & Sons Ltd. The stamps were printed on the Jumelle press in photogravure; cover, stubs and interleaves were printed in lithography.

*Composition.* One pane of six and three panes each of nine stamps: Pane UWB29 (9 × 18p. phosphorised (advanced coated) paper); Pane UWB30 (9 × 13p. centre band); Pane UWB31 (1p. and 2 × 13p. band at right arranged *se-tenant* with 3 × 18p. two bands and 26p. *se-tenant* with 2 × 18p. with two bands); Pane UWB32 (6 × 13p. centre band)

| | | | |
|---|---|---|---|
| DX8 (3.3.87) | FCP/PVAD or Phosphorised paper | 321,100 | 20·00 |
| DX8 | First Day Cover | | 8·00 |

The Post Office first day cover was issued with Pane UWB31 cancelled by a special First Day postmark at the Philatelic Bureau, Edinburgh or Falmouth, Cornwall.

*Withdrawn:*   2.3.88

Type DX9
(*Illustration reduced actual size* 162 × 97 *mm.*)

The Post Office issued this booklet in connection with the *Financial Times* to mark the centenary of the newspaper. Lithography was employed for the first time to print the stamp panes. The interleaves, also in lithography, give a background history of the *Financial Times* which first appeared on 13 February 1888. It replaced the weekly *London Financial Guide* but, due to competition for increased circulation, the early years were very difficult. To make the newspaper distinct from its main competitor the paper was changed to a pinkish hue in 1893. By 1920 the *Financial Times* had established itself as the leading newspaper of its type. The first international edition was published in Frankfurt in 1979 and, from 1985, also in the United States. The booklet was designed by The Partners Ltd., and Mike Barden wrote the text. The booklet and stamps were printed in lithography by Questa.

*Composition.* Two panes each of six and nine stamps: Pane UHP1 (9 × 18p. phosphorised (advanced coated) paper/PVAD gum); Pane UHP2 (6 × 13p. FCP/PVA centre band); Pane UHP3 (3 × 13p. band at right, 3 × 13p. band at left *se-tenant* with 18p., 22p. and 34p. FCP/PVA with two bands); Pane UHP4 (6 × 18p. phosphorised (advanced coated) paper/PVAD gum)

| | | | |
|---|---|---|---|
| DX9 (9.2.88) | FCP/PVA or Phosphorised paper/PVAD gum | 262,200 | 20·00 |
| DX9 | First Day Cover | | 8·00 |

The Post Office first day cover was issued with the *se-tenant* Pane UHP3 cancelled by a special First Day postmark at the Philatelic Bureau, Edinburgh or London, E.C.4.

*Withdrawn:*   8.2.89

Type DX10

(*Illustration reduced actual size* 162 × 97 *mm.*)

The front cover features the Firth of Forth railway bridge which was opened in 1890 and on the 12 interleaves is an illustrated history of the Scots by Roddy Martine. The booklet was designed by Tayburn and both stamps and interleaves were printed in lithography by Questa.

*Composition.* Two panes of six, one of nine stamps and *se-tenant* pane including label: Pane XDS1 (9 × 19p. phosphorised (advanced coated) paper/PVAD gum); Pane XDS2 (6 × 14p. FCP/PVA band to right of centre); Pane XDS3 (5 × 14p. band at left arranged *se-tenant* with 19p. and 23p. FCP/PVA with two bands); Pane XDS4 (6 × 19p. phosphorised (advanced coated) paper/PVAD gum)

DX10 (21.3.89)  FCP/PVA or Phosphorised paper/PVAD gum          286,775          15·00
   *a.* Additional Pane XDS3   ..   ..   ..   ..   ..
   *b.* Pane XDS3 omitted ..   ..   ..   ..   ..
DX10                                                              First Day Cover          7·50

The Post Office first day cover was issued with the *se-tenant* Pane No. XDS3 cancelled by a special First Day postmark at the Philatelic Bureau, Edinburgh or Inverness.

*Withdrawn:*  20.3.90

Type DX11

(*Illustration reduced actual size* 162 × 97 *mm.*)

The booklet cover shows the Life Guards in their ceremonial dress, ever popular with tourists to London. For the first time the prestige booklet contains panes of special and definitive stamps. The panes are printed in photogravure by Harrison and the multicoloured interleaves with text are in lithography. The back cover shows the entrance to the Palm Court at Alexandra Palace, venue of the "Stamp World London 90" International Stamp Exhibition (3–13 May). The booklet was designed by David Driver and picture research by Sara Driver.

*Composition.* One pane of four, two panes of six and one *se-tenant* pane of eight stamps with centre label showing exhibition logo: Pane WP824 (4 × 20p. Alexandra Palace on phosphorised (advanced coated) paper); Pane WP801 (6 × 20p. Penny Black Anniversary on phosphorised (advanced coated) paper); Pane UWB33 (2nd, 50p., 1st, 15p., label, 20p., Machin and NVI and 15p., 29p., 20p. Penny Black Anniversary on fluorescent coated paper, stamps with 2 bands (excluding 2nd and 15p. which have band at right); Pane WP802 as Pane WP801

| | | |
|---|---|---|
| DX11 (20.3.90) FCP/PVAD or Phosphorised paper/PVAD gum | | 12·00 |
| DX11 | First Day Cover | 7·50 |

The Post Office first day cover was issued with the *se-tenant* Pane No. UWB33 cancelled by a special First Day postmark at the Philatelic Bureau, Edinburgh or Tower Hill, London E.C.3.
Pane No. WP824 is known postmarked at Enfield with first day of issue cancellation dated 6 February 1990. Pane UWB33 exists on cover with both 6 February and 20 March dates due to the use of an unchanged datestamp after it had been used for the 20p. greetings stamps of the 6 February 1990.

*Sold out:*   12.90

# B.    Folded Booklets (1976–90)

## General Notes

The Swedish-style folded booklets comprise a cover with printed information and a single pane of stamps affixed by its selvedge and folded over. The panes may contain two or more values arranged vertically intended for use in vending machines or horizontal panes comprising the current values for first and second class mail for sale over post office counters. Illustrations of untrimmed sheets of the different forms of make-up are given in the Perforators Appendix I.

When the 10p. folded booklets were introduced in March 1976 only a few machines had been modified to issue them. However they were only of limited use since they contained insufficient stamps to frank more than one letter and a 50p. booklet was introduced in January 1977. This was intended for issue through vending machines but it was not until April 1977 that a few machines were converted to take a 50p. coin at a few trial sites and only 100 machines had been converted by the end of 1978. However, all machines were due to be converted by the end of 1979 and the 10p. booklet was phased out in August 1981.

The different editions may be distinguished by the "going to press" dates given in relation to the information about postal rates. The first date given is that printed on the cover and the second is the date of issue. Pictorial covers were introduced in February 1978 with a different theme for each booklet series. From 1987 the Counter booklets were gradually replaced by Barcode booklets.

Further notes are given under Sub-section B of Section UE, where the folded booklet panes in photogravure are listed in detail. See also Section UH for panes printed in lithography. Panes including the Penny Black Anniversary stamps are listed in Section W (photo and litho).

**PAPER AND GUM.** Panes issued before February 1980 had phosphor bands on FCP/PVAD except for the 10p. pane of ten issued 3 October 1979 which was on "All over" phosphor paper. The first pane containing stamps for the first class letter rate to be issued on phosphorised (fluorescent coated) paper was the 12p. pane of ten, issued 4 February 1980. This paper has since been used for all panes which only contain stamps for first class letters, except in cases where the fluorescent additive was omitted in error. Panes containing stamps of mixed denominations or second class only continued to be printed on FCP/PVAD with phosphor bands. One exception was the *se-tenant* pane from the £4 Royal Mint booklet which was printed on phosphorised (advanced coated) paper as no second class rate stamps were included in that pane. The first counter booklet containing stamps for the first class letter rate to be printed on this paper was issued on 14 April 1987 in the £1·80 booklet No. FU3.

**Quantities issued.** These figures are supplied by the Post Office and refer to the quantities issued.

**PRICES.** Again we must stress that prices quoted here are for booklets containing panes with average perforations whereas the same panes with good perforations and listed according to perforator types are quoted at higher rates in Section UE.

For folded Christmas and 1989 Greetings booklets see Nos. FX1/10.

## 10p. Booklets
### For Sale in Automatic Slot Machines

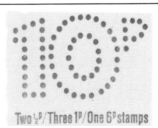

Type FA1

This booklet was pre-released by the Edinburgh Bureau on 5 March and panes exist postmarked 8 and 9 March.

*Cover*. Printed in dull rose on very pale lavender

*Composition*. One pane of six: Pane UMFB1 or 2 (horizontal pair of ½p. *se-tenant* with 6p. and 1p., *se-tenant* with pair of 1p.)

## APPENDIX J    Folded Booklets—10p.

---

*Experimental Series, Type* FA1, *designed by Post Office artists*

| | | |
|---|---|---|
| FA1 November 1975 (10.3.76) | 2,380,360 | 60 |
| FA2 March 1976 (9.6.76) | 18,343,150 | 80 |
|   *a.* Miscut pane  ..   ..   ..   ..   ..   .. | | |
|   *b.* Pale lavender omitted from cover  ..   ..   ..   .. | | £100 |
| FA3 JUNE 1977 (13.6.77) | 16,130,900 | 70 |
|   *a.* Miscut pane  ..   ..   ..   ..   ..   ..   .. | | 6·50 |

---

Type FA2
Farm Buildings Series.   Des. Norman Battershill

---

*Cover.* Printed in bistre-brown and turquoise-blue

*Composition.* One pane of five: Pane UMFB7 (½p. *se-tenant* with label at right printed "remember the postcode" in same colour; ½p. *se-tenant* with 1p.; 7p. *se-tenant* with 1p.—all values with centre band)

*Type* FA2, *Farm Buildings*

| | | |
|---|---|---|
| FA4 No. 1. Oast houses (January 1978) (8.2.78) | 7,411,800 | 60 |
|   *a.* Miscut pane  ..   ..   ..   ..   ..   .. | | 55·00 |
| FA5 No. 2. Northern Ireland (January 1978) (3.5.78) | 7,393,575 | 60 |
|   *a.* Miscut pane  ..   ..   ..   ..   ..   .. | | 70·00 |
| FA6 No. 3. Yorkshire (July 1978) (9.8.78) | 5,388,675 | 80 |
|   *a.* Turquoise-blue omitted from cover ..   ..   ..   .. | | £110 |
| FA7 No. 4. Wales (October 1978) (25.10.78) | 3,569,775 | 60 |
| FA8 No. 5. Scotland (December 1978) (10.1.79) | 5,871,200 | 60 |
|   *a.* Miscut ..   ..   ..   ..   ..   ..   .. | | 13·00 |
| FA9 No. 6. Sussex (March 1979) (4.4.79) | 5,370,825 | 60 |
|   *a.* Miscut ..   ..   ..   ..   ..   ..   .. | | £225 |

*Withdrawn or sold out:*

| | | | | | | | | |
|---|---|---|---|---|---|---|---|---|
| FA1 .. | .. | 7.76 | FA4 .. | .. | 6.78 | FA7 .. | .. | 3.79 |
| FA2 .. | .. | 1.10.77 | FA5 .. | .. | 11.78 | FA8 .. | .. | 11.79 |
| FA3 .. | .. | 30.6.78 | FA6 .. | .. | 2.79 | FA9 .. | .. | 11.79 |

---

Type FA3
"London 1980" Int. Stamp Exhibition. Des. Hamper and Purssell

---

*Cover.* Printed in red and blue

*Composition.* One pane of three: Panes UMFB11 or 12 (label *se-tenant* vertically with 8p., label printed "be properly addressed use the postcode" and pair of 1p., all values with one centre band)

*Type* FA3 *"London 1980" International Stamp Exhibition*

| | | | | | | | | | |
|---|---|---|---|---|---|---|---|---|---|
| FA10 | No. 1. London 1980 (August 1979) (17.10.79) (*with* FA11) | | | | | | 19,737,686 | 50 |
| | *a.* Miscut | .. | .. | .. | .. | .. | .. | .. | 7·00 |
| FA11 | as last (January 1980) (12.1.80) | | | | | | | 50 |
| | *a.* Miscut. Pane UMFB11 ("Jumelle") | | .. | .. | .. | .. | .. | 3·50 |
| | *b.* Miscut. Pane UMFB12 (Chambon) | | .. | .. | .. | .. | .. | £250 |

Miscut panes show the postcode label at right.

*Withdrawn or sold out:*

| | | | | |
|---|---|---|---|---|
| FA10 | .. | .. | .. | 8.81 |
| FA11 | .. | .. | .. | 30.4.82 |

## 50p. Booklets

**Intended for Sale in Automatic Slot Machines as and when 10p. Machines were converted**

All booklets were sold at the cover price of 50p., although some contain stamps to a greater value.

Type FB1

*Cover.* Printed in maroon and pale blue

*Composition.* One pane of ten: Pane UMFB3 or 4 (½p. (2); 1p. (2); 8½p. (4); 6½p. side band (2)). The pane is folded twice.

*Type* FB1, *designed by Post Office artists*

| | | | |
|---|---|---|---|
| FB1A Pane UMFB3 with 6½p. at left (band right) (March 1976) (26.1.77) } | 701,344 | 2·50 |
| FB1B Pane UMFB4 with 6½p. at right (band left) (March 1976) (26.1.77) } | | 2·00 |

**Contents Changed**

*Cover.* Chestnut and stone

*Composition.* One pane of eight: Pane UMFB5 or 6 (1p. (2); 9p. (3); 7p. side band (3))

Type FB1 but with values altered

| | | | |
|---|---|---|---|
| FB2A Pane UMFB5 with 7p. at left (band at right) (June 1977) (13.6.77) } | 335,825 | 4·00 |
| FB2B Pane UMFB6 with 7p. at right (band at left) (June 1977) (13.6.77) } | | 2·50 |

Type FB2
Commercial Vehicles Series. Des. John Ireland

*Cover*. Printed in olive-yellow and grey

*Composition*. As for No. FB2
> A. Pane UMFB5 with 7p. at left (band at right)
> B. Pane UMFB6 with 7p. at right (band at left)

*Type* FB2, *Commercial Vehicles*

|  |  | A | B |
|---|---|---|---|
| FB3 No. 1. Clement-Talbot van (January 1978) (8.2.78) | 179,950 | 4·00 | 3·50 |
| FB4 No. 2. Austin Cape taxi (January 1978) (3.5.78) | 310,975 | 4·00 | 2·75 |
| FB5 No. 3. Morris Royal Mail (July 1978) (9.8.78) | 147,950 | 4·50 | 2·75 |
| FB6 No. 4. Guy Electric dustcart (October 1978) (25.10.78) | 217,950 | 5·00 | 3·00 |
| FB7 No. 5. Albion van (December 1978) (10.1.79) | 155,550 | 5·50 | 2·75 |
| FB8 No. 6. Leyland Fire engine (March 1979) (4.4.79) | 532,798 | 4·00 | 2·75 |

**Contents Changed**

*Composition*. One pane of seven: Pane UMFB9 or 10 (2p. (2) *se-tenant* with label printed "don't forget the postcode"; 8p. side band (2); 10p. 2 bands (3))
> A. Pane UMFB9  with 8p. at left (band at right)
> B. Pane UMFB10 with 8p. at right (band at left)

*Type* FB2, *Commercial Vehicles*

|  |  | A | B |
|---|---|---|---|
| FB9 No. 6. Leyland Fire Engine (August 1979) (28.8.79) | 592,620 | 2·25 | 2·00 |

*Withdrawn or sold out:*

| | | | | | |
|---|---|---|---|---|---|
| FB1 .. .. .. 10.77 | FB4 .. .. .. 2.79 | FB7 .. .. .. 9.79 |
| FB2 .. .. .. 10.78 | FB5 .. .. .. 9.79 | FB8 .. .. .. 1.80 |
| FB3 .. .. .. 7.79 | FB6 .. .. .. 12.79 | FB9 .. .. .. 10.79 |

Veteran Car Series. Des. Basil Smith

*Cover*. Printed in orange-red and reddish lilac

*Composition*. As Nos. FB9A/B
> A. Pane UMFB9  with 8p. at left (band at right)
> B. Pane UMFB10 with 8p. at right (band at left)

*Type* FB2, *Showing Automobiles*

|  |  | A | B |
|---|---|---|---|
| FB10 No. 1. 1907 Rolls-Royce Silver Ghost (August 1979) (3.10.79) | 485,925 | 2·00 | 2·00 |
| *a.* Miscut .. .. .. .. .. .. .. | | — | |

**Contents Changed**

*Composition.* One pane of seven: Panes UMFB14/15 (FB11A/B) or UMFB16/17 (FB12A/13B) (2p. (3) *se-tenant* with label printed "don't forget the postcode", 10p. side band (2); 12p. 2 bands (2))
      A. Pane UMFB14 or 16 with 10p. at left (band at right)
      B. Pane UMFB15 or 17 with top at right (band at left)

*Type* FB2, *Showing Automobiles*

|  |  | A | B |
|---|---|---|---|
| FB11 No. 2. 1908 Grand Prix Austin (January 1980) (4.2.80) | 1,690,384 | 2·00 | 2·00 |
| FB12 No. 3. 1903–5 Vauxhall (May 1980) (25.6.80) | 1,292,256 | 2·00 | 2·00 |
| FB13 No. 4. 1897–1900 Daimler (July 1980) (24.9.80) | 1,419,896 | 2·00 | 2·00 |

**Contents Changed**

*Composition.* One pane of six: Pane UMFB19 or 20 (½p., 1p., 14p. *se-tenant* with 11½p. side band (3))
      A. Pane UMFB19 with 11½p. at left (band at right)
      B. Pane UMFB20 with 11½p. at right (band at left)

*Type* FB2, *Showing Automobiles*

|  |  | A | B |
|---|---|---|---|
| FB14 No. 5. 1896 Lanchester (January 1981) (26.1.81) .. .. | 3,342,150 | 2·25 | 2·25 |
|     *a.* Miscut .. .. .. .. .. .. | | — | |
| FB15 No. 6. 1913 Bullnose Morris (January 1981) (18.3.81) .. | 202,825 | 2·25 | 2·25 |

*Withdrawn or sold out:*

| FB10 | .. .. | 2·80 | FB12 | .. .. | 12·80 | FB14 | .. .. | 11·81 |
|---|---|---|---|---|---|---|---|---|
| FB11 | .. .. | 9·80 | FB13 | .. .. | 4·81 | FB15 | .. .. | 12·81 · |

Type FB16
Follies Series. Des. Richard Downer

*Cover.* Printed in brown and orange-brown

*Composition.* As for No. FB14
      A. Pane UMFB19 with 11½p. at left (band at right)
      B. Pane UMFB20 with 11½p. at right (band at left)

*Type* FB16, *Follies*

|  |  | A | B |
|---|---|---|---|
| FB16 No. 1. Mugdock Castle (January 1981) (6.5.81) | 3,723,925 | 2·50 | 2·50 |

*Withdrawn:* 12.81

**Contents Changed**

*Composition.* One pane of eight: Pane UMFB23 or 24 (2½p. 2 bands (3), 4p. 2 bands (2) *se-tenant* with 11½p. side band (3))

      A. Pane UMFB23 with 11½p. at left (band at right)
      B. Pane UMFB24 with 11½p. at right (band at left)

*Type* FB16, *Follies*

|  |  | A | B |
|---|---|---|---|
| FB17 No. 1. Mugdock Castle (January 1981) (26.8.81) | 1,767,975 | 6·00 | 7·00 |
| FB18 No. 2. Mow Cop Castle (January 1981) (30.9.81) | 1,769,575 | 6·00 | 6·50 |

**Contents Changed**

*Composition.* One pane of eight: Pane UMFB26 or 27 (½p.; 3p. two bands (4) *se-tenant* with 12½p. side band (3))

      A. Pane UMFB26 with 12½p. at left (band at right)
      B. Pane UMFB27 with 12½p. at right (band at left)

*Type* FB16, *Follies*

|  |  | A | B |
|---|---|---|---|
| FB19 No. 3. Paxton's Tower (February 1982 (1.2.82) | 5,398,900 | 2·75 | 2·75 |
|   *a.* Miscut  ..   ..   ..   ..   .. | | £500 | £500 |
| FB20 No. 4. Temple of the Winds (February 1982) (6.5.82) | 3,436,275 | 2·75 | 2·75 |
| FB21 No. 5. Temple of the Sun (February 1982) (11.8.82) | 2,355,350 | 3·00 | 3·00 |
| FB22 No. 6. Water Garden (February 1982) (6.10.82) | 3,403,200 | 3·00 | 3·00 |

*Withdrawn or sold out:*

| FB17 | .. | .. | 11.81 | FB19 | .. | .. | 1.83 | FB21 | .. | .. 11.8.83 |
|---|---|---|---|---|---|---|---|---|---|---|
| FB18 | .. | .. | 5.82 | FB20 | .. | .. | 6.5.83 | FB22 | .. | .. 5.10.83 |

Type FB23
Rare Farm Animals Series. Des. Harry Titcombe

*Cover.* Printed in black and bright green

*Composition.* As for No. FB19

      A. Pane UMFB26 with 12½p. at left (band at right)
      B. Pane UMFB27 with 12½p. at right (band at left)

*Type* FB23, *Rare Farm Animals*

|  |  | A | B |
|---|---|---|---|
| FB23 No. 1. Bagot Goat (February 1982) (16.2.83) | 405,275 | 2·75 | 3·00 |

**Contents Changed**

*Cover.* Printed in black and bright green

*Composition.* One pane of eight: Pane UMFB31 (1p. (2); 3½p. (3) *se-tenant* with 12½p. (3) centre band)

*Type* FB23, *Rare Farm Animals*

| | | |
|---|---|---|
| FB24 No. 2. Gloucester Old Spot Pig (April 1983) (5.4.83) | 7,304,754 | 6·50 |
| *a.* Miscut .. .. .. .. .. .. .. .. | | £150 |
| *b.* Corrected rate .. .. .. .. .. .. .. | | 6·50 |
| FB25 No. 3. Toulouse Goose (April 1983) (27.7.83) | 3,753,500 | 6·50 |
| FB26 No. 4. Orkney Sheep (April 1983) (26.10.83) | 9,981,000 | 6·50 |

The corrected rate reads, "36p. for 200 g" instead of "37p. for 200 g"

*Withdrawn or sold out:*

| | | | | | |
|---|---|---|---|---|---|
| FB23 | .. | .. 15.2.84 | FB25 | .. | .. 26.7.84 |
| FB24 | .. | .. 1.84 | FB26 | .. | ..25.10.84 |

Type FB27
Orchid Series. Des. Peter Morter

*Cover.* Printed in yellow-green and lilac

*Composition.* One pane of eight: Pane UMFB34 (1p. (3); 4p. (2) *se-tenant* with 13p. (3) centre band)

*Type* FB27, *Orchids*

| | | |
|---|---|---|
| FB27 No. 1. *Dendrobium nobile* (September 1984) (3.9.84) | 9,325,500 | 4·00 |
| FB28 No. 2. *Cypripedium calceolus* (September 1984) (15.1.85) | 3,761,600 | 4·00 |
| FB29 No. 3. *Bifrenaria* (September 1984) (23.4.85) | 4,810,850 | 4·00 |
| FB30 No. 4. *Cymbidium* (September 1984) (23.7.85) | 2,789,500 | 4·00 |

*Withdrawn:*

| | | | | | |
|---|---|---|---|---|---|
| FB27 | .. | .. 2.9.85 | FB29 | .. | .. 22.4.86 |
| FB28 | .. | .. 14.1.86 | FB30 | .. | .. 22.7.86 |

Type FB31
Des. Michael Thierens Design Ltd.

*Cover.* Printed in red and black

*Composition.* One pane of three: Pane UFB38 (17p. two bands (3) with *se-tenant* label printed
"Please use the postcode" all with multiple double lined star underprint in blue)

*Type* FB31
FB31 Pillar box design (November 1985) (4.11.85)　　　　　　10,485,275　　　3·00

*Withdrawn:* 3.11.86

Type FB32
Pond Life Series. Des. Peter Morter

*Cover.* Printed in dull blue and emerald

*Composition.* As for No. FB31

*Type* FB32, *Pond Life*
FB32 No. 1. Emperor Dragonfly (November 1985) (20.5.86)　　　　　—　　　2·75
FB33 No. 2. Common Frog (November 1985) (29.7.86)　　　5,213,148　　　2·75
　　*a.* Pane UFB39 (no underprint) (12.8.86)　　..　　..　　..　　　　　　2·75

*Withdrawn:*
　　　　　　FB32　　..　　..　19.5.87 ┃ FB33*a*　　..　　..　11.8.87
　　　　　　FB33　　..　　..　28.7.87 ┃

**517**

Type FB34
Roman Britain Series. Des. Norman Battershill

*Cover.* Printed in brown-ochre and Indian red

*Composition.* One pane of six: Pane UMFB39 (1p. (2); 12p. (4) centre band).

*Type* FB34, *Roman Britain*
FB34 No. 1. Hadrian's Wall (November 1985) (29.7.86)          304,640          7·00

*Withdrawn:* 28.7.87


**Contents Changed**
*Cover.* Printed in dull blue and emerald
*Composition.* One pane of six: Pane UMFB40 or 40*b* (1p.; 5p. (2) *se-tenant* with 13p. (3) all centre band)
*Type* FB32, *Pond Life*
FB35 No. 3. Moorhen (No imprint date) (20.10.86)          362,643          3·25
FB36 No. 4. Giant Pond and Great Ramshorn Snails (October
1986) (27.1.87)                                           289,417          3·25

*Withdrawn:*
          FB35      ..      .. 19.10.87  |  FB36      ..      .. 26.1.88


**Contents Changed**
*Composition.* One pane of four: Pane UMFB42 or 42*c* (1p. side-band at left; 13p. one side-band at right; 18p. two bands (2))
*Type* FB34, *Roman Britain*
FB37 No. 2. Roman Theatre of Verulamium, St. Albans (No
imprint date) (20.10.86)                                  9,273,036        2·50
FB38 No. 3. Portchester Castle, Hampshire (October 1986)
(27.1.87)                                                 3,369,484        2·50

*Withdrawn:*
          FB37      ..      .. 19.10.87  |  FB38      ..      .. 26.1.88

Type FB39
Bicentenary of Marylebone Cricket Club Series. Des. Patricia Howes

*Cover.* Printed in brown and dull ultramarine

*Composition.* As for No. FB37. One pane of four: Pane UMFB42*c* (1p. band at left, 13p. band at right with 18p. 2 bands (2))

*Type* FB39, *MCC Bicentenary*

| | | |
|---|---|---|
| FB39 No. 1. Father Time weathervane (October 1986) (14.4.87) | 5,498,000 | 2·50 |
| FB40 No. 2. Ashes urn and embroidered velvet bag (October 1986) (14.7.87) | 4,293,075 | 2·50 |
| FB41 No. 3. Lord's Pavilion and wrought iron decoration on roof (October 1986) (29.9.87) | 5,036,525 | 2·50 |
| FB42 No. 4. England team badge and new stand at Lord's (October 1986) (26.1.88) | 3,752,950 | 2·50 |

Nos. FB39/40 exist with panes in the original phosphor ink. *Price for* FB39, £6 *and* FB40, £200.

*Withdrawn:*

| | | | | | | | |
|---|---|---|---|---|---|---|---|
| FB39 | .. | .. | 13.4.88 | FB41 | .. | .. | 28.9.88 |
| FB40 | .. | .. | 13.7.88 | FB42 | .. | .. | 25.1.89 |

Type FB43
Botanical Gardens Series. Des. Graham Evernden

*Cover.* Printed in ultramarine and rose-red

*Composition.* As for No. FB35. One pane of six: Pane UMFB40*b* or 41 with vertical sides imperf. (1p., 5p. (2), 13p. (3) centre band)

*Type* FB43, *Botanical Gardens*

FB43 No. 1. Rhododendron "Elizabeth", Bodnant (October
    1986) (14.4.87) (ultramarine and rose-red cover)               700,000      2·50

FB44 No. 2. *Gentiana sino-ornata*, Edinburgh (October 1986)
    (14.7.87) (deep ultramarine and cobalt cover)            271,875      2·50

FB45 No. 3. *Lillum auratum*, Mount Stuart (October 1986)
    (29.9.87) (dull ultramarine and orange-yellow)         1,693,325      2·50
   *a.* Corrected inscription (30.10.87)     ..    ..    ..                    2·50

FB46 No. 4. *Strelitzia reginae*, Kew (October 1986) (26.1.88)
    (dull ultramarine and yellow-orange)              664,975      2·50

No. FB45*a* shows correct spelling of Mount Stewart.

*Withdrawn:*

|  |  |  |  |  |  |  |  |
|---|---|---|---|---|---|---|---|
| FB43 | .. | .. | 13.4.88 | FB45/*a* | .. | .. | 28.9.88 |
| FB44 | .. | .. | 13.7.88 | FB46 | .. | .. | 25.1.89 |

Type FB47
London Zoo. Drawings by children from Byron Infants School, Croydon

*Composition.* As for No. FB37. One pane of four: Pane UMFB42*c* (1p. band at left, 13p. band at right with 18p. 2 bands (2))

*Type* FB47, *London Zoo*
FB47 No. 1. Pigs design (October 1986) (12.4.88) (black and rose
    cover)                                          1,268,900      2·50

**Contents Changed**

*Composition.* As for No. FB35. One pane of six: Pane UMFB41 (1p., 5p. (2), 13p. (3) centre band) with vertical sides imperf.

*Type* FB47, *London Zoo*
FB48 No. 2. Birds design (October 1986) (12.4.88) (black and
    yellow cover)                                   756,150      2·50

**Contents Changed**

*Composition.* As for No. FB37. One pane of four: Pane UMFB42*c* (1p. band at left, 13p. band at right with 18p. 2 bands (2))

*Type* FB47, *London Zoo*
FB49 No. 4. Elephants design (October 1986) (5.7.88) (black and
    grey cover)                                   133,450      2·50

*Withdrawn:*

|  |  |  |  |  |  |  |  |
|---|---|---|---|---|---|---|---|
| FB47 | .. | .. | 11.4.89 | FB49 | .. | .. | 4.7.89 |
| FB48 | .. | .. | 11.4.89 | | | | |

Type FB50

Marine Life Series. Des. Peter Morter

*Composition.* As for No. FB35. One pane of six: Pane UMFB41 (1p., 5p. (2), 13p. (3) centre band) with vertical sides imperf.

*Type* FB50, *Marine Life*
FB50 No. 1. Parasitic anemone on Common whelk shell
   (October 1986) (5.7.88) (blue and orange-brown cover)           91,950        2·50

*Withdrawn:* 4.7.89

Type FB51

Gilbert and Sullivan Operas Series. Des. Lynda Gray

*Cover.* Printed in red and black

*Composition.* One pane of three: Pane UMFB45 (14p. side band *se-tenant* vertically with label printed "Please use the postcode" and 19p. 2 bands (2))

*Type* FB51, *Gilbert and Sullivan*
FB51 No. 1. *The Yeomen of the Guard* (5.9.88)             9,971,300      2·75
   *a.* Miscut pane    ..      ..      ..      ..    ..      ..
FB52 No. 2. *The Pirates of Penzance* (24.1.89)            4,535,950      2·75
FB53 No. 3. *The Mikado* (25.4.89)                     3,685,225      2·75
*Withdrawn:*

| | | | | | | |
|---|---|---|---|---|---|---|
| FB51 | .. | .. | 4.9.89 | FB53 | .. | .. 24.4.90 |
| FB52 | .. | .. | 23.1.90 | | | |

Changed back to Marine Life Type FB50

*Composition.* As for No. FB51
FB54 No. 2. Common Hermit Crab (18.7.89) (blue and orange-
   brown cover)                             1,999,675      3·25

    No. FB54 was first issued containing panes printed on the Jumelle press. The booklet subsequently appeared on 8 August 1989 with panes printed on the Chambon machine. Panes from the two printings may be distinguished by the clear cut holes of the Chambon and gummed side residue left by the Jumelle APS rotary perforator. Prices are the same for either printing.

*Withdrawn:* 30.4.90

Type FB55
Aircraft Series. Des. Peter Hutton

*Cover*. Printed in turquoise-green and light brown

*Composition*. One pane of three: Pane UMFB47 (15p. side band (2) *se-tenant* with label printed "Please use the postcode" and 20p. 2 bands)

*Type* FB55, *Aircraft*
FB55 No. 1. HP42, Armstrong Whitworth "Atalanta" and De
    Havilland "Dragon Rapide" (2.10.89)                        2,332,200        2·25
   No. FB55 was incorrectly inscribed "Atlanta".

As before, but containing Penny Black Anniversary pane No. WP797

FB56 No. 2. Vickers "Viscount 806" and De Havilland "Comet
   4" (30.1.90)                                                2·25

**Contents Changed**

*Cover*. Printed in turquoise-green and light brown

*Composition*. One pane of three: Pane UFB69 (label (without bands) *se-tenant* vertically with 17p. (deep blue) with band at right and vertical pair of 17p. with band at left, label printed "Please use the postcode")

*Type* FB55, *Aircraft*
FB57 No. 3. BAC "1-11" and "VC10" (4.9.90)                              75

*Withdrawn:*
            FB55     ..    ..   1.10.90  |  FB56     ..    ..  29.1.91

## 65p. Booklets

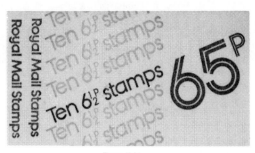

Type FC1

*Cover*. Printed in turquoise-blue and pale buff

*Composition*. One pane of ten: Pane UFB1 or 2 (10 × 6½p. centre band)
   A. Pane UFB1 with selvedge at left
   B. Pane UFB2 with selvedge at right

*Type* FC1, designed by Post Office artists

|  |  | A | B |
|---|---|---|---|
| FC1 (March 1976) (14.7.76) | 5,947,235 | 8·00 | 6·00 |
| *a*. Miscut pane     ..    ..    ..    ..    ..    ..    .. | | 10·00 | 7·50 |

*Withdrawn:* 12.6.78

## 70p. Booklets

*Cover*. Printed in purple-brown and dull rose

*Composition*. One pane of ten: Pane UFB5 or 6 (10 × 7p. centre band)
   A. Pane UFB5 with selvedge at left
   B. Pane UFB6 with selvedge at right

*Type* FC1

|  |  | A | B |
|---|---|---|---|
| FD1 (June 1977) (13.6.77) | 6,536,825 | 5·00 | 4·50 |
| *a*. Miscut pane     ..    ..    ..    ..    ..    ..    .. | | 7·00 | 8·00 |

Type FD1
*(Illustration reduced to ⅔ actual size)*
Country Crafts Series. Des. Eric Stemp

*Cover*. Printed in grey-green and red-brown

*Composition*. As for No. FD1
 A. Pane UFB5 with selvedge at left
 B. Pane UFB6 with selvedge at right

*Type* FD1, *Country Crafts*

|  |  | A | B |
|---|---|---|---|
| FD2 No. 1. Horse-shoeing (January 1978) (8.2.78) | 2,642,050 | 10·00 | 4·00 |
| *a*. Miscut pane  ..    ..    ..    ..    ..    ..    .. |  | 6·00 | 6·00 |
| FD3 No. 2. Thatching (January 1978) (3.5.78) | 186,525 | 50·00 | 4·00 |
| FD4 No. 3. Dry-stone-walling (July 1978) (9.8.78) | 499,950 | £110 | 4·00 |
| FD5 No. 4. Wheel making (October 1978) (25.10.78) | 1,499,875 | 9·00 | 5·00 |
| FD6 No. 5. Wattle fence making (December 1978) (10.1.79) | 1,701,175 | 18·00 | 10·00 |
| *a*. Miscut  ..    ..    ..    ..    ..    ..    ..    .. |  | † | £140 |

Type FD2
*(Illustration reduced to ⅔ actual size)*
Kedleston Hall. Des. Fritz Wegner

Official Opening of Derby Mechanised Letter Office

*Cover*. Printed in pale yellow-green and lilac

*Composition*. As for No. FD1
 A. Pane UFB5 with selvedge at left
 B. Pane UFB6 with selvedge at right

*Type* FD2, *Kedleston Hall*

|  |  | A | B |
|---|---|---|---|
| FD7 (December 1978) (5.2.79) | 76,475 | 7·00 | 7·00 |

On sale only in the Derby Head Post Office area to promote postcode publicity, and also at the Philatelic Bureau and philatelic sales counters.

Change back to Country Crafts Type FD1

|  |  | A | B |
|---|---|---|---|
| FD8 No. 6. Basket Making (March 1979) (4.4.79) | 1,128,425 | 6·00 | 5·00 |

*Withdrawn or sold out:*

| | | | | | | | | | |
|---|---|---|---|---|---|---|---|---|---|
| FD1 | .. | .. | .. | 7.79 | FD4 .. | .. | .. | 7.81 | FD7 .. | .. | .. | 4.79 |
| FD2 | .. | .. | .. | 4.80 | FD5 .. | .. | ·.. | 11.80 | FD8 .. | .. | .. | 12.80 |
| FD3 | .. | .. | .. | 5.80 | FD6 .. | .. | .. | 7.79 | | | | |

## 80p. Booklets

Type FE 1
*(Illustration reduced to $\frac{2}{3}$ actual size)*
Military Aircraft Series. Des. Peter Hutton

*Cover.* Printed in blue and grey

*Composition.* One pane of ten: Pane UFB9 or 10 (10 × 8p. centre band)
        A. Pane UFB9  with selvedge at left
        B. Pane UFB10 with selvedge at right

*Type* FE1 *Military Aircraft*

|  |  | A | B |
|---|---|---|---|
| FE1 No. 1. BE 2B, 1914 and Vickers Gun Bus, 1915 (August 1979) (3.10.79) | 3,220,390 | 3·25 | 3·00 |

*Withdrawn:* 2.82

## 85p. Booklets

*Cover.* Printed in light yellow-olive and brownish grey

*Composition.* One pane of ten: Pane UFB3 or 4 (10 × 8½p. two bands)
        A. Pane UFB3 with selvedge at left
        B. Pane UFB4 with selvedge at right

*Type* FC1

|  |  | A | B |
|---|---|---|---|
| FF1 (March 1976) (14.7.76) | 5,021,770 | 5·50 | 5·50 |
|   *a.* Miscut pane    ..    ..    ..    ..    ..    .. | | 10·00 | 25·00 |

*Withdrawn:* 12.6.78

## 90p. Booklets

*Cover*. Printed in deep grey-blue and cobalt

*Composition*. One pane of ten: Pane UFB7 or 8 (10 × 9p. two bands)
    A. Pane UFB7 with selvedge at left
    B. Pane UFB8 with selvedge at right

*Type* FC1

|  |  | A | B |
|---|---|---|---|
| FG1 (June 1977) (13.6.77) | 5,005,175 | 4·50 | 5·50 |
|   *a*. Miscut pane    ..    ..    ..    ..    .. |  | 12·00 | 7·00 |

Type FG1
*(Illustration reduced to ⅔ actual size)*
British Canals Series. Des. Ronald Maddox

*Cover*. Printed in yellow-olive and new blue

*Composition*. As for No. FG1
    A. Pane UFB7 with selvedge at left
    B. Pane UFB8 with selvedge at right

*Type* FG1, *British Canals*

|  |  | A | B |
|---|---|---|---|
| FG2 No. 1. Grand Union (January 1978) (8.2.78) | 1,707,950 | 17·00 | 6·00 |
|   *a*. Miscut pane   ..   ..   ..   ..   ..   ..   .. |  | 22·00 | 8·00 |
| FG3 No. 2. Llangollen (January 1978) (3.5.78) | 2,052,700 | 5·00 | £250 |
| FG4 No. 3. Kennet & Avon (July 1978) (9.8.78) | 1,491,875 | 14·00 | 8·00 |
| FG5 No. 4. Caledonian (October 1978) (25.10.78) | 1,374,050 | 5·00 | 6·00 |
| FG6 No. 5. Regents (December 1978) (10.1.79) | 2,004,775 | 16·00 | 7·00 |
|   *a*. Pane in cover moved one stamp row to left and folded   .. |  | 18·00 | † |
|   *b*. Miscut pane    ...    ...    ...    ...    ...    ... |  | † | £375 |

No. FG6*a*. was issued because part of the printing had the postal rate notices in the cover placed to the left. In order not to obscure all the notice inside the right-hand cover, the pane was placed left by one stamp row.

Type FG2
*(Illustration reduced to ⅔ actual size)*
Tramway Museum, Crich. Des Fritz Wegner

Official Opening of Derby Mechanised Letter Office.

*Cover.* Printed in violet-blue and rose

*Composition.* As for No. FG1
    A. Pane UFB7 with selvedge at left
    B. Pane UFB8 with selvedge at right

*Type FG2, Tramway Museum, Crich*

|  |  | A | B |
|---|---|---|---|
| FG7 (December 1978) (5.2.79) | 76,450 | 8·00 | 8·00 |

On sale only in the Derby Head Post Office area to promote postcode publicity, and also at the Philatelic Bureau and philatelic sales counters.

Change back to British Canals Type FG1

|  |  | A | B |
|---|---|---|---|
| FG8 No. 6. Leeds and Liverpool (March 1979) (4.4.79) | 2,362,475 | 4·00 | 4·00 |
| *a.* Miscut  .. | | 40·00 | † |

*Withdrawn or sold out:*

| FG1 .. | .. | .. | 7.78 | FG4 .. | .. | .. 12.80 | FG7 .. | .. | .. 4.79 |
|---|---|---|---|---|---|---|---|---|---|
| FG2 .. | .. | .. | 2.78 | FG5 .. | .. | .. 12.80 | FG8 .. | .. | .. 2.82 |
| FG3 .. | .. | .. | 5.80 | FG6 .. | .. | .. 11.80 | | | |

## £1 Booklets
**For Counter Sale**

Type FH1
*(Illustration reduced to ⅔ actual size)*
Industrial Archaeology Series. Des. Norman Battershill

*Cover.* Printed in red and green

*Composition.* One pane of ten: Pane UFB11 or 12 (10 × 10p. "all over" phosphor)

    A. Pane UFB11 with selvedge at left
    B. Pane UFB12 with selvedge at right

*Type FH1, Industrial Archaeology*

|  |  | A | B |
|---|---|---|---|
| FH1 No. 1. Ironbridge, Telford, Salop (August 1979) (3.10.79) | 3,550,120 | 4·00 | 4·00 |
|   *a.* Miscut pane .. .. .. .. .. .. .. |  | 10·00 | 5·50 |

Military Aircraft Series

*Cover.* Printed in blue and grey

*Composition.* (As for No. FH1 but 10 × 10p. centre band)

    A. Pane UFB13 with selvedge at left
    B. Pane UFB14 with selvedge at right

*Type FE1, Military Aircraft*

|  |  | A | B |
|---|---|---|---|
| FH2 No. 2. Sopwith Camel and Vickers Vimy (January 1980) (4.2.80) | 4,015,070 | 4·00 | 4·00 |
|   *a.* Miscut pane .. .. .. .. .. .. |  | 24·00 | 22·00 |
| FH3 No. 3. Hawker Fury* and Handley Page Heyford (May 1980) (25.6.80) | 602,250 | 4·00 | 4·00 |
| FH4 No. 4. Hurricane and Wellington (July 1980) (24.9.80) | 732,100 | 4·00 | 4·00 |

*The aircraft shown is a Hawker Hart.

*Withdrawn or sold out:*

| FH1 .. | .. | .. | 2.82 | FH3 .. | .. | .. | 30.4.82 |
|---|---|---|---|---|---|---|---|
| FH2 .. | .. | .. | 30.4.82 | FH4 .. | .. | .. | 30.4.82 |

## £1 Booklets
### For Sale in Automatic Slot Machines

All booklets were sold at the cover price of £1, although some contain stamps to a greater value.

Type FH5
Musical Instruments Series. Des. Martin Newton and Stanley Paine

*Cover.* Printed in scarlet and black

*Composition.* One pane of six: Pane UFB42 (6 × 17p. phosphorised (fluorescent coated) paper)

*Type FH5, Musical Instruments*

| FH5 No. 1. Violin (November 1985) (29.7.86) | 300,100 | 4·75 |
|---|---|---|

*Withdrawn:* 28.7.87

### Contents Changed

*Composition.* One pane of six: Pane UMFB43 or 43*b* (13p. side-band at left; 18p. (two bands (5))

| FH6 No. 2. French horn (No imprint date) (20.10.86) | 586,268 | 4·75 |
|---|---|---|
| FH7 No. 3. Bass clarinet (October 1986) (27.1.87) | 298,008 | 4·75 |

*Withdrawn:*

| FH6 | .. | .. | 19.10.87 | FH7 | .. | .. | 26.1.88 |
|---|---|---|---|---|---|---|---|

**528**

Type FH8
Sherlock Holmes Series. Des. Andrew Davidson

---

*Cover.* Printed in bright scarlet and grey-black

*Composition.* As for No. FH6. One pane of six: Pane UMFB43*b* or 44 with vertical sides imperf. (13p. band at right with 18p. 2 bands (5))

*Type* FH8, *Sherlock Holmes*
| | | |
|---|---|---|
| FH8  No. 1 *A Study in Scarlet* (October 1986) (14.4.87) | 263,950 | 4·75 |
| FH9  No. 2 *The Hound of the Baskervilles* (October 1986) (14.7.87) | 771,925 | 4·75 |
| FH10 No. 3. *The Adventure of the Speckled Band* (October 1986) (29.9.87) | 1,624,625 | 4·75 |
| FH11 No. 4. *The Final Problem* (October 1986) (26.1.88) | 875,475 | 4·75 |

*Withdrawn:*

| | | | | | |
|---|---|---|---|---|---|
| FH8 | .. | .. 13.4.88 | FH10 | .. | .. 28.9.88 |
| FH9 | .. | .. 13.7.88 | FH11 | .. | .. 25.1.89 |

London Zoo. Drawings by children from Byron Infants School, Croydon

*Composition.* As for No. FH10. One pane of six: Pane UMFB44 (13p. band at right with 18p. 2 bands (5)) with vertical sides imperf.

*Type* FB47, *London Zoo*
| | | |
|---|---|---|
| FH12 No. 3. Bears design (October 1986) (12.4.88) (black and brown cover) | 2,130,100 | 4·75 |

*Withdrawn:* 11.4.89

---

Type FH13
Charles Dickens. Des. Liz Moyes

---

*Cover.* Printed in orange-red and maroon

*Composition.* As for No. FH10. One pane of six: Pane UMFB44 (13p. band at left with 18p. 2 bands (5)) with vertical sides imperf.

*Type* FH13, *Charles Dickens*
FH13 No. 1. *Oliver Twist* (October 1986) (5.7.88)                           409,375                    4·75

**Contents Changed**

*Composition.* One pane of six: Pane UMFB46 (14p. band at right (2) with 19p. two bands (4)) with vertical sides imperf.

*Type* FH13, *Charles Dickens*
FH14 No. 2. *Nicholas Nickleby* (5.9.88)                                  3,284,975                  4·00
FH15 No. 3. *David Copperfield* (24.1.89)                                 4,687,225                  4·00

**Contents Changed**
Stamps printed in lithography by Walsall

*Composition.* One pane of six: Pane UMLP1 (14p. band at right (2) with 19p. two bands (4)) with vertical sides imperf.

*Type* FH13, *Charles Dickens*
FH16 No. 4. *Great Expectations* (September 1988) (25.4.89)               1,904,000                  4·00

*Withdrawn:*

| | | | | | | |
|---|---|---|---|---|---|---|
| FH13 | .. | .. | 4.7.89 | FH15 | .. | .. 23.1.90 |
| FH14 | .. | .. | 4.9.89 | FH16 | .. | .. 24.4.90 |

Marine Life Series. Des. Peter Morter

*Cover.* Printed in turquoise-green and scarlet

*Composition.* As for No. FH14. One pane of six: Pane UMFB46 (14p. band at right (2) with 19p. two bands (4)) with vertical sides imperf.

*Type* FB50, *Marine Life*
FH17 No. 3. Edible Sea Urchin, Common Starfish (18.7.89)                  916,675                    4·00

*Withdrawn:* 30.4.90

Type FH18
Mills Series. Des. Jeremy Sancha

*Cover*. Grey-black and grey-green

*Composition*. One pane of five: Pane UFB68 (5 × 20p. phosphorised (advanced coated) paper with *se-tenant* label printed "Please use the postcode") with vertical sides imperf.

*Type* FH18, *Mills*
FH18 No. 1. Wicken Fen, Ely (2.10.89)                    2,938,810              3·25

As before but experimental glossy card cover containing Penny Black Anniversary pane No. WP810, printed in lithography by Walsall with vertical sides imperf.

*Type* FH18, *Mills*
FH19 No. 1. Wicken Fen, Ely (30.1.90) (bottle-green and pale
   green cover)                                                                    3·25
   No. FH19 was an experimental printing to test a new cover card. This appears glossy when compared with Nos. FH18 and FH20.

As before but changed back to matt card cover containing Penny Black Anniversary pane No. WP798, printed in photogravure by Harrison with vertical sides imperf.

*Type* FH18, *Mills*
FH20 No. 2. Click Mill, Orkney (20.1.90) (grey-black and bright
   green cover)                                                                   3·25

**Contents Changed**

*Cover*. Printed in light blue and buff

*Composition*. One pane of five: Pane UMFB48 (17p. (2) right band, 22p. (3) two bands *se-tenant* with labels (3) printed "Please use the postcode")

*Type* FH18, *Mills*
FH21 No. 3. Jack and Jill Mills, Clayton, Sussex (4.9.90)                  1·50

*Withdrawn or sold out:*

|  |  |  |  |  |  |  |
|---|---|---|---|---|---|---|
| FH18 | .. | .. | 1.10.90 | FH20 | .. | .. 29.1.91 |
| FH19 | .. | .. | 10.90 |  |  |  |

## £1·15 Booklets

*Cover.* Printed in blue and grey

*Composition.* One pane of ten: Pane UFB17 or 18 (10 × 11½p. centre band)
      A. Pane UFB17 with selvedge at left
      B. Pane UFB18 with selvedge at right

*Type* FE1, *Military Aircraft*

|  |  |  | A | B |
|---|---|---|---|---|
| FI1 No. 5. Spitfire and Lancaster (January 1981) (26.1.81) | 3,074,480 | | 4·00 | 4·00 |
| FI2 No. 6. Lightning and Vulcan (January 1981) (18.3.81) | 1,176,400 | | 4·00 | 4·00 |

Type F13
(*Illustration reduced to ⅔ actual size*)
Museums Series. Des. Ronald Maddox

*Cover.* Printed in turquoise-green and blue

*Composition.* As for No. FI1
      A. Pane UFB17 with selvedge at left
      B. Pane UFB18 with selvedge at right

*Type* FI3, *Museums*

|  |  | A | B |
|---|---|---|---|
| FI3 No. 1. Natural History Museum, London (January 1981) (6.5.81) | 652,425 | 4·00 | 4·00 |
| FI4 No. 2. National Museum of Antiquities of Scotland (January 1981) (30.9.81) | 960,600 | 4·00 | 4·00 |

*Withdrawn or sold out:*

| FI1 .. | .. | .. 30.4.82 | FI3 .. | .. | .. 30.4.82 |
|---|---|---|---|---|---|
| FI2 .. | .. | .. 30.4.82 | FI4 .. | .. | .. 5.82 |

## £1·20 Booklets

*Cover.* Printed in red and green

*Composition.* One pane of ten. Pane UFB15 or 16 (10 × 12p. phosphorised paper)
      A. Pane UFB15 with selvedge at left
      B. Pane UFB16 with selvedge at right

*Type* FH1, *Industrial Archaeology*

|  |  | A | B |
|---|---|---|---|
| FJ1 No. 2. Beetle Mill, Ireland (January 1980) (4.2.80) | 4,398,445 | 4·00 | 4·00 |
| *a.* Miscut .. .. .. .. .. .. .. | | 8·00 | 7·00 |
| FJ2 No. 3. Tin Mines, Cornwall (May 1980) (25.6.80) | 1,850,625 | 4·00 | 4·00 |
| FJ3 No. 4. Bottle Kiln, Gladstone, Stoke-on-Trent (July 1980) (24.9.80) | 677,200 | 4·00 | 4·00 |

*Withdrawn:* Nos. FJ1/3 30.4.82

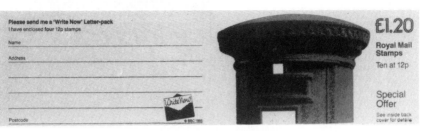

Type FJ4
(*Illustration reduced to ⅔ actual size*)

Des. Michael Thierens Design Ltd.

*Cover.* Printed in pale red and yellow-green

Composition. One pane of ten: Pane UFB40 or UFB41 (10 × 12p. centre band)
   A. Pane UFB40 with selvedge at left
   B. Pane UFB41 with selvedge at right

*Type* FJ4, *Pillar box*

| | | | A | B |
|---|---|---|---|---|
| FJ4 "Write Now", Letter-pack (14.1.86) | | 3,942,575 | 5·00 | 5·00 |

*Withdrawn:* 13.1.87

Type FJ5
(*Illustration reduced to ⅔ actual size*)

National Gallery. Des. Ronald Maddox

*Cover.* Printed in magenta and blue-green

*Composition.* One pane of ten: Pane UFB40 or UFB41 (10 × 12p. centre band)
   A. Pane UFB40 with selvedge at left
   B. Pane UFB41 with selvedge at right

*Type* FJ5, *National Gallery, London*

| | | A | B |
|---|---|---|---|
| FJ5 National Gallery, London (November 1985) (29.4.86) | 3,398,855 | 5·00 | 5·00 |

*Withdrawn:* 28.4.87

**533**

**UNCERTAIN? INDECISIVE?**    **£1.20**

*maybe*

THREAD LEAD-IN

Indicates a writer
who is uncertain
and indecisive.

Send off for your booklet to
discover the secrets of handwriting. ▶

**Royal Mail
Stamps**

Ten at 12p

**Special
Offer
for four
12p stamps**
See inside back
cover for details

Type FJ6

(*Illustration reduced to ⅔ actual size*)

Des. Trickett and Webb Ltd.

*Cover*. Printed in bright orange and bright blue

*Composition*. As for No. FJ5

    A. Pane UFB40 with selvedge at left
    B. Pane UFB41 with selvedge at right

*Type FJ6, Handwriting*

|  |  | A | B |
|---|---|---|---|
| FJ6 "Maybe" (November 1985) (29.7.86) | 551,825 | 2·50 | 2·50 |

*Withdrawn*: 28.7.87

## £1·25 Booklets

*Cover*. Printed in turquoise-green and blue

*Composition*. One pane of ten: Pane UFB21 or 22 (10 × 12½p. centre band)

    A. Pane UFB21 with selvedge at left
    B. Pane UFB22 with selvedge at right

*Type FI3, Museums*

|  |  | A | B |
|---|---|---|---|
| FK1 No. 3. Ashmolean Museum, Oxford (February 1982) (1.2.82) | 3,824,248 | 4·00 | 4·00 |
| FK2 No. 4. National Museum of Wales, Cardiff (February 1982) (6.5.82) | 3,343,589 | 4·00 | 4·00 |
| FK3 No. 5. Ulster Museum, Belfast (February 1982) (11.8.82) | 483,600 | 4·00 | 4·00 |
| FK4 No. 6. Castle Museum, York (February 1982) (6.10.82) | 933,124 | 4·00 | 4·00 |

*Withdrawn or sold out:*

| FK1 .. | .. | .. 1.83 | FK3 .. | .. | .. 11.8.83 |
|---|---|---|---|---|---|
| FK2 .. | .. | .. 6.5.83 | FK4 .. | .. | .. 5.10.83 |

GWR Isambard
Kingdom Brunel
First of four
illustrations by
Stanley Paine on
Railway Engines.
Printed by
Harrison &
Sons Limited

**£1.25**

**Royal Mail
Stamps**

Ten at 12½p

Type FK5

(*Illustration reduced to ⅔ actual size*)
Railway Engines Series. Des. Stanley Paine

*Cover.* Printed in red and blue-green

*Composition.* As for No. FK1
    A. Pane UFB21 with selvedge at left
    B. Pane UFB22 with selvedge at right

*Type FK5, Railway Engines*

|  |  | A | B |
|---|---|---|---|
| FK5 No. 1. GWR *Isambard Kingdom Brunel* (February 1982) (16.2.83) | 170,950 | 6·00 | 5·00 |
| FK6 No. 2. LMS Passenger Tank Engine (April 1983) (5.4.83) | 4,103,942 | 6·00 | 6·00 |
|   *a.* Corrected rate (see note after No. FB26) .. .. | | 30·00 | 30·00 |
| FK7 No. 3. L.N.E.R. *Mallard* (April 1983) (27.7.83) | 1,224,525 | 6·00 | 6·00 |
| FK8 No. 4. SR/BR *Clan Line* (April 1983) (26.10.83) | 3,973,725 | 6·00 | 6·00 |

*Withdrawn:*

| | | | | | | | |
|---|---|---|---|---|---|---|---|
| FK5 .. | .. | .. 15.2.84 | FK7 .. | .. | .. 26.7.84 |
| FK6 .. | .. | .. 4.4.84 | FK8 .. | .. | .. 25.10.84 |

## £1·30 Booklets

Type FL1
*(Illustration reduced to ⅔ actual size)*
Postal History Series. Des. John Gibbs

*Composition.* One pane of ten: Pane UMFB21 or 22 (11½p. side band (4); 14p. (6)).
    A. Pane UMFB21 with selvedge at left
    B. Pane UMFB22 with selvedge at right

*Type FL1, Postal History*

|  |  | A | B |
|---|---|---|---|
| FL1 No. 1. The Penny Black, 1840/41 (April 1981) (6.5.81) (red and black cover) | 1,736,525 | 5·00 | 5·00 |
| FL2 No. 2. The Downey Head, 1911 (September 1981) (30.9.81) (red and green cover) | 104,875 | 7·00 | 20·00 |

*Withdrawn or sold out:*

| | | | | | |
|---|---|---|---|---|---|
| FL1 .. | .. | .. 5.82 | FL2 .. | .. | .. 7·82 |

Type FL3
(*Illustration reduced to ⅔ actual size*)
Trams Series. Des. John Thirsk

---

*Cover.* Printed in yellow-orange and purple

*Composition.* One pane of ten: Pane UFB30 or 31 (10 × 13p. centre band)
    **A.** Pane UFB30 with selvedge at left
    **B.** Pane UFB31 with selvedge at right

*Type FL3, Trams*

|  | | A | B |
|---|---|---|---|
| FL3 No. 1. Swansea/Mumbles Railway Car No. 3 (September 1984) (3.9.84) | 5,038,525 | 5·00 | 5·00 |
| FL4 No. 2. Glasgow, Car Nos. 927, 1194 (September 1984) (15.1.85) | 2,192,375 | 5·00 | 5·00 |
| FL5 No. 3. Blackpool, Car No. 717 (September 1984) (23.4.85) | 1,665,925 | 5·00 | 5·00 |
| FL6 No. 4. London, Cars No. 120 and "D" Class (September 1984) (23.7.85) | 863,850 | 5·00 | 5·00 |

*Withdrawn:*

| | | | | | | | |
|---|---|---|---|---|---|---|---|
| FL3 | .. | .. | 2.9.85 | FL5 | .. | .. | 22.4.86 |
| FL4 | .. | .. | 14.1.86 | FL6 | .. | .. | 22.7.86 |

---

Type FL7
(*Illustration reduced to ⅔ actual size*)
Des. Ann Morrow

*Cover.* Printed in rose-red and lemon

*Composition.* As for No. FL3
>  A. Pane UFB30 with selvedge at left
>  B. Pane UFB31 with selvedge at right

*Type FL7, Books for Children*

|  |  | A | B |
|---|---|---|---|
| FL7  Teddy bears design (No imprint date) (20.10.86) | 5,881,285 | 5·00 | 5·00 |

*Withdrawn:* 19.10.87

Type FL8
(*Illustration reduced to ⅔ actual size*)

*Cover.* Printed in light green and bright blue

*Composition.* As for No. FL3
>  A. Pane UFB30*b* with selvedge at left
>  B. Pane UFB31*b* with selvedge at right

*Type FL8 "Keep in touch"*

|  |  | A | B |
|---|---|---|---|
| FL8  Handclasp and envelope (October 1986) (27.1.87) | 1,536,477 | 5·00 | 5·00 |

*Withdrawn:* 26.1.88

Type FL9
(*Illustration reduced to ⅔ actual size*)
"Ideas for your Garden". Des. Hannah Firmin

*Cover.* Printed in bistre and orange-brown

*Composition.* As for No. FL3
>  A. Pane UFB30*b* with selvedge at left
>  B. Pane UFB31*b* with selvedge at right

*Type FL9, "Ideas for Your Garden"*

|  |  | A | B |
|---|---|---|---|
| FL9  Conservatory design (October 1986) (14.4.87) | 3,185,925 | 5·00 | 5·00 |

*Withdrawn:* 13.4.88

Type FL10
(*Illustration reduced to ⅔ actual size*)

"Brighter Writer". Des. Trickett and Webb Ltd.

*Cover.* Printed in orange and bright reddish violet

*Composition.* As for No. FL3
  A. Pane UFB30*b* with selvedge at left
  B. Pane UFB31*b* with selvedge at right

*Type* FL10, *"Brighter Writer"*

| | | A | B |
|---|---|---|---|
| FL10 Flower design (October 1986) (14.7.87) | 1,373,650 | 5·00 | 5·00 |

*Withdrawn:* 13.7.88

Type FL11
(*Illustration reduced to ⅔ actual size*)
"Jolly Postman". Des. Eric Stemp

*Cover.* Printed in pale blue and deep blue

*Composition.* As for No. FL3
  A. Pane UFB30*b* with selvedge at left
  B. Pane UFB31*b* with selvedge at right

*Type* FL11, *"Jolly Postman"*

| | | A | B |
|---|---|---|---|
| FL11 Boy drawing design (October 1986) (29.9.87) | 3,400,575 | 5·00 | 5·00 |

*Withdrawn:* 28.9.88

538

Type FL12
(*Illustration reduced to ⅔ actual size*)

Bicentenary of Linnean Society. Des. Ted Hughes

*Cover.* Printed in blue and claret

*Composition.* As for No. FL3
    A. Pane UFB30*b* with selvedge at left
    B. Pane UFB31*b* with selvedge at right

*Type* FL12, *Linnean Society*

|  |  | A | B |
|---|---|---|---|
| FL12 Mermaid, fish and insect (from "Hortus Sanitatis" 1497) (October 1986) (26.1.88) | 2,936,875 | 5·00 | 5·00 |

*Withdrawn:* 25.1.89

Type FL13
(*Illustration reduced to ⅔ actual size*)

Recipe Cards. Des. Hannah Firmin

*Cover.* Printed in brown and green

*Composition.* As for No. FL3
    A. Pane UFB30*b* with selvedge at left
    B. Pane UFB31*b* with selvedge at right

*Type* FL13, *Recipe Cards*

|  |  | A | B |
|---|---|---|---|
| FL13 Vegetables design (October 1986) (12.4.88) | 1,844,150 | 5·00 | 5·00 |

*Withdrawn:* 11.4.89

Type FL14

*(Illustration reduced to ⅔ actual size)*

"Children's Parties". Des. Trickett and Webb Ltd.

*Cover.* Printed in blue-green and bright purple

*Composition.* As for No. FL3
      A. Pane UFB30*b* with selvedge at left
      B. Pane UFB31*b* with selvedge at right

*Type FL14, "Children's Parties"*

| | | A | B |
|---|---|---|---|
| FL14  Balloons and streamers design (October 1986) (5.7.88) | 493,650 | 5·00 | 5·00 |

*Withdrawn:* 4.7.89

## £1·40 Booklets

*Cover.* Printed in red and green

*Composition.* One pane of ten: Pane UFB19 or 20 (10 × 14p. phosphorised (fluorescent coated) paper)
      A. Pane UFB19 with selvedge at left
      B. Pane UFB20 with selvedge at right

*Type FH1, Industrial Archaeology*

| | | A | B |
|---|---|---|---|
| FM1 No. 5. Preston Mill, Scotland (January 1981) (26.1.81) | 2,668,453 | 5·00 | 5·00 |
| FM2 No. 6. Talyllyn Railway, Tywyn (January 1981) (18.3.81) | 192,600 | 5·00 | 5·00 |
|   *a.* Miscut pane  ..  ..  ..  ..  ..  ..  .. | | † | £650 |

*Withdrawn:* Nos. FM1/2 30.4.82

Type FM3

*(Illustration reduced to ⅔ actual size)*

Nineteenth-century Women's Costume. Des. Eric Stemp

*Cover.* Printed in dull blue and claret

*Composition.* As for No. FM1
    A. Pane UFB19 with selvedge at left
    B. Pane UFB20 with selvedge at right

*Type* FM3, *Nineteenth-century Women's Costume*

| | | A | B |
|---|---|---|---|
| FM3 No. 1. 1800–1815 (January 1981) (6.5.81) | 3,489,275 | 5·00 | 5·00 |
| FM4 No. 2. 1815–1830 (January 1981) (30.9.81) | 779,600 | 5·00 | 5·00 |

*Withdrawn:*

        FM3   ..   ..   5·82  |  FM4   ..   ..   7·82

Type FM5
(*Illustration reduced to ⅔ actual size*)

"Pocket Planner". Des. Allan Drummond

*Cover.* Printed in grey-black and yellow

*Composition.* One pane of ten: Pane UFB57 or 58 (10 × 14p. centre band)
    A. Pane UFB57 with selvedge at left
    B. Pane UFB58 with selvedge at right

*Type* FM5, "*Pocket Planner*"

| | | A | B |
|---|---|---|---|
| FM5 "Legal Charge" design (5.9.88) | 4,980,200 | 5·00 | 5·00 |

*Withdrawn:* 4.9.89

Type FM6
(*Illustration reduced to ⅔ actual size*)

William Henry Fox Talbot. Des. Debbie Cook

This booklet was issued to mark the 150th anniversary of Fox Talbot's Report on the Photographic Process to the Royal Society.

*Cover.* Printed in reddish orange and black

*Composition.* One pane of ten: Pane UFB57 or 58 (10 × 14p. centre band)
    A. Pane UFB57 with selvedge at left
    B. Pane UFB58 with selvedge at right

*Type* FM6, *William Henry Fox Talbot*

| | | A | B |
|---|---|---|---|
| FM6 | Photographs and darkroom equipment (September 1988) (24.1.89) | | |
| | | 5·00 | 5·00 |

539,200 (under A/B: 5·00 5·00)

*Withdrawn:* 23.1.90

## £1·43 Booklets

*Composition.* One pane of ten: Pane UMFB28 or 29 (12½p. side band (4); 15½p. two bands (6))
    A. Pane UMFB28 with selvedge at left
    B. Pane UMFB29 with selvedge at right

*Type* FL1, *Postal History*

| | A | B |
|---|---|---|
| FN1 No. 3. James Chalmers, 1782–1853 (1.2.82) (orange and turquoise-blue cover)    1,861,150 | 5·00 | 5·00 |
|    *a.* Miscut pane    ..    ..    ..    ..    ..    ..    .. | | |
| FN2 No. 4. Edmund Dulac, 1882–1953 (6.5.82) (brown and red cover)    2,047,410 | 5·00 | 5·00 |
|   Nos. FN1/2 are inscribed February 1982. | | |

Type FN3
(*Illustration reduced to ⅔ actual size*)
The *Golden Hinde.* Des. John Gardner

"The Holiday Postcard Stamp Book".

*Cover.* Printed in turquoise-blue and purple

*Composition.* As for No. FN1
    A. Pane UMFB28 with selvedge at left
    B. Pane UMFB29 with selvedge at right

*Type* FN3, *Golden Hinde*

| | A | B |
|---|---|---|
| FN3 (February 1982) (12.7.82)    2,943,350 | 5·00 | 6·00 |

This special promotion was in operation until 30 September 1982. During this period the Post Office undertook to refund 10p. for each voucher which was returned to the address printed on the back cover of the booklet. The offer was made during the holiday season to promote the sale of postcards when the voucher would be handed to the retailer as part payment for six or more postcards.

Change back to Postal History Series Type FL1

|  |  | A | B |
|---|---|---|---|
| FN4 No. 5. Forces' Postal Service Centenary (21.7.82) (grey and violet cover) | 182,200 | 5·50 | 5·50 |
| FN5 No. 6. The £5 Orange (6.10.82) (orange and black cover) | 94,875 | 5·50 | 5·50 |
| FN6 No. 7. Postmark History (16.2.83) (bright scarlet and deep dull blue cover) | 69,575 | 5·50 | 5·50 |

Nos. FN4/6 are inscribed February 1982.

*Withdrawn or sold out:*

| FN1 | .. | .. | .. | 1.83 | FN3 .. | .. | .. 12.7.83 | FN5 .. | .. | .. 5.10.83 |
|---|---|---|---|---|---|---|---|---|---|---|
| FN2 .. | .. | .. 6.5.83 | | | FN4 .. | .. | .. 21.7.83 | FN6 .. | .. | .. 15.2.84 |

NOTE: For booklet inscribed "£1·45" showing Lyme Regis, Dorset cover, see Type FR2 under £1·60 Booklets.

## £1·46 Booklets

*Composition.* One pane of ten: Pane UMFB32 or 33 (12½p. side band (4); 16p. two bands (6))

    A. Pane UMFB32 with selvedge at left
    B. Pane UMFB33 with selvedge at right

*Type FL1, Postal History*

|  |  | A | B |
|---|---|---|---|
| FO1 No. 8. Seahorse High Values (March 1983) (5.4.83) (blue and green cover) | 2,536,452 | 10·00 | 10·00 |
| *a.* Corrected rate (see note after No. FB26) .. .. .. | | 10·00 | 10·00 |
| FO2 No. 9. Parcel Post Centenary (May 1983) (27.7.83) (turquoise-blue and carmine cover) | 692,275 | 10·00 | 10·00 |
| FO3 No. 10. Silver Jubilee of Regional Stamps (June 1983) (26.10.83) (dull green and reddish violet cover) | 850,850 | 10·00 | 10·00 |

*Withdrawn:*

| FO1 | .. | .. | 4.4.84 | FO3 | .. | .. 25.10.84 |
|---|---|---|---|---|---|---|
| FO2 | .. | .. | 26.7.84 | | | |

## £1·50 Booklets

"Write Now", Letter-pack. Des. Michael Thierens Design Ltd.

*Cover.* Printed in red and ultramarine

*Composition.* One pane of ten: Pane UMFB37 or 38 (12p. side band (4); 17p. two bands (6))

    A. Pane UMFB37 with selvedge at left
    B. Pane UMFB38 with selvedge at right

*Type FJ4, Pillar box*

|  |  | A | B |
|---|---|---|---|
| FP1 "Write Now", Letter-pack (14.1.86) | 2,603,275 | 5·50 | 5·50 |

*Withdrawn:* 13.1.87

National Gallery, London

*Cover.* Printed in violet and vermilion

*Composition.* One pane of ten: Pane UMFB37 or UMFB38 (12p. side band (4); 17p. two bands (6))

    A. Pane UMFB37 with selvedge at left
    B. Pane UMFB38 with selvedge at right

*Type FJ5, National Gallery, London*

|  |  | A | B |
|---|---|---|---|
| FP2 National Gallery, London (November 1985) (29.4.86) | 1,097,275 | 5·50 | 5·50 |

*Withdrawn:* 28.4.87

Handwriting, "No.". Des. Trickett and Webb Ltd.

*Cover*. Printed in blue-green and bright blue

*Composition*. As for No. FP2
> A. Pane UMFB37 with selvedge at left
> B. Pane UMFB38 with selvedge at right

*Type FJ6, Handwriting*

|  |  | A | B |
|---|---|---|---|
| FP3 "No" (November 1985) (29.7.86) | 406,700 | 5·50 | 5·50 |

*Withdrawn:* 28.7.87

---

## £1·54 Booklets

*Composition*. One pane of ten: Pane UMFB35 or 36 (13p. side band (4); 17p. two bands (6))
> A. Pane UMFB35 with selvedge at left
> B. Pane UMFB36 with selvedge at right

*Type FL1, Postal History*

|  |  | A | B |
|---|---|---|---|
| FQ1 No. 11. To Pay Labels (July 1984) (3.9.84) (reddish purple and pale blue cover) | 2,883,325 | 7·00 | 7·00 |
| FQ2 No. 12. Embossed Stamps (September 1984) (15.1.85) (yellow-green and blue cover) | 411,825 | 7·00 | 7·00 |
| FQ3 No. 13. Queen Victoria Surface-Printed stamps (September 1984) (23.4.85) (blue-green and carmine cover) | 331,450 | 7·00 | 7·00 |
| FQ4 No. 14. 350 Years of Service to the Public (September 1984) (23.7.85) (deep brown and orange-red cover) | 383,300 | 7·00 | 7·00 |

*Withdrawn:*

| FQ1 | .. | .. | 2.9.85 | FQ3 | .. | .. | 22.4.86 |
|---|---|---|---|---|---|---|---|
| FQ2 | .. | .. | 14.1.86 | FQ4 | .. | .. | 22.7.86 |

---

## £1·55 Booklets

*Cover*. Printed in claret and dull blue

*Composition*. One pane of ten: Pane UFB23 or 24 (10 × 15½p. phosphorised (fluorescent coated) paper)

> A. Pane UFB23 with selvedge at left
> B. Pane UFB24 with selvedge at right

*Type FM3, Nineteenth Century Women's Costume*

|  |  | A | B |
|---|---|---|---|
| FR1 No. 3. 1830–1850 (February 1982) (1.2.82) | 4,313,350 | 5·50 | 5·50 |
| FR2 No. 4. 1850–1860 (February 1982) (6.5.82) | 3,768,843 | 5·50 | 5·50 |
| *a.* Claret omitted from cover .. .. .. .. .. | £450 |  |  |
| FR3 No. 5. 1860–1880 (February 1982) (11.8.82) | 489,450 | 5·50 | 5·50 |
| FR4 No. 6. 1880–1900 (February 1982) (6.10.82) | 2,383,359 | 5·50 | 5·50 |

*Withdrawn or sold out:*

| FR1 .. | .. | .. | 1.83 | FR3 .. | .. | .. | 11.8.83 |
|---|---|---|---|---|---|---|---|
| FR2 .. | .. | .. | 6.5.83 | FR4 .. | .. | .. | 5.10.83 |

## £1·60 Booklets

Type FS1
(*Illustration reduced to ⅔ actual size*)
Des. Carol Wilkin

"Birthday Box" Stamp Booklet.

*Cover*. Printed in magenta and red-orange

*Composition*. One pane of ten: Pane UFB25 or UFB26 (10 × 16p. phosphorised (fluorescent coated) paper)

        A. Pane UFB25 with selvedge at left
        B. Pane UFB26 with selvedge at right

*Type FS1, "Birthday Box" Design*

|  |  | A | B |
|---|---|---|---|
| FS1 (No imprint date) (5.4.83) | 4,335,537 | 6·00 | 6·00 |
| *a*. Rates altered and "February 1983" imprint date   ..   .. |  | 15·00 | 35·00 |

    This was a special promotion by the Post Office, to increase the sale of stamp booklets. In exchange for any three back covers from Royal Mail stamp booklets the Post Office would despatch a box which contained specially printed birthday reminder cards. The offer, limited to one per household, closed on 31 March 1984.
    For a note on the corrected rate see after No. FB26.

*Withdrawn or sold out: 7.83*

Type FS2
(*Illustration reduced to ⅔ actual size*)
British Countryside Series. Des. Ronald Maddox

Special Discount Booklet (sold at £1·45).

*Cover.* Printed in greenish blue and ultramarine

*Composition.* One pane of ten: UFB27 or UFB28 (10 × 16p. phosphorised (fluorescent coated) paper with double lined "D" in blue printed *over* the gum)

      A. Pane UFB27 with selvedge at left
      B. Pane UFB28 with selvedge at right

*Type* FS2, *British Countryside*

|  |  | A | B |
|---|---|---|---|
| FS2 No. 1. Lyme Regis, Dorset (April 1983) (10.8.83) | 4,427,800 | 6·75 | 6·75 |
|   *a.* Miscut  ..    ..    ..    ..    ..    ..    ..    .. |  | £1800 | † |

*Withdrawn:* 20.9.83

**Contents Changed**

*Cover.* Printed in dull green and violet

*Composition.* One pane of ten: UFB25 or UFB26 (10 × 16p. phosphorised (fluorescent coated) paper)

      A. Pane UFB25 with selvedge at left
      B. Pane UFB26 with selvedge at right

*Type* FS2 but inscribed "£1·60" at top right

|  |  | A | B |
|---|---|---|---|
| FS3 No. 2. Bibury, Gloucestershire (April 1983) (21.9.83) | 10,235,225 | 6·00 | 6·00 |

*Withdrawn:* 20.9.84

Type FS4
(*Illustration reduced to ⅔ actual size*)
Des. Martin Newton

"Write it" Stamp Booklet.

*Cover.* Printed in vermilion and ultramarine

*Composition.* One pane of ten: UFB25 or UFB26 (10 × 16p. phosphorised (fluorescent coated) paper)

      A. Pane UFB25 with selvedge at left
      B. Pane UFB26 with selvedge at right

*Type* FS4, *"Write it" Design*

|  |  | A | B |
|---|---|---|---|
| FS4 (April 1983) (14.2.84) | 2,499,850 | 6·00 | 6·00 |

   The Post Office undertook to donate, to the Stars Organisation for Spastics, five pence for each charity wallet ordered. The special wallet was designed to hold credit cards, season tickets and stamp books. It was obtained from the Post Office by sending the booklet cover and two 16p. stamps to a Freepost address. The offer, limited to one per household, closed on 30 April 1984.

*Withdrawn or sold out:* 11.84

## £1·70 Booklets

Type FT1
(*Illustration reduced to ⅔ actual size*)
Social Letter Writing Series. Des. George Hardie

*Cover.* Printed in rose and deep claret

*Composition.* One pane of ten: Pane UFB34 or 35 (10 × 17p. phosphorised (fluorescent coated) paper)
        A. Pane UFB32 with selvedge at left
        B. Pane UFB33 with selvedge at right

*Type* FT1, *Social Letter Writing*

|  |  | A | B |
|---|---|---|---|
| FT1 No. 1. Love Letters (September 1984) (3.9.84) | 7,918,100 | 7·00 | 7·00 |

*Withdrawn:* 2.9.85

Social Letter Writing Series continued. Des. George Hardie

Special Discount Booklet (sold at £1·55)

*Cover.* Printed in turquoise-blue and deep claret

*Composition.* One pane of ten: UFB36 or UFB37 (10 × 17p. phosphorised (fluorescent coated) paper with double lined "D" in blue printed *over* the gum)
        A. Pane UFB36 with selvedge at left
        B. Pane UFB37 with selvedge at right

*Type* FT1, *Social Letter Writing*

|  |  | A | B |
|---|---|---|---|
| FT2 No. 2. Letters abroad (September 1984) (5.3.85) | 4,041,950 | 7·00 | 7·00 |

*Withdrawn:* 6.4.85 or 8.4.85 in Scotland

**Contents Changed**

*Cover.* Printed in bright blue and deep claret

*Composition.* One pane of ten: UFB34 or UFB35 (10 × 17p. phosphorised (fluorescent coated) paper)
        A. Pane UFB34 with selvedge at left
        B. Pane UFB35 with selvedge at right

*Type* FT1, *Social Letter Writing*

|  |  | A | B |
|---|---|---|---|
| FT3 No. 3. Fan Letters (September 1984) (9.4.85) | 6,794,325 | 6·50 | 6·50 |

*Withdrawn:* 8.4.86

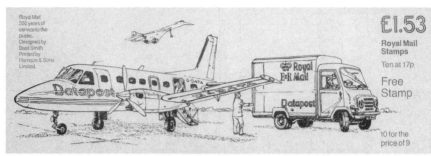

Type FT4
(*Illustration reduced to ⅔ actual size*)
Datapost Service. Des. Basil Smith

Royal Mail 350 Years of Service to the Public

Special Discount Booklet (sold at £1·53)

*Cover.* Printed in rosine and bright blue

*Composition.* One pane of ten stamps No. W626: Pane WP627 (10 × 17p. on phosphorised paper with multiple double lined "D" underprint). Folded twice between rows 1/2 and 3/4 with selvedge at top only.

*Type* FT4, *Royal Mail 350 Years of Service to the Public*

FT4  Datapost Service (September 1984) (30.7.85)                    5,057,600            9·00

*Withdrawn:* 31.8.85

Type FT5 (without "BBC 1985" below "Write Now" envelope)
(*Illustration reduced to ⅔ acutal size*)
Social Letter Writing Series continued

*Cover.* Printed in black and bright scarlet
*Composition.* As for No. FT3
        A. Pane UFB34 with selvedge at left
        B. Pane UFB35 with selvedge at right

*Type* FT5, *Pillar box*

|  | A | B |
|---|---|---|
| FT5 No. 4. Write Now, Letter-pack (8.10.85)          9,248,775 | 6·50 | 6·50 |
| *a.* Revised rates (2nd class (60g) 12p.) ..    ..    ..    .. | 8·00 | 8·00 |

    No. FT5*a* has the "BBC 1985" copyright on the outer back cover as shown on £1·20 booklet Type FJ4.

*Withdrawn:* 7.10.86

National Gallery, London

*Cover*. Printed in blue-green and blue

*Composition*. One pane of ten: Pane UFB32 or UFB33 (10 × 17p. phosphorised (fluorescent coated) paper)
      A. Pane UFB34 with selvedge at left
      B. Pane UFB35 with selvedge at right

*Type* FJ5, *National Gallery, London*

|  |  | A | B |
|---|---|---|---|
| FT6 National Gallery, London (November 1985) (29.4.86) | 7,125,411 | 6·50 | 6·50 |

*Withdrawn:* 28.4.87


Handwriting, "Yes". Des. Trickett and Webb Ltd.

*Cover*. Printed in red and bright blue

*Composition*. As for No. FT6
      A. Pane UFB34 with selvedge at left
      B. Pane UFB35 with selvedge at right

*Type* FJ6, *Handwriting*

|  |  | A | B |
|---|---|---|---|
| FT7 "Yes" (November 1985) (29.7.86) | 658,816 | 6·50 | 6·50 |

*Withdrawn:* 28.7.87


## £1·80 Booklets


Books for Children

*Cover*. Printed in new blue and orange-brown

*Composition*. One pane of ten: Pane UFB43 or 44 (10 × 18p. phosphorised (fluorescent coated) paper)
      A. Pane UFB43 with selvedge at left
      B. Pane UFB44 with selvedge at right

*Type* FL7, *Books for Children*

|  |  | A | B |
|---|---|---|---|
| FU1 Rabbits design (No imprint date) (20.10.86) | 7,317,187 | 7·00 | 7·00 |

*Withdrawn:* 19.10.87


"Keep in Touch"

*Cover*. Printed in magenta and bright blue

*Composition*. As for No. FU1
      A. Pane UFB43 with selvedge at left
      B. Pane UFB44 with selvedge at right

*Type* FL8, *"Keep in Touch"*

|  |  | A | B |
|---|---|---|---|
| FU2 Handclasp and envelope (October 1986) (27.1.87) | 7,079,571 | 7·00 | 7·00 |

*Withdrawn:* 26.1.88

"Ideas for your Garden"

*Cover*. Printed in claret and brown-olive

*Composition*. One pane of ten: Pane UFB45 or 46 (10 × 18p. phosphorised (advanced coated) paper)
       A. Pane UFB45 with selvedge at left
       B. Pane UFB46 with selvedge at right

*Type FL9, "Ideas for your Garden"*

| | | A | B |
|---|---|---|---|
| FU3 Garden path design (October 1986) (14.4.87) | 1,432,372 | 7·00 | 7·00 |

*Withdrawn:* 13.4.88

"Brighter Writer"

*Cover*. Printed in turquoise-green and reddish orange

*Composition*. As for No. FU3
       A. Pane UFB45 with selvedge at left
       B. Pane UFB46 with selvedge at right

*Type FL10, "Brighter Writer"*

| | | A | B |
|---|---|---|---|
| FU4 Berries and leaves design (October 1986) (14.7.87) | 2,886,475 | 7·00 | 7·00 |

*Withdrawn:* 13.7.88

"Jolly Postman"

*Cover*. Printed in deep blue and claret

*Composition*. As for No. FU3
       A. Pane UFB45 with selvedge at left
       B. Pane UFB46 with selvedge at right

*Type FL11, "Jolly Postman"*

| | | A | B |
|---|---|---|---|
| FU5 Girl drawing design (October 1986) (29.9.87) | 6,945,450 | 7·00 | 7·00 |
|    *a.* Miscut pane  ..   ..   ..   ..   ..   ..   .. | | † | £110 |

*Withdrawn:* 28.9.88

Bicentenary of Linnean Society

*Cover*. Printed in dull yellow-green and dull claret

*Composition*. As for No. FU3
       A. Pane UFB45 with selvedge at left
       B. Pane UFB46 with selvedge at right

*Type FL12, Linnean Society*

| | | A | B |
|---|---|---|---|
| FU6 Wolf and birds (from "Hortus Sanitatis" 1497) (October 1986) (26.1.88) | 3,969,575 | 7·00 | 7·00 |
|    *a.* Inside cover text of FL12 (four 13p. stamps)  ..   .. | | 9·00 | 9·00 |
|    *b.* Miscut pane  ..   ..   ..   ..   ..   ..   .. | | £110 | † |

    FU6*a* inside cover has the special offer text of the £1·30 booklet No. FL12. The offer in FU6 refers to four 18p. stamps

*Withdrawn:* 25.1.89

Recipe Cards

*Cover*. Printed in claret and Indian red

*Composition*. As for No. FU3
    A. Pane UFB45 with selvedge at left
    B. Pane UFB46 with selvedge at right

*Type* FL13, *Recipe Cards*

| | | A | B |
|---|---|---|---|
| FU7 Fruits, pudding and jam design (October 1986) (12.4.88) | 5,950,150 | 7·00 | 7·00 |

*Withdrawn:* 11.4.89

"Children's Parties"

*Cover*. Printed in violet and rosine

*Composition*. As for No. FU3
    A. Pane UFB45 with selvedge at left
    B. Pane UFB46 with selvedge at right

*Type* FL14, *"Children's Parties"*

| | | A | B |
|---|---|---|---|
| FU8 Balloons and party hats design (October 1986) (5.7.88) | 472,550 | 7·00 | 7·00 |

*Withdrawn:* 5.7.89

## £1·90 Booklets

"Pocket Planner"

*Cover*. Printed in yellow-green and magenta

*Composition*. One pane of ten: Pane UFB59 or 60 (10 × 19p. phosphorised (advanced coated) paper)
    A. Pane UFB59 with selvedge at left
    B. Pane UFB60 with selvedge at right

*Type* FM5, *"Pocket Planner"*

| | | A | B |
|---|---|---|---|
| FV1 "Marriage Act" design (5.9.88) | 6,816,575 | 6·00 | 6·00 |

*Withdrawn:* 4.9.89

William Henry Fox Talbot

*Cover*. Printed in emerald and black

*Composition*. As for No. FV1
    A. Pane UFB59 with selvedge at left
    B. Pane UFB60 with selvedge at right

*Type* FM6, *William Henry Fox Talbot*

| | | A | B |
|---|---|---|---|
| FV2 W. H. Fox Talbot with camera and Lacock Abbey (September 1988) (24.1.89) | 758,950 | 6·00 | 6·00 |

*Withdrawn:* 23.1.90

## 1978. £1·60 Christmas Booklet

Type FX1
*(Illustration reduced to ⅔ actual size)*
Des. Jeffery Matthews

*Cover.* Printed in rose-red and sage-green

*Composition.* One pane of twenty: Pane UMFB8 (10 × 9p. two bands and 10 × 7p. centre band, folded twice with selvedge at left only)

*Type* FX1

| | | |
|---|---|---|
| FX1  (August 1978) (15.11.78) | 1,111,660 | 4·00 |

*Sold out:* 3.79

## 1979. £1·80 Christmas Booklet

Type FX2
*(Illustration reduced to ⅔ actual size)*
Des. Phillip Sharland

*Cover.* Printed in red and green

*Composition.* One pane of twenty: Pane UMFB13 (10 × 10p. two bands and 10 × 8p. centre band, folded twice with left selvedge only)

*Type* FX2

| | | |
|---|---|---|
| FX2  (October 1979) (15.11.79) | 1,018,315 | 4·75 |
| *a.* Miscut  ..    ..    ..    ..    ..    ..    .. | | 80·00 |

*Withdrawn:* 30.4.82

## 1980. £2·20 Christmas Booklet

Type FX3
*(Illustration reduced to ⅔ actual size)*
Des. Eric Fraser

*Cover.* Printed in red and blue

*Composition.* One pane of twenty: Pane UMFB18 (10 × 12p. two bands and 10 × 10p. centre band, folded twice with left selvedge only)

*Type* FX3

| | | |
|---|---|---|
| FX3 (September 1980) (12.11.80) | 787,108 | 6·00 |

*Withdrawn:* 30.4.82

## 1981. £2·55 Christmas Booklet

Type FX4
*(Illustration reduced to ⅔ actual size)*
Des. Bill Sanderson

*Cover.* Printed in red and deep blue

*Composition.* One pane of twenty: Pane UMFB25 (10 × 14p. two bands and 10 × 11½p. centre band, folded twice with left selvedge only)

*Type* FX4

| | | |
|---|---|---|
| FX4 (January 1981) (11.11.81) | 683,600 | 8·00 |
|    *a.* Miscut  ..    ..    ..    ..    ..    ..    ..    .. | | £700 |

*Withdrawn:* 10.82

## 1982. £2·80 Christmas Booklet (sold at a discount rate of £2·50)

Type FX5
(*Illustration reduced to ⅔ actual size*)
Des. Andrew Davidson

*Cover.* Printed in dull claret and blue-green

*Composition.* One pane of twenty: Pane UMFB30 (10 × 15½p. two bands and 10 × 12½p. centre band, folded twice with left selvedge only)

*Type* FX5 *Christmas Mummers*
FX5 (February 1982) (10.11.82)                    4,971,475              12·00

*Sold out:* Soon after issue

## 1983. £2·50 Christmas Booklet (sold at a discount rate of £2·20)

Type FX6
(*Illustration reduced to ⅔ actual size*)
Des. Barbara Brown

*Cover.* Printed in brown-lilac and yellow

*Composition.* One pane of twenty: Pane UFB29 (20 × 12½p. centre band with a double lined blue star underprint, folded twice with left selvedge only)

*Type* FX6 *Pantomimes*
FX6 (April 1983) (9.11.83)                        6,063,875              7·00
  *a.* Miscut   ..   ..   ..   ..   ..   ..   ..   ..                £1800

*Withdrawn:* 24.12.83

## 1984. £2·60 Christmas Booklet (sold at a discount rate of £2·30)

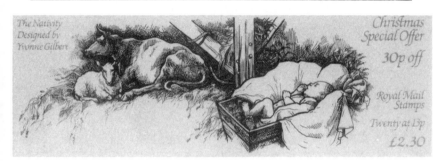

Type FX7
(*Illustration reduced to ⅔ actual size*)
Des. Yvonne Gilbert

---

The sheet make-up was twenty-two horizontal rows of ten stamps in each.

*Cover*. Printed in red-orange and light brown

*Composition*. One pane of twenty Christmas stamps No. W602: Pane WP603 (20 × 13p. one 4 mm. band (to right) with multiple double lined blue star underprint, folded four times and with left selvedge only

*Type* FX7 *The Nativity*
| | | |
|---|---|---|
| FX7 (September 1984) (20.11.84) | 6,195,825 | 10·00 |
|   *a*. Miscut .. .. .. .. .. .. .. .. | | 15·00 |

*Withdrawn:* 24.12.84

---

## 1985. £2·40 Christmas Booklet

---

Type FX8
(*Illustration reduced to ⅔ size*)
Des. Adrian George

---

The sheet make-up was twenty-two horizontal rows of ten stamps each.

*Cover.* Printed in bright blue and rose

*Composition.* One pane of twenty Christmas stamps No. W642: Pane WP643 (20 × 12p. one 4 mm. band at right with multiple double lined blue star underprint, folded four times between rows 2/3, 4/5, 6/7 and 8/9 with left selvedge only)

*Type* FX8, *The Pantomime*

FX8  (19.11.85)                                3,105,950              8·00

*Withdrawn:* 18.11.86

---

## 1986. £1·30 Christmas Booklet (sold at discount rate of £1·20)

Type FX9
(*Illustration reduced to ⅔ actual size*)
Des. Lynda Gray

---

*Cover.* Printed in red and dull blue-green

*Composition.* One pane of ten: Pane UFB32 or UFB33 (10 × 13p. centre band with a single double lined star underprint in blue)
   A. Pane UFB32 with selvedge at left
   B. Pane UFB33 with selvedge at right

*Type* FX9, *Shetland Yule cakes*

|  | A | B |
|---|---|---|
| FX9 (No imprint date) (2.12.86) | 10·00 | 6·00 |

*Withdrawn:* 24.12.86

## 1989. £1·90 Greetings Booklet

Type FX10
(*Illustration reduced to ⅔ actual size*)

Des. Lewis Moberly

*Cover*. Multicoloured. Inscription at right in rose-red

*Composition*. One pane of ten: Pane UJP6 (10 × 19p. (Nos. UJ1/5(2)) and twelve labels (3 × 4) all
  on phosphorised (advanced coated) paper, folded three times with left selvedge)

*As Type* FX10, *various elements*
FX10  Greetings design (September 1988) (31.1.89)                2,705,225          28·00

   The cover of No. FX10 shows an overall pattern of elements taken from the stamp designs. Due to
the method of production the position of these elements varies from cover to cover.

*Withdrawn:* 30.1.90

## C.   Barcode Machin Booklets (1987–90)

### General Notes

A new style of booklet was issued as an experiment on 4 August 1987. The booklets had a number of new features and they were available from the Philatelic Bureau, philatelic counters and Post Offices in Bristol, Nottingham, Preston and York areas. These were to offer the barcode booklets for at least six months, during which time counter booklets were withdrawn.

By the beginning of 1990 barcode booklets were available nationwide and had replaced the previous folded counter booklets at Post Offices.

**PRICES.** Since it is necessary to examine the contents prices are for booklets that have been opened carefully. Tests are being made to introduce covers with peelable adhesive.

**LAMINATED COVERS.** Printed in scarlet, lemon and black these were specially laminated to provide protection and to allow for the window at the top right to show one stamp from the pane inside the booklet. Another important feature is the bar and letter codes on the outside back cover. Printed in black, the first covers had letter codes in the bottom right-hand corner of each booklet. By tucking the front cover into a flap cut from the back it is possible to retain the stamps safely; at first a square tab then a round tab was used for the flap. Evidently the round tab reduced scuffing. Variations in the yellow strip at right are known but these are not listed.

**ERRORS IN MAKE-UP.** These are not, at present, listed and collectors should take expert advice before purchase. Some panes are attached by peelable adhesive while the early Harrison panes would show any attempt at fraud since these were well affixed to the cover. Other attempts at moving panes from their original covers can be checked under ultra violet light.

**ILLUSTRATIONS.** The illustrations of the covers are ½ size.

### 52p. Booklets

Type GA1
Des. Design House Consultants

*Cover.* As Type GA1, with cellophane window, printed by Harrison
    A. Letter code E. Barcode 5 014721 100036
    B. Letter code F. Barcode 5 014721 200033

*Composition.* One pane of four: Pane UFB47 (4 × 13p. centre band) with margins all round

*Type* GA1, *square tab*

|  | A | B |
|---|---|---|
| GA1  (Inscribed 20 October 1986) (4.8.87) | 2·25 | 2·25 |
|   *a.* Round tab (3.88)  ..   ..   ..   ..   ..   .. | 4·25 | 4·25 |

*Quantities Issued:* Nos. GA1/*a* 876,400 (E); 423,350 (F)
*Withdrawn:* 11.4.89

## 56p. Booklets

*Cover.* As Type GA1, with cellophane window, printed by Harrison
    A. Letter code O. Barcode 5 014721 100098
    B. Letter code P. Barcode 5 014721 200095

*Composition.* One pane of four: Pane UFB52 (4 × 14p. centre band) with margins all round

*Type GA1, round tab*

|  | A | B |
|---|---|---|
| GB1 (23.8.88) | 2·50 | 2·50 |

As before, but cover printed by Walsall

|  | A | B |
|---|---|---|
| GB2 (11.10.88) | 2·50 | 2·50 |

*Quantities Issued:* No. GB1 284,500 (O); 123,950 (P); Nos. GB2/4 3,131,225
*Withdrawn:*
      GB1   ..   ..   4.9.89 | GB2   ..   ..   10.10.89

Type GA2
Des. Design House Consultants

*Cover.* As Type GA2, with stamp printed in deep blue, by Harrison
    Barcode 5 014721 200095
*Composition.* One pane of four: Pane UFB61 (4 × 14p. centre band) with horizontal edges imperforate

*Type GA2, round tab*
GB3 (Inscribed 5 September 1988) (11.10.88)          3·00

*Withdrawn:* 28.2.90

As before, but cover printed by Walsall and pane by Harrison

    Barcode 5 014721 100098

*Composition.* One pane of four: Pane UFB66 (4 × 14p. centre band), imperforate on three sides

*Type GA2, round tab*
GB4 (Inscribed 5 September 1988) (24.1.89)          3·00

*Withdrawn:* 28.2.90

**559**

## 72p. Booklets

*Cover.* As Type GA1, with cellophane window, printed by Harrison
    A. Letter code A. Barcode 5 014721 100012
    B. Letter code B. Barcode 5 014721 200019

*Composition.* One pane of four: Pane UFB48 (4 × 18p. phosphorised (advanced coated) paper) with margins all round

*Type* GA1, *square tab*

|  | A | B |
|---|---|---|
| GC1 (Inscribed 20 October 1986) (4.8.87) | 3·00 | 3·00 |
|   *a.* Round tab (3.88) .. .. .. .. .. .. | 12·00 | 15·00 |

*Quantities Issued:* Nos. GC1/*a* 876,400 (A); 423,350 (B)

*Withdrawn:* 11.4.89

## 76p. Booklets

*Cover.* As Type GA1, with cellophane window, printed by Harrison
    A. Letter code K. Barcode 5 014721 100074
    B. Letter code L. Barcode 5 014721 200071

*Composition.* One pane of four: Pane UFB53 (4 × 19p. phosphorised (advanced coated) paper) with margins all round

*Type* GA1, *round tab*

|  | A | B |
|---|---|---|
| GD1 (23.8.88) | 3·50 | 3·50 |

*Quantities Issued:* No. GD1 353,600 (K); 126,150 (L)
*Withdrawn:* 4.9.89

As before, but cover printed by Walsall and pane by Harrison

    A. Letter code K. Barcode 5 014721 100074
    B. Letter code L. Barcode 5 014721 200071

*Composition.* One pane of four: Pane UFB53 (4 × 19p. phosphorised (advanced coated) paper) with margins all round

*Type* GA1, *round tab*

|  | A | B |
|---|---|---|
| GD2 (11.10.88) | 3·50 | 3·50 |

*Quantity Issued:* Nos. GD2/4 5,326,725

*Withdrawn:* 10.10.89

As before, but cover as Type GA2 and contents changed

*Cover.* As Type GA2, with stamp printed in bright orange-red by Harrison
    Barcode 5 014721 200071

*Composition.* One pane of four: Pane UFB62 (4 × 19p. phosphorised (advanced coated) paper) with horizontal edges imperforate

*Type* GA2, *round tab*

| GD3 (Inscribed 5 September 1988) (11.10.88) | 4·00 |
|---|---|

*Withdrawn:* 28.2.90

As before, but cover printed by Walsall and pane by Harrison

Barcode 5 014721 100074

*Composition.* One pane of four: Pane UFB67 (4 × 19p. phosphorised (advanced coated) paper), imperforate on three sides

*Type* GA2, *round tab*

GD4 (Inscribed 5 September 1988) (24.1.89)                                       4·00

*Withdrawn:* 28.2.90

---

## £1.04 Booklets

*Cover.* As Type GA1, with cellophane window, printed by Harrison
  A. Letter code I. Barcode 5 014721 100050
  B. Letter code J. Barcode 5 014721 200057

*Composition.* One pane of four: Pane UFB49 (4 × 26p. (type II) phosphorised (advanced coated) paper) with margins all round

*Type* GA1, *square tab*

|                                                         | A     | B     |
|---------------------------------------------------------|-------|-------|
| GE1 (Inscribed 20 October 1986) (4.8.87)                | 18·00 | 18·00 |
| *a.* Round tab (3.88)   ..   ..   ..   ..   ..   ..      | 18·00 | †     |

*Quantities Issued:* Nos. GE1/*a* 273,900 (I); 145,025 (J)
*Withdrawn:* 11.4.89

---

## £1·08 Booklets

*Cover.* As Type GA1, with cellophane window, printed by Harrison
  A. Letter code S. Barcode 5 014721 100111
  B. Letter code T. Barcode 5 014721 200118

*Composition.* One pane of four: Pane UFB54 (4 × 27p. phosphorised (advanced coated) paper) with margins all round

*Type* GA1, *round tab*

|                                             | A     | B    |
|---------------------------------------------|-------|------|
| GF1 (23.8.88)                               | 4·00  | 4·00 |
| *a.* Incorrect cover ..   ..   ..   ..   ..   ..   .. | 4·50  | †    |

No. GF1*a* has the postage rate leaflet advert omitted from the inside cover above the Harrison imprint.

*Quantities Issued:* Nos. GF1/*a* 90,650 (S); 54,500 (T)
*Withdrawn:* 4.9.89

As before, but cover as Type GA2 and contents changed

*Cover.* As Type GA2, with stamp printed in chestnut by Harrison
  Barcode 5 014721 200118

*Composition.* One pane of four: Pane UFB63 (4 × 27p. phosphorised (advanced coated) paper) with horizontal edges imperforate

*Type* GA2, *round tab*

GF2 (Inscribed 5 September 1988) (11.10.88)                                       4·75

*Quantity Issued:* 424,700
*Withdrawn:* 28.2.90

## £1·16 Booklets

Type GA3
Redrawn Crown (small)
Des. Design House Consultants

*Cover.* As Type GA3, with stamp printed in deep mauve, by Walsall
Barcode 5 014721 100166

*Cover.* As Type GA3, with stamp printed in deep mauve, by Walsall Barcode 5 014721 100166

*Composition.* One pane of four: Pane ULP3 (4 × 29p. two bands), imperforate on three sides, printed in lithography by Walsall

*Type GA3, round tab*

GG1 (2.10.89)                                                                 3·50

*Quantity Issued:* 77,560
*Withdrawn:* 1.10.90

As before, but contents changed

*Composition.* One pane of four: Pane ULP4 (4 × 29p. phosphorised (advanced coated) paper) imperforate on three sides, printed in lithography by Walsall

*Type GA3, round tab*

GG2 (17.4.90)                                                                 3·50

*Withdrawn:* 16.4.91

## £1·24 Booklet

Type GA4
Redrawn Multicoloured Crown on White Background

*Cover.* As Type GA4, with stamp printed in ultramarine, by Walsall
Barcode 5 014721 100227

*Composition.* One pane of four: Pane ULP5 (4 × 31p. phosphorised (advanced coated) paper) with horizontal edges imperforate, printed in lithography by Walsall

*Type GA4, round tab*

GH1 (17.9.90)                                                                 1·90

## £1·30 Booklets

Type GA5
Des. Design House Consultants

*Cover.* As Type GA5, with cellophane window, printed by Harrison
    A. Letter code G. Barcode 5 014721 100043
    B. Letter code H. Barcode 5 014721 200040

*Composition.* One pane of ten: Pane UFB50 (10 × 13p. centre band) with margins all round

*Type* GA5, *square tab*

| | A | B |
|---|---|---|
| GI1 (Inscribed 20 October 1986) (4.8.87) | 4·50 | 4·50 |
|   *a.* Round tab (3.88)    ..    ..    ..    ..    ..    .. | 6·00 | 6·00 |

*Quantities Issued:* Nos. GI1/*a* 468,450 (G); 517,150 (H)
*Withdrawn:* 11.4.89

## £1·40 Booklets

*Cover.* As Type GA5, with cellophane window, printed by Harrison
    A. Letter code Q. Barcode 5 014721 100104
    B. Letter code R. Barcode 5 014721 200101

*Composition.* One pane of ten: Pane UFB55 (10 × 14p. centre band) with margins all round

*Type* GA5, *round tab*

| | A | B |
|---|---|---|
| GJ1 (23.8.88) | 6·00 | 6·00 |

*Quantities Issued:* No. GJ1 264,800 (Q); 311,475 (R)
*Withdrawn:* 4.9.89

As before, but contents changed

*Cover.* As Type GA5, with cellophane window, printed by Questa
    A. Letter code Q. Barcode 5 014721 100104
    B. Letter code R. Barcode 5 014721 200101

*Composition.* One pane of ten: Pane ULP1 (10 × 14p. short centre band) printed in lithography by Questa

*Type* GA5, *round tab*

| | A | B |
|---|---|---|
| GJ2 (11.10.88) | 6·00 | 6·00 |

*Quantity Issued:* Nos. GJ2/4 8,502,100
*Withdrawn:* 10.10.89

**563**

Type GA6
Des. Design House Consultants

*Cover.* As Type GA6, with stamp printed in deep blue, by Harrison
  Barcode 5 014721 200101 (11.10.88)
  Barcode 5 014721 100104 (5.89)

*Composition.* One pane of ten: Pane UFB64 (10 × 14p. centre band) with horizontal edges imperforate

*Type* GA6, *round tab*

GJ3 (Inscribed 5 September 1988) (11.10.88)                                                             6·00
  *a.* Barcode changed (5.89)       ..       ..       ..       ..       ..                              6·00

As before, but stamp printed by Questa

        Barcode 5014721 100104

*Composition.* One pane of ten: Pane ULP1 (10 × 14p. short centre band) printed in lithography by Questa

*Type* GA6, *round tab*

GJ4 (11.10.88)                                                                                         6·00

*Withdrawn:* Nos. GJ3/*a* and GJ4, 28.2.90

## £1·80 Booklets

*Cover.* As Type GA5, with cellophane window, printed by Harrison
  A. Letter code C. Barcode 5 014721 100029
  B. Letter code D. Barcode 5 014721 200026

*Composition.* One pane of ten: Pane UFB51 (10 × 18p. phosphorised (advanced coated) paper) with margins all round

|                                                          | A    | B    |
|----------------------------------------------------------|------|------|
| *Type* GA5, *square tab*                                 |      |      |
| GK1 (Inscribed 20 October 1986) (4.8.87)                 | 6·50 | 6·50 |
| *a.* Round tab (3.88)     ..     ..     ..   ..     ..    ..  | 7·50 | 7·50 |

*Quantities Issued:* Nos. GK1/*a* 581,650 (C); 799,025 (D)
*Withdrawn:* 11.4.89

## £1·90 Booklets

*Cover.* As Type GA5, with cellophane window, printed by Harrison
    A. Letter code M. Barcode 5 014721 100081
    B. Letter code N. Barcode 5 014721 200088

*Composition.* One pane of ten: Pane UFB56 (10 × 19p. phosphorised (advanced coated) paper) with margins all round

*Type* GA5, *round tab*

|  | A | B |
|---|---|---|
| GL1 (23.8.88) | 7·00 | 7·00 |

*Quantities Issued:* No. GL1 266,550 (M); 297,000 (N)
*Withdrawn:* 4.9.89

As before, but cover printed by Questa
    A. Letter code M. Barcode 5 014721 100081
    B. Letter code N. Barcode 5 014721 200088

*Composition.* One pane of ten: Pane ULP2 (10 × 19p. phosphorised (advanced coated) paper) printed in lithography by Questa

*Type* GA5, *round tab*

|  | A | B |
|---|---|---|
| GL2 (11.10.88) | 7·00 | 7·00 |

*Quantity Issued:* Nos. GL2/4 13,777,700
*Withdrawn:* 10.10.89

As before, but cover as Type GA6 and contents changed

*Cover.* As Type GA6, with stamp printed in bright orange-red by Harrison
    Barcode 5 014721 200088 (11.10.88)
    Barcode 5 014721 100081 (6.89)

*Composition.* One pane of ten: pane UFB65 (10 × 19p. phosphorised (advanced coated) paper) with horizontal edges imperforate

*Type* GA6, *round tab*

| | |
|---|---|
| GL3 (Inscribed 5 September 1988) (11.10.88) | 7·00 |
|   *a.* Barcode changed (6.89) .. .. .. .. .. | 7·00 |

As before, but cover printed by Questa

    Barcode 5 014721 100081

*Composition.* One pane of ten: Pane ULP2 (10 × 19p. phosphorised (advanced coated) paper) printed in lithography by Questa

*Type* GA6, *round tab*

| | |
|---|---|
| GL4 (11.10.88) | 7·00 |

*Withdrawn:* Nos. GL3/*a* and GL4, 28.2.90

# D. Barcode NVI Booklets (1989–90)

## General Notes

The first barcode booklets containing Machin stamps with no value indicated were issued on 22 August 1989, when 56p., 76p., £1·40 and £1·90 appeared. These were subsequently sold at increased postal rates from 2 October. The following year the 60p., 80p., £1·50 and £2 booklets were released and from 17 September 1990 were sold at the revised postal rates.

Notes describing the laminated covers, errors of make-up and prices in Section C apply here. All booklet covers have round tabs.

**ILLUSTRATIONS.** The illustrations of the covers are ½ size.

## 56p. Booklet

Type HA1
Des. Design House Consultants

*Cover.* As Type HA1, with stamp printed in bright blue, by Walsall
Barcode 5 014721 100142

*Composition.* One pane of four: Pane UIP7 (4 × 2nd. centre band) imperforate on three sides, printed in lithography by Walsall

*Type* HA1

HA1 (sold at 60p. from 2.10.89) (22.8.89)                                                    3·00

*Quantity Issued:* 355,350
*Withdrawn:* 21.8.90

## 60p. Booklets

*Cover.* As Type HA1, with stamp printed in bright blue, by Walsall
Barcode 5 014721 100142

*Composition.* One pane of four: Pane UIP2 (4 × 2nd. centre band) imperforate on three sides, printed in photogravure by Harrison

*Type* HA1

HB1 (28.11.89)                                                                            3·50

*Quantity Issued:* 411,840
*Withdrawn:* 14.9.90

Type HA2
Redrawn Multicoloured Crown on White Background

*Cover.* As Type HA2, with stamp printed in deep blue, by Walsall
   Barcode 5 014721 100203

*Composition.* One pane of four: Pane UIP8 (4 × 2nd. centre band) with horizontal edges
   imperforate, printed in lithography by Walsall

*Type* HA2

HB2 (sold at 68p. from 17.9.90) (7.8.90)                                                          90

## 76p. Booklet

*Cover.* As Type HA1, with stamp printed in brownish black, by Walsall
   Barcode 5 014721 100128

*Composition.* One pane of four: Pane UIP10 (4 × 1st. two bands) imperforate on three sides,
   printed in lithography by Walsall

*Type* HA1

HC1 (sold at 80p. from 2.10.89) (22.8.89)                                                    3·50

*Quantity Issued:* 544,210
*Withdrawn:* 21.8.90

## 80p. Booklets

*Cover.* As Type HA1, with stamp printed in brownish black, by Walsall
   Barcode 5 014721 100128

*Composition.* One pane of four: Pane UIP5 (4 × 1st. phosphorised (advanced coated) paper)
   imperforate on three sides, printed in photogravure by Harrison

*Type* HA1

HD1 (5.12.89)                                                                                       5·00

*Quantity Issued:* 667,750
*Withdrawn:* 14.9.90

As before, but cover as Type HA2 and contents changed

*Cover.* As Type HA2, with stamp printed in bright orange-red by Walsall
   Barcode 5 014721 100180

*Composition.* One pane of four: Pane UIP11 (4 × 1st. phosphorised (advanced coated) paper) with
   horizontal edges imperforate, printed in lithography by Walsall

*Type* HA2

HD2 (sold at 88p. from 17.9.90) (7.8.90)                                                     1·25
   *a.* Error Pane UIP11*a*   ..      ..      ..      ..      ..      ..              7·00

**567**

**£1·40 Booklets**

Type HA3
Des. Design House Consultants

*Cover.* As Type HA3, with stamp printed in bright blue, by Harrison
Barcode 5 014721 100159

*Composition.* One pane of ten: Pane UIP1 (10 × 2nd. centre band) with horizontal edges imperforate

*Type* HA3

HE1 (sold at £1·50 from 2.10.89) (22.8.89)                                        5·00
 *a.* Inside cover with new rates (sold at £1·50) (2.10.89)      ..               5·50

*Quantity Issued:* Nos. HE1/*a* and HE2 650,000
*Withdrawn:*

   HE1     ..     ..  21.8.90 │ HE1*a*   ..     ..  14.9.90

As before, but cover printed by Questa

      Barcode 5 014721 100159

*Composition.* One pane of ten: Pane UIP13 (10 × 2nd. short centre band) printed in lithography by Questa

*Type* HA3

HE2 (sold at £1·50 from 2.10.89) (19.9.89)                                        5·00

*Withdrawn:* 14.9.90


**£1·50 Booklets**

Type HA4
Redrawn Multicoloured Crown on White Background

*Cover.* As Type HA4, with stamp printed in deep blue, by Harrison
    Barcode 5 014721 100210

*Composition.* One pane of ten: Pane UIP3 (10 × 2nd. centre band) with horizontal edges imperforate

*Type* HA4

HF1 (sold at £1·70 from 17.9.90) (7.8.90)                    2·25


As before, but cover printed by Questa

    Barcode 5 014721 100210

*Composition.* One pane of ten: Pane UIP14 (10 × 2nd. short centre band) printed in lithography by Questa

*Type* HA4

HF2 (sold at £1·70 from 17.9.90) (7.8.90)                    2·25


As before, but cover printed by Walsall

    Barcode 5 014721 100210

*Composition.* One pane of ten: Pane UIP9 (10 × 2nd. centre band) printed in lithography by Walsall, with horizontal edges imperforate

*Type* HA4

HF3 (sold at £1·70 from 17.9.90) (7.8.90)                    2·25


## £1·90 Booklets


*Cover.* As Type HA3, with stamp printed in brownish black, by Harrison
    Barcode 5 014721 100135

*Composition.* One pane of ten: Pane UIP4 (10 × 1st. phosphorised (advanced coated) paper) with horizontal edges imperforate

*Type* HA3

HG1 (sold at £2 from 2.10.89) (22.8.89)                    7·00
    *a.* Inside cover with new rates (sold at £2) (2.10.89)  ..      ..        7·00

*Quantity Issued:* Nos. HG1/*a* and HG2 757,500
*Withdrawn:*

            HG1      ..      ..   21.8.90 | HG1*a*      ..      ..   14.9.90


As before, but cover printed by Questa

    Barcode 5 014721 100135

*Composition.* One pane of ten: Pane UIP15 (10 × 1st. phosphorised (advanced coated) paper) printed in lithography by Questa

*Type* HA3

HG2 (sold at £2 from 2.10.89) (19.9.89)                    7·00

*Withdrawn:* 14.9.90

## £2 Booklets

*Cover.* As Type HA4, with stamp printed in bright orange-red, by Harrison
Barcode 5 014721 100197

*Composition.* One pane of ten: Pane UIP6 (10 × 1st. phosphorised (advanced coated) paper) with horizontal edges imperforate

*Type* HA4

HH1 (sold at £2·20 from 17.9.90) (7.8.90)                                    3·00


As before, but cover printed by Questa

Barcode 5 014721 100197

*Composition.* One pane of ten: Pane UIP16 (10 × 1st. phosphorised (advanced coated) paper) printed in lithography by Questa

*Type* HA4

HH2 (sold at £2·20 from 17.9.90) (7.8.90)                                    3·00


As before, but cover printed by Walsall

Barcode 5 014721 100197

*Composition.* One pane of ten: Pane UIP12 (10 × 1st. phosphorised (advanced coated) paper) printed in lithography by Walsall, with horizontal edges imperforate

*Type* HA4

HH3 (sold at £2·20 from 17.9.90) (7.8.90)                                    3·00

# E.   Barcode Penny Black Anniversary Booklets (1990)

These booklets all have laminated covers, printed in scarlet, yellow and black. The panes either consist of four or ten stamps and booklet covers show the stamp printed in bright blue (15p.) or brownish black (20p.).

For other booklets containing Penny Black Anniversary stamps see, Nos. FB56 (50p.), FH19/20 (£1) and DX11 (£5 London Life prestige booklet).

### 60p. Booklet

Type JA1
Des. Design House Consultants

---

*Cover.* As Type JA1, with stamp printed in bright blue, by Walsall
    Barcode 5 014721 100159

*Composition.* One pane of four: Pane WP808 (4 × 15p. centre band) imperforate on three sides, printed in lithography by Walsall

*Type* JA1

| | |
|---|---:|
| JA1 (30.1.90) | 3·00 |
|     *a.* Queen Victoria's head in cream      ..      ..      ..      .. | 6·00 |

*Withdrawn:* 29.1.91

---

### 80p. Booklets

---

*Cover.* As Type JA1, with stamp printed in brownish black and cream, by Walsall
    Barcode 5 014721 100128

*Composition.* One pane of four: Pane WP809 (4 × 20p. phosphorised (advanced coated) paper) imperforate on three sides and printed in lithography by Walsall

*Type* JA1

| | |
|---|---:|
| JB1 (30.1.90) | 4·00 |

*Withdrawn:* 29.1.91

As before, but cover printed by Walsall and pane by Harrison

    Barcode 5 014721 100128

*Composition.* One pane of four: Pane WP803 (4 × 20p. phosphorised (advanced coated) paper) imperforate on three sides and printed in photogravure by Harrison

*Type* JA1

| | |
|---|---:|
| JB2 (17.4.90) | 4·00 |

*Withdrawn:* 16.4.91

## £1·50 Booklets

Type JA2
Des. Design House Consultants

*Cover.* As Type JA2, with stamp printed in bright blue, by Harrison
Barcode 5 014721 100159

*Composition.* One pane of ten: Pane WP799 (10 × 15p. centre band) with horizontal edges imperforate

*Type* JA2

JC1 (30.1.90)                                                                                  4·50

*Withdrawn:* 29.1.91

As before, but cover printed by Questa

Barcode 5 014721 100159

*Composition.* One pane of ten: Pane WP813 (10 × 15p. short centre band) printed in lithography by Questa

*Type* JA2

JC2 (17.4.90)                                                                                  4·50

*Withdrawn:* 16.4.91

As before, but cover printed by Walsall

Barcode 5 014721 100159

*Composition.* One pane of ten: Pane WP811 (10 × 15p. centre band) imperforate on three sides and printed in lithography by Walsall

*Type* JA2

JC3 (12.6.90)                                                                                  5·25

## £2 Booklets

*Cover.* As Type JA2, with stamp printed in brownish black and cream, by Harrison
Barcode 5 014721 100135

*Composition.* One pane of ten: Pane WP800 (10 × 20p. phosphorised (advanced coated) paper) with horizontal edges imperforate

*Type* JA2

JD1 (30.1.90)                                                                                  6·00

*Withdrawn:* 29.1.91

As before, but cover with stamp printed in brownish black by Questa
  Barcode 5 014721 100135

*Composition.* One pane of ten: Pane WP814 (10 × 20p. phosphorised (advanced coated) paper) printed in lithography by Questa

*Type* JA2

JD2 (17.4.90)                                                                                            6·00

*Withdrawn:* 16.4.91


As before, but with stamp printed in brownish black and cream by Walsall
  Barcode 5 014721 100135

*Composition.* One pane of ten: Pane WP812 (10 × 20p. phosphorised (advanced coated) paper) printed in lithography by Walsall

*Type* JA2

JD3 (12.6.90)                                                                                            3·00


# F.   Barcode Booklets containing Greetings stamps (1990)

**£2 Booklet**

Type KX1
(*Illustration reduced to ⅔ actual size*)
Des. Michael Peters and Partners Limited

*Cover.* As Type KX1, with cut-out window. Printed in scarlet, yellow and black on surfaced card
  Barcode 5 014721 100173

*Composition.* One pane of ten not attached by selvedge: Pane UKP17 (10 × 20p. Nos. UK7/16, with two bands) with margins all round and folded between rows 3/4. Separate sheet (3 × 4) of greetings labels with margins all round

*Type* KX1

KX1 "Smile" design (6.2.90)                                                                5·00

*Withdrawn:* 5.2.91

# G.    Barcode Booklets containing Christmas stamps (1990)

## £3·40 Booklet

Type LX1
(*Illustration reduced to ½ actual size*)
Des. Andrew Davidson

*Cover*. Laminated and printed in scarlet, lemon, blue and black by Harrison
Barcode 5 014721 100234

*Composition*. One pane of twenty Christmas stamps No. W847: Pane WP852 (20 × 17p. one centre
band), folded five times and with left selvedge only. Horizontal edges imperforate

*Type* LX1, *Snowman, round tab*

LX1 (13.11.90)                                                                                                                5·25

# Further Reading

**Awcock, P. G.** *Automatic Letter Sorting in the United Kingdom.* (1985. 7th Edn. The Author, Haywards Heath.)

**Dagnall, H.** *The Mechanised Sorting of Mail.* (1976. The Author, Leicester.)

**Mackay, James A.** *The Parcel Post of the British Isles.* (1982. The Author, Dumfries.)

**Mackay, James A.** *Registered Mail of the British Isles.* (1983. The Author, Dumfries.)

**Mackay, James A.** *Scottish Postmarks 1693–1978.* (1978. The Author, Dumfries.)

**Mackay, James A.** *English and Welsh Postmarks since 1840.* (1980. The Author, Dumfries.)

**Mackay, James A.** *Surcharged Mail of the British Isles.* (1984. The Author, Dumfries.)

**Mackay, James A.** *British Stamps.* (1985. Longman Group Ltd, London.)

**Mackay, James A.** *Machine Cancellations of Scotland.* (1986. The Author, Dumfries.)

**Mackay, James A.** *Official Mail of the British Isles.* (1983. The Author, Dumfries.)

**Mackay, James A.** *Postal History Annual.* (From 1979. The Author, Dumfries.)

**Muir, Douglas N. and Robinson, Martin.** *An Introduction to British Postal Mechanisation.* (1980. Postal Mechanisation Study Circle, Pinner, Middx. Supplements 1981 & 1983.)

**Myall, D. G. A.** *The Bookmark Catalogue of British Decimal Postage Stamp Books.* (1975. GB Decimal Stamp Book Study Circle. Supplement 1983.)

**Myall, D. G. A.** *The Deegam Se-tenant Catalogue of G.B. Elizabethan Definitives.* (1979. The Author, Bridport, Dorset.)

**Myall, D. G. A.** *The Deegam Catalogue of Elizabethan Coil Leaders.* (1987. The Author, Bridport, Dorset.)

**Parsons, Cyril R. H., Peachey, Colin G. and Pearson, George.** *Slogan Postmarks of the Seventies.* (1980. The Authors, London).

**Pask, Brian and Peachey, Colin G.** *Twenty Years of First Day Postmarks: The story and details of "First Day of Issue" Postmarks used by the British Post Office from 1963 to 1983.* (1983. British Postmark Society, Hemel Hempstead, Herts.)

**Pearson, George R.** *Special Event Postmarks of the United Kingdom.* (1984. 3rd Edn. British Postmark Society, London.)

**Reynolds, Paul.** *The Machine Cancellations of Wales 1905–1985.* (1985. Welsh Philatelic Society, Swansea.)

**Rigo de Righi, A. G.** *The Stamp of Royalty; British Commonwealth Issues for Royal Occasions, 1935–1972.* (1973. The National Postal Museum, London.)

**Rose, Stuart.** *Royal Mail Stamps—A Survey of British Stamp Design.* (1980. Phaidon Press, Oxford.)

**Whitney, J. T.** *Collect British Postmarks.* (1987. 4th Edn. The Author, Benfleet, Essex.)

**Wijman, J. J.** *Postage Stamps of Great Britain and their History.* (1986. The Author, Netherlands.)

## PHILATELIC PERIODICALS DEVOTED TO GREAT BRITAIN
## STAMPS AND POSTMARKS

*The Bookmark* (The GB Decimal Stamp Book Study Circle.)

*British Philatelic Bulletin* (From 1963) (The Post Office, London) (title was *Philatelic Bulletin*, 1963–83.)

*British Postmark Bulletin* (From 1971) (The Post Office, London) (title was *Postmark Bulletin*, 1971–84.)

*British Postmark Society Quarterly Bulletin* (From 1958) (British Postmark Society.)

*Gibbons Stamp Monthly* (*British Stamps* supplement from October 1981, January, April and July 1982, monthly since October 1982.)

*Guidec* (The British Decimal Stamps Study Circle.)

*The GB Journal* (From 1956) (The Great Britain Philatelic Society, London.)

*The Philatelist/Philatelic Journal of Great Britain* (From 1981) (The P.J.G.B., 1891–1980, was wholly devoted to Great Britain after March 1966.) (Christie's Robson Lowe Ltd., London.)

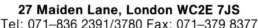

# INTERESTED IN MACHINS?

## Then you need the Stanley Gibbons Uvitec Micro Ultra Violet Lamp.

As all GB collectors know, the current 'Machin' definitives have been through quite a number of changes since they were first issued; with some of the combinations of paper, gum and phosphor type being extremely hard to find.

Unfortunately not all of these desirable items can be spotted with the naked eye, many of them requiring the aid of a shortwave ultra violet lamp for positive identification.

Following exhaustive research and tests Stanley Gibbons believe that they have come up with the perfect answer to the 'Machin' collectors prayer.

**The Stanley Gibbons Uvitec Micro Short Wave Ultra Violet Lamp.**
MODERN – designed for today's collector and produced by the leading manufacturer of UV lamps in Britain.
EFFECTIVE – detects phosphors, paper and ink variations, fakes, forgeries and repairs.
SAFE – the specially designed hood protects the eyes from direct UV light.
SMART and ROBUST – well designed plastic casing built to withstand regular use.
CONVENIENT – battery powered, ideal for taking to stamp shops and fairs.
EASY TO USE – simple press button, on-off operation.
SMALL and LIGHT – slips easily into the pocket. Weighs less than 6oz (with batteries) and therefore suitable for prolonged use.
VERSATILE – comes with its own detachable viewing hood allowing effective daylight use. Suitable for studying individual stamps or for 'sweeping'.
CLEAR INSTRUCTIONS – are provided with every lamp.
THE PRICE – not only one of the best ultra violet lamps on the market but also one of the least expensive.